Documenta Q

Reconstructions of Q
Through Two Centuries of Gospel Research
Excerpted, Sorted, and Evaluated

General Editors

James M. Robinson
Claremont Graduate University

Paul Hoffmann
University of Bamberg

John S. Kloppenborg Verbin
University of St. Michael's College

Managing Editors

Stanley D. Anderson
Robert A. Derrenbacker, Jr.
Christoph Heil
Thomas Hieke
Steven R. Johnson
Milton C. Moreland

The Database
of the
International Q Project

Q 7:1-10
The Centurion's Faith in
Jesus' Word

Steven R. Johnson

Volume Editor
Steven R. Johnson

PEETERS
Leuven – Paris – Sterling, VA
2002

The Greek text of the *Novum Testamentum Graece*, 27th edition 1993 is used with permission of the Deutsche Bibelgesellschaft, Stuttgart.

Library of Congress Cataloging-in-Publication Data

Johnson, S. R. (Steven R.)
  Q 7:1-10 : the centurion's faith in Jesus' Word / Steven R. Johnson ; volume editor, Steven R. Johnson.
    p. cm. -- (Documenta Q)
  Includes bibliographical references mand indes.
  ISBN 9042910798 (Peeters Leuven : alk. paper) -- ISBN 2877236048 (Peeters France : alk. paper)
    1. Q hypothesis (Synoptics criticism) 2. Bible. N.T. Gospels--Criticism, interpreta-tions, etc. I. Title: At head of title: Database of the International Q Project. II. Title. IV. Series.

BS2555.J65 2002
226'.066--dc21   2001055173

BS
2555.2
. J65
2002

ISBN 90-429-1079-8 (Peeters Leuven)
ISBN 2-87723-604-8 (Peeters France)
D. 2002/0602/6

© PEETERS, Bondgenotenlaan 153, B-3000 Leuven, Belgium, 2002

Introduction

The existence of Q was first included in a hypothesis to account for the Synoptic data in 1838, by Christian Hermann Weiße in *Die evangelische Geschichte kritisch und philosophisch bearbeitet*. This has been the predominant view since 1863, when Heinrich Julius Holtzmann published *Die synoptischen Evangelien: Ihr Ursprung und geschichtlicher Charakter*. Since then scholars have debated the exact wording of individual sayings in Q in a vast body of literature published in several languages and scattered among journals, commentaries and monographs for over a century. The literature has in effect become overwhelming and hence inaccessible.

Many scholars have made no effort to move behind Matthew's and Luke's divergences to establish the wording of Q itself, but have merely designated verses as those "behind" which the Q text lurked. This is perhaps the most disconcerting effect of the absence of any manuscript evidence for Q itself, for such a procedure leaves Q nowhere really accessible to serious detailed discussion.

While fraught with various uncertainties, the reconstruction of Q is not in fact as hopeless or hypothetical a project as is sometimes imagined. A comparison of Matthew and Luke in the double tradition indicates that there is verbatim or near-verbatim agreement in approximately fifty percent of the words. Additionally, in a significant number of instances, it is reasonably clear that one Evangelist has intervened in Q, for example, transporting a saying to a new location where it can function in a Markan pericope, or furnishing it with a framework that belongs to the conceptual interests of that Evangelist. In such cases, the history of scholarship reflects a near-unanimous verdict in favor of the other Evangelist.

Of course there are cases where it is not possible to reconstruct a given Q wording with certainty. But any actual papyrus has lacunae that can be filled only with a certain degree of probability or not at all, and yet the more certain parts of the text fully deserve publication. So also the text of Q, though not extant on papyrus, is eminently worthy of being critically reconstructed and published, to the extent this can be done with a reasonable degree of probability.

Often only a passing observation as to which Evangelist altered the Q wording at a single divergence in a given saying has led to the inference that the whole saying was to be reconstructed according to the other Evangelist. But in textual criticism we have learned that one scribal error does not necessarily mean that the same scribe is in error at the next divergent reading.

Hence each text must be divided into variation units delimiting precisely the extent to which a divergence at one point, e.g. in the choice of a preposition, brings with it of necessity other divergences, e.g. the case of the preposition's object, and on the other hand the extent to which the surrounding context is not of necessity drawn into that error, i.e. is not part of that same variation unit. Hence the sayings of Q have here been analyzed into their respective variation units, each of which involved a discrete decision on the part of the diverging Evangelist and hence a discrete decision on our part in the effort to reconstruct the original wording of Q.

When one Evangelist can be seen to have altered the text of Q, this does not imply necessarily that the other Evangelist has preserved the Q reading. Both may in fact have altered Q (just as at times both altered Mark). Hence at each variation unit one must to a degree analyze each Evangelist separately, deciding largely in terms of that Gospel alone whether that Evangelist has preserved or altered the Q text, leaving it a relatively open question, to be analyzed in a logically distinct operation, whether the other Evangelist has or has not retained the Q wording.

The discussion of a given variation unit can best be understood in the chronological sequence of the history of scholarship. It is not only relevant to establish who first represented a given point of view that then came to be widely cited. Rather, it is also important to be able to place a given opinion within the context of the conscious or unconscious assumptions of a given generation or school of thought. Divergences in wording between Matthew and Luke have been explained on the assumption that Jesus on different occasions presented the same saying, but with the normal fluctuations of each "performance"; or that Matthew and Luke used different translations of an original Aramaic saying; or that the transmitting communities shaped sayings to fit their varying situations; or that the redactors introduced their own stylistic and theological preferences. Such factors may always deserve consideration, but in a given epoch may have been weighed very differently. This subjectivity of a given generation or school of thought becomes more apparent as one studies the history of the problem in chronological order.

Such considerations have been constitutive in the way the material has here been organized. The texts of Matthew, Q and Luke are presented in parallel columns (along with any Markan parallels), with sigla delimiting each variation unit, which in turn is numbered, so that each can be investigated seriatim in the database of scholarly literature that follows. When there are Markan parallels, they are printed in a column to the left of Matthew (when the closer parallel is Matthew) or to the right of Luke (when the closer parallel is Luke), at times both, aligned so as to facilitate the identification of the parallel formulations, but without sigla. Parallel material of John 4:46b-53 is printed in the far right-hand column.

Each variation unit is presented in four sequences, each in chronological order: Those who have presented reasons to the effect that Luke has preserved the text of Q; next those who have argued that Luke has not preserved the text of Q; then those who have advocated Matthew as preserving the text of Q; and finally those who have contested that Matthew equals Q. Footnotes to quotations in the database are included only when relevant to the issue at hand. The presentation is basically conservative, in that it is primarily designed to make accessible what the scholarly tradition has produced thus far. But it is also itself critically creative, in that the analysis of the scholarly literature is followed by Evaluations in which members of the project have brought to expression their own conclusions. The user is then free to move forward into one's own creative use of the scholarly tradition.

This undertaking grew out of the Q Seminar of the Society of Biblical Literature (1985—1989), which then was reconstituted by the Research and Publications Committee of the Society of Biblical Literature as the International Q Project. The team of over forty members has met just before the Annual Meeting of the SBL at the convention site, and then in second and third annual meetings at the project's centers, Claremont, CA, USA; Bamberg, Germany; and Toronto, Canada. The procedure has been that for each pericope one member collected and sorted the scholarly literature and wrote a first Evaluation. Then one or more other members responded with their own Evaluations. All this was distributed in advance of a project meeting so that the resultant divergences could be discussed and resolved at such a session. The results of each year's meetings appeared the the fall issue of the *Journal of Biblical Literature* the following year (1990—1995, 1997). Thus the critical text of Q became promptly accessible. *Documenta Q* incorporates this text in the discussion of each variation unit.

From the beginning it was assumed that the project would be open-ended, to stay abreast of ongoing scholarship, much as Bible translations and critical texts of the Greek New Testament are never "final," but are no sooner published than the next revision is already underway. An Editorial Board of the International Q Project is in charge of this continuing revision, of which *Documenta Q* is itself a major result: The refinement of the formatting of variation units, the supplementing of the scholarly literature, the reformulations of the Evaluations, the General Editors' establishment of a revised critical text (published also in *The Critical Edition of Q: Synopsis including the Gospels of Matthew and Luke, Mark and Thomas, with English, German, and French Translations of Q and Thomas,* Leuven: Peeters; Minneapolis: Fortress Press, 2000), and the Managing Editors' publication of this massive database in individual volumes of *Documenta Q*, are the fruit of this continuing research.

The future volumes are to appear as they become ready, from the discussion of the problem of an *Incipit* and the sayings of John in Q 3, to the conclusion

of Q with the prophecy of the judging of the twelve tribes of Israel by Jesus'
followers (Q 22:28, 30). Lucan chapter and verse numeration is used as a con-
venience and a mere convention.

It is hoped that *Documenta Q* will become a standard tool to facilitate all Q
research of the future.

The work of the International Q Project has been aided by grants from
Claremont Graduate University, the Deutsche Forschungsgemeinschaft, the
Deutscher Akademischer Austauschdienst, the Institute for Antiquity and
Christianity, the Social Sciences and Humanities Research Council of Canada,
and the Society of Biblical Literature's Research and Publications Committee,
for all of whose support we are very grateful.

The critical text of Q used here is that adopted by the General Editors, pre-
supposing the work of the International Q Project. The original Evaluations
have been updated and those of the General Editors composed in an informal
dialogue of those involved. When the critical text differs from the decision of
the International Q Project published in *JBL*, the original decision is recorded
in the critical apparatus with the abbreviation IQP and the date of the meeting at which the decision was made. Minority views among the General Editors are also recorded in the critical apparatus, identified by initials: JMR, PH,
or JSKV.

The Greek text is that of the *Novum Testamentum Graece*, 27th edition
1993, edited by Barbara Aland et al., Deutsche Bibelgesellschaft, Stuttgart.
We thank Prof. Dr. Barbara Aland and Dr. Joachim Lange for their coopera-
tion in this undertaking.

Just prior to the Bibliography at the conclusion of the volume the resultant
critical text of Q 7:1-10 is printed, without the many formatting sigla that
may well distract the general reader, though with the sigla indicating instances
of serious uncertainty in establishing the text. Then this Greek text is followed
by English, German and French translations, with the English and German
provided by the General Editors, and the French by Frédéric Amsler, to whom
we would like to express our gratitude for this assistance, as well as his assistance in providing the French translation of the front matter.

Einleitung

Die Existenz von Q wurde erstmals im Rahmen einer Hypothese vertreten,
die Christian Hermann Weiße 1838 in seiner Studie "Die evangelische
Geschichte kritisch und philosophisch bearbeitet" zur Lösung der synoptischen Frage entwickelte. Durch Heinrich Julius Holtzmanns Untersuchung:
"Die synoptischen Evangelien. Ihr Ursprung und geschichtlicher Charakter"

(1863) setzte sich die Annahme, daß die Evangelisten Matthäus und Lukas neben Markus eine zweite Quelle ("Q") in ihren Evangelien verarbeitet haben, in der Synoptikerforschung weithin durch. In einer unüberschaubaren Zahl von Studien, die seit mehr als hundert Jahren in verschiedenen Sprachen und verstreut in verschiedenen Zeitschriften, Kommentaren und Monographien veröffentlicht wurden, wird seitdem über den exakten Wortlaut der einzelnen Sprüche in Q gestritten. Die Literatur ist überwältigend und heute kaum noch zu erfassen.

Viele Forscher versuchten nicht, jenseits der Verschiedenheiten von Matthäus und Lukas den Wortlaut von Q selbst zu rekonstruieren, sondern nannten einfach Verse, "hinter" denen der Q-Text zu vermuten ist. Dies ist vielleicht die unglücklichste Wirkung der Tatsache, daß es von Q selbst keine handschriftliche Überlieferung gibt. Denn durch eine solche Vorgehensweise wird der Text von Q einer ernsten, detaillierten Diskussion entzogen.

Obwohl sie mit einigen Unsicherheiten belastet bleibt, ist die Rekonstruktion von Q jedoch kein so hoffnungsloses oder hypothetisches Projekt, wie es manchem erscheint. Ein Vergleich von Matthäus und Lukas zeigt, daß etwa fünfzig Prozent der Sprüche, die beide überliefern, wörtlich oder nahezu wörtlich übereinstimmen. Außerdem kann in einer bedeutenden Zahl von Fällen nachgewiesen werden, daß ein Evangelist in seine Q-Vorlage eingegriffen hat, indem er zum Beispiel einen Spruch an eine neue Stelle innerhalb der markinischen Akoluthie versetzte, oder indem er einem Spruch einen Rahmen oder einen Wortlaut gab, der von seinen eigenen Interessen bestimmt war. In solchen Fällen ermöglicht die Geschichte der Forschung ein nahezu einstimmiges Urteil darüber, daß der jeweils andere Evangelist Q bewahrt hat.

Natürlich kommt es auch vor, daß der ursprüngliche Wortlaut von Q nicht mit Sicherheit rekonstruiert werden kann. Aber jeder Papyrus hat Lücken, die nur mit einem bestimmten Grad an Wahrscheinlichkeit (oder auch gar nicht) gefüllt werden können. Dennoch verdienen es die sicheren Teile des Textes, veröffentlicht zu werden. So ist auch der Text von Q, wenngleich er nicht als Papyrus vorliegt, wertvoll genug, kritisch rekonstruiert und veröffentlicht zu werden—in dem Umfang, wie dies mit einem begründeten Grad an Wahrscheinlichkeit getan werden kann.

Oft führte die beiläufige Beobachtung, daß der eine Evangelist den Wortlaut eines Q-Spruchs in einer einzigen Variante geändert hat, zu der Meinung, daß man in der Rekonstruktion des ganzen Spruches dem Wortlaut des anderen Evangelisten folgen müsse. Aber schon die Textkritik lehrt, daß ein Schreibfehler nicht zu der Folgerung zwingt, derselbe Schreiber müsse sich auch bei der nächsten Textvariante geirrt haben. Daher sind die Textvarianten so zu bestimmen, daß sie das Ausmaß der Abweichung präzise abgrenzen. Die Wahl einer Präposition bedingt zum Beispiel notwendigerweise weitere

Abweichungen, wie etwa den Casus des präpositionalen Objekts. Andererseits können Abweichungen, die sich nicht gegenseitig bedingen, auch nicht demselben Variantenbereich zugeordnet werden. Daher sind die einzelnen Varianten in den Q-Sprüchen so definiert worden, daß sie eine gesonderte Beurteilung der Unterschiede zwischen beiden Evangelisten und damit auch eine gezielte Entscheidung bei der Rekonstruktion des ursprünglichen Wortlauts von Q ermöglichen.

Wenn sich nachweisen läßt, daß ein Evangelist den Q-Text geändert hat, impliziert dies noch nicht notwendig, daß der andere Evangelist den Q-Wortlaut bewahrt hat. Beide können nämlich ihre Q-Vorlage verändert haben (wie beide manchmal auch Markus nicht wörtlich übernommen haben). Daher muß bei jeder Variante jeder Evangelist für sich allein analysiert werden. Es ist so weit wie möglich im Rahmen des jeweiligen Evangeliums zu entscheiden, ob es Q bewahrt oder verändert hat. Dabei bleibt es eine zunächst offene Frage, die in einem eigenen Verfahren zu behandeln ist, ob das andere Evangelium den Q-Wortlaut erhalten hat oder nicht.

Die Diskussion einer bestimmten Variante kann am besten anhand der chronologischen Abfolge der Forschungsgeschichte erfaßt werden. Diese zeigt nicht nur, wer zuerst ein bestimmtes Argument vertreten hat, das später weithin einfach übernommen wurde. Sie ist auch wichtig für die Einordnung eines bestimmten Arguments in den Kontext der bewußten oder unbewußten Voraussetzungen, die in der jeweiligen Forschergeneration oder Forschungsrichtung geherrscht haben. Unterschiede im Wortlaut bei Matthäus und Lukas wurden zum Beispiel damit erklärt, daß Jesus bei verschiedenen Gelegenheiten denselben Spruch, jedoch mit den Abweichungen, wie sie bei jeder neuen "Verwendung" üblich sind, gebrauchte; oder daß Matthäus und Lukas verschiedene Übersetzungen eines ursprünglich aramäischen Spruches verwendeten; oder daß die überliefernden Gemeinden die Sprüche ihren unterschiedlichen Situationen anpaßten; oder daß die Redaktoren ihren eigenen stilistischen und theologischen Präferenzen folgten. Solche Faktoren verdienen immer Beachtung, sie können aber in einer bestimmten Forschungsepoche sehr unterschiedlich gewichtet worden sein. Diese Subjektivität einer jeweiligen Forschergeneration oder Schule wird deutlicher sichtbar, wenn man die Geschichte eines Problems in seiner chronologischen Folge studiert.

Solche Überlegungen waren grundlegend für die Art und Weise, wie das Material in den *Documenta Q*-Bänden präsentiert wird. Die Texte von Matthäus, Q und Lukas sind in parallelen Spalten angeordnet (zusammen mit eventuellen Parallelen aus dem Markus- oder Thomasevangelium). Numerierte Siglen grenzen jede Variante so ab, daß in der folgenden Datenbasis der wissenschaftlicher Literatur eine jede von ihnen der Reihe nach untersucht werden kann. Sind markinische Parallelen vorhanden, werden sie in einer

Spalte links von Matthäus geboten, wenn sie dem matthäischen Text näher-
stehen. Entsprechen sie mehr dem lukanischen Text, stehen sie in einer Spalte
rechts von Lukas. Gelegentlich stehen die markinischen Parallelen sowohl
links vom matthäischen, als auch rechts vom lukanischen Text, und zwar zei-
lenangepaßt, damit die parallelen Formulierungen leichter gefunden werden
können. Der Markus-Text wird allerdings ohne Siglen angeführt. Paralleler
Stoff von Johannes 4:46-53 steht in einer Spalte ganz rechts.

Jede Variante wird in der Datenbasis in chronologischer Folge in vier
Schritten vorgestellt: Zunächst werden jene Forscher zitiert, die Gründe vorbringen, daß Lukas den Q-Text bewahrt habe; dann die, die argumentieren,
daß Lukas den Q-Text nicht erhalten habe; dann die, die in Matthäus den Q-
Text erkennen; schließlich die, die sich gegen Matthäus aussprechen. Fußno-
ten in den Zitaten werden in der Datenbasis nur wiedergegeben, wenn sie für
das jeweilige Argument relevant sind. Die Präsentation der Forschungsgeschichte ist ihrem Wesen nach konservativ, da sie vor allem die bisherigen
Ergebnisse der wissenschaftlichen Diskussion zugänglich machen möchte.
Allerdings möchte die Reihe *Documenta Q* auch kritisch und kreativ sein. Die
Präsentation der Forschungsgeschichte wird daher von Evaluationen abgeschlossen, in denen die Mitglieder des Internationalen Q-Projekts ihre eigenen
Urteile abgeben. Der Leserin bzw. dem Leser ist es freigestellt, auf dieser Basis
weiterzuarbeiten und selbst kreativen Gebrauch von der Forschungsgeschichte
zu machen.

Das vorliegende Unternehmen erwuchs aus dem Q-Seminar der *Society of
Biblical Literature* (1985–1989), das 1989 von dem *Research and Publications
Committee* der *Society of Biblical Literature* als „Internationales Q-Projekt" wie-
dergegründet wurde. Das Team von über vierzig Mitgliedern hat sich jeweils
vor der Jahrestagung der SBL am Kongreßort getroffen, zum Teil auch in
zweiten und dritten jährlichen Tagungen an den Zentren des Q-Projekts,
nämlich in Claremont, CA (USA), Bamberg (Deutschland) und Toronto
(Kanada). Folgendes Verfahren wurde dabei gewählt: Für jeden Textabschnitt
sammelte ein Mitglied die wissenschaftliche Literatur, ordnete sie und schrieb
dann eine erste Evaluation. Darauf antworteten ein oder zwei Mitglieder mit
eigenen Evaluationen. Die Stellungnahmen wurden vor der Projekt-Tagung
allen Mitgliedern zugänglich gemacht, über die verbliebenen Meinungsunter-
schiede wurde bei der Tagung diskutiert und entschieden. Die Resultate der
Tagungen eines Jahres wurden jeweils in der folgenden Herbstausgabe des
Journal of Biblical Literature (1990–1995, 1997) veröffentlicht. *Documenta Q*
enthält diesen Text jeweils in der Diskussion der entsprechenden Variante.

Von Beginn an wurde davon ausgegangen, daß das Projekt sich zeitlich
nicht begrenzen läßt. Es ist auf die weitergehende Forschung hin offen. Ähnlich sind auch Bibelübersetzungen und kritische Ausgaben des griechischen

Neuen Testaments niemals "endgültig"; in der Regel hat die nächste Revision schon begonnen, wenn eine neue Auflage gedruckt wird. Ein Herausgeberkreis des Internationalen Q-Projekts ist für die kontinuierliche Revision verantwortlich, von der *Documenta Q* selbst ein wichtiges Resultat darstellt: Die Verbesserung der Formatierung der Varianten, die Ergänzung der wissenschaftlichen Literatur, die Revision der Evaluationen, die Publikation der Datenbasen in eigenen *Documenta Q*-Bänden durch die Managing Editors sowie die Herstellung eines revidierten kritischen Q-Textes durch die Hauptherausgeber sind Früchte dieser weitergehenden Arbeit. Die von den Hauptherausgebern verantwortete Q-Rekonstruktion ist unter dem Titel *The Critical Edition of Q: Synopsis including the Gospels of Matthew and Luke, Mark and Thomas, with English, German, and French Translations of Q and Thomas* (Leuven: Peeters; Minneapolis: Fortress Press, 2000) veröffentlicht.

Die künftigen *Documenta Q*-Bände erscheinen gemäß Manuskripteingang und werden schließlich von der Diskussion eines *Incipit* und den Worten des Johannes in Q 3 bis zum Schluß von Q mit der Ankündigung, daß die Nachfolger Jesu über die zwölf Stämme Israels richten werden (Q 22:28, 30), den gesamten Q-Text behandeln. Die Benennung der Q-Stellen nach lukanischer Kapitel- und Verszahl dient der Vereinfachung und ist reine Konvention.

Es ist zu hoffen, daß die *Documenta Q*-Reihe ein Standardwerk wird, welches die künftige Q-Forschung erleichtert.

Die Arbeit des Internationalen Q-Projekts wurde unterstützt durch Fördermittel der Claremont Graduate University, der Deutschen Forschungsgemeinschaft, des Deutschen Akademischen Austauschdienstes, des Institute for Antiquity and Christianity, des Social Sciences and Humanities Research Council of Canada und dem Research and Publications Committee der Society of Biblical Literature. Für all diese Unterstützung sind wir sehr dankbar.

Der kritische Q-Text, der hier wiedergegeben wird, stammt von den Hauptherausgebern, die die Arbeit des Internationalen Q-Projekts voraussetzen. Die ursprünglichen Evaluationen wurden aktualisiert und überarbeitet, die der Hauptherausgeber wurden in einem informellen Dialog erarbeitet. Wenn der kritische Q-Text von dem Urteil des Internationalen Q-Projekts, das in *JBL* veröffentlicht wurde, abweicht, wird diese Entscheidung im kritischen Apparat mit der Abkürzung IQP und dem Jahr der Tagung, bei der die Entscheidung getroffen wurde, vermerkt. Minderheitsmeinungen unter den Hauptherausgebern werden ebenfalls mit den jeweiligen Initialen (JMR, PH oder JSKV) im kritischen Apparat angeführt.

Der griechische Text entstammt dem *Novum Testamentum Graece*, 27. Auflage 1993, herausgegeben von Barbara Aland und anderen, Deutsche Bibelgesellschaft, Stuttgart. Wir danken Prof. Dr. Barbara Aland und Dr. Joachim Lange für ihre Kooperation in diesem Unternehmen.

Vor der Bibliographie am Ende des Bandes ist der rekonstruierte kritische Text von Q 7:1-10 wiedergegeben. Dabei wurde auf zahlreiche Formatierungs-Siglen, die einen nicht an den Details interessierten Leser leicht ablenken können, verzichtet. Allerdings sind Siglen enthalten, die erkennen lassen, wo die Rekonstruktion unsicher ist. Der griechische Q-Text wird durch englische, deutsche und französische Übersetzungen ergänzt; die englische und deutsche Übersetzung wurde von den Hauptherausgebern angefertigt, die französische von Frédéric Amsler, dem wir für seine Hilfe danken, insbesondere für die Übersetzung der Einleitung.

Introduction

L'existence de Q a été postulée, pour la première fois, dans le cadre d'une hypothèse qui cherchait à rendre compte du problème synoptique et qui a été émise en 1838 par Christian Hermann Weisse dans *Die evangelische Geschichte kritisch und philosophisch bearbeitet*. Cette hypothèse est devenue l'opinion dominante à partir de 1863, date à laquelle Heinrich Julius Holtzmann publia *Die synoptischen Evangelien: Ihr Ursprung und geschichtlicher Charakter*. Depuis lors, les savants ont discuté la formulation exacte de chaque sentence susceptible d'appartenir à Q et, en plus d'un siècle, ils ont constitué un vaste corpus littéraire rédigé dans plusieurs langues et dispersé dans des revues, des commentaires et des monographies. La masse écrasante de cette littérature l'a rendue inaccessible.

Bien des savants se sont contentés de signaler des versets "derrière" lesquels le texte de Q devait se cacher, mais n'ont pas fait l'effort d'aller au-delà des divergences entre Matthieu et Luc pour reconstituer la formulation même de Q. C'est sans doute l'effet le plus déconcertant de l'absence de tout témoin manuscrit de Q que d'aboutir à une manière de procéder qui rende Q nulle part véritablement accessible pour une discussion de détail sérieuse.

Bien que truffée de difficultés diverses, la reconstitution de Q n'est en réalité pas une entreprise aussi désespérée ou hypothétique qu'on l'imagine parfois. Une comparaison de Matthieu et de Luc, en tradition double, laisse voir des accords verbaux ou presque verbaux pour près de cinquante pour cent des mots. En outre, pour un nombre significatif de cas, il est assez clair que l'un des évangélistes est intervenu sur Q, en déplaçant, par exemple, une sentence à un autre endroit pour lui faire remplir telle fonction particulière dans une péricope de Marc ou en l'enrichissant d'une structure qui corresponde à ses intérêts conceptuels de théologien. Dans de tels cas, l'histoire de la recherche rend un jugement quasi unanime en faveur de l'autre évangéliste.

Il y a toutefois des cas où il n'est pas possible de reconstituer la formulation de Q avec certitude. Mais n'importe quel papyrus, aujourd'hui, a aussi des lacunes, qui peuvent être comblées, soit avec un certain degré de probabilité seulement, soit pas du tout; et pourtant, les parties sûres du texte méritent pleinement d'être publiées. Il en va de même pour le texte de Q qui, sans être attesté par un papyrus, mérite au plus haut point d'être reconstitué critiquement et publié, dans la mesure où il peut être offert avec un degré raisonnable de probabilité.

Parfois, une simple retouche, apportée par un évangéliste à la formulation de Q, occasionne une divergence dans une sentence donnée et peut faire croire que toute la sentence doive être reconstituée d'après l'autre évangéliste. Mais en critique textuelle, nous avons appris qu'une erreur de scribe ne signifiait nullement que le même scribe commettrait aussi une faute au lieu divergent suivant. C'est pourquoi chaque texte doit être divisé en lieux variants. Cette méthode permet d'évaluer avec précision, d'une part, dans quelle mesure une divergence sur un point (par exemple le choix d'une préposition) entraîne nécessairement d'autres divergences (par exemple le cas de l'objet régi par cette préposition); et d'autre part, dans quelle mesure le contexte environnant n'est pas lui aussi, par nécessité, mêlé à cette erreur (c'est-à-dire ne fait pas partie de ce même lieu variant). Pour cette raison, les sentences de Q sont analysées ici en fonction de leurs lieux variants. Chacun d'eux suppose, en effet, une discrète modification du texte de Q de la part des évangélistes et implique, du même coup, une décision discrète de notre part pour reconstituer la formulation originale de Q.

Lorsqu'on peut constater qu'un évangéliste a modifié le texte de Q, cela n'implique pas nécessairement que l'autre évangéliste ait préservé la bonne lecture de Q, car les deux peuvent avoir modifié Q (exactement comme parfois Matthieu et Luc ont tous deux modifié Marc). Pour chaque lieu variant, on doit, par conséquent, analyser, jusqu'à un certain point, chaque évangéliste séparément, en fondant sa décision pour une bonne part sur un seul évangile, et voir si tel évangéliste a préservé ou modifié le texte de Q, en laissant la question relativement ouverte et digne d'être analysée selon une opération logiquement distincte, de savoir si l'autre évangéliste a retenu ou non la formulation de Q.

C'est en suivant l'ordre chronologique de l'histoire de la recherche que l'on comprend le mieux la discussion d'un lieu variant donné. Ce type de présentation n'a pas pour seul but d'établir qui a, le premier, défendu un point de vue que l'on a ensuite largement cité. Elle a pour objectif principal d'offrir la possibilité de placer une opinion donnée dans le contexte des présupposés conscients ou inconscients de telle génération ou de telle école de pensée. Les divergences de formulation entre Matthieu et Luc ont été expliquées de diverses manières. On a soutenu que Jésus avait présenté en différentes occasions la même sentence, mais avec les fluctuations normales dues aux circonstances particulières;

ou que Matthieu et Luc avaient utilisé différentes traductions d'un original en araméen; ou que les communautés qui avaient transmis les sentences les avaient modelées pour qu'elles correspondent à la diversité de leurs situations; ou que les rédacteurs avaient apposé leur griffe stylistique et théologique. De tels facteurs sont toujours dignes de considération, mais selon les époques, ils ont pu avoir un poids très différent. Cette subjectivité d'une génération ou d'une école de pensée apparaît plus nettement si on étudie l'histoire du problème en suivant l'ordre chronologique.

De telles considérations ne sont pas indépendantes de la façon dont la matière a été organisée ici. Les textes de Matthieu, Q et Luc sont présentés en colonnes parallèles (avec en regard les parallèles de Marc), avec des sigles qui délimitent chaque lieu variant et une numérotation suivie des variantes, de sorte que chacune d'elles puisse être examinée séparément dans la base de données contenant la littérature savante qui est fournie ensuite. Lorsqu'il y a des parallèles chez Marc, ceux-ci sont imprimés dans la colonne à gauche de Matthieu (si le parallèle le plus proche est Matthieu) ou dans celle à droite de Luc (si le parallèle le plus proche est Luc), ou parfois dans les deux, disposés de manière à faciliter l'identification de formulations parallèles, mais sans sigles. Le texte parallèle chez Jean 4:46-53 est imprimé dans la colonne extérieure droite.

Chaque lieu variant est présenté en quatre sections, lesquelles suivent toujours l'ordre chronologique: en premier lieu viennent les auteurs qui ont avancé des arguments pour démontrer que Luc avait préservé le texte de Q; puis ceux qui ont estimé que Luc n'avait pas préservé le texte de Q; ensuite ceux qui ont plaidé que Matthieu avait préservé le texte de Q; et enfin ceux qui ont contesté que Matthieu était égal à Q. Les notes de bas de page attachées aux citations ont été incluses dans la base de données seulement lorsqu'elles concernaient le problème en question. La présentation est fondamentalement conservatrice, dans la mesure où elle est destinée prioritairement à rendre accessible ce que la tradition érudite a produit jusqu'ici. Mais elle est aussi en elle-même critiquement créative, puisque l'analyse de cette littérature savante est suivie d'évaluations, dans lesquelles les membres du projet sont amenés à exprimer leur propres conclusions. Les lecteurs sont ensuite libres d'aller plus loin dans leur propre usage créatif de la tradition érudite.

Cette entreprise est issue du *Q Seminar* de la *Society of Biblical Literature* (1985–1989), qui a été ensuite remodelé par le *Research and Publications Committee* de la *Society of Biblical Literature* en *International Q Project*. L'équipe, qui compte plus de quarante membres, avait l'habitude de se retrouver juste avant le Congrès annuel de la *SBL* sur le même site et, par la suite, lors d'une deuxième et d'une troisième rencontre annuelle dans les trois centres responsables du projet, à Claremont en Californie, à Bamberg en Allemagne et à

Toronto au Canada. La procédure suivie veut que, pour chaque péricope, un membre récolte et trie la littérature savante, puis rédige une première évaluation. Ensuite, un ou plusieurs autres membres répondent en formulant leur propre évaluation. Tous ces documents sont distribués avant chaque réunion de manière à ce que les divergences puissent être discutées et aplanies lors des sessions. Les résultats de chaque réunion annuelle ont été publiés l'année suivante (1990—1995, 1997) dans la livraison d'automne du *Journal of Biblical Literature*. Ainsi, le texte critique de Q est devenu rapidement accessible. Les volumes de la série des *Documenta Q* intègrent ce texte dans la discussion de chaque lieu variant.

Dès le début, il a été clair que le projet serait sans fin, pour rester en prise avec le développement de la science, à l'image des traductions de la Bible ou des éditions critiques du Nouveau Testament grec, qui ne sont jamais définitives, mais qui, à peine publiées, ont déjà leur prochaine révision en chantier. Le Comité éditorial de l'*International Q Project* a la charge de poursuivre cette révision, dont les volumes des *Documenta Q* constituent en eux-mêmes le principal résultat: le perfectionnement de la mise en forme des lieux variants, l'intégration de la littérature savante, la reformulation des évaluations, l'établissement par les *General Editors* d'un texte critique révisé (publié aussi en un seul volume, *The Critical Edition of Q: Synopsis including the Gospels of Matthew and Luke, Mark and Thomas, with English, German, and French Translations of Q and Thomas*, Leuven: Peeters; Minneapolis: Fortress Press, 2000), et la publication par les *Managing Editors* de l'énorme base de données dans les volumes séparés des *Documenta Q* sont les fruits de cette recherche en cours.

Les prochains volumes paraîtront dès qu'ils seront prêts, en partant de la discussion du problème de l'*Incipit* et des sentences de Jean en Q 3, pour aboutir à la conclusion de Q avec la prophétie sur le jugement des douze tribus d'Israël par les compagnons de Jésus (Q 22:28, 30). La numérotation des chapitres et des versets suit celle de Luc par commodité et par simple convention.

Il est à souhaiter que les volumes des *Documenta Q* deviennent l'outil de travail standard pour faciliter toute recherche future sur Q.

Le travail de l'*International Q Project* a bénéficié des subventions de la *Claremont Graduate University*, de la *Deutsche Forschungsgemeinschaft*, du *Deutscher Akademischer Austauschdienst*, de l'*Institute for Antiquity and Christianity*, du *Social Sciences and Humanities Research Council of Canada*, du *Society of Biblical Literature's Research and Publications Committee*, et nous leur sommes particulièrement reconnaissants de leur soutien.

Le texte critique de Q utilisé ici est celui qui a été adopté par les *General Editors*, sur la base du travail de l'*International Q Project*. Les premières évaluations ont été mises à jour et celles des *General Editors*, élaborées au cours de dialogues informels, y ont été intégrées. Lorsque le texte critique diffère de la décision de l'*International Q Project* publié dans le *JBL*, la décision précédente est rappelée dans l'apparat critique avec l'abréviation IQP et la date de la rencontre lors de laquelle la décision a été prise. Les opinions minoritaires parmi les *General Editors* sont aussi rappelées dans l'apparat critique avec les initiales: JMR, PH ou JSKV.

Le texte grec est celui du *Novum Testamentum Graece*, 27ᵉ édition 1993, de Barbara Aland et al., Deutsche Bibelgesellschaft, Stuttgart. Nous remercions la Prof. Dr. Barbara Aland et le Dr. Joachim Lange de leur coopération dans cette entreprise.

Juste avant la bibliographie à la fin du volume, le texte critique de Q 7:1-10 est imprimé sans aucun sigle qui puisse distraire le lecteur non spécialiste, bien que certains sigles indiquent les lieux marqués d'une sérieuse incertitude quant à l'établissement du texte. Le texte grec est accompagné d'une traduction anglaise, allemande et française. Les traductions anglaise et allemande sont des *General Editors* et la traduction française de Frédéric Amsler, qui a également traduit la présente introduction et auquel nous aimerions exprimer notre reconnaissance pour son aide.

Preface of the Volume Editor

The following *Documenta Q* fascicle is a completely revised and greatly expanded version of a database first compiled by Saw Lah Shein of Claremont Graduate University and subsequently discussed and debated by members of the International Q Project at a meeting in Claremont, California, the week of 23-27 May, 1994. The results of that meeting were published the following year as:

> "The International Q Project: Work Sessions 23-27 May, 22-26 August, 17-18 November 1994." By M.C. Moreland and J.M. Robinson. *Journal of Biblical Literature* 114 (1995): 475-485, esp. 478-479.

As with all of the fascicles of the *Documenta Q Series, Q 7:1-10: The Centurion's Faith in Jesus' Word* is the product of the dedicated and thoughtful work of many people and organizations. With my apologies for overlooking anyone, I would like to recognize some of those involved in this volume.

When I took over the authorship of this database, I was greatly aided by the Q bibliography database compiled by the New Testament faculty of Bamberg University—Thomas Hieke and Christoph Heil were especially helpful in this regard, but in other ways as well. James M. Robinson provided further research assistance in the course of revising his evaluations. Furthermore, he undertook the odious task of thoroughly proofreading my preliminary typescript in the summer of 2000—*before* I had proofread the hardcopy myself. The reader cannot appreciate the value of his work.

Very soon into the editing aspect of the project, I realized that my old Mac Classic was, alas, not up to the task. J. Harold Ellens graciously stepped in, however, and provided the means for the Institute for Antiquity and Christianity of CGU to purchase a Macintosh G3 computer for just this purpose. Jon Ma. Asgiersson, then Director of the Institute, often provided me with needed assistance as I began my work. And, while I was teaching as an Instructor at California State University, Fullerton (and living in Northern California), my department chair, Benjamin L. Hubbard, assisted me in my Q work by providing me with a teaching assistant, who took some of the grading burden off my shoulders and allowed me some time for library work. Thank you, Kitty Callanan.

Lycoming College has been of great assistance these last two years. I would like to thank especially Marlene Neece of Snowden Library for her forbearance, considering all of the Interlibrary Loan requests she has processed for me. She claims I am reintroducing her to the language of her German forefathers and foremothers.

Finally, I am always appreciative of the patient support of my beloved spouse, Ellen Davis, and the always enthusiastic support of my parents, Bob and Lois Johnson.

Williamsport, June 2002   *Steven R. Johnson*

Table of Contents

Grades Used by the International Q Project

The International Q Project uses a letter grade {A}, {B}, {C}, {D}, or {U} to indicate the relative degree of certainty for each decision. {A} and {B} grades are considered convincing enough to be printed without qualification as part of the reconstructed Q text. {A} represents "virtual certainty": all of the good arguments are on one side of the decision. {B} represents "a convincing probability": there may be good arguments on both sides of the question, but the arguments on one side clearly outweigh the arguments on the other side. {C} represents "a hesitant possibility," with significant enough doubt that in the reconstructed text the reading is placed in double brackets (see below). The {D} grade is a way of indicating the decision towards which one is inclined, but without enough certainty to include the reading in the text. An undecided grade {U} indicates that the data is not clear enough to make an informed decision.

Die vom Internationalen Q-Projekt benutzten Wahrscheinlichkeitsgrade

Das Internationale Q-Projekt verwendet die Buchstaben {A}, {B}, {C}, {D} oder {U}, um die relativen Wahrscheinlichkeitsgrade für jede Entscheidung anzugeben. {A} und {B} kennzeichnen Entscheidungen, die so überzeugend sind, daß sie ohne weitere Qualifikation als Teil des rekonstruierten Q-Textes gedruckt werden. {A} indiziert "mit an Sicherheit grenzender Wahrscheinlichkeit": Alle ernsthaften Argumente sprechen für diese Textentscheidung. {B} bedeutet eine "überzeugende Wahrscheinlichkeit": Es mag zwar ernsthafte Argumente für beide überlieferten Textfassungen geben, aber die Argumente für einen Evangelisten überwiegen klar die für den anderen. Mit {C} wird eine "schwache Wahrscheinlichkeit" gekennzeichnet, die einen nicht unbedeutenden Zweifel signalisiert. Die Lesart wird daher im rekonstruierten Text mit doppelten eckigen Klammern versehen (siehe unten). Eine Entscheidung mit {D} zeigt an, daß hier Gründe zugunsten der Lesart genannt werden können, die Wahrscheinlichkeit für sie aber nicht ausreicht, um sie in der Rekonstruktion zu berücksichtigen. {U} bedeutet, daß die vorgebrachten Argumente nicht ausreichen, eine begründete Entscheidung zu treffen; die Lesart der betreffenden Variante bleibt unentschieden.

Degrés de probabilité utilisés par l'*International Q Project*

L'*International Q Project* recourt à des lettres {A}, {B}, {C}, {D} ou {U} pour exprimer le degré relatif de certitude pour chaque décision. {A} et {B} sont considérés comme suffisamment assurés pour être imprimés tels quels comme parties intégrantes du texte reconstitué de Q. {A} représente une "certitude virtuelle": tous les bons arguments vont dans le sens de la décision prise. {B} représente une "forte probabilité": il peut y avoir de bons arguments pour et contre la décision prise, mais les arguments qui l'appuient sont nettement plus lourds que ceux qui l'invalident. {C} représente une "probabilité moyenne" qui reflète un doute suffisamment fort pour que le texte reconstitué soit placé dans des doubles crochets droits (voir plus bas). Le degré de probabilité {D} indique qu'il y a des arguments en faveur d'une leçon, mais qu'ils sont trop faibles pour qu'on inclue cette leçon dans le texte. Le sigle {U}, pour "undecided", indique que les données ne sont pas assez claires pour permettre une décision fondée.

Sigla Used in the Greek Text

[αβγ] Square brackets in the text of Luke and Q enclose words or letters found in Luke but not in Matthew.

(αβγ) Parentheses in the text of Matthew and Q enclose words or letters found in Matthew but not in Luke.

ſ ι The sigla ſ and ι surround transpositions in the order of Matthew's and Luke's shared material. The relative position where one evangelist has placed the indicated material is shown in the other Gospel by the sigla ſ ι, enclosing no text. The sigla are retained at both locations in the reconstructed Q text so as to indicate what the other alternative was. No space between ſ and ι means that this position was rejected with a certainty of {A} or {B}. Space between ſ and ι means that this position has been rejected with a certainty of only {C} or {D}, or is undecided {U} (in which case one finds Luke's position by default). For example,

ſαβγι⁵ χψω ſι⁵   means that "αβγ" is at Q's position with an {A} or {B} grade;

ſαβγι⁵ χψω ſ ι⁵   means that "αβγ" is at Q's position with a {C} or {D} grade, or the problem is undecided {U}, in which case the Lukan position is followed.

1 2 3 ...	Small raised numerals following the closing siglum are used to number the variation units within a verse. The numbers are normally included only after the closing siglum. However, when another variation unit falls within the position markers S and l, the number precedes the first position marker as well as following the last position marker, so that the numeration of the variation unit marked by S and l may use a smaller number than the numeration of the other variation unit inside the position markers.
$^{0}/$ ... $\backslash^{0}$	Variation unit number zero is reserved for the discussion about whether or not a relatively large unit of text is to be included in the Q text. When the reason for including variation unit number zero is significant dissimilarity between Matthew and Luke, slashes are used to indicate the extent of the material being discussed. When the reason for including variation unit number zero is Markan overlap, Matthean Sondergut, or Lukan Sondergut, then braces, parentheses, or square brackets, respectively, are used to indicate the extent of the material being discussed.
⟦ ⟧	Double brackets are used in the reconstructed Q text to enclose reconstructions that are uncertain (i.e., {C} grades).
	Double brackets enclose verse references when the whole verse or unit is graded {C}.
	Issues of order are excepted from using double brackets, i.e., ⟦S⟧, ⟦l⟧, or ⟦Sl⟧ does not occur.
[ ] ( )	When square brackets or parentheses enclose text that has no parallel in the other Gospel, empty brackets and parentheses (with space between them) are used at the equivalent position in the other Gospel to indicate the location of the difference between the texts.
[] ()	When it has been decided with a grade of {A} or {B} that the words in question do not belong in Q, the brackets or the parentheses are retained in the reconstructed Q text, but the space between them is removed, thus marking the place in Q where the relevant note occurs, while indicating that no text is assumed to occur here.
⟦[]⟧ ⟦()⟧	When it has been decided with a grade of {C} that the words in question do not belong in Q, the brackets or the parentheses are retained in the reconstructed Q text, the space between them is removed, and double brackets are placed around the brackets or parentheses: ⟦()⟧ or ⟦[]⟧.
[ ] ( )	When there is text only in Matthew or only in Luke: If it is still undecided, {U}, whether the text is in Q, or decided pro *or* con with a grade no higher than {D}, the space is retained, since no strong opinion for eliminating a reading has been established.

[()]   When there is diverging text both in Matthew and in Luke: If it is
[[()]]   decided that neither the text of Matthew nor of Luke was in Q, the
[( )]   space is removed: [()] for a grade of {A} or {B}, [[()]] for a grade of
              {C}. But when it is decided with a grade of {D} or it is left unde-
              cided, {U}, that neither the text of Matthew nor of Luke was in Q,
              the space is retained, since no strong opinion for eliminating a
              reading has been established: [( )].

Q 7:1,2,3   If it has been decided that a verse or unit is not in Q, the numera-
              tion is marked through (i.e., Q 7:1, 2̶, 3 means that Luke 7:2 is not
              in Q, but Luke 7:1, 3 par. is).

⟨ ⟩   The text is an emendation found as such neither in Matthew nor in
              Luke.

« »   When double pointed brackets are used in the translations, they
              indicate a gist or a train of thought, or the most probable terms,
              though the Greek text could not be reconstructed.

..   In the unformatted text of Q, and in translations of Q, two dots
              indicate that the probability of some text being in Q is graded as
              {D}, or is left undecided.

Die im griechischen Text verwendeten Siglen

[αβγ]   Eckige Klammern im Text von Lukas und Q umschließen Worte
              oder Buchstaben, die in Lukas vorhanden sind, aber nicht in Mat-
              thäus.

(αβγ)   Runde Klammern im Text von Matthäus und Q umschließen
              Worte oder Buchstaben, die in Matthäus vorhanden sind, aber
              nicht in Lukas.

ſ ʅ   Die Siglen ſ und ʅ bezeichnen Abweichungen in der Abfolge des
              von Matthäus und Lukas gebotenen Textes. Die relative Position,
              an der ein Evangelist das damit gekennzeichnete Material plaziert
              hat, wird in dem anderen Evangelium durch die Siglen ſ ʅ (ohne
              Text) angezeigt. Die Siglen stehen an beiden Positionen im rekon-
              struierten Q-Text, um so die Alternativen zu verdeutlichen. Steht
              kein Leerzeichen zwischen ſ und ʅ, so bedeutet das, daß diese Posi-
              tion mit einer Wahrscheinlichkeitsgrad von {A} oder {B} zurückge-
              wiesen wurde. Ein Leerzeichen zwischen ſ und ʅ bedeutet, daß
              diese Position mit einer Wahrscheinlichkeitsgrad von {C} oder {D}
              zurückgewiesen wurde oder unentschieden blieb. Wenn keine Ent-
              scheidung möglich ist ({U}), wird als Konvention die lukanischen
              Position gefolgt. Zum Beispiel:

ˢαβγˡ⁵ χψω ˢˡ⁵   bedeutet, daß sich "αβγ" in der Q-Position mit
                     einer Wahrscheinlichkeitsgrad von {A} oder {B}
                     befindet.

ˢαβγˡ⁵ χψω ˢ ˡ⁵   bedeutet, daß sich "αβγ" in der Q-Position mit
                     einer Wahrscheinlichkeitsgrad von {C} oder {D}
                     befindet. Wenn hier die Lukas-Position gedruckt
                     wurde, kann dies auch bedeuten, daß die Positi-
                     onsfrage unentschieden {U} blieb.

1 2 3 …   Kleine, hochgestellte Zahlen bezeichnen die Nummer der Variante
           innerhalb eines Verses. Die Nummern stehen üblicherweise nur
           nach dem schließenden Sigel. Wenn allerdings eine andere Vari-
           ante innerhalb die Positionszeichen ˢ und ˡ fällt, wird die hochge-
           stellte Nummer vor den öffnenden und hinter den schließenden
           Positionszeichen eingefügt. Die Varianten-Zahl der Positionszei-
           chen kann daher kleiner sein als die Zahl der Variante, die inner-
           halb der Positionszeichen steht.

⁰/ … \⁰   Die Varianten-Nummer Null ist für die Diskussion reserviert, ob
           eine relativ große Texteinheit in Q stand oder nicht. Wenn der
           Grund für die Diskussion dieser Variante darin liegt, daß Matthäus
           und Lukas signifikant voneinander abweichen, zeigen die Schräg-
           striche den Umfang des Materials an, das diskutiert wird. Liegt der
           Grund für die Diskussion darin, daß eine Doppelüberlieferung von
           Q und Markus oder matthäisches beziehungsweise lukanisches Son-
           dergut vorliegen, dann zeigen jeweils geschweifte oder runde bezie-
           hungsweise eckige Klammern den Umfang des Materials an, das
           diskutiert wird.

⟦ ⟧   Doppelte eckige Klammern umschließen Q-Texte, die mit schwa-
           cher Wahrscheinlichkeit, d.h. mit Grad {C}, rekonstruiert wurden.
           Doppelte eckige Klammern umschließen Verszahlen, wenn der
           ganze Vers oder die ganze Einheit mit der Wahrscheinlichkeit {C}
           Q zugeordnet wurde.
           Angaben über die Position werden nicht mit doppelten eckigen
           Klammern gekennzeichnet: ⟦ˢ⟧, ⟦ˡ⟧ oder ⟦ˢˡ⟧ kommen also nicht
           vor.

[ ] ( )   Wenn eckige oder runde Klammern Textteile umschließen, die
           keine Parallele in dem anderen Evangelium haben, stehen leere
           eckige beziehungsweise runde Klammern (mit einem Leerzeichen
           dazwischen) an der entsprechenden Stelle im anderen Evangelium,
           um die Position der Abweichung zwischen den Textteilen zu kenn-
           zeichnen.

[] () Wenn mit der Wahrscheinlichkeit {A} oder {B} entschieden wurde, daß die fraglichen Worte nicht zu Q gehören, bleiben die eckigen oder runden Klammern im rekonstruierten Q-Text stehen, aber das Leerzeichen innerhalb der Klammern fällt weg. Damit wird die Position markiert, wo sich die relevante Variante befindet, wobei jedoch angenommen wird, daß hier kein Text in Q stand.

[[]] Wenn mit der Wahrscheinlichkeit {C} entschieden wurde, daß die
[()] fraglichen Worte nicht zu Q gehören, bleiben die eckigen oder runden Klammern im rekonstruierten Q-Text gleichfalls ohne das Leerzeichen stehen, aber doppelte eckige Klammern umschließen die eckigen beziehungsweise runden Klammern: [[]] oder [()].

[ ] ( ) Wenn es nur in Matthäus oder nur in Lukas einen Text gibt und es unentschieden ist, ob der Text in Q stand ({U}), oder falls die Entscheidung pro oder contra nicht mit einer höheren Wahrscheinlichkeit als {D} gefällt wurde, bleibt das Leerzeichen erhalten, da die Argumente nicht stark genug waren, die Lesart Q abzusprechen.

[()] Wenn bei Matthäus und Lukas ein jeweils unterschiedlicher Text
[[()]] steht und entschieden wurde, daß weder der matthäische noch der
[( )] lukanische Text in Q stand, bleiben runde und eckige Klammern im rekonstruierten Q-Text ohne das Leerzeichen stehen: [()] für einen Wahrscheinlichkeitsgrad {A} oder {B}, [[()]] für den Wahrscheinlichkeitsgrad {C}. Wenn allerdings mit dem Wahrscheinlichkeitsgrad {D} entschieden oder mit Unentschieden {U} die Entscheidung offengelassen wurde, ob die matthäische oder die lukanische Textfassung in Q stand, bleibt das Leerzeichen erhalten, da die Argumente nicht stark genug waren, beide Fassungen Q abzusprechen: [( )].

Q 7:1,~~2~~,3 Wurde entschieden, daß ein Vers oder eine Einheit nicht in Q stand, ist die Verszahl durchgestrichen. Q 7:1, ~~2~~, 3 bedeutet zum Beispiel, daß Lk 7:2 nicht in Q stand, im Gegensatz zu Lk 7:1, 3 par.

‹ › Spitze Klammern umschließen einen emendierten Text, der als solcher weder in Matthäus noch in Lukas zu finden ist.

« » Wenn doppelte spitze Klammern in den Übersetzungen gebraucht werden, umschreiben sie das Gemeinte, den Gedankengang oder die wahrscheinlichsten Begriffe, obwohl der griechische Q-Text nicht rekonstruiert werden konnte.

.. In dem unformatierten griechischen Q-Text und in Übersetzungen des Q-Textes bedeuten zwei Punkte, daß ein Text mit der Wahrscheinlichkeit {D} in Q stand oder daß es unentschieden blieb ({U}), ob ein Text in Q stand.

Sigles utilisés dans le texte grec

[αβγ]   Les crochets droits dans le texte de Luc et de Q encadrent des mots ou des lettres trouvés dans Luc, mais pas dans Matthieu.

(αβγ)   Les parenthèses dans le texte de Matthieu et de Q encadrent des mots ou des lettres trouvés dans Matthieu, mais pas dans Luc.

ᔕ ᔕ   Les sigles ᔕ et ᔕ signalent des divergences dans l'ordre du matériel commun à Matthieu et à Luc. La position relative dans laquelle un évangéliste a placé le matériel signalé est indiquée dans l'autre évangile par les sigles ᔕ ᔕ, sans texte à l'intérieur. Ces sigles sont reproduits aux deux endroits dans le texte reconstitué de Q, de manière à indiquer quelle est l'autre possibilité. L'absence d'espace entre ᔕ et ᔕ signifie qu'il s'agit de la position rejetée avec un degré de probabilité {A} ou {B}. Une espace entre ᔕ et ᔕ signifie qu'il s'agit de la position rejetée avec un degré de certitude {C} ou {D}, ou que le cas ne peut pas être tranché {U} (dans ce cas, on trouve, par défaut, la position de Luc). Par exemple,

     ᔕαβγᔕ⁵ χψω ᔕᔕ⁵   signifie que "αβγ" est à cette place dans Q avec un degré de probabilité {A} ou {B};

     ᔕαβγᔕ⁵ χψω ᔕ ᔕ⁵   signifie que "αβγ" est à cette place dans Q avec un degré de probabilité {C} ou {D} ou que le problème ne peut pas être tranché {U}, auquel cas, c'est la place occupée dans Luc qui est reprise.

1 2 3...   Les chiffres de petite taille en exposant, qui suivent le sigle de fermeture, sont utilisés pour numéroter les lieux variants à l'intérieur d'un verset. Ces chiffres sont normalement insérés seulement après le sigle de fermeture. Cependant, lorsqu'un nouveau lieu variant se trouve à l'intérieur d'un passage marqué par ᔕ et ᔕ, le chiffre précède le sigle d'ouverture et suit le sigle de fermeture, de manière à ce que la numérotation du passage signalé par ᔕ et ᔕ puisse utiliser un chiffre plus petit que celui du lieu variant qui s'y trouve inséré.

⁰/... \⁰   Le lieu variant zéro est réservé à la discussion de la présence dans Q d'une portion relativement large de texte. Lorsque la raison pour inclure un lieu variant zéro provient d'une dissemblance entre Matthieu et Luc, des barres obliques sont utilisées pour délimiter le matériel en discussion. Lorsque la raison pour inclure un lieu variant zéro est un recoupement avec Marc ou avec du bien propre de Matthieu ou du bien propre de Luc, on utilise alors respectivement des accolades, des parenthèses et des crochets droits pour délimiter le matériel en discussion.

⟦ ⟧   Les doubles crochets droits sont utilisés dans la reconstitution du texte de Q pour encadrer des restitutions incertaines (par exemple de degré de probabilité {C}).

Les doubles crochets droits encadrent un verset, lorsque tout le verset ou l'unité est marqué du degré de probabilité {C}.

Pour les problèmes relatifs à l'ordre, le double crochet droit n'est pas utilisé; par exemple ⟦ʃ⟧, ⟦ᒿ⟧ ou ⟦ʃᒿ⟧ n'apparait pas.

[ ] ( )   Lorsque les crochets droits ou les parenthèses encadrent un texte qui n'a pas de parallèle dans l'autre évangile, des crochets droits ou des parenthèses vides (avec seulement une espace entre eux) sont néanmoins reproduits dans l'autre évangile, à l'endroit correspondant, pour indiquer la localisation de la différence entre les textes.

[] ()   Lorsqu'il a été décidé avec un degré de probabilité {A} ou {B} que les mots en question n'appartenaient pas à Q, les crochets droits ou les parenthèses sont maintenus dans le texte reconstitué de Q, mais l'espace entre eux est supprimée. Ainsi se trouve indiqué l'endroit dans Q où la note correspondante apparaît, quand bien même on suppose l'absence de texte à cet endroit.

⟦[]⟧   Lorsqu'il a été décidé avec un degré de probabilité {C} que les mots
⟦()⟧   en question n'appartenaient pas à Q, les crochets droits ou les parenthèses sont maintenus dans le texte reconstitué de Q, mais l'espace entre eux est supprimée et des doubles crochets droits sont placés de part et d'autre des crochets droits ou des parenthèses: ⟦()⟧ ou ⟦[]⟧.

[ ] ( )   Si le texte ne se trouve que dans Matthieu ou que dans Luc, et qu'il n'y a pas de décision quant à la présence ou non de ce texte dans Q {U}, ou s'il y a une décision pour, mais avec un degré de probabilité non supérieur à {D}, l'espace est maintenue, tant qu'aucune opinion déterminante pour l'élimination de la leçon n'a été établie.

[()]   S'il y a divergence par rapport à Q tant du texte de Matthieu que
⟦[()]⟧   de celui de Luc, et qu'il est décidé que ni le texte de Matthieu ni
[( )]   celui de Luc ne figurent dans Q, l'espace est supprimée: [()] pour un degré de probabilité {A} ou {B}, ⟦[()]⟧ pour un degré de probabilité {C}. Mais s'il est décidé avec un degré de probabilité {D}, ou simplement pas décidé {U}, que ni le texte de Matthieu ni le texte de Luc ne figurent dans Q, l'espace est maintenue, tant qu'aucune opinion déterminante pour l'élimination de la leçon n'a été établie: [( )].

Q 7:1,2̶,3   S'il a été décidé qu'un verset ou qu'une unité n'était pas dans Q, le numéro est inscrit en caractères barrés (par exemple, Q 7:1,2̶,3 signifie que Luc 7:2 n'est pas dans Q, mais que Luc 7:1, 3 par. l'est).

‹ ›   Le texte est une conjecture et ne se trouve comme tel ni dans Mat-
            thieu ni dans Luc.

« »   Lorsque des guillemets sont utilisés dans les traductions, ils indi-
            quent un contenu possible ou un enchaînement d'idées ou le terme
            le plus probable, bien que le texte grec ne puisse être reconstitué.

..   Dans le texte non mis en forme de Q et dans les traductions de Q,
            deux points de suite indiquent que la probabilité du texte se trou-
            vant dans Q est marquée du degré de probabilité {D} ou demeure
            non décidée {U}.

Other Sigla and Abbreviations

BDF = Blass, F., A. Debrunner, and R.W. Funk (ed. and trans.)—see Bibliography

BDR = Blass, F., A. Debrunner, and F. Rehkopf (ed.)—see Bibliography

ET = English Translation

FT = French Translation

GT = German Translation

IQP = International Q Project

KG = Kühner, R. and B. Gerth—see Bibliography

LSJ = Liddell-Scott-Jones—see Bibliography

R or ^{R} = Redactor (also MattR and LukeR)

Red = Redaktion = Redaction

red = redaktionell = redactional

sek = sekundär = secondary (usually implying a redacted text)

Sg = Sondergut = special source material (of Luke or Matthew, not derived from Mark or Q)

Trad = Tradition

trad = traditionell = traditional

Bussmann 1925, 1929
   L = Luke
   R = Redenquelle = speech source (i.e., Q)

Dauer 1984
   (a.)u.St. = (an) unsere(r) Stelle = (at) our position/location (in the gospel text)

Easton 1926
   L = Lukan special source = Sondergut

Gagnon 1993
   The following is copied verbatim from Gagnon, pp. 714-715, but without italics for the bracketed letters. Brackets are the author's.
   "1. [M] and [L] = definite redaction by Matthew or Luke, respectively, of a Marcan source (an 'A' rating). This category primarily applies to a word in Matthew or Luke which appears in a *verse* paralleled in Mark but without occurrence of the identical word in the Marcan parallel. Such words can be safely regarded as the evangelist's own additions to the text of Mark.

2. [M?] and [L?] = likely Matthean or Lucan redaction of a Marcan source ('B' rating). These sigla primarily refer to a word which appears in a Matthean or Lucan *pericope* which, as a pericope, has at least a partial Marcan or Q parallel but for which there is no parallel verse and no parallel word. Such words lie in the gray area between so-called special material (i.e., whole pericopes peculiar to a given Gospel) and relatively clear additions to Mark.

3. [MQ] and [LQ] = likely Matthean or Lucan redactions to Q material (a 'B-' to 'C+' rating). Primarily included under this heading is any word which occurs only in Matthew or only in Luke within a pericope which has a parallel in that other Gospel (and not in Mark) but which is probably to be attributed to the evangelist's redaction. ...

4. [S] = words found in so-called special material (a 'C' rating), without prejudging whether the particular word used was traditional or due to the evangelist's redaction. The symbol simply denotes that the word or phrase appears *in a pericope* that lacks any parallel material in the other Gospels for any substantial portion of that pericope. Where further clarification is necessary, [MS] and [LS] will be employed to make explicit the Gospel to which the special material belongs.

5. [QM] and [QL] = likely Q material (a 'D' rating). These sigla refer to a word which occurs only in Matthew, or only in Luke, within a pericope which has a parallel in the other Gospel of this pair (and not in Mark) and which probably belongs to their shared source.

6. [Q] = definite derivation from Q (an 'E' rating). Such a word appears in both Matthew and Luke (but not in Mark) in a Q pericope, at roughly the same point in the text and in roughly the same context.

7. [Mk] = definite derivation from Mark (an 'E' rating). ...

30/5/25 + 3 = 30 times in Matthew, 5 times in Mark, 25 times in Luke, and 3 times in Acts; an additional indication of 2 occurrences in John would produce the series 30/5/25 + 3/2."

Gnilka 1986
  E = the Evangelist (Matthew)

Haupt 1913
  Q^3 = ethische Didascalia, Gemeindelehre = ethical instruction, community teaching

Hirsch 1941
  Lu I = die leicht erweiterte Fassung von Q, die Luk unmittelbar vorgelegen hat = the slightly revised and enlarged form of Q from which Luke worked

Lu II = die Sondervorlage des Luk, die bei Matth unbenutzt geblieben ist = Q^{Luke} (a pre-Lukan recension of Q)

Holtzmann 1863

Λ = Urmatthäus = Q

A = Urmarkus

Jeremias 1980

sNT = sonst im NT = elsewhere in the NT

→ 1,63 Red = (1) reference to the Lukan text where fuller treatment of the word or phrase in question is given, and (2) Jeremias' judgment on whether the word or phrase is tradition or redaction.

Parker 1953

K = "*progonos koinos* ('common ancestor')" = a source common to Matthew and Mark. Parker argues that Matthew uses this source, which lies behind Mark but is not Mark itself, along with Q and M.

Schenk 1987

+ x, where x is a number, means that Matthew added the word in question x times to the source.

− y, where y is a number, means that Matthew eliminated the word in question y times from the source.

A–Mt z, where z is a number, indicates Matthean material that has no parallel in the other gospels.

Example: "= (Mk 5 − 2 + 15) + (Q 2 + 6) + (A–Mt 7)."

This means that Matthew took the word over from Mark 5 times, omitted it from Markan material 2 times, and added it to Markan material 15 times; Matthew took the word over from Q twice, and added it to Q material 6 times; Matthew also has the word in 7 other places.

+Q or +Mk means that the text in question comes from either Q or Mark.

Example: "[Matt] 7,28 (+Q); 11,1 (+Q); 13,53 (+Mk); 19,1 (+Mk); 26,1 (+Mk)"

Schniewind 1914

L = Lukan Sondergut

Schulz 1972

fin = *finitum* = adjacent

Schürmann 1969
  S = Sondergut

Simons 1880
  Λ and Q. = Q (Λ = Holtzmann 1863 above; Q. = B. Weiß 1876's Quelle)

Wegner 1985
  The following is taken verbatim from Wegner, pp. ix-x, with an English
  translation in brackets (semicolons are replaced by equal signs).
  "acc   = übernimmt/übernommen von der Mk-Vorlage. [takes/taken
                over from Mark]
  add   = fügt hinzu/hinzugefügt zur Mk-Vorlage. [adds/added to the
                Markan source]
  (a)uSt   = (an) unsere(r) Stelle. [(at) our position]
  Bespr   = Besprechung. [discussion]
  diff   = im Unterschied zu. [differing from, in distinction to]
  Ev(v)   = Evangelium (-ien). [gospel(s)]
  (im) gNT   = (im) gesamten Neuen Testament. [(in the) entire New Testa-
                ment]
  HP   = Die rekonstruierte Fassung der ursprünglichen Hauptmann-
                sperikope. [Wegner's reconstructed version of the original Q
                centurion pericope] …
  Mt; Lk usw. = Die Endredaktoren der entsprechenden Evangelien. [the
                final redactors of the corresponding gospels]
  mt; lk usw. = matthäisch; lukanisch usw. [Matthean; Lukan; etc.]
  MtEv; MkEv usw. = Matthäusevangelium, Markusevangelium usw. [the
                gospels]
  mt (lk) Mk-Stoff = der von dem ersten oder dritten Evangelisten verarbei-
                tete Mk-Stoff. [Markan material that has been incorporated,
                but worked over, by Matthew or Luke] …
  om   = läßt aus/ausgelassen von. [omits/omitted from]
  par   = in Übereinstimmung mit; dasselbe kann aber auch durch
                einen diagonalen Strich (/) bezeichnet werden. [parallel to, in
                agreement with; the same can also be indicated by a slash (/)]
  Q   = Q-Überlieferung: Der Traditionsstoff der mt/lk Doppelüber-
                lieferungen, die entweder im MkEv nicht oder nur in einer
                von dem Mt- und Lk-Text abweichenden Textgestalt zu
                finden ist. [The Q tradition: material of the Matthean/Lukan
                double-tradition, which is not found in Mark or in
                Matthew or Luke alone.] …
  Q 7,28a; 8,5-10.13 = per. aus der Q-Quelle. [Wegner's Q versification] …

QMt (QLk) = Worte, die nur in der Q-Überlieferung des Mt (oder Lk) zu finden sind, trotz Parallelüberlieferung bei Lk (oder Mt). [Words found only in the Q tradition of Matthew (or Luke), in spite of a parallel tradition in Luke (or Matthew).] ...

Rez   = Rezensent bzw. Rezension. [reviewer, etc. review] ...

(im) SNT = (im) sonstigen Neuen Testament. [(in the) rest/remainder of the New Testament]

Sv(v)   = Sondervers(e). [verse(s) from Sondergut]

Stat   = Statistik; stat = statistisch. [statistics; statistical] ...

u.a.   = und andere; unter anderem. [and others; among others]

u.E.   = unseres Erachtens. [in our opinion]

u.M.n.   = unserer Meinung nach; s.M.n. = seiner Meinung nach. [in our/his opinion]

urspr   = ursprünglich. [original]"

Weiß, B. 1901, 1907, 1908
Bem = Bemerke = Remark
L = see J. Weiß 1892 below

Weiß, J. 1892
L = "dem Lk eigenthümliche Ueberlieferung (L)" = "Lukan special tradition"
LQ = a *Vorlage* of Luke in which Q was reworked in the spirit of L and enlarged with material from L

Weiß, J. 1907
S = the special traditions of Luke *or* the Sondergut of Matthew

Wellhausen 1904b
D = Codex Bezae

Q 7:1, 2̶, 3, 4̶-6̶a̶, 6b-9, ?10?
The Centurion's Faith in Jesus' Word

Database Author
Steven R. Johnson

Evaluators
Paul Hoffmann
Steven R. Johnson
John S. Kloppenborg Verbin
James M. Robinson
Saw Lah Shein

Q 7:1

Mark 7:24a	Matt 15:21	Matt 7:28a; 8:5a	Q 7:1
		7:28a [0]/ (Καὶ ἐγένετο ὅτε)[1] ἐ(τέλε)[2]σεν (ὁ Ἰησοῦς)[3] [ ][4] τ(οὺς λόγους τούτους)[4] [ ][5],	[0]/ [[(καὶ ἐγένετο ὅτε)[1]]] ἐ[[[πλήρω][2]]]σεν ( )[3] [][4] τ(οὺς λόγους τούτους)[4] [][5],
		\[0]	\[0]
Ἐκεῖθεν δὲ ἀναστὰς ἀπῆλθεν εἰς τὰ ὅρια Τύρου.	Καὶ ἐξελθὼν ἐκεῖθεν ὁ Ἰησοῦς ἀνεχώρησεν εἰς τὰ μέρη Τύρου καὶ Σιδῶνος.	8:5a Εἰσ(ε)[6]λθ(ό)[6]ν(τος δὲ αὐτοῦ)[6] εἰς Καφαρναούμ.	εἰσ[ῆ][6]λθ[ε][6]ν()[6] εἰς Καφαρναούμ.

IQP 1994: / \[0] in Q {C}.
IQP 1994: [][1] ( )[1] ἐ[[[πλήρω][2]]]σεν; JMR: (καὶ ἐγένετο ὅτε)[1] ἐ(τέλε)[2]σεν.
IQP 1994: ()[3]; JSK: ( )[3] Luke = Q {D}; PH: ( )[3] indeterminate; JMR: [[(ὁ Ἰησοῦς)[3]]].
IQP 1994: τ[[(οὺς λόγους τούτους)[4]]].

[0] Is Luke 7:1a par. Matthew 7:28a in Q?
[1] Luke's ἐπειδή or Matthew's καὶ ἐγένετο ὅτε.
[2] Luke's ἐπλήρωσεν or Matthew's ἐτέλεσεν.
[3] Matthew's ὁ Ἰησοῦς.
[4] Luke's πάντα τὰ ῥήματα αὐτοῦ or Matthew's τοὺς λόγους τούτους.
[5] Luke's εἰς τὰς ἀκοὰς τοῦ λαοῦ.
[6] Luke's εἰσῆλθεν or Matthew's εἰσελθόντος δὲ αὐτοῦ (See also Mark 1:21a parr.).

Q 7:1

Luke 7:1	Lukan Doublet	Mark 2:1a	John 4:46b
⁰/			
[᾿Επειδὴ]¹			
ἐ[πλήρω]²σεν			
⟨ ⟩³			
⟦πάντα]⁴			
τ[ὰ ῥήματα			
αὐτοῦ]⁴			
[εἰς τὰς ἀκοὰς			
τοῦ λαοῦ]⁵,			
\⁰			
εἰσ[ῆ]⁶λθ[ε]⁶ν( )⁶		καὶ εἰσελθὼν	καὶ ἦν τις βασιλικὸς
		πάλιν	οὗ ὁ υἱὸς ἠσθένει
εἰς Καφαρναούμ.		εἰς Καφαρναοὺμ	ἐν Καφαρναούμ.

Q 7:1[0]: Is Luke 7:1a par. Matthew 7:28a in Q?

In Q

B. Weiß 1876, 224: "(V. 28.) Die Schilderung des Eindrucks dieser Rede wird mit einer abschließenden Formel eingeleitet, welche, da dieselbe Luc. 7,1 offenbar wörtlich umschrieben wird, bereits in der apostolischen Quelle gestanden haben muß."

J. Weiß 1892, 398-399[2]: "Denn [Lk 7,1] ist ja zweifellos eine Übersetzungsvariante zu [399] Mt 7,28."

B. Weiß 1898, 164: "Die Umschreibung dieser Übergangsformel [Matt 7:28a] in Lk 7:1 deutet darauf hin, daß dieselbe aus der Quelle stammt."

Hawkins 1899, 165: "As to whether that formula which we seem to discern in those five verses of Matthew [7:28; 11:1; 13:53; 19:1; 26:1] was due to an editor of the Gospel who himself made these compilations, or whether he brought it in from the Logia with some collections which already existed there, it is difficult to form an opinion. Two points may be noted in favour of the latter alternative: (1) Lk vii. 1 ἐπειδὴ ἐπλήρωσεν πάντα τὰ ῥήματα αὐτοῦ is so closely parallel in substance, though not in words, to Mt vii. 28 καὶ ἐγένετο ὅτε ἐτέλεσεν ὁ Ἰησοῦς τοὺς λόγους τούτους as to suggest a common origin for them both; and (2) there is nothing distinctively Matthaean in the wording of the formula: on the contrary, ἐγένετο, followed by a finite verb, is only found in these 5 places in Matthew, while it occurs 22 times in Luke (also twice in Mark and nowhere else in N.T.)."

B. Weiß 1901, 382: "Dieser Übergang ist nur eine in luk. Stil übersetzte Wiedergabe des Abschlusses der Bergrede in Mt 7:28 und zeigt, daß diese Übergangsformel aus Q herrührt."

von Harnack 1907, 54: "Sehr wichtig ist, daß Matth. 7,28 und 8,5 bei Luk. 7,1 eine Parallele haben; denn daraus folgt mit Sicherheit, daß auch in Q große Teile der Bergpredigt zusammengestanden haben und daß darauf die Heilungsgeschichte in Kapernaum folgte. Aber die Form der Aussage haben beide geändert. ... Also muß man leider darauf verzichten, hier den ursprünglichen Wortlaut vor den Worten εἰσῆλθεν εἰς Καφαρναούμ herzustellen."

von Harnack 1907, ET 1908, 74: "It is a most important point that St. Matt. vii. 28 and viii. 5 have a parallel in St. Luke vii. 1; for from this it follows with certainty that even in Q large portions of the Sermon on the Mount occurred together, and that the Sermon was followed by the Cure of the Centurion's Servant in Capernaum. But both evangelists have altered the wording here. ... There seems, therefore, no hope of recovering the original wording of the source before the words εἰσῆλθεν εἰς Καφαρναούμ."

Loisy 1907, 645: "Il semble que les deux évangélistes ont lu tous deux une formule de transition qui reliait le discours à un récit; et ce récit devait être l'histoire du centurion de Capharnaüm."

B. Weiß 1907, 242: "Genau dasselbe Quellenverhältnis zeigt der Eingang der Geschichte vom Hauptmann zu Kapharnaum, die doch Lukas nach der wörtlichen Übereinstimmung von 7,6-9 mit Mt. 8,8-10 sicher aus Q entnahm."

J. Weiß 1907, 300: "'Als Jesus diese Worte vollendet hatte', so schließen bei Matthäus (vgl. auch Lk. 7,1) viele Reden Jesu; es war dies wohl eine Schlußformel in Q."

B. Weiß 1908, 14²²: "Daß diese Übergangsformel dem Matth. eigentümlich (Harnack [1907] 54 [ET 74]), läßt sich durchaus nicht erweisen, da sie den noch erkennbaren Abschnitten seines Evangeliums durchaus nicht entspricht, und überall (11,1. 13,53. 19,1. 26,1) nur nach größeren Redestücken vorkommt, die nachweislich in Q standen, also ebensogut in Q selbst von diesen zu den eingeschalteten Erzählungsstücken übergeleitet haben kann (bem. das ὅτε, das außer dieser Formel noch 9,25. 12,3. 13,26.48. 21,34. Lk. 17,22. 22,35 nachweislich in Q vorkommt und nur Mt. 21,1. 27,31 von der Hand des Evangelisten nach Mrk., und zu dem τελεῖν Lk. 22,37."

14-16: Reconstruction: "Καὶ ἐγένετο ὅτε ἐτέλεσεν ὁ Ἰησοῦς τοὺς λόγους τούτους, κατέβη ἀπὸ τοῦ ὄρους. ... [15] καὶ εἰσῆλθεν εἰς Καφαρναούμ. καὶ ἑκατόνταρχος παρεκάλει αὐτὸν λέγων· κύριε, ὁ παῖς μου βέβληται ἐν τῇ οἰκίᾳ παραλυτικός, δεινῶς βασανιζόμενος. καὶ λέγει αὐτῷ· ἐγὼ ἐλθὼν θεραπεύσω αὐτόν. καὶ ὁ ἑκατόνταρχος εἶπεν· κύριε, οὐκ εἰμὶ ἱκανὸς ἵνα μου ὑπὸ τὴν στέγην εἰσέλθῃς· ἀλλὰ εἰπὲ λόγῳ καὶ ἰαθήσεται ὁ παῖς μου· καὶ γὰρ ἐγὼ ἄνθρωπός εἰμι ὑπὸ ἐξουσίαν, ἔχων ὑπ' ἐμαυτὸν στρατιώτας, καὶ λέγω τούτῳ· πορεύθητι, καὶ πορεύεται, καὶ ἄλλῳ· ἔρχου, καὶ ἔρχεται, καὶ τῷ δούλῳ μου· ποίησον τοῦτο, καὶ ποιεῖ. ἀκούσας δὲ ὁ Ἰησοῦς ἐθαύμασεν καὶ τῷ ἀκολουθοῦντι αὐτῷ ὄχλῳ εἶπεν· λέγω ὑμῖν, οὐδὲ ἐν τῷ Ἰσραὴλ τοσαύτην πίστιν [16] εὗρον· καὶ εἶπεν ὁ Ἰησοῦς τῷ ἑκατοντάρχῃ· ὕπαγε, ὡς ἐπίστευσας γενηθήτω σοι. καὶ ἰάθη ὁ παῖς ἐν τῇ ὥρᾳ ἐκείνῃ."

Wendling 1908, 106: "Es ist zuzugeben, daß diese Formeln auf Q [Mt 5,1f.//Lc 6,20; Mt 7,28//Lc 7,1] zurückgehen können, wenn nämlich die λόγοι Ἰησοῦ dort schon irgend eine biographische Einrahmung gehabt haben. Ebenso gut ist es aber denkbar, daß Lc hier den Mt variiert. Durch folgende Erwägung scheint mir diese Möglichkeit zur Wahrscheinlichkeit zu werden."

Bartlett 1911, 328: "[The Q Sermon's] epilogue in Lk vii. 1, 'As soon as he fulfilled all his words into the ears of the people, he entered into Capernaum,' agrees in substance with the epilogue in Mt vii. 28a, along with the opening clause of viii. 5. These probably stood together in Matthew's Q, but were separated to admit matter found in Mk i. 22, 40-4."

Streeter 1911, 148: "It is noticeable also that after each of Matthew's five blocks of discourse occurs a slightly varying formula καὶ ἐγένετο ὅτε ἐτέλεσεν ὁ Ἰησοῦς (Mt vii. 28; xi. 1; xiii. 53; xix. 1; xxvi. 1),—a formula indicating, be it noted, the *resumption* of a narrative, and therefore due to the editor, though the *first* instance of it, which perhaps suggested to him the others, may have occurred in his source Q, connecting the Great Sermon with the *narrative* of the healing of the Centurion's Servant (cf. Mt vii. 28 = Lk vii. 1)."

Castor 1912, 28-29: "The common beginning and ending [to the Q Sermon] which we have found is a strong indication that some source, containing not mere fragmentary sayings but a real discourse, stood back of both the accounts, Matthew's and Luke's. This is confirmed by the relation of the whole discourse to the following narrative of the centurion's servant. The connection is not easily accounted for in any other [29] way. Luke 7:1 combines Matt. 7:28 and 8:5; and the cleansing of the leper, Matt. 8:1-4, is generally recognized as an insertion of Matthew from Mark. In this account of the centurion's servant, so closely connected in both Gospels with the preceding sermon, literary evidence again demonstrates the presence of a common source."

40: "It has already been pointed out that Luke's introduction here, 7:1, combines Matthew's conclusion to the Sermon on the Mount with his introduction to this incident, and that therefore the account of the centurion stood in this same connection in Q."

222-224: English reconstruction: "And it came to pass, when he finished his words, he went to Capernaum. [223] ...

"Matt. 8:5-10, 13; Luke 7:1-10.—A certain centurion's servant was sick. (When he heard concerning Jesus, he sent to him elders of the Jews, asking him to come and save his servant. They came to Jesus and besought him, saying, He is worthy that thou shouldest do this for him; for he loves our nation and he built the synagogue for us. And Jesus went with them. And then, when he was not far from the house, the centurion sent friends,) saying, Lord, I am not worthy that thou shouldest come under my roof; but only say the word and my servant shall be healed. For I myself am a man under authority with soldiers under me; and I say to this one, Go, and he goes; [224] and to another, Come, and he comes; and to my servant, Do this, and he does it. When Jesus heard, he marvelled, and said to those who followed, Verily, I say to you, I have not found so great faith, no, not in Israel. And they who were sent, returning to the house, found the servant whole."

McNeile 1915, 99: "The phrase is somewhat similar in Lk. vii. 1a, and may have been suggested here by Q."

Klostermann 1919, 448: "Diese Überleitung entspricht Mt 7,28a καὶ ἐγένετο ὅτε ἐτέλεσεν ὁ Ἰησοῦς τοὺς λόγους τούτους + Mt 8,5 εἰσελθόντος δὲ αὐτοῦ εἰς Καφαρναούμ."

Loisy 1924, 214: "La transition qui, dans la source commune, rattachait au discours l'histoire du centurion de Capharnaüm a été mieux gardée dans Luc que dans Matthieu."

Streeter 1924, 262: "It is just possible that Matthew may have found the formula ["It came to pass when Jesus had finished these sayings that ..."] in Q, for a phrase rather like it occurs after Luke's Sermon on the Plain in a context parallel to the occurrence of the formula in Matthew after the Sermon on the Mount (Lk. vii. 1 = Mt. vii. 28). But, if it stood in Luke's copy of Q, there also it would have done so as a formula of transition from discourse to narrative; for in Luke it occurs between the Great Sermon and the story of the Centurion's Servant. It would seem likely, then, that Matthew found the formula in Q, and thought it a convenient one to repeat whenever he had occasion to mark a similar transition from a long discourse to narrative."

Marriott 1925, 50: "Lk. 7:1 is substantially, though not verbally, parallel to Mt. 7:28a, and very possibly comes from the connecting link in Q between the Sermon and the healing of the centurion's servant."

Easton 1926, 94: "(1) Cf. Mt 7:28; 8:5a. A Q transition verse, into which Mt has inserted (7:29-8:4) Mk 1:22, 40-45."

Crum 1927, 138: Crum places Matt 7:28a, 8:5 with Luke 7:1, but does not attempt to reconstruct the original transitional phrase.

von Dobschütz 1928, 341: "Bei Matthäus findet sich bekanntlich an 5 Stellen die Formel: 'und es geschah, nachdem Jesus diese Worte vollendet hatte', Kap 7,28; 11,1; 13,53; 19,1; 26,1. Matthäus bezeichnet damit deutlich den Abschluß seiner 5 großen Redegruppen. Man hat nun geglaubt, diese 5 Stellen schon seiner Quelle, den Logien, zuweisen zu können, die danach fünfteilig gewesen wären, und man hat damit in Verbindung gebracht, daß des Papias bekanntes Werk 'Auslegung der Herrenworte' in 5 Bücher zerfiel. Dabei ist wieder übersehen, daß Matthäus die Formel zu wiederholen liebt. An der einen Stelle der ersten, war sie ihm in der Tat durch seine Quelle geboten. Das zeigt der Vergleich von Mt 7,28 mit Lc 7,1. An keiner der anderen Stellen bietet Lukas eine solche Parallele zu der Formel bei Matthäus."

Bussmann 1929, 56: "Vielleicht hat also eine ganz kurze Notiz vor εἰσῆλθεν εἰς Καφαρναούμ über das Ende der Rede in R gestanden; wie sie aber gelautet hat, ist unmöglich zu bestimmen."

Klostermann 1929, 85-86: "Diese Ueberleitung entspricht [86] z. T. dem Abschluß der Rede in Q, vgl. Mt 7,28a καὶ ἐγένετο ὅτε ἐτέλεσεν ὁ Ἰησοῦς τοὺς λόγους τούτους, z. T. Mt 8,5 εἰσελθόντος δὲ αὐτοῦ εἰς Καφαρναούμ."

Schmid 1930, 251: "Nun gesteht auch Simons [1880, 42] wenigstens die Möglichkeit zu, daß das Zusammentreffen der beiden Evangelisten auch auf eine gemeinsame Quelle zurückgeführt werden kann, in welcher die Hauptmannsperikope unmittelbar auf die Bergpredigt folgte. Und diese Möglichkeit wird zur Wahrscheinlichkeit durch den Umstand, daß Lk hier und nur hier mit Mt die fast stereotype Wendung gebraucht, die der erste Evangelist auch bei vier weiteren Redeabschnitten als Übergangsformel von der Rede zur Erzählung anbringt. Es ist eine naheliegende Vermutung, die jedenfalls nicht als unhaltbar erklärt werden kann, daß diese formelhafte Wendung hier schon in der Quelle stand, von Mt aber selbständig am Schluß der vier weiteren Reden wiederholt wurde."

Bultmann 1931, 361-362: "Der Abschluß der Feldrede 7,1 [362] ist wohl nach Q gebildet: ἐπειδὴ ἐπλήρωσεν πάντα τὰ ῥήματα αὐτοῦ εἰς τὰς ἀκοὰς τοῦ λαοῦ ... (vgl. Mt 7,28)."

Bultmann 1931, ET 1968, 337: "The conclusion to the Sermon on the Plain is in all probability modeled on Q: ἐπειδὴ ἐπλήρωσεν πάντα τὰ ῥήματα αὐτοῦ εἰς τὰς ἀκοὰς τοῦ λαοῦ ... (cp. Matt. 7:28)."

Grundmann 1961, 155: "Sowohl die Übereinstimmung sowie die Aufeinanderfolge von Bergpredigt und Centurio bei beiden—vgl. Einleitung Luk. 7,1 mit Matth. 7,28a und 8,5—weist darauf hin, daß wir es bei diesem Bericht mit einer dritten Q-Folge zu tun haben."

Schürmann 1969, 391: "V 1a bringt Luk die gleiche Überleitungswendung nach der Predigt am Berge wie Mt 7,28a, was für eine gemeinsame Vorlage mit gleicher Akoluthie spricht."

Morganthaler 1971, 304: "Wenn Lk die Bergpredigt schließt mit den Worten: ἐπειδὴ ἐπλήρωσεν πάντα τὰ ῥήματα αὐτοῦ εἰς τὰς ἀκοὰς τοῦ λαοῦ, so ist dies zwar nicht wörtlich aber sachlich identisch mit Mt 7,28: καὶ ἐγένετο ὅτε ἐτέλεσεν ὁ Ἰησοῦς τοὺς λόγους τούτους. Die Mt-Formulierung wollte er vielleicht gerade deshalb nicht übernehmen, weil sie eine der bekanntesten Formeln ist, die Lk als reinen Mt-Rahmen nie übernommen hat; er wollte sie möglicherweise auch deshalb nicht übernehmen, weil sie hier bei Mt nur Einleitung zu dem verschobenen Mk-Text Mk 1,21f ist, den er Lk 4,31f in der genauen Mk-Taxis bereits so wiedergegeben hat (mitsamt der Ortsangabe εἰς Καφαρναούμ). Es ist sehr wohl möglich, daß Lk 7,1 Q-Stoff ist."

Schramm 1971, 41[1]: "Vgl. nur noch 7,1—durch Mt 7,28a als Traditionselement erwiesen."

Schulz 1972, 236: "Mt 8,5/Lk 7,1b zeigen Übereinstimmungen bei beiden Evangelisten: εἰσελθεῖν, Καφαρναούμ, ἑκατόνταρχος (bei Lk V 2)."

Schweizer 1973, 123: "Die Formel in V. 28a ist wohl im Anschluß an eine schon in Q vorliegende Wendung (Lk. 7,1) gebildet."

Schweizer 1973, ET 1975, 192: "The formula in verse 28a is probably patterned after a phrase that was already present in Q (Luke 7:1)."

Pesch and Kratz 1976, 77: "Ursprünglich an die Bergpredigt anschließend (so auch noch im lukanischen Zusammenhang, vgl. Lk 7,1) ist sie von Mattäus in den Wunderzyklus eingeordnet worden."

80: "Die Erzählung vom Hauptmann von Kafarnaum folgte in der Logienquelle, wie Lk 7,1 = Mt 7,28a verrät, auf die Bergpredigt. Sie ist in Kafarnaum
lokalisiert (Lk 7,1 = Mt 8,5)."

Polag 1977, 17: "Wegen der Schlußwendung zur Bergrede, die unmittelbar
zur Hauptmannsperikope überleitet (Lk 7,1a par Mt), kann vermutet werden,
daß überhaupt Rahmenelemente mit Überleitungscharakter auf die späte
Redaktion zurückgehen. Es gibt auch Anzeichen, daß die Einleitungswendun-
gen in der ganzen Sammlung überarbeitet worden sind."

Marshall 1978, 279: "The opening verse [Luke 7:1] forms a transition
from the Sermon; its closeness in form to Mt. 7:28a; 8:5a, shows that it has
been taken from a common source, but each Evangelist has modified it in his
own way."

Muhlack 1979, 41: "Lukas' Rückverweis auf die Feldrede (Lk 7,1) stimmt
inhaltlich mit dem letzten Abschnitt der Bergpredigt überein (Mt 7,28.29).
Da jedoch in seinem Evangelium der Bericht von der Heilung eines Lepra-
kranken (Mt 8,1-4) ihre letzten Sätze von dem Bericht über den Hauptmann
von Kapernaum trennt, folgen beide Perikopen noch unverbunden aufeinan-
der."

Polag 1979, 38: Brackets indicate text that Polag includes in Q with a
degree of confidence ("vermutlich") that is less than probability ("wahrscheinlich") and greater than mere possibility ("möglich"). The vertical line indicates
substantial Lukan material not in Q.

Mt		Lk
7,28	Καὶ ἐγένετο ὅτε ἐτέλεσεν ὁ Ἰησοῦς τοὺς λόγους τούτους,	7,1
8,5a	εἰσῆλθεν εἰς Καφαρναούμ.	
8,5b.6	Ἑκατοντάρχης δὲ [παρεκάλεσεν αὐτὸν | λέγων· κύριε, ὁ παῖς μου βέβληται ἐν τῇ οἰκίᾳ παραλυτικὸς δεινῶς βασανιζόμενος.	7,2-6a
8,7	καὶ λέγει αὐτῷ· ἐγὼ ἐλθὼν θεραπεύσω αὐτόν.	
8,8	καὶ ἀποκριθεὶς ὁ ἑκατοντάρχης ἔφη·] κύριε, οὐκ εἰμὶ ἱκανός, ἵνα ὑπὸ τὴν στέγην μου εἰσέλθῃς· ἀλλὰ εἰπὲ λόγῳ καὶ ἰαθήσεται ὁ παῖς μου·	7,6b
		7,7
8,9	καὶ γὰρ ἐγὼ ἄνθρωπός εἰμι ὑπὸ ἐξουσίαν, ἔχων ὑπ' ἐμαυτὸν στρατιώτας, καὶ λέγω τούτῳ· πορεύθητι, καὶ πορεύεται, καὶ ἄλλῳ· ἔρχου, καὶ ἔρχεται, καὶ τῷ δούλῳ μου· ποίησον τοῦτο, καὶ ποιεῖ.	7,8
8,10	ἀκούσας δὲ ὁ Ἰησοῦς ἐθαύμασεν καὶ εἶπεν τοῖς ἀκολουθοῦσιν·	7,9

[ἀμὴν] λέγω ὑμῖν·
οὐδὲ ἐν τῷ Ἰσραὴλ τοσαύτην πίστιν εὗρον.

8,13   [καὶ ἰάθη ὁ παῖς αὐτοῦ ἐν τῇ ὥρᾳ ἐκείνῃ.]   7,10.''

Schmithals 1980, 90: "In Mat. 7,28/Luk. 7,1a hat sich auch der Übergang von Rede zu Erzählung, wie er sich in Q fand, erhalten."

Schenk 1981, 37: German reconstruction:
"Q:

> Nachdem Jesus seine ganze Grundsatzrede beendet hatte,
>> ging er nach Kafarnaum hinein.
> Da bat ihn ein nichtjüdischer Befehlshaber einer Hundertschaft
>> um Hilfe: 'Mein Sklave liegt gelähmt in meinem Haus.'
> Jesus sagte zu ihm:
>> 'Ich werde kommen, um ihn zu heilen.'
> Doch der Befehlshaber erwiderte:
>> 'Herr, ich habe kein Recht darauf,
>> daß du in mein Haus kommst.
>> Doch wenn du ein Machtwort sprichst,
>> dann wird mein Sklave geheilt werden.
>> Denn das ist ja bei mir gegenüber den Soldaten,
>> die ich unter mir habe, genauso, obwohl ich doch—
>> im Gegensatz zu dir—nur unter fremdem Befehl stehe:
>> Befehle ich einem: "Geh!"—dann geht er,
>> und einem anderen: "Komm!"—dann kommt er,
>> und meinem Sklaven: "Tu das!"—dann tut er's.'
> Als Jesus das hörte, staunte er und sagte zu denen,
>> die schon in seiner Nachfolge waren:
>> 'Ich versichere euch:
>> Nicht einmal in Israel habe ich so großes Zutrauen gefunden.'
> Und zu dem Befehlshaber sagte Jesus: 'Geh!'
> Und sein Sklave wurde geheilt."

Denaux 1982, 315: "Q: Mt 7,28a—Lk 7,1a."

Guelich 1982, 414: "Matthew redactionally concludes the Sermon with a brief summary composed of two elements drawn from two separate sources. First, he used, 'When Jesus finished these words,' a statement occurring at the end of all five of his discourse sections. ... The roots of this summary may well stem from the Q tradition underlying the Sermon's conclusion now found in Luke 7:1, 'When Jesus completed all his sayings,' which Matthew then reworked into his own formula."

416: "Luke 7:1 has a content parallel [to Matt 7:28a] in better Greek style (Ἐπειδὴ ἐπλήρωσεν). The presence of this conclusion in Luke 7:1 and the following Lucan pericope of the Centurion in 7:2-10, par. Matt 8:5-13, strongly suggest that a similar conclusion had terminated the Q Sermon. ... Matthew may well reflect the earlier form of the conclusion which Luke has stylistically improved."

Gundry 1982, 136: "At first, Luke 7:1a provides a parallel: 'when he completed all his words in the hearing of the people.' Matthew rewords the statement. He draws καὶ ἐγένετο, a Semitism occurring in Matthew only in these concluding formulas, from the last clause in the tradition of the preceding parable, where he omitted it in his revision (v 27; cf. Luke 6:49b)."

Schürmann 1982, 136: "Nach fast allgemeiner Überzeugung finden wir Umfang und Akoluthie ... der sogenannten 'Bergpredigt' der Redenquelle Lk 6,20-49 par. Mt 5,1-7,27 (von Matthäus bedeutend erweitert) weitgehend in Lk, wobei bei beiden Evangelisten Lk 6,12-16(17) par. Mt voranging und Lk 7,1.2-10 par. Mt 7,28; 8,5-10.13 folgte."

Vassiliadis 1982, 386: Luke 7:1a/Matt 7:28 is included in Vassiliadis' appendix as the end of a discrete block of Q material with the title "The ending of Jesus' teaching."

Dauer 1984, 110: "Lk V. 1a entspricht sachlich Mt 7,28a. Wir haben hier offensichtlich den Schluß der Berg- bzw. Feldpredigt aus Q vor uns: ... Die sprachlichen Differenzen gehen auf Kosten lk bzw. mt Redaktion."

Strecker 1984, 179: "Durch das feierliche, der LXX-Sprache entlehnte καὶ ἐγένετο ('und es geschah') nimmt Matthäus die zu Anfang der Bergpredigt beschriebene Situation wieder auf. Schon in der Q-Quelle stand am Schluß der Rede eine Formel, wie sie ähnlich die Parallele Lk 7,1a bezeugt."

Luz 1985, 415: "Lk 7,1a macht wahrscheinlich, daß auch in der Logienquelle an dieser Stelle eine ähnliche Abschlußwendung stand."

Luz 1985, ET 1989, 455: "Luke 7:1a makes it probable that there was a similar concluding clause in the Sayings Source at this place."

Wegner 1985, 102: "Die in Lk 7,1a erscheinende Überleitungswendung von der Bergpredigt zur Hauptmannsperikope stimmt sachlich mit Mt 7,28a überein. Da nun Mt 7,28b.f deutlich von Mk 1,22 (vgl. Lk 4,32) abhängen und Mt 8,2-4 hinsichtlich der Mk-Akoluthie wohl den Abschnitt Mk 1,40-45 antizipiert, ist zu vermuten, daß bereits in der Q-Vorlage des Mt und Lk eine Mt 7,28a/Lk 7,1a ähnliche Überleitungswendung von der Bergpredigt zum Hauptmannsbericht vorlag."

270-271: "(Urspr Übergangswendung von der Bergpredigt zur HP: Q [Matt] 7,28a)

"Καὶ ἐγένετο ὅτε ἐτέλεσεν ὁ Ἰησοῦς τοὺς λόγους τούτους...

"(Text der urspr HP: Q [Matt] 8,5-10.13)

"V 5:   εἰσῆλθεν εἰς Καφαρναούμ. καὶ [ἀκούσας περὶ αὐτοῦ]
              ἦλθεν πρὸς αὐτὸν ἑκατοντάρχης παρακαλῶν αὐτὸν

 V 6:   καὶ λέγων· ὁ παῖς μου βέβληται ἐν τῇ οἰκίᾳ παραλυτικός,
              δεινῶς βασανιζόμενος.

V 7:   καὶ εἶπεν αὐτῷ· ἐγὼ ἐλθὼν θεραπεύσω αὐτόν;
V 8:   καὶ ἀποκριθεὶς ὁ ἑκατοντάρχης ἔφη·
          κύριε, οὐκ εἰμὶ ἱκανὸς ἵνα ὑπὸ τὴν στέγην μου εἰσέλθῃς,
          ἀλλὰ εἰπὲ λόγῳ καὶ ἰαθήσεται ὁ παῖς μου.
V 9:   καὶ γὰρ ἐγὼ ἄνθρωπός εἰμι ὑπὸ ἐξουσίαν, ἔχων ὑπ’ ἐμαυτὸν
          στρατιώτας, καὶ λέγω τούτῳ· πορεύθητι, καὶ πορεύεται,
          καὶ ἄλλῳ· ἔρχου, καὶ ἔρχεται, καὶ τῷ δούλῳ μου· ποίησον
          τοῦτο, καὶ ποιεῖ. [271]
V 10:   ἀκούσας δὲ ὁ Ἰησοῦς ἐθαύμασεν καὶ εἶπεν τοῖς ἀκολουθοῦσιν·
          ἀμὴν λέγω ὑμῖν· παρ’ οὐδενὶ τοσαύτην πίστιν ἐν
          τῷ Ἰσραὴλ εὗρον.
V 13:   καὶ εἶπεν τῷ ἑκατοντάρχῃ· ὕπαγε, [ὁ παῖς σου ἐσώθη].
          [καὶ ἀπελθὼν εἰς τὴν οἰκίαν εὗρεν τὸν παῖδα ἰαθέντα].”

Brackets around Greek text indicate a degree of uncertainty (usually stated as "möglich") in his reconstruction.

Gnilka 1986, 283: "Man darf annehmen, daß E bereits in der Jüngerunterweisungsrede in Q eine abschließende Bemerkung las, wie Lk 7,1 nahelegt. Denn Lk bietet an keiner anderen Stelle eine vergleichbare Abschlußform. Wie diese allerdings in Q aussah, ist kaum noch zu rekonstruieren, da Lk 7,1 lk geprägt erscheint, vielleicht mit Ausnahme des ἐπλήρωσεν im Sinn von 'zu Ende bringen.'"

Syreeni 1987, 76: "The two-source theory gives an unconstrained explanation for these observations: Matthew has combined Mk and Q. Mk's contribution is evident in the anaphoric prolongation 7:28b-29, while the influence of Q is traceable in 7:28[a]; 8,5. The underlying Q text cannot be reconstructed verbatim, but obviously Luke has rendered its essential content: having ended these sayings (*anaphora*), Jesus went to Capernaum (*cataphora*). This brief note would in Q link Jesus' inaugural speech and the healing at Capernaum. Since Matthew did not place the Capernaum episode right after the Sermon on the Mount but first recorded a Markan healing story in 8:1-4, he was not able to use the cataphoric part of the Q link until 8:5.

"The Q document at Matthew's disposal thus seems to have contained a two-part transitional link between a lengthy *speech* and a *narrative*-like sequence."

Davies and Allison 1988, 724: "Immediately following the parable of the two builders Luke has this: 'After he had ended all his sayings in the hearing of the people...' The sentence must be judged editorial. But so must Mt 7:28-29. This means that if Q contained a concluding line for the sermon on the plain, its wording is forever lost. All one can say is that such a closing sentence, if it did exist, may have combined a remark about Jesus finishing his words with a notice of his going on to Capernaum (cf. Mt. 7:28; 8:5; Lk 7:1)."

Kloppenborg 1988, 50: "The lack of significant agreement between Matthew and Luke, coupled with the presence of Matthean and Lukan elements and Markan influence suggests that both evangelists have thoroughly reworked Q at this point."

Wiefel 1988, 142-143: "Die Einleitung, die von der Feldrede zum Heilungswunder überleitet, enthält die dem Lukas eigene Ausdrucksweise (πληροῦν, vgl. 22,16; εἰς τὰς ἀκοάς, vgl. 1,44; Apg. 17,20), andererseits läßt sie als Hörerkreis der Rede das Volk (λαός) erkennen. Daß hier die Feldrede im Unterschied zu Luk. 6,20 als Volksunterweisung erscheint, könnte auf Q zurückgehen, [143] wo eine abschließende und überleitende Wendung enthalten war, die in Matth. 7,28 und Luk. 7,1 mit je unterschiedlicher Akzentuierung aufgenommen wurde."

Bovon 1989, 347[13]: "Lukas verwendet das Wort πληρόω zwar häufig, aber nirgendwo sonst für das Ende einer Rede; vgl. Apg 13,25, wo es für das Ende des Lebens, das mit einem (Wett)lauf verglichen wird, gebraucht ist. Vermeidet er τελέω (Mt 7,28) wegen des folgenden τελευτᾶν in Lk 7,2?"

Bovon 1989, FT 1991, 340[13]: "Luc utilise souvent πληρόω, mais jamais ailleurs pour la fin d'un discours; cf. Ac 13,25 pour l'achèvement d'une vie, comparée à une course. Evite-t-il τελέω (Mt 7,28) à cause de τελευτᾶν (Lc 7,2)?"

Kosch 1989, 223: "Vielfach wird vermutet, daß hinter Lk 6,20a; Mt 5,1f eine Q-Einleitung zur programmatischen Rede steht, der in Lk 7,1; Mt 7,28f eine Schlußwendung entspricht."

227: "Als zusätzliches Argument für die Existenz einer Einleitung, welche die Präsenz von Volksscharen erwähnte, wird auf die Übereinstimmung von Lk 7,1 mit Mt 7,28 verwiesen, welche die Existenz einer Abschlußwendung nahelegt."

229-230: "Sowohl in Lk (7,1a) als auch bei Mt (7,28f) folgt der programmatischen Rede eine *Abschlußwendung*. Diese Abschlußwendungen stimmen zwar der Sache nach überein, weichen aber im Wortlaut stark [230] voneinander ab. In bezug auf 7,28f kann mit Sicherheit gesagt werden, daß allenfalls 7,28a aus Q stammen kann, 7,28b-29 hängt deutlich von Mk 1,22 ab."

Nolland 1989, 315: "The similarity (but not verbal) of the opening clause to Matt 7:28a suggests that Luke is here reflecting a traditional termination for the great sermon."

Catchpole 1992, 518 [1993, 281]: "At the beginning of the centurion tradition ... a link lies beneath the surface of Matt 7,28a; 8,5a/Luke 7,1."

521-522 [1993, 285-286]: "At the one end of the story, it is not difficult to envisage the Q transition as καὶ ἐγένετο ὅτε ἐτέλεσεν ὁ Ἰησοῦς τοὺς λόγους τούτους, εἰσῆλθεν εἰς Καφαρναούμ, thus matching OT precedents (Num 16:31; Jer 26:8 and especially Deut 32:45), and taking seriously the

Matthew/Luke agreements in substance: (i) a time clause referring to (ii) the completion of (iii) the sayings of Jesus in (iv) the hearing of the audience, followed by (v) a movement into Capernaum. Similar formulations in Matt 11:1; [522] 13:53; 19:1 and 26:1 do not negate this proposal, since there are several examples of Matthew's repeated [286] usage of phrases attested singly in one of his sources.[17]"

522 [286][17]: "'There shall be weeping and gnashing of teeth' (Q 13:28) became the prototype for five other Matthaean occurrences: Matt 13:42, 50; 22:13; 24:51 diff Luke 12:46; and Matt 25:30 diff Luke 19:27. The 'little ones' (Mark 9:42) became the source of the characteristic Matthaean discipleship terminology. The Marcan reference to 'your Father who is in heaven' (Mark 11:25) stimulated many such Matthaean references."

521, 522, 527, 533, 539 [285, 286, 292, 299, 307]: Catchpole's complete reconstruction of Q: "καὶ ἐγένετο ὅτε ἐτέλεσεν ὁ Ἰησοῦς τοὺς λόγους τούτους, εἰσῆλθεν εἰς Καφαρναούμ. [527, 292] καὶ ἦλθεν αὐτῷ ἑκατοντάρχης παρακαλῶν αὐτὸν καὶ λέγων· ὁ παῖς μου ἐν τῇ οἰκίᾳ δεινῶς βασανιζόμενος μέλλει τελευτᾶν. λέγει αὐτῷ· ἐλθὼν θεραπεύσω αὐτόν. [533, 299] ἀποκριθεὶς δὲ ὁ ἑκατοντάρχης εἶπεν· κύριε, οὐκ εἰμὶ ἱκανὸς ἵνα μου ὑπὸ τὴν στέγην εἰσέλθῃς· ἀλλὰ εἰπὲ λόγῳ, καὶ ἰαθήσεται ὁ παῖς μου. καὶ γὰρ ἐγὼ ἄνθρωπός εἰμι ὑπὸ ἐξουσίαν, ἔχων ὑπ' ἐμαυτὸν στρατιώτας, καὶ λέγω τούτῳ· πορεύθητι, καὶ πορεύεται, καὶ ἄλλῳ· ἔρχου, καὶ ἔρχεται. καὶ τῷ δούλῳ μου· ποίησον τοῦτο, καὶ ποιεῖ. [539, 307] ἀκούσας δὲ ὁ Ἰησοῦς ἐθαύμασεν καὶ εἶπεν τοῖς ἀκολουθοῦσιν· λέγω ὑμῖν, παρ' οὐδενὶ τοσαύτην πίστιν ἐν τῷ Ἰσραὴλ εὗρον. [522, 286] καὶ εἶπεν ὁ Ἰησοῦς τῷ ἑκατοντάρχῃ· ὕπαγε, ὡς ἐπίστευσας γενηθήτω σοι. καὶ ἰάθη ὁ παῖς ἐν τῇ ὥρᾳ ἐκείνῃ."

Sevenich-Bax 1993, 161-162: "Zwar läßt sich die Konstruktion mit ἐπειδή und damit zugleich die Vorstellung eines [162] zeitlichen Nacheinanders vordergründig der lukanischen Redaktion zuweisen, doch lehrt ein Blick in die matthäische Parallele, daß wohl auch bereits die Logienquelle zwischen der Predigt am Berg und der Erzählung vom Hauptmann eine dem Lukas vergleichbare Überleitungswendung geboten hat: Dem Vers Lk 7,1a korrespondiert nämlich Vers Mt 7,28a. Dieser ist bei Matthäus durch Markusstoff ergänzt (Mt 7,28b.29; vgl. Mk 1,22). Streicht man den redaktionellen Nachtrag Mt 7,28b.29 sowie den ebenfalls sekundären Einschub Mt 8,1-4 (vgl. Mk 1,40-45), dann erhält man mit Mt 7,28a einen Halbvers, der nach Ergänzung verlangt. Diese ist in der Abfolge der Logienquelle erst wieder mit Mt 8,5a gegeben, genau der Vers, der auch bei Lukas die Überleitungswendung zum Abschluß bringt (Lk 7,1b). Das heißt: Die Verse Lk 7,1a und 7,1b par. sind einander zugeordnet und nicht voneinander abgrenzbar."

173: "Oben war bereits darauf aufmerksam gemacht worden, daß Lk 7,1 par. die Funktion einer Überleitung von der Predigt am Berg zur Szene in Kapharnaum hat. Die zweite Hälfte des Verses Lk 7,1b//Mt 8,5aα wird dabei sowohl die Ortsangabe 'Kapharnaum' als auch das Verb 'εἰσέρχομαι' enthalten haben, da beides von Matthäus und Lukas übereinstimmend bezeugt ist."

238: Reconstruction: "Lk 7,1-10//Mt 7,28a; 8,5-13

Lk 7,1a par.	Καὶ ἐγένετο ὅτε <u>ἐτέλεσεν (ἐπλήρωσεν)</u> ὁ Ἰησοῦς τοὺς λόγους τούτους,
Lk 7,1b par.	εἰσῆλθεν εἰς Καφαρναούμ.
Lk 7,2 par.	Ἑκατοντάρχης δὲ παρεκάλεσεν αὐτὸν λέγων·
	ὁ παῖς μου βέβληται ἐν τῇ οἰκίᾳ παραλυτικός,
	δεινῶς βασανιζόμενος.
Mt 8,7.8a	λέγει αὐτῷ·
(vgl. Lk 7,6)	ἐγὼ ἐλθὼν θεραπεύσω αὐτόν.
	ἀποκριθεὶς δὲ ὁ ἑκατόνταρχος ἔφη·
Lk 7,6c par.	κύριε, οὐκ εἰμὶ ἱκανὸς
	ἵνα ὑπὸ τὴν στέγην μου εἰσέλθῃς·
Lk 7,7b par.	ἀλλὰ εἰπὲ λόγῳ,
	καὶ ἰαθήσεται ὁ παῖς μου.
Lk 7,8 par.	καὶ γὰρ ἐγὼ ἄνθρωπός εἰμι ὑπὸ ἐξουσίαν,
	ἔχων ὑπ' ἐμαυτὸν στρατιώτας,
	καὶ λέγω τούτῳ·
	πορεύθητι,
	καὶ πορεύεται,
	καὶ ἄλλῳ·
	ἔρχου,
	καὶ ἔρχεται,
	καὶ τῷ δούλῳ μου·
	ποίησον τοῦτο,
	καὶ ποιεῖ.
Lk 7,9 par.	ἀκούσας δὲ ὁ Ἰησοῦς ἐθαύμασεν
	καὶ εἶπεν τοῖς ἀκολουθοῦσιν·
	<u>(ἀμὴν)</u> λέγω ὑμῖν,
	οὐδὲ ἐν τῷ Ἰσραὴλ τοσαύτην πίστιν εὗρον.
Lk 7,10 par.	<u>καὶ εἶπεν ὁ Ἰησοῦς τῷ ἑκατοντάρχῃ·</u>
	ὕπαγε, ὡς ἐπίστευσας γενηθήτω σοι.
	καὶ ἰάθη ὁ παῖς ἐν τῇ ὥρᾳ ἐκείνῃ."

Parentheses and underlining indicate a degree of uncertainty in the reconstruction.

Gagnon 1994b, 135: Reconstruction: "Καὶ ἐγένετο ὅτε ἐτέλεσεν ὁ Ἰησοῦς τοὺς λόγους τούτους, εἰσῆλθεν εἰς Καφαρναούμ. ἀκούσας δὲ περὶ αὐτοῦ, ἑκατοντάρχης, οὗ ὁ παῖς αὐτοῦ κακῶς ἔχων ἤμελλεν τελευτᾶν, ἦλθεν πρὸς αὐτὸν παρακαλῶν αὐτὸν καὶ λέγων· κύριε, οὐκ εἰμὶ ἱκανὸς ... καὶ ἀπελθὼν εἰς τὴν οἰκίαν εὗρεν τὸν παῖδα ἰαθέντα.[8]"

135⁸: "And when Jesus finished these words, he entered Capernaum. Now upon hearing about him, a centurion, whose boy was sick and about to die, came to him imploring him and saying, 'Lord, I am not fit...' [there follows here the dialogue in Matt 8.8-10]. And when he went back to his house he found the boy healed." Brackets are Gagnon's.

International Q Project 1995, 478-479: Double-brackets indicate an uncertain {C} vote; pointed brackets indicate an emended text not found in Matthew or Luke—see section on sigla (pp. xxiii-xxx)

"Q 7:1
… ἐ⟦πλήρω⟧σεν ⟦τοὺς λόγους τούτους⟧ εἰσῆλθεν εἰς Καφαρναούμ.

Q 7:2-4
7:3 προσῆλθεν αὐτῷ ἑκατόνταρχος
7:4 παρακαλῶν αὐτὸν καὶ λέγων·
7:2 ὁ παῖς μου ⟦κακῶς ἔχων⟧ .. . καὶ λέγει αὐτῷ· ἐγὼ ἐλθὼν θεραπεύσω αὐτόν.

~~Q 7:5~~

Q 7:6
καὶ ἀποκριθεὶς ὁ ἑκατοντάρχ...ς ἔφη κύριε, οὐκ εἰμὶ ἱκανὸς ἵνα μου ὑπὸ τὴν στέγην εἰσέλθῃς·

Q 7:7
ἀλλὰ εἰπὲ λόγῳ, καὶ ἰαθή⟦σεται⟧ ὁ παῖς μου.

Q 7:8
καὶ γὰρ ἐγὼ ἄνθρωπός εἰμι ὑπὸ ἐξουσίαν, ἔχων ὑπ' ἐμαυτὸν στρατιώτας, καὶ λέγω τούτῳ· πορεύθητι, καὶ πορεύεται, καὶ ἄλλῳ· ἔρχου, καὶ ἔρχεται, καὶ τῷ δούλῳ μου· ποίησον τοῦτο, καὶ ποιεῖ.

Q 7:9
ἀκούσας δὲ ὁ Ἰησοῦς ἐθαύμασεν καὶ εἶπεν τ⟦οῖς⟧ ἀκολουθοῦ⟦σιν⟧· λέγω ὑμῖν, οὐδὲ ἐν τῷ Ἰσραὴλ τοσαύτην πίστιν εὗρον.

Q 7:10
καὶ ⟦⟧ ⟨..⟩.

Q 7:1
… he ended ⟦these⟧ sayings, he entered Capharnaum.

Q 7:2-4
A centurion came to him, beseeching him and saying, My boy ⟦is sick⟧ … And he said to him, I will come and heal him.

~~Q 7:5~~

Q 7:6
The centurion answered him, Lord, I am not worthy for you to come under my roof;

Q 7:7
but only say the word, and my boy ⟦will be⟧ healed.

Q 7:8
For I am a man under authority, with soldiers under me; and I say to one, Go, and he goes, and to another, Come, and he comes, and to my slave, Do this, and he does it.

Q 7:9
When Jesus heard him, he marveled, and said to ⟦those who⟧ followed, I say to you, not even in Israel have I found such faith.

Q 7:10
⟨..⟩."

Allison 1997, 77-78: "When one adds that Matthew omitted very lit-[78]tle of Mark, and that Luke, aside from the major omission [78] of Mk

6:48-8:26, also omitted very little of Mark, we may infer that probably neither omitted very much of Q. That this generalization holds for the SM [Matthew's Sermon on the Mount] and SP [Luke's Sermon on the Plain] in particular is confirmed by the circumstance that, apart from the woes (Lk 6:24-26) and two short proverbs (Lk 6:39-40), all of the units in the SP have parallels in the SM; and even the two proverbs appear elsewhere in Matthew (10:24-25; 15:14). Indeed, all of the materials common to the SM and SP, with the sole exception of the golden rule, are in the same order:

Lk 6:20a cf. Mt 5:1-2
Lk 6:20b-23 cf. Mt 5:3-12 …
Lk 7:1 cf. Mt 7:28-8:1."

Not in Q

Holtzmann 1901, 226: "Epilog. Mt 7,28.29. Entsprechend der Vorbemerkung 5,1.2 rundet Mt dieses Prachtstück seiner Composition ab mit einer Schlußbemerkung über den Eindruck der Rede."

Müller 1908, 47: In a chart of sources, Müller identifies Matt 7:28 as Matthean and Luke 7:1a as Lukan.

Haupt 1913, 80: "Da Mt und Lc dies Erzählungsstück gleich nach der Bergpredigt bringen, so entsteht der Schein, daß es in der Quelle mit dieser verbunden gewesen sei. Das war aber nicht der Fall. Die Formel, die am ehesten auf solche Verbindung weisen könnte (Mt 7,28 = Lc 7,1) stammt nicht aus der Quelle sondern gehört den Evangelisten an (für Mt cf. 11,1; 13,53; 19,1; 26,1 und für Luc cf. Act. 17,20). Wenn die Hauptmannserzählung bei beiden auf die Bergpredigt folgt (doch cf. Mt 8,1-4), so rührt das daher, daß nach der Bergpredigt dies der nächste größere Zusatz in Q³ war. Denn zugegeben, daß es bei den Stücken von Q³ sich überall um Zusätze handelt, so kann die Hauptmannserzählung mit der ihr folgenden Rede nur ein Zusatz zur Heilung der Kananäerin gewesen sein, da in der Grundschrift (G) das Thema einer Wirksamkeit Jesu unter den Heiden überhaupt nur an dieser Stelle behandelt ist (bem. auch, wie Mt den Schluß der Hauptmannserzählung genau nach dem der Kananäerin gestaltet 8,13 = 15,28)."

Taylor 1926, 150: "With the similitude of the two men who built their houses, one upon the rock and the other upon sand, the Sermon concludes ([vi.]47-9). It is followed by an editorial passage which leads on to the story of the Healing of the Centurion's Servant: 'After he had ended all his sayings in the ears of the people, he entered into Capernaum' (vii.1)."

Manson 1937, 63: "It is almost certain that the dialogue alone belongs to Q. The narrative framework is supplied independently by Mt. and Lk."

Fuchs 1971, 52: "Mt 7,28; 11,1; 13,53; 19,1 und 26,1 sind erst von Mt formuliert und in dieser Prägung keiner Quelle entnommen.[6]"

52[6]: "Ein Vergleich der Perikopen, zu denen die angeführten Texte die Einleitung bzw. den Abschluß bilden, mit dem entsprechenden Mk- und Lk-Stoff würde das von dritter Seite in den meisten Fällen bestätigen."

Zeller 1982, 398-399: "Erzählende Abschlußwendungen sind in Q nicht [399] (mehr?) ausfindig zu machen, wenn die sachliche Übereinstimmung zwischen Mt 7:28a und Lc 7,1a möglicherweise auf Zufall beruht."

Zeller 1982, ET 1994, 120: "It is now difficult to know whether there were any narrative conclusions in Q ... since, for example, the agreement in content between Matt 7:28a and Luke 7:1a is probably coincidental."

Sato 1988, 24[24]: "Die Q-Zugehörigkeit der Schlußbemerkung zur programmatischen Rede (Lk 7,1a/Mt 7,28a) ist noch weniger wahrscheinlich zu machen. Es gibt hier keine Übereinstimmung im Wortlaut, sondern nur eine vage inhaltliche Assoziation. Ausserdem sind die zwei Verse jeweils ganz und gar redaktionell formuliert."

Evaluations

Shein 1998: In Q {C}.
Most of the scholars consulted consider Q to have contained a phrase linking the Sermon on the Plain/Mount to the narrative about the healing of the centurion's son. The phrase in Luke and Matthew is content-wise the same and, notably, for what immediately follows in Matthew's verse, he depends on Mark. At the same time, scholars find it almost impossible to reconstruct the exact wording due to the lack of verbatim agreement between Luke and Matthew. There are no detailed arguments offered against the phrase—only a few scholars judge it editorial. While Haupt considers the opening phrase in Matthew redactional, Hawkins points out that ἐγένετο with a finite verb is more typical in Luke. In other words, there is a double attestation even though agreement is not verbatim. Yet, if only for the lack of verbatim agreement one is cautioned to a grade no higher than {C} for Q.

Johnson 2000: In Q {B}.
Objections to Q containing a transitional statement between the Q Sermon and the Centurion story spring from the lack of verbatim agreement between Matthew and Luke and the fact that both Gospels provide what are typical narrative transitions between pericopes of unlike genre (Manson). More specifically, Matthew's conclusion in particular is seen as just one of a set of five formulaic conclusions to major speech units (Haupt, Fuchs), with similarity between Matt 7:28a and Luke 7:1a a mere coincidence (Zeller).

Despite the lack of verbatim agreement, however, the substance of the transitions is virtually identical (Hawkins). Overlooked in objections to a Q transition is the fact that this agreement in substance includes not only Q 7:1a—the conclusion to the Sermon—but extends to the mention of Jesus' entry into Capharnaum in 7:1b (Harnack, Pesch and Kratz). If Matt 8:5a (Luke 7:1b) is accepted as Q material, then there can be no strong objection to the first half of the formula (Matt 7:28a par. Luke 7:1a) being original in substance as well.

To the objection that Matthew is simply using a redactional formula, it is noted that, apart from the other four formulaic speech conclusions, none of the language in Matt 7:28a is typically Matthean (Hawkins). For this reason, many have concluded that the statement in Matt 7:28a was traditional and became the basis for the subsequent formulaic speech-narrative transitions (Streeter, Dobschütz). This conclusion has ramifications for the reconstruction of the transition statement in Q.

Robinson 2000: In Q {B}.

It is too striking a coincidence to assume that both Matthew and Luke introduced here redactionally a reference to Jesus finishing his sayings and proceeding on his way. Though Matthew does so at the end of each discourse, Luke does so only here. Hence the Lukan parallel argues strongly for something having been here in Q.

The Matthean formulation recurs (with but slight fluctuation due to the differences in the discourses) at the conclusion of the five major Matthean discourses. But, rather than the formula being simply a Mattheanism, it seems to be an instance, like several others, where Matthew has appropriated Q idiom.

Other instances of Matthew appropriating the language of Q: ὀλιγόπιστος (Q 12:28 = Matt 6:30; Matt 8:26; 14:31; 16:8) and ὁ κλαυθμὸς καὶ ὁ βρυγμός (Q 13:28 = Matt 8:12; Matt 13:42, 50; 22:13; 24:51; 25:30). Since in these cases the Q instance is in Luke as well as in Matthew, it is clear that it is a Q expression that is appropriated by Matthew and repeated in the first case three times and in the second case five times. Hence it has come to be considered typically Matthean, though derived from Q. Matthew also took over from Q the "eschatological/prophetic correlative" (Q 11:40; 17:24, 26, 30) in Matt 13:40-41. Similarly Q 7:1a = Matt 7:28a is repeated by Matthew four times (Matt 11:1; 13:53; 19:1; 26:1), so as to become typically Matthean, without thereby eliminating the option of having come from Q. (This is all the more normal if the Matthean community is a product of the Q community.)

The formula is in two parts: The first refers to when Jesus has completed these sayings: (7:28a; 19:1 καὶ ἐγένετο ὅτε ἐτέλεσεν ὁ Ἰησοῦς τοὺς λόγους τούτους; 26:1... πάντας τοὺς λόγους τούτους; 11:1... διατάσσων τοῖς δώδεκα μαθηταῖς αὐτοῦ; 13:53... τὰς παραβολὰς ταύτας). Here Luke 7:1a deviates somewhat, but in a different way from the minor deviations within Matthew: ἐπειδὴ ἐπλήρωσεν πάντα τὰ ῥήματα αὐτοῦ εἰς τὰς ἀκοὰς τοῦ λαοῦ.

Then, in the second part, it is said that Jesus went on to the next thing, expressed in the aorist (Matt 11:1 μετέβη; Matt 13:53 μετῆρεν; Matt 19:1 μετῆρεν; in Matt 26:1, Jesus resumes speaking εἶπεν). In the present case, the formula is interrupted by a Matthean interpolation (Matt 7:28b-8:4), no doubt to document first of all that Jesus' teaching did fulfill the law and the prophets (Matt 7:12), since Jesus tells the healed leper to show himself to the priest "and offer the gift that Moses commanded" (Matt 8:4).

Only then does the formula reach its natural conclusion. As a result of the interpolation, it is shifted by Matthew into a genitive absolute (εἰσελθόντος δὲ αὐτοῦ εἰς Καφαρναούμ), followed by the aorist to express the action of the Centurion (προσῆλθεν αὐτῷ). Here it is Luke who actually retains the standard aorist finite verb of Jesus moving on (Luke 7:1 εἰσῆλθεν εἰς Καφαρναούμ). If thus the second part of the formula is here documented by Luke, without interpolation and hence in purer form than in Matt 8:5a (to judge by the other four Matthean instances), it must have been in Q, and not just be a Matthean creation.

In view of the fluctuations, the exact wording in Q is less certain, and needs to be examined in detail in the subsequent variation units.

Kloppenborg 2000: In Q (with emendations): {A} for 7:1b < >⁰; {C} for 7:1a < >⁰.

Hoffmann 2001: In Q {B}.

Q 7:1¹: Luke's ἐπειδή or Matthew's καὶ ἐγένετο ὅτε.

Luke = Q: [᾿Επειδή]¹

Pro

Morganthaler 1971, 304: See Q 7:1⁰, In Q (p. 8).

Wegner 1985, 115: "*Pro*: a. Die temporale Verwendung von ἐπειδή ist dem Lk nicht geläufig. b. Die Konjunktion wird von Mt kein einziges Mal in seinem Evangelium verwendet, er könnte sie also leicht ersetzt haben. c. Die in Mt 7,28a entsprechende Konjunktion ὅτε verwendet Lk 10x in der Apg und vielleicht 2x als Eintragung in seinem Mk-Stoff, weshalb eine Streichung durch ihn nicht unbedingt zu erwarten wäre. d. Das mt ὅτε könnte vom Evangelisten selbst stammen, denn auch gegenüber Mk setzt Mt es 2x ein." Elsewhere, Wegner decides for Luke = Q, Con (p. 22) and Matt = Q, Pro (pp. 23-24).

Syreeni 1987, 88⁴: "Luke's two-part link is more likely to represent Q's wording."

Merklein 1994, 97: "Die bei Lukas noch erhaltene Einleitung (7,1: 'Nachdem er alle seine Worte vor den Ohren des Volkes vollendet hatte ...') läßt noch erkennen, woher Matthäus die Anregung zu seinen stereotypen Redeschlüssen hat (siehe oben zu Mt 7,28)."

Con

Wellhausen 1904b, 26: "᾿Επειδή 7,1 ist unhaltbar; D hat καὶ ἐγένετο ὅτε."

von Harnack 1907, 54: "Der Lukastext ... erweist sich durch das ἐπειδή als sekundär (es steht bei Matth., Mark. und Joh. niemals, bei Luk. aber [Ev. und Act.] 5 mal)."

von Harnack 1907, ET 1908, 74: "The Lukan text is shown to be secondary by ἐπειδή (never occurring in St. Matthew, St. Mark, and St. John; five times, however, in St. Luke's gospel and Acts)."

B. Weiß 1908, 14²²: "Daß sie Luk. auch hier in Q las [...] folgt daraus, daß er das ἐγένετο ὅτε durch sein ἐπειδή ersetzt, das auch Harnack [see above] für lukanisch erklärt."

14: Reconstruction. For complete text see Q 7:1⁰ In Q (p. 5).

Castor 1912, 42: "Most of the linguistic differences seem due to Luke's literary changes. Luke 7:1a is a Lukan paraphrase for Matt. 7:28a. ᾿Επειδή, ἐπλήρωσεν, ῥήματα, εἰς τὰς ἀκοάς are all characteristic of Luke."

Easton 1926, 95: "῾Ρῆμα and λαός are 'Lukan,' and ἐπειδή (13:46, three times in Acts, not in Mk or Mt) and εἰς τὰς ἀκοάς (Acts 17:20) are likewise to be referred to Lk."

Bussmann 1929, 56: "Die Formel des Mt ἐγένετο ὅτε ἐτέλεσεν ist auch sonst bei ihm 11,1; 13,53; 19,1; 26,1 zu finden, aber ἐπλήρωσεν πάντα τὰ ῥήματα ist spezifisch lukanisch, eben ἐπειδή und εἰς τὰς ἀκοάς."

Busse 1977, 146: "Lukas favorisiert die lectio difficilior ἐπειδή im Gegensatz zu den anderen Evangelisten im kausalen Sinn, obwohl in dieser Überleitung eine temporale Konjunktion wie ὡς eher angebracht ist. Seiner Ansicht nach kann Jesus nur aufgrund der Feldpredigt seine missionarische Aktivität in Kapharnaum fortsetzen. Sein dortiges Auftreten steht mit seinen vorhergehenden Worten auch in einem kausalen Zusammenhang."

Gatzweiler 1979, 307-308: "Le v. 1 assure la transition entre le discours dans la plaine (6,20-49) et notre histoire: son caractère [308] rédactionnel est patent."

Jeremias 1980, 151: "Red ἐπειδή: kommt im NT außer bei Paulus (fünfmal) nur im lk Doppelwerk vor: Lk 7,1; 11,6/Apg 13,46; 14,12; 15,24."

Gundry 1982, 136: "Instead of ἐπειδή, which is probably a Lukanism, we read the more usual ὅτε."

Dauer 1984, 110: "Auch die Formulierung bei *Lk* dürfte redaktionell sein: zu ἐπειδή vgl—außer 5mal bei Pls—Lk 7,1 u.St.; 11,6; Apg 13,46; 14,12; 15,24."

Luz 1985, 415: "Wieweit sich Mt an Q gehalten hat, ist aber kaum mehr erkennbar, da Lk 7,1a ganz lukanisch ist.[4]"

415[4]: "Lk sind in 7,1 ἐπειδή, πάντα τὰ ῥήματα, εἰς τὰς ἀκοάς (vgl. Apg 17,20)."

Luz 1985, ET 1989, 455: "How far Matthew followed Q can hardly be recognized, since Luke 7:1a is completely Lukan.[4]"

455[4]: "The following expressions are Lukan in 7:1: ἐπειδή, πάντα τὰ ῥήματα, εἰς τὰς ἀκοάς (cf. Acts 17:20)."

Wegner 1985, 105[13]: "Immerhin wird man fragen müssen, ob Lk das mt periphrastische καὶ ἐγένετο (+ ὅτε) nicht durch sein Äquivalent ἐπειδή sek ersetzt haben könnte."

115: "*Contra*: a. ἐπειδή ist sonst in Q nicht mehr belegt; Q bevorzugt es vielmehr, Temporalsätze durch Partizipialkonstruktionen wiederzugeben. b. ἐπειδή erscheint bei Lk gehäuft, was wohl dazu berechtigt, ihm auch (ausnahmsweise) die Verwendung des Wortes im temporalen Sinne zuzuschreiben."

122-123: "'Επειδή scheint uns auf Grund der hohen Belegzahl innerhalb des lk Doppelwerkes als sehr wahrscheinlich von Lk selbst in Lk 7,1a eingefügt. Dafür spricht auch, daß ἐπειδήπερ als ntl. hapax legomenon ebenfalls aus seiner Hand stammt (Lk [123] 1,1)."

Davies and Allison 1991, 18[32]: "Luke's hand is revealed by word statistics. ἐπειδή: Mt: 0; Mk: 0; Lk: 2; Acts: 3."

Gagnon 1993, 715: "It should be noted that Lucan redaction can ... be seen in the transition phrase in v 1a, 'when he completed all his words in the hearing of the people.'"

Sevenich-Bax 1993, 161-162: See Q 7:1⁰ In Q (p. 15).

International Q Project 1995, 478: Reconstruction. For complete text see Q 7:1⁰ In Q (p. 16).

Matt = Q: (Καὶ ἐγένετο ὅτε)¹

Pro

Hawkins 1899, 165: "There is nothing distinctively Matthaean in the wording of the formula: on the contrary, ἐγένετο, followed by a finite verb, is only found in these 5 places in Matthew, while it occurs 22 times in Luke (also twice in Mark and nowhere else in N.T.)."

B. Weiß 1908, 14²²: See Q 7:1⁰ In Q (p. 5).

14: Reconstruction. For complete text see Q 7:1⁰ In Q (p. 5).

Streeter 1911, 148: See Q 7:1⁰ In Q (p. 6).

Castor 1912, 222-224: Reconstruction. For complete text see Q 7:1⁰ In Q (p. 6).

Streeter 1924, 262: See Q 7:1⁰ In Q (p. 7).

von Dobschütz 1928, 341: See Q 7:1⁰ In Q (p. 7).

Polag 1979, 38: Reconstruction. For complete text see Q 7:1⁰ In Q (pp. 9-10).

Luz 1985, 415⁵: "Ἐγένετο ὅτε ist nicht mt."

Luz 1985, ET 1989, 455⁵: "Ἐγένετο ὅτε is not Matthean."

Wegner 1985, 104-105: For καὶ ἐγένετο: *"Pro:* a. Mt zeigt keine Bevorzugung der Wendung innerhalb seiner Bearbeitung des Mk-Stoffes.

"b. Mt hat die Tendenz, festgeprägte Wendungen aus Mk oder Q red in seinem Ev zu wiederholen. Da καὶ ἐγένετο innerhalb einer solchen Wendung auftaucht (= καὶ ἐγένετο ὅτε ἐτέλεσεν ὁ Ἰησοῦς τοὺς λόγους τούτους o.ä.) und diese sachlich bei Lk nur gegenüber Mt 7,28a eine Parallele hat (= Lk [105] 7,1a: ἐπειδὴ ἐπλήρωσεν πάντα τὰ ῥήματα ...), ist damit zu rechnen, daß der erste Evangelist in 11,1; 13,53; 19,1 und 26,1 red wiederholt, was er trad in seiner Q-Vorlage—eben Mt 7,28a—bereits vorfand."

107-108: For ὅτε: *"Pro:* a. Eindeutig von Mt bevorzugt wird ὅτε lediglich in der formelhaften Wendung καὶ ἐγένετο + ὅτε + ἐτέλεσεν ὁ Ἰησοῦς. ... Besteht bei Mt 11,1; 13,53; 19,1 und 26,1 zu Recht ein Verdacht auf red Bildung, da ja weder Mk noch Lk zu diesen Stellen eine Parallele bieten, so könnte Mt es in 7,28a sehr wohl trad vorgefunden haben, und entsprechend seiner auch anderswo belegbaren red Wiederholungen von Mk- und Q-Formeln dann später von sich aus sekundär eingesetzt haben."

[108] "b. Diese Möglichkeit wird teilweise durch den Befund bei dem dritten Evangelisten unterstützt, denn erstens ist bei ihm ὅτε kein Vorzugswort, es könnte daher leicht ersetzt oder ausgelassen worden sein, zweitens wird ὅτε in der Wendung καὶ ἐγένετο ὅτε niemals von ihm gebraucht, und drittens steht das dem mt ὅτε entsprechende ἐπειδή in Lk 7,1a unter Verdacht lk Red."

122: "Das mt Verfahren gegenüber mk ἐγένετο spricht nicht gerade für eine mt Verfasserschaft der Wendung. Eher könnte schon ὅτε auf Mt zurückgehen, da er es 2x dem Mk-Text hinzufügt. Doch ist dann unklar, warum Mt es nicht auch außerhalb der Redeschlüsse mit καὶ ἐγένετο verbindet. Καὶ ἐγένετο ὅτε kann daher in 7,28a für vor-mt gehalten werden."

123: "Man wird daher das mt καὶ ἐγένετο ὅτε als ursprüngliche Lesart in Q betrachten können."

126: "Die Wahrscheinlichkeit, daß Mt die ursprünglichere Fassung enthält, stimmt auch mit seinem sonstigen Verfahren überein, ursprünglich in Mk oder Q vorgefundene Formeln mehrmals redaktionell innerhalb seines Ev zu verwenden. Man wird daher mit der Ursprünglichkeit der Abschlußformel καὶ ἐγένετο ὅτε ἐτέλεσεν ὁ Ἰησοῦς (τοὺς λόγους τούτους) in 7,28a, kaum aber in 11,1; 13,53; 19,1 und 26,1 rechnen können, da letztere Stellen durch das Fehlen sachlicher Parallelen in Lk und Mk mit großer Wahrscheinlichkeit von Mt selbst stammen."

270: Reconstruction. For complete text see Q 7:1⁰ In Q (pp. 11-12).

Schenk 1987, 440: "Davon entfallen 5 auf die stereotype Weiterführungswendung nach Reden Jesu καὶ ἐγένετο ὅτε ἐτέλεσεν ὁ Ἰησοῦς + Akk. (bzw. 11,1 ein nachgestelltes Pt. conj.). Diese Wendung ist keine reine Abschlußwendung und vor allem kein Trenner, sd. ein Verbinder der temporalen Weiterführung. ... Die erste Stelle 7,28 (+Q) dürfte in Struktur und Funktion von Q übernommen sein, da Lk 7,1 einen analogen Übergang hat und außerdem das hier gegenüber Lk fehlende 'alle' dann bei Mt typischerweise an der letzten Stelle 26,1 auftaucht."

Kosch 1989, 230: "Wegner [1985, 102-126] hat die beiden Abschlußwendungen sehr detailliert auf die Frage hin geprüft, was von ihnen allenfalls auf Q zurückgeführt werden kann. Dabei kommt er zum Schluß, daß die mt Formulierung ursprünglicher ist.

"Sato [1988, 24²⁴; see Q 7:1⁰ Not in Q (p. 18)] dagegen äußert die Auffassung, daß beide Verse 'jeweils ganz und gar redaktionell formuliert (sind)'. Auch diese Auffassung ließe sich mit den Analysen von Wegner [103-114] vereinbaren, der in Mt 7,28a kein Element auszumachen vermag, das sicher nicht red ist. Allerdings unterschätzt Sato m.E. das Gewicht der Tatsache, daß Lk 7,1a und Mt 7,28a sachlich übereinstimmen und beachtet zu wenig, daß es eine Eigenart des mt Redaktionsverfahrens ist, ursprünglich in Q oder Mk auftretende Formeln häufig zu wiederholen, was für die Annahme spricht, daß

Mt die Schlußwendung 7,28a aus Q übernommen und red als Übergangsformel am Abschluß seiner fünf großen Reden in 11,1; 13,53; 19,1 und 26,1
aufgegriffen hat. Ohne letzte Gewißheit zu haben, kann davon ausgegangen
werden, daß in Q Mt 7,28a (Lk 7,1b) *kai egeneto hote etelesen ho Iēsous tous
logous toutous* (*eisēlthen eis Kapharnaum*) von der programmatischen Rede zur
Perikope vom Hauptmann von Kafarnaum überleitete."

Catchpole 1992, 521-522 [1993, 285-286]: See Q 7:1⁰ In Q (pp. 13-14).

Sevenich-Bax 1993, 175: "Aber auch die Einleitung mit καὶ ἐγένετο ist
nicht typisch matthäisch: Matthäus verwendet sie einzig in den Abschlußwendungen der 5 Redekompositionen. Davon sind wohl 4 Belege redaktionell.
An der vorliegenden Stelle kann die Konstruktion aber auf Q zurückgehen,
zumal das Verb γίνομαι der Logienquelle auch sonst bekannt ist (vgl. Mt
11,21//Lk 10,13; Mt 11,26//Lk 10,21), wenngleich nicht in derselben temporalen Verwendung. Die Tatsache, daß das bei Lukas gebotene ἐπειδή in der
Logienquelle als Gliederungssignal keine Rolle spielt, von Lukas aber—als
einzigem Evangelisten!—fünfmal gebraucht wird, spricht zusätzlich zugunsten
des bei Matthäus bezeugten Wortlautes."

238: Reconstruction. For complete text see Q 7:1⁰ In Q (p. 15).

Gagnon 1994b, 135: Reconstruction. For complete text see Q 7:1⁰ In Q
(p. 15).

Con

Simons 1880, 42: "Aber Lc. 7,1 ἐπεὶ δὲ ἐπλήρωσεν τὰ ῥήματα αὐτοῦ ist
wörtliche Umschreibung des bekannten Matthäischen Schlußstrichs καὶ
ἐγένετο ὅτε ἐτέλεσεν τοὺς λόγους τούτους, s. Mt 7,28; 11,1; 13,53; 19,1; 26,1;
dieser muß darum nach W. [B. Weiß 1876, 224] der Q. angehört haben.
Wenn aber auch Mt. καὶ ἐγένετο mit asyndetisch folgendem Verbum nur in
dieser Formel, den Plural von λόγος sonst 'nur in den Reden der Q.' und τελεῖν
nur noch zweimal 'in ganz anderem Sinne' (aber ist nicht 10,23 der Sinn doch
derselbe wie hier?) schreibt, ... so beweist das noch nicht die Herkunft dieser
Formel aus Λ, vielmehr wird sie, da Mt. sie regelmäßig braucht, wo er aus den
verschiedensten Elementen gebildete Redekompositionen abschließt, Eigen-
tum des 1. Evangelisten und bei diesem von Lc. gelesen sein."

Holtzmann 1901, 226: See Q 7:1⁰ Not in Q (p. 17).

von Harnack 1907, 54: "Die Form der Aussage haben beide geändert;
denn ἐγένετο ὅτε ἐτέλεσεν ist ein oft wiederholter Ausdruck des Matth. (s. 11,1;
13,53; 19,1; 26,1), und ... zeigt ... den sekundären Charakter des Matthäus-
textes an dieser Stelle."

von Harnack 1907, ET 1908, 74: "Both evangelists have altered the wording here; for ἐγένετο ὅτε ἐτέλεσεν is a phrase that is often repeated by

St. Matthew (vide xi. 1, xiii. 53, xix. 1, xxvi. 1) and … shows the secondary character of the text of St. Matthew at this point."

Easton 1926, 94-95: "Mt's 'it came to pass when Jesus had finished these words' is a set Matthæan phrase (Mt 19:1; 26:1; cf 11:1; 13:53) and its insertion, together with the [95] addition of clauses from Mk, must have disarranged Q's wording seriously."

Bussmann 1929, 10: "Holtzmann [1901, 226] … [meint] Matthäus habe mit Bewußtsein die Stoffe kunstvoll geordnet und eingeschoben, wie die 7,28; 11,1; 13,53; 19,1; 26,1 vorkommende Formel καὶ ἐγένετο ὅτε ἐτέλεσεν ὁ Ἰησοῦς τοὺς λόγους τούτους zeige."

56: "Die Formel des Mt ἐγένετο ὅτε ἐτέλεσεν ist auch sonst bei ihm 11,1; 13,53; 19,1; 26,1 zu finden."

Parker 1953, 176: "Matt. 7:28-29; Mark 1:22. In Mark this precedes a passage that Matthew lacks, and in Matthew it follows a discourse that Mark lacks. K did have part of the Sermon on the Mount and probably did not have the Markan story. Hence Matthew's arrangement is more likely to be that of K."

195: Reconstruction of Parker's 'K' source: "Matt. 7:28. And it came to pass, when Jesus ended these words…." Parker argues that Luke 7:1-10 represents the text of Q.

Fuchs 1971, 51-52: "Der Text enthält eine Abschlußformel, die hier wie auch bei Mt 7,28; 13,53; 19,1 und 26,1 den jeweils vorausgehenden Abschnitt als Einheit zusammenfaßt und sich in mehreren Punkten als mt Redaktion verrät. Am überzeugendsten wirkt wohl die sofort auffallende gleiche Formulierung: [52]

"7,28:   καὶ ἐγένετο ὅτε ἐτέλεσεν ὁ Ἰησοῦς τοὺς λόγους τούτους
                 ἐξεπλήσσοντο …

11,1:   καὶ ἐγένετο ὅτε ἐτέλεσεν ὁ Ἰησοῦς διατάσσων τοῖς δώδεκα
                 μαθηταῖς αὐτοῦ, μετέβη ἐκεῖθεν …

13,53:   καὶ ἐγένετο ὅτε ἐτέλεσεν ὁ Ἰησοῦς τὰς παραβολὰς ταύτας,
                 μετῆρεν ἐκεῖθεν.

19,1:   καὶ ἐγένετο ὅτε ἐτέλεσεν ὁ Ἰησοῦς τοὺς λόγους τούτους,
                 μετῆρεν ἀπὸ τῆς Γαλιλαίας καὶ ἦλθεν …

26,1:   καὶ ἐγένετο ὅτε ἐτέλεσεν ὁ Ἰησοῦς πάντας τοὺς λόγους τούτους,
                 εἶπεν τοῖς μαθηταῖς αὐτοῦ·

"Alle fünf Stellen haben die gleiche Gliederung: καὶ ἐγένετο, ὅτε ἐτέλεσεν ὁ Ἰησοῦς, Objekt, neuer Satz, beginnend mit dem Verb. Nur bei 11,1 weicht die Formulierung des Objektes etwas ab, was sich aus der Sache selbst ergibt, da Mt 10 nicht bloß Reden, sondern auch Aufträge enthält.

"Der gleiche Wortlaut ist an diesen Stellen nicht unbewußter Mt-Stil, sondern absichtlich gewählt, um die Redeblöcke des Mt-Ev aus dem übrigen Text kräftig herauszuheben. Gerade dieses Vorgehen, das mit dem Gesamtkonzept des Evangeliums zusammenhängt, sichert in anderer Weise den Schluß noch stärker, der sich auch schon aus dem bloßen stereotypen Text ergeben hatte: Mt 7,28; 11,1; 13,53; 19,1 und 26,1 sind erst von Mt formuliert und in dieser Prägung keiner Quelle entnommen."

Gundry 1982, 136: "Matthew rewords the statement. He draws καὶ ἐγένετο, a Semitism occurring in Matthew only in these concluding formulas, from the last clause in the tradition of the preceding parable, where he omitted it in his revision (v 27; cf. Luke 6:49b)."

Dauer 1984, 110: "Von *Matthäus* stammt die Neuformulierung καὶ ἐγένετο ὅτε ἐτέλεσεν, die in redaktionellen Bildungen wie 11,1; 13,53; 19,1; 26,1 wiederkehrt."

Wegner 1985, 105: For καὶ ἐγένετο: "*Contra*: a. Abgesehen von Mt 7,28a lassen sich in Q keine weiteren Belege für die Wendung καὶ ἐγένετο finden, wohl aber für isoliertes καί und γένεσθαι.

"b. Bei Lk erscheint καὶ ἐγένετο gehäuft, weshalb er es kaum ausgelassen haben würde, falls es zum Bestand seiner Vorlage in 7,1a gehört hätte."

108: For ὅτε: "Ὅτε wurde von Mt 2x gegenüber dem Mk-Stoff red eingefügt, so daß auch gegenüber Q mit diesem Verfahren gerechnet werden muß.

"b. In Q erscheint ὅτε auch anderswo nirgends sicher belegt.

"c. Wie Harnack [1907, 113 (ET 160)] bereits herausstellte, sind in Q Temporalsätze weder mit ὅτε noch mit ὡς belegt; diese werden vielmehr durch einfache Partizipialkonstruktionen oder (1x!) durch den Genitivus absolutus wiedergegeben. Diesem Befund entsprechend, wären eigentlich zu unserer Stelle eher Formulierungen in der Art von καὶ τελέσας ὁ Ἰησοῦς κτλ. / τελέσας δὲ ὁ Ἰησοῦς oder καὶ τελέσαντος τοὺς λόγους τούτους κτλ. und dergleichen zu erwarten." Elsewhere, Wegner decides for Matt = Q, Pro, for καὶ ἐγένετο ὅτε (pp. 23-24).

Schenk 1987, 132: "Ἐγένετο ὅτε ἐτέλεσεν ὁ Ἰησοῦς τ(οὺς λόγου)ς τ(ούτου)ς: Mt 5: Mk 0; Lk 0 +0. Der Konjunktionalsatz wird in der festen Autorwendung, mit der er weniger die Rede abschließt als das Folgende verbindend angeschlossen einleitend markiert, bei Mt mit ὅτε angeschlossen, wo Lk in vergleichbaren Konstruktionen immer ὡς verwendet ...: 7,28 (+Q); 11,1 (+Q); 13,53 (+Mk); 19,1 (+Mk); 26,1 (+Mk)." But see Schenk 1987 at Matt = Q, Pro (p. 24).

Syreeni 1987, 75: "Any reader of Matthew's Gospel, in trying to structure the whole of this product linearly or otherwise, is sure to pay attention to the five καὶ ἐγένετο expressions in vv. 7:28f; 11:1; 13:53f; 19:1; 26:1f. Individual variations notwithstanding, the common features of these verses are easy to recognize: (a) the Semitic narrative phrase καὶ ἐγένετο followed by (b) an anaphoric reference to the antecedent speech (ὅτε ἐτέλεσεν ὁ Ἰησοῦς + obj.), (c) a brief note of transition, e.g., with μετέβη/μετῆρεν, (d) a cataphoric introduction to the narrative to follow, e.g., with a final infinitive (11:1) or ἐλθεῖν (13:54a; 19:1). The opening phrase (a) and the anaphoric reference (b) recur most uniformly and constitute the *formulaic expression*. The first (7:28f) and the last (19:1) in the linear series deviate more from the common scheme than do the three inner members. The formulaic expression, however, ties the five occurrences firmly together. The reader can readily observe their literary function: they mark shifts from conspicuous speech sections to narrative.

"The set of five καὶ ἐγένετο markers is clearly Matthew's literary device, for only the first occurrence has partial parallels in Mk and Luke:

[Syreeni lays out the texts of Matt 7:28-29, Luke 7:1 and Mark 1:22 side-by-side]."

76: "The Q document at Matthew's disposal ... seems to have contained a two-part transitional link between a lengthy *speech* and a *narrative*-like sequence.[4] Possibly it was this linkage that gave Matthew the idea for his καὶ ἐγένετο markers, even though he, guided by his other principal source, precisely here let the marker function somewhat differently. If so, then we have here an instance of Matthew's *modeling* technique, which ... is one of the hallmarks of his redaction. In all events, the evangelist has used his formulaic expression very creatively. So far as one can detect, there is no marked division into speech and narrative sequences in Q in general, nor can a five-fold or six-fold outline, marked by a recurrent formal link, be imposed on Q."

88[4]: "The καὶ ἐγένετο phrase ... was hardly used in Q. The phrase does not seem to occur elsewhere in Q, and the wording is rather heavy in this connection."

Davies and Allison 1988, 82: "Καὶ ἐγένετο + finite verb: see [Matt] 7:28; 8:26; 9:10; 11:1; 13:53; 19:1; 26:1—all redactional."

Merklein 1994, 95: "V. 28a ist stereotyp für den Abschluß matthäischer Redekompositionen: 'Und es geschah, als Jesus diese Worte vollendet hatte, ...' (vgl. 11,1; 13,53; 19,1; 26,1)."

Evaluations

Shein 1998: Neither Luke nor Matt = Q {C}, [[()]¹].

'Επειδή is Lukan and Matthew also is proven to have a redactional tendency to conclude various discourses by the phrase καὶ ἐγένετο ὅτε (7:28; 11:1; 13:53; 19:1; 26:1). Therefore both introductions can be attributed to an editorial insertion. Hawkins' observation about Luke's frequent use of ἐγένετο with a finite verb does not disqualify the formulaic use of the phrase in Matthew as his redaction. Fuchs considers this use to serve the purpose of emphasizing the discourse material in his gospel. Yet, something must have stood in Q, hence {C}.

Johnson 2000: Matt = Q {B}, (καὶ ἐγένετο ὅτε)[1].

If one concludes that Q had a transition statement that concluded the Q Sermon and brought Jesus into Capharnaum, then it remains to determine the text of that transition. It is not sufficient to simply observe that the corresponding expressions in this variation unit are each used five times by the respective authors and give up on reconstructing Q (e.g., Harnack). Rather, the fact that the Matthean and Lukan transition statements as a whole correspond in substance suggests that one should consider both the text of the individual variations units and the statements as wholes when reconstructing the individual variation units.

In the case of Luke, Luke's use of ἐπειδή in a variety of contexts suggests that Lukan vocabulary is being used here. It is elsewhere not used in a Q context. Likewise, as is shown elsewhere in the database, the entire Lukan statement ἐπειδὴ ἐπλήρωσεν πάντα τὰ ῥήματα αὐτοῦ εἰς τὰς ἀκοὰς τοῦ λαοῦ is replete with Lukan vocabulary (Castor, Easton).

The case for Matthew is more complicated. Apart from the other four Matthean speech-to-narrative transition statements, ἐγένετο ὅτε (Luz) and ἐγένετο followed by a finite verb are not common to Matthew (Hawkins). Also, the argument that five uses of the expression indicate the secondary character of the expression here (Harnack) is vitiated—even contradicted—by the fact that the latter four uses (Matt 11:1; 13:53; 19:1; 26:1) are conscious and formulaic repetitions of the first (7:28a). Repeated use of a formula is not an indication of typical Matthean vocabulary. On the contrary, Wegner observes that Matthew has the tendency to use and repeat fixed expressions from Mark and Q. *If* this is the case for Q 7:1[1], then it strengthens the case for Matthew's text in Q 7:1[2-5] as well.

Wegner does ask why Luke, who uses ἐγένετο followed by a finite verb 22 times, would not use Q here. Gundry answers the question by claiming that ἐγένετο wasn't in Q—Matthew replaced Q 7:1's ἐπειδή with ἐγένετο ὅτε from the previous sentence (Q 6:49; cf. Luke 6:49). But Gundry's argument cuts both ways: Luke typically varies vocabulary and is just as likely to have replaced the καὶ ἐγένετο ὅτε of Q 7:1 with ἐπειδή in order to avoid repetition of the καὶ ἐγένετο that he uses in the previous sentence—Luke 6:49.

Robinson 2000: Matt = Q {B}, (καὶ ἐγένετο ὅτε)[1].

The Lukan formulation is so full of Lukanisms that it does not come into consideration.

Hawkins points out that ἐγένετο with a finite verb is only in Matthew in this formula, but in Luke 22 times. This supports the formula having come to Matthew from Q. (Davies and Allison inaccurately add Matt 8:26; 9:10, where different constructions are involved.) Hence it is hard to attribute this fixed formula to Matthew himself. It must be the Q formula.

The fact that this formulation is not elsewhere in Matthew than at the conclusion of the five Matthean discourses is strong evidence it was in Q. Hawkins (170-171) shows that it is characteristic of Matthew to adopt Markan and Q formulae and repeat them, with our idiom being his last (nineteenth) illustration. So to remove it from Q on the grounds that it is Matthean seems to be less likely than that Matthew adopted a Q idiom.

It would have required a strong Matthean preference for him to have changed from the Q idiom, had that been ἐπειδή, to this non-Matthean idiom all five times he used it to conclude a discourse.

The fact that Luke changes this formula again and again (see Q 7:1²⁻⁵) suggests that here, too, it is Luke who changed.

Kloppenborg 2000: Matt = Q {C}, ⟦(καὶ ἐγένετο ὅτε)¹⟧.

Hoffmann 2001: Matt = Q {C}, ⟦(καὶ ἐγένετο ὅτε)¹⟧.

Da von den Synoptikern nur Lukas ἐπειδή gebraucht, temporal an unserer Stelle, kausal in Lk 11,6; Apg 13,46; 14,12; 15,24 (vgl. auch Lk 1,1 ἐπειδήπερ), liegt lukanische Redaktion nahe (vgl. BDR [BDF] §455,1; 456,3, zum klassischen Sprachgebrauch KG II, 131, 445b, 460).

Mit ὅτε eingeleitete Temporalsätze sind bei jedem der drei Synoptiker— allerdings meist in unterschiedlichen Kontexten—12mal belegt. Matthäus übernimmt sie aus der Markusvorlage 3mal (Mt 12,3; 21,1; 27,31), 7mal läßt er sie dort weg (Mt 8,16; 13,10; 15,15; 16,9.10; 26,17; 27,55), 2mal ersetzt er sie durch Partizipialkonstruktionen (Mt 13,6; 14,6), 4mal fügt er ὅτε-Sätze in diese ein (Mt 9,25; 13,35; 19,1; 21,34), als redaktionelle Bildungen sind auch Mt 11,1 und 26,1 zu beurteilen, im Sondergut finden sie sich 2mal (Mt 13,26.48).

Auffallend ist, daß die Formulierung von Mt 7,28/Q 7,1 καὶ ἐγένετο ὅτε von Matthäus noch 4mal—sicher redaktionell—in den Redeabschlüssen Mt 11,1; 13,53; 19,1; 26,1 verwendet wird (LXX: 16 Belege). Gestattet dies den Schluß, daß die Wendung auch in Q 7,1 redaktionell ist? Oder hat sich Matthäus bei der Formulierung der übrigen Abschlußwendung von seiner Q-Vorlage inspirieren lassen? Da die lukanische Parallele ἐπειδή höchstwahrscheinlich redaktionell ist, ist Letzteres—falls man nicht wie z.B. Sato (1988, 24²⁴) beide Fassungen als redaktionell beurteilen will—die wahrscheinlichere Lösung. Bestätigt wird dies durch den lukanischen Gebrauch von ὅτε.

Lukas übernimmt nur 1mal einen ὅτε-Satz aus der Markusvorlage, 2mal läßt er ihn ganz weg (Lk 8,6.9), 4mal gestaltet er ihn um (Lk 6,3; 22,14; 23,33). Redaktionelle Bildungen liegen auch in Lk 4,25; 17,22 und 22,35 vor, dazu kommen noch vier weitere Sondergutbelege (Lk 2,21.22.42; 15,30). Aus Q dürfte in 13,35 ἕως ἥξει ὅτε stammen. In der Apostelgeschichte finden sich zehn Belege. Dieser Befund zeigt, daß Lukas insgesamt sehr frei in der Verwendung von ὅτε ist.

Aufschlußreich für die Beurteilung von Q 7,1 ist, daß die Konstruktion ἐγένετο ὅτε sich bei Lukas nicht findet. Für eine analoge Zeitangabe gebraucht er in Lk 1,23.41; 2,15; 19,29 allerdings ἐγένετο ὡς (vgl. BDR §455,2; LXX: 79 Belege). Für ein temporales ὡς finden sich im Evangelium insgesamt 13, in der Apostelgeschichte 29 Belege, im Markusevangelium dagegen nur ein, im Matthäusevangelium kein Beleg. Außerdem verwendet er für temporale Angaben in Verbindung mit ἐγένετο einen mit ἐν τῷ eingeleiteten substantivierten Infinitiv in Lk 1,8; 2,6; 3,21; 5,1.12; 9,18.29.33.51; 11,1.27; 14,1; 17,11.14; 18,35; 19,15.29 (hier ersetzt er damit Mk 11,1 ὅτε das Mt 21,1 übernimmt); 24,4.15.30.51; Apg 19,1 (vgl. BDR §404,1 mit Anm. 5: unattisch, LXX-Einfluß. LXX: 38 Belege). Diese Verbindung findet sich bei den Synoptikern sonst nur noch in Mk 4,4, in den Parallelen Mt 13,4 und Lk 8,5 wird das ἐγένετο gestrichen. Insgesamt gebrauchen ἐν τῷ mit Infinitiv Matthäus 3mal, Markus 2mal, Lukas 32mal, die Apostelgeschichte 7mal.

Die Übersicht zeigt die Variabilität der lukanischen Ausdrucksweise und macht insgesamt deutlich, daß er—aus welchen Gründen auch immer—auch andere Konstruktionen wählen kann. Das spricht für die Annahme, daß er Q 7,1 redaktionell verändert hat.

Q 7:1²: Luke's ἐπλήρωσεν or Matthew's ἐτέλεσεν.

Luke = Q: [ἐπλήρωσεν]²

Pro

Schmid 1930, 252: "Mag nun Lk in allen abweichenden Worten sekundär sein, so stammt doch der ungriechische Ausdruck ἐπλήρωσεν ... εἰς τὰς ἀκοὰς τοῦ λαοῦ doch nicht vom Evangelisten."

Morganthaler 1971, 304: See Q 7:1⁰ In Q (p. 8).

Guelich 1982, 416: "Luke most likely has the earlier verb to 'complete' (πληρόω), a verb that has a much too technical 'fulfillment' connotation for Matthew, especially when used with reference to the spoken word. ... Consequently, the evangelist exchanged the theologically pregnant *to fulfill* for *to finish* (τελέω) with its more neutral meaning and used the verb to express its basic meaning in this context of bringing the discourse material to an end."

Gundry 1982, 136: "Ἐπλήρωσεν becomes ἐτέλεσεν (5,2) in order that πληρόω might be reserved for the notion of fulfillment."

Luz 1985, 415⁴: "Vorlk könnte πληρόω (in der Bedeutung 'beendigen') sein."

Luz 1985, ET 1989, 455⁴: "Πληρόω (in the meaning 'conclude') could be pre-Lukan."

Wegner 1985, 116-117: "Pro: a. Mt verwendet πληρόω nicht im profanen Sinne von 'vollenden'/'beendigen', könnte es also ersetzt haben. b. Das in Mt 7,28a entsprechende τελέω könnte zwar von Mt aus einer in Q stehenden Übergangsformel übernommen worden sein, doch [117] zeigt zugleich eine relativ hohe Anzahl von Beispielen, in denen Mt Formeln wiederholt, die weder durch Mk noch Q gedeckt sind, daß es sehr wohl auch unter Verdacht seiner eigenen Red steht. c. Lk verwendet τελέω zwar nicht häufig, doch setzt er es immerhin vermutlich 1x in seinem Mk-Stoff (18,31b), 1x im Sg (2,26) und 1x in der Apg (13,29) von sich aus ein." But see Wegner at Luke = Q, Con (pp. 33-34).

Sand 1986, 158: "Das wohl ursprüngliche 'erfüllen' (so Lk) hat Mt durch 'beenden' ersetzt."

Merklein 1994, 97: "Die bei Lukas noch erhaltene Einleitung (7,1: 'Nachdem er alle seine Worte vor den Ohren des Volkes vollendet hatte ...') läßt noch erkennen, woher Matthäus die Anregung zu seinen stereotypen Redeschlüssen hat (siehe oben zu Mt 7,28)."

International Q Project 1995, 478: Reconstruction. For complete text see Q 7:1⁰ In Q (p. 16).

Con

B. Weiß 1908, 14²²: "Besonders das ἐπλήρωσεν—εἰς τὰς ἀκοάς Lk. 7,1 ist sicher nicht von Luk. geprägt; nur wird derselbe nach seiner Vorstellung von dem Auditorium der Bergrede (vgl. Anm. 1) das τῶν μαθητῶν in τοῦ λαοῦ verwandelt haben. Es hatte also in L die Bergrede auch einen feierlichen Schluß, wie sie in 6,20 einen feierlichen Eingang hatte, obwohl wir den Anfang desselben nicht mehr herzustellen vermögen. Luk. hat in Reminiszenz an Mt. 7,28 daraus den Übergang zur folgenden Erzählung gebildet."

115: Reconstruction: Weiß's "L" source: "Ἐπλήρωσεν πάντα τὰ ῥήματα αὐτοῦ εἰς τὰς ἀκοάς."

Castor 1912, 42: "Most of the linguistic differences seem due to Luke's literary changes. Luke 7:1a is a Lukan paraphrase for Matt. 7:28a. Ἐπειδή, ἐπλήρωσεν, ῥήματα, εἰς τὰς ἀκοάς are all characteristic of Luke."

Bussmann 1929, 56: See Q 7:1¹ Luke = Q, Con (p. 22).

Busse 1977, 146³: "Auch sonst zeigt dieser Teilvers stilistisch Redaktion an: Das Verb πληρόω kennen zwar alle Synoptiker (16mal Mt; 2mal Mk; 9mal Lk und 16mal Apg). Doch wo es Lk verwendet, hat es bei den Korreferenten keine Parallelen: Lk 1,20; 2,40; 3,5 LXX-Zitat; 4,21; 7,1; 9,31; 21,24; 22,16; 24,44."

Marshall 1978, 279: "Πάντα τὰ ῥήματα αὐτοῦ, a Lucan phrase, corresponds to Mt. τούς λόγους τούτους."

Gatzweiler 1979, 307-308: "Le v. 1 assure la transition entre le discours dans la plaine (6,20-49) et notre histoire: son caractère [308] rédactionnel est patent."

Jeremias 1980, 151: "Red ... ἐπλήρωσεν: Der Gebrauch von πληρόω im rein profanen Sinne von 'beendigen' ist kennzeichnend für das lk Doppelwerk: Lk 7,1/Apg 7,23.30; 9,23; 12,25; 13,25; 14,26; 19,21; 24,27, sonst im NT nur Mk 1,15; Joh 7,8."

Dauer 1984, 110: "Auch die Formulierung bei *Lk* dürfte redaktionell sein: ... zu πληρόω schreibt Jeremias [1980, 151]: 'Der Gebrauch von πληρόω im rein profanen Sinne von "beendigen" ist kennzeichnend für das lk Doppelwerk'; vgl. dazu Lk 7,1 u.St.; Apg 7,23.30; 9,23; 12,25; 13,25; 14,26; 19,21; 24,27—sonst im NT: Mk 1,15; Joh 7,8."

Wegner 1985, 117: "Contra: a. πληρόω weist anderswo keine weiteren Belege in Q auf. b. In der Bedeutung 'beenden', 'vollenden' wird es von Lk bevorzugt. c. Mt bevorzugt zwar die Verwendung von πληρόω im Sinne der Schrifterfüllung, benutzt aber zugleich dieses Verb auch in anderer Bedeutung, weshalb nicht anzunehmen ist, daß er es in der Bedeutung 'vollenden'/'beenden' ablehnen würde, falls es ihm so vorgelegen hätte."

123: "Lk verwendet es zwar auch von sich aus vermutlich 3x redaktionell (Lk 2,39; 18,31b und Apg 13,29), doch wird πληρόω im Vergleich zu τελέω deutlich von ihm bevorzugt. Hinzu kommt, daß auch πληρόω im Sinne von 'vollenden', 'beendigen' von Lk oft benutzt wird."

Gnilka 1986, 283: See Q 7:1⁰ In Q (p. 12).

Wiefel 1988, 142-143: "Die Einleitung, die von der Feldrede zum Heilungswunder überleitet, enthält die dem Lukas eigene Ausdrucksweise (πληροῦν, vgl. 22,16; εἰς τὰς ἀκοάς, vgl. 1,44; Apg. 17,20)."

Nolland 1989, 315: "Luke has reformulated in his own language (πληροῦν means 'to finish' in Acts 12:35; 14:26; 19:21; for εἰς τὰς ἀκοάς [lit., 'into the ears'] see Acts 17:20 and cf. at Luke 1:44; for πάντα τὰ ῥήματα, 'all the words,' cf. at Luke 1:65)."

Davies and Allison 1991, 18³²: "Luke's hand is revealed by word statistics. … πληρόω with profane sense: Mt: 0; Mk: 1; Lk: 1; Acts: 8."

Gagnon 1993, 715: "It should be noted that Lucan redaction can … be seen in the transition phrase in v 1a, 'when he completed all his words in the hearing of the people.'"

Sevenich-Bax 1993, 174: "Schwierig stellt sich die Beurteilung der ersten Vershälfte dar: Das Verb πληρόω ist ebenso gut lukanisch³ wie die Formulierung 'πάντα τὰ ῥήματα' und 'εἰς τὰς ἀκοὰς τοῦ λαοῦ'. Deshalb wird Lk 7,1a zu Recht der lukanischen Redaktion zugewiesen."

174³: "Lkev: 9mal + Apg: 15mal. Allerdings auch bei Matthäus 16mal (Markus: 2mal)."

Gagnon 1994b, 135: Reconstruction. For complete text see Q 7:1⁰ In Q (p. 15).

Matt = Q: (ἐτέλεσεν)²

Pro

Hawkins 1899, 32: "Words and Phrases characteristic of St. Matthew's Gospel: … πληρόω." The implication is that Matthew would have used πληρόω (Luke 7:1) had it been in the source.

B. Weiß 1908, 14²²: See Q 7:1⁰ In Q (p. 5).

14: Reconstruction. For complete text see Q 7:1⁰ In Q (p. 5).

Streeter 1911, 148: See Q 7:1⁰ In Q (p. 6).

Castor 1912, 222: Reconstruction. For complete text see Q 7:1⁰ In Q (p. 6).

Streeter 1924, 262: See Q 7:1⁰ In Q (p. 7).

von Dobschütz 1928, 341: See Q 7:1⁰ In Q (p. 7).

Polag 1979, 38: Reconstruction. For complete text see Q 7:1⁰ In Q (pp. 9-10).

Schenk 1981, 37: Reconstruction. For complete text see Q 7:1⁰ In Q (p. 10).

Wegner 1985, 109-110: "Pro: a. τελέω wird von Mt in seiner Bearbeitung des Mk-Stoffes niemals red hinzugefügt.

"b. Mt könnte das Verb in 7,28a bereits trad vorgefunden und es von sich aus, entsprechend seiner Tendenz, Mk- und Q-Formeln zu wiederholen, in 11,1; 13,53; 19,1 und 26,1 red eingefügt haben.

"c. Das in Lk 7,1a auftauchende Synonym πληρόω gebraucht der erste Evangelist 16x in seinem Ev, weshalb kaum anzunehmen ist, daß er es in 7,28a durch τελέω ersetzte.

[110] "d. Das lk πληρόω steht unter dem Verdacht der lk Red, was vor allem die hohe Belegzahl in der Apg nahelegt."

123: "Hier wird wiederum das mt Wort vorzuziehen sein. Für seine Ursprünglichkeit spricht: 1. Mt verwendet es im Sinne der Beendigung einer Rede nur in seine fünf festgeprägten Redeschlüssen. 2. Im Gegensatz zu πληρόω taucht es vermutlich noch 2x in Q auf (Mt 10,23 om Lk und Lk 12,[50] om Mt). 3. Lk verwendet es zwar auch von sich aus vermutlich 3x redaktionell (Lk 2,39; 18,31b und Apg 13,29), doch wird πληρόω im Vergleich zu τελέω deutlich von ihm bevorzugt. Hinzu kommt, daß auch πληρόω im Sinne von 'vollenden', 'beendigen' von Lk oft benutzt wird. 4. Mt, der im Vergleich mit dem LkEv πληρόω fast doppelt so oft einsetzt, würde es kaum übergehen, falls er es in 7,28a vorgefunden hätte."

126: See Q 7:1¹ Matt = Q, Pro (p. 24).

270: Reconstruction. For complete text see Q 7:1⁰ In Q (pp. 11-12).

Kosch 1989, 230: See Q 7:1¹ Matt = Q, Pro (pp. 24-25).

Catchpole 1992, 521-522 [1993, 285-286]: See Q 7:1⁰ In Q (pp. 13-14).

Sevenich-Bax 1993, 175: "Anders liegt der Fall allerdings bei der Vokabel τελέω: Wie auch das Verb πληροῦν ist τελέω in der Logienquelle an keiner weiteren Stelle sicher nachzuweisen. Auch kann man nicht gut behaupten, daß Matthäus πληροῦν in jedem Fall bevorzugt hätte, hätte er es in seiner Quelle vorgefunden. Hier muß nämlich beachtet werden, daß das Verb πληρόω in seiner Theologie ausschließlich zur Konstatierung der Erfüllung der Schrift dient. Letztendlich wird man zwischen den Vokabeln τελέω und πληρόω keine sichere Entscheidung treffen können: Beide Evangelisten verwenden πληρόω häufiger als τελέω. Kann man Lukas—gegenüber Matthäus—dennoch eine Vorliebe für πληρόω nachsagen und von daher die Sekundarität der lukanischen Formulierung begründen, so trifft nicht weniger zu, daß Matthäus an der vorliegenden Stelle kaum πληρόω eingesetzt hätte, da es in seinem Evangelium spezifische Bedeutung hat."

Gagnon 1994b, 135: Reconstruction. For complete text see Q 7:1⁰ In Q (p. 15).

Con

Simons 1880, 42: See Q 7:1¹ Matt = Q, Con (p. 25).

Holtzmann 1901, 226: See Q 7:1⁰ Not in Q (p. 17).

von Harnack 1907, 54 (ET 1908, 74): See Q 7:1¹ Matt = Q, Con (pp. 25-26).

Wellhausen 1904a, 33: "Der Übergang ὅτε ἐτέλεσεν ist besonders bei Mt beliebt."

Easton 1926, 94-95: See Q 7:1¹ Matt = Q, Con (p. 26).

Schmid 1930, 252: See Q 7:1² Luke = Q, Pro (p. 32).

Parker 1953, 176, 195: See Q 7:1¹ Matt = Q, Con (p. 26).

Fuchs 1971, 51-52: See Q 7:1¹ Matt = Q, Con (pp. 26-27).

Gundry 1982, 136: "Ἐπλήρωσεν becomes ἐτέλεσεν (5,2) in order that πληρόω might be reserved for the notion of fulfillment."

Dauer 1984, 110: "Von *Matthäus* stammt die Neuformulierung καὶ ἐγένετο ὅτε ἐτέλεσεν, die in redaktionellen Bildungen wie 11,1; 13,53; 19,1; 26,1 wiederkehrt."

Luz 1985, 415⁵: "Τελέω kommt nur noch 2x trad. vor; der Evangelist könnte das Wort gewählt haben, um das 'christologische' πληρόω zu vermeiden."

Luz 1985, ET 1989, 455⁵: "Τελέω occurs only two more times in the tradition; the evangelist might have chosen the word in order to avoid the 'Christological' πληρόω."

Wegner 1985, 110: "Contra: a. τελέω ist innerhalb von Q an keiner anderen Stelle *sicher* belegt. Die Belegstellen, die außer Mt 7,28a für Q noch in Frage kämen—Mt 10,23 und Lk 12,50—sind in der Forschung stark umstritten. …

"b. Die Statistik zeigt zwar, daß Lk τελέω nur selten verwendet, doch könnte es in Lk 2,39—wofür der Vergleich mit Apg 13,29 spricht—und 18,31b aus seiner Hand stammen. Das aber heißt, daß Lk es in 7,1a kaum gestrichen haben würde, falls er es in Q vorgefunden hätte." But see Wegner at Matt = Q, Pro (p. 35).

Gnilka 1986, 283-284: "Mt 7,28a ist durch E gestaltet. Dafür spricht nicht nur die [284] viermalige Wiederholung der Formel, sondern auch ihre Anlehnung an Dt 31,1: 'Als Mose all diese Worte vollendet hatte' (vgl. 31,24; 32,44-46). Die Verwendung des Kompositums συνετέλεσεν in Dt ist kein Argument gegen diese Annahme. Die Anlehnung an Dt, die wir bereits wiederholt und vor allem in 4,25 feststellen konnten, erhärtet sie vielmehr."

Sand 1986, 158: "Das wohl ursprüngliche 'erfüllen' (so Lk) hat Mt durch 'beenden' ersetzt."

Brooks 1987, 53: "In vocabulary, the use of *teleō* stands out. The word regularly occurs as part of an ending to discourse material in Matthew in the phrase *hote etelesen ho Iēsous* 'when Jesus had finished' (7.28; 11.1; 13.53;

19.1; 26.1). Two other uses of the word occur in unparalleled material. At 17.24, the meaning is 'to pay (a tax)'. In 10.23b, the meaning appears to be 'to end' or 'to finish'.

"In the clear redactional uses of *teleō*, the action to be finished is specified by a supplementary participle, which may be either implied by the context or supplied explicitly. ... In 7.28; 13.53; 19.1; 26.1, the reader would understand either *legōn* or *lalōn*."

Schenk 1987, 132: See Q 7:1¹ Matt = Q, Con (p. 27).

Merklein 1994, 95: "V. 28a ist stereotyp für den Abschluß matthäischer Redekompositionen: 'Und es geschah, als Jesus diese Worte vollendet hatte, ...' (vgl. 11,1; 13,53; 19,1; 26,1)."

Evaluations

Shein 1998: Luke = Q {C}, ἐ[[πλήρω]²]σεν.

While πληρόω is typically Lukan, τελέω is part of the Matthean formula. However it seems likely that there was some such verb in this context and therefore the grade {C}.

Johnson 2000: Matt = Q {D}, ἐ( )²σεν.

Neither πληρόω nor τελέω is found in any other Q texts (Wegner), except where πληρόω is inserted by Matthew in Matt 23:32 (cf. Matt 23:29-32 par Luke 11:47-48).

The primary argument for Luke's ἐπλήρωσεν is the argument that Matthew would most likely replace it with a less theologically-loaded term, ἐτέλεσεν (Guelich, Gundry). Matthew's 14 redactional uses of πληρόω in the sense of fulfilling the scriptures compared to only two other uses—one probably from a source (13:48) and the other in reference to completing the apostasy of Israelite ancestors (23:32)—are significant. Only Matt 23:32 approximates the meaning of πληρόω as used in Luke 7:1. At the same time, the other two uses suggest that Matthew is not bound to one technical use of the word, but uses it with nearly the breadth of meaning found in Luke-Acts. Also, the verb is used often and in several different ways by Luke and would appear to be Lukan vocabulary (Castor, Busse, Jeremias).

Both Luke and Matthew use τελέω with different nuances, suggesting that Luke would not have been averse to using τελέω if it existed in Q. At the same time, Luke only uses it five times in Luke-Acts, and Matthew only twice apart from the formula transition phrase. Therefore τελέω is not Matthean vocabulary.

It is likely that the transitional phrase of Q 7:1a was largely Matthean in appearance (see Q 7:1¹,³⁻⁵). Yet, the argument from general to particular appears to be weakened by lack of supporting arguments in this particular case. A weak but valid argument also exists for Matthean replacement of πληρόω.

Robinson 2000: Matt = Q {B}, ἐ(τέλε)²σεν.

Luke's verb πληρόω in the meaning "to bring to an end" is typically Lukan. There is no particular reason for assuming the Lukan πληρόω was the Q verb here. Πληρόω does not occur in Q. Matt 23:32 interpolates it into Q 11:48 (without the distinctively Matthean meaning of "fulfill," but rather meaning "make complete"). As Matt 13:48 also illustrates, Matthew was not limited to the fulfillment-meaning of πληρόω. He could have retained it here, if it were in the Q formula. His rare and untechnical usage of τελέω does not suggest he would have favored it as an emendation of the formula all five times, if the formula had used πληρόω.

Matthew uses τελέω only twice (10:23; 17:24) outside of this formula, and in different meanings, so that its consistent use in the formula suggests it came with the formula to Matthew.

Kloppenborg 2000: Luke = Q {C}, ἐ⟦[πλήρω]²⟧σεν.

Hoffmann 2001: Luke = Q {C}, ἐ⟦[πλήρω]²⟧σεν.

Die Möglichkeit, daß Matthäus seine Schlußwendung bereits in Q hier vorgefunden und nur ihre häufige Anwendung auf seine Redaktion zurückgeht (vgl. Robinson) ist nicht auszuschließen. Für die Ursprünglichkeit des lukanischen ἐπλήρωσεν spricht jedoch, daß Matthäus—mit Ausnahme von 13,48—das Verb sonst qualifiziert theologischer Bedeutung verwendet (15mal). Er könnte es also deswegen hier durch das allgemeinere τελέω (insgesamt 7 Belege) ersetzt und so in die Abschlußwendungen seiner Redekompositionen aufgenommen haben. Lukas gebraucht beide Verben sowohl theologisch qualifiziert im Sinn der Schrifterfüllung als auch in der allgemeinen Bedeutung "beenden" bzw. "vollmachen, vollenden" (τελέω 4mal im Evangelium, 1mal in der Apostelgeschichte; πληρόω 9mal im Evangelium, 16mal in der Apostelgeschichte). Insofern reicht das relativ häufige Vorkommen von πληρόω im lukanischen Doppelwerk nicht aus, lukanische Herkunft hier zu begründen. Wahrscheinlicher ist es, daß Matthäus als Abschlußwendung καὶ ἐγένετο ὅτε ἐπλήρωσεν in Q vorfand und mit Rücksicht auf seinen spezifischen Gebrauch von πληρόω änderte.

Q 7:1³: Matthew's ὁ Ἰησοῦς.

Luke = Q: ( )³

Pro

Con

B. Weiß 1908, 115: Reconstruction: Weiß's "L" source. For complete text see Q 7:1² Luke = Q, Con (p. 33).

Wegner 1985, 120: "Die Tatsache, daß er es gegenüber der Mk-Vorlage nur 1x einträgt, dagegen aber 19x ausläßt, macht es wahrscheinlich, daß er auch in Lk 7,1a ein ursprüngliches Ἰησοῦς durch das Pronomen αὐτοῦ sekundär ersetzte. Diese Wahrscheinlichkeit wird zusätzlich noch dadurch verstärkt, daß Lk überhaupt Eigennamen und Substantive mehrmals durch das Pronomen wiedergibt."

Matt = Q: (ὁ Ἰησοῦς)³

Pro

B. Weiß 1908, 14²²: See Q 7:1⁰ In Q (p. 5).
14: Reconstruction. For complete text see Q 7:1⁰ In Q (p. 5).
Streeter 1911, 148: See Q 7:1⁰ In Q (p. 6).
Streeter 1924, 262: See Q 7:1⁰ In Q (p. 7).
von Dobschütz 1928, 341: See Q 7:1⁰ In Q (p. 7).
Polag 1979, 38: Reconstruction. For complete text see Q 7:1⁰ In Q (pp. 9-10).
Schenk 1981, 37: Reconstruction. For complete text see Q 7:1⁰ In Q (p. 10).
Wegner 1985, 112: "Pro: a. Ἰησοῦς erscheint in Q mehrmals belegt.
"b. Im Vergleich mit Mt läßt Lk Ἰησοῦς weit öfter gegenüber Mk aus.
"c. Das Analogon αὐτός in Lk 7,1a wird von Q zwar auch mehrmals in den obliquen Kasus für Jesus verwendet, doch tauchen die von Mt und Lk zugleich gedeckten Belege ausschließlich innerhalb einer Perikope, nämlich in der Versuchungsgeschichte auf."
124: "Träfe dies auch für die Hauptmannsgeschichte zu, so könnte das mt Ἰησοῦς eine Reminiszenz der Verwendung dieses Namens zu Beginn der ursprünglichen Erzählung sein. Sicheres läßt sich freilich nicht mehr ermitteln."
126: See Q 7:1¹ Matt = Q, Pro (p. 24).
270: Reconstruction. For complete text see Q 7:1⁰ In Q (pp. 11-12).

Kosch 1989, 230: See Q 7:1¹ Matt = Q, Pro (pp. 24-25).

Catchpole 1992, 521-522 [1993, 285-286]: See Q 7:1⁰ In Q (pp. 13-14).

Sevenich-Bax 1993, 238: Reconstruction. For complete text see Q 7:1⁰ In Q (p. 15).

Gagnon 1994b, 135: Reconstruction. For complete text see Q 7:1⁰ In Q (p. 15).

Con

Simons 1880, 42: See Q 7:1¹ Matt = Q, Con (p. 25).

Holtzmann 1901, 226: See Q 7:1⁰ Not in Q (p. 17).

Castor 1912, 222: Reconstruction. For complete text see Q 7:1⁰ In Q (p. 6).

Easton 1926, 94-95: See Q 7:1¹ Matt = Q, Con (p. 26).

Schmid 1930, 252: See Q 7:1² Luke = Q, Pro (p. 32).

Parker 1953, 176, 195: See Q 7:1¹ Matt = Q, Con (p. 26).

Fuchs 1971, 51-52: See Q 7:1¹ Matt = Q, Con (pp. 26-27).

Morganthaler 1971, 304: See Q 7:1⁰ In Q (p. 8).

Gundry 1982, 136: "Characteristically, Matthew inserts the name of Jesus to clarify the subject."

Wegner 1985, 111: "Das relativ häufige Auftauchen von Ἰησοῦς in QMt (9x) stimmt mit dem mt Verfahren gegenüber Mk überein, wo die Zahl der mt Eintragungen ebenfalls sehr hoch ist (59x!). Die mt Bearbeitung der Mk-Vorlage berechtigt also, auch in QMt weitgehend mit mt Red zu rechnen, wo immer die Lk-Parallele Ἰησοῦς nicht enthält. Dies legt sich auch dadurch nahe, daß Mt überhaupt das Subjekt gegenüber Mk des öfteren präzisiert."

112: "Gegen die Ursprünglichkeit in Q spricht vor allem die Tatsache, daß Mt eine starke Vorliebe für die Einfügung von Ἰησοῦς in seiner Mk-Bearbeitung zeigt."

120: "Mt zeigt eine starke Tendenz, Ἰησοῦς in seiner Mk-Vorlage einzufügen, könnte also in 7,28a ein ursprüngliches Pronomen durchaus sek durch Ἰησοῦς ersetzt haben." But see Wegner at Matt = Q, Pro (p. 39).

Schenk 1987, 132: See Q 7:1¹ Matt = Q, Con (p. 27).

Davies and Allison 1991, 18: "Also typical is the naming of the subject (αὐτοῦ): Jesus is always named first in the Matthean healing narratives."

Merklein 1994, 95: "V. 28a ist stereotyp für den Abschluß matthäischer Redekompositionen: 'Und es geschah, als Jesus diese Worte vollendet hatte, …' (vgl. 11,1; 13,53; 19,1; 26,1)."

International Q Project 1995, 478: Reconstruction. For complete text see Q 7:1⁰ In Q (p. 16).

Evaluations

Shein 1998: Luke = Q {A}, ()³.

Wegner's observation is not convincing against the heavily attested inclination in Matthew to include the name of Jesus.

Johnson 2000: Matt = Q {C}, ⟦(ὁ Ἰησοῦς)³⟧.

Ἰησοῦς does not occur often in Q, but it does occur at least five times in Q 4-9. It occurs at the beginning of The Temptations of Jesus (Q 4:1—following the Q 3 Baptist material and possibly Jesus' baptism), at least twice when Jesus responds to Satan (Q 4:8, 12; cf. Luke 4:4 par), once here at Q 7:9 where he responds to the centurion's faithful actions, and once at Q 9:58 in Jesus' interaction with potential followers (in a pericope that serves as a narrative transition between This Generation and the Children of Wisdom [Q 7:31-35] and the Q mission speech [Q 10:2-16]). Having Jesus' name mentioned in this transitional statement, at the beginning of The Centurion's Faith in Jesus' Word, would be consistent with other minimal Q uses of Jesus' name.

The evidence for redactional omission (Luke) or insertion (Matthew) of the name is inconclusive: Luke commonly omits the name from Markan material (Wegner), but Matthew commonly adds the name as well (Gundry, Wegner).

Problematic is Davies' and Allison's statement that "Jesus is always named first in the Matthean healing narratives"—and is therefore redactional here. But Matt 7:28a precedes the Markan healing of Matt 8:1-4, not the Centurion story. Jesus' name does not arise in Matthew's version of The Centurion's Faith in Jesus' Word until his statement of amazement in Matt 8:10. Indeed, unless one includes Luke's two delegations in Q, Jesus' name would not assuredly appear in Q—subsequent to The Temptations of Jesus—until Q 7:9, well near the end of the centurion story.

Matthew's use of the name in the subsequent transition statements (11:1; 13:53; 19:1; 26:1) therefore appears to result from use of traditional material in 7:28a (Q 7:1a).

Robinson 2000: Matt = Q {C}, ⟦(ὁ Ἰησοῦς)³⟧.

In collections of sayings (and in the "remember" formula found in Acts and elsewhere) there was at the incipit and/or explicit an identification of Jesus as the speaker, as in the incipit of Thomas and probably of Q. In contrast to Thomas, there is not a quotation formula with each saying, but the identity of the speaker is clearly intended as Jesus (except for John's sayings, distinguishable as such).

Since there is no naming of Jesus at the beginning of the Sermon, and only one documented in The Centurion's Faith in Jesus' Word, it would have been useful for it to be here in Q. Luke's αὐτοῦ replacing Q's τούτους may be a reminiscence of "Jesus" in Q. The Sermon ended with an appeal to hear and do "my" sayings, not just to call *me* "Lord, Lord." The identity of the speaker is essential, to carry this much authoritative weight. Hence to follow this peroration with the "completing" formula naming Jesus is reasonable. This sensitivity to refer to sayings and to Jesus is what is at work I think also in the conjectured incipit.

"Jesus" is part of the formula Matthew uses all 5 times, in consistency with the other instances of an identification at the beginning or end of a collection of sayings. It thus seems to belong to the tradition out of which the formula arose, and not simply to be a Matthean trait. Hence one may assume it was here in the formula in Q, in spite of its absence from Luke 7:1. See also its normal presence in the "words" formula (Q 7:1⁴).

Yet Matthew often inserts Jesus' name. This calls for some caution.

Kloppenborg 2000: Luke = Q {D}, ( )³.

Hoffmann 2001: Indeterminate {U}, ( )³.

Q 7:1⁴: Luke's πάντα τὰ ῥήματα αὐτοῦ or Matthew's τοὺς λόγους τούτους.

Luke = Q: [πάντα τὰ ῥήματα αὐτοῦ]⁴

Pro

Castor 1912, 222: Reconstruction: for αὐτοῦ only. For complete text see Q 7:1⁰ In Q (p. 6).

Schmid 1930, 252: See Q 7:1² Luke = Q, Pro (p. 32).

Morganthaler 1971, 304: See Q 7:1⁰ In Q (p. 8).

Schenk 1981, 37: Reconstruction. For complete text see Q 7:1⁰ In Q (p. 10).

Wegner 1985, 118: "Pro: Von Lk wird das mt Analogon λόγος mehrmals in den Mk-Stoff eingefügt und gehäuft in der Apg verwendet, wodurch die Annahme einer lk Streichung unwahrscheinlich wird."

120: "Auf Jesus bezogen taucht αὐτός in den obliquen Kasus mehrmals in Q auf, und zwar innerhalb der Versuchungsgeschichte." But see Wegner at Luke = Q, Con (p. 45).

Merklein 1994, 97: "Die bei Lukas noch erhaltene Einleitung (7,1: 'Nachdem er alle seine Worte vor den Ohren des Volkes vollendet hatte ...') läßt noch erkennen, woher Matthäus die Anregung zu seinen stereotypen Redeschlüssen hat (siehe oben zu Mt 7,28)."

Con

Hawkins 1899, 21: "Words and Phrases characteristic of St. Luke's Gospel: ... ῥῆμα."

von Harnack 1907, 54: "Der Lukastext ... erweist sich ... als sekundär ... durch das πάντα τὸ ῥήματα (es steht bei Matth., Mark., Joh. niemals, bei Luk. aber noch 3mal)."

von Harnack 1907, ET 1908, 74: "The Lukan text is shown to be secondary by ... πάντα τὰ ῥήματα (never occurring in St. Matthew, St. Mark, and St. John; thrice again in St. Luke)."

B. Weiß 1908, 14²²: "Daß sie Luk. auch hier in Q las [...] folgt daraus, daß er das ἐγένετο ὅτε durch sein ἐπειδή ersetzt, das auch Harnack [see Q 7:1¹ Luke = Q, Con (p. 21)] für lukanisch erklärt. Dies gilt aber keineswegs von dem πάντα τὰ ῥήματα, das nach Lk. 1,65. 2,51 (vgl. auch 2,19) auch in L stand."

115: Reconstruction: Weiß's "L" source. For complete text see Q 7:1² Luke = Q, Con (p. 33).

Castor 1912, 42: "Most of the linguistic differences seem due to Luke's literary changes. Luke 7:1a is a Lukan paraphrase for Matt. 7:28a. Ἐπειδή, ἐπλήρωσεν, ῥήματα, εἰς τὰς ἀκοάς are all characteristic of Luke."

222: Reconstruction. For complete text see Q 7:1⁰ In Q (p. 6).

Cadbury 1920, 187: "The following changes [by Luke] may be recorded without more particular explanation. Many of them are probably improvements in clearness, or in elegance or exactness of expression: ... Mt. 7,28 λόγους—Lk 7,1 ῥήματα (Q)."

Easton 1926, 95: See Q 7:1[1] Luke = Q, Con (p. 21).

Bussmann 1929, 56: See Q 7:1[1] Luke = Q, Con (p. 22).

Fuchs 1971, 175[6]: "Bei Mk kommt der Ausdruck πᾶν ῥῆμα bzw. τοῦτο τὸ ῥῆμα überhaupt nicht vor; bei Mt erscheint nur in 4,4; 12,36 und 18,16 die Verbindung πᾶν ῥῆμα, die aus dem AT stammt, wie die Zitate aus Dt 8,3 (Mt 4,4) und Dt 19,15 (Mt 18,16) zeigen. Lk dagegen hat mehrere sehr nahe verwandte Stellen: ... Lk 2,51 und 7,1: πάντα τὰ ῥήματα."

Busse 1977, 146[3]: "Ferner kennt nur Lk den Plural πάντα τὰ ῥήματα in Lk 1,65; 2,51; Apg 5,20, zumal ῥῆμα eine luk. Vorzugsvokabel ist. Das ist nicht nur wortstatistisch (5mal Mt, 19mal Lk, 14mal Apg) nachweisbar. Wiederum verwendet die Korreferenten das Substantiv immer ohne direkte Parallele bei Lk."

Gatzweiler 1979, 307-308: "Le v. 1 assure la transition entre le discours dans la plaine (6,20-49) et notre histoire: son caractère [308] rédactionnel est patent."

Jeremias 1980, 54: "'Ρῆμα: Schon die Statistik lehrt, daß ῥῆμα ein lukanisches Vorzugswort ist: von den 67 neutestamentlichen Belegen (Mt 5, Mk 2, Lk 19/Apg 14, Joh 12, Pls 8, sNT 7) steht die Hälfte (33) im Doppelwerk. Es kommt hinzu, daß Lukas die Vokabel im Markusstoff nicht nur beließ (Lk 9,45a = Mk 9,32; vgl. Lk 22,61 𝔓[69.75] B ℵ = Mk 14,72), sondern außerdem an drei Stellen in ihn einfügte (Lk 9,45c; 18,34; 20,26). Doch wäre es voreilig, wollte man daraufhin die restlichen 14 Belege für ῥῆμα, die der Nicht-Markusstoff des Evangeliums bietet, ohne weitere Nachprüfung sämtlich der lukanischen Redaktion zuweisen; denn hier mahnt die Feststellung zur Vorsicht, daß von diesen 14 Belegen 9 der Kindheitsgeschichte zugehören, also ῥῆμα schon zu deren Vorzugsworten gehört haben wird. Eine Zuweisung von ῥῆμα an Lukas bedarf also, jedenfalls für Lk 1-2, zusätzlicher Argumente. An diesen fehlt es nun allerdings nicht. So ist für den lukanischen Gebrauch von ῥῆμα kennzeichnend: a) die Wendung πάντα τὰ ῥήματα (im NT nur Lk 1,65; 2,19.51; 7,1/Apg 5,20...)."

71: "Πάντα τὰ ῥήματα ταῦτα: im Nt nur Lk 1,65; 2,19; ... Die Wendung ist ganz lukanisch (zu ῥῆμα = 'Sache' etc. → 1,37 Red ...; zur rhetorischen Verstärkung durch πᾶς → 1,10 Red)."

151: "Red ... πάντα τὰ ῥήματα: Die Wendung ist lukanisch → 1,65 Red ...; zum missionstheologischen Gebrauch von τὰ ῥήματα ('die Verkündigung') → 1,37 Red."

Guelich 1982, 415-417: See Guelich at Matt = Q, Pro (p. 46).

Dauer 1984, 110: "Auch die Formulierung bei *Lk* dürfte redaktionell sein: ... Die Wendung πάντα τὰ ῥήματα ist nach Jeremias [1980, 151] 'lukanisch'."

Luz 1985, 415, 415⁴ (ET 1989, 455, 455⁴): See Q 7:1¹ Luke = Q, Con (p. 22).

Wegner 1985, 118: "Con: a. Lk benutzt πᾶς mit Vorliebe, könnte es daher sehr wohl selbst eingefügt haben. b. Die 30 Eintragungen in dem Mk-Stoff zeigen, daß auch Mt eine Vorliebe für πᾶς hat, so daß eine sekundäre Streichung durch ihn für unwahrscheinlich gehalten werden muß."

119: "Con: a. Während ῥῆμα in Q sonst nicht mehr erscheint, taucht das in Mt 7,28a entsprechende λόγος bei drei weiteren Q-Belegen auf. b. ῥῆμα könnte aus der Feder des Lk stammen, wie seine Einfügungen im Mk-Stoff und die Belege der Apg zeigen. c. Da Mt dieses Wort aus seinem Sg und Mk-Stoff 3x übernahm und es von sich aus 1x im Mk-Stoff und wahrscheinlich 1x in QMt einfügte, wäre eigentlich zu erwarten, daß er es auch in Mt 7,28a übernehmen würde, falls seine Q-Vorlage es enthalten hätte. ...

"Der Gesamtausdruck πάντα τὰ ῥήματα begegnet innerhalb des NT ausschließlich im lk Doppelwerk, nämlich in 2,51, auSt [Luke 7:1] und in Apg 5,20; außerdem noch mit zusätzlichem ταῦτα in Lk 1,65 und 2,19. D.h.: 3x im Sg, 1x in QLk und 1x in Apg. Für Jeremias [1980, 71] ist diese Wendung 'ganz lukanisch', was sowohl aus der lk Vorliebe für rhetorische Verstärkung durch πᾶς [1980, 30] als auch aus der Tatsache hervorgeht, daß von den drei ersten Evangelisten nur Lk ῥῆμα im missionstheologischen Sinne von 'Verkündigung' in 7,1a und anderen Stellen des Evangeliums und der Apg verwendet [1980, 54]."

120: See Q 7:1³ Luke = Q, Con (p. 39).

124: "Isoliert betrachtet ist auf Grund des Befundes in Q eine Entscheidung zwischen πάντα und τούτους rein statistisch kaum möglich, denn sowohl für das Demonstrativum als auch für das Adjektiv weist Q mehrere Belege auf (οὗτος: 20x und πᾶς: 14x). Der Q-Text hätte somit entweder πάντας τοὺς λόγους oder τοὺς λόγους τούτους gelautet. Weiter führt aber die Beobachtung, daß der Gesamtausdruck πάντα τὰ ῥήματα im gNT ausschließlich innerhalb des lk Doppelwerkes auftaucht (Lk 1,65; 2,19.51; 7,1 und Apg 5,20), so daß auch bezüglich des πάντα mit der Annahme einer lk Red aus guten Gründen gerechnet werden kann. Dies legt sich schließlich auch auf Grund der lk Eintragungen von πᾶς in den Mk-Stoff nahe. Mt, der πᾶς ebenfalls mit Vorliebe in seine Mk-Vorlage einfügt, würde es übrigens kaum gestrichen haben!"

Nolland 1989, 315: See Q 7:1² Luke = Q, Con (p. 34).

Davies and Allison 1991, 18³²: "Luke's hand is revealed by word statistics. ... πάντα τὰ ῥήματα: Mt: 0; Mk: 0; Lk: 4."

Catchpole 1992, 521-522 [1993, 285-286]: See Q 7:1⁰ In Q (pp. 13-14).

Gagnon 1993, 715: "It should be noted that Lucan redaction can ... be seen in the transition phrase in v 1a, 'when he completed all his words in the hearing of the people.'"

Sevenich-Bax 1993, 174: "Schwierig stellt sich die Beurteilung der ersten Vershälfte dar: Das Verb πληρόω ist ebenso gut lukanisch wie die Formulierung 'πάντα τὰ ῥήματα'⁴ und 'εἰς τὰς ἀκοὰς τοῦ λαοῦ'. Deshalb wird Lk 7,1a zu Recht der lukanischen Redaktion zugewiesen."

174⁴: "Der Gesamtausdruck πάντα τὰ ῥήματα wird im gesamten NT ausschließlich im lukanischen Doppelwerk verwendet."

Matt = Q: (τοὺς λόγους τούτους)⁴

Pro

B. Weiß 1908, 14: Reconstruction. For complete text see Q 7:1⁰ In Q (p. 5).

Streeter 1924, 262: See Q 7:1⁰ In Q (p. 7).

von Dobschütz 1928, 341: See Q 7:1⁰ In Q (p. 7).

Polag 1979, 38: Reconstruction. For complete text see Q 7:1⁰ In Q (pp. 9-10).

Guelich 1982, 416-417: "The object of this verb, *these words,* (τοὺς λόγους τούτους), also differs from Luke's 'all his sayings' (πάντα τὰ ῥήματα αὐτοῦ). Whether Matthew's [417] phrase, which picks up the same phrase of 7:24, 26, or Luke's, which statistically appears more frequently in Luke-Acts (19x in Luke, 12x in Acts; cf. 5x in Matt, 2x in Mark), occurred in the tradition lies beyond our control, since Luke demonstrates no redactional bias either way. Matthew does use ῥῆμα on occasion but usually referring to a word or statement (e.g., 12:36; 26:75; 27:14). The similar use of ῥῆμα to refer to a longer discourse in Acts 2:14; 5:20; 10:22, 44 may tip the scale in favor of Matthew's having the more original phrase."

Wegner 1985, 112: "Pro: a. λόγος ist in Q mehrmals belegt. b. Ein Q-Beleg (Mt 7,24/Lk 6,47) erscheint im unmittelbaren Kontext von Mt 7,28a/Lk 7,1a. c. Das dem λόγος entsprechende ῥῆμα in Lk 7,1a ist in Q sonst nicht belegt und steht außerdem auch noch unter Verdacht lk Red."

113: "Pro: a. οὗτος wird oftmals in Q verwendet. b. Das von Lk parallel verwendete πᾶς könnte aus seiner Red stammen. c. Mt ist in der Verwendung von πᾶς keineswegs zurückhaltend, würde es also kaum beseitigen wenn Q es ihm in 7,28a geboten hätte."

124: "1. Für die Ursprünglichkeit von λόγος ist u.E. der Befund in Q ausschlaggebend: Q benutzt es im Gegensatz zu ῥῆμα nicht nur auch an weiteren Stellen (Mt 7,24; 8,8 und 12,32 par Lk), sondern vor allem im unmittelbar vorangehenden (Mt 7,24/Lk 6,47) und folgenden (Mt 8,8/Lk 7,7) Kontext.

Die Ursprünglichkeit liegt aber auch auf Grund der Verwendung von ῥῆμα bei Mt nahe, der das Wort mehrmals aus seinen Quellen übernimmt und nachweislich 1x (27,14) von sich aus in seinen Mk-Stoff einfügt."

125: "Stimmt dieses Ergebnis, so muß noch einmal kurz auf das Demonstrativum τούτους eingegangen werden. Oben äußerten wir nämlich die Vermutung, das Wort sei unter Einfluß der mt Red in 7,24.26 verwendet. Gegen diese Erklärung spricht aber, daß der Verweis auf vorhergehende Worte—in unserem Falle auf Worte der vorangestellten Bergpredigt—durch adjektivische oder pronominale Näherbestimmung eigentlich eher zu erwarten ist als ein bloßer Hinweis nach der Art von τοὺς λόγους. Das aber bedeutet, daß bei Annahme einer Red hinsichtlich der adjektivischen Näherbestimmung, wie sie oben als wahrscheinlich dargelegt wurde, die Traditionalität der pronominalen Näherbestimmung (τούτους) durchaus für annehmbar erscheint. Dafür spricht auch der Q-Befund, worin οὗτος nicht weniger als 20x sicher belegt ist. Bei dieser Annahme hätte aber dann nicht mit Red in 7,24.26 eine sek Hinzufügung von τούτους in 7,28a bedingt, sondern eher das Gegenteil wäre der Fall: ein Demonstrativum, das urspr am Schluß der Bergpredigt stand, hätte die mt Formulierung des Schlußgleichnisses Mt 7,21-17 beeinflußt.

"So ergibt sich hinsichtlich beider Wendungen in Mt und Lk, daß die mt Formulierung (τοὺς λόγους τούτους) wiederum die ursprünglichere ist, wobei sich der Wortlaut des LkEv hinreichend durch die Annahme eines lk Ersatzes für die von Q gebotene Wendung erklären läßt."

126: See Q 7:1¹ Matt = Q, Pro (p. 24).

270: Reconstruction. For complete text see Q 7:1⁰ In Q (pp. 11-12).

Kosch 1989, 230: See Q 7:1¹ Matt = Q, Pro (pp. 24-25).

Catchpole 1992, 521-522 [1993, 285-286]: See Q 7:1⁰ In Q (pp. 13-14).

Sevenich-Bax 1993, 174-175: "Die matthäische Fassung steht allerdings gleichfalls unter dem Verdacht redaktioneller Überarbeitung, da Matthäus die Formulierung, wie sie Mt 7,28a vorliegt, an vier Stellen als Abschlußwendung weiterer Redekompositionen einsetzt (Mt 11,1; 13,53; 19,1; 26,1f.). Bei näherer Betrachtung zeigt sich jedoch, daß diese Tatsache nicht unbedingt einer Herkunft der Formulierung aus der Logienquelle widersprechen muß; dies v.a. dann, wenn sich nachweisen läßt, daß Matthäus vom Wortmaterial her näher an Q liegt. Letzteres trifft insbesondere für die Vokabel λόγος zu, die im Unterschied zu ῥῆμα nicht nur an weiteren Stellen für Q belegt ist, sondern auch im unmittelbar vorangehenden und folgenden [175] Kontext (Lk 6,47//Mt 7,24; Lk 7,7//Mt 8,8)."

176: "Daß die Struktur der Aussage Mt 7,28a im Matthäusevangelium in vier gleichlautenden Wendungen aufgegriffen wird, die jeweils zudem in der Funktion stehen, das Ende einer Redekomposition anzuzeigen, erklärt sich dann so, daß Matthäus eine zunächst in der Tradition gefundene Wendung für seine Zwecke aufnimmt und sie sich für die weitere Gestaltung seines Evangeliums zunutze macht."

238: Reconstruction. For complete text see Q 7:1⁰ In Q (p. 15).

Gagnon 1994b, 135: Reconstruction. For complete text see Q 7:1⁰ In Q (p. 15).

International Q Project 1995, 478: Reconstruction. For complete text see Q 7:1⁰ In Q (p. 16).

Con

B. Weiß 1876, 288: "Auch von der zweiten größeren Rede, die der Evangelist mitheilt, leitet er mit der gleichen Formel, wie 7,28, zum Fortgang seiner Darstellung über, nur daß an die Stelle des τοὺς λόγους τούτους mit dem gut griechischen Partizip der Hinweis darauf tritt, daß es sich in dieser Rede um spezielle Verordnungen für die zwölf Jünger (vgl. 10,1) gehandelt hatte. Ausdrücklich aber wird der Faden des zeitlichen Zusammenhangs zerschnitten, wenn der Evangelist berichtet, daß Jesus fortging von dort, wo er den Jüngern die Anweisungen gegeben, um zu lehren und zu verkündigen in ihren Städten."

Simons 1880, 42: See Q 7:1¹ Matt = Q, Con (p. 25).

Holtzmann 1901, 226: See Q 7:1⁰ Not in Q (p. 17).

Easton 1926, 94-95: See Q 7:1¹ Matt = Q, Con (p. 26).

Parker 1953, 176, 195: See Q 7:1¹ Matt = Q, Con (p. 26).

Fuchs 1971, 51-52: See Q 7:1¹ Matt = Q, Con (pp. 26-27). Fuchs does specify this, but implies it in his alignment of the texts (cf. Matt 13:53; 19:1; 26:1).

Gundry 1982, 126: "Instead of 'all his words' we read 'these words,' which echoes vv 24 and 26."

Luz 1985, 415: "V28a zeigt das erste Vorkommen einer mt Abschlußformulierung, die am Ende sämtlicher Reden mit geringen Variationen³ begegnen wird (11,1; 13,53; 19,1; 26,1). Der Evangelist hebt dadurch die fünf großen Reden seines Evangeliums gegenüber anderen Jesusreden heraus."

415³: "26,1 faßt mit πάντας τοὺς λόγους τούτους alle fünf Reden zusammen."

Luz 1985, ET 1989, 455: "Verse 28a shows the first occurrence of a Matthean concluding formula which will occur at the end of all discourses, with small variations (11:1; 13:53; 19:1; 26:1).³ The evangelist in this way distinguishes the five great discourses of his Gospel from other discourses of Jesus."

455³: "Matthew 26:1 brackets with πάντας τοὺς λόγους τούτους all five discourses."

Wegner 1985, 113: "Contra: a. Mt zeigt keine Vorliebe für ῥῆμα, könnte es also leicht ersetzt haben. b. Wie die Statistik zeigt, ist Lk gegenüber λόγος keineswegs zurückhaltend: Sein häufiger Gebrauch in der Apg und die Eintragungen im Mk-Stoff sprechen vielmehr gegen die Annahme einer sekundären Streichung oder Ersatz in Lk 7,1a. ...

"Ergebnis: mt Red möglich/wahrscheinlich. ...

"Für eine mt Red könnte abgesehen von der Statistik auch der unmittelbare Kontext sprechen, wo ja Mt in 7,24.26 τοὺς λόγους mit dem Demonstrativum τούτους bringt, während Lk in den entsprechenden Stellen 1x nur das Substantiv bietet (6,47) und in 6,49 weder das Substantiv noch das Demonstrativum bringt. Es liegt daher nahe, daß Mt in 7,28a auf das red τούτους von 7,24.26 zurückgreift." But see Wegner at Matt = Q, Pro (pp. 46-47).

Schenk 1987, 132: See Q 7:1¹ Matt = Q, Con (p. 27).

337: "Da auch die mt Schüler nur dieselben Worte weitergeben, konnte 10,14 (+Mk) auch für sie der Plur. von 7,24.26.28 renominalisiert werden."

388: "λόγους τούτους: Mt 5: Mk 0: Lk 2: 7,24.26.28 (+Q)."

Sevenich-Bax 1993, 176¹: "Matthäus hat aber wohl das Demonstrativum τούτους—als anaphorischen Verweis auf die Bergpredigt—sekundär zugesetzt. Das gleiche Verfahren war auch schon Mt 7,24.26 zu beobachten."

Merklein 1994, 95: "V. 28a ist stereotyp für den Abschluß matthäischer Redekompositionen: 'Und es geschah, als Jesus diese Worte vollendet hatte, ...' (vgl. 11,1; 13,53; 19,1; 26,1)."

Evaluations

Shein 1998: Matt = Q {C}, ⟦(τοὺς λόγους τούτους)⁴⟧.

There is no argument for Luke's πάντα τὰ ῥήματα αὐτοῦ in favor of its inclusion in Q. It is Lukan. Wegner's observation about Q's use of ῥήμα and λόγος is convincing as well as for its attribute "these." Yet, the possibility of Matthean redaction—an observation supported by other occurrences of this phrase in Matthew—cautions against its inclusion with a grade higher than {C}.

Johnson 2000: Matt = Q {B}, (τοὺς λόγους τούτους)⁴.

Matthew's demonstrative pronoun οὗτος and noun λόγος are common in Q (Wegner); the same cannot be said for Luke's noun ῥῆμα (Sevenich-Bax).

The only arguments for Luke are that Luke had no clear and obvious reason to omit λόγος from Q (Wegner) and that Matthew's τοὺς λόγους τούτους echoes the same in Matt 7:24, 26 (cf. Lk 6:47, 49) (Gundry). Yet, the phrase πάντα τὰ ῥήματα αὐτοῦ is decidedly Lukan (Harnack)—especially in the way it is used theologically (Jeremias)—as is the word ῥῆμα (Hawkins, Cadbury, Busse). Matthew also uses ῥῆμα on occasion—even πᾶς and ῥῆμα together—so there is no obvious reason to suggest Matthean replacement of ῥῆμα (Wegner).

On the other hand, Matthew's vocabulary is found in Q (Wegner; Sevenich-Bax) and is consistent with the use of the plural of ὁ λόγος in Q 6:47 (and 6:49; cf. Matt 7:26) (cf. Schenk). Matthew's only other uses of this phrase are in the formulaic transitional phrases of 19:1 and 26:1, which are most likely based on Matt 7:28a (Q 7:1a).

Robinson 2000: Matt = Q {B}, (τοὺς λόγους τούτους)[4].

Three out of five of the conclusions to discourses in Matthew include this expression (and the contents of the other two discourses make sense of Matthew—in these instances—having departed from the formula). Hence it is formulaic. Λόγοι is the designation for sayings of Jesus from the beginning, and indeed in the immediately preceding context (Q 6:47, 49). It occurs (in the singular) in the present healing story (Q 7:7), and is indeed the connecting link between the Sermon and The Centurion's Faith in Jesus' Word. Thus λόγοι/λόγος is apparently the term that had established itself as the oldest reference to collections of sayings of Jesus. Hence it is the term one would expect here. See also the incipit of the Gospel of Thomas, which, like the present text, includes the demonstrative adjective: οὗτοι οἱ λόγοι .... See also the (forthcoming) discussion of the incipit of Q in Documenta Q, and already a preprint: "The *Incipit* of the Sayings Gospel Q," *Hommage à Étienne Trocmé: Revue d'Histoire et de Philosophie Religieuses* 75 (1995) 9-33; esp. 19-28: The "recalling" formula indicates that the earliest way to refer to Jesus' sayings used the idiom "the words of the Lord Jesus": Acts 20:35 μνημονεύειν τε τῶν λόγων τοῦ κυρίου Ἰησοῦ ὅτι αὐτὸς εἶπεν· 1Clem 13,1 μεμνημένοι τῶν λόγων τοῦ κυρίου Ἰησοῦ, οὓς ἐλάλησεν διδάσκων ...; cf. also Polycarp, Phil 2,3 μνημονεύοντες δὲ ὧν εἶπεν ὁ κύριος διδάσκων, where the "remembering" formula is present without the noun. The opening of the *Didache* attests the same language, when (1,3) it gives as "the way of life" the quotation of Jesus' two laws of love plus the Golden Rule, for which he then provides an interpretation ("teaching"—compare Mark 4:34, where ἐπέλυεν corresponds to the synonym ἐπίλυσις, a riddle's "resolution"; and Qumran's technical term "Pesher"). The "teaching" is called "the teaching of these words" (τούτων δὲ τῶν λόγων ἡ διδαχὴ ἐστιν αὕτη), followed by a collection of Jesus' sayings that are referred to by the technical term "these words."

Πάντα τὰ ῥήματα is distinctively Lukan language.

There is no equivalent in the Matthean formula for Luke's πάντα, except τούτους, which is a somewhat different nuance. But Luke's synonym τὰ ῥήματα for τοὺς λόγους strengthens the assumption that one or the other was in Q.

Kloppenborg 2000: Matt = Q {B}, (τοὺς λόγους τούτους)[4].

Hoffmann 2001: Matt = Q {B}, (τοὺς λόγους τούτους)[4].

Q 7:1⁵: Luke's εἰς τὰς ἀκοὰς τοῦ λαοῦ.

Luke = Q: [εἰς τὰς ἀκοὰς τοῦ λαοῦ]⁵

Pro

Schmid 1930, 252: "Mag nun Lk in allen abweichenden Worten sekundär sein, so stammt doch der ungriechische Ausdruck ἐπλήρωσεν … εἰς τὰς ἀκοὰς τοῦ λαοῦ doch nicht vom Evangelisten.²"

252²: "Abgesehen von dem lukanischen λαός (3,15.18; 6,16; 8,47; 9,13; u.ö.)."

Morganthaler 1971, 304: See Q 7:1⁰ In Q (p. 8).

Wegner 1985, 121: "Was die Wahrscheinlichkeit der Ursprünglichkeit in Q betrifft, so steht dieser vor allem der Befund im MtEv entgegen, da Mt ἀκοή keineswegs zurückhaltend gebraucht." But see Wegner at Luke = Q, Con (pp. 52-53).

Kosch 1989, 230-231: "Ernsthafter als dies bei Wegner geschieht, muß jedoch gefragt werden, ob Q an dieser Stelle nicht auch einen Hinweis auf das Volk als Auditorium Jesu enthielt, denn die Wendung *eis akoas tou laou* (Lk 7,1a) hat zwar in Mt 7,28a keine Entsprechung, doch fällt auf, daß Mt in 7,28b diff Mk 1,22 die *ochloi* erwähnt, die über Jesu Lehre erstaunt [231] waren. Zudem ist es problematisch, *eis tas akoas* aufgrund der einzigen Parallele in Apg 17,20 und trotz der Beobachtung, 'daß Lk isoliertes *akoē* zu vermeiden pflegt', als lk zu bezeichnen. Daß Mt es hier—entgegen seiner Gewohnheit, *akoē* aus seinen Vorlagen zu übernehmen—ausläßt, könnte damit zusammenhängen, daß der Verweis auf das Auditorium Jesu aus Q durch die Verknüpfung mit Mk 1,22 als überschüssig entfiel." See Kosch at Emendation = Q (p. 54).

Merklein 1994, 97: "Die bei Lukas noch erhaltene Einleitung (7,1: 'Nachdem er alle seine Worte vor den Ohren des Volkes vollendet hatte …') läßt noch erkennen, woher Matthäus die Anregung zu seinen stereotypen Redeschlüssen hat (siehe oben zu Mt 7,28)."

Con

B. Weiß 1908, 14²²: See Q 7:1² Luke = Q, Con (p. 33).

14: Reconstruction. For complete text see Q 7:1⁰ In Q (p. 5).

115: Reconstruction: Weiß's "L" source. For complete text see Q 7:1² Luke = Q, Con (p. 33).

Castor 1912, 42: "Most of the linguistic differences seem due to Luke's literary changes. Luke 7:1a is a Lukan paraphrase for Matt. 7:28a. Ἐπειδή, ἐπλήρωσεν, ῥήματα, εἰς τὰς ἀκοάς are all characteristic of Luke."

222: Reconstruction. For complete text see Q 7:1⁰ In Q (p. 6).

Easton 1926, 95: See Q 7:1¹ Luke = Q, Con (p. 21).

Bussmann 1929, 56: See Q 7:1¹ Luke = Q, Con (p. 22).

Schmid 1930, 252²: "Abgesehen von dem lukanische λαός (3,15.18; 6,17; 8,47; 9,13 u.ö.)."

Conzelmann 1954, 153¹: "Der Leiblingsausdruck des Lc ist freilich eindeutig λαός. Er ist schon im Ev. vielfach in Quellenstücken eingesetzt: Lc 6,17; 8,47; 18,43; 19,47; 20,9.19.26; 21,38; 23,35. Dabei überwiegt die vulgäre Bedeutung: Lc 1,21; 3,15; 3,18; 7,1; 8,47; 20,1.9.45 usw."

Conzelmann 1954, ET 1960, 164¹: "Luke's favourite expression is certainly λαός. In the Gospel he often inserts it in passages from sources, e.g. Luke vi,17; viii,47; xviii,43; xix,47; xx,9,19,26; xxi,38; xxiii,35. It is generally used for the common people; cf. Luke i,21; iii,15; iii,18; vii,1; viii,47; xx,1,9,45; etc."

Busse 1977, 146³: "Ebenso erinnert die Wendung εἰς τὰς ἀκοάς an Apg 17,20 (vgl Apg 28,26), die Haenchen [1956, 457] im Gegensatz zu εἰς ὦτα φέρω als hellenistisch bestimmt. Der Genitiv τοῦ λαοῦ bezieht sich auf Lk 6,17 zurück, wo die Wendung red. bestimmbar wird. Denn auch λαός ist eine luk. Vorzugsvokabel."

Polag 1979, 38: Reconstruction. For complete text see Q 7:1⁰ In Q (pp. 9-10).

Jeremias 1980, 151: "Red ... εἰς τὰς ἀκοάς: mit εἰς und Plural im NT nur im lk Doppelwerk (Lk 7,1; Apg 17,20). —τοῦ λαοῦ: lk Vorzugswort → 1,10 Red."

Schenk 1981, 37: Reconstruction. For complete text see Q 7:1⁰ In Q (p. 10).

Dauer 1984, 110: "Auch die Formulierung bei *Lk* dürfte redaktionell sein: ... Schließlich muß man auch die Wendung εἰς τὰς ἀκοάς τοῦ λαοῦ für lk Redaktion erachten; denn λαός ist ein Lieblingsausdruck des Lukas; εἰς τὰς ἀκοάς begegnet uns zwar nur noch Apg 17,20; vgl. aber εἰς τὰ ὦτα Lk 1,44; Apg 11,22 und ἐν τοῖς ὠσίν Lk 4,21."

Strecker 1984, 179: "Der erste Evangelist verbindet Q- und Markustradition. Waren in Q die ὄχλοι ('Volksmenge') als Hörer der Rede vorausgesetzt (vgl. Lk 7,1a; Mt 5,1), so berichtet auch Markus von der Wirkung der Lehre Jesu (Mk 1,22.27)."

Luz 1985, 415, 415⁴ (ET 1989, 455, 455⁴): See Q 7:1¹ Luke = Q, Con (p. 22).

Wegner 1985, 121: "Die Tatsache, daß Lk nach Reden mehrmals auf ein 'Hören' verweist, dürfte darauf hindeuten, daß wir es in diesem Falle mit einer Bildung des dritten Evangelisten zu tun haben. ...

"Ergebnis: lk Red wahrscheinlich."

122: "Die statistischen Angaben zeigen, das mit einem Q-Verweis auf das λαός am Abschluß der Bergpredigt kaum zu rechnen ist. Auf eine lk Red auSt weist vor allem die Tatsache hin, daß Lk bereits zu Beginn der Bergpredigt λαός in die Mk Vorlage einsetzte (vgl. Lk 6,17 mit Mk 3,7), so daß die Wiederholung dieses Wortes auch in 7,1a mit großer Wahrscheinlichkeit aus seiner Hand stammen wird. Dies legt sich um so mehr nahe, als ja auch Mt mit der Verwendung von λαός keineswegs zurückhaltend ist, wie aus der Statistik hervorgeht. Bestätigt werden diese Beobachtungen nicht zuletzt von Q selbst, das nicht λαός sondern ὄχλος verwendet (vgl. Lk 7,24 und 11,4 par Mt!)."

125-126: "Für diese Wendung ist die Annahme einer lk Red sehr wahrscheinlich. Dies geht vor allem daraus hervor, daß Mt weder ἀκοή noch λαός gegenüber Mk zu vermeiden pflegt. Aber auch der Befund in Q spricht dafür, wo weder ἀκοή noch λαός anderswo belegt erscheinen, und wo statt λαός vielmehr ὄχλος verwendet wird. Schließlich zeigt der Befund in Lk selbst, daß die Wendung sehr wahrscheinlich von ihm stammt: Erstens taucht εἰς τὰς ἀκοάς im gNT nur innerhalb des lk Doppelwerkes auf [126] (Lk 7,1a und Apg 17,20) und zweitens ist λαός bekanntlich ein von Lk bevorzugtes Wort."

270: Reconstruction. For complete text see Q 7:1⁰ In Q (pp. 11-12).

Wiefel 1988, 142-143: "Die Einleitung, die von der Feldrede zum Heilungswunder überleitet, enthält die dem Lukas eigene Ausdrucksweise (πληροῦν, vgl. 22,16; εἰς τὰς ἀκοάς, vgl. 1,44; Apg. 17,20)."

Nolland 1989, 315: See Q 7:1² Luke = Q, Con (p. 34).

Davies and Allison 1991, 18³²: "Luke's hand is revealed by word statistics. ... εἰς + τὰς ἀκοάς: Mt: 0; Mk: 0; Lk: 1; Acts: 1. λαός: Mt: 14; Mk: 2; Lk:36; Acts: 48."

Catchpole 1992, 521-522 [1993, 285-286]: See Q 7:1⁰ In Q (pp. 13-14).

Gagnon 1993, 715: "It should be noted that Lucan redaction can ... be seen in the transition phrase in v 1a, 'when he completed all his words in the hearing of the people.'"

Sevenich-Bax 1993, 174: "Schwierig stellt sich die Beurteilung der ersten Vershälfte dar: Das Verb πληρόω ist ebenso gut lukanisch wie die Formulierung 'πάντα τὰ ῥήματα' und 'εἰς τὰς ἀκοὰς τοῦ λαοῦ'.⁵ Deshalb wird Lk 7,1a zu Recht der lukanischen Redaktion zugewiesen."

174⁵: "Ἀκοή mit εἰς und im Plural nur im lukanischen Doppelwerk. Auch λαός ist lukanisches Vorzugswort (Mtev: 14mal; Mkev: 2mal; Lkev: 36mal + Apg: 42mal)."

238: Reconstruction. For complete text see Q 7:1⁰ In Q (p. 15).

Gagnon 1994b, 135: Reconstruction. For complete text see Q 7:1⁰ In Q (p. 15).

International Q Project 1995, 478: Reconstruction. For complete text see Q 7:1⁰ In Q (p. 16).

Matt = Q: [ ]⁵

Pro

Con

Emendation = Q: εἰς <>⁵ ἀκοὰς τοῦ ὄχλου⁵

Kosch 1989, 231: "Daß das in Q nicht bezeugte *laos* mit hoher Wahrscheinlichkeit auf Lk zurückgeht, trifft zu, doch ist zu fragen, ob Lk hier nicht das in Q sicher bezeugte *ochlos* (oder *ochloi*, vgl. Mt 7,28b diff Mk 1,22) durch das von ihm bevorzugte *laos* ersetzt, wie er es auch an 5 Stellen in seinem Mk-Stoff tut, so daß in Q *kai egeneto hote etelesen ho Iēsous tous logous toutous eis akoas tou ochlou* (oder *tōn ochlōn*) gestanden hätte."

Evaluations

Shein 1998: Matt = Q {A}, []⁵.
The phrase εἰς τὰς ἀκοὰς τοῦ λαοῦ is entirely bound to Lukan redaction and there is no evidence to argue for its inclusion in Q.

Johnson 2000: Matt = Q {B}, []⁵.
Only Schmid presents a viable argument for Luke, and even that argument is rebuffed (Busse). Yet, even Schmid (and Kosch) has to admit that λαός is decidedly Lukan here (Kosch pleads for εἰς τὰς ἀκοάς, but replaces λαός with ὄχλος).

It is weak to argue Lukan vocabulary for εἰς τὰς ἀκοάς on the basis of one other use (Acts 17:20) in the Lukan text (Jeremias), but Dauer and Wiefel offer examples of similar expressions used by Luke in four other places.

The lack of this phrase in Matt 11:1; 13:53; 19:1; and 26:1 tell against its existence in Matthew's formulaic paradigm, 7:28a (Q 7:1a).

Robinson 2000: Matt = Q {B}, []⁵.
The vocabulary is typically Lukan and is not found in Q. It is attached to Lukan redaction, indicating a redactional context.

Kloppenborg 2000: Matt = Q {A}, []⁵.

Hoffmann 2001: Matt = Q {A}, []⁵.

Q 7:1⁶: Luke's εἰσῆλθεν or Matthew's εἰσελθόντος δὲ αὐτοῦ. (See also Mark 1:21a parr.)

Luke = Q: [εἰσῆλθεν] ( )⁶

Pro

von Harnack 1907, 54: "Also muß man leider darauf verzichten, hier den ursprünglichen Wortlaut vor den Worten εἰσῆλθεν εἰς Καφαρναούμ herzustellen."

91: "M 7,28; 8,5-10.13; L 7,1-10.

"[Nachdem er diese Worte gesprochen hatte], εἰσῆλθεν εἰς Καφαρναούμ καὶ προσῆλθεν αὐτῷ ἑκατόνταρχος παρακαλῶν αὐτὸν (6) καὶ λέγων· κύριε, ὁ παῖς μου βέβληται ἐν τῇ οἰκίᾳ παραλυτικός, δεινῶς βασανιζόμενος. (7) λέγει αὐτῷ· ἐγὼ ἐλθὼν θεραπεύσω αὐτόν. (8) ἀποκριθεὶς δὲ ὁ ἑκατόνταρχος ἔφη· κύριε, οὐκ εἰμὶ ἱκανὸς ἵνα μου ὑπὸ τὴν στέγην εἰσέλθῃς· ἀλλὰ μόνον εἰπὲ λόγῳ, καὶ ἰαθήσεται ὁ παῖς μου. (9) καὶ γὰρ ἐγὼ ἄνθρωπός εἰμι ὑπὸ ἐξουσίαν, ἔχων ὑπ' ἐμαυτὸν στρατιώτας, καὶ λέγω τούτῳ· πορεύθητι, καὶ πορεύεται, καὶ ἄλλῳ· ἔρχου, καὶ ἔρχεται, καὶ τῷ δούλῳ μου· ποίησον τοῦτο, καὶ ποιεῖ. (10) ἀκούσας δὲ ὁ Ἰησοῦς ἐθαύμασεν καὶ εἶπεν τοῖς ἀκολουθοῦσιν· [ἀμὴν] λέγω ὑμῖν, οὐδὲ ἐν τῷ Ἰσραὴλ τοσαύτην πίστιν εὗρον. [[(13) καὶ εἶπεν ὁ Ἰησοῦς τῷ ἑκατοντάρχῃ· [ὕπαγε,] ὡς ἐπίστευσας γενηθήτω σοι. καὶ ἰάθη ὁ παῖς ἐν τῇ ὥρᾳ ἐκείνῃ.]]" Brackets around text indicate uncertainty of reconstruction. Double-brackets indicate indecision—see Q 7:?10?⁰ Undecided (p. 361).

von Harnack 1907, ET 1908, 74: "There seems ... no hope of recovering the original wording of the source before the words εἰσῆλθεν εἰς Καφαρναούμ."

131-132: "(St. Matt. vii. 28; viii. 5-10, 13; St. Luke vii. 1-10)

"[After He had spoken these words] εἰσῆλθεν εἰς Καφαρναούμ κτλ. [See text above]."

B. Weiß 1908, 15²⁴: "Die Erzählung begann mit dem καὶ εἰσῆλθεν εἰς καφ. Lk. 7,1, das nur Mt. 8,2 in den ihm so beliebten gen. abs. verwandelt ist, ... was hier durch das ihm ebenso charakteristische προσῆλθεν αὐτῷ notwendig wurde."

15: Reconstruction. For complete text see Q 7:1⁰ In Q (p. 5).

Bartlett 1911, 329: "[Use of a source other than Mark] is confirmed by the very form 'Nazara' [Luke 4:16], ... which seems the more vernacular form, but occurs elsewhere only at the same point in Matthew (iv. 13, probably = his Q). It is not what we should expect from Luke himself; and the simple style of the opening, 'And he came to Nazara' (cf. the similar εἰσῆλθεν εἰς Καφαρναούμ in vii. 1 ...), ... suggests a primitive type of narrative like the Q tradition."

Castor 1912, 222: Reconstruction. For complete text see Q 7:1⁰ In Q (p. 6).

Morganthaler 1971, 304: See Q 7:1⁰ In Q (p. 8).

Polag 1979, 38: Reconstruction. For complete text see Q 7:1⁰ In Q (pp. 9-10).

Schenk 1981, 37: Reconstruction. For complete text see Q 7:1⁰ In Q (p. 10).

Dauer 1984, 110: "Lk V. 1b entspricht Mt 8,5a; in Lk ist die ursprüngliche Formulierung erhalten, da der Genitivus absolutus in Perikopenanfängen häufig auf Matthäus zurückgeht."

Wegner 1985, 127: "Der Lk-Text wird also in diesem Falle gegenüber der mt Formulierung vorzuziehen sein, so daß der Q-Wortlaut wohl, wie in Lk, aus εἰσῆλθεν εἰς Καφαρναούμ bestand."

270: Reconstruction. For complete text see Q 7:1⁰ In Q (pp. 11-12).

Kosch 1989, 230: See Q 7:1¹ Matt = Q, Pro (pp. 24-25).

Catchpole 1992, 521-522 [1993, 285-286]: See Q 7:1⁰ In Q (pp. 13-14).

Lindars 1992, 204: "In Jn 4,46 the alteration of Jesus' movements explains ἦλθεν for the original εἰσῆλθεν."

210: "In order to facilitate comparison, I give here a tentative reconstruction of the source based on the critical evaluation of the form in all three Gospels which has just been made. All the words are found in one or other of the three texts except [ἐγγίζοντος].

"εἰσῆλθεν ὁ Ἰησοῦς εἰς Καφαρναούμ. καὶ ἦν τις ἑκατόνταρχος οὗ ὁ παῖς κακῶς ἔχων ἤμελλεν τελευτᾶν. ἀκούσας δὲ περὶ τοῦ Ἰησοῦ, ἀπῆλθεν πρὸς αὐτὸν καὶ παρεκάλεσεν αὐτὸν ἵνα ἐλθὼν ἰάσηται αὐτοῦ τὸν παῖδα. ὁ δὲ Ἰησοῦς ἐπορεύετο σὺν αὐτῷ. ἤδη δὲ αὐτοῦ [ἐγγίζοντος] τῇ οἰκίᾳ, λέγει πρὸς αὐτὸν ὁ ἑκατόνταρχος· κύριε, οὐκ εἰμὶ ἱκανὸς ἵνα μου ὑπὸ τὴν στέγην εἰσέλθῃς· ἀλλὰ μόνον εἰπὲ λόγῳ, καὶ ἰαθήσεται ὁ παῖς μου. καὶ γὰρ ἐγὼ ἄνθρωπός εἰμι ὑπὸ ἐξουσίαν, ἔχων ὑπ' ἐμαυτὸν στρατιώτας, καὶ λέγω τούτῳ· πορεύθητι, καὶ πορεύεται, καὶ ἄλλῳ· ἔρχου, καὶ ἔρχεται, καὶ τῷ δούλῳ μου· ποίησον τοῦτο, καὶ ποιεῖ. ἀκούσας δὲ ταῦτα ὁ Ἰησοῦς ἐθαύμασεν αὐτὸν καὶ στραφεὶς τῷ ἀκολουθοῦντι αὐτῷ ὄχλῳ εἶπεν. ἀμὴν λέγω ὑμῖν, παρ' οὐδενὶ τοσαύτην πίστιν ἐν τῷ Ἰσραὴλ εὗρον. καὶ εἶπεν ὁ Ἰησοῦς τῷ ἑκατοντάρχῃ· ὕπαγε, ὡς ἐπίστευσας γενηθήτω σοι. καὶ ἰάθη ὁ παῖς ἐν τῇ ὥρᾳ ἐκείνῃ."

Sevenich-Bax 1993, 174: "So wird sowohl die Partikel δέ als auch die Konstruktion mit dem Genitivus absolutus auf Matthäus zurückzuführen sein. Damit ist die lukanische Formulierung 'εἰσῆλθεν εἰς Καφαρναούμ' als ursprünglich vorauszusetzen."

238: Reconstruction. For complete text see Q 7:1⁰ In Q (p. 15).

Gagnon 1994b, 135: Reconstruction. For complete text see Q 7:1⁰ In Q (p. 15).

Landis 1994, 17 [Individual verse reconstructions follow Landis' discussions on pp. 7, 9, 10, 11, 12, 13, and 17.]: Ellipsis and parentheses are from

Landis. "Im folgenden soll nun unsere Rekonstruktion der Q-Fassung als ganze wiedergegeben werden:

"(8,5) εἰσῆλθεν εἰς Καφαρναούμ. καὶ ἦλθεν πρὸς αὐτὸν ἑκατοντάρχης παρακαλῶν αὐτὸν (6) καὶ λέγων· κύριε, ὁ παῖς μου... (κατάκειται;) δεινῶς βασανιζόμενος. (7) καὶ λέγει αὐτῷ· ἐγὼ ἐλθὼν θεραπεύσω αὐτόν; (8) καὶ ἀποκριθεὶς ὁ ἑκατοντάρχης ἔφη· κύριε, οὐκ εἰμὶ ἱκανὸς ἵνα ὑπὸ τὴν στέγην μου εἰσέλθῃς, ἀλλὰ εἰπὲ λόγῳ, καὶ ἰαθήσεται ὁ παῖς μου. (9) καὶ γὰρ ἐγὼ ἄνθρωπός εἰμι ὑπὸ ἐξουσίαν, ἔχων ὑπ' ἐμαυτὸν στρατιώτας, καὶ λέγω τούτῳ· πορεύθητι, καὶ πορεύεται, καὶ ἄλλῳ· ἔρχου, καὶ ἔρχεται, καὶ τῷ δούλῳ μου· ποίησον τοῦτο, καὶ ποιεῖ. (10) ἀκούσας δὲ ὁ Ἰησοῦς ἐθαύμασεν καὶ εἶπεν τοῖς ἀκολουθοῦσιν· λέγω ὑμῖν, οὐδὲ ἐν τῷ Ἰσραὴλ τοσαύτην πίστιν εὗρον. (13) καὶ εἶπεν τῷ ἑκατοντάρχῃ· ὕπαγε, (Heilungszusage, Bericht von der Heilung) ἐν τῇ ὥρᾳ ἐκείνῃ."

International Q Project 1995, 478: Reconstruction. For complete text see Q 7:1⁰ In Q (p. 16).

Reed 1995, 20: "The next and final spatial reference in a narrative section occurs in Q 7:1 to introduce the story of the Capernaum centurion: 'He entered Capernaum.'[13]"

32[13]: "Wegner [1985, 126-127] identifies the Matthean genitive absolute as redactional: this form occurs only once in Q (7:24), and Matthew uses it frequently in this immediate setting (in Matt 8:5-10 as well as 8:1 and 8:28). Furthermore, Matthew could be carrying over the Markan genitive absolute from Mark 2:1 after inserting the cleansing of the leper in between the sermon and the reference to the centurion (Matt 8:1-4/Mark 1:40-45)."

Con

Allen 1907, 73: "In Lk. also, if we allow that Capharnaum was the natural place for the miracle, there was an obvious reason for inserting 7:1 between the Sermon and the miracle." However, Allen continues by listing other possibilities, including the possibility that Luke used a source that Matthew coincidentally agreed with.

Matt = Q: (Εἰσελθόντος δὲ αὐτοῦ)⁶

Pro

Fuchs 1971, 110[77a]: "In [Matt] 5,1; 8,5; 14,15; 17,14; 21,23 und 24,3 geht ein Gen. abs. der Formel voraus, z.T. ist diese Konstruktion aber wiederum schon in den Quellen enthalten."

Con

Allen 1907, 73: "In Mt 8:5 Εἰσελθόντος δὲ αὐτοῦ εἰς Καφαρναούμ may be purely editorial. The editor places immediately after the Sermon Mk.'s narrative of the leper, 8:1-4. He now wishes to continue with the story of the centurion's servant. Capharnaum was the obvious place in which to locate this, cf. Mt 4:13, especially as the editor intends to continue with Mk 1:29-31, which did take place in Capharnaum. He was therefore obliged to insert a statement of the return to that city somewhere, and 8:5 was an obvious opportunity for doing so."

von Harnack 1907, 54: "Die Form der Aussage haben beide geändert; ... der hinzugefügte Genit. abs. (εἰσελθόντος αὐτοῦ) zeigt ... den sekundären Charakter des Matthäustexts an dieser Stelle."

von Harnack 1907, ET 1908, 74: "Both evangelists have altered the wording here; ... the genitive absolute (εἰσελθόντος αὐτοῦ), which is added, likewise shows the secondary character of the text of St. Matthew at this point."

Lagrange 1923, cxiv: "Nous savons d'avance que dans Mt., après un génitif absolu posant la situation, quelqu'un se présentera viii, 5. Ces génetifs absolus nous ont paru tout à fait révélateurs du style de Mt."

Klostermann 1927, 73: "Εἰσελθόντος δὲ αὐτοῦ ... εἰς Καφαρναούμ: durch die Verknüpfungsarbeit des Mt sieht noch der Wortlaut der Quelle hindurch vgl. Lc' εἰσῆλθεν εἰς Καφαρναούμ."

Parker 1953, 63-65: "The Centurion's Boy (Matt. 8:5ff.; Luke 7:1ff.)

"As with the temptation stories, we have here what seems to be a clear case of conflation by the compiler of Matthew. To show this, it is necessary to consider the story in sections.

"*a*) Matt. 8:5 And when he was entered into Capernaum, THERE CAME unto him a centurion, BESEECHING him, 6 and saying, Lord, my servant lieth in the house SICK OF THE PALSY, grievously tormented.

"*b*) 7 And he saith unto him, I will come and heal him. 8 And the centurion answered and said, Lord, I am not worthy that thou shouldst come *under my roof:* but only say the word, and my servant shall be healed. 9 For I also am a man *under authority,* having *under myself* soldiers: and I say to this one, Go, and he goeth; and to another, Come and he cometh; and to my *servant,* Do this, and he doeth it. 10 And when Jesus heard it, [64] he marveled, and said to them that followed, Verily I say unto you, I have not found so great faith, *no, not* in Israel.

"*c*) 11 And I say unto you, that many *shall come* from the east and the west, and shall sit down with Abraham, and Isaac, and Jacob, in the kingdom of heaven: 12 but the sons of the kingdom shall be cast forth into the outer darkness: there *shall be* weeping and gnashing of teeth.

"*d*) 13 And Jesus said unto the centurion, GO THY WAY; as thou hast believed, SO BE IT DONE unto thee. And the servant was healed IN THAT HOUR.

"We comment on each of these portions in turn. (*a*) Out of 23 (Greek) words in Matthew and 72 in Luke 7:1-5, only 6 are even partly common to both. In Matthew the centurion's child (*pais*) is ill; in Luke, his slave. In Matthew the centurion comes to Jesus; in Luke he sends Jewish leaders. Matthew has a marked K vocabulary, with no Q words at all; but Luke has *doulos* (slave) and the typically Q word *axios* (worthy). (*b*) Unlike the preceding, this is almost identical with Luke 7:6-9; and here Matthew has a strong Q vocabulary. (*c*) This is found in Luke at another place (Luke 13:28, 29). Here again Matthew uses typical Q expressions. (*d*) But in a passage that has *no* parallel in Luke, Matthew reverts to K vocabulary again, with expressions that are most unlike Q. Thus, where Luke has a marked Q style throughout, Matthew has it only in the part (vss. 7-12) that is actually paralleled in the Third Gospel. Elsewhere his usage is strongly K.

"Now note that at Matt. 8:7 Jesus says, 'I will come and heal him,' but only in Luke (7:6) does he actually set out. Indeed, Matthew's verse 13 contradicts verse 7! Still more significantly, note that Matt. 8:5, 6, 13 forms a complete story by itself:

"And when he was entered into Capernaum, there came unto him a centurion, beseeching him, and saying, Lord, my child lieth in the house sick of the palsy, grievously tormented. And Jesus said unto the centurion, Go thy way; as thou hast believed, so be it done unto thee. And the child was healed in that hour.

"It is remarkable that this shorter narrative carries all the features that have caused the longer passage to be likened to John 4:46ff.:

"And there was a certain nobleman, whose son was sick at Capernaum. When he heard that Jesus was come … he went unto him, and besought him that he would come down, and heal his son … Jesus saith unto him, Go thy way; thy son liveth. The man believed … his son lived … the fever left him … at that hour. [Ellipses are Parker's.]

"[65] Equally striking in many respects is the similarity to Matt. 15:21ff. (cf. Mark 7:24ff.):

"And Jesus … withdrew into the parts of Tyre and Sidon. And behold, a Canaanitish woman came out from those borders, and cried, saying, Have mercy on me … my daughter is grievously vexed with a devil. … Then Jesus answered and said unto her, O woman, great is thy faith: be it done unto thee even as thou wilt. And her daughter was healed from that hour. [Ellipses are Parker's.]

"In each case, Jesus arrives at a destination. A parent (Matthew: a gentile parent) comes seeking aid for his child who is grievously ill. Jesus speaks the word. The parent has faith. The child is healed, at a distance, in the same hour.

"Thus Matt. 8:5, 6, 13 is complete and homogeneous by itself. It lacks the Q usage that appears in the rest of the passage and throughout the Lukan story. It is very unlike Luke, whereas verses 7-12 are closely paralleled in Luke. And, unlike verses 7-12, verses 5, 6, and 13 exhibit a strong, positive K vocabulary. The true Q account of the centurion's slave is in Luke. Matthew has expanded an originally independent K story, about a centurion's child, by two additions from Q (7-10; 11, 12). Matthew's ambiguous *pais* may have been chosen by the editor to cover both K's *huios* (son) and Q's *doulos* (slave). Assignment: to Q, Matt. 8:7-12, but Luke 7:1-10; to K, Matt. 8:5, 6, 13."

Schulz 1972, 236³⁹⁹: "Die Konstruktion mit gen abs (εἰσελθόντος αὐτοῦ) könnte allerdings mt sein."

Gundry 1982, 141: "Matthew reduces the independent clause concerning Jesus' entering Capernaum (so Luke) to a genitive absolute."

Dauer 1984, 101: "Typisch mt ist die hier vorliegende formelhafte Einführung, die so oder in ähnlicher Weise auch andernorts im 1. Evangelium erscheint und mit der Matthäus häufig eine ausführlichere Einleitung des Mk ersetzt hat.

"(1) Zu dieser formelhaften Einführung gehört der Genitivus absolutus zu Beginn einer Erzählung, den Matthäus zwar häufig aus seiner Mk-Vorlage übernimmt, den er aber auch diff Mk oder an redaktionellen Stellen schreibt."

Wegner 1985, 126: "Wenn Mt statt εἰσῆλθεν den Gen. abs. εἰσελθόντος δὲ αὐτοῦ bringt, so ist dies wohl auf seinen Einschub von Mk 1,22.40-45 (vgl. Mt 7,28f; 8,1-4) innerhalb der urspr Q-Akoluthie, die nach der Bergpredigt unmittelbar die Hauptmannserzählung brachte, zurückzuführen."

127: "Für den red Charakter der Konstruktion in Mt 8,5a spricht auch ihre mehrmalige red Verwendung im unmittelbaren Kontext von Mt 8,5-10, wie aus Mt 8,1.28 hervorgeht (vgl. auch Mt 8,16). Auch die Beobachtung von Fuchs [1971, 110⁷⁷], nach der Gen. abs. 6x einer sicherlich von Mt geprägten Formel (προσέρχεσθαι + αὐτῷ + Substantiv) vorangestellt begegnet (vgl. 5,1; 8,5; 14,15; 17,14; 21,23 und 24,3), könnte für den red Charakter der Konstruktion auSt herangezogen werden. Die Tatsache, daß die Formulierung des Gen. abs. hier mit δέ erscheint, paßt übrigens angesichts der mt Bevorzugung dieser Konjunktion gegenüber Mk ganz zu seinem Stil."

Luz 1990, 12: "V 5a erinnert an den später weggelassenen Vers Mk 2,1 [καὶ εἰσελθὼν πάλιν εἰς Καφαρναούμ]."

Luz 1990, ET 2001, 8: "Verse 5a is reminiscent of Mark 2:1 that is going to be omitted later [καὶ εἰσελθὼν πάλιν εἰς Καφαρναούμ]."

Davies and Allison 1991, 18: "The form, participle + δέ + αὐτοῦ/αὐτῶν + preposition is a redactional feature.³¹"

18³¹: "Cf. 8:1; 17:22, 24; 24:3; 27:19."

Sevenich-Bax 1993, 173-174: "Allerdings ist Matthäus durch den Einschub Mt 8,1-4 genötigt, den Neueinsatz [174] mit Mt 8,5 deutlicher zu akzentuieren. So wird sowohl die Partikel δέ als auch die Konstruktion mit dem Genitivus absolutus auf Matthäus zurückzuführen sein."

Gagnon 1994b, 136: "In my estimation, Matthew has ... adjusted the entrance- and encounter-phrases of his source to the stereotyped Matthean formula of introduction (genitive-absolute construction + προσῆλθεν αὐτῷ)."

Landis 1994, 6: "Der Genetivus absolutus εἰσελθόντος δὲ αὐτοῦ ist wohl mt Redaktion, vielleicht bedingt durch den Einschub von 8,1-4 aus Mk 1,40-45 in die (bei Lk erhaltene) Q-Akoluthie. Der Genetivus absolutus ist bei Q äußerst selten, wird hingegen von mt gerade im Umfeld dieser Perikope mehrmals redaktionell eingetragen (8,1.28). Typisch für den ersten Evangelisten ist auch die Verbindung eines Genetivus absolutus mit der Formel προσῆλθεν αὐτῷ. Für Q ist also die von Lk überlieferte finite Verbform εἰσῆλθεν und ein Anschluß des Folgenden mit καί anzunehmen."

Evaluations

Shein 1998: Luke = Q {C}, ⟦εἰσῆλθεν ()⁶⟧.

Both Luke and Matthew use the verb εἰσέρχομαι, but Matthew's construction with genitive absolute is typically Matthean. There are few arguments offered against the Lukan reading. Luke's indicative remains as the Q reading only because of the clearly attested Matthean redactional style.

Johnson 2000: Luke = Q {B}, εἰσῆλθεν ()⁶.

The database is almost equally divided between arguments for Luke's aorist verb and arguments against Matthew's genitive absolute. The fundamental observation is that Matthew's inclusion of the healing of the paralytic interrupts the transition formula and leads Matthew to rewrite Matt 8:5a as a genitive absolute (Allen et al.). The genitive absolute construction is considered to be Matthean style (Gagnon), as is the construction of participle + δέ + αὐτοῦ/αὐτῶν (Davies and Allison). Lindars sees John's ἦλθεν as being explained by Luke's εἰσῆλθεν being found in oral tradition.

There are almost no arguments put forth against Luke and for Matthew. A {B} vote seems is too low for this variation unit, but is in accordance with the vote at 7:1⁰.

Robinson 2000: Luke = Q {B}, εἰσῆλθεν ()⁶.

The Matthean interpolation (Matt 7:28b-8:4) makes the Matthean resumption of Q with the genitive absolute appropriate. It occurs in a typically Matthean redactional syntax.

The repetitive Matthean formula does not end with the statement that Jesus finishing the sayings, but continues with an aorist verb reporting that Jesus moved on (see variation unit ⁰ above). The only exception is Matt 26:1, where the aorist verb reports him continuing to speak, in spite of the formula terminating a discourse. The Matthean interpolation thus intervenes in the present instance before the formula is actually completed. The completion of the formula is deferred to Matt 8:5a, after the interpolation, where it is hence only Luke that retains the aorist indicative referring to Jesus moving on. There are here no distinctively Lukan traits, and hence the Lukan reading no doubt was the completion of the formula ending the Q Sermon and opening the Q story of The Centurion's Faith in Jesus' Word.

Since Matthew uses the same verb εἰσέρχομαι as does Luke, and some verb of motion to introduce εἰς Καφαρναούμ is needed, the Lukan reading is what one would expect.

The reference to Capharnaum is not redactional, not only because the reference to Capharnaum is in both Matthew and Luke—i.e., in minimal Q— but also because it is in John 4:46b, where it is also not redactional (the redactional transition ends with John 4:46a), but an inherent part of the story. It is the location of the official, rather than being mentioned redactionally as a place Jesus came into (as in John 4:46a).

Kloppenborg 2000: Luke = Q {B}, εἰσῆλθεν ()⁶.

Hoffmann 2001: Luke = Q {B}, εἰσῆλθεν ()⁶.

Q 7:~~2~~, 3, ~~4~~ 6a

Mark 7:25-27	Matt 15:22-23a, 25-26	Matt 8:5b-7	Q 7:~~2~~, 3, ~~4~~ 6a
		8:5b ⌜ ⌟¹	7:~~2~~ ⌜⌟¹
7:25 ἀλλ' εὐθὺς ἀκούσασα γυνὴ περὶ αὐτοῦ,	15:22 καὶ ἰδοὺ γυνὴ Χαναναία ἀπὸ τῶν ὁρίων ἐκείνων ἐξελθοῦσα ἔκραζεν λέγουσα· ἐλέησόν με, κύριε υἱὸς Δαυίδ·	[ ]²	7:3 [[[]²]]
ἧς εἶχεν τὸ θυγάτριον αὐτῆς πνεῦμα ἀκάθαρτον,	ἡ θυγάτηρ μου κακῶς δαιμονίζεται. 15:23a ὁ δὲ οὐκ ἀπεκρίθη αὐτῇ λόγον.		
ἐλθοῦσα προσέπεσεν πρὸς τοὺς πόδας αὐτοῦ· 7:26 ἡ δὲ γυνὴ ἦν Ἑλληνίς, Συροφοινίκισσα τῷ γένει·	15:25 ἡ δὲ ἐλθοῦσα προσεκύνει αὐτῷ	(προσῆλθεν)³ [ ]⁴ αὐτ(ῷ)⁴ ¹⌜ἑκατόνταρχ(ος)⁵ ⌟¹ [ ]³	(<>³ἦλθεν)³ []⁴ αὐτ(ῷ)⁴ ¹⌜ἑκατόνταρχ[[(ο)⁵]](ς)⁵ ⌟¹ []³
καὶ ἠρώτα αὐτὸν ἵνα	λέγουσα·	(παρακαλ)⁶ῶν αὐτὸν 8:6 (καὶ λέγων·)⁷	(παρακαλ)⁶ῶν αὐτὸν [[(καὶ λέγων·)⁷]]
	κύριε,	(κύριε,)⁸	()⁸
τὸ δαιμόνιον ἐκβάλῃ ἐκ τῆς θυγατρὸς αὐτῆς.	βοήθει μοι.	¹⌜ (ὁ παῖς)⁹ (μου)⁷ (βέβληται ἐν τῇ οἰκίᾳ παραλυτικός)¹⁰, (δεινῶς βασανιζόμενος)¹¹. ⌟¹	¹⌜ (ὁ παῖς)⁹ [[(μου)⁷ [κακῶς ἔχ]¹⁰<ει>¹⁰ [()]¹¹. ⌟¹
7:27 καὶ ἔλεγεν αὐτῇ· ἄφες πρῶτον χορτασθῆναι τὰ τέκνα, οὐ γάρ ἐστιν καλὸν λαβεῖν	15:26 ὁ δὲ ἀποκριθεὶς εἶπεν· οὐκ ἔστιν καλὸν λαβεῖν	8:7 (καὶ λέγει αὐτῷ· ἐγὼ)⁷ ἐλθὼν (θεραπεύσ)¹²(ω)⁷ (αὐτόν;)¹²	(καὶ λέγει αὐτῷ· ἐγὼ)⁷]] ἐλθὼν (θεραπεύσ)¹²[[(ω)⁷]] (αὐτόν;)¹²
		[ ]¹³	7:4 []¹³
τὸν ἄρτον τῶν τέκνων καὶ τοῖς κυναρίοις βαλεῖν.	τὸν ἄρτον τῶν τέκνων καὶ βαλεῖν τοῖς κυναρίοις.		
			7:~~5~~
			7:~~6~~a

uke 7:2-6a	Luke 8:41-42a	Mark 5:22-23	John 4:46b-48
:2 ¹⁵ Ἑκατοντάρχ[ου δέ ινος]⁵ ιοῦλος]⁹ ικῶς ἔχων]¹⁰ μελλεν τελευτᾶν]¹¹, ς ἦν αὐτῷ ἔντιμος]⁹. ὶ¹			4:46b Καὶ ἦν τις βασιλικὸς οὗ ὁ υἱὸς ἠσθένει ἐν Καφαρναούμ.
.3 [ἀκούσας δὲ ιρὶ τοῦ Ἰησοῦ]²			4:47 οὗτος ἀκούσας ὅτι Ἰησοῦς ἥκει ἐκ τῆς Ἰουδαίας εἰς τὴν Γαλιλαίαν
πέστειλεν]³	8:41 καὶ ἰδοὺ ἦλθεν ἀνὴρ ᾧ ὄνομα Ἰάϊρος καὶ οὗτος	5:22 Καὶ ἔρχεται εἷς τῶν ἀρχισυναγώγων,	ἀπῆλθεν
ρὸς]⁴ αὐτ[ὸν]⁴ ὶ¹ ρεσβυτέρους ὶν Ἰουδαίων]³	ἄρχων τῆς συναγωγῆς ὑπῆρχεν, καὶ πεσὼν παρὰ τοὺς πόδας τοῦ Ἰησοῦ	ὀνόματι Ἰάϊρος, καὶ ἰδὼν αὐτὸν πίπτει πρὸς τοὺς πόδας αὐτοῦ	πρὸς αὐτὸν
ρωτ]⁶ῶν αὐτὸν πως]⁷ ,⁸ ὶ¹	παρεκάλει αὐτὸν εἰσελθεῖν εἰς τὸ οἶκον αὐτοῦ, 8:42a ὅτι θυγάτηρ μονογενὴς ἦν αὐτῷ ὡς ἐτῶν δώδεκα	5:23 καὶ παρακαλεῖ αὐτὸν πολλὰ λέγων ὅτι τὸ θυγάτριόν μου	καὶ ἠρώτα ἵνα
7	καὶ αὐτὴ ἀπέθνῃσκεν.	ἐσχάτως ἔχει,	
θὼν ,ασώσῃ τὸν δοῦλον τοῦ.]¹²		ἵνα ἐλθὼν ἐπιθῇς τὰς χεῖρας αὐτῇ ἵνα σωθῇ καὶ ζήσῃ.	καταβῇ καὶ ἰάσηται αὐτοῦ τὸν υἱόν ἤμελλεν γὰρ ἀποθνήσκειν.
4 [οἱ δὲ παραγενόμενοι ὸς τὸν Ἰησοῦν ρεκάλουν αὐτὸν ουδαίως λέγοντες ε ἄξιός ἐστιν ᾧ παρέξῃ ῦτο· 5 ἀγαπᾷ γὰρ τὸ ἔθνος ῶν καὶ τὴν συναγωγὴν τὸς ᾠκοδόμησεν ἡμῖν. 6a ὁ δὲ Ἰησοῦς ορεύετο σὺν αὐτοῖς.]¹³			4:48 εἶπεν οὖν ὁ Ἰησοῦς πρὸς αὐτόν· ἐὰν μὴ σημεῖα καὶ τέρατα ἴδητε, οὐ μὴ πιστεύσητε.

Q 7:2, 3, 4-6a

JSK: ⌐ ⌐¹ indeterminate.
IQP 1994: 7:3 []² (προσῆλθεν)³.
JSK: 7:3 [ ]² Luke = Q {D}.
JSK: 7:3 [[πρὸς]⁴] αὐτ[[όν]⁴].
IQP 1994: 7:3 ἐκατόνταρχ( )⁵ς; JSK: ἐκατόνταρχ[<η>]⁵(ς)⁵.
IQP 1994: 7:3 (καὶ λέγων·)⁷ ()⁸ ¹⌐ (ὁ παῖς)⁹ (μου)⁷ [[κακῶς ἔχων]¹⁰] [ ]¹¹. ⌐¹
(καὶ λέγει αὐτῷ· ἐγὼ)⁷ ἐλθὼν (θεραπεύσω)¹²(ω)⁷ (αὐτόν)¹² (ending in a period
rather than a question mark); JSK the same, but with a question mark.
JMR: 7:3 [()]¹¹.

Text Critical Note: The phrase ἐγὼ ἐλθὼν θεραπεύσω αὐτόν can be punctuated
either as a statement or as a question.

¹ Does the sequence of the pericope present the situation of the centurion,
   the sick person, and the illness in an introductory narration (Luke), or in
   a brief introduction to the opening dialogue (Matthew)?
² Luke's ἀκούσας δὲ περὶ τοῦ Ἰησοῦ.
³ Luke's ἀπέστειλεν ... πρεσβυτέρους τῶν Ἰουδαίων or Matthew's προσῆλθεν.
⁴ Luke's πρὸς αὐτόν or Matthew's αὐτῷ.
⁵ Luke's ἐκατοντάρχου δέ τινος or Matthew's ἐκατόνταρχος.
⁶ Luke's ἐρωτῶν αὐτόν or Matthew's παρακαλῶν αὐτόν (See also Luke 7:4
   παρακάλουν αὐτόν).
⁷ Luke's ὅπως with indirect discourse or Matthew's direct discourse: καὶ
   λέγων· ... μου ... καὶ λέγει αὐτῷ· ἐγὼ ...-ω.
⁸ Matthew's κύριε.
⁹ Luke's δοῦλος ..., ὃς ἦν αὐτῷ ἔντιμος or Matthew's ὁ παῖς.
¹⁰ Luke's κακῶς ἔχων or Matthew's βέβληται ἐν τῇ οἰκίᾳ παραλυτικός (See
   also Luke 7:6b ἀπὸ τῆς οἰκίας).
¹¹ Luke's ἤμελλεν τελευτᾶν or Matthew's δεινῶς βασανιζόμενος.
¹² Luke's διασώσῃ τὸν δοῦλον αὐτοῦ· or Matthew's θεραπεύσ- αὐτόν;.
¹³ Is Luke 7:4-6a in Q?

Q 7:2, 3, 4-6a¹: Does the sequence of the pericope present the situation of the centurion, the sick person, and the illness in an introductory narration (Luke), or in a brief introduction to the opening dialogue (Matthew)?

Luke = Q: The situation is presented in an introductory narration.

Pro

Castor 1912, 223: Reconstruction. For complete text see Q 7:1⁰ In Q (p. 6).

Ellis 1966, 117: "Probably Matthew telescopes the narrative and, in Semitic fashion, corporately identifies the representatives with the centurion or 'army captain' … Luke retains the more detailed account in order to bring into fuller focus the personality of the captain and, perhaps, to enhance the parallel with the story of the first Gentile Christian (Ac. 10)."

Dauer 1984, 99-104: See Q 7:2, 3, 4-6a¹ Matt = Q, Con (pp. 73-75).

110: "Er [Lk 7,2] entspricht sachlich Mt V. 6. Die Form bei Lk, nach der die Krankheit des Knechtes in einer Erzählnotiz angegeben wird, ist gegenüber Mt, wo die Krankheitsschilderung in das Wort des Hauptmanns aufgenommen ist, ursprünglicher."

Lindars 1992, 210: Reconstruction. For complete text see Q 7:1⁶ Luke = Q, Pro (p. 56).

Gagnon 1994b, 135: Reconstruction. For complete text see Q 7:1⁰ In Q (p. 15).

Con

Held 1960, 183: "Lukas hat dem Gespräch aus einer anderen Quelle eine ausführliche und eigenartige Einleitung gegeben (Lk. 7,2-6a),³ die er durch einen eingeschobenen Satz (Lk. 7,7a) kunstvoll mit dem Dialog verknüpft.⁴"

183³: "Die Quelle des Lukas ist nach W. Bussmann [1929, 57] an der Verschiedenheit der verwandten Worte zu erkennen. Q (mit Mt. gemeinsam): παῖς, ἱκανός; Lukas-Sonderquelle: δοῦλος, ἄξιος."

183⁴: "Vgl. die Stichwortverbindung: (7,4) ἄξιος (7,7) ἠξίωσα."

221-223: See Q 7:2, 3, 4-6a⁷ Matt = Q, Con (pp. 154-155).

Held 1960, ET 1963, 194: "Luke, from another source, has given the conversation a detailed and unique introduction (Luke 7:2-6a)¹ which he has skillfully linked with the dialogue² by means of the insertion of a sentence (Luke 7:7a)."

194¹: "Luke's source can be recognized according to W. Bussmann [1929, 57] by the difference in the words he uses. Q (along with Matthew): παῖς, ἱκανός; Luke's special source: δοῦλος, ἄξιος."

194²: "Cf. the combination of the catchwords: (7:4) ἄξιος (7:7) ἠξίωσα."
233-235: See Q 7:2, 3, 4-6a⁷ Matt = Q, Con (pp. 155-156).

Dodd 1963, 191: "Luke, on the other hand, has expanded the opening part of the narrative in such a way as to alter the whole picture. In his version the centurion never appears in person; his striking utterance about the authority exercised by one who is himself under authority is merely reported by friends who come to intercede, and it is the friends who on returning find the patient restored to health."

Wilson 1973, 31: "Ellis [1966, 117] thinks that Luke's is the more original version and that Matthew's is a telescoping of it which 'corporately identifies the representatives with the centurion.' It is more probable, however, that Luke has added these details both to bring into focus the personality of the centurion and his faith, and to enhance the parallel with the narrative of Cornelius, the first Gentile Christian (Acts 10-11)."

Busse 1977, 146: "Lukas gestaltet die Bittrede des Hauptmanns (Mt 8,5) in eine Situationsschilderung V 2 um, die er stilistisch elegant mit dem Imperfekt von ihrem Kontext abhebt."

150-151: "Die radikale [Lukan] Neubearbeitung der traditionellen Ereignisse um einen heidnischen Hauptmann in Kapharnaum hat ihre ursprüngliche Form gesprengt. Dem Charakter der Logienquelle entsprechend lag dort der formale Schwerpunkt auf dem Dialog zwischen Hauptmann und Jesus, dessen Höhepunkt Jesus selbst durch die Einbeziehung seiner Begleitung (Mt 8,10) in das Gespräch signalisierte. Die Schilderung der Handlungsabfolge wurde zugunsten des Dialogs vernachlässigt. Diese Disproportion beseitigt Lukas vollkommen.

"Schon die Umwandlung der direkten Rede, in der bei Mt 8,5 die Krankheitsgeschichte des Kindes entfaltet wird, in eine objektivierende Exposition zeigt die neue luk. Formintention, die Redelastigkeit zu beseitigen und aus der Perikope eine echte Erzählung zu formen. Deshalb wählt der Evangelist auch einen ebenso objektivierenden Abschluß V 10. Darüber hinaus findet der Dialog des Hauptmanns mit Jesus unter Vermittlung zweier Gesandtschaften statt, deren Einschub in die Vorlage das erzählerische Potential beträchtlich erweitert.

"Deshalb konnte Bultmann [1931, 39] die traditionelle Perikope nicht unter die 'stilgerechten Wundergeschichten' einordnen, sondern [151] behandelt sie in einem Anhang zu den Apophthegmata zusammen mit der inhaltlich verwandten Erzählung von der Syrophönizierin Mk 7,24-31, die bei Lukas ausfällt. Die luk. Fassung steht nach den von Bultmann mitentwickelten Formkriterien einer Wundergeschichte bedeutend näher als die ursprüngliche Fassung: Die einleitende Situationsangabe V 1², die in eine Krankheitsschilderung übergeht V 2³, das darauf folgende Heilswirken des Wundertäters, um zum Schluß mit dem Erfolg der Heilung (V 10) und einem Bericht (Chorschluß) über die Reaktion der Anwesenden die Wundergeschichte ausklingen zu lassen, diese abgerundete Form einer stilgerechten Wundergeschichte ist in der luk. Fassung größtenteils wiedererkennbar. Doch fehlt das Element des Heilswirkens (vgl Mt 8,13) und die Akklamation."

151[2]: "Die Einleitung hebt die Wort-Tat-Relation hervor."

151[3]: "Auch dieser Bestandteil ist eigenwillig überformt."

Polag 1979, 38: Reconstruction. For complete text see Q 7:1[0] In Q (pp. 9-10).

Luz 1990, 13: "Ob die lk Einleitung 7,2-6a auf eine Rezension von Q (Q[Lk]) oder auf lk Red. zurückgeht, kann hier offenbleiben."

Luz 1990, ET 2001, 8-9: "We may leave open here the question whether the Lukan introduction [9] 7:2-6a is due to a recension of Q (Q[Lk]) or to Lukan redaction."

Sevenich-Bax 1993, 176: "Die autoriale Schilderung der Not hängt bei Lukas mit der Einführung zweier Gesandtschaften (Lk 7,3-6) zusammen. Da die Bitte des Hauptmanns erst durch diese übermittelt wird, muß der Leser zuvor über die Situation informiert werden. Dies kann aber nur durch den Erzähler geschehen."

Dunderberg 1994, 85: See Q 7:2, 3, 4-6a[3] Luke = Q, Con (pp. 114-115).

Landis 1994, 5-6: "Bei Lk verläuft die Einleitung bis zur demütigen Vertrauenserklärung des Hauptmanns ungleich windungsreicher: In breiter Erzählung—nicht wie bei Mt in knappem Dialog—wird zunächst die Situation geschildert: Der Knecht des Hauptmanns—hier wird die Bezeichnung δοῦλος statt des mehrdeutigen Wortes παῖς verwendet—ist nicht nur krank, sondern gar dem Tode nahe. Der ἑκατοντάρχης schickt zunächst, als er von Jesus hört, eine Gesandtschaft von jüdischen Ältesten, um diesen zu bitten, zu ihm zu kommen und seinen Knecht zu retten. Die πρεσβύτεροι bemühen sich eifrig, die judenfreundliche Haltung des Hauptmanns und sein gottesfürchtiges Handeln herauszustellen und so allfällige Bedenken Jesu gegenüber dem Umgang mit einem Nichtjuden zu zerstreuen. Jesus, offensichtlich von den Argumenten der Ältesten überzeugt, geht mit ihnen. Jetzt aber besinnt sich der Hauptmann seltsamerweise plötzlich anders und schickt eine weitere Gesandtschaft (diesmal von φίλοι) zu Jesus. Dieser soll nun doch nicht in sein Haus kommen. Die Abwehr des Kommens Jesu wird mit denselben Worten wie bei Mt ausgedrückt, und auch die Begründung ist bei beiden Evangelisten praktisch identisch. Nun passen die Worte des Hauptmanns wohl gut in die mt Erzählung—dort war von Jesus ja nie ein Besuch im Haus des Heiden verlangt worden; zum lk Kontext hingegen, wo der Wundertäter ausdrücklich um sein Kommen gebeten worden war, stehen sie in starker Spannung, und zwar nicht nur in inhaltlicher, sondern auch in formaler Hinsicht: So wirkt es merkwürdig, daß die φίλοι die Botschaft des Hauptmanns in der 1. Pers. Sing.

ausrichten (bei Mt werden die Sätze von ihrem Urheber selber gesprochen). Auch ist nun plötzlich von einem παῖς die Rede statt von einem δοῦλος wie vor und auch nach den Worten des Hauptmanns (bei Mt wird dagegen immer παῖς verwendet).

"Alle diese Brüche und Spannungen lassen erkennen, daß Erzähl- und Dialogteil in Lk 7,1-10 ursprünglich nicht zusammengehört haben können, daß sie vielmehr erst sekundär zusammengestellt wurden. Demgegenüber erscheint Mt 8,5-13 als klare, einheitliche Erzählung mit logischem Aufbau, der [6] von Anfang an auf die Pointe des Gesprächs in V.8-10 hinzielt. Der Mt-Text bewahrt also wohl auch in seinem erzählenden Rahmen zum zen- tralen Dialog in etwa die vorgegebene Fassung der Logienquelle, währenddem bei Lk nur das Zwiegespräch V.6c-9 (und wahrscheinlich die Einleitung der Geschichte in V.1b, die ungefähr der mt Version in 8,5 entspricht aus Q über- nommen, der Rest aber hinzugefügt ist."

Neirynck 1995, 180: "En ce qui concerne Lc 7,2-6b.7a. je me range du côté de D. Catchpole. Je crois en effet qu'il y a de bonnes raisons pour y voir une rédaction lucanienne[21]. Qui tient la (seule) délégation des anciens des Juifs pour traditionnelle, dans la source Q ou dans une Q élargie, ... se voit confronté avec la difficulté d'un centurion qui fait demander à Jésus de venir (v. 3) et qui se rétracte par après (Q). La théorie de Landis [1994] permet d'échapper à cette difficulté: il considère Lc 7,2-5 comme le début d'un récit de miracle complètement indépendant de Q. Mais dans ce cas c'est la suite du récit qui fait problème. Landis n'a d'autre solution que le recours à Jn 4,50 (la parole de guérison) et Jn 4,51 (cf. Lc 7,6b). Ce n'est qu'une 'Vermutung' ([p.] 26), mais, par anticipation, elle risque de compromettre l'exégèse de Jn 4,46-54."

180[21]: "[Catchpole 1992, 532; 1993, 298], on 'the Intermediaries': 'Given the formal, verbal and theological relationships…, it can be inferred without risk that Luke 7,3-6a.7a do indeed owe their existence to LukeR. They did not belong to Q or to any pre-Lucan recension of Q'."

Matt = Q: The situation is presented in a brief introduction to the opening dialogue.

Pro

Bleek 1862, 347-348: "Es frägt sich nun aber, wessen Bericht hier der genauere ist. Hier scheint nun für den des Lucas die größere Ausführlichkeit zu sprechen, und wenn wir bloß diese beiden Berichte hätten, würden wir uns die Sache so denken können, daß der des Lucas der ursprünglichere wäre und daß Matthäus daraus den seinigen in die Kürze zusammengezogen hätte, zumal da Matthäus auch sonst überhaupt ein überwiegendes Interesse für Reden Christi kundgibt und vergleichungsweise weniger darauf ausgeht, deren Veranlassungen mit allen einzelnen Umständen genau zu berichten. ... Doch läßt sich auf der anderen Seite nicht leugnen, daß hier die Erzählung des Matthäus einen einfacheren natürlicheren Charakter an sich trägt, was weniger mit Lucas der Fall ist, namentlich mit Dem, was dieser über die zwiefache förmliche Gesandtschaft des Hauptmannes an Jesum erzählt. ... Wird aber dieses angenommen [that John 4:47-54 is a variation of the same story], was auch mir überwiegend wahrscheinlich ist, so schließt des Matthäus Darstellung sich an die Johanneische enger an und läßt sich leichter mit ihr vereinigen, als die des Lucas; und so werden wir auch dadurch veranlaßt, jene im Allgemeinen für die [348] ursprünglichere zu halten und es so anzusehen, daß daraus die des Lucas erst durch eine spätere Erweiterung in der Über-lieferung hervorgegangen ist."

von Harnack 1907, 55: "Wenn irgendwo, so ist in dieser Perikope deutlich, daß, was Luk. anders als Matth. hat oder über ihn hinaus, nicht aus Q stammt, daß also Matth. die Quelle ursprünglicher wiedergibt."

von Harnack 1907, ET 1908, 76: "In this section at least it is obvious that all traits in St. Luke different from or in addition to St. Matthew do not pro-ceed from Q, and that St. Matthew thus transmits the source in the more original form."

Crum 1927, 138: "The Centurion's Servant at Capernaum

Mt. viii.	5.	There came unto him a centurion, saying,	Lk. vii.	2
	6.	Lord, my servant lieth in the house, grievously tormented.		
	7.	And he saith unto him, I will come and heal him.		
	8.	And the centurion said, Lord, I am not worthy that thou shouldest come under my roof: but say the word and my servant shall be healed.		6
				7
	9.	For I also am a man under authority, having under myself soldiers: and I say to this one, Go, and he goeth; and to another, Come, and he cometh; and to my servant, Do this, and he doeth it.		8
	10.	And when Jesus heard it, he marvelled, and said to them that followed, Verily, I say unto you, I have not found so great faith, no, not in Israel.		9

13.   And Jesus said unto the centurion, Go
       thy way; as thou hast believed, so be it
       done unto thee. And the servant was   (10)
       healed in that hour."

Polag 1979, 38: Reconstruction. For complete text see Q 7:1⁰ In Q (pp. 9-10).

Judge 1989, 487: "The suggestion that Q contained only the dialogue with a brief introduction is appealing."

Luz 1990, 13: "Die Einleitung wird in Lk 7,2-6a sehr verschieden überliefert. Der fromme heidnische Hauptmann schickt jüdische Älteste als Gesandte zu Jesus. Während hier der Lukastext sehr stark red. gefärbt ist, überliefert Mt vermutlich den Q-Text ziemlich wörtlich."

Luz 1990, ET 2001, 8: "In Luke 7:2-6a the introduction is quite different. There the pious gentile centurion sends Jewish elders to Jesus as intermediaries. While Luke's text is highly redacted, Matthew presumably gives the Q text somewhat literally."

Catchpole 1992, 527 [1993, 292]: Reconstruction. For complete text see Q 7:1⁰ In Q (pp. 13-14).

Sevenich-Bax 1993, 238: Reconstruction. For complete text see Q 7:1⁰ In Q (p. 15).

Dunderberg 1994, 85: "Mt bietet einen logisch fortlaufenden Bericht, in dem das Wort Jesu betont wird, wie es auch in Q zu erwarten wäre."

Landis 1994, 7, 17: Reconstruction: εἰσῆλθεν εἰς Καφαρναούμ. καὶ ἦλθεν πρὸς αὐτὸν ἑκατοντάρχης παρακαλῶν αὐτόν. For complete text see Q 7:1⁶ Luke = Q, Pro (p. 57).

International Q Project 1995, 478: Reconstruction. For complete text see Q 7:1⁰ In Q (p. 16).

Con

Parker 1953, 63-65: See Q 7:1⁶ Matt = Q, Con (pp. 58-60).

Morganthaler 1971, 223: "Dann werden wir gut tun, von der Annahme auszugehen, daß sowohl V 11f (Q) wie V 2f (S) Mt-Intarsien sind und ihnen Lk 7,2-6a als ursprüngliches Q-Element zum Opfer fällt. ...

"Dem würde die Übernahme von Lk 13,28f in 8,11f nicht unbedingt widersprechen. Die allfällige Kürzung um Lk 7,2-6a (67 Worte) wiegt die Aufnahme von 13,28f (47 Worte) und des S-Stückes Mt 8,6f (19 Worte) auf."

Dauer 1984, 98: "Es ist wenig wahrscheinlich, daß die Erweiterung der Erzählung gegenüber Mt durch die beiden Gesandtschaften von Lukas selber stammt, der damit die Demut des Mannes herausstellen oder nach dem Vorbild von Apg 10 die Heidenmission rechtfertigen wollte."

99-100: "Mt 8,5-8a—*eine andere (ursprünglichere, heidenchristliche) Fassung der Q-Erzählung oder das Produkt mt Kürzung und Überarbeitung?* [The absence of Luke's Jewish delegation does not make the Matthean Q text Gentile Christian. This dimension of Dauer's question, based on Haenchen 1959a, can be ignored.]

"Diese Frage läßt sich bei näherem Zusehen m. E. nur im letzten Sinn beantworten. M.a.W. Mt 8,5-8a ist das Ergebnis mt Redaktion. Dafür sprechen im einzelnen:

"a) Beobachtungen zur mt Bearbeitung mk Heilungsgeschichten [This approach makes sense only on the unexamined presupposition that a Q healing story would be like a Markan healing story, and hence the briefer Matthean form (compared with Luke 7:1-10) would have to presuppose a longer, Mark-like Q text.]

"(1) Matthäus kürzt seine Mk-Vorlage:

"Vgl. hierzu Mt 8,14f diff Mk 1,29ff (I); Mt 8,16f diff Mk 1,32ff (II); Mt 9,28-34 diff Mk 5,1-20 (III); Mt 9,1-8 diff Mk 2,1-12 (IV); Mt 9,18-26 diff Mk 5,21-43 (V); Mt 14,13-21 diff Mk 6,30-44 (VI); Mt 15,32-39 diff Mk 8,1-10 (VII); Mt 17,14-20 diff Mk 9,14-29 (VIII).

"In diesem Zusammenhang ist es äußerst aufschlußreich, daß neben sonstigen Kürzungen besonders die Anfänge dieser Erzählungen vom 1. Evangelisten mehr oder weniger stark gerafft werden, wie die Beispiele I, III, IV, VII, VIII zeigen.

"(2) Matthäus schaltet Nebenpersonen aus oder drängt sie in den Hintergrund: vgl. Mt 8,14f diff Mk 1,29ff: er übergeht die bei Mk erwähnten Jünger und ihre Intervention für die Schwiegermutter des Petrus. —Mt 9,20-22 diff Mk 5,25-34: er streicht die bei Mk aufgeführte Menge, an die sich Jesus wendet, bzw. die Jünger, die Jesu Frage beantworten. —Mt 9,23 diff Mk 5,35-37: er unterläßt die bei Mk berichtete Ankunft von Leuten aus dem Hause des Synagogenvorstehers; er sagt auch nichts von den drei speziellen Jüngern, die Jesus in das Haus des Mannes begleiten. —Mt 9,25 diff Mk 5,40: er läßt die Eltern des Kindes und die Jesus begleitenden Jünger aus. — Mt 9,27-31 diff Mk 10,48f: die Menge ist bei der 1. Blindenheilung völlig übergangen. —Mt 20,31f diff Mk 10,48f: in der 2. Blindenheilung ist die Menge in ihrer Rolle stark zurückgedrängt. [100] —Mt 17,14 diff Mk 9,14ff: auch hier wird die Bedeutung der Menge heruntergespielt. —Mt 17,17 diff Mk 9,20-24: das Gespräch zwischen Jesus und dem Vater des epileptischen Jungen ist ausgelassen (ebenso bei Lk)."

101-104: "Typisch mt ist die hier vorliegende <u>formelhafte</u> Einführung, die so oder in ähnlicher Weise auch andernorts im 1. Evangelium erscheint und mit der Matthäus häufig eine ausführlichere Einleitung des Mk ersetzt hat.

"(1) Zu dieser formelhaften Einführung gehört der Genitivus absolutus zu Beginn einer Erzählung, den Matthäus zwar häufig aus seiner Mk-Vorlage übernimmt, den er aber auch diff Mk oder an redaktionellen Stellen schreibt:... [A long list of examples are given.].

"(2) 'Die Verbindung der Formen von προσέρχεσται und λέγειν ist offensichtlich eine feste Formel des Matthäus zur Einleitung von Gesprächen' [Held 1960, 216].

"Eine Tabelle der einschlägigen Stellen ist hierfür sehr aufschlußreich:

"Mt 8,5f   : ... <u>προσῆλθεν</u> <u>αὐτῷ</u> ... παρακαλῶν <u>αὐτὸν</u>
                  <u>καὶ</u> <u>λέγων</u>

Mt 8,2   : ... <u>προσελθὼν</u> προσεκύνει αὐτῷ
               <u>λέγων</u>
               (diff Mk 1,40)

Mt 9,18b   : ... <u>προσελθὼν</u> προσεκύνει αὐτῷ
               <u>λέγων</u>
               (diff Mk 5,22) [102]

Mt 9,20f   : ... <u>προσελθοῦσα</u> ὄπισθεν ...
               (ἔλεγεν γὰρ ἐν ἑαυτῇ)
               (diff Mk 5,27f)

Mt 9,28   : ... <u>προσῆλθον</u> <u>αὐτῷ</u> οἱ τυφλοὶ
               <u>καὶ</u> <u>λέγει</u> αὐτ. ὁ Ἰησ.

Mt 17,14f   : ... <u>προσῆλθεν</u> αὐτῷ ... γονυπετῶν <u>αὐτὸν</u>
               <u>καὶ</u> <u>λέγων</u>
               (diff Mk 9,17).

"Diese Beispiele stammen alle aus Einleitungen zu Heilungsgeschichten. Besonders wichtig ist die letztgenannte Stelle Mt 17,14b—eine mt Umbildung von Mk 8,17—die fast wörtlich, auch mit dem den Satz beginnenden Genitivus absolutus, Mt 8,5b entspricht.

"Außer in Einleitungen zu Heilungsgeschichten verwendet Matthäus auch sonst noch häufig die formelhafte Wendung προσέρχεσται ... λέγειν, besonders bei Einführungen zu Gesprächen zwischen Jesus und anderen:...

"Nicht zu vergessen ist in diesem Zusammenhang—worauf schon oben hingewiesen wurde—daß an etlichen Stellen die stereotype Formel des Matthäus eine <u>ausführlichere</u> Einführung des Mk ersetzt, so in Mt 8,2; 9,19b; 9,20; 17,14b.

"Das berechtigt uns wiederum zu der Annahme, daß auch im vorliegenden Fall Mt 8,5-8a der 1. Evangelist die stereotype Einleitungsformel anstelle einer ausführlicheren Hinführung in die Erzählung vom Hauptmann von Kafarnaum gesetzt hat, m.a.W. daß nicht in Mt, sondern viel eher in Lk die ursprüngliche Q-Fassung zu finden ist.

[103] "c) Zur Arbeitsweise des Matthäus gehört es auch, daß er bisweilen erzählerische Angaben des Mk in direkte Reden umwandelt; besonders auf-schlußreich hierfür sind die beiden ersten der folgenden Stellen: [The texts of Mark 3:2 par. Matt 12:10; Mark 7:25 par. Matt 15:22; and Mark 8:32 par. Matt 16:22, are presented in a table.]

"In ähnlicher Weise könnte Matthäus auch im vorliegenden Fall eine erzäh-lerische Angabe, die den Zustand des Kranken schilderte und die jener bei Lk ähnlich gewesen sein mag, in die Bitte des Vaters umgeformt haben.

"Unser Verdacht verstärkt sich noch, wenn man sieht, daß hier einige mt Wendungen vorliegen: Das Partizip λέγων (λέγουσα) zur Einführung einer Rede ist zwar 'gemein-synoptisch, wird aber von Matthäus bevorzugt ange-wandt' [Trilling 1964, 67].... [104] Freilich ist auch bei einer Rückverwand-lung der direkten Rede bei Mt in eine Erzählnotiz noch ein großer Unter-schied zwischen den Krankheitsschilderungen des Mt und Lk: nach Mt V. 6 liegt der Knecht gelähmt zuhause und leidet große Schmerzen – nach Lk V. 2 ist der Knecht krank und nahe daran zu sterben."

Lindars 1992, 204: "After making the opening words a genitive absolute, [Matthew] brings the centurion to Jesus without any explanation of the cir-cumstances, which then have to be included in the centurion's request."

Gagnon 1994b, 136: "In my estimation, Matthew has ... converted the narrative description of the boy's illness into direct discourse to place greater attention on the personal interaction of the centurion and Jesus."

Evaluations

Johnson 2000: Matt = Q, {B}.

There is very little direct discussion of this variation unit in the database. Most of the arguments address the broader differences between Matthew and Luke in Q 7:2, 3, 4-6a. Indeed, it is largely assumed that this issue is tied to the question of whether Q had embassies (Luke) or had Jesus deal directly with the centurion (Matthew).

No one specifically speaks in favor of Luke's introductory narration. On the contrary, Busse sees Luke's introduction as a movement away from what was in essence a pronouncement story built around an apophthegm of Jesus (Q) and toward a full-blown miracle story (Luke)—hence the immediate descrip-tion of the illness. Despite the baggage of Bultmann's form-critical distinctions attached to Busse's argument, it is clear that what little introductory narrative exists elsewhere in Q is used to set up dialogue between Jesus and others. Luke 7:1-4b would represent the longest stretch of narrative material in Q—eclips-ing even Q 4:1-3a, the introduction to The Temptations of Jesus—and this variation unit would appear to be connected to a Lukan tendency in this pericope to move away from dialogue with Jesus and toward a greater emphasis on the faith of the Gentile centurion.

Bleek sees in Matthew's brief introduction a more natural character to the story, not a shortening of the narrative. He anticipates Dauer's argument that this is a case of Matthew typically abbreviating miracle stories. However, neither argument is appropriate as Matthew's version is not the shorter narrative in this particular variation unit. More pertinent is Dauer's observation that Matthew sometimes changes Markan narration to direct speech (see also Held at 7:2, 3, 4-6a³ Matt = Q, Con [p. 121]). This argument is especially pertinent when Matthew's reworking of Mark 7:25-26—the introduction to the story of the Syro-Phoenician woman—is considered.

Also to be considered is the issue of the substantial subsequent variations between Matthew and Luke in Q 7:2-7. If Luke has added the two delegations—and I think the evidence is weighted heavily in that direction—then this variation unit could represent the beginning of a thoroughgoing alteration of the narrative on the part of Luke. Clearly, a connection to the redaction of Q 7:2-7—be it Matthean abbreviation or Lukan expansion—though not logically necessary, is more relevant than a connection to Matthew's previous creation of the genitive absolute in Matt 8:5a (Dauer, Lindars), a change that was necessitated by the insertion of the healing of the lame person between Matt 7:28a and 8:5a (Q 7:1a and 1b), but which did not require further redaction to the narrative.

While Matthean tendency toward direct speech in introductions must be considered, consideration of the style of Q as a whole suggests that Matthew's text is closer to Q style than Luke's. Luke changed Q in order to move away from direct confrontation between Jesus and the centurion and as preparation for the introduction of the first embassy.

Robinson 2000: Matt = Q {B}.

The generally recognized redactional nature of the two delegations in Luke has of necessity led to a Lukan reorganization of the beginning of the pericope. For if in Q, as in Matthew, the problem of the sick boy is introduced first in the request for help, but in Luke that request is made by the first delegation, some explanation must precede the sending of that delegation as to why the delegation was sent at all. Hence the narrative introduction of Luke 7:2 stating the problem is required by the secondary Lukan interpolations of the two delegations.

The solution to this basic problem is facilitated by a form-critical comparison with the other healings from a distance (John 4:46b-54 and Mark 7:24-30). In the case of John, it is a parallel version of the same healing; in the case of Mark, it is a quite different healing, yet with a remarkably parallel structure to that found in Luke 7:1-10. The shared structure in the case of John might be explained by a postulated dependence of John on the Q pericope (be it on the Q, Matthean, or Lukan text, or on some oral derivative), though no one of these theories has yet gained wide acceptance and indeed they tend to be mutually exclusive. But in the case of Mark no such literary relationship can be maintained, so that here one must clearly postulate a shared oral narrative form, which could also be used to explain John 4:46b-54.

To judge by John 4:46b-47a and Mark 7:25-26a, the opening narrative formula in a healing from a distance consists of a person who appeals to Jesus on behalf of the sick person, the definition of the sick person's relation to that figure, and the illness involved. The basic issue is whether this standard form-critical form for introducing a healing from a distance has been inserted into the Q text by Luke, or whether Matthew has reduced this narrative introduction into the dialogue form.

In the case of the Syro-Phoenician woman, Matthew replaced the narrative purpose clause of her coming to Jesus (Mark 7:26b: ἵνα τὸ δαιμόνιον ἐκβάλῃ ἐκ τῆς θυγατρὸς αὐτῆς) with direct discourse (Matt 15:25b): λέγουσα· κύριε, βοήθει μοι. This is quite parallel to the situation of Matt 8:6 (καὶ λέγων· κύριε, ὁ παῖς μου βέβληται ἐν τῇ οἰκίᾳ παραλυτικός, δεινῶς βασανιζόμενος), whereas Luke 7:3c: ὅπως ἐλθὼν διασώσῃ τὸν δοῦλον αὐτοῦ is nearer to Mark. Luke in turn is also quite similar here to John 4:47c: ἵνα καταβῇ καὶ ἰάσηται αὐτοῦ τὸν υἱόν, ἤμελλεν γὰρ ἀποθνῄσκειν (cf. Luke 7:2: ἤμελλεν τελευτᾶν).

One must thus make a difficult decision, as to whether Matthew has changed Q's narration into dialogue, or whether Luke has changed Q's dialogue into narration. In view of the way in which Luke has clearly rewritten the later parts of the story (see Q 7:2, 3, 4-6a⁷, Q 7:6b-c², Q 7:?10?⁰ and Q 7:?10?⁴), also in the direction of the standard miracle story of a healing from a distance, it is probable that Luke is also responsible for the change in the same direction at the beginning of the story. Matthew's proclivity to change from narrative to dialogue (Held [Q 7:2, 3, 4-6a³ Matt = Q, Con], Dauer, Gagnon) may be one of the several points where Matthew follows the proclivity of Q. For one would expect (see Busse above) Q itself to have told the story in the dialogue form, rather than in the full-blown form of narrating a miracle story, which then Matthew would have had to change into a dialogue form more suitable to Matthew—but also to Q. The extensive discussion of Matthew favoring the abridgement of narrative detail in Markan miracle stories and preferring dialogue to narration seems to fit Matthew, but this may well be one of the dimensions in which Matthew continues the policy of Q. (See my Evaluation of Q 7:1⁰ for other instances.)

The Matthean version is really not a shortening of the beginning of the pericope, since the details in Luke 7:2 all have their equivalents in Matt 8:5b-

6. The shortening has to do with the two delegations, where it is not Matthew who has shortened, but Luke who has expanded. See Q 7:2, 3, 4-6a³ᶠᶠ.

The Lukan delegation of elders is secondary, and to this extent the Lukan sequence is secondary. But it seems to be form-critically standard, to judge by the Syro-Phoenician Woman and John 4's version of the Centurion, as well as Luke 7, that the parent comes to Jesus in view of a stated illness of the child, and that this narration precedes the explicit appeal to Jesus to help. Hence the stating of the nature of the illness is not needed in the appeal to Jesus, since it is already made explicit in the opening narration. Therefore the decision is whether this form-critical argument favoring the Lukan sequence outweighs the Matthean sequence based on the secondary nature of the Lukan delegation. Of course Luke would have tended, even without the delegation, to favor the narrative opening in the form-critical sequence of a *Fernheilung*, just as Matthew would have favored the focus on the dialogue (which leads some to prefer the Lukan sequence). The result is that the preference for the Matthean sequence is not compelling.

Kloppenborg 2000: Indeterminate {U}.

Hoffmann 2001: Matt = Q {B}.
Wenn Konsens darüber besteht, daß die Delegation der Ältesten bei Lukas redaktionell ist, dann geht auch die Änderung der Exposition der Erzählung auf ihn zurück. Daher ist m.E. der Grad {B} gerechtfertigt.

Q 7:2, 3, 4-6a²: Luke's ἀκούσας δὲ περὶ τοῦ Ἰησοῦ.

Luke = Q: [ἀκούσας δὲ περὶ τοῦ Ἰησοῦ]²

Pro

Castor 1912, 223: Reconstruction. For complete text see Q 7:1⁰ In Q (p. 6).

Fitzmyer 1981, 651: "Hearing about Jesus. This undoubtedly refers to his reputation as a miracle-worker (4:37). This detail is preserved in John 4:47, and may well have been part of pre-Lucan tradition."

Wegner 1985, 50-52: "Nur Lk und Joh berichten von einem ἀκούειν περὶ Ἰησοῦ des Hauptmanns. Mt läßt ihn dagegen gleich die Bitte durch eine Schilderung der Not formulieren (Mt 8,5b.f). Hat der erste Evangelist die Erwähnung des ἀκούειν infolge seines Kürzungsverfahrens ausgelassen oder handelt es sich bei Lk und Joh um erzählerische Zusätze?

"Indizien, die dafür sprechen, daß die Erwähnung des ἀκούειν urspr sein könnte, sind folgende:

"1. Die Q-Quelle, die diese Geschichte enthielt, benutzt ἀκούειν keineswegs mit Zurückhaltung: Harnack [1907, 103; ET, 147] rechnet mit 13 [51] Belegen in dieser Quelle, von denen nach Gaston [1973, 68] 10 gleichzeitig im Lk- und Mt-Text bezeugt sind. Von der Stat her wäre also innerhalb von Q die Verwendung von ἀκούειν am Anfang der Hauptmannsperikope durchaus möglich. Dies wird noch zusätzlich dadurch erhärtet, daß auch in der Erzählung von der Anfrage des Täufers und Jesu Antwort (Mt 11,2-6 par Lk 7,18-23) die Q-Tradenten sehr wahrscheinlich ebenfalls ἀκούειν zu Beginn der Erzählung verwendeten, wie die Einleitung in Mt 11,2 nahelegt: ὁ δὲ Ἰωάννης ἀκούσας ἐν τῷ δεσμωτηρίῳ τὰ ἔργα τοῦ Χριστοῦ κτλ.! [The IQP omits the ἀκούσας clause from Q, while the editors of the *Critical Edition of Q* include ὁ Ἰωάννης [πάντων τούτον ...]] (Robinson et al. 2000, 118-119).]

"2. Noch schwerwiegender ist, daß der erste Evangelist an 2/3 Stellen die Erwähnung eines ἀκούειν περὶ Ἰησοῦ innerhalb der von ihm bearbeiteten Mk-Vorlage überging: so unzweideutig gegenüber dem ἀλλ' εὐθὺς ἀκούσασα γυνὴ περὶ αὐτοῦ von Mk 7,25a (vgl. Mt 15,22) und dem ἀκούσασα περὶ τοῦ Ἰησοῦ von Mk 5,27a (vgl. Mt 9,20); gegenüber dem καὶ ἀκούσας ὅτι Ἰησοῦς ὁ Ναζαρηνός ἐστιν von Mk 10,47a (vgl. Mt 9,27) gilt dasselbe, freilich nur insofern, als Mt 9,27-31 neben Mt 20,29-34 für eine zweite mt Bearbeitung von Mk 10,46-52 zu gelten hat, also nicht als mt Sondergut zu betrachten ist.

"Diese Indizien [of Matthew's omission of the ἀκούσας clause] werden aber dadurch relativiert, daß das Verbum ἀκούειν sowohl im JohEv (59x) als auch im LkEv (65x) relativ gut belegt ist und daher eine red Bildung durch beide

Evangelisten nicht prinzipiell ausgeschlossen werden kann. Dies gilt insbesondere für die Wendung ἀκούειν + [52] περί (Lk 7,3), die der dritte Evangelist nicht nur 4x in der Apg verwendet (vgl. Apg 9,13; 11,22; 24,24 und 28,15), sondern auch noch 3x in seinem Ev, davon in Lk 9,9 deutlich in red Bildung gegenüber Mk 6,16!

"Zusammenfassend läßt sich sagen: Der lk und joh Hinweis auf ein ἀκούειν περὶ Ἰησοῦ des Hauptmanns könnte durchaus einen urspr Zug der Hauptmannsperikope dargestellt haben, den der erste Evangelist sek ausließ; eine letzte Sicherheit ist freilich deshalb nicht mehr erreichbar, weil ἀκούειν auch als Hinzufügung von Lk oder/und Joh denkbar ist."

170: "Statistisch läßt V 3a keine sichere Entscheidung zu. Vielleicht klingt bei ἀκούσας δὲ περὶ τοῦ Ἰησοῦ ein urspr bereits in Q erwähnter Zug an, wie Joh 4,47a und die Tatsache, daß Mt auch die mk Erwähnung einer Kunde von Jesus in Mk 7,25 übergeht, nahelegen."

Nolland 1989, 314: "Bultmann's suggestion [1931, 39; ET, 38] that the account of the centurion and his slave is a variation on that of the healing of the Syrophoenician woman's daughter (Mark 7:24-30) is quite unbelievable, but it is possible that the stories with their similar motifs were at some stage transmitted as a pair. If this were so, it would favor an original form for the centurion episode which included Luke 7:3-5."

Lindars 1992, 204: "In Jn 4,47 ἀκούσας comes from the source, as shown by the Lucan parallel."

210: Reconstruction. For complete text see Q 7:1⁶ Luke = Q, Pro (p. 56).

Con

Simons 1880, 42: "Lc. V. 3, 4, 5 sind vom Evangelisten eingeschoben."

von Harnack 1907, 91 (ET 1908, 131): Reconstruction. For complete text see Q 7:1⁶ Luke = Q, Pro (p. 55).

B. Weiß 1908, 15: Reconstruction. For complete text see Q 7:1⁰ In Q (p. 5).

Schniewind 1914, 17: "Lk. 7, 3: ἀκούσας δὲ περὶ τοῦ Ἰησοῦ soll bedeuten, ... daß also in L das Ereignis auf den ersten Besuch Jesu in Kapernaum verlegt werde. ... Denn unsere Perikope wäre die erste Erwähnung von Kapernaum (nicht nur in 'L', sondern) auch in Q, gerade nach Mt., denn Mt. 4, 13 ist wohl Parallele zu Mk. 1, 21, schriftstellerisch umgestellt, stammt jedenfalls nicht aus Q."

Crum 1927, 138: Reconstruction. For complete text see Q 7:2, 3, 4-6a¹ Matt = Q, Pro (pp. 71-72).

Schulz 1972, 237-238: "Die Vv 3-6a bei Lk haben keine Parallele bei Mt und sind lk Erweiterung der Geschichte vom [238] Hauptmann.[410] Auch sachlich erweist sich der Einschub als sek."

238[410]: "Ἀκούειν ist bei Lk gehäuft (Ev 65mal; Apg 89mal); die Konstruktion ἀκούσας + Verb fin findet sich im Ev ca 4mal trad; ca 5mal red und mehrmals in Apg; ἀκούειν περί kommt bei Lk im Ev 2mal trad und in 9,9 red vor, außerdem 4mal in Apg."

Busse 1977, 147-149: "Die Schilderung der beiden Gesandtschaften V 3-6a, von Harnack [1907, 55; ET, 76)] schon als späterer Zusatz erkannt, läßt sich stilkritisch [148] präzise als luk. Zusatz bestimmen.¹ Die stilistische Analyse wird besonders dort relevant, wo Lukas den [149] Hauptmann charakterisiert."

148¹: "Für V 3 hat Schulz [see above] statistische Kriterien zusammengetragen, um ihn als red. zu bestimmen. ἀκούω, ἀποστέλλω wie πρεσβύτεροι τῶν Ἰουδαίων sind sicher luk. Gerade die Korrelation der Motive 'Hören' und 'Senden' (vgl Lk 7,20; Apg 8,14; 9,38; 13,15) verrät Lk. Ebenso verkürzt er den Dialog."

152: "Nach der—wie bei Lukas gewöhnlich—die Ausgangssituation schildernden Exposition wird das die eigentliche Handlung einleitende und die Erzählung weiterführende καὶ ἰδού vermißt. An dessen Stelle steht die Wendung ἀκούσας δέ in V 3, die in V 9 noch einmal aufgegriffen wird. Lukas strebt in dieser Erzählung keine direkte Interaktion, sondern eine von anderen vermittelte Kommunikation an. Ein Zusammentreffen der Hauptpersonen soll auf jeden Fall vermieden werden. Diese Variation der sonst bei Lukas gemäßen Form einer Wundergeschichte ermöglicht eine Fernheilungserzählung."

Marshall 1978, 280: "Ἀκούω περί is a Lucan combination."

Gatzweiler 1979, 308: "Fidèle à lui-même Lc amplifie la narration en signalant que le centurion se décide à sa démarche suite à la réputation faite à Jésus (v. 3)."

Neirynck 1979, 109-110: See Q 7:2, 3, 4-6a³ Luke = Q, Con (p. 107).

Polag 1979, 38: Reconstruction. For complete text see Q 7:10 In Q (pp. 9-10).

Schenk 1981, 37: Reconstruction. For complete text see Q 7:10 In Q (p. 10).

Wegner 1985, 51-52: "Diese Indizien [of Matthean omission of the phrase] werden aber dadurch relativiert, daß das Verbum ἀκούειν sowohl im JohEv (59x) als auch im LkEv (65x) relativ gut belegt ist und daher eine red Bildung durch beide Evangelisten nicht prinzipiell ausgeschlossen werden kann. Dies gilt insbesondere für die Wendung ἀκούειν + [52] περί (Lk 7,3), die der dritte Evangelist nicht nur 4x in der Apg verwendet (vgl. Apg 9,13; 11,22; 24,24 und 28,15), sondern auch noch 3x in seinem Ev, davon in Lk 9,9 deutlich in red Bildung gegenüber Mk 6,16!"

170: "Was Ἰησοῦς betrifft, so schien uns die gehäufte Verwendung dieses Namens innerhalb von Lk 7,3-6 (3x) gegen die Annahme einer lk Verfasserschaft des gesamten Abschnittes zu sprechen, da ja Lk ihn im Vergleich mit Mt und Mk zurückhaltend benutzt. Demgegenüber könnte das relativ häufige Auftauchen von Ἰησοῦς im lk Sg darauf hinweisen, daß der dritte Evangelist in 7,3-6 unter Einfluß von Tradition aus seinem Sg steht."

Schnelle 1987, 103: "Lukas hat in einem weit größeren Maß als Matthäus die Q-Vorlage umgestaltet. Auf seine Redaktion gehen die Situationsschilderung in V.2 … zurück."

Schnelle 1987, ET 1992, 89: "Luke has reshaped the Q version of the story much more thoroughly than Matthew. His redaction produced the description of the situation in v. 2."

Catchpole 1992, 527 [1993, 292]: Reconstruction. For complete text see Q 7:1⁰ In Q (pp. 12-13).

531 [297]: "Given so extensive a correspondence [between Mark 5,21-43 and Q 7,1-10] it is readily understandable that Luke should move over from the one story to the other a series of details. … From ἀκούσασα περὶ τοῦ Ἰησοῦ, sandwiched inside the Jairus tradition (Mark 5,27), there develops ἀκούσας δὲ περὶ τοῦ Ἰησοῦ/αὐτοῦ in Luke 7,3. It is striking that there are no other exact ἀκούσας περὶ τοῦ Ἰησοῦ/αὐτοῦ formulations anywhere else in the synoptic tradition except in Mark 7,25, part of the Syro-Phoenician woman tradition."

Sevenich-Bax 1993, 238: Reconstruction. For complete text see Q 7:1⁰ In Q (p. 15).

Landis 1994, 7, 17: Reconstruction. For complete text see Q 7:1⁶ Luke = Q, Pro (p. 57).

21: Landis argues that ἀκούω περί comes from Lukan *Sondergut*.

International Q Project 1995, 478: Reconstruction: indeterminate vote. For complete text see Q 7:1⁰ In Q (p. 16).

Matt = Q: [ ]²

Pro

Con

Parker 1953, 63-65: See Q 7:1⁶ Matt = Q, Con (pp. 58-60).

Lindars 1992, 204: "It is probable that Matthew has suppressed this item for the sake of brevity."

210-211: "The extent of Matthew's abbreviation can be realized when the same introductory material is compared. … The reduction has been achieved in the following manner: … the information that the centurion heard of Jesus' reputation [211] before going to him has been omitted."

Gagnon 1994b, 136: "In my estimation, Matthew has ... omitted the non-essential remark 'upon hearing about him.'[13]"

136[13]: "Note the presence of corresponding remarks in Luke and John, as well as Matthew's omission of the similar participial clause from Mark's account of the Syrophoenician woman (Mark 7.25!) and other accounts in Mark (5.27!; 6.2, 29; 12.28; 14.11 par.; though Matthew also adds it on seven occasions)."

Emendation = Q: ἀκούσας <>[2] περὶ <αὐτοῦ>[2]

Wegner 1985, 270: Reconstruction: "[ἀκούσας περὶ αὐτοῦ]" [Square brackets indicate uncertainty.]. For complete text see Q 7:1[0] In Q (pp. 11-12).

Emendation = Q: ἀκούσας δὲ περὶ <αὐτοῦ>[2]

Gagnon 1994b, 135: Reconstruction. For complete text see Q 7:1[0] In Q (p. 15).

Evaluations

Johnson 2000: Indeterminate {U}.

In favor of Luke's reading is the use of ἀκούσας in John 4:47 with the same meaning (Fitzmyer, Wegner) and Matthew's tendency to omit the motif. In contrast to claims such that the addition of this motif is indicative of Luke's treatment of *Fernheilungen* (Busse), I am leery of making general, form-critical statements about how Matthew or Luke treat distant healing stories—especially when there are only two recorded in the Gospels (three, if John 4:46b-53 is included as having an independent transmission history).

Against Luke's reading is the fact that Luke loves this expression (Schulz). Also, while Gagnon admits that Matthew omits the expression from Mark six times, he notes that Matthew also adds variants of the motif in other places. Perhaps more significant, if Ἰησοῦς is in Q at 7:1a (see 7:1[3]: the IQP omits it; the editors of the *Critical Edition of Q* are divided; I include it), then it is redundant here. Likewise, if Luke omitted it from Q 7:1a, he may have replaced it here as the introductory occurrence of Jesus' name in the story.

Ἀκούω is Q vocabulary, but the motif does not appear to occur elsewhere in Q. In short, either Matthew omits the motif as unnecessary or Luke, as he is wont to do, adds it. A decisive argument is lacking for addition or omission.

Robinson 2000: Matt = Q {C}, [[]²].

Since John 4:47 also has ἀκούσας in the same position and with the same meaning, it may have been in the oral tradition of this healing. Moreover, the similar formulation at the same position and with the same function in Mark 7:25 could indicate that it was part of the form for introducing stories of a healing from a distance, to the effect that it was by hearing about Jesus that the encounter was instigated: John 4:47a οὗτος ἀκούσας ὅτι Ἰησοῦς ...; Mark 7:25 ἀλλ' εὐθὺς ἀκούσασα γυνὴ περὶ αὐτοῦ,... Luke 7:3 ἀκούσας δὲ περὶ τοῦ Ἰησοῦ ....

Matthew does have a proclivity to eliminate the introductory participle "hearing" (Gagnon). But in some cases this is not at the opening of healing stories: In Mark 6:2 par. Matt 13:54 it has to do with hearing Jesus in the synagogue. In Mark 6:29 par. Matt 14:12 it is a matter of John's disciples hearing he had been executed. In Mark 12:28 par. Matt 22:34 it is a matter of a scribe hearing Jesus debating with Jewish authorities. In Mark 14:11 par. Matt 26:15 the chief priests hear that Judas is available.

But this Matthean trait also occurs in healing stories. In the case of the healing of the daughter of the Syro-Phoenician woman (Mark 7:25 par. Matt 15:22), Matthew reads καὶ ἰδοὺ γυνὴ ... ἔκραζεν for Mark's ἀλλ' εὐθὺς ἀκούσασα γυνὴ περὶ αὐτοῦ. In the case of the woman with a hemorrhage (Mark 5:27 par. Matt 9:20), Matthew reads προσελθοῦσα instead of Mark's ἀκούσασα περὶ τοῦ Ἰησοῦ, ἐλθοῦσα. In the case of blind Bartimaeus in Jericho (Mark 10:47 par. Matt 9:27), Matthew omits Mark's ἀκούσας. Yet when Matthew repeats this healing (Matt 20:30) he reads ἀκούσαντες (the plural since Matthew has two blind persons). So in this case Matthew is on both sides of the discussion, and the instance in Matt 9:27 could be explained in view of the major reduction of the narration and Matthew's vested interest in varying the two accounts of the same tradition.

This survey of Matthean usage indicates he could also have omitted it from Q 7:3: ἀκούσας δὲ περὶ τοῦ Ἰησοῦ ἦλθεν ... par. Matt 8:5b: προσῆλθεν....

To postulate this standard trait of the healings from a distance to be in the Q pericope, whereas the other narrative traits are secondary, weakens the case for including it in Q. Yet, in Q it would not be in the same sentences that are secondary (Luke 7:2, 3b), but in Q would introduce the text of dialogue. Even though Luke has changed the verb (from ἦλθεν to ἀπέστειλεν) so as to introduce the first delegation, ἀκούσας may have been here in Q introducing the centurion coming to Jesus. For a motivation explaining the centurion's unusual action, since he was a Gentile, as was the Syro-Phoenician woman (which begins: ἀλλ' εὐθὺς ἀκούσασα γυνὴ περὶ αὐτοῦ), would be appropriate. The fact that in Luke ἀκούσας begins the Lukan interpolation about the delegation does not make it part of that interpolation. For, in any case, it modifies the subject of a finite verb, which is not only here in the interpolation (ἀπέστειλεν), but also at the same place in Q (ἦλθεν, see Q 7:2, 3, 4-6a³). Q could hence have begun: ἀκούσας ἦλθεν.

Subsequent to Busse writing in favor of Matt = Q, others (e.g. Dauer and Gagnon 1994b) wrote thinking Matthew abbreviated Q. So Busse's argument has been weakened, though not necessarily overturned.

Kloppenborg 2000: Luke = Q {D}, [ ]².

Hoffmann 2001: Matt = Q {C}, [[]²].
Die Streichung des Motivs durch Matthäus in Mt 9,20; 15,22 legt hier zunächst einen redaktionellen Eingriff nahe. Mt 9,27 läßt sich dagegen nur mit Vorbehalt als Beleg hierfür anführen, denn einerseits "hört" der Blinde nach Mk 10,47 nur, daß es Jesus ist, der vorüberzieht, andererseits übernimmt Matthäus in 20,30 dieses Motiv, welches er bei der Doppelung der Erzählung in 9,27 wegließ. An allen genannten Stellen erfolgt die Streichung jedoch im Rahmen einer gezielten und umfassenden Bearbeitung der Markus-Vorlagen. Eine vergleichbare Textsituation liegt in Q 7,3 nicht vor. Welches Interesse sollte Matthäus hier an der Streichung gehabt haben? In Mt 11,2: "Johannes hört im Gefängnis von den Werken des Christus" übernimmt Matthäus das Motiv des Hörens wahrscheinlich aus Q (nach der Editio Critica las Q 7,18 ἀκούσας περὶ πάντων τούτων [Robinson et al. 2000, 118].) Auch sonst setzt Matthäus voraus, daß sich die Kunde von Jesus verbreitet (4,24; 9,26.31).

Für einen redaktionellen Zusatz der Wendung ἀκούειν περὶ τοῦ Ἰησοῦ spricht, daß Lukas nicht nur die Präposition περί häufig verwendet (Matthäus 28, Markus 22, Lukas 45, Apostelgeschichte 72 Belege), sondern vor allem die Wendungen περὶ (τοῦ) Ἰησοῦ/αὐτοῦ oder (τὸ) περὶ (τοῦ) Ἰησοῦ/αὐτοῦ u.ä.— vor allem in Verbindung mit Wörtern des Sagens—bevorzugt gebraucht (Lk 2,28; 4,37; 5,15; 7,17; 22,37; 24,19.27.44; Apg 18,25; 22,18; 23,11.15; 28,31). In Verbindung mit ἀκούω ist die Wendung noch in Lk 9,9; 23,8 belegt (vgl. auch den allgemeinen Gebrauch von ἀκούειν περί in Lk 16,2; Apg 9,13; 11,22; 17,32; 24,24).

Die Angabe stellt zudem in Lk 7,3 ein notwendiges Element der lukanischen Fassung der Erzählung dar. Denn es muß dem Leser plausibel gemacht werden, wie der Centurio dazu kommt, zu diesem Jesus eine Delegation mit der Heilungsbitte zu schicken. Lukas bindet mit der Angabe die Begebenheit in den übergreifenden Erzählzusammenhang seiner Jesus Darstellung ein. In den vorangehenden Texten weist er gezielt auf die Verbreitung der Kunde "über Jesus" hin (Lk 4,14: φήμη ... περὶ αὐτοῦ 4,37: ἦχος περὶ αὐτοῦ [diff. Mk 1,28: ἡ ἀκοὴ αὐτοῦ]; 5,15: ὁ λόγος περὶ αὐτοῦ [ebenso 7,17] vgl. noch 4,23: ὅσα ἠκούσαμεν γενόμενα εἰς τὴν Καφαρναούμ ...).

Mit Joh 4,47 kann die Ursprünglichkeit des Lukastextes kaum begründet werden, denn dort geht es nur darum, daß der Vater "hört, daß Jesus aus Judäa nach Galiläa kommt". Charakteristisch für Lukas ist aber gerade das περὶ τοῦ Ἰησοῦ.

Ein Vergleich mit anderen Heilungsgeschichten zeigt, daß eine solche Motivation der Heilungsbitte in ihnen kein notwendiger Bestandteil ist. Oft genug wird davon ausgegangen, daß sich jemand unmittelbar an Jesus wendet.

Im Zusammenhang von Q haben wir zudem das Problem, daß—im Unterschied zu Lukas—von Heilungtaten Jesu noch nicht die Rede war. Die Wundererzählung dient in Q wahrscheinlich gerade auch dazu, die in Q 7,18-23 folgende Anfrage des Täufers vorzubereiten und—nach der großen Rede Jesus—ein Beispiel für Jesu Heilungen zu geben. Nach dem Q-Zusammenhang hätte der Centurio nur von dieser Rede gehört haben können. Was sollte ihn dann veranlassen, aufgrund dessen, was er "über Jesus" gehört hatte, diesen um eine Heilung zu bitten? Ich gebe zu, daß in einer isoliert überlieferten Erzählung ein solches umfassenderes Wissen vom Erzähler für die Akteure seiner Erzählung einfach vorausgesetzt werden kann, plausibel wird eine solche Angabe jedoch erst in dem übergreifenden Erzählzusammenhang, wie ihn die Evangelien bieten. Ich kann nicht ganz ausschließen, daß in Q erwähnt war, der Centurio habe von Jesu Kommen gehört. Daher nur der Wahrscheinlichkeitsgrad {C}. Die Wendung περὶ τοῦ Ἰησοῦ scheint mir jedoch lukanisch zu sein.

Q 7:2, 3, 4-6a³: Luke's ἀπέστειλεν ... πρεσβυτέρους τῶν Ἰουδαίων or Matthew's προσῆλθεν.

Luke = Q: [ἀπέστειλεν ... πρεσβυτέρους τῶν Ἰουδαίων]³

Pro

H. Meyer 1864, 218: "Welchem der beiden Evangelisten der Vorzug der Ursprünglichkeit gebühre, ist zu Gunsten nicht des Matth., sondern des *Lukas* zu entscheiden, dessen specielle Angaben im Verlauf der Sache ... nur mit Gewaltthätigkeit der traditionellen Erweiterung zugewiesen werden können; sie tragen durchaus das Gepräge der geschichtlichen und psychologischen Ursprünglichkeit, und am wenigsten bedurfte es ihrer Erfindung zur mehrern Hervorhebung der Demuth des Mannes, welche nach Matth. nicht weniger groß und rührend ist."

H. Meyer 1864, ET 1884, 179: "The question as to which of the two evangelists the preference in point of originality is to be accorded, must be decided not in favor of Matthew, but of *Luke*, whose special statements in the course of the incident ... cannot, except in an arbitrary way, be ascribed to an amplifying tendency; they bear throughout the stamp of historical and psychological originality, and nothing would have been more superfluous than to have invented them for the sake of giving greater prominence to the man's humility, which is brought out quite as fully and touchingly in Matthew's narrative."

Hawkins 1899, 195: "Luke may have retained the original narrative in its fullness, while Matthew, after his manner, shortened it: —Lk vi.17a(?); vii. 3a, 4, 5, 6, 7a; 10; 20, 21."

Castor 1912, 41-42: "Although the two accounts agree so closely in the conversation reported, the preceding narrative is given in very different forms. Matthew's form is more condensed and simpler, but not necessarily more original. That a gentile centurion should send Jewish elders to Jesus is most natural; nor is it strange that he should remain by the bedside instead of coming out himself. Nor again is it absurd that the friends should give his message in his own words; it would only be so if Jesus answered them as if addressing him, but this he does not. There is a respect here for Jewish prejudices which seems primitive. Nothing distinctively Lukan can be found in the standpoint of these additions, nor is there any indication that they were added to magnify the miracle. The theory of an assimilation of this narrative to Mark 5:21-43 does not commend itself. Moreover, Matthew's tendency to condense pure narration is established by his use of Mark. It is [42] possible, therefore, that Luke is closer to Q despite the nearly unanimous verdict of the critics in favor of Matthew." But see Castor at Q 7:~~2~~, 3, ~~4-6a~~³ Luke = Q, Con (p. 95).

163: "Whether Luke has made any additions in Sec. 4 [Luke 7:1-10] is doubtful."

223: Reconstruction. For complete text see Q 7:1⁰ In Q (p. 6).

Schmid 1930, 252-253: "Daß aber die besprochenen Übereinstimmungen tatsächlich auf eine gemeinsame schriftliche Vorlage zurückgehen und nicht von Lk direkt aus Mt übernommen wurden, wird sofort klar, wenn man die beiden Versionen der Hauptmannsperikope nebeneinander stellt. Hier läßt sich nachweisen, daß Lk die vollständigere und damit auch ursprünglichere Darstellung hat, die von Mt verkürzt worden ist. Während nämlich nach Mt der heidnische Hauptmann persönlich zu Jesus kommt, läßt Lk ihn überhaupt nicht, wenigstens nicht 'auf der Bühne' mit Jesus zusammenkommen, sondern die πρεσβύτεροι τῶν 'Ιουδαίων als Fürsprecher schicken. Allerdings erklärt man vielfach die Mt-Darstellung als die allein mögliche und darum ursprüngliche, weil 'die lange Rede, die nach Lk angeblich die Freunde halten, schlechterdings nur in den Mund des Hauptmanns selbst paßt' [Harnack 1907, 55; ET, 76]. Allein diese Begründung ist hinfällig. Castor [1912, 41] sagt [253] dagegen mit Recht: 'That a gentile centurion should send Jewish elders to Jesus is most natural; nor is it strange that he should remain by the bedside instead of coming out himself. Nor again is it absurd that the friends should give his message in his own words; it would only be so if Jesus answered them as if addressing him, but this he does not. There is a respect here for Jewish prejudices which seems primitive'. … Daß gerade der Heidenchrist Lk diesen 'judaistischen' Zug, wonach der Nichtjude nur durch Vermittlung der Juden zu Jesus gelangen kann, eigens hinzugefügt hätte, ist, selbst wenn er ihn in irgend einer Sonderquelle gefunden hätte, ganz unwahrscheinlich und entspricht nicht seiner sonstigen Praxis."

Schmid 1951, 118: "Die zwischen V. 6 und V. 3 vorhandene Spannung braucht nicht durch die Annahme einer Sinnesänderung des Hauptmanns, gegen die auch V. 8 spricht, behoben zu werden. Die Bitte, persönlich zu kommen, kann auch erst von den Ältesten der Juden ausgesprochen worden sein, ohne dem Wunsch des Hauptmanns selbst zu entsprechen. Sein demütiges Wort, das in die kirchliche Liturgie Aufnahme gefunden hat, klingt nicht bloß, wenn es, wie bei Matthäus, von ihm persönlich zu Jesus gesprochen wurde, natürlich."

Schmid 1956, 163: "Vor allem geht der Lukas-Bericht darin über den des Matthäus hinaus, daß der Hauptmann es als Heide nicht wagt, persönlich zu Jesus zu kommen, sondern ihn durch 'Älteste der Juden' bitten läßt, seinen Knecht durch sein auch in die Ferne wirksames Machtwort gesund zu machen."

Grundmann 1968, 249-250: See Q 7:~~2~~, 3, ~~4-6a~~³ Matt = Q, Con (pp. 121-122).

Siegman 1968, 189: "I submit that we may reconstruct the incident as follows: the centurion first sent the Jewish elders to Jesus; they persuade Him to come with them. As they near the house, the centurion *personally* comes out to meet Jesus and bids Him inconvenience Himself no further."

Derrett 1973, 175: "The Centurion must have met Jesus personally, perhaps after some introduction by respectable Jews."

Frankemölle 1974, 112-113: "Der umständlichen, primären lk Gestaltung, wonach Jesus 'auf Bitten jüdischer Presbyter hin sich ... mit den Heiden [113] eingelassen' hat, setzt Mt den direkten Kontakt[151] des Heiden mit Jesus voraus."

113[151]: "Auf die Vorschrift des Gesetzes, kein heidnisches Haus zu betreten, die in der lk Tradition noch ein Problem ist, braucht Mt als Theologe einer Heidenkirche keine Rücksicht mehr zu nehmen."

Theissen 1974, 183 (ET 1983, 182-183): See Q 7:6b-c² Luke = Q, Con (pp. 247-248).

Pesch and Kratz 1976, 80: "Die Doppelung des Gesandschaftsmotivs dürfte ursprünglich sein, die Vereinfachung in Mt par (und Joh par) eine sekundäre Kürzung. Ursprünglich erörtert die Wundergeschichte wohl das Problem der Aufnahme von 'Gottesfürchtigen', d.h. der jüdischen Synagoge nahestehenden Heiden, in das Christentum. Juden werden zu Fürsprechern für den Heiden gemacht, der Jesus durch seinen Glauben überzeugt."

Gundry 1982, 141: "In [Matt 8:5] προσῆλθεν replaces ἀπέστειλεν (so Luke). This substitution accords with the dropping of the delegation and with Matthew's fondness for his verb, which connotes Jesus' dignity (38,6)."

Dauer 1984, 94: "Schon diese Beobachtungen an der Verwendung mk Erzählgutes im 3. Evangelium, die doch deutlich und unmißverständlich die lk Arbeitsweise zeigt, machen es äußerst unwahrscheinlich, daß Lukas von sich aus die beiden Gesandtschaften eingefügt hätte, wenn ihm ein Bericht vorgelegen hätte, der dem mt glich oder sehr ähnlich gewesen war."

105-106: See Dauer at Matt = Q, Con (pp. 123-124).

Bovon 1989, 346: "Matthäus vereinfacht oft das Szenarium der Wunderberichte; die beiden Gesandtschaften gehen also nicht zwangsläufig auf die lukanische Redaktion zurück."

347: "Wahrscheinlich ist die erste Gesandtschaft trotz der lukanischen Formulierung traditionell. Möglich ist ebenso, daß Lukas zwei Varianten kennt: die von Q und eine andere. Bei Johannes blieb die Erinnerung an eine Gesandtschaft erhalten, freilich in einer anderen Funktion (Joh 4,51).

"Zur Grundstruktur des Q-Berichts gehört also die Situation des Kranken in Kafarnaum, der Hilferuf des Hauptmannes (vielleicht durch Vermittlung einer Gesandtschaft), die lange Rede des Hauptmannes, seine Bewunderung durch Jesus und die Heilung. Unsicher ist, ob Jesus nur zögert, nicht gleich mitkommt und dadurch die Rede des Hauptmannes verursacht (Q und Matthäus) oder ob dieser erst kurz vor dem Eintreffen Jesu herbeieilt und in diesem Zusammenhang seine Rede beginnt (vorlukanische Überlieferung). Im zweiten Fall wäre die erste Gesandtschaft traditionell."

Bovon 1989, FT 1991, 339: "Matthieu—on le sait—a tendance à simplifier et ramasser le scénario des récits de miracle, de sorte qu'on ne peut jurer que la présence de deux délégations successives soit due à la plume de Luc. ...

"La première délégation vient probablement de la tradition, en dépit des retouches rédactionnelles. Il est également possible que Luc connaisse deux variantes de l'histoire, l'une étant celle de Q. Jean a gardé le souvenir d'une délégation, mais il lui fait jouer un rôle un peu différent (Jn 4,51).

"Font donc partie du récit de base dans Q: l'habitat du malade à Capharnaüm, l'appel au secours du centurion (transmis sans doute par une délégation), le long discours de l'officier, l'admiration de Jésus et la guérison. Mais on ne sait pas si Jésus hésite à venir et suscite ainsi le discours persuasif de l'officier (Matthieu et Q) ou si l'officier, sorti de chez lui peu avant l'arrivée de Jésus, tient alors son discours (état de la tradition avant Luc), auquel cas la première délégation est traditionnelle."

Nolland 1989, 314: See Q 7:2, 3, 4-6a² Luke = Q, Pro (p. 80).

316: "Matthew, who has the centurion speak directly to Jesus, has nothing corresponding to vv 3-6a. Despite the degree of Lukan language in these verses ... it is not unlikely that the Jewish delegation already had a role in the tradition prior to Luke ... and that this has disappeared in the Matthean abbreviation."

Schnackenburg 1991, 79: "Die Erzählung selbst hat er auf das Gespräch zwischen dem Hauptmann und Jesus (ähnlich wie beim Aussätzigen) konzentriert und die vielleicht ursprüngliche Intervention der jüdischen Ältesten (Lk 7,3-6) weggelassen."

Con

Strauss 1836, 101-103: "Hauptsächlich aber die doppelte Gesandtschaft bei Lukas ist nach Schleiermacher etwas, das nicht leicht erdacht wird. Wie, wenn sich dieser Zug vielmehr sehr deutlich als einen erdachten zu erkennen gäbe? Während bei Matthäus der Hauptmann Jesum auf sein Erbieten, mit ihm gehen zu wollen, durch die Einwendung zurückzuhalten sucht: κύριε, οὐκ εἰμὶ ἱκανός, ἵνα μου ὑπὸ τὴν στέγην εἰσέλθῃς, läßt er bei Lukas durch die abgesandten Freunde noch hinzusetzen: διὸ οὐδὲ ἐμαυτὸν ἠξίωσα πρὸς σὲ ἐλθεῖν, womit deutlich genug der Schluß angegeben ist, auf welchem diese Gesandtschaft beruht. Erklärte sich der Mann für unwürdig, daß Jesus zu ihm komme, dachte man, so hat er wohl auch sich selbst nicht für würdig gehalten, zu Jesu zu kommen; eine Steigerung seiner Demuth, durch welche sich auch hier der Bericht des Lukas als der secundäre zu erkennen gibt. Den ersten Anstoß zu dieser Gesandtschaft scheint übrigens das andere Interesse gegeben zu haben, die Bereitwilligkeit Jesu, in des Heiden Haus zu gehen, durch eine vorgängige Empfehlung desselben zu motiviren. Das ist ja das Erste, was die πρεσβύτεροι τῶν Ἰουδαίων, nachdem sie Jesu den Krankheitsfall berichtet, hinzusetzen, ὅτι ἄξιός ἐστιν ᾧ παρέξει τοῦτο· ἀγαπᾷ γὰρ τὸ ἔθνος ἡμῶν κ.τ.λ., ähnlich, wie gleichfalls bei Lukas, in der A. G. 10,22, die Boten des Cornelius dem Petrus, um ihn zu einem Gang in dessen Haus zu vermögen, auseinandersetzen, daß er ein ἀνὴρ δίκαιος καὶ φοβούμενος τὸν θεόν, [102] μαρτυρούμενός τε ὑπὸ ὅλου τοῦ ἔθνους τῶν Ἰουδαίων sei. Daß die doppelte Gesandtschaft nicht ursprünglich sein kann, erhellt am deutlichsten daraus, daß durch dieselbe die Erzählung des Lukas alle Haltung verliert. Bei Matthäus hängt Alles wohl zusammen: der Hauptmann zeigt Jesu zuerst nur den Zustand des Kranken an, und überläßt entweder ihm selber, was er nun thun wolle, oder es kommt ihm, ehe er seine Bitte stellt, Jesus mit seinem Anerbieten, sich in sein Haus zu begeben, zuvor, was nun der Hauptmann auf die bekannte Weise ablehnt. Welches Benehmen dagegen, wenn nach Lukas der Centurio Jesu zuerst durch die jüdischen Ältesten sagen läßt, er möchte kommen (ἐλθών) und seinen Knecht heilen, hierauf aber, wie Jesus wirklich kommen will, gereut es ihm wieder, ihn dazu veranlaßt zu haben, und er begehrt nur ein wunderthätiges Wort von ihm. Daß die erste Bitte nur von den Ältesten, nicht von dem Centurio ausgegangen sei, diese Auskunft läuft den ausdrücklichen Worten des Evangelisten entgegen, welcher durch die Wendung: ἀπέστειλε—πρεσβυτέρους—ἐρωτῶν αὐτόν die Bitte als vom Hauptmann selber ausgegangen darstellt; daß aber dieser mit dem ἐλθών nur gemeint haben sollte, Jesus möchte sich in die Nähe seines Hauses begeben, und nun wie er gesehen, daß Jesus sogar in sein Haus treten wolle, dieß abgelehnt habe, wäre doch wohl zu ungereimt, als daß man es dem sonst verständigen Manne zutrauen könnte, von welchem aber ebendeshalb noch weniger eine so wetterwendische Umstimmung zu erwarten ist, wie sie im Texte des Lukas liegt. Der ganze Übelstand wäre vermieden worden, wenn Lukas der ersten Gesandtschaft, wie Matthäus dem Centurio selbst, zuerst nur die directe oder indirecte Bitte um Heilung überhaupt, und dann, nachdem Jesus sich erboten, in das Haus des Kranken sich zu begeben, noch derselben ersten Gesandtschaft das bescheidene Ablehnen dieses Anerbietens in den Mund gelegt hätte. Allein er glaubte, den Entschluß Jesu, in das Haus [103] zu gehen, durch eine ebendahin zielende Bitte motiviren zu müssen, und indem ihm nun die Tradition noch ein Verbitten dieser persönlichen Bemühung Jesu an die Hand gab: so sah er sich außer Stande, Bitten und Verbitten denselben Personen zu leihen, und mußte daher eine zweite Gesandtschaft veranstalten; wodurch aber der

Widerspruch nur scheinbar vermieden ist, indem ja beide Gesandtschaften von dem Einen Centurio abgeschickt sind."

Strauss 1836, ET 1855, 516-517: "Especially the double message in Luke is, according to Schleiermacher, a feature very unlikely to have been invented. How if, on the contrary, it very plainly manifested itself to be an invention? While in Matthew the centurion, on the offer of Jesus to accompany him, seeks to prevent him by the objection: *Lord, I am not worthy that thou shouldest come under my roof,* in Luke he adds by the mouth of his messenger, *wherefore neither thought I myself worthy to come unto thee,* by which we plainly discover the conclusion on which the second embassy was founded. If the man declared himself unworthy that Jesus should come to him, he cannot, it was thought, have held himself worthy to come to Jesus; an exaggeration of his humility by which the narrative of Luke again betrays its secondary character. The first embassy seems to have originated in the desire to introduce a previous recommendation of the centurion as a motive for the promptitude with which Jesus offered to enter the house of a Gentile. The Jewish elders after having informed Jesus of the case of disease, add, *that he was worthy for whom he should do this, for he loveth our nation and has built us a synagogue*: a recommendation the tenor of which is not unlike what Luke (Acts x. 22) makes the messengers of Cornelius say to Peter to induce him to return with them, namely, that the centurion was a *just man, and one that feareth God, and in good report among all the nation of the Jews.* That the double embassy cannot have been original, appears the most clearly from the fact, that by it the narrative of Luke loses all coherence. In Matthew all hangs well together: the centurion first describes to Jesus the state of the sufferer, and either leaves it to Jesus to decide what he shall next do, or before he proffers his request Jesus anticipates him by the offer to go to his house, which the centurion declines in the manner stated. Compare with this his strange conduct in Luke: he first sends to Jesus by the Jewish elders the request that he will come and heal his servant, but when Jesus is actually coming, repents that he has occasioned him to do so, and asks only for a miraculous word from Jesus. The supposition that the first request proceeded solely from the elders and not from the centurion runs counter to the express words of the evangelist, who by the expressions: ἀπέστειλε—πρεσβυτέρους—ἐρωτῶν αὐτόν, *he sent—the elders—beseeching him,* represents the prayer as coming from the centurion himself; and that the latter by the word ἐλθών meant only that Jesus should come into the neighbourhood of his house, declined this as too great a favour,—is too absurd a demeanour to attribute to a man who otherwise appears sensible, and of whom for this reason so capricious [517] a change of mind as is implied in the text of Luke, was still less to be expected. The whole difficulty would have been avoided, if Luke had put into the mouth of the first messengers, as

Matthew in that of the centurion, only the entreaty, direct or indirect, for a cure in general; and then after Jesus had offered to go to the house where the patient lay, had attributed to the same messengers the modest rejection of this offer. But on the one hand, he thought it requisite to furnish a motive for the resolution of Jesus to go into the Gentile's house; on the other, tradition presented him with a deprecation of this personal trouble on the part of Jesus: he was unable to attribute the prayer and the deprecation to the same persons, and he was therefore obliged to contrive a second embassy. Hereby, however, the contradiction was only apparently avoided, since both embassies are sent by the centurion."

Bleek 1862, 347-348: See Q 7:2, 3, 4-6a¹ Matt = Q, Pro (pp. 70-71).

Holtzmann 1863, 78: "Die andere Differenz, daß nach Matthäus der Hauptmann Jesu entgegenläuft, während er nach Lucas zuerst Älteste, dann Freunde schickt, könnte zwar auch so erklärt werden wollen, daß Matthäus, wie sonst auch, die Geschichtserzählung verkürzt und vereinfacht habe; in der That aber hat Lucas hier verändert."

220: "An die Stelle von A Mt. 8, 1.5-10. 13 hat Lucas ... eine ausgebildetere Tradition gesetzt, in welcher teils die Bescheidenheit des Hauptmanns mehr betont, teils der ganze Vorfall unter einen Gesichtspunkt gebracht worden ist, von dem aus es unzulässig schien, daß Jesus in unmittelbare Berührung mit Heiden tritt. Die schriftstellerische Form ist dieser Tradition von Lucas gegeben; sie berührt sich daher teils mit A Mr. 5, 35 = Lc. 8, 49, teils mit der Act. 10 enthaltenen Geschichte des Cornelius."

B. Weiß 1876, 229: "Im Übrigen hat Luc. den Eingang der Erzählung ganz umgegossen, da er einer spezielleren Überlieferung folgend, die Synagogenältesten, bei denen der Centurio sich durch den Neubau ihrer Synagoge beliebt gemacht hat, bei Jesu für denselben Fürsprache thun läßt (v. 3-5)."

B. Weiß 1878, 364: "Von dieser Vermittlung weiß die ältere Quelle nichts, und wenigstens das ἐλθών kann ihnen nach V. 6 der Hauptmann nicht aufgetragen haben, da die Annahme Meyer's [1867, 355-356; ET, 344-345], daß der Hauptmann sich nachher eines andern besonnen, weil sein Vertrauen gestiegen, bloße Ausflucht ist."

Simons 1880, 42: "Lc. V. 3, 4, 5 sind vom Evangelisten eingeschoben."

J. Weiß 1892, 399: "Die Sendung der Stadt-πρεσβύτεροι ... gehört der Sonderüberlieferung an."

Wernle 1899, 86: "Leider verrät gerade diese Einleitung so deutlich wie möglich den Lc als Verfasser durch den Ausdruck 'Die Ältesten der Juden' 7,3."

Holtzmann 1901, 344: "Wie aber 8,49 eine Gesandtschaft aus dem Hause des Vaters in die Handlung eingreift, so bedient sich 7,3 der Centurio zunächst einiger *Ältesten*, d.h. Stadtvorsteher, *der Juden*, die er zu Jesus schickt mit dem Ersuchen, ὅπως ἐλθών (das ist aber ganz gegen die 7,6.7 zu Tage tretende Absicht und Gesinnung des Heiden, daher wohl Nachwirkung des anders gemeinten ἐλθών Mt 8,7) διασώσῃ (durchrette, durchbringe) τὸν κτλ."

B. Weiß 1901, 383: See Q 7:6b-c² Luke = Q, Con (pp. 242-243).

384: Weiß argues below that the first embassy is from L (not Q), while the second embassy is a creation of the Lukan redactor. "Stand diese Entschuldigung schon in L, so kann sie nur die Anbringung der Bitte V. 3 durch die Stadtältesten motivirt haben, und nicht erst die Sendung der Freunde; sie trennt offenbar die beiden Hälften von Mt 8,8, woher sogar das ὁ παῖς μου aufgenommen, obwohl Lk nach V. 2 von einem δοῦλος erzählte. Natürlich nahm es Lk in diesem Sinne; aber der Wechsel des Ausdrucks von derselben Hand ist unmöglich. Bem. noch den dem εἰπέ konformiten Imper. ἰαθήτω.—V. 8 wörtlich, wie Mt 8,9, nur mit dem erläuternden τασσόμενος (Röm 13,1). Unnöthiger Weise nimmt man an dem Prt. Praes. Anstoß, weshalb Hofm. [Hofmann 1878, 179]. es durch ἔχων—στρατ. erläutern sein läßt (der mit den mir untergebenen Kriegern an einen Posten gestellt wird), wozu ja das folgende κ. τ. δούλῳ μ. schlechterdings nicht paßt, und Hhn. [Hahn 1892, 462-463] als Zwischensatz faßt.... Es bezeichnet doch einfach, daß auch er im Dienste immer wieder unter Oberbefehl gestellt wird, und darum wisse, was gehorchen heißt. Daß diese Worte, so lebensvoll sie bei Mt im Munde des Hauptmanns sind, so unmöglich im Munde der Freunde, bedarf keines Nachweises. Bem., wie hier der Hauptmann nur einen Privatsklaven hat (τ. δοῦλ. μ.), während nach V. 2 offenbar mehrere, da der kranke von ihm besonders geschätzt war."

B. Weiß 1904, 242: "Schon in der ältesten Überlieferung schloß sich an die Bergrede die Erzählung vom Hauptmann zu Kapernaum an (vgl. Mtth. 8,1.5). Auch hier geht Jesus unmittelbar nach Vollendung derselben nach Kapernaum. Aber Lukas befaß in der ihm eigentümlichen Überlieferung noch einen reicheren Bericht über diese Geschichte, dem er besonders in der ersten Hälfte folgt. Hier war es ein sonderlich wertgeschätzter Knecht des Hauptmanns, dessen Krankheit zwar nicht näher bezeichnet wird, der aber bereits in den letzten Zügen lag. Hier hält sich der heidnische Hauptmann nicht einmal für würdig, Jesu selbst mit seiner Bitte zu nahen, sondern sendet die Stadtältesten zu ihm, um die Errettung des Knechtes aus der letzten Todesnot zu erbitten."

B. Weiß 1904, ET 1906, 56: "In the oldest tradition the Sermon on the Mount was followed by the account of the centurion of Capernaum (cf. Matt. viii. 1-5). According to this tradition Jesus goes to the city immediately after finishing His address. But Luke possessed in his special source of information fuller details of this history which he follows, especially in the first part of his account. He describes that it was an especially useful servant of the centurion, whose sickness is not, however, more closely described, but who was already at the point of death. Here the Gentile centurion does not even consider himself worthy of approaching the Lord personally with his petition, but he sends the elders of the city to Him, to ask Him to save his servant in his great danger."

von Harnack 1907, 55: "Die beiden Gesandtschaften an Jesus (statt daß der Hauptmann selbst kommt) sind späterer Zusatz. Das geht schlagend 1. daraus hervor, daß die lange Rede, die nach Luk. angeblich die Freunde halten, schlechterdings nur in den Mund des Hauptmanns selbst paßt, 2. daß auch bei Joh. (4,46ff.) der Hauptmann (βασιλικός) selbst kommt."

56: "Διασώζειν kann als ein lukanisches Wort in Anspruch genommen werden, sowie der Wechsel ἀπέστειλεν (v. 3) und ἔπεμψεν (v. 6)."

von Harnack 1907, ET 1908, 76: "The two deputations to our Lord (in place of the personal interview of the centurion) are a later addition. This is strikingly shown (1) by the fact that the long speech which St. Luke assigns to the friends is intelligible and appropriate only if it was spoken by the centurion himself, and (2) because also in St. John (iv. 46ff.) the centurion (βασιλικός) comes himself."

77: "Διασώζειν can be claimed as Lukan, as well as the alternation between ἀπέστειλεν (verse 3) and ἔπεμψεν (verse 6)."

B. Weiß 1907, 242: "Vor allem kommt Mt. 8,5 ff. der Hauptmann selbst und klagt über das Elend seines Sohnes, ohne eine Bitte zu wagen, so daß erst Jesus sein Kommen zur Heilung anbieten muß, während er nach Lk. 7,3 ff. die Stadtältesten schickt, die in seinem Namen bitten (ἐρωτῶν, vgl. Joh. 4,47), er möge kommen und den Knecht durch die Todesnot hindurchretten, und diese Bitte mit einer Empfehlung des Hauptmanns unterstützen, die mit ihren konkreten Details allein schon jeden Verdacht ausschließt, als handle es sich nur um eine Ausmalung des Lukas."

J. Weiß 1907, 448: "Die Bergrede wird fast wörtlich so beschlossen, wie bei Matthäus. Die Geschichte, die von V. 6 an ganz wie bei Matthäus ... verläuft, hat bei Lukas einige Zusätze: die doppelte Botschaft und die starke Zurückhaltung des Hauptmanns fügt zu dem kühnen Glauben des Mannes noch den Zug der außerordentlichen Demut hinzu. Die Vertretung der Synagogen-Gemeinde von Kapernaum stellt ihm ein glänzendes Zeugnis aus; er erscheint wie Kornelius (Apg. 10,1ff.) als ein Proselyt."

Castor 1912, 42: "On a priori grounds we should hardly expect the longer narrative [Luke 7:3-6a] to belong to that source, and it may be that Luke has supplemented Q with information from other sources." But see Castor at Q Luke = Q, Pro (p. 88).

Patton 1915, 144: "Burton [1904, 46; see Q 7:2, 3, 4-6a[13] Matt = Q, Con (pp. 231-232).] alleges that Matthew's omission of the item of the messengers is characteristic of him, with his tendency to condensation. But that the messengers were not in the original story, but were added by Luke (or his source) and not omitted by Matthew, is plain from the fact that the conversation, even in Luke, is based upon the supposition that the centurion had made his request in person. In Luke's vss. 3-6, which contain the account of the sending of the messengers, there are at least five Lucan words (ἔντιμος, παραγενό-μενοι, σπουδαίως, μακράν, ἀπέχοντος). These occur in the portion of the story unparalleled in Matthew. But there are also three such Lucan words in the two following verses, where the story of Luke runs quite closely parallel to that of Matthew (διό, ἠξίωσα, τασσόμενος). The changing of a detail, even an important detail, in the narrative part of such a section, especially when contrasted with general faithfulness to the source in that part containing the words of Jesus, would be characteristic of Luke."

145: "These facts cannot be said to throw much light on whether Luke is here to be charged with the verses in which these words occur, or whether they may have stood in his source. But considering the extremely close agreement between Luke's vss. 7b-9 and Matthew's vss. 8b-10 (note especially the εἰπὲ λόγῳ, unparalleled elsewhere), the best conclusion may be that the story stood in Q, much as it now stands in Matthew, and that Luke, perhaps having heard this other version of the story, has himself altered the narrative part of it."

Klostermann 1919, 448; 1929, 86: "Das persönliche Kommen des heidni-schen Hauptmanns, der irgendwie von Jesus gehört hat, wird ersetzt durch die Sendung von jüdischen πρεσβύτεροι d.h. Gemeindevertretern, … die Jesu Kommen und seine Hilfe vermitteln sollen."

Loisy 1924, 215: See Q 7:2, 3, 4-6a⁹ Luke = Q, Con (p. 169).

216: "Au lieu de solliciter lui-même auprès de Jésus la guérison de son malade, le centurion délègue les anciens de la synagogue, les personnes les plus notables de la communauté, pour le prier de venir: cette requête est en contra-diction avec les sentiments que l'officier va témoigner dans quelques instants par l'organe de ses amis, mais elle correspond à l'intention que Jésus témoi-gnait dans le récit original (cf. Mt viii, 7), avant que le centurion lui dît d'opé-rer la guérison sans prendre la peine de se déranger."

Bussmann 1925, 11: "Man müßte sonst annehmen, daß Mt an den einen Stellen kritischer als L verfahren sei und an den anderen wie der L. Wie ist es z.B. zu erklären, daß L in der Geschichte vom Hauptmann von Kapernaum (7,1-10) die Erweiterung geben kann gegenüber Mt, daß er erst Fürbitter sen-det, dann Freunde, dann es sei schon zu spät und den kleinen hierzu passen-den Einschub: διὸ οὐδὲ ἐμαυτὸν ἠξίωσα πρὸς σὲ ἐλθεῖν, der doch eine Duplette zum vorhergehenden Verse bildet."

Easton 1926, 96: "The divergence at the beginning is very considerable; in Mt the centurion comes himself, in Lk he sends deputies. An abbreviation of Q by Mt … is hardly possible, for the rather pointless character of these verses is unlike Q, which ordinarily does not waste a word. On the other hand, an expansion of Q by Lk seems incredible. ...

"The most plausible assumption is that Lk had the material in a parallel account, and he felt bound to give it for historic completeness. ...

"The words of the centurion's message may, indeed, have been learned by heart by his emissaries, but they would certainly be more natural in his own mouth. Perhaps the circle in which L originated felt that any dealing on Christ's part with Gentiles required explanation, particularly dealings that included such superlative praise. So the explanation grew up that this Gentile was an extraordinary benefactor of Israel and most humble in the presence of Jews. Reminiscences of the Jairus story seem to have aided in putting this interpretation into narrative form; ... both the ruler of the synagogue and its founder appeal for aid in sickness."

97: "'Of the Jews' may be Lk's addition."

Montefiore 1927, 423-424: "Luke ... makes diverse changes [424] in the story of the centurion. The centurion sends the Jewish elders to Jesus instead of coming himself."

Bussmann 1929, 56: "Bei Mt erklärt Jesus auf die Erzählung des Haupt-manns, er wolle hingehen ihn zu heilen, bei L aber, und das erzählt einge-hend der Einschub bei L, wird eine Gesandtschaft vom Hauptmann gesandt."

Creed 1930, 100: "The chief difference between Mt. and Lk. is that in Mt. the centurion himself comes to Jesus with his petition, whereas in Lk. he approaches him through two successive embassies—first, elders of the Jews, and secondly, friends. This seems artificial, and there can be no doubt that Mt. gives the story in a more original form. The words of the centurion (6b-8) are in place when the centurion speaks himself; they are not in place when repeated by his friends, who, as Wellh. [Wellhausen 1904b, 27] says, appear to have learnt the centurion's words by heart. It seems possible that the symbolic character of the centurion, as typifying Gentile believers, has encouraged the expansion of the story as given in Lk."

Bultmann 1931, 39: "Es scheint doch, daß auch Lk die Geschichte in einer Form las, in der deutlich war, daß Jesu Bedenken überwunden werden mußte; aber da er den Dialog nicht mehr klar verstand, teilte er die Rolle des Überre-dens den πρεσβύτεροι zu, die nun andere Argumente bringen müssen, die Lk für einleuchtender hielt."

Bultmann 1931, ET 1968, 39: "It also seems that Luke had the story in a form in which it was plain that Jesus' scruples had to be overcome; though, since he no longer clearly understood the dialogue, he gave the persuasive role to the πρεσβύτεροι, who had to adduce other arguments, which to Luke seemed more illuminating."

Hauck 1934, 93: "Die Verse 2-6a (Bittgesandtschaft), welche eine Erweiterung gegenüber Mt darstellen, sind wohl eine Überlieferungsvariante (Bericht II [= a Jewish-Christian source used by Luke]), welche Lk in den ersten Bericht (I [= Q]) eingearbeitet hat."

Kiddle 1935, 170: "[Luke] mentions [the centurion] as being the first to be dealt with under the new law ... and says that this Gentile actually sent elders of the Jews to come and save his servant, and that these elders assured Jesus that 'he is worthy that thou shouldest do this for him'.¹"

170¹: "Since Lk.'s account from vii 8 is almost exactly the same as that in Mt., it is probable that the long introduction which makes the narrative so clumsy was inserted by him."

Manson 1937, 63: "It is almost certain that the dialogue alone belongs to Q. The narrative framework is supplied independently by Mt. and Lk."

64: "It may be noted that the participation of the Jewish elders is hardly consistent with the subsequent statement, 'I have not found such faith in Israel.'"

Hirsch 1941, 89: "Sachlich bedeuten sie eine Veränderung der Geschichte, wie sie Luk sich an Markustexten da, wo nicht eine markusfremde Vorlage ihn bestimmte, nirgends erlaubt hat. Es sind folgende: a) Der Hauptmann spricht nicht selbst mit Jesus, sondern schickt erst die jüdische Gemeindebehörde, dann Freunde zu Jesus (Luk 7,2-6a). Bei der Bestellung durch die Freunde fällt auf, daß sie in einer ausführlichen Darlegung so reden, als ob sie der Hauptmann selber wären. ... Wir fanden schon einmal in der Sonderfassung von Q bei Luk judenchristliche Prägung .... hier ist sie noch deutlicher. Und hier kann niemand bezweifeln, daß nicht Q selbst, sondern die von Luk benutzte Umarbeitung und Erweiterung von Q, Lu I, diese bewußt judenchristliche Prägung getragen hat. Damit sind Lu I und Lu II deutlich geschieden. Lu II hat in der Geschichte von Jesu Verwerfung in Nazareth verraten, daß er über die Grenzen des Judentums weit hinausschaut." Hirsch assumes that Matthew represents the most original version of Q, and that Luke works from Lu II, a revised and expanded version of Q (Lu I).

Jeremias 1956, 25-26 (ET 1958, 30): See Q 7:2, 3, 4-6a⁷ Matt = Q, Pro (p. 151).

Leaney 1958, 141: "This part of the story is peculiar to Luke. On no other occasion in the gospels are elders called 'elders of the Jews' and the full explanatory phrase suggests that Luke had Gentile readers in mind. ...

"It is likely that Luke has himself invented the detail of the sending of the elders, knowing that the synagogue had been built at the instance of a centurion and using this as an opportunity to introduce into the days of Jesus' ministry a character like Cornelius (Acts x). The construction of the story bears this out: in verse 3 the centurion sends to ask Jesus to come but in verse 6 (from Q) tells him that it is not necessary for him to come. Luke has also added an apology for the centurion's not coming to Jesus himself (7a), but it cannot be regarded as a very satisfactory explanation from a man with so earnest a request and so great respect for the Lord. The story in Matt. viii. 5-13 is free from these contradictions."

Haenchen 1959a, 25-26 [1965, 84-85]: "Warum die beiden Delegationen eingeführt [by a post-Q, pre-Lukan redactor] worden sind, ist klar: Die erste soll die Würdigkeit des Mannes durch seine Verdienste um die Judenschaft begründen, die er selbst Jesus gegenüber nicht gut geltend machen konnte. Also mußten hier die 'Ältesten der Juden' bemüht werden. Aber wenn nun [26, 85] Jesus, dieser Bitte folgend, zum Haus des Centurio aufbrach, dann drohte dessen Glaubenswort—wie es die Tradition doch bot—unmöglich zu werden: Der Hauptmann konnte doch Jesus nicht an der Schwelle seines Hauses mit den Worten empfangen: 'Ich bin nicht würdig, daß du unter mein Dach trittst; sprich nur ein Wort!' Also mußte der Erzähler wohl oder übel eine zweite Delegation aufbieten, die Jesus noch unterwegs antreffen kann."

Haenchen 1959b, 496: "The writer could not simply bring in the centurion's alms to the poor: neither could the officer himself mention his own merits, nor had the poor any opportunity to bear witness before Jesus. So the writer introduces Jewish elders. They can tell all that is in favour of the centurion: he loves the Jewish nation, and he has built the synagogue in Capernaum. Yet this insertion of the Jewish elders is very clumsy." Haenchen argues for a post-Q, pre-Lukan redaction of the story.

Held 1960, 185: "So kommt der Heide nicht selbst zu Jesus, da er sich nach seinen eigenen Worten für unwürdig hält (Lk. 7,7a, von Lukas selbst eingefügt). Vielmehr sendet er eine Gesandtschaft von jüdischen Ältesten, die aber gerade seine Würdigkeit hervorheben (Lk. 7,4)."

Held 1960, ET 1963, 195: "The Gentile man does not himself come to Jesus, since, according to his own words, he regards himself as unworthy (Luke 7:7a, inserted by Luke). He sends rather a deputation of Jewish elders, who, however, make a point of emphasizing his worthiness (Luke 7:4)."

Grundmann 1961, 155: "Die Erzählung vom Centurio in Kapernaum findet sich auch im Matthäus-Evangelium. Der Vergleich ergibt, daß bei Lukas zwei Berichte miteinander verbunden sind; während nach dem Bericht des Matthäus der Centurio Jesus begegnet, verkehrt er hier durch eine doppelte Gesandtschaft mit ihm, wobei das direkte Gespräch zwischen beiden bei Matthäus in den Mund vom Mittelsleuten gelegt wird. Die Veränderung ist so stark, wie sie bei keinem der Berichte, die Lukas aus Markus übernimmt, vorgenommen ist. Das legt den Gedanken nahe, daß Lukas die Verbindung nicht selbst vollzogen, sondern vorgefunden hat. Die Verbindung wird auch durch sprachliche Beobachtungen belegt. Für den beiden Evangelisten gemeinsamen

Grundbericht ist für den Kranken παῖς (Luk. 7,7; Matth. 8,6.8.13), für den nur dem Lukas eigenen Bericht δοῦλος gegeben (Luk. 7,2.3.10); für den Ausdruck der Würdigkeit liest der Grundbericht ἱκανός (Luk. 7,6; Matth. 8,8), während der Sonderbericht ἄξιος liest (Luk. 7,4; vgl. auch in ἀξιόω 7,7). So ergibt sich eine weitgehende Übereinstimmung zwischen Luk. 7,7-9 und Matth. 8,8-10, die bis in sprachliche Einzelheiten geht, während die Einleitung (7,1-6) und der Schluß (7,10) bei Lukas sich auch sprachlich von Matthäus unterscheiden. Sowohl die Übereinstimmung sowie die Aufeinanderfolge von Bergpredigt und Centurio bei beiden—vgl. Einleitung Luk. 7,1 mit Matth. 7,28a und 8,5—weist darauf hin, daß wir es bei diesem Bericht mit einer dritten Q-Folge zu tun haben. Dann entsteht die Frage, wie es zur Verschmelzung des Grundberichtes aus Q mit dem lukanischen Sonderbericht gekommen ist. Hat ihn Lukas seinem Sondergut entnommen und mit dem Q-Bericht verschmolzen? Da solche Arbeit des Lukas sonst nicht zu beobachten ist, erscheint diese Auskunft wenig wahrscheinlich; zudem trägt der Sonderbericht einen stark judenchristlichen Charakter, strenger als Matthäus selbst, aber das Sondergut des Lukas zeigt universalistische Züge. Diese Erwägungen legen die Auskunft Hirschs [1941, 88-90] nahe, daß Lukas in einer überarbeiteten Ausgabe von Q, Hirschs Lu I, den Bericht bereits zusammengefügt vorgefunden hat." Grundmann 1961 is included in the Luke = Q, Con section because he considers the longer Lukan material to be part of an expanded version of Q—see Hirsch 1941 above. However, see Grundmann 1968 at Matt = Q, Con (pp. 121-122), where he argues for a Matthean abbreviation of the Q narrative.

Dodd 1963, 191: See Q 7:2, 3, 4-6a¹ Luke = Q, Con (p. 68).

Lampe 1965, 168: "The centurion never comes face to face with Jesus. Here, other motives help to determine the Lukan form of the story: Jesus does not have direct dealings with Gentiles in the pre-Resurrection period, and it is through the mediation of Jewish elders that communication is established between this Gentile and Jesus in the first instance. Luke seems to have made an artificial reconstruction of the tradition."

Delobel 1966, 456: "Nous considérons les vv. 1-6a comme une composition lucanienne. Nous avons déjà remarqué que Luc aime les délégations de personnes intermédiaires, tels les envoyés de Jean-Baptiste dans *Lc.*, VII, 24, et les envoyés aux Samaritains dans IX, 52."

Harrington 1967, 116: "The Sermon on the Mount had been spoken in the hearing of Israel ('the people'); it may be that in turning immediately to the episode of the centurion Luke wishes to foreshadow the Gentile mission. This may explain why (unlike Matthew) Jesus does not meet the centurion: according to the plan of Luke in Acts, the Gentile mission is to follow the Ascension."

Talbert 1967, 491-492: "In Luke 7:1-10 we find a Q tradition (cf. Matthew 8:5-13) to which the Evangelist has added vv. 3-6a. Thus, we have a story of a [492] pious centurion who sends others to secure assistance for him. The point of the tradition as it stands here is the centurion's faith as contrasted with Israel's lack of faith (v. 9). This tradition, as it has been adapted by Luke, sounds remarkably like the Cornelius episode in Acts 10:11. It would seem that Luke has introduced into Jesus' Galilean ministry a character like Cornelius."

Lührmann 1969, 57³: "Bei Lk redet der Hauptmann freilich durch jüdische Übermittler, ein wohl gegenüber Q sekundärer Zug."

Schürmann 1969, 397: "Der Ausspruch harmoniert in der vorliegenden Form nicht mehr so gut mit der Fürsprache der jüdischen Ältesten VV 3ff und scheint eine spätere Verschärfung erfahren zu haben. Auch 'der Ausdruck "Älteste der Juden" verrät den heidenchristlichen Schriftsteller'. Wahrscheinlich war es aber erst Luk selbst, der die Presbyter durch den Genitiv seinen Lesern verdeutlichte. So verrät eine im Kern palästinenische Erzählung eine leichte heidenchristliche und lukanische Redaktion."

P. Meyer 1970, 410: "The secondary character of Luke's use of the 'elders' is widely recognized."

Schnider and Stenger 1971, 61-62: Schnider and Stenger preface their rationale for Lukan redaction by setting it against Haenchen's theory (1959a,b) of a pre-Lukan, Jewish-Christian source that accounts for some of the differences between Matthew and Luke. "Doch scheint eine solche Begründung allzu gesucht und die wahre Bedeutung des 'Gesandtenmotivs' zu verdecken. Man muß nur aufmerksam auf das Gefälle der Erzählung achten. Gewiß preisen die Gesandten den Mann. Er liebt das Volk und hat [62] Verdienste um es (Lk 7,5). Deshalb ist er in den Augen der Gesandtschaft der Bitte würdig (ἄξιός ἐστιν Lk 7,4). Doch die Selbsteinschätzung des Mannes widerspricht dem Urteil der Gesandtschaft: 'Ich habe mich nicht für würdig gehalten (οὐδὲ ἐμαυτὸν ἠξίωσα Lk 7,7)!' 'Würdig' ist das Stichwort, das uns die Bedeutung der zweifachen Gesandtschaft erschließt. Dadurch, daß er einerseits im Urteil der anderen als ἄξιος dasteht, sich selber aber, indem er das Wort verneinend wieder aufnimmt, nicht so einschätzt, wird der Kontrast zwischen dem Fremdurteil und der Selbsteinschätzung betont. Durch den Kontrast aber tritt seine Selbsteinschätzung als eindrucksvolles Beispiel von Demut hervor. Dem selben Zweck dient die zweifache Gesandtschaft; denn nicht nur durch das, was die Gesandten sagen, sondern schon durch ihr Auftreten, wird der Centurio als demütig und bescheiden charakterisiert. Er wagt es nicht selbst zu Jesus zu gehen, sondern schickt zweimal Gesandte aus, um sich an Jesus zu wenden. Dann aber liegt hier nicht 'ungeschickte' Erzählungskunst vor, die man Lukas nicht zutrauen dürfe, sondern gerade das

Gegenteil. Bis jetzt ist kein Grund sichtbar geworden, warum Lukas eine besondere, judenchristlich vorgeformte Vorlage benutzt haben soll; vielmehr weist die angewandte Erzählkunst auf Lukas selber, was auch wortstatistische Beobachtungen bestätigen."

Schramm 1971, 40-42: See Q 7:2̶, 3, 4̶-6a⁷ Luke = Q, Con (p. 149).

Danker 1972, 91-92: "In Luke the centurion sends word through interme-diaries. Through this shape of the story Luke is able to show that even Jewish leaders [92] recognize Jesus' power and urge him to use it for the benefit of a Gentile. The gesture fits Luke's Jew-to-Gentile theme and his concern to establish continuity between Israel and the Gentiles (cf. Acts 10:35)." But see Danker at Matt = Q, Con (p. 122).

George 1972, 70: "Comme on l'a déjà senti dans le commentaire, l'inter-vention de ces intermédiaires entraîne plusieurs difficultés dans le récit de Luc: la demande du v. 6 s'accorde mal avec celle du v. 3; le message des vv. 6-8 serait mieux placé sur les lèvres du centurion, comme chez Mt 8,8-9, que sur celles de ses envoyés; et, comme on va le voir, c'est sans doute l'absence du centurion qui amène Luc à ne pas rapporter la 'parole de guérison' de Mt 8,13. Ces divers traits suggèrent que les deux envois d'intermédiaires n'appar-tiennent pas à la forme originelle du récit."

76: "Ce qui intéresse Luc dans ce récit, ce n'est pas la Loi, dont il n'a pas parlé dans le discours précédent, mais la rencontre du païen avec Jésus. Il sait combien il est difficile pour un païen d'être accueilli par un Juif. Il montre aussi dans les Actes que l'Évangile est parvenu aux païens par l'intermédiaire d'Israël: tous les premiers prédicateurs ont été des Juifs, et dans toute ville païenne ils ont toujours commencé leur prédication dans la synagogue. Luc y pense sans doute quand il montre les 'anciens des Juifs' intervenant auprès de Jésus en faveur du païen. S'il insiste sur la bienveillance du centurion pour les païens (7,5), c'est probablement moins pour montrer ses mérites que pour évoquer les bons rapports entre Juifs et païens, qu'il est soucieux de montrer dans l'Eglise naissante (Ac 11,22-24.27-30; 15,1-35; 21,17-26, si différents de l'image que nos donne Paul)."

Jervell 1972, 120-121: "When Jesus heals a non-Jew, or rather listens to and grants [121] a prayer from a Gentile, Luke must offer a defense, by refer-ring to the Gentile's close relationship to Israel (7:5). Luke's concern is obvi-ously not to heighten the miraculous element. The Jewish leaders who appear play quite another role, and they would be unnecessary if this were his inten-tion. Luke's reworking of this account shows that it is hardly accidental that he does not retell the story of the healing of the Canaanite woman (Mark 7:25ff; Matt. 15:21ff.). It is not sufficient merely to mention that the account lies within 'the great omission.' Rather it is all too clear that Luke consciously wants to limit Jesus' activity to the Jews."

Schulz 1972, 237-238: "Die Vv 3-6a bei Lk haben keine Parallele bei Mt und sind lk Erweiterung der Geschichte vom [238] Hauptmann.⁴¹⁰ Auch sachlich erweist sich der Einschub als sek.⁴¹¹"

238⁴¹⁰: "Ἀποστέλλειν πρός wird von Lk im Ev 7,20 red gebraucht, außerdem 5mal in Apg; πρεσβύτερος für die jüdischen Presbyter findet sich 7mal in Apg (πρεσβύτεροι τῶν Ἰουδαίων auch Apg 25,15)."

238⁴¹¹: "Die Erzählung erfährt durch die zweimalige Gesandtschaft bei Lk eine ungewöhnliche Komplizierung, die gegenüber dem direkten Vorbringen des Anliegens durch den Hauptmann bei Mt formgeschichtlich deutlich sek Züge zeigt. Zudem entstehen in der Lk-Fassung durch den Einschub der Vv 3-6a Unklarheiten, die das Ganze sehr konstruiert erscheinen lassen. Nur wenn Jesus zunächst zu kommen zögert (so Mt), ist das demütige Bekenntnis des Hauptmannes sinnvoll. ... Nach V 3 soll Jesus kommen, um den Knecht zu heilen—und nachdem er die Presbyter begleitet hat, muß er erfahren, daß sich der Hauptmann nun doch für unwürdig hält, Jesus ins Haus kommen zu lassen; V 6b wirkt nun überhaupt nicht mehr motiviert: Die Erklärung des Hauptmanns, er sei nicht würdig, Jesus in sein Haus kommen zu lassen, ist sinnvoll nur, wenn Jesus vorher die Bitte des Hauptmanns abgewiesen hat, dieser seine Unwürde nun eingesteht und dann dennoch mit der Bitte um ein bloßes Wort Jesu dessen Hilfe auch auf Distanz erwartet. Endlich wirkt auch die Art, wie die Freunde in V 6 das Wort des Hauptmanns in der I. Person vorbringen, sehr konstruiert und trägt deutlich die Zeichen der Umarbeitung an sich. Lk könnte bei der Überarbeitung Anklänge aus der Jairus-Geschichte aufgenommen haben."

Derrett 1973, 175: "The word *elders* Luke caught up from Exod. xviii 18 Pal. Targ."

Lange 1973, 42⁵⁰: See Q 7:2, 3, 4-6a⁷ Luke = Q, Con (p. 149).

Wilson 1973, 31: See Q 7:2, 3, 4-6a¹ Luke = Q, Con (p. 68).

Busse 1977, 147-149: "Die Schilderung der beiden Gesandtschaften V 3-6a, von Harnack [1907 55; ET, 76] schon als späterer Zusatz erkannt, läßt sich stilkritisch [148] präzise als luk. Zusatz bestimmen.¹ Die stilistische Analyse wird besonders dort relevant, wo Lukas den [149] Hauptmann charakterisiert."

148¹: "Für V 3 hat Schulz [1972, 238⁴¹⁰; see above] statistische Kriterien zusammengetragen, um ihn als red. zu bestimmen. ἀκούω, ἀποστέλλω wie πρεσβύτεροι τῶν Ἰουδαίων sind sicher luk. Gerade die Korrelation der Motive 'Hören' und 'Senden' (vgl. Lk 7,20; Apg 8,14; 9,38; 13,15) verrät Lk. Ebenso verkürzt er den Dialog."

151-152: "Eine weitere formale Besonderheit dieser Wundererzählung liegt in ihrer Dramatik. Schon die Krankheitsschilderung des auf den Tod erkrankten Knechts vermittelt den Eindruck äußerster Dringlichkeit, sich um sofortige Hilfe zu bemühen. Die Lage spitzt sich durch die Einführung der beiden Gesandtschaften noch weiter zu. Lukas nützt jede Gelegenheit aus, die Dramatik zu steigern. Die Ältesten bitten Jesus 'eifrig', dem Mann zu helfen, und erwecken—von Lukas bewußt im durativen Imperfect erzählt—den Eindruck der Zeitvergeudung. Danach wird Jesus—von Lukas durch die Wahl der Litotes οὐ μακράν emphatisch und ironisch zugleich dramatisiert—kurz vor dem Ziel von der zweiten Gesandtschaft angehalten. Lukas verlängert diesen Spannungsbogen mit dem Fortfall des Heilungswortes bis zum Schluß. Die Spannung löst sich erst mit dem pointierten Abschluß der Erzählung, 'sie fanden den Knecht gesund'. Der Spannungsbogen erreicht aber seinen Höchstwert in der Botschaft des Hauptmanns, er werde vollkommen auf das Wort Jesu vertrauen. Die Erzählung wir zu einer stilgerechten Wundergeschichte.

[152] "Der Formintention dienen auch die V 3-6. Sie geben der Erzählung erst ihren spezifischen Charakter und haben Lukas veranlaßt, die traditionelle Geschichte nach ihnen auszurichten. Schon die Umgestaltung der Exposition zu einer doppelten Situationsschilderung, in der mit der imperfektivischen Erzählweise die Situation im Haus des Hauptmanns von dem Einzug Jesu in die Stadt abgegrenzt wird, läßt keinen direkten Kontakt der beiden Hauptakteure zu. Deshalb hat in V 3ff der Hauptmann auch die Initiative zu ergreifen, um Jesus um Hilfe zu bitten."

Ernst 1977, 238: "Mt bevorzugt die direkte Rede Jesu am Anfang (8,6ff.) und am Schluß der Perikope (8,13), Lk schaltet dagegen als Mittler die 'Ältesten der Juden' und Freunde ein."

Schneider 1977, 165: "Bei Lk hingegen erscheint die Vermittlertätigkeit der 'Ältesten' (VV 3-5) und der 'Freunde' des Hauptmanns (V 6) als mögliche Erweiterung gegenüber Q."

Jacobson 1978: 66: "Luke has sought to avoid a direct encounter between Jesus and a Gentile, thereby developing the 'unworthiness' motif already present in Q (Lk 7:6/Mt 8:8). The centurion is never allowed to meet Jesus. Instead, hearing of Jesus, he sends a delegation of Jewish elders (!) to plead on his behalf. Jesus agrees to come, but before he gets to the house, the centurion sends another (!) delegation (of 'friends') to tell Jesus that he should not come after all since he is not 'worthy.' Moreover, there is no need to come anyway; if only Jesus will say the word, the servant will be healed. These delegations are almost surely products of Luke's own mind; moreover, they seem to reflect his theology.[126]"

115[126]: "Luke uses the device of a centurion sending a delegation also in Acts 10. There, too, the delegation stresses the exemplary piety of the centurion. … The Jews' pleading on behalf of a benevolent friend is also typically Lukan. … Also note the delegation in Lk 7:18ff."

Marshall 1978, 280: "The addition τῶν Ἰουδαίων (cf. 23:3, 37, 38, 51) is natural in a story dealing with Jewish-gentile relationships and is probably intended by Luke to stress this aspect of the story."

Martin 1978, 17-18: "Luke's account is clearly secondary, and his detail of the elders and friends who act as intermediaries [18] is given, not primarily to pick up the theme of the Gentiles' indebtedness to Israel, but to give an independent attestation of the Roman's integrity, worthiness, and humility as a part of his (that is, Luke's) interest in presenting the Gentiles in a favorable light. He has an eye on a ruling purpose, stated in his preface (Luke 1:1-4), to commend the Christian message to Theophilus. But, at a deeper level, in order to endorse the legitimacy of the preaching to the Gentiles, he wants to demonstrate how the church of his generation came genetically out of 'true Israel,' of which this Gentile soldier, like Cornelius in Acts, is an illustrious example (cf. Acts 10:34,35)."

Gatzweiler 1979, 308: "La nouveauté lucanienne à proprement parler consiste évidemment dans l'évocation des diverses délégations expédiées par le centurion auprès de Jésus (vv. 3-6). … Dans la version lucanienne la requête du centurion se voit à la fois amplifiée et dramatisée. Elle porte la marque de la prière: le verbe prier est utilisé à plusieurs reprises (vv. 3 et 4); l'intervention des anciens prend la forme classique de la prière d'intercession; enfin l'attitude du centurion exprimée tant dans sa démarche que dans son discours est tout empreinte de confiance, de persévérance et d'humilité."

Muhlack 1979, 40-41: Aside from underlining common elements, Muhlack does not indicate which text is from Q when those common elements differ in wording. "Ein Vergleich ihrer Perikopen zeigt jedoch schon im den ersten Versen auch den Unterschied, der ihre Darstellungsweise insgesamt kennzeichnet.

"Mt 8,5-7	Lk 7,1-6
Ἐπελθόντος δὲ αὐτοῦ εἰς Καφαρναοὺμ	Ἐπειδὴ ἐπλήρωσεν πάντα τὰ ῥήματα [αὐτοῦ] εἰς τὰς ἀκοὰς τοῦ λαοῦ, εἰσῆλθεν εἰς Καφαρναούμ.
[41] προσῆλθεν αὐτῷ ἑκατόνταρχος	[41] 2. Ἑκατοντάρχου δέ τινος δοῦλος κακῶς ἔχων ἤμελλεν τελευτᾶν, ὅς ἦν αὐτῷ ἔντιμος. 3. ἀκούσας δὲ περὶ τοῦ Ἰησοῦ ἀπέστειλεν πρὸς αὐτὸν πρεσβυτέρους
παρακαλῶν αὐτὸν καὶ λέγων· 6. κύριε, ὁ παῖς μου βέβληται ἐν τῇ οἰκίᾳ παραλυτικὸς κακῶς βασανιζόμενος.	τῶν Ἰουδαίων ἐρωτῶν αὐτὸν ὅπως ἐλθὼν διασώσῃ τὸν δοῦλον αὐτοῦ. 4. οἱ δὲ παραγενόμενοι

πρὸς τὸν Ἰησοῦν παρεκάλουν
αὐτὸν σπουδαίως, λέγοντες ὅτι
ἄξιός ἐστιν ᾧ παρέξῃ τοῦτο.
5. ἀγαπᾷ γὰρ τὸ ἔθνος ἡμῶν καὶ
τὴν συναγωγὴν αὐτὸς ᾠκοδόμησεν
ἡμῖν.

7. λέγει αὐτῷ· ἐγὼ ἐλθὼν   6. Ὁ δὲ Ἰησοῦς ἐπορεύετο σὺν
θεραπεύσω αὐτόν;   αὐτοῖς.

"Gemeinsame Elemente des Matthäus- und des Lukas-Evangeliums ____.
"Ergänzungen des Lukas ………."

41-42: "Lukas dagegen blickt bei der Ankunft Jesu in Kapernaum auf die Feldrede zurück. Sein Handeln verwirklicht seine Predigt.

[42] "Vom Beginn seiner Tätigkeit in Galiläa an, erscheint Jesu Verkündigung in Einheit mit seinem Tun. Die Folge der Heilung für den Hauptmann von Kapernaum auf die Feldrede verstärkt diese Tendenz. Die Erfüllung der Bitte eines Heiden bedeutet an dieser zentralen Stelle einen ersten, andeutenden Hinweis auf das Gottesreich.

"Unter diesem Gesichtspunkt formt Lukas die Erzählung um. Der Hauptunterschied zu der bei Matthäus überlieferten einfacheren Geschichte liegt darin, daß dort der Centurio selbst mit Jesus spricht, Lukas dagegen eine Gesandtschaft aus den πρεσβύτεροι der Synagoge an Jesus einführt. … Lukas sieht die Erzählung im Zusammenhang des ganzen Evangeliums, das bereits auf die Apostelgeschichte vorbereitet. Das Evangelium richtet sich zunächst allein an das Volk Israel. Erst die christliche Mission erfaßt auch die Heiden.

"Der Centurio Cornelius ist zwar ein φοβούμενος τὸν θεόν (Apg 10,2), doch unbeschnitten wie jeder Heide. Trotzdem kommt Petrus seinem Wunsche, das Evangelium zu vernehmen, nach. Er reist nach Cäsarea (Apg 10,21). Mit seiner Predigt im Hause des Cornelius beginnt sich die Verheißung der Propheten, in der Endzeit werde sich der Ruf Gottes auch an die Heiden wenden (vgl. Apg 10,43), zu erfüllen. Dieser Gedanke, der die Diskussion des Apostelkonzils wie die Heidenmission selbst bestimmt, ist bereits in der Erzählung von dem Hauptmann von Kapernaum im Evangelium angedeutet.

"Den Wunsch des Hauptmanns von Kapernaum, Jesus möge seinem Diener helfen, suchen seine Gesandten mit seiner Sympathie für die Juden zu begründen: sogar eine Synagoge habe er bauen lassen (Lk 7,5). Zu ihrer Bitte für den Heiden muß Jesus Stellung nehmen. Er begleitet die Boten des Centurio auf dem Weg zu dessen Hause (Lk 7,6)."

43: "Lukas' Gedanke, das Anliegen des Centurio unter die Obhut jüdischer πρεσβύτεροι zu stellen, dagegen entspricht seinem Verständnis der Mission in der Apostelgeschichte. Unter diesem Gesichtspunkt gewinnt der Glaube des Hauptmanns von Kapernaum für Lukas eine besondere Bedeutung."

Neirynck 1979, 109-110: "Le récit matthéen se situe d'emblée dans la perspective du miracle à distance. En effet, le centurion ne demande pas à Jésus de venir chez lui, mais l'invoque seulement pour son serviteur malade (Mt 8,5-6). À quoi Jésus répond en proposant d'aller le guérir (v. 7); le centurion décline l'offre ... (v. 8). Lc, au contraire, intercale entre le début du récit (7,1-2/Mt 8,5-6) et la parole du centurion à Jésus (vv. 6b-8/Mt 8,8-9) toute une mise en scène inspirée sans doute en partie du récit marcien de la résurrection de la fille de Jaïre[191] et qui présente Jésus [110] comme accédant à la demande des envoyés du centurion qu'il se rende chez celui-ci (Lc 7,3 ἐλθὼν διασώσῃ ... v. 6 ὁ δὲ Ἰησοῦς ἐπορεύετο σὺν αὐτοῖς; cf. Mc 5,24a). Ce n'est qu'arrivé οὐ μακρὰν ... ἀπὸ τῆς οἰκίας que Jésus est arrêté par les 'amis' dépêchés en second lieu par le centurion. D'où une relative incohérence avec le motif initial du miracle à distance intégralement conservé par Mt où Jésus n'a pas à se déplacer du tout. Lc aboutit à une solution moyenne: Jésus ne va quand même pas jusque chez le centurion, mais opère la guérison 'non loin de la maison'."

109[191]: "Lc 7,2ss

2	ἑκατοντάρχου δέ τινος		

Mc 5,22ss.

22	εἷς τῶν ἀρχισυναγώγων
23	... καὶ παρακαλεῖ αὐτὸν ...

Lc:
2 ἑκατοντάρχου δέ τινος
   δοῦλος
   κακῶς ἔχων ἤμελλεν τελευτᾶν ...
3 ἐρωτῶν αὐτὸν
   ὅπως
   ἐλθὼν
   διασώσῃ τὸν δοῦλον αὐτοῦ.
6 ὁ δὲ Ἰησοῦς ἐπορεύετο
   σὺν αὐτοῖς.
   ἤδη δὲ αὐτοῦ οὐ μακρὰν
   ἀπέχοντος ἀπὸ τῆς οἰκίας
   ἔπεμψεν φίλους
   ὁ ἑκατοντάρχης
   λέγων αὐτῷ·
   κύριε, μὴ σκύλλου.

Mc:
22 εἷς τῶν ἀρχισυναγώγων
23 ... καὶ παρακαλεῖ αὐτὸν ...
   τὸ θυγάτριόν μου
   ἐσχάτως ἔχει,
   ἵνα
   ἐλθὼν...
   ἵνα σωθῇ καὶ ζήσῃ.
24 καὶ ἀπῆλθεν
   μετ' αὐτοῦ.
35 ἔρχονται
   ἀπὸ τοῦ ἀρχισυναγώγου
   λέγοντες ὅτι ...
   τί ἔτι σκύλλεις τὸν
   διδάσκαλον;

"La double ambassade des 'anciens des Juifs' (v. 3), puis des 'amis' (v. 6) envoyés par le centurion et le va-et-vient que cela évoque présentent des analogies avec le récit de Mc où la première intervention de Jaïre (Mc 5,22-23) est suivie d'une seconde où des gens arrivent de chez lui pour dire que la venue de Jésus était désormais inutile (5,35). Le trajet de Jésus vers la maison du centurion a pu être suggéré par la parole du récit traditionnel οὐ γὰρ ἱκανός εἰμι ἵνα ὑπὸ τὴν στέγην μου εἰσέλθῃς ; d'où la réutilisation du motif de la maison fourni par le récit de la résurrection de la fille de Jaïre. Dans sa version, Lc insiste aussi par rapport à Mc sur l'entrée de Jésus dans la maison:

Mc 5,23.37		Lc 8,41.51	
23	παρακαλεῖ αὐτὸν πολλὰ ...	41	παρεκάλει αὐτὸν
	ἵνα ἐλθὼν ...		εἰσελθεῖν εἰς τὸν οἶκον
			αὐτοῦ,
37	καὶ	51	ἐλθὼν δὲ εἰς τῆν οἰκίαν
	οὐκ ἀφῆκεν		οὐκ ἀφῆκεν
	οὐδένα μετ' αὐτοῦ συνακολουθῆσαι ...		εἰσελθεῖν τινα σὺν αὐτῷ ...

"Lc 8,51 concentre et anticipe ce qui est dit un peu plus loin en Mc 5,38 (καὶ ἔρχονται εἰς τὸν οἶκον).39 (καὶ εἰσελθών). En faisant intercéder les Juifs en sa faveur, il souligne l'identité païenne du centurion, en même temps que ses bonnes dispositions (ἄξιός ἐστιν au v. 4 nuançant οὐ γὰρ ἱκανός εἰμι au v. 6). La même thématique se retrouve en Ac 10-11: le centurion Corneille est présenté sous un jour très favorable (Ac 10,2) et il envoie des messagers à Pierre (10,5-8)."

Jeremias 1980, 152: "Red ... πρεσβυτέρους τῶν Ἰουδαίων: Diese Wendung kommt im NT nur in den beiden Teilen des Doppelwerks vor: Lk 7,3 und Apg 25,15; sie ist lukanisch."

Schmithals 1980, 91: "In Zusammenhang damit steht der bemerkenswerte Eingriff in die Vorlage, den Lukas mit V.3-5 vornimmt: Es kommt zu keiner direkten Begegnung zwischen Jesus und dem heidnischen Hauptmann! Der Hauptmann, der sich ähnlich wie später sein gottesfürchtiger Kollege Kornelius (Apg. 10,1ff.) bereits der jüdischen Frömmigkeit geöffnet hatte, bedient sich der Vermittlung angesehener Juden, wie Lukas im Anschluß an die formale Vorlage 8,49/Mark. 5,35 berichtet. Darum bedarf es in V.6 der weiteren Sendung der Freunde, welche Jesus die Demut des heidnischen Hauptmanns mit dessen eigenen Worten kundtun—ein erzählerisch wenig geschickter Zug, weil die Freunde reden, als hätten sie die Worte, die nur in den Mund des Hauptmanns passen, auswendig gelernt."

Beare 1981, 207: "In Luke, the recognition of the centurion's inferiority is carried further by his use of intermediaries and his explanation—'I did not count myself worthy to come to you in person' (Lk. 7:7)."

Fitzmyer 1981, 649: "If the double delegation sent to Jesus were part of 'Q,' its omission by Matthew would be more difficult to explain than to regard it as a Lucan compositional addition to the 'Q' form."

650: "The Lucan additions bring it about that it is not a simple pronouncement-story. The elders have been introduced to provide a background for the centurion's own statement about his authority (*exousia*, v. 8) and his recognition of Jesus' authority (v. 7b). ... The double delegation, introduced by Luke, is clearly a literary device to build up the suspense for the pronouncement of Jesus."

Schweizer 1982, 86: "Hätte Lukas nach mündlicher Tradition oder in Angleichung an Apg 10,2.5.22 (s. zu Apg 10,1-48) V.3-6a gebildet und durch 7a (im Kontrast zu 4b) mit seiner Vorlage verbunden."

Schweizer 1982, ET 1984, 131: "Luke, drawing on oral tradition or Acts 10:2,5,22, composed vss. 3-6a and linked them with his archetype by means of vs. 7a (in contrast to vs. 4b)."

Haapa 1983, 71: "Die lukanischen Erweiterungen sind in ganz anderem Geiste geschrieben. Hier spricht man von der Liebe zu 'unserem Volk', vom Synagogenbau und vom Ziehen Jesu mit den Ältesten der Juden zum Hause des Hauptmanns, um dessen schwerkranken Knecht aus dem Tode zu erretten. Es fehlt der ursprüngliche Dialog. Jesus und der Hauptmann begegnen sich überhaupt nicht. Statt dessen sendet der Bittsteller zwei Gesandtschaften."

Schneider 1984, 165: "Bei Lk hingegen erscheint die Vermittlertätigkeit der 'Ältesten' (VV 3-5) und der 'Freunde' des Hauptmanns (V 6) als mögliche Erweiterung gegenüber Q."

Zeller 1984, 37: "Er berichtete von Jesu Kommen nach Kafarnaum, dem Hauptmann und seinem schwerkranken Burschen, der Bitte des Hauptmanns—die beiden Gesandtschaften bei Lk sind redaktionell—um Heilung."

Gnilka 1986, 299: "Das Wort des Hauptmanns ... muß von diesem selbst gesprochen sein. Auch nach Q kommt er Jesus entgegen. Ob von der Delegation der jüdischen Ältesten in Q zu lesen war, ist umstritten. Doch dürfte auch sie von Lk eingefügt sein, da bei Mt die dramatische Entwicklung folgerichtig verläuft[6]."

299[6]: "Nach Theissen [1974, 183], war in Q von einer Gesandtschaft die Rede. Die daraus bei Mt resultierende Ungeschicklichkeit: Erst bittet der Hauptmann Jesus zu kommen; unmittelbar darauf erklärt er sich für unwürdig, daß Jesus komme, kann ich nicht entdecken. Einmal wird in V 6 die Bitte zu kommen nicht ausgesprochen, zum anderen ist die in V 7 enthaltene Ablehnung zu beachten."

Schnelle 1987, 103: "Lukas hat in einem weit größeren Maß als Matthäus die Q-Vorlage umgestaltet. Auf seine Redaktion gehen ... die zweifache Gesandtschaft in V. 3-6a ... zurück."

103[96]: "E. Haenchen [1959a, 25-26 (1965, 84-85)] hält die doppelte Gesandtschaft für eine 'verunglückte Bearbeitung' der Q-Überlieferung durch judenchristliche Kreise auf vorlukanischer Ebene (auch A. Dauer [1984, 93-94] hält die doppelte Gesandtschaft für vorlukanisch). Diese Annahme ist unzutreffend, weil sowohl der sprachliche Befund als auch das theologische Interesse auf lukanische Redaktion schließen lassen. ... Diese Kritik gilt auch G. Theissen [1974, 183] der lediglich die zweite Gesandtschaft auf Lukas zurückführen will."

Schnelle 1987, ET 1992, 89: "Luke has reshaped the Q version of the story much more thoroughly than Matthew. His redaction produced ... the two sets of messengers in vv. 3-6a."

89⁹⁶: "Haenchen [1959a, 25-26 (1965, 84-85)] regards the two sets of messengers as a 'failed revision' of the Q tradition by Jewish Christian circles at a pre-Lukan stage of development. ... Dauer [1984, 93-94] also considers the two sets of messengers pre-Lucan. ... This idea is inaccurate, because both the language and the theological interest point to Lukan redaction. ... This criticism applies also to Theissen [1974, 183], who wishes to assign only the second set of messengers to Luke."

Sellin 1987, 30-31: "Die Q-Fassung der Perikope vom 'Hauptmann zu Kafarnaum' rekonstruiert D. [Dauer 1984, 76-115], was den Erzählrahmen betrifft, nach Lk 7,1-10 anstatt nach Mt 8,5-13. Da die vorjohanneische Fassung aber in der Struktur Mt 8,5-13 entspricht, sei sie von der redaktionell gestrafften Mt-Form abhängig. Zu Unrecht bestreitet D. ..., daß die doppelte Gesandtschaft in Lk 7,3ff auf Lukas zurückgeht. Zumindest die erste in V. 3-6a ist ganz lukanisch motiviert: Die Beziehung eines Heiden zu Jesus wird durch Anhänger des Heilsvolkes vermittelt und durch eine soziale Tat gerechtfertigt (vgl. Apg 10,2). Auch hat D. Mühe, vorlukanische Stilelemente in V. 3-6a zu finden:

"In V. 3a sei lediglich der Zusatz '(Älteste) der Juden' lukanisch, 'der Rest des Halbverses wird aus Q stammen' (113—ohne Begründung). Die Konstruktion mit *axios* sei für Lk ungewöhnlich. In der Tat—nur ist sie für das gesamte NT ungewöhnlich (Latinismen begegnen aber auch sonst in Lk/Apg—vgl. Bl.-D.-Rehkopf, §5 [BDF §3.5b]). *agapaō* hielt selbst Jeremias für lukanisch. Den Singular *to ethnos* (auf das Heilsvolk bezogen) kennt nur Lukas (Lk 23,2; Apg 10,22; 24,2.10). *poreuesthai* (luk. Vorzugswort) begegnet zweimal in Apg [31] auch mit syn. Nur *elthōn diasōsē* und *parakalō* in V. 3b und 4 stammen tatsächlich aus Q. Beweis dafür ist aber gerade ihr Vorkommen in der Mt-Parallele!

"Das heißt: Die Q-Fassung ähnelte der Mt- und nicht der Lk-Fassung."

Sato 1988, 55: "Zwischen V. 3 und V. 6b besteht eine inhaltliche Inkongruenz. Dies ist eindeutig durch sekundäres Auftreten der jüdischen 'Ältesten' sowie der Freunde des Hauptmanns verursacht worden. Auch die parallele Erzählung in Joh 4,46-53, die der Szenerie von Mt 8,5-10.13 entspricht, bestätigt den sekundären Charakter der Lukas-Version. Diese Erweiterung wird aber im ganzen kaum lukanisch sein; sie stammt wahrscheinlich von Q-Lukas."

Wiefel 1988, 141: "Während nach dem Bericht des Matthäus der Centurio selbst Jesus begegnet, verkehrt er hier durch eine doppelte Gesandtschaft mit Jesus, wobei an Stelle des bei Matthäus berichteten Gesprächs zwischen Jesus und dem Centurio die Bitte der ausgesandten Mittelsleute steht. Die Veränderung ist so stark, daß sich die Gestaltung des vorliegenden Stücks deutlich von der Bearbeitung jener Abschnitte abhebt, bei denen Lukas

Erzählstoffe aus Markus übernommen und redigiert hat. Das legte die Folgerung nahe, daß bei Lukas zwei Berichte miteinander verbunden sind: der mit Matthäus gemeinsame Grundbericht aus Q und ein Sonderbericht."

Bovon 1989, 346[10]: "Schulz, S. [1972, 238[410]] zeigt jedoch, daß das Vokabular der VV 3-6a sehr lukanisch ist."

348-349: "Die erste Gesandtschaft[26] bringt den Hilferuf des Hauptmannes zum Ausdruck und zeigt diskret auf, daß der Offizier die vom Gesetz verlangte Trennung [349] zwischen Juden und Nicht-Juden respektiert (vgl. Apg 10,28)."

348[26]: "Die Gesandtschaft wird sichtlich für die nichtjüdischen Leser vorgestellt (vgl. 'die Ältesten der Juden' [v. 3]; 'unser Volk' [v. 5])."

Bovon 1989, FT 1991, 339[10]: "S. Schulz [1972, 238[410]] montre toutefois que le vocabulaire des v. 3-6a est très lucanien."

341: "La première délégation[26] exprime l'appel au secours du centurion et laisse discrètement entendre que cet officier respecte la séparation voulue par la Loi entre Juifs et non Juifs (cf. Ac 10, 28)."

341[26]: "La délégation est présentée à l'intention de lecteurs manifestement non juifs (cf. 'des anciens des Juifs', v. 3; 'notre peuple', v. 5).

Judge 1989, 487: "The Gentile's approach to Jesus through a delegation of respected Jews followed by the friends who come to say μὴ σκύλλου corresponds with Jairus' respectful request and the delegation from the house who say it is not necessary to bother Jesus further. ... By having the Jews intercede for the centurion Luke has underlined his Gentile identity as well as his favorable disposition ('he is deserving' in v. 4 nuances 'I am not worthy' in v. 6). We discover this same motif operating in Acts' story of Cornelius. Notice also the correspondence between the Syrophoenician and the centurion in 'hearing about' Jesus (Mk 7:25; Lk 7:3)."

Gnilka 1990, 127-128[34]: "Die beiden Gesandtschaften, erst Älteste der Juden, dann Freunde, sind als lk anzusehen. Das Demutswort, das hier die Freunde überbringen, paßt letztlich nur in den Mund des [128] Hauptmanns. Die vermittelnde Delegation der Juden ist mit der 'heilsgeschichtlichen Sicht' des Lk gut zu vereinbaren."

Gnilka 1990, ET 1997, 121[98]: "The two delegations, first elders of the Jews and then friends, have to be viewed as Lukan. In the final analysis the expression of humility, here brought by the friends, is appropriate only if voiced by the centurion. The mediating delegation of the Jews can be reconciled well with Luke's 'salvation-history perspective.'"

Riniker 1990, 62: "Sur ce point déjà, nous nous séparons de A. Dauer [1984, 87-98, 116], qui pense que le récit lucanien, avec les deux délégations des vv. 3-6 et 10, représente le texte de la source Q. Ce qui le fait aller dans ce sens—et sur ce point, nous croyons qu'il a entièrement raison—c'est la difficulté d'attribuer à Luc les nombreux traits du récit lucanien qui le distinguent de celui de Matthieu. A mes yeux, le texte pré-lucanien que Dauer reconstitue n'est autre que la forme spécifique qu'a prise la source Q avant d'arriver chez l'évangéliste (QLc), ou bien le résultat du développement de la source Q dans le milieu du Sondergut lucanien. C'est à cette couche pré-rédactionnelle qu'appartiennent la plupart des éléments qui distinguent le récit de l'évangile de Luc de celui de la source Q, en particulier les deux délégations."

Crossan 1991, 326: "The story of 119 *Distant Boy Cured* ... appears in John 4:46b-53 and in the *Sayings Gospel Q* at Luke 7:1-2[3-5]6-10 and Matthew 8:5-10, 13. In that latter case Luke 7:3-5 is probably his own creation."

328: "In this instance Matthew 8:5-10, 13 must be the version in the *Sayings Gospel Q* and Luke 7:3-6a his own creative redaction. By its insertion, on the one hand, Jesus and a Gentile believer never come directly into contact with each other, and, on the other, the Gentile God-fearers of the Acts of the Apostles and especially the centurion of Acts 10:1-11:18 receive a proleptic presence. Luke, in other words, adds on a symbolic specification in preparation for his own vision of the Gentile mission."

Crossan 1991, GT 1994, 431: "Die Erzählung von dem aus der Ferne geheilten Knaben findet sich bei Johannes 4,46b-53 und, der Spruchquelle Q entnommen, bei Lukas 7,1-2.6-10 sowie bei Matthäus 8,5-10.13. Die Verse 3-5 bei Lukas 7 sind vermutlich eigene Erfindung des Apostels."

433: "Während Matthäus 8,5-10.13 offenbar die Überlieferung der Spruchquelle Q wiedergibt, hat Lukas den Abschnitt 7,3-6a wohl aus eigener Erfindung gestaltet. ... Mittels dieser Erfindung wird verhindert, daß Jesus und der heidnische Gläubige einander persönlich begegnen, zugleich erscheint uns dieser von ferne Glaubende als Vorläufer der heidnischen Gottesfürchtigen in der Apostelgeschichte und namentlich des Centurions Cornelius, von dem in 10,1-11.18 berichtet ist. So dient das von Lukas der Überlieferung Hinzugefügte dazu, seine eigene Auffassung der Heidenmission vorzubereiten."

Catchpole 1992, 520 [1993, 284]: "The verbal overlap [between Matt 7,28a; 8,5-13 par Luke 7,1-10; 13,28-29] is intense, the only contrary impression being created by the most probably LukeR intervention with the delegation of Jewish elders."

531-532 [297-298]: "Given so extensive a correspondence [between Mark 5:21-43 and Q 7:1-10] it is readily understandable that Luke should move over from the one story to the other a series of details. [532, 298] ... From the double approach to Jesus, first by Jairus and then by members of his household (Mark 5,22, 35), there develops the idea of the double approach by the elders and the friends in Luke 7,3, 6."

Jacobson 1992, 108-109: "Luke's redactional work may have altered the narrative portion of the story radically; this would account for the rarity of verbal agreement with Matthew's narrative. Luke has sought to avoid a direct encounter between Jesus and a gentile, thereby developing the 'unworthiness' motif already present in Q 7:6. The centurion is never allowed to meet Jesus. Instead, hearing of Jesus he sends a delegation of Jewish elders (!) to plead on his behalf. Jesus agrees to come, but before he gets to the house the centurion sends another (!) delegation (of 'friends') to tell Jesus that he should not come after all, since the centurion is not 'worthy.' There is no need to come anyway; if only Jesus will say the word, the servant will be healed. These delegations are surely products of Luke's own mind and hence of his theology."

Lindars 1992, 205: "Luke's evidence fails at this point because of his insertion of the deputation of Jews."

208: See Q 7:2, 3, 4-6a¹³ Emendation = Q (p. 232).

Gagnon 1993, 713⁵: "Other commentators have suggested that the double delegation (or at least the delegation of Jewish elders) traces back to Q and that Matthew excised the motif because it conflicted with his negative stance toward 'their synagogues.' Such a view founders, however, when one considers (1) the version without any delegation in John 4:46b-54; (2) the rarity of an omission of such major characters by Matthew elsewhere; (3) the narrative stinginess of sayings sources; and (4) the literary and linguistic tensions between Luke's narrative frame and the common core dialogue."

719: "In v 3, the words ἀποστέλλω (ἀποστέλλω πρός: not at all in [S]) and ἐρωτάω could derive from Luke or his special source, but derive more probably from Luke; the expression 'elders of the Jews' (not in [S]) and the word διασώζω (also not in [S]) almost certainly derive from Luke himself. ...

"The word ἀποστέλλω (22/20/26 + 24) elsewhere appears in Luke in [L] 2x (4:43; 19:32), [LQ] 3x (7:20; 14:32; 19:14), [S] 6x, [QL] 1x (10:1), [Q] 6x, and [Mk] 6x; note its frequency in Acts and Luke's trademark alternation of it with πέμπω in Luke 20:10-13; Acts 10:5,8; 11:29-30; 15:22,25,27,33. The combination of ἀποστέλλω + πρός + person occurs only 3x in Luke and with only weak support for Lucan redaction (but none for [S]! 7:20 [LQ]; 13:34 [Q]; 20:10 [Mk]); however, it does appear 5x in Acts (8:14; 9:38; 11:11,30; 13:15; in 11:11 it occurs in a speech)."

730: "It is my opinion that the function of Luke 7:3-7a coheres well with Luke's redactional themes elsewhere.

"... The intervention of the Jewish elders on behalf of the Gentile centurion absolves Christ (and thus Luke's community) of any blame for religious fraternization with uncircumcised Gentiles. The social setting behind this apology is probably to be located in charges which local Jews are bringing, or might bring, before Roman magistrates: charges that Christians are persons bent on destroying Judaism and that, as such, they are inciting the Jews to unrest and shattering the peace and stability of the whole body politic (see Luke 23:2; Acts 17:6; 18:12-13; 21:28; 24:2,5). Luke responds by asserting that the kinds of people (including Gentiles) found in his community had demonstrated their love (not their hate) for the Jewish people in their pre-Christian life and that they thus merited the approval of the Jews (see Acts 10:2; 24:12,17; 25:10; 28:17,19). Luke may also be responding to a criticism by Jewish Christians opposed to close contact with Gentile Christians free of the law (see Acts 11:1-18; chap. 15; 21:20-24)."

Sevenich-Bax 1993, 166: "Die Vermittlung zwischen dem Hauptmann und Jesus durch eine jüdische Delegation (Lk 7,3-6a) steht in Spannung zu der polemischen Aussage von Vers 9, die den Glauben des Heiden gegen den Israels ausspielt. Auch weist bereits der Ausdruck 'Älteste der Juden' auf den heidenchristlichen Schriftsteller hin, 'der seine Zuhörer in einen für sie fremden Kulturkreis einführt' [quoting Ernst 1977, 239]."

167-168: "In dem theologischen Verständnis des Lukas spielt Israel als ursprünglicher Empfänger der Heilsoffenbarung eine grundlegende Rolle für die Entwicklung und das Selbstverständnis des Christentums. Daß in der Geschichte vom Hauptmann von Kapharnaum ausgerechnet Juden zwischen Jesus und dem Heiden vermitteln, hat mit diesem für Lukas wesentlichen Gedanken zu tun. Dabei ist darauf hinzuweisen, daß das Thema 'Vermittlung' bei Lukas einen eigenen Stellenwert hat, wie schon die Komposition des Reiseberichts zu erkennen gibt: Dort ereignet sich nämlich die Vermittlung des Evangeliums (als Offenbarungsträger) in einer Kette von Reisen und Reden, ein Schema, das im übrigen auch in der Apostelgeschichte verwendet wird. 'Vermittlung' hat bei Lukas aber nicht nur einen quasi formalen Stellenwert (als Vermittlung des Evangeliums). Der Begriff wird in der von Lukas dargebotenen Interaktion von Juden und Heiden auch inhaltlich gefüllt (in soteriologischer und ekklesiologischer Hinsicht). Dies ist besonders deutlich in der Apostelgeschichte, wo dieses Thema mehrfach aufgegriffen [168] wird."

168-169: Sevenich-Bax presents corollary examples in the Acts of the Apostles of Luke's treatment of the theme of the relationship between Jews and gentiles.

169: "Die Verse Lk 7,3-6b sind demzufolge der lukanischen Redaktion zuzuweisen. Zugleich wird man dann aber auch Lk 7,7a als sekundär ausgrenzen müssen, da dieser Vers offensichtlich in Zusammenhang mit der Einfügung Lk 7,3-6b steht."

Dunderberg 1994, 85-86: "Doch gibt es auch Unterschiede zwischen den beiden synoptischen Erzählungen. Während Mt den Mann Jesus direkt anreden läßt (Mt 8,6), kommen zwei Gesandtschaften in der lukanischen Fassung (Lk 7,3-6) vor. ...

"Wegen der Unterschiede zwischen Mt und Lk gibt es keinen Konsens darüber, welche dieser beiden Versionen der Q-Fassung nähersteht. Mt bietet einen logisch fortlaufenden Bericht, in dem das Wort Jesu betont wird, wie es auch in Q zu erwarten wäre. Dagegen ist allerdings angeführt, daß Lk die markinischen Wundererzählungen normalerweise nur leicht bearbeitet. So sei es unwahrscheinlich, daß Lk den Wunderbericht von Q durch die beiden Gesandtschaften erweitert hätte. Die kürzere Fassung bei Mt sei auch als Verkürzung der ursprünglichen Erzählung zu erklären, denn Mt pflegt auch die markinischen Wundererzählungen zu verkürzen.

"Die beiden letzten Einwände bleiben jedoch zu allgemein. Einerseits kann auch Lk seine Traditionen stark bearbeiten; andererseits kann man sich auf die Verkürzungstendenz als eine allgemeingültige Regel der mt Redaktion nicht berufen. Von Gewicht ist hier die andere Fernheilungsgeschichte bei Mt (15,21-28). Sie ist aus Mk 7,24-30 entnommen; doch hat Mt gerade sie *verlängert*. Deswegen versteht sich nicht von selbst, daß Mt hier die andere [86] Fernheilung durch die Auslassung der beiden Gesandtschaften wesentlich gekürzt hätte."

87-88: "In einigen neueren Arbeiten wird dafür plädiert, daß die erste oder beide Gesandtschaften (Lk 7,3-6) schon in Q vorkamen.[70] Doch ist die lk Prägung [88] auch in diesem Abschnitt kaum zu übersehen. Hier steht uns die folgende Auflistung der lk Merkmale von Dauer zur Verfügung:

τῶν 'Ιουδαίων (V. 3)—ἐρωτῶν αὐτὸν ὅπως (V. 3)—παραγενόμενοι πρὸς τὸν 'Ιησοῦν (V. 4)—ἤδη δὲ αὐτοῦ ἀπὸ μακρὰν ἀπέχοντος ἀπὸ τῆς οἰκίας (V. 6).

"Schon im Hinblick auf diese Auflistung ist es fraglich, ob sich eine frühere Quelle hinter Lk 7,3-6 überhaupt begründen läßt. Obwohl das ἤδη δὲ αὐτοῦ ἀπὸ μακρὰν ἀπέχοντος ἀπὸ τῆς οἰκίας in V. 6 lk ist, kann es aus seinem Erzählzusammenhang nicht herausgenommen werden. Denn die Sendung der 'Freunde' setzt schon Jesu Kommen in die Nähe voraus (ähnlich Lk 15,20). Folglich wäre die zweite Gesandtschaft ohne die lk Zwischenbemerkung ἤδη δὲ αὐτοῦ ἀπὸ μακρὰν ἀπέχοντος ἀπὸ τῆς οἰκίας unmotiviert. Darüber hinaus ist nicht nur der Anfang von V. 6 durch lukanische Wendungen geprägt. Auch die Vokabeln πέμπειν und φίλος kommen bei Lk deutlich häufiger vor als bei Mt und Mk.[72]"

87[70]: "Für die Ursprünglichkeit der ersten Gesandtschaft plädieren z.B. Bovon [1989, 347] und Schnackenburg [1991, 79], während Ernst [1977, 238] eine vorlk Erweiterung annimmt."

88[72]: "Πέμπειν: Mt 4 Mk 1 Lk 10 (Apg 11); φίλος: Mt 1 Mk 0 Lk 15 (Apg 3)."

88-89: "Dies hat zur Folge, daß zumindest die zweite Gesandtschaft (V. 6) eine lk Bildung ist. Läßt man sie weg, wird die lk Erzählung allerdings noch problematischer. Schon in der heutigen Gestalt der Erzählung fällt der Widerspruch auf, daß der Hauptmann erst indirekt um das Kommen Jesu bittet, ihn aber daraufhin nicht aufnimmt. Aus der Auslassung der zweiten Gesandtschaft ergäbe sich eine Szene mit einer noch deutlicheren Spannung: Jesus käme mit den Ältesten zum Hauptmann, der jetzt die Worte an ihn direkt richten würde: κύριε, μὴ σκύλλου, οὐ γὰρ ἱκανός εἰμι κτλ. Die Szene wäre kaum mehr sinnvoll: der Mann weigert sich, Jesus aufzunehmen, obwohl er schon mit ihm redet!

"Außerdem sind die dem dritten Evangelisten zugeschriebenen Merkmale aus Lk 7,3-5 nicht zu streichen. In V. 3 können die lukanischen Worte ἐρωτῶν αὐτὸν ὅπως von der Fortsetzung ἐλθὼν διασώσῃ τὸν δοῦλον αὐτοῦ kaum getrennt werden. Es wäre zwar möglich, daß die Erzählung keine direkte Bitte enthielt (vgl. Mt 8,6), aber nur unter der Voraussetzung, daß V. 4a als Ganzes zur früheren Erzählung gehört. Allerdings wurden die Worte οἱ δὲ παραγενόμενοι πρὸς τὸν Ἰησοῦν in V. 4a schon in der obengenannten Auflistung als lukanischer Einschub angesehen, und wohl zu Recht. Es kommen noch [89] weitere Beobachtungen über die lk Redaktion in V. 3-5 hinzu. Lk gebraucht das Verb παρέχειν häufiger als Mk und Mt.[74] Die Zusammenstellung von παρακάλειν, λέγειν und ὅτι taucht in der Apg sogar viermal auf (2,40; 16,9.15; 27,33). Auch das Wort ἔθνος ist für das Lk und vor allem für die Apg typisch,[75] und zwar als Bezeichnung für das israelitische Volk.[76]"

89[74]: "Mt 1 Mk 1 Lk 4 (Apg 5)."

89[75]: "Mt 15 Mk 6 Lk 13 Apg 43."

89[76]: "Unter dieser Bedeutung kommt das Wort im NT außer Joh 11,48.50-52; 18,35; 1Petr 2,9 nur in dem lukanischen Doppelwerk vor (Lk 7,5; 23,2; Apg 10,22; 24,2.10.17; 26,4; 28,19 ...)."

89: "Diese Beobachtungen sprechen dafür, daß erst Lk die beiden Gesandtschaften in die Geschichte eingebracht hat. Die beiden Gesandtschaften sind nicht nur in erzählerischer Hinsicht problematisch, sondern weisen auch stilistisch auf die redaktionelle Tätigkeit des Lk hin.

"Fazit: Mt steht dem Wortlaut der Q näher als Lk."

Gagnon 1994a, 124-125: "The argument put forward by Dauer [1984, 115] and others that the double- (or single-) delegation motif was present already in *Matthew's* Q source has its own special problems. In my opinion, it is the least plausible of all the solutions to the problem of the origin of the double-delegation motif. Here I will merely allude to four critical problems with this proposal. First, through a comparison with the variant account in John 4:46b-54 and with Mark's closely related story about a distance healing (the Syrophoenician woman, Mark 7:24-30), it is possible to reconstruct a coherent account of a *direct* encounter between the centurion and Jesus which enables one to explain in simplest terms the tradition-historical development of the story. Secondly, although Matthew frequently abbreviates Mark's miracle stories, at no time does Matthew completely eliminate characters who play

a role as significant as the one played by the elders of the Jews in the centurion pericope. Thirdly, the narrative attention given to the two delegations in
Luke 7:3-6 is more extensive than the brief narrative frames that normally
accompany stories in sayings collections such as the reconstructed Q and the
Gospel of Thomas.

"Finally, the literary and linguistic tensions between Luke's narrative frame
and the common core dialogue indicate that the double-delegation motif is
secondary. Here special mention can be made of: (i) the substitution in 7:3-
6b, 10 of synonyms for words found in the common sayings core; (ii) the
high incidence of vocabulary and style foreign to Q in Luke's narrative frame;
(iii) the fact that the delegation of friends preserves the centurion's first-person
speech (in contrast to the third-person speech of the elders); and (iv) the contradiction between the request in 7:3 that Jesus *should* 'come' and the statement in 7:6c par. that Jesus *should not* [125] come."

127: "As for the evidence to be culled from the vocabulary and style of
Luke 7:3-6b, 7a, only a few brief remarks can be made here. In the most
meticulous analysis thus far of the subject, Wegner [1985, 161-206, 238-39,
243-45] concluded that the language employed for the double-delegation
motif points to an origin in Luke's special source. But even Wegner could only
single out two constructions in vv. 3-6a, 7a which he regarded 'mit hoher
Wahrscheinlichkeit' as not stemming from Lucan redaction (ἀγαπᾷ ... καὶ ...
ᾠκοδόμησεν (7:5) and μακρὰν ἀπέχειν (7:6). All other words and phrases he
acknowledges as at least possibly deriving from Lucan redaction, although he
expressed special doubts about the high frequency with which the name
Ἰησοῦς was employed (3 times)."

134-135: "The social situation which issues in the motif of the Jewish delegation in 7:3-6a is probably to be located in the trouble which Jewish communities might create for Christians at the hands of civil authorities.
Throughout the second half of Acts, Jews repeatedly incite Gentiles against
Christians: at Pisidian Antioch, they stir up the leading citizens of the city
(13:50); at Lystra, the crowds (14:19); at Thessalonica, the whole city with
the help of local 'ruffians' (17:5-7); [135] and at Beroea, the crowds (17:13).
At Corinth, 'the Jews made a united attack on Paul' (18:12) without inciting
the general populace; and in Jerusalem, 'Jews from Asia' roused the Jews in
Jerusalem (21:27-30). Paul and his associates are brought before civil authorities at Thessalonica (17:6-7), Corinth (18:12-13), and Caesarea (first before
Felix, ... then before Festus and Agrippa II)."

136: "The prominence given to this theme in the second half of Acts suggests that Luke's community faces—or at least anticipates facing—such
charges from a neighboring Jewish community and fears the political reper-
cussions arising from such charges. By arguing that they are not enemies of

the Jews but in every sense of the word are themselves 'Jewish,' Luke's community hopes to convince local magistrates that the conflict between Christians and Jews is an 'in-house' squabble, not worthy of any major punishment (a decision which civil authorities frequently reach in Acts: 18:14; 23:29; 25:18-19; 26:31). It is within such a setting that the delegation of Jewish elders in Luke 7:3-6a becomes comprehensible. The centurion at Capernaum, like Cornelius, represents the ideal type of Gentile in Luke's community—a Gentile who is not out to menace the Jewish community but whose pre-Christian life provides proof of the fact that he 'loves our *ethnos*' (7:5)."

144: "The strongest argument for Lucan redaction is simply that the double-delegation motif embodies significant Lucan themes. The intervention of the Jewish elders on behalf of the centurion underscores the compatibility of the Gentile mission with the Jewish heritage on the basis of the pro-Jewish attitude of Gentile converts to the Christian faith."

Gagnon 1994b, 141: "The door to Matthean shortening of a Q version with the double delegation is nailed shut by the fact that the double-delegation motif in Luke does not fit very smoothly over the common core dialogue in Q. By both linguistic and literary standards this motif looks secondary. ... The remark in Luke 7.3 that the centurion 'sent to him elders of the Jews, requesting him *to come* and heal his slave' stands in obvious tension with the core dialogue ('I am not worthy for you to enter under my roof but speak a word ...'). All of these signs indicate a revision of the Q account."

Landis 1994, 21: Landis argues that ἀποστέλλω πρός and πρεσβυτέρους τῶν Ἰουδαίων come from Lukan *Sondergut*.

Meier 1994, 722: "Luke emphasizes the Gentile origin of the centurion by having a delegation of Jewish elders intercede with Jesus for him on the grounds that the centurion 'loves our nation and personally built the synagogue for us' (Luke 7:5). This Jewish delegation, as well as a second delegation sent by the centurion from his house, may well be a Lucan creation."

769¹⁹³: See Meier at Matt = Q, Pro (p. 120).

Merklein 1994, 100: "Gegenüber der matthäischen Version (Q) ist die Gesandtschaft verdoppelt: Zuerst schickt der Hauptmann 'Älteste der Juden' (V. 3), dann 'Freunde' (V. 6). Der Hauptmann selbst kommt nicht. Dies unterstreicht seinen Glauben. Der Hauptmann wird in spezifischer Weise charakterisiert: als Freund und Wohltäter des jüdischen Volkes, der sogar die Synagoge gestiftet hat (VV. 4f), als demütig-frommer Mann (V. 7) und als gläubiger Mensch (VV. 7f.9). Lukas zeichnet das Bild des gottesfürchtigen Heiden. Darin spiegelt sich ein Stück urchristlicher Missionsgeschichte. Die heidenchristliche Kirche setzt sich wesentlich aus solchen 'Gottesfürchtigen' zusammen, die schon vorher mit dem Judentum sympathisierten, ... aber nicht konvertiert waren."

Reed 1995, 23: "One would think that 'Israel' was more preferable to Galileans than the more southern designation 'Judaean' (*Ioudaioi*), which does not occur in Q at all.³¹"

34³¹: "The *presbyterous tōn Ioudaiōn* in Q 7:3 is certainly Lukan. Surprisingly, Wegner (1985, 166) considers Lukan redaction here only 'not impossible,' in spite of the fact that *Ioudaiōn* would be a hapax legomenon in Q."

Neirynck 1996, 455: "I can agree with D's view [Dunderberg 1994, 85-89] on Lukan redaction in Lk 7,1-10 (87-89): ἤμελλεν τελευτᾶν (in v. 2), the two delegations (vv. 3-6) and the conclusion (v. 10)."

Matt = Q: (προσῆλθεν)³

Pro

Bleek 1862, 347-348: See Q 7:2, 3, 4-6a¹ Matt = Q, Pro (pp. 70-71).

von Harnack 1907, 91 (ET 1908, 131): Reconstruction (Harnack adds καὶ before προσῆλθεν). For complete text see Q 7:1⁶ Luke = Q, Pro (p. 55).

Crum 1927, 138: Reconstruction. For complete text see Q 7:2, 3, 4-6a¹ Matt = Q, Pro (pp. 71-72).

Haenchen 1959a, 23 [1965, 82]: "Beginnen wir mit der *Vorlage des Matthäus*. Nach ihr findet das Ereignis in Kapernaum statt. Ein Centurio, Offizier des Herodes Antipas ... kommt zu Jesus."

Strecker 1962, 99: "Matthäus bietet im Anfang die ursprüngliche Gestalt; denn gegenüber dem sofortigen Auftreten des Zenturio ist die Absendung von Ältesten und deren Argumentation bei Lukas sekundär."

P. Meyer 1970, 410: "Matthew reproduces Q's text."

Sabourin 1975, 154: "In Matthew's version the freshness of the original encounter seems preserved: the centurion himself speaks to Jesus, while in Luke he communicates through interpreters. The laborious, even confusing narrative of Luke (esp. in v. 6) would indicate that he transmits a preexistent composite narrative he found in his source, while the Q version alone would be preserved in Mt."

Schmithals 1980, 90: "Die Q-Fassung der Erzählung hat Matthäus in 8,5-10.13, insgesamt gesehen, besser als Lukas bewahrt. Läßt sich auch der Anfang der Geschichte aus V. 1b-6 und Mat. 8,5-8 im einzelnen nicht sicher rekonstruieren, so war doch in Q erzählt, daß Jesus, nach Kapernaum kommend, von dem heidnischen Hauptmann persönlich um Hilfe für seinen kranken (bei Lukas todkranken) Knecht (oder Sohn) gebeten wurde."

Schenk 1981, 37: Reconstruction. For complete text see Q 7:1⁰ In Q (p. 10).

Schnelle 1987, 102: "Matthäus steht am Anfang der Q-Überlieferung näher als Lukas. Dies ergibt sich aus ... dem unmittelbaren Auftreten und der direkten Rede des Centurio."

Schnelle 1987, ET 1992, 88: "At the beginning, Matthew is closer to Q than is Luke. This is seen from ... the immediate appearance and direct address of the centurion."

Riniker 1990, 62: "La forme que ce texte avait dans la source Q est pour l'essentiel mieux conservée chez Matthieu (8,5-10.13)[59], qui ne l'a que peu retouchée."

62[59]: "L'argument décisif est que la parole de foi du centurion est placée— chez Luc—dans la bouche des messagers (Lc 7,6 contre Mt 8,8)."

Crossan 1991, 328: "In this instance Matthew 8:5-10, 13 must be the version in the Sayings Gospel Q and Luke 7:3-6a his own creative redaction."

Crossan 1991, GT 1994, 433: "Während Matthäus 8,5-10.13 offenbar die Überlieferung der Spruchquelle Q wiedergibt, hat Lukas den Abschnitt 7,3-6a wohl aus eigener Erfindung gestaltet."

Sevenich-Bax 1993, 167: "Die matthäische Kurzfassung entspricht in der knappen narrativen Entfaltung der Szenerie der auch sonst in der Logienquelle zu beobachtenden Akzentverteilung, die mehr Gewicht auf das gesprochene Wort legt."

Meier 1994, 769[193]: "I think that Schulz [1972, 236-240] and Fitzmyer [1981, 648-649] make a good case for the position that, apart from the redactional insertion in Matt 8:11-12, Matthew's version of the story is closer to the Q form than is Luke's version. In particular: (1) Matthew and John agree that the petitioner comes to Jesus and speaks face-to-face with him; neither knows anything of the two Lucan delegations."

International Q Project 1995, 478: Reconstruction. For complete text see Q 7:1⁰ In Q (p. 16).

Con

Hawkins 1899, 7: "Words and Phrases characteristic of St. Matthew's Gospel: ... προσέρχομαι."

195: "Luke may have retained the original narrative in its fullness, while Matthew, after his manner, shortened it: —Lk vi.17a(?); vii. 3a, 4, 5, 6, 7a; 10; 20, 21."

B. Weiß 1908, 15[24]: See Q 7:1⁶ Luke = Q, Pro (p. 55).

Schmid 1930, 253: "Auf der anderen Seite entspricht aber gerade das Fehlen der vermittelnden jüdischen Ältesten bei Mt dem Verfahren des ersten Evangelisten."

Parker 1953, 63-65: See Q 7:1⁶ Matt = Q, Con (pp. 58-60).

Schmid 1956, 163: "Daß hier Matthäus die Erzählung durch Ausschaltung der Nebenpersonen verkürzt und nicht umgekehrt der Heidenchrist Lukas den 'judaistischen' Zug erst hinzugedichtet hat, nach welchem der Nichtjude nur durch Vermittlung der Juden zu Jesus gelangen kann, ist um so wahrscheinlicher, als Matthäus auch in 9,18-26 ebenso verfährt."

Held 1960, 216: "Die Verbindung von προσέρχεσθαι und λέγειν [ist] in der Tat eine stereotype Formel des Matthäus zur Einleitung von Reden und Gesprächen. Der Blick auf die synoptischen Parallelstellen belehrt darüber, daß er sie einerseits in kurze Gesprächseinleitungen einfügt, andererseits aber mit ihrer Hilfe vorhandene Sätze umformt oder durch sie eine reichhaltigere, anschaulichere Einleitung des Markus ersetzt. ...

"So ergibt sich im Matthäusevangelium eine gewisse Parallelität zwischen den Einleitungen der Heilungsgeschichten einerseits und der Streit- und Schulgespräche andererseits, zumal da das Wort προσέρχεσθαι häufig in den Wundergeschichten von einer wörtlichen Rede (Mt. 8,2; 9,18) oder von einem regelrechten Gespräch (Mt. 8,5; 9,20; 17,14) gefolgt ist. Hier wie dort ist die Verbindung von προσέρχεσθαι und λέγειν eine Formel zur Gesprächseinleitung und hat keine erzählerische Aufgabe, bewirkt vielmehr eine Typisierung. Sie will offenbar das Interesse von dem individuell-einmaligen Ereignis auf die im folgenden enthaltene allgemeine Lehre bzw. Verkündigung richten."

Held 1960, ET 1963, 228: "The combination of προσέρχεσθαι and λέγειν is, in fact, a stereotyped formula of Matthew's for the introduction of speeches and conversations. ... On the one hand, he inserts them into brief introductions to conversations, but on the other he refashions existing sentences by means of them or displaces by them a richer more vivid Markan introduction. ...

"Thus there issues in Matthew's Gospel a certain parallelism between the introductions of the healing stories on the one hand and the controversy and scholastic conversations on the other, especially as the word προσέρχεσθαι is frequently followed in the miracle stories by a quotation (Matt. 8:2; 9:18) or by a normal conversation (Matt. 8:5; 9:20; 17:14). In both the combination of προσέρχεσθαι and λέγειν has become a formula for introducing a conversation and has no descriptive function, but rather gives the impression of conformity to a type. The intention is obviously to direct attention from the individual unique event to the general doctrine, or rather, proclamation contained in what follows."

Ellis 1966, 117: See Q 7:2, 3, 4-6a¹ Luke = Q, Pro (p. 67).

Grundmann 1968, 249-250: "Sie [die Hauptmannperikope] hat gewiß in der Spruchquelle eine einfachere Form gehabt, als Lukas sie bietet, es muß jedoch angesichts des Befundes der Aufnahme anderer Wundererzählungen bei Matthäus, bei denen der Vergleich mit Markus und Lukas möglich ist, damit gerechnet werden, daß Matthäus auch hier Erzählungspartien gekürzt und eine starke Konzentration auf das Gespräch vorgenommen hat. ... [250] ... Er bestimmt den Inhalt des Gesprächs zwischen Jesus und dem Centurio, so daß er 'nicht nur eine sachlich-theologische Bedeutung für das Verständnis der Wundergeschichten hat, sondern auch förmlich ihr gestaltendes Prinzip enthält' [Held 1960, 228]. Die unverkennbare Konzentration auf das Gespräch veranlaßt R. Bultmann [1931, 70; ET 66], sie mit Recht jenen Heilungsgeschichten zuzurechnen, die 'nicht als Wundergeschichten erzählt' werden, sondern 'im Stil des Apophthegmas' geformt sind; 'der Erzähler begnügt sich, wie in szenischen Bemerkungen, Rede und Gegenrede zu verteilen' [Lohmeyer 1962, 157]. Diese aber hat zu viel eigenes Gewicht, als daß man sie nur als Variante zur Erzählung von der Syrophönizierin ansehen könnte und beide als ideale Szenen, entstanden in der hellenistischen Gemeinde, zu betrachten gezwungen wäre. Mögen in der Tat erzählerische Parallelen erkennbar sein, gerade die Gespräche tragen einen so eigenen Charakter, daß sie nicht einfach der Erfindung einer Gemeinde zugerechnet werden können."

Fuchs 1971, 116-117: "Neben προσέρχεσθαι + αὐτῷ und ἐλθεῖν (bzw. ἔρχεσθαι) in der Verbindung mit εἰς τὴν οἰκίαν ist auch die Verknüpfung von ἔρχεσθαι mit προσέρχεσθαι ein bei Mt mehrfach verwendetes Stilmittel. An vier Stellen geht ἔρχεσθαι (bei 8,5 εἰσέρχεσθαι) dem Verb προσέρχεσθαι voraus, wobei das Simplex jeweils in der Konstruktion des Gen. Abs. verwendet wird: Mt 8,5; 9,28; 17,14.24; 21,23. Da diese Konstruktion sonst nicht in den Evangelien vorkommt, drängt sich die Annahme einer Mt-Redaktion umso mehr auf.—Die Parallelen werden jeweils zum Vergleich der mt Bearbeitung angeführt.

"1) Mt 8,5:   εἰσελθόντος δὲ αὐτοῦ εἰς Καφαρναοὺμ *προσῆλθεν αὐτῷ* ἑκατόνταρχος παρακαλῶν... [117]

Lk 7,1-2:   ... εἰσῆλθεν εἰς Καφαρναούμ. ἑκατοντάρχου δέ τινος δοῦλος κακῶς ἔχων ἔμελλεν τελευτᾶν.

2) Mt 9,28:   ἐλθόντι δὲ εἰς τὴν οἰκίαν *προσῆλθον αὐτῷ* οἱ τυφλοί ...

3) Mt 17,14:   καὶ ἐλθόντων πρὸς τὸν ὄχλον *προσῆλθεν αὐτῷ* ...

Mk 9,14-15:   καὶ ἐλθόντες πρὸς τοὺς μαθητὰς εἶδον ... καὶ προστρέχοντες ἠσπάζοντο αὐτόν.

Lk 9,37:   ... κατελθόντων αὐτῶν ἀπὸ τοῦ ὄρους συνήντησεν αὐτῷ ὄχλος πολύς.

"Bei 8,5 und 17,14 ist besonders deutlich ersichtlich, daß Mt dem Text seinen Stil aufdrückt, weil er das Wort προσέρχεσθαι erst in den Text einsetzen muß."

Danker 1972, 92: "Matthew is concerned to show that the apostles replace Jerusalem's hierarchy as teaching authority; therefore he naturally omits reference to any Jewish delegation." But see Danker at Luke = Q, Con (p. 102).

Schulz 1972, 236: "Προσῆλθεν αὐτῷ ist eindeutig Zusatz des Mt."

236[398]: "Προσέρχεσθαι ca 35mal red; Mk 5mal; Lk 10mal; Apg 10mal."

Lange 1973, 479: "Προσέρχομαι erscheint bei Mattäus—abgesehen von unserer Stelle—noch 52mal (Mk 6mal; Lk 10mal). Abgesehen von unserer Stelle, ist es in 21 Fällen rein redaktionell[1]."

479¹: "Mt 4,3.11; 5,1; 8,5.19.25; 13,10; 15,12.30; 17,7.19; 18,1; 24,1.3; 26,17.50.60.60.73; 28,2.9."

Howard 1975, 171: "Mt streicht das Motiv der Gesandtschaft überhaupt und konzentriert sich auf Jesu Hilfsbereitschaft (und den Gang zum Hause des Hauptmanns) in V. 7."

Pesch and Kratz 1976, 77: "Die Vereinfachung der Handlung (Streichung der zweifachen Gesandtschaft) sowie die Einfügung des Drohspruchs vv 11f geht sicherlich auf das Konto des mattäischen Redaktors. Bei Mattäus ist aus der Erzählung eine klar und übersichtlich aufgebaute Wundergeschichte geworden, die fast ausschließlich in der besprochenen Welt spielt; Mattäus liebt die Stilisierung von Wundergeschichten zum Gespräch (von daher wird auch die Einfügung des Drohwortes verständlich). Auch die Konzentration auf die Hauptpersonen, der das Auftreten der beiden Gesandtschaften zum Opfer fällt, ist mattäische Eigenart."

80: See Pesch and Kratz at Luke = Q, Pro (p. 89).

Gundry 1982, 141: "Because the centurion is prototypical of Gentile Christian believers, Matthew does not care to have Jewish elders glorify him for loving their nation and building their synagogue (Luke 7:3-5). In Matthew, God has transferred the kingdom of heaven to another 'nation' (21:43), and the synagogue is designated '*their* synagogue' in opposition to the church (5,0). Therefore Matthew omits the part of the story concerning the delegation of Jewish elders. The centurion now appears to approach Jesus directly. … In v 5 προσῆλθεν replaces ἀπέστειλεν (so Luke). This substitution accords with the dropping of the delegation and with Matthew's fondness for his verb, which connotes Jesus' dignity (38,6)."

Dauer 1984, 101-102: See Q 7:2, 3, 4-6a¹ Matt = Q, Con (pp. 73-74).

105-106: "Der Rahmen von Mt 8,5-13 ist im wesentlichen das Produkt mt Redaktion. Deswegen ist es unzulässig, mit Haenchen [1959a (1965)] in der [106] Frage nach der ursprünglichen Gestalt der Perikope von der mt Version aus eine ursprünglich heidenchristliche, von judenchristlichen Zusätzen freie Erzählung zu postulieren. Es ist im Gegenteil viel wahrscheinlicher, daß Matthäus in etwa dieselbe Form vorgelegen hat, wie sie uns jetzt noch in Lk 7,1-10 erhalten ist. Der 1. Evangelist hat diese Erzählung gekürzt und überarbeitet, wie er es auch bei Heilungsgeschichten aus seiner Mk-Vorlage getan hat. Damit erreichte er eine entscheidende Konzentration auf das Wesentliche: auf das große Glaubenswort des heidnischen Hauptmanns und das Lob, das Jesus diesem spendet.

"Freilich wird Matthäus nicht nur um dieser Konzentration willen die Gesandtschaften ausgelassen haben. ein weiterer Grund wird mitentscheidend gewesen sein: seine scharfe Kritik am ungläubigen Judentum."

Wegner 1985, 127-128: "Προσῆλθεν αὐτῷ. Diese Wendung gehört sehr wahrscheinlich der mt Red an. Darauf deutet nicht nur das gehäufte Vorkommen von προσέρχομαι in Mt hin, sondern vor allem seine stereotype Verwendung zu [128] Beginn der Heilungsgeschichten. Überhaupt ist die Wendung mit προσέρχομαι (auch -θεν, -θόντες o.ä.) + αὐτῷ (oder der Dativ der Person) + Substantiv (im Sing. oder Plur.) eine von Mt sehr beliebte Konstruktion, wie Fuchs [1971, 100-111] einleuchtend herausstellte. Daß wir es hier mit mt Formulierung zu tun haben, zeigt nicht zuletzt auch der Befund in Q, wo προσέρχεσθαι an keiner weiteren Stelle verwendet wird. Schließlich wird es auch Lk kaum gelesen haben, da er es nur 1x aus seinem Mk-Stoff ausläßt, dagegen aber 5x red einfügt."

132: "Eindeutig mt Red schien uns das Compositum προσέρχομαι zu entstammen, das möglicherweise das Simplex ἔρχομαι seiner Vorlage ersetzte."

O'Donnell 1988, 75: "Matthew uses a construction for introducing participants into the story. The pattern of προσέρχομαι in the aorist indicative, αὐτῷ, and a nominative subject occurs fifteen times in Matthew."

Nolland 1989, 314: "Matthew frequently abbreviates and simplifies the tradition that he uses and may have omitted the delegation of Jewish elders."

Luz 1990, 13⁶: "Matthäismen ... sind in V 5-7: Προσέρχομαι, λέγων, κύριε, λέγει ... evt. βασανίζομαι, ἐλθών."

Luz 1990, ET 2001, 8⁶: "Mattheisms in vv. 5-7 are ...: προσέρχομαι, λέγων, κύριε, λέγει ..., perhaps βασανίζομαι, ἐλθών."

Davies and Allison 1991, 19: "Προσῆλθεν is Matthean, as is the sentence structure.³⁵ Luke, with the exception perhaps of adjectival τις, probably comes closer to Q."

19³⁵: "Προσέρχ[ο]μαι + αὐτῷ + subject + participle: Mt: 12-13; Mk: 0; Lk: 0."

19: "Pace Schulz [1972, 237], Matthew has probably turned indirect speech (so Luke and Jn 4.47) into direct speech, as in 26.1-2 diff. Mk 14.1. This puts the Jewish elders in Luke = Q out of the picture and requires certain other changes, such as the omission of Lk 7:4-5."

Catchpole 1992, 522 [1993, 286]: See Catchpole at Emendation = Q: <ἦλθεν> (p. 128).

Lindars 1992, 204-205: "Matthew's προσῆλθεν αὐτῷ accords with Matthean usage, and so has less claim to originality than John's ἀπῆλθον πρὸς αὐτόν, [205] which is very common in Matthew, used rarely by Mark and Luke, but found elsewhere in John only at 12,21."

Gagnon 1993, 719: For προσῆλθεν, see Q 7:2, 3, 4-6a⁴ Luke = Q, Pro (p. 132).

Hagner 1993, 202: "Rather than coming directly to Jesus himself (as in Matthew), the centurion sends 'elders of the Jews' on his behalf, who present his credentials as a God-fearer (ἄξιος, 'worthy') who loves the Jews and had built a synagogue for them (7:3-5). Matthew does not mention that the centurion was a friend of the Jews, thus sharpening the grace toward a Gentile as a Gentile."

Even in the second part of the Lukan version (7:6-8), the words of the centurion's humility and his authority over others, in very close verbal agreement with Matthew, are delivered by φίλοι, 'friends,' and not by the centurion himself. Matthew thus appears to have abbreviated Q considerably to emphasize the faith of the centurion and the direct contact and acceptance of the Gentile by Jesus."

Sevenich-Bax 1993, 178: "Insgesamt ist in den Versen Lk 7,2//Mt 8,5aβ.b.6 also an Änderung durch Lukas zu denken. Doch sind auch Matthäus redaktionelle Eingriffe nachzuweisen: So ist die mit προσῆλθεν αὐτῷ umschriebene Annäherung an den Wundertäter wohl auf Matthäus zurückzuführen. Die Vokabel προσέρχομαι gehört nicht nur zu den matthäischen Vorzugsvokabeln.⁴ Auffällig ist darüberhinaus, daß gerade die Konstruktion mit dem Dativ der Person typisch matthäisch ist,⁵ wobei in sechs Fällen der Dativ das Subjekt eines Genitivus absolutus wiederholt, wie es auch in der vorliegenden Textstelle der Fall ist."

178⁴: "Mtev: 52mal; Mkev: 5mal; Lkev: 10mal + Apg: 10mal."

178⁵: "Mtev: 26mal; Mkev: keinmal; Lkev: 1mal + Apg: 5mal."

Gagnon 1994b, 135: "There are essentially three arguments adduced in favour of Matthean abbreviation of a Q account containing mention of one or more delegations. First, evidence of widespread Matthean redaction can be found for the narrative frame of the story in 8.5-8a, 13 (not to mention the insertion of the Q saying at vv. 11-12). Secondly, Matthew shows a tendency elsewhere to abbreviate the text of Mark and to reduce the presence of unnecessary characters. Thirdly, Matthew would have had an excellent motive for deleting the account about the Jewish elders, since it conflicted with Matthew's aim to sharpen the criticism of Jewish unbelief." But see Gagnon 1994b at Luke = Q, Con (p. 118).

136: "In my estimation, Matthew has ... adjusted the entrance- and encounter-phrases of his source to the stereotyped Matthean formula of introduction (genitive-absolute construction + προσῆλθεν αὐτῷ)."

Landis 1994, 6: "Προσῆλθεν αὐτῷ ἑκατόνταρχος ist eine typisch mt Formulierung. Bei Q kommt προσέρχομαι sonst nie vor, hingegen ausgesprochen häufig bei Mt, v.a. am Anfang von Heilungsgeschichten. Besonders oft erscheint bei Mt die Reihenfolge προσέρχομαι + Pers. im Dativ + Substantiv."

Undecided

Marshall 1978, 277-278: "The problem is that in Mt. the centurion approaches Jesus personally with his request for help, while in Lk. he sends two groups of intermediaries, the second of which delivers his message in the first person singular form. Luke's version is thus more complicated, if not actually improbable: it is odd that having requested Jesus to come to his house, the centurion then attempts to dissuade him, and that as a result Jesus and the centurion never meet. The following points are relevant: 1. [278] Matthew has a well-known tendency to abbreviate his sources (Mt. 9:2, 18ff.; 11:2f.). It is at least as probable that he has abbreviated here as that Luke has creatively expanded the story. 2. The centurion's speech to Jesus sounds better on his own lips than if committed to memory by the messengers, and Jesus' praise of him would be more reasonable if he were present. ... Nevertheless, the procedure is perfectly credible. For messengers reciting a memorised message see 2 Ki. 19:20-34, ... and for gentiles approaching Jesus through intermediaries see Jn. 12:20ff.; cf. Acts 10. ... 3. The idea of an embassy could have been borrowed from [Luke] 8:49 where a messenger comes to tell Jairus that his daughter has died. But it is worth noting that, since Matthew omits this detail, it could be argued there also that Luke has introduced a characteristic motif, were it not that Luke is known to be dependent on Mk. there. In the present case also Luke could be dependent on his source. In any case, the function of the messengers in the two stories is different. 4. A weightier point is that the expansion demonstrates the piety of the centurion (cf. Acts 10:2, 34f.) and provides an example of faith in Jesus without having seen him (cf. 1 Pet. 1:8; Naaman, 2 Ki. 5:10). This could well be due to Lucan redaction. ... But the fact that Jesus welcomes such a God-fearer perhaps reflects the concerns of the primitive church rather than of Luke himself, to whom the gentile mission was a reality. ... 5. The language of the 'insertion' is Lucan (Schulz [1972], 238[410]). Moreover, the use of third person narrative in 7:2 instead of the incorporation of this information in the centurion's own request to Jesus (Mt. 8:6) could be a Lucan alteration, since the insertion prevented him from using the first person style at this point; elsewhere too it is Luke's habit to assemble basic information at the beginning of a story (5:17). On the other hand, there are some un-Lucan features in the style, and it can be argued that the inclusion of two sets of messengers is too awkward to be attributed to Luke. ... The balance between these arguments is very even. The linguistic evidence slightly favours the case for Lucan insertion, but it is hard to see why Luke should have altered the story to such an extent without some basis in his sources. The view that Luke has combined two sources is improbable. It is more likely that the story appeared in different forms in two versions of Q, and/or that Matthew has abbreviated it, but the possibility of Lucan expansion cannot by excluded."

Emendation = Q: <>³

B Weiß 1908, 15: Reconstruction. For complete text see Q 7:1⁰ In Q (p. 5).

Polag 1979, 38: Reconstruction. For complete text see Q 7:1⁰ In Q (pp. 9-10). **Sevenich-Bax** 1993, 238: Reconstruction. For complete text see Q 7:1⁰ In Q (p. 15).

Emendation = Q: <>³ἦλθεν

Wegner 1985, 128-129: "Ist der red Charakter der Wendung [προσῆλθεν αὐτῷ] deutlich, so muß noch gefragt werden, ob Mt diese Konstruktion neu oder lediglich als Ersatz für eine andere schuf. Die Lk-Parallele führt in dieser Frage nicht weiter, denn die Einführung der Gesandtschaften bedingt den Gebrauch von ἀποστέλλω und πέμπω in Lk 7,3.6. Anders aber der joh Parallelvers (4,47b), der ebenfalls das Gehen des βασιλικός zu Jesus mit einem Kompositium von ἔρχομαι beschreibt: ἀπῆλθεν πρὸς αὐτόν. Diese parallele Schilderung des Auftretens des Hilfsbedürftigen in Joh 4,47b deutet also eher auf einen Ersatz als auf einen Zusatz hin. Dafür spricht auch, daß überhaupt das Auftreten des Hilfsbedürftigen zum festen Motiv der Wundergeschichten gehört. Vielleicht ist es sogar möglich, die wahrscheinlich von Mt ersetzte Wendung zu präzisieren. Dazu seien zunächst einige Stellen aus Mk zum Vergleich mit der mt Bearbeitung aufgeführt:

Mk 1,40:   καὶ ἔρχεται πρὸς αὐτὸν λεπρός ...
Mt 8,2:   καὶ ἰδοὺ λεπρὸς προσελθών ...
Mk 5,22:   καὶ ἔρχεται εἷς τῶν ἀρχισυναγώγων ...
Mt 9,18:   ἰδοὺ ἄρχων εἷς προσελθών ...
Mk 5,27:   ἐλθοῦσα ἐν τῷ ὄχλῳ ὄπισθεν ἥψατο ...
Mt 9,20:   προσελθοῦσα ὄπισθεν ἥψατο ...

"Alle diese Stellen schildern jeweils das uns hier interessierende Motiv vom Auftreten des Hilfsbedürftigen. Προσέρχομαι [129] dient dabei ständig als Ersatz für das Simplex ἔρχομαι. Da dieses Simplex in Q auch sonst belegt ist, liegt die Vermutung nahe, daß Mt mit der Wendung προσῆλθεν αὐτῷ in Mt 8,5b möglicherweise das Simplex ἦλθεν + πρὸς αὐτόν ersetzt hat.

"Als Ergebnis kann daher festgestellt werden: προσῆλθεν αὐτῷ ist sehr wahrscheinlich mt Red einer vor-mt Konstruktion, die wohl aus ἦλθον und πρός + Akk. der Person bestand."

132: See Wegner at Matt = Q, Con (p. 124).

270: Reconstruction. For complete text see Q 7:1⁰ In Q (pp. 11-12).

Catchpole 1992, 522 [1993, 286]: "The standard MattR προσῆλθεν and the Lucan favourite παραγίνομαι[18] probably replace an ἔρχομαι formulation, supported by the redactional Luke 7:1 and by the frequency with which such a MattR replacement takes place.[19]"

522 [286][18]: "Statistics: 3—1—8 + 20."

522 [286][19]: "See Matt 8,2; 9,14.18.20; 14,12; 21,33; 22,23; 26,7; 26,69."

527 [292]: Reconstruction: "καὶ ἦλθεν αὐτῷ ἑκατοντάρχης." For complete text see Q 7:1⁰ In Q (p. 14).

Gagnon 1994b, 135: Reconstruction: "ἦλθεν πρὸς αὐτὸν παρακαλῶν αὐτόν." For complete text see Q 7:1⁰ In Q (p. 15).

Landis 1994, 6-7: "Es stellt sich die Frage, ob προσῆλθεν αὐτῷ Zusatz des Mt oder Ersatz für eine andere Formulierung in Q ist. Die zweite Möglichkeit erscheint aus verschiedenen Gründen als wahrscheinlicher: Zunächst einmal muß ja wohl das Auftreten des Hilfesuchenden irgendwie geschildert worden sein; es gehört zum festen Schema von Wundergeschichten. Außerdem ist beim Vergleich von Mt mit seinen Mk-Vorlagen zu beobachten, daß mt προσέρχομαι immer mk ἔρχομαι ersetzt. [7] Das Simplex ist für Q belegt. Es ist daher gut möglich, daß Mt auch an dieser Stelle die von ihm bevorzugte Formulierung mit dem Kompositum als Ersatz für eine Wendung mit dem Simplex in seiner Vorlage gebraucht hat. Für Q wäre dann etwa die Konstruktion ἦλθεν πρὸς αὐτόν anzunehmen."

7, 17: Reconstruction: "καὶ ἦλθεν πρὸς αὐτὸν ἑκατοντάρχης." For complete text see Q 7:1⁶ Luke = Q, Pro (p. 57).

Emendation = Q: <ἀπ>³ἦλθεν

Lindars 1992, 210: Reconstruction. For complete text see Q 7:1⁶ Luke = Q, Pro (p. 56).

211: "Luke has ... introduced the deputation of Jewish elders in vv. 3-5. This has necessitated changing ἀπῆλθεν πρὸς αὐτὸν καὶ παρεκάλει αὐτόν (cf. Jn 4,47) to ἀπέστειλεν πρὸς αὐτὸν πρεσβυτέρους τῶν Ἰουδαίων ἐρωτῶν αὐτόν."

Evaluations

Johnson 2000: Matt = Q {B} (with emendation), (<>ἦλθεν)³.

As this variation unit is the axis on which much of the discussion of the original form of the centurion pericope has turned since at least as far back as Friedrich Schleiermacher, a brief summary of the database is called for.

The debate does not divide itself neatly into a discussion for or against Matthew or Luke; discussion in the database usually includes consideration of the second Lukan delegation (Q 7:6b-c²) and often includes the question of Lukan *Sondergut*. For example, while most of the database authors argue for the two delegations deriving from Lukan redaction (e.g. Strauss, Holtzmann, Harnack, Patton, Loisy), many others propose that Luke's additional material comes from a source other than Matthew's Q, such as Lukan *Sondergut* (e.g. J. Weiß, Bussmann, Easton, Hauck, Wegner; cf. B. Weiß) or a revised edition of Q (e.g. Hirsch, Haenchen, Grundmann, Sato). The latter positions arise from some vocabulary that is not clearly Lukan (see Q 7:2, 3, 4-6a¹³ Luke = Q, Con [pp. 232-233]) as well as recognition that Luke does not tend to expand the narrative material of Markan miracle stories. Also, while there are a number of authors who argue for the two delegations deriving from Q (e.g. H. Meyer, Castor, Schmid, Gundry, Dauer), still others accept only the first delegation of Jewish leaders in Q (e.g. Siegman, Theissen, Davies and Allison, Bovon, Nolland; cf. Schweizer, who accepts the *second* delegation as Q, but not the first). The latter position is usually an attempt to preserve the Jewish delegation as traditional while recognizing the problem of a second delegation speaking for the centurion in the first person singular.

There are very few arguments in favor of Luke's ἀποστέλλω and first delegation. These arguments include the intuitive notions that the narrative shows the "stamp of originality" (H. Meyer), sounds "natural," and shows a "respect here for Jewish prejudices which seems primitive" (Castor). The primary argument for Luke is Matthew's tendency to abbreviate miracle stories (e.g. Burton, Hawkins, Nolland). However, with the inclusion of Matt 8:11-12 (Q 13:28-29), Matthew's version of the story is as long as Luke's. The one other substantial difference in the length of the narratives comes with the block of material in Luke 7:3-6b. Yet, a strong theological rationale for Matthean abbreviation here is lacking. Danker suggests that Matthew "is concerned to show that the apostles replace Jerusalem's hierarchy as teaching authority; therefore he naturally omits reference to any Jewish delegation." Gundry goes as far as to suggest that Matthew wants to eliminate references to Jews altogether. Yet, Matthew retains mention of the "leader of the synagogue" (Mark's Jairus) in Matt 9:18 (cf. 9:23), and the elders in Luke 7:3 function as local community leaders and as emissaries, not as the primary authority figures of the story. Pesch and Kratz and Davies and Allison point to Matthew's preferences for stylizing stories as dialogues and for direct speech over indirect speech. The force of these arguments is mitigated by the fact that these preferences are indicative of Q (and *Gos. Thom.* as well—Gagnon 1994a). Other arguments are similarly problematic (cf. Hagner, Gagnon 1994b).

On the other hand, evidence of and strong arguments for Lukan expansion abound. For example, ἀπέστειλεν πρός and πρεσβυτέρους τῶν Ἰουδαίων are Lukan terms and motifs (Schulz, Sellin, Gagnon 1994a). John does not have an initial delegation—the royal official meets Jesus face-to-face. As for a rationale, the insertion of Jewish community leaders as representatives of a Roman centurion who asks for Jesus' help fits squarely with Luke's theme of presenting potential Gentile believers in a positive light in relation to Judaism (Gagnon)—in this the centurion foreshadows the god-fearer Cornelius in Acts. It has also been argued that Luke intentionally avoids narrating direct contact between Jesus and Gentiles prior to the resurrection (George, Lampe, Harrington).

The second delegation in Luke presents serious problems for this variation unit. The existence of the first delegation almost requires the existence of the second (Q 7:6b-c²), unless the first delegation originally gave *both* speeches in Q (Luke 7:4b-5 and 7:6c-8)—and the first speech is important for explaining why Jewish community elders would be speaking for a Gentile centurion in the first place (Q 7:2, 3, 4-6a¹³). But the first person form of the centurion's speech in Q 7:6c-8 makes this unlikely, because what would have been rehearsed speech in fact *follows* Jesus' response of coming with them (minimal Q; cf. Matt 8:7a, which is not necessarily a positive response) and is not part of the initial petition for help. If, along with the second delegation (Q 7:6b-c²), one jettisons the first speech and the plea to come as Lukan redaction (almost requiring Q 7:2, 3, 4-6a⁶,¹² Matt = Q, Pro)—and μὴ σκύλλου must go as well, since it assumes a positive response of Jesus' *coming*, yet is part of the rehearsed speech (see Q 7:6b-c⁶)—then one moves closer to Matthew's dialog being the part of the Q narrative, with the remaining possibility that a Jewish delegation dialogues with Jesus in place of the centurion throughout. In light of the first person voice of the Q speech, this is ridiculous. But including the second delegation in Q is even more problematic because it necessarily carries with it the baggage of other significant variation units that contain obvious Lukanisms (Q 7:2, 3, 4-6a¹³; Q 7:6b-c⁴⁻⁷; Q 7:7¹ is actually more dependent upon inclusion of the first delegation). To summarize, it appears to be a case of all or nothing. Either both delegations with their attendant variation units were in Q, or none at all. So a decision for or against Luke = Q here partly determines decisions for a host of subsequent variation units. At the same time, the problems of these subsequent variations also impact a decision here.

Matthew's προσέρχομαι is another issue. It is clear that Matthew favors the word (e.g. Hawkins, Held, Fuchs). The verb is not otherwise found in Q. It is also clear that if representatives were not sent, then the centurion probably came to Jesus. John's ἀπέρχομαι supports the tradition having a form of ἔρχομαι (Lindars even proposes John's verb). Wegner's emendation resolves the dilemma. He also demonstrates Matthew's tendency to change Markan ἔρχομαι to προσέρχομαι. This is one of those rare cases where an emendation stands out as the clear and obvious text of Q.

Robinson 2000: Matt = Q {B} (with emendation), (<>ἦλθεν)³.

In John 4:47 the official himself comes to Jesus, as in Matthew.

The Lukan alternative ἀπέστειλεν is part of the delegation motif, which was not in Q.

The story of Cornelius the centurion and his delegation in Acts 10-11:18 is a similar Lukan narration. There (Acts 10:28) the need for such a delegation from Luke's point of view is made explicit.

The formulation οἱ πρεσβύτεροι τῶν Ἰουδαίων recurs in Acts 25:15. It is hence Lukan.

The argument reported (but not embraced) by Dunderberg that Luke leaves Markan healing narratives largely unchanged while Matthew abbreviates them, cannot be used for a precedent as to how they would handle a healing narrative (better: dialogue) in Q. For Luke is nearer Mark, and hence would have little to change, whereas Matthew is further from Mark, and hence would have more to change. Conversely Luke is further from Q, and hence would have more to change than he had in the case of Mark, and Matthew is nearer to Q and hence would have less to change than he had in the case of Mark.

The delegation of disciples interpolated into the narration of John's question about the Coming One in Q 7:19-20 is also Lukan redaction. The narration of the delegation in the present instance is thus typically Lukan.

In Acts 10:28, προσέρχεσθαι is used for what a Jew may not do with regard to one of another race (cf. Bovon, 348-349). Q may have avoided such a pointed affront as προs- may imply, and hence have read only ἦλθεν.

It is unclear whether Luke's preposition πρός (see Q 7:2, 3, 4-6a⁴) is simply an instance of Luke's preference for that preposition, or is his transferral of the prefix προσ- from the verb (which he does not use at all), which would thus be an indirect attestation for προσέρχεσθαι. But this argument has little force, in view of Luke's preference for the preposition πρός.

Since we come down on the overall side of Matt = Q, in spite of Matthean traits that we decide are also Q traits, it is a bit inconsistent to vote against the prefix προσ- on the grounds it is typically Matthean. But προσέρχομαι is nowhere else in Q.

Kloppenborg 2000: Matt = Q {B} (with emendation), (<>ἦλθεν)³.

Hoffmann 2001: Matt = Q {B} (with emendation), (<>ἦλθεν)³.

Q 7:2, 3, 4-6a⁴: Luke's πρὸς αὐτόν or Matthew's αὐτῷ.

Luke = Q: [πρὸς αὐτόν]⁴

Pro

Wegner 1985, 128-129: See Q 7:2, 3, 4-6a³ Emendation = Q: <ἦλθεν>³ (p. 127). 270: Reconstruction. For complete text see Q 7:1⁰ In Q (pp. 11-12).

Nolland 1989, 314: See Q 7:2, 3, 4-6a² Luke = Q, Pro (p. 80).

Lindars 1992, 210: Reconstruction. For complete text see Q 7:1⁶ Luke = Q, Pro (p. 56).

Gagnon 1993, 719: "I agree with Wegner [1985, 128-129] in viewing the πρὸς αὐτόν in 7:3 as part of the original Q text (reading Matthew's stereotypical προσῆλθεν αὐτῷ as a replacement for ἦλθεν πρὸς αὐτόν)."

Gagnon 1994b, 135: Reconstruction. For complete text see Q 7:1⁰ In Q (p. 15).

Landis 1994, 7: "Für Q wäre dann etwa die Konstruktion ἦλθεν πρὸς αὐτόν anzunehmen."

7, 17: Reconstruction. For complete text see Q 7:1⁶ Luke = Q, Pro (p. 57).

Con

B. Weiß 1907, 242: See Q 7:2, 3, 4-6a³ Luke = Q, Con (p. 95).

Schulz 1972, 237-238: See Q 7:2, 3, 4-6a³ Luke = Q, Con (p. 103).

Muhlack 1979, 41: For complete text of Lukan expansions, see Q 7:2, 3, 4-6a³ Luke = Q, Con (pp. 105-106).

Neirynck 1979, 109-110: See Q 7:2, 3, 4-6a³ Luke = Q, Con (pp. 107-108).

Schnelle 1987, 103: "Lukas hat in einem weit größeren Maß als Matthäus die Q-Vorlage umgestaltet. Auf seine Redaktion gehen die Situationsschilderung in V.2 ... zurück."

Schnelle 1987, ET 1992, 89: "Luke has reshaped the Q version of the story much more thoroughly than Matthew. His redaction produced the description of the situation in v. 2."

Crossan 1991, 326, 328 (GT 1994, 431, 433): See Q 7:2, 3, 4-6a³ Luke = Q, Con (p. 112).

Matt = Q: (αὐτῷ)⁴

Pro

von Harnack 1907, 91 (ET 1908, 131): Reconstruction. For complete text see Q 7:1⁶ Luke = Q, Pro (p. 55).

Catchpole 1992, 527 [1993, 292]: Reconstruction: "καὶ ἦλθεν αὐτῷ ἑκα-τοντάρχης." For complete text see Q 7:1⁰ In Q (p. 14).

International Q Project 1995, 478: Reconstruction. For complete text see Q 7:1⁰ In Q (p. 16).

Con

Parker 1953, 63-65: See Q 7:1⁶ Matt = Q, Con (pp. 58-60).

Schulz 1972, 236: "Προσῆλθεν αὐτῷ ist eindeutig Zusatz des Mt."

Gundry 1982, 141: "In v 5 προσῆλθεν replaces ἀπέστειλεν (so Luke). This substitution accords with the dropping of the delegation and with Matthew's fondness for his verb, which connotes Jesus' dignity (38,6)."

O'Donnell 1988, 75: "Matthew uses a construction for introducing participants into the story. The pattern of προσέρχομαι in the aorist indicative, αὐτῷ, and a nominative subject occurs fifteen times in Matthew."

Davies and Allison 1991, 19: See Q 7:~~2~~, 3, ~~4-6~~a³ Matt = Q, Con (p. 124).

Lindars 1992, 204-205: See Q 7:~~2~~, 3, ~~4-6~~a³ Matt = Q, Con (p. 124).

Gagnon 1994b, 136: "In my estimation, Matthew has ... adjusted the entrance- and encounter-phrases of his source to the stereotyped Matthean formula of introduction (genitive-absolute construction + προσῆλθεν αὐτῷ)."

Neither Luke nor Matthew

B. Weiß 1908, 15: Reconstruction. For complete text see Q 7:1⁰ In Q (p. 5).

Fuchs 1971, 116-117: See Q 7:~~2~~, 3, ~~4-6~~a³ Matt = Q, Con (p. 122).

118: "Ein weiteres Kennzeichen des Lk an dieser Stelle ist πρὸς αὐτόν. Lk setzt πρός 165mal, davon nur einmal nicht (19,37) mit Akkusativ, Mk hat es nur 63mal (einmal nicht mit Akkusativ: 5,11), Mt 41mal. Auch die Stellen, in denen πρὸς αὐτόν erscheint, überwiegen deutlich bei Lk: ... Lk 1,13; 2,48; 3,12; 4,4.40; 5,33; 7,3.6.20.40; 8,4.19; 9,50.57.62; 10,26; 11,1.5.39; 18,3.40; 19,5.9.39; 20,2; 21,38; 24,18 (27)."

Polag 1979, 38: Reconstruction. For complete text see Q 7:1⁰ In Q (pp. 9-10).

Sevenich-Bax 1993, 238: Reconstruction. For complete text see Q 7:1⁰ In Q (p. 15).

Evaluations

Robinson 2000: Matt = Q {B}, (αὐτῷ)⁴

Though the dative αὐτῷ with προσῆλθεν is typically Matthean, it is logically needed to connect the Centurion with Jesus, and thus to launch the story.

This is clearly the reason for beginning by pointing out to whom the Centurion came.

Matthew's αὐτῷ is preferable to Luke's πρὸς αὐτόν, for in Q it goes with Matthew's Q verb ἐλθών, rather than with Luke's redactional verb ἀπέστειλεν.

Luke uses πρός another time redactionally in the interpolation of the delegation: The delegation παραγενόμενοι πρός (Luke 7:4). Compare the similar redactional delegation Luke 7:20: παραγενόμενοι δὲ πρὸς αὐτόν. Furthermore ἀποστέλλειν πρός is typically Lukan (redactionally Luke 7:20; Acts 5x; πέμπειν πρός Luke 7:19).

Kloppenborg 2000: Luke = Q {C}, [[πρὸς αὐτόν]⁴]

Johnson 2001: Matt = Q {C}, [[(αὐτῷ)⁴]]
It could very well be that Matthew finds πρός in Q and attaches it to the immediately preceding ἦλθεν (Wegner), changing the accusative pronoun to the dative. John also has πρὸς αὐτόν. On the other hand, Luke has a strong preference for the use of πρὸς αὐτόν (Fuchs).

Robinson suggests that because Matthew's subsequent αὐτῷ is in Q, the dative pronoun here belongs in Q. However, the subsequent αὐτῷ does not as much belong with ἐλθών as it does with λέγει—there really is no connection between the two pronouns as they function with very different verbs.

As Matthew's redactional propensity for προσέρχομαι from ἔρχομαι doesn't require a contiguous πρός as a prompt (though we face a similar situation in Matt 8:19 par Luke 9:57 [Q]), and since Luke's redactional preference for πρός is certain, the arguments lean in favor of Q = Matthew's αὐτῷ. However, the presence of the preposition in both texts makes me somewhat less than sure about my decision.

Hoffmann 2001: Matt = Q {B}, (αὐτῷ)⁴

Q 7:2, 3, 4-6a⁵: Luke's ἑκατοντάρχου δέ τινος or Matthew's ἑκατόνταρχος.

Luke = Q: [ἑκατοντάρχου δέ τινος]⁵

Pro

Castor 1912, 223: Reconstruction. For complete text see Q 7:1⁰ In Q (p. 6).

Dauer 1984, 112: "Wenn es stimmt, daß ἤμελλεν τελευτᾶν auf Lukas zurückgeht, dann wird es in der lk Vorlage geheißen haben: ἑκατοντάρχου δέ τινος παῖς κακῶς ἔχει."

Davies and Allison 1991, 19: "Luke, with the exception perhaps of adjectival τις, probably comes closer to Q."

Landis 1994, 19-20: "Einziges deutliches Anzeichen für eine redaktionelle Überarbeitung dieses Verses durch Lk ist die Art der Einführung des Bittstellers: ἑκατοντάρχου δέ [20] τινος. Sie ist mit ihrer Verbindung von δέ und dem Indefinitpronomen τις typisch lk. Die stilistische Prägung des Ausdrucks durch Lk legt die Vermutung nahe, daß auch die Nennung und Bezeichnung des Bittstellers als solche von Lk in die Vorlage eingetragen worden ist." Landis argues for ἑκατοντάρχης and against Luke's δὲ τινος. See Landis at Emendation = Q: <καὶ>⁵ ἦλθεν αὐτῷ (or πρὸς αὐτὸν) ἑκατοντάρχ<η>⁵ς (p. 138).

Con

Hawkins 1899, 47: "Words and Phrases characteristic of St. Luke's Gospel: ... τις, with nouns."

von Harnack 1907, 56: "Es dem Stil des Luk. entspricht ... τις hinzuzusetzen (vgl. Matth. v. 5 und Luk. v. 2)."

von Harnack 1907, ET 1908, 77: "It is in the style of St. Luke to add τις (cf. St. Matthew verse 5 and St. Luke verse 2)."

Schulz 1972, 236: "Die Konstruktion ἑκατοντάρχου δέ τινος ist lk. ⁴⁰¹" 236⁴⁰¹: Ev 38mal; Apg 63mal."

Neirynck 1979, 109-110: See Q 7:2, 3, 4-6a³ Luke = Q, Con (pp. 107-108).

Jeremias 1980: 151: "Red ἑκατοντάρχου: Getreu seiner Abneigung gegen Fremdworte (→ 10,18 Trad ...) schreibt Lukas nie das lateinische κεντυρίων (im NT nur Mk 15,39.44f.), sondern konsequent die griechische Form ἑκατοντάρχης (Lk 3/Apg 13 mal). —τινος: Adjektivisches τις ist markantes Kennzeichen für Lukas → 1,5 Red."

Schnelle 1987, 103: "Lukas hat in einem weit größeren Maß als Matthäus die Q-Vorlage umgestaltet. Auf seine Redaktion gehen die Situationsschilderung in V.2 ... zurück."

Schnelle 1987, ET 1992, 89: "Luke has reshaped the Q version of the story much more thoroughly than Matthew. His redaction produced the description of the situation in v. 2."

Gagnon 1993, 715: "It should be noted that Lucan redaction can ... be seen in the δέ τινος and δοῦλος of v 2a, '*now a slave of a certain* centurion.'"

Matt = Q: (ἑκατόνταρχος)⁵

Pro

von Harnack 1907, 91 (ET 1908, 131): Reconstruction. For complete text see Q 7:1⁶ Luke = Q, Pro (p. 55).

Schenk 1981, 37: Reconstruction. For complete text see Q 7:1⁰ In Q (p. 10).

Schenk 1987, 205: "In der Vermeidung das mk Latinismus κεντυρίων hat [Matt] 27,54 (+Mk) die att.-griech. Übersetzung (-ος) eingesetzt, die er auch Q-Mt 8,5.8 (=Lk, der aber die von ihm bevorzugte hell.-griech. Form auf -ης hat) hat, während er V. 13 (+Q) auch ohne Bedenken zu dieser hell.-griech. Form wechseln kann."

Schnelle 1987, 102: "Matthäus steht am Anfang der Q-Überlieferung näher als Lukas."

Schnelle 1987, ET 1992, 88: "At the beginning, Matthew is closer to Q than is Luke."

Lindars 1992, 204: See Lindars at Emendation = Q: <καὶ ἦν τις>⁵ ἑκατόν-ταρχος <οὗ>⁵ ὁ παῖς (p. 138).

International Q Project 1995, 478: Reconstruction. For complete text see Q 7:1⁰ In Q (p. 16).

Con

B. Weiß 1898, 167¹: "Tsch [Tischendorf] liest V. 5 u. 8 nach ℵ allein ἑκα-τοντάρχης, das offenbar nach V. 13 konformirt ist, wie dort die Rcpt. (nach Δ) ἑκατοντάρχῳ schreibt. Die von ἄρχω abgeleiteten Worte gehen im NT und bei den Späteren gewöhnlich nach der 1. Dekl.; doch hat sich die ältere Form auf -αρχος auch sonst erhalten, und rührt wohl im Unterschiede von V. 13 von der Hand des Evangelisten her."

Parker 1953, 63-65: See Q 7:1⁶ Matt = Q, Con (pp. 58-60).

Gundry 1982, 141: "Matthew reduces the independent clause concerning Jesus' entering Capernaum (so Luke) to a genitive absolute and makes the centurion rather than his servant the subject of the sentence."

Wegner 1985, 129: "Das Wort ist für Q durch die Lk-Parallele in Lk 7,2 und 7,6 (vgl. Mt 8,8) gesichert. In Mt 8,13 kann es red oder trad sein.

"Welche Endung (-αρχος oder -άρχης?) gebrauchte aber die urspr Erzählung? Der Vergleich von Mt 27,54 (= ἑκατόνταρχος) und Lk 23,47 (= ἑκατοντάρχης) mit Mk 15,39 (= κεντυρίων) zeigt, daß sowohl in Lk 7,(2.)6 die Endung -άρχης als auch in Mt 8,5.8 die Endung -αρχος red gebildet sein könnten. Da im Mt-Text aber zumindest einmal (= 8,13) auch die hellenistische Endungs-bildung[11] gebraucht wird, ist sie u.E. der Endung -αρχος vorzuziehen."

129[11]: "Diese Endung bevorzugt Lk, bei dem -αρχος nur in Apg 22,25 und als sek Lesart einiger Hss in 28,16 begegnet. Im NT ist, abgesehen von ἑκατόνταρχος und χιλίαρχος, ebenfalls die Endung -άρχης für die Bildung von Substantiven mit ἄρχειν charakteristisch: vgl. z.B. ἐθνάρχης, πατριάρχης, πολιτάρχης u. a."

270: Reconstruction. See below, Emendation = Q.

Davies and Allison 1991, 19: "Προσῆλθεν is Matthean, as is the sentence structure."

19[35]: "Προσέρχομαι + αὐτῷ + subject + participle: Mt: 12-13; Mk: 0; Lk: 0."

Landis 1994, 7: "Bei der griechischen Bezeichnung für 'Hauptmann' differieren bei Mt und Lk die Endungen: Mt hat ἑκατόνταρχος, Lk ἑκατον-τάρχης. Da Mt aber in 8,13 auch zur Endung -ης übergeht, ist sie eher als ursprünglich anzusehen."

Emendation = Q: <καὶ>[5] ἑκατόνταρχος

B. Weiß 1908, 15: Reconstruction: "καὶ ἑκατόνταρχος." For complete text see Q 7:1[0] In Q (p. 5).

Emendation = Q: ἑκατοντάρχ<η>[5]ς δέ <>[5]

Polag 1979, 38: Reconstruction: "ἑκατοντάρχης δέ." For complete text see Q 7:1[0] In Q (pp. 9-10).
Sevenich-Bax 1993, 238: Reconstruction: "ἑκατοντάρχης δέ." For complete text see Q 7:1[0] In Q (p. 15).

Emendation = Q: ἑκατοντάρχ<η>[5]ς <>[5]

Wegner 1985, 270: Reconstruction: "ἑκατοντάρχης." For complete text see Q 7:1[0] In Q (pp. 11-12).

Emendation = Q: <χιλίαρχος>[5]

Evans 1990, 343: "In Matthew there is slight textual evidence for *chiliarchos* = 'ruler of a thousand', i.e. a cohort, the equivalent of the Roman military tribune, ... and *centurion* could represent a downgrading by Luke in the interests of his story which has affected Matthew's text."

Emendation = Q: <καὶ>⁵ ἦλθεν αὐτῷ (or πρὸς αὐτὸν) ἑκατοντάρχ<η>⁵ς

Catchpole 1992, 527 [1993, 292]: Reconstruction: "καὶ ἦλθεν αὐτῷ ἑκα-τοντάρχης." For complete text see Q 7:1⁰ In Q (p. 14).
Landis 1994, 7, 17: Reconstruction: "καὶ ἦλθεν πρὸς αὐτόν ἑκατοντάρχης." For complete text see Q 7:1⁶ Luke = Q, Pro (p. 57).

Emendation = Q: <καὶ ἦν τις>⁵ ἑκατόνταρχος <οὗ>⁵ ὁ παῖς

Lindars 1992, 204: "John's καὶ ἦν τις may well be original, as it is a good narrative opening (cf. Jn 1,6; 11,1). If so, Luke has improved the style by using the genitive. Matthew as usual abbreviates the source. After making the opening words a genitive absolute, he brings the centurion to Jesus without any explanation of the circumstances, which then have to be included in the centurion's request."
210: Reconstruction. For complete text see Q 7:1⁶ Luke = Q, Pro (p. 56).

Emendation = Q: ἑκατοντάρχ<η>⁵ς <οὗ>⁵ ὁ παῖς αὐτοῦ

Gagnon 1994b, 135: Reconstruction: "ἀκούσας δὲ περὶ αὐτοῦ, ἑκατον-τάρχης οὗ ὁ παῖς αὐτοῦ ... ἦλθεν." For complete text see Q 7:1⁰ In Q (p. 15).

Evaluations

Robinson 2000: Matt = Q {B}, for the nominative case; Matt = Q {C}, for the ending: ἑκατόνταρχ⟦(ο)⁵⟧(ς)⁵.
Regarding the case: The healing story in Q is about the centurion's faith in Jesus' word, not just about a boy getting healed (but see Q 7:22). Luke 7:2 begins with the centurion only in a genitive, and resumes at the end of the verse with a reference back to him in the dative. The nominative is given over to the boy. But even here the syntax is awkward, with ὃς ἦν αὐτῷ ἔντιμος appended belatedly at the end of the verse. Luke 7:3 reverts to the nominative for the centurion, probably reflecting the original story, but creating in Luke an awkward transition, in the unmediated shift from the nominative referring to the boy ὃς ἦν αὐτῷ ἔντιμος to the nominative referring to the centurion ἀκούσας. Hence Matthew's nominative begins the story more naturally (with which John 4:46b and Mark 7:25 agree).
The use of τις is Lukan (Schulz; Jeremias).

Regarding the ending: -ης in Luke 7:6 and Matt 8:13 stands over against -ος in Matt 8:5, 8. The redactional usage of the two Evangelists elsewhere, Matt 27:54 (-ος) and Luke 23:47 (-ης), indicates that the Evangelists prefer the same forms they use here (assuming that the genitive in Luke 7:2, which obscures the declension, is intended by him as the first declension used at Luke 7:6). But there is one exception: The use of Luke's preferred -ης in Matt 8:13 against Matthew's preferred -ος poses a problem, since Matthew clearly fluctuates.

Q 7:2, 8 (6?), 10 may have consistently referred to the centurion with -ης, though Matt 8:5b, 8 changed to his preferred -ος. Or, if Matt 8:13 is not in Q (see Q 7:?10?[20]), one would have in Matt 8:13 a Matthean reminiscence of the spelling -ης, which had been assimilated to Matthew's preferred usage -ος in Matt 8:5b, 8. Or Matt 8:13 could be simply a Matthean fluctuation. The redactional inconsistency would be analogous to Luke referring to the boy as δοῦλος in Luke 7:2-3,10, but yielding to Q's παῖς in Luke 7:7 (see Q 7:2, 3, 4-6a[9]). But of course Q, too, could have been inconsistent. Given the fluidity, it may be unwise to depart, in Q 7:3, from the only attestation one has, Matthew's -ος.

The fact that the ending -ης occurs in the redactional verse Matt 8:13 but not in the pre-Matthean verses Matt 8:5, 8 suggests that the pre-Matthean—i.e., Q—text read -ος. If Matthew had changed in the first two instances, against the Q text, he would hardly have introduced the rejected ending into his redactional conclusion.

Johnson 2000: Matt = Q {B}, for the nominative case; Matt = Q {C}, for the ending: ἑκατόνταρχ⟦(ο)⁵⟧(ς)⁵.

Kloppenborg 2000: Matt = Q {B}, for the nominative case; Luke = Q {C}, for the ending: ἑκατοντάρχ⟦<η>⁵⟧(ς)⁵.

Hoffmann 2001: Matt = Q {B}, for the nominative case; Matt = Q {C}, for the ending: ἑκατόνταρχ⟦(ο)⁵⟧(ς)⁵.

Wenn die Exposition des Lukas sekundär ist, dann ist es auch der Genitiv. Zur Frage ἑκατοντάρχης oder ἑκατόνταρχος siehe Q 7:6b-c³.

Q 7:2, 3, 4-6a⁶: Luke's ἐρωτῶν αὐτόν or Matthew's παρακαλῶν αὐτόν (See also Luke 7:4 παρεκάλουν αὐτόν).

Luke = Q: [ἐρωτῶν αὐτόν]⁶

Pro

Castor 1912, 223: Reconstruction. For complete text see Q 7:1⁰ In Q (p. 6).

Con

Bleek 1862, 347-348: See Q 7:2, 3, 4-6a¹ Matt = Q, Pro (pp. 70-71).

B. Weiß 1876, 229: "Nur in dem ἐλθών v. 3, das ihnen wenigstens nach v. 6 unmöglich aufgetragen sein kann, und in dem παρεκάλουν v. 4, welches das lucanische ἐρωτᾶν (v. 3 und noch 15mal bei Luc.) ablöst, zeigt sich vielleicht noch ein Nachklang der Urrelation."

J. Weiß 1892, 399: "Die Sendung der Stadt-πρεσβύτεροι ... gehört der Sonderüberlieferung an; ebenso ἐρωτᾶν = bitten."

Hawkins 1899, 18: "Words and Phrases characteristic of St. Luke's Gospel: ... ἐρωτάω."

Easton 1910, 161: "Of the [nine] cases [of ἐρωτάω] in Lc., 8:37 is a Lucan insertion in Mc. 5:17. The other eight (or nine) (5:3; 7:3, 4 [text dubious], 36; 11:37; 14:18, 19, 32; 16:27) are all L."

Schulz 1972, 237-238: "Die Vv 3-6a bei Lk haben keine Parallele bei Mt und sind lk Erweiterung der Geschichte vom [238] Hauptmann.⁴¹⁰ Auch sachlich erweist sich der Einschub als sek."

238⁴¹⁰: "Ἐρωτᾶν ist bei Lk stark gehäuft (Ev ca 9mal trad; ca 5mal red; Apg 7mal; dagegen Mk 3mal; Mt 4mal—verbunden mit ὅπως auch Lk 11,37 red)."

Busse 1977, 148¹: "V 3b zeigt red. Beeinflussung. Die Verbindung von ἐρωτᾶν mit ὅπως findet sich bei ihm in 11,37 und Apg 23,10 und 25,3."

152-153: "Darum muß auch die normale kniefällige Bitte um Hilfe (vgl Lk 5,12) der neuen Form angepaßt werden. Lukas gelingt dies mit einem wahren literarischen Kabinettstück. In den folgenden Versen 3-6 variiert Lukas die antike Petitionsform. Sie ist mit den drei Petitionsverben ἀξιόω, ἐρωτάω und παρακαλέω konstituiert. Darüber hinaus hat V 3 eine spezifisch formale Gliederung erfahren. Zuerst wird eine notwendige Hintergrundinformation gegeben, der Hauptmann habe die Ältesten der Juden zu Jesus gesandt. Darauf folgt das Petitionsverb ἐρωτάω mit einer genauen Darstellung dessen, was von Jesus erbeten wird. Dies alles paßt ausgezeichnet zur standardisierten

Form einer hellenistischen Petition. Nach der Analyse von Terence Mullins [1962, 46] besteht sie aus drei Elementen: 'The three basic elements of a petition are the background, the petition verb and the desired action. ... They are necessary to the constitution of the petition as "form" in literature of this period.' Eingepaßt [153] in den Erzählzusammenhang und aus diesem Grund überformt variiert Lukas ohne Zweifel die hellenistische Form einer Petition in V 3."

Neirynck 1979, 109-110: See Q 7:2, 3, 4-6a³ Luke = Q, Con (pp. 107-108).

Jeremias 1980, 152: "Red ... ἐρωτῶν ... ὅπως: In der Bedeutung, 'bitten' wird ἐρωτάω im lk Doppelwerk teils durch nachfolgenden Infinitiv (Lk 5,3; 8,37/Apg 3,3; 10,48; 16,39; 18,20; 23,18), teils durch ὅπως (Lk 7,3; 11,37/Apg 23,20), teils durch ἵνα (Lk 7,36; 16,27) ergänzt. Wie wir → 2,26 Red ... gesehen haben, ist die Konstruktion mit Infinitiv und mit ὅπως lukanisch."

Dauer 1984, 113-114: "Hier spricht ἐρωτᾶν in der Bedeutung 'bitten' für lk Formulierung: Lk 10mal; Apg 6mal; sonst: Mt 1mal; Mk 1mal; Joh 11mal; Johbr 2mal; Pls 4mal. Von diesen zehn Fällen im 3. Evangelium ist es mit Sicherheit oder großer Wahrscheinlichkeit redaktionell: Lk 4,38 diff Mk 1,30; Lk 8,37 diff Mk 5,17; ferner Lk 5,3; 7,36; 11,37; Lk 14,18.19.32; 16,27 stammt aus Sondergut bzw. aus einer anderen Version [114] des Gleichnisses vom Gastmal.—Wichtig ist auch, daß nur Lukas ἐρωτᾶν mit ὅπως konstruiert: Lk 7,3 u.St.; 11,37; Apg 23,20, wenn es auch auffällt, daß Lukas nur a.u.St. das Participium coniunctum ἐρωτῶν gebraucht. So wird man sagen dürfen, daß auch hier die Formulierung ἐρωτῶν αὐτὸν ὅπως von ihm stammt, möglicherweise als Ersatz für λέγων ἵνα."

Wegner 1985, 167: "In der hier in Frage kommenden Bedeutung 'bitten' erscheint es bei Lk außer auSt noch 1x als add zu Mk (8,37), 2x eventuell in QLk (14,18f), sonst aber nur noch im Sg: vgl. 5,3; (7,3?); 7,36; 11,37; 14,32 und 16,27. Man wird daher eine Vorliebe des lk Sg für ἐρωτάω in der Bedeutung 'bitten' annehmen dürfen. Freilich zeigt die Apg in 3,3; 10,48; 16,39; 18,20 und 23,18.20, daß auch dem dritten Evangelisten das Verb in dieser Bedeutung vertraut war."

Riniker 1990, 62-63[62]: "La liste des interventions lucaniennes que dresse A. Dauer [1984, 113-116] ne me paraît contestable que sur deux points. ... (b) 7,3 ἐρωτῶν αὐτὸν ὅπως. ... Comme on ne peut pas éliminer [63] cette partie de la phrase traditionnelle, A. Dauer propose de la remplacer—au niveau de la tradition lucanienne—par λέγων ἵνα (p. 114). Mais la statistique du vocabulaire n'impose nullement cette construction. Des dix occurrences de ἐρωτάω au sens de 'prier' dans l'évangile de Luc, A. Dauer (p. 113 s. [see above]) en attribue cinq à la rédaction lucanienne et quatre au Sondergut traditionnel (Lc 14,18.19.32; 16,27). Pourquoi ne pas prendre Lc 7,3 comme cinquième occurrence traditionnelle? Dans le cas de 7,3, la proposition de A. Dauer est improbable."

Crossan 1991, 326, 328 (GT 1994, 431, 433): See Q 7:2, 3, 4-6a³ Luke = Q, Con (p. 112).

Lindars 1992, 205: "Both evangelists [Luke and John] frequently use ἐρωτάω, whereas παρακαλέω is never used by John and Luke uses it in the sense of making a request only in Lk 8,31.32.41, where he is reproducing Mark."

Gagnon 1993, 719-720: "As for ἐρωτάω (4/3/15 + 7/26 or 27), there are three clear instances where Luke has substituted ἐρωτάω for a different word in Mark: 4:38 [L] (Mark: λέγουσιν); 8:37 [L] (Mark: παρακαλεῖν); 19:31 [L] (Mark: εἴπῃ). Luke retains the only Marcan use of the word (cf. Mark 4:10, albeit Luke uses the related form ἐπερωτάω). In the face of this and the ample use in Acts, the evidence for ἐρωτάω as a term of Luke's special source (see Luke 5:3; 7:36; 11:37?; 14:32; 16:27, all [S] but perhaps Luke's wording) must be judged less convincing than for its belonging to Lucan redaction. Moreover, ἐρωτάω is combined with ὅπως in indirect discourse elsewhere in the [720] NT only in Luke 11:37 [LQ] and Acts 23:20. Now it is true that ἐρωτάω appears in the Johannine version of the story (John 4:47), suggesting that the use of the word in Luke 7:3 goes back to Q. However, there are also no clear Q uses of ἐρωτάω (cf. Luke 14:18-19 [LQ]) and the word is a favorite of John's (albeit eight occurrences are found in Fortna's reconstructed Signs Source)."

Sevenich-Bax 1993, 169: See Q 7:2, 3, 4-6a³ Luke = Q, Con (p. 114).

Dunderberg 1994, 88: "In V. 3 können die lukanischen Worte ἐρωτῶν αὐτὸν ὅπως von der Fortsetzung ἐλθὼν διασώσῃ τὸν δοῦλον αὐτοῦ kaum getrennt werden. Es wäre zwar möglich, daß die Erzählung keine direkte Bitte enthielt (vgl. Mt 8,6), aber nur unter der Voraussetzung, daß V. 4a als Ganzes zur früheren Erzählung gehört. Allerdings wurden die Worte οἱ δὲ παραγενό-μενοι πρὸς τὸν Ἰησοῦν in V. 4a schon in der obengenannten Auflistung als lukanischer Einschub angesehen, und wohl zu Recht."

Landis 1994, 21: Landis argues that ἐρωτάω with ὅπως comes from Lukan *Sondergut*.

Matt = Q: (παρακαλῶν αὐτόν)⁶

Pro

Bleek 1862, 347-348: See Q 7:2, 3, 4-6a¹ Matt = Q, Pro (pp. 70-71).

von Harnack 1907, 91 (ET 1908, 131): Reconstruction. For complete text see Q 7:1⁶ Luke = Q, Pro (p. 55).

B. Weiß 1908, 15²⁴: "Daraus ergab sich auch die Umgestaltung des dem Eingang der vorigen Erzählung genau entsprechenden παρεκάλει αὐτὸν λέγων in παρακαλῶν καὶ λέγων."

15: Reconstruction. See B. Weiß at Emendation = Q: <καὶ>⁶ παρεκάλ<ει>⁶ [or <εσεν>⁶] αὐτόν (pp. 145-146).

Schulz 1972, 236: "Παρακαλεῖν fehlt sonst bei Mt, dürfte also schon in Q gestanden haben, um so mehr, als in dieser Geschichte Lk starke Eingriffe vorgenommen hat und Mt insgesamt Q näher steht. Da sich in Mt V 5 sonst keine mt Spracheigentümlichkeiten nachweisen lassen, wird er ungefähr Q wiedergeben."

Schenk 1981, 37: Reconstruction. For complete text see Q 7:1⁰ In Q (p. 10).

Wegner 1985, 37-38: "Im Bericht von Lk und Joh erscheint zunächt eine Schilderung der Not (Lk 7,2; Joh 4,46b), nach der jeweils die Bitte des Hauptmanns (durch Stellvertreter: Lk!) in *indirecter und direkter Rede* (Lk 7,3 und Joh 4,47 bzw. Lk 7,4 und Joh 4,49) folgt. Bei Mt fallen dagegen die Schilderung der Not und die Bitte zusammen, d.h. die Schilderung der Not erscheint bei ihm [38] in Form einer Bitte (παρακαλῶν) vom Hauptmann selbst in direkter Rede (Mt 8,6) vorgetragen. Es fragt sich: Hat Mt zusammengefaßt/gekürzt, oder muß bei Lk und Joh mit einer späteren, differenzierenden Erweiterung gerechnet werden?

"a. Die Verwendung von παρακαλεῖν ist in Mt 8,5 ein wenig befremdend, denn eigentlich erwartet man, dem Verb entsprechend, die Formulierung einer konkreten Bitte; statt dessen wird aber lediglich die Krankheit mit ihren Nebenwirkungen beschrieben (Mt 8,6). Es fällt nun freilich sofort auf, daß beim ersten Evangelisten eine derartige Verwendung des Verbs sonst an keiner anderen Stelle belegt ist. Vielmehr folgt dem mt 'παρακαλεῖν für *bittendes Ersuchen um Hilfe*'³ überwiegend in direkter (8,31; 18,29 und 26,53) oder indirekter (8,34 und 14,36) Rede der Inhalt der Bitte; ist das nicht der Fall, so wird—wie in 18,32—der Inhalt zumindest durch den unmittelbaren Kontext (vgl. 18,29) deutlich vorausgesetzt. In Anbetracht dieses Befundes wird man wohl sagen können, daß die Verwendung von παρακαλεῖν mit Schilderung der Not *ohne konkrete Angabe des Inhalts der Bitte*, wie es in Mt 8,5f begegnet, kaum vom ersten Evangelisten selbst stammen wird."

38³: "Vgl. Schmitz [1954, 792; ET, 794)]."

40-41: "b. Mt bringt—anders als Lk und Joh—die in Form einer Bitte geschilderte Not ausschließlich in direkter Rede. Nun macht Held [1960, 222-223] darauf aufmerksam, daß bei Mt fast alle Heilungswunder 'nach kurzer formelhafter Einleitung mit einer direkten Rede' einsetzen, und stellt fest, 'daß die in direkter Rede an Jesus gerichtete Bitte ein wesentlicher Baustein der Wunderheilung im Matthäusevangelium ist'. Es wäre demnach zu erwägen, ob die direkte Anrede in Mt 8,6 nicht erst sek vom ersten Evangelisten stammt, der dann etwa eine urspr, in Erzählform erhaltene Angabe über die Natur der Krankheit später als direkte Anrede in den Mund des Hauptmanns gelegt hätte. Dafür spräche, daß Mt auch sonst Erzählung durch Rede ersetzt. Ein gewichtiges Argument gegen diese Annahme liefert freilich die Eingangswendung καὶ λέγων, die in diesem Falle von Mt stammen müßte: Die stat Analyse zeigt nämlich, daß diese Konstruktion nicht charakteristisch für den ersten Evangelisten ist, zumal er sie häufig in seiner Mk-Bearbeitung zugunsten des bloßen Partizips übergeht. Stammt aber die Einleitungswendung nicht von Mt, so ist die Wahrscheinlichkeit, daß die ihr folgende direkte Rede ebenfalls dem ersten Evangelisten bereits trad vorlag, um so größer! In dieselbe Richtung weist übrigens [41] der Befund in den anderen Wundergeschichten der Synoptiker, denn auch bei ihnen erscheint die Bitte hilfesuchender Personen an Jesus überwiegend in direkter Rede formuliert. ...

"Zusammenfassend zu den Punkten a. und b. läßt sich folgendes sagen: Die besprochenen Differenzen zwischen Mt einerseits und Lk und Joh andererseits lösen sich nicht dadurch, daß man annimmt, Mt habe eine urspr in indirekter Rede formulierte Bitte (vgl. etwa Lk 7,3; auch Joh 4,47) übergangen, um sogleich durch die Anwendung der direkten Rede in V 6 auf das Gespräch als dem gewichtigeren Teil der Geschichte aufmerksam zu machen. Vielmehr stellte es sich als wahrscheinlich heraus, daß der erste Evangelist eine konkrete Angabe des Inhalts der Bitte, wie sie aus Lk 7,3 oder Joh 4,47 hervorgeht, in der von ihm benutzten Vorlage nicht vorfand; außerdem schienen die seltsame Verwendung von παρακαλεῖν in Mt 8,5 und die von Mt sonst eher vermiedene Einleitungswendung zu V 6 (= καὶ λέγων!) darauf hinzudeuten, daß der erste Evangelist in den Vv 5b.6 auf Trad fußt. Ferner konnte noch beobachtet werden, daß die Verwendung eines Verbums des Bittens ohne nachfolgende konkrete Angabe seines Inhalts, wie beim mt παρακαλεῖν in 8,5, im Laufe der Überlieferung eher eine Tendenz aufweist, durch eben eine solche Angabe ergänzt zu werden, als das Gegenteil. Es muß daher zumindest mit der Möglichkeit gerechnet werden, daß Lk 7,3 überlieferungsgeschichtlich gegenüber Mt 8,5.(6) einem späteren Stadium zuzuweisen ist."

270: Reconstruction. For complete text see Q 7:1⁰ In Q (pp. 11-12).

Schenk 1987, 400: "Sonst im *Akt.* der *dringenden Bitte* erzählend 4mal an Jesus gerichtet 8,5 (=Q).31.34 (=Mk); 14,35 (=Mk)."

Catchpole 1992, 527 [1993, 292]: Reconstruction. For complete text see Q 7:1⁰ In Q (p. 14).

Lindars 1992, 205: "Luke and John agree in the use of ἐρωτάω against Matthew παρακαλῶν αὐτόν, which, however, is more likely to be original." See Lindars at Emendation = Q: <καὶ>⁶ παρεκάλ<ει>⁶ [or <εσεν>⁶] αὐτόν (p. 146).

Gagnon 1993, 720: "Since Matt 8:5 and Luke 7:4 agree on the use of the word παρακαλέω and Matthew shows no special preference for that word, it is more likely that παρακαλέω rather than ἐρωτάω stood in the Q text."

722-723: "I regard παρακαλῶν (Matt 8:5) as belonging to the Q text; this accounts for Luke's use of παρεκάλουν in 7:4 (9/9/7 + 22; elsewhere in Q perhaps Matt 5:4 [QM]). Matthew shows no preference for παρακαλέω. He adopts the word from Mark 3 times but also omits it 3 times (Mark 1:40; 5:23; 7:32; each of which has to do with petitioning for a miracle). Otherwise παρακαλέω appears in Matthew in [S] 3x (2:18 in an OT citation; 18:29,32) [723] and in [M?] only once (26:53)."

Sevenich-Bax 1993, 178: For the form of the verb, see Sevenich-Bax at Emendation = Q: παρεκάλ<εσεν>⁶ αὐτόν (p. 146).

Gagnon 1994b, 135: Reconstruction. For complete text see Q 7:1⁰ In Q (p. 15).

Landis 1994, 7: "Der Ausdruck παρακαλῶν αὐτόν bei Mt ist wohl traditionell, denn παρακαλέω wird vom ersten Evangelisten nie redaktionell eingesetzt."

7, 17: Reconstruction. For complete text see Q 7:1⁶ Luke = Q, Pro (p. 57).

International Q Project 1995, 478: Reconstruction. For complete text see Q 7:1⁰ In Q (p. 16).

Con

Allen 1907, 76-77: "It is curious that the editor should omit παρακαλῶν in [77] Mk v. 40 and insert it here. Perhaps he thought it more suitable in view of the long appeal which here follows, than in reference to the short sentence of v. 2."

Parker 1953, 63-65: See Q 7:1⁶ Matt = Q, Con (pp. 58-60).

Frankemölle 1974, 112: "Das Thema des Glaubens hat Mt gegenüber dem Stoff in der Logienquelle Q entschieden herausgestellt, indem er die Tradition—wie auch an anderen Stellen—strafft und kürzt, sie zugleich aber durch einen redaktionell bearbeiteten Einleitungs- (8,5 παρακαλῶν) und Schlußvers (8,13 ὡς ἐπίστευσας), vor allem durch den Zusatz 8,11f ... von der Wundergeschichte weg in verstärktem Maße zu einer Glaubensperikope gestaltet."

Gundry 1982, 141: "Παρακαλῶν and λέγων come from the account of the Jewish elders' plea to Jesus (see Luke 6:4)."

Davies and Allison 1991, 19: See Q 7:2̶, 3, 4̶-6̶a³ Matt = Q, Con (p. 124).

Emendation = Q: <καὶ>⁶ παρεκάλ<ει>⁶ [or <εσεν>⁶] αὐτόν

B. Weiß 1908, 15²⁴: See B. Weiß at Matt = Q, Pro (p. 143).

15: Reconstruction: "καὶ παρεκάλει αὐτόν λέγων." For complete text see Q 7:1⁰ In Q (p. 5).

Lindars 1992, 205: See Lindars at Matt = Q, Pro (p. 144).

210: Reconstruction: "καὶ παρεκάλεσεν αὐτόν." For complete text see Q 7:1⁶ Luke = Q, Pro (p. 56).

211: "Luke has ... introduced the deputation of Jewish elders in vv. 3-5. This has necessitated changing ἀπῆλθεν πρὸς αὐτὸν καὶ παρεκάλει αὐτόν (cf. Jn 4,47) to ἀπέστειλεν πρὸς αὐτὸν πρεσβυτέρους τῶν Ἰουδαίων ἐρωτῶν αὐτόν."

Emendation = Q: <>⁶

Crum 1927, 138: Reconstruction. For complete text see Q 7:2, 3, 4-6a¹ Luke = Q, Pro (pp. 71-72).

Emendation = Q: παρεκάλ<εσεν>⁶ αὐτόν

Polag 1979, 38: Reconstruction: "παρεκάλεσεν αὐτόν." For complete text see Q 7:1⁰ In Q (pp. 9-10).

Sevenich-Bax 1993, 178: "Mit der Einfügung der finiten Form von προσέρχομαι sowie der sekundären Formulierung des Verses Mt 8,5aα [See Sevenich-Bax at Q 7:2, 3, 4-6a³ Matt = Q, Con (p. 125) and Q 7:1⁶ Matt = Q, Con (p. 61)] wird des weiteren die partizipiale Abfassung des Verbs παρακαλέω zusammenhängen. Daß diese Vokabel für den Wortlaut der Perikope in der Logienquelle vorauszusetzen ist, ergibt sich dabei aus der verwandten Formulierung bei Lukas (vgl. Lk 7,4), der die Aussage allerdings aufgrund der Einführung der Delegation durch die vorangehenden Verben ἀποστέλλω und ἐρωτάω vermitteln muß."

238: Reconstruction: "παρεκάλεσεν αὐτὸν λέγων." For complete text see Q 7:1⁰ In Q (p. 15).

Evaluations

Johnson 2000: Matt = Q {B}, (παρακαλ)⁶ῶν αὐτόν.

Neither verb is found in minimal Q material. However, it is found in Matthew here and in Luke 7:4.

The only argument in favor of Luke's verb is the presence of ἐρωτάω in John 4:47. However, ἐρωτάω is both Lukan (Easton, Jeremias, Dauer) and Johannine (Lindars, Gagnon 1993) vocabulary (Luke-Acts 23x; John 20x). It is John's standard verb for profane request (cf. αἰτέω for prayer). Matthew is not averse to the verb, omitting it from Markan material twice, but taking it over once, adding it to Markan material once, and replacing ἐπερωτάω (a Markan stylistic preference) with it twice.

Παρακαλέω is not particularly Matthean (Matt 9x; Mark 9x). It is quite common in Luke-Acts (30x) and its presence in Q 7:2 here may explain its subsequent use by Luke in 7:4. John never uses παρακαλέω, preferring ἐρωτάω for profane request. This would explain John's agreement with Luke in the choice of the verb.

Robinson 2000: Matt = Q {B}, (παρακαλ)⁶ῶν αὐτόν.

Mark 7:26b uses ἠρώτα. Matthew omits this, in omitting the whole Markan explanation of who the woman is (Matt 15:25), but strengthens Mark's προσέπεσεν to read προσεκύνει, thus combining the motifs of coming and exhorting. Luke 7:3 uses ἐρωτῶν, but then in Luke 7:4 uses a reminiscence of the Q verb παρεκάλουν.

Luke's formulation ἐρωτῶν αὐτὸν ὅπως ἐλθὼν διασώσῃ τὸν δοῦλον αὐτοῦ is quite parallel to the language of John 4:47b: ἠρώτα ἵνα καταβῇ καὶ ἰάσηται αὐτοῦ τὸν υἱόν, ἤμελλεν γὰρ ἀποθνῄσκειν (cf. Luke 7:2: ἤμελλεν τελευτᾶν). This would suggest that this participial phrase was in Q, if it were not for the almost equally similar formulation in Mark 7:26b: καὶ ἠρώτα αὐτὸν ἵνα τὸ δαιμόνιον ἐκβάλῃ ἐκ τῆς θυγατρὸς αὐτῆς. Thus it seems quite possible that it is a motif in the oral presentation of healing stories. (It is less likely to be that Luke is dependent on Mark, with the Johannine parallel only coincidental or dependent on Luke, while reverting to the customary ἵνα of Mark 7:26.) The verb ἐρωτάω is typical of Luke but not of Q. διασῴζω is distinctively Lukan (see Q 7:2, 3, 4-6a¹²). As in Luke 7:3, δοῦλος is a Lukan replacement for παῖς (Q 7:7). See Q 7:2, 3, 4-6a¹².

Kloppenborg 2000: Matt = Q {B}, (παρακαλ)⁶ῶν αὐτόν.

Hoffmann 2001: Matt = Q {B}, (παρακαλ)⁶ῶν αὐτόν.

Q 7:2, 3, 4-6a⁷: Luke's ὅπως with indirect discourse or Matthew's direct discourse: καὶ λέγων· ... μου ... καὶ λέγει αὐτῷ· ἐγὼ ...-ω.

Luke = Q: [ὅπως]⁷

Pro

Castor 1912, 223: Reconstruction. For complete text see Q 7:1⁰ In Q (p. 6).

Schmid 1930, 252: "Hier läßt sich nachweisen, daß Lk die vollständigere und damit auch ursprünglichere Darstellung hat, die von Mt verkürzt worden ist. Während nämlich nach Mt der heidnische Hauptmann persönlich zu Jesus kommt, läßt Lk ihn überhaupt nicht."

Nolland 1989, 314: See Q 7:2, 3, 4-6a² Luke = Q, Pro (p. 80).

315-316: "In Matthew the centurion explains his own situation to Jesus. In Luke the situation is made known in the narrative. Either evangelist could be responsible [316] for the change, but the frequency of Matthew's redactional introduction of Κύριε ('Lord'; ...), Luke's double deletion of κακῶς ἔχειν, 'to be ill,' from his Markan source at 4:40, and perhaps also the similarity between Luke's 'he was about to die' and John's phrase in 4:47 (the English equivalent is identical but the Greek varies slightly), and even Matthew's possible borrowing of the word 'paralytic' from Mark 2:3, favor the originality of Luke's form."

Con

Holtzmann 1901, 344: See Q 7:2, 3, 4-6a³ Luke = Q, Con (pp. 93-94).

von Harnack 1907, 55: "Die lange Rede, die nach Luk. angeblich die Freunde halten, schlechterdings nur in den Mund des Hauptmanns selbst paßt."

von Harnack 1907, ET 1908, 76: "The long speech which St. Luke assigns to the friends is intelligible and appropriate only if it was spoken by the centurion himself."

Cadbury 1920, 79-80: "A number of instances may be quoted where Luke by omission, by combination, or by putting into indirect form, considerably shortens the dialogue of his source. [80] ... Matt 8,6 (Q) καὶ λέγων· κύριε, ὁ παῖς μου βέβληται ... 7 λέγει αὐτῷ ἐγὼ ἐλθὼν θεραπεύσω αὐτόν.—Luke 7,3 ἐρωτῶν αὐτὸν ὅπως ἐλθὼν διασώσῃ τὸν δοῦλον αὐτοῦ."

Klostermann 1929, 86: "Ὅπως ἐλθὼν διασώσῃ (luk.) κτλ.: hier will der Hauptmann noch, was er v. 6 nicht mehr will—natürlicher Mt."

Hirsch 1941, 89: See Q 7:2, 3, 4-6a³ Luke = Q, Con (p. 98).

Jeremias 1956, 26⁹⁷: "Lukas hat, um diese scharfe Ablehnung [Matt 8:7] zu umgehen, die Einleitung der Geschichte völlig neu gefaßt (7,2-6a.7a)."

Jeremias 1956, ET 1958, 30[3]: "In order to avoid this harsh refusal [Matt 8:7], Luke has completely recast the introduction to the story (7.2-6a, 7a)."

Schramm 1971, 40-42: "Daß auch in Lk 7,1-10 Quellenkombination vorliegt, ist evident. In den Versen 6c-9, die bis in Einzelheiten mit Mt 8,8-10 übereinstimmen, ist ein Grundbericht [Q] greifbar, der vom παῖς (Lk 7,7; Mt 8,6.8.13) des Centurio erzählte. Lk 7,1-6b und 10 dagegen sind durch terminologische [41] —hier ist durchweg vom δοῦλος des Hauptmanns die Rede— und inhaltliche Charakteristika von diesem Grundbericht unterschieden und als Teil einer abweichenden Ausprägung der Geschichte ausgewiesen. ...

"Besonderes Kennzeichen der 7,1-6b.10 [42] vorliegenden Lk-S-Fassung war der indirekte Verkehr zwischen Jesus und dem Hauptmann. Die jüdischen Ältesten erbitten die Hilfe (V 3), Freunde wehren Jesu Kommen ab (v 6b). Lk läßt sie sich dabei des Wortes bedienen, das nach dem Grundbericht der Hauptmann selbst spricht (Mt 8,8f.)."

Schulz 1972, 237: "Aber wahrscheinlicher ist doch, daß die Umformung der direkten Rede zu einem bloß erzählenden Bericht das Werk des Lk ist und mit dem lk Einschub Vv 3-6 zusammenhängt."

237-238: "Die Vv 3-6a bei Lk haben keine Parallele bei Mt und sind lk Erweiterung der Geschichte vom [238] Hauptmann.[410] Auch sachlich erweist sich der Einschub als sek."

238[410]: "Ἐρωτᾶν ist bei Lk stark gehäuft (Ev ca 9mal trad; ca 5mal red; Apg 7mal; dagegen Mk 3mal; Mt 4mal—verbunden mit ὅπως auch Lk 11,37 red)."

Lange 1973, 42[50]: "Mt 8,7 ist erstaunt oder entrüstet abweisende Frage. ... Der hierin gelegene oder empfundene Anstoß könnte alsbald zu dem erbaulich vermittelnden Ausbau geführt haben, wie Lk 7,3-5 ihn bietet. Diese Entwicklung ist mir wahrscheinlicher als die These, Matthäus habe die bei Lk erhaltene ältere Gestalt gekürzt ... und ihr den so anstößigen Auftakt gegeben. Für die Deutung von Mt 8,7 im Sinn einer abweisenden Frage und für die Ursprünglichkeit eines solchen Anfangs der Perikope spricht m.E. Mk 7,24-30 vgl. V. 27. Es ist gerade eine Pointe der alten Erzählung, daß der Glaube des Heiden gerade am Widerstand (des Juden) Jesu(s) wächst, so erstaunliche 'Lösungen' sieht und darin sein Format offenbart. ...—Matthäus läßt die ursprüngliche Härte betont stehen und sich vor dieser den Glauben des Hauptmanns erheben."

Busse 1977, 143: "Weiterhin läßt sich die Bearbeitung konsequent aus der ursprünglichen Fassung ableiten. Dort (Mt 8,7 = Q) reagiert Jesus auf das Ansinnen, als Jude einem Heiden helfen zu sollen (vgl Mk 7,27f.), mit einer abweisenden Frage. Sie kann der Anstoß gewesen sein, mit den Delegationen, die einen direkten Kontakt zwischen Jesus und dem Mann verhindern, das Kommen Jesu (Lk 7,6) zugunsten des Hauptmanns zu motivieren."

148[1]: "V 3b zeigt red. Beeinflussung. Die Verbindung von ἐρωτᾶν mit ὅπως findet sich bei ihm in 11,37 und Apg 23,10 und 25,3."

Muhlack 1979, 43: "Die Perikope bezweckt nicht mehr allein, den Glauben des Centurio zu zeigen. Wegen seiner Botschaft an Jesus fehlen Worte wie Matthäus' ἐγὼ θεραπεύσω αὐτόν; sie sind nur dem Centurio selbst, nicht seinen Boten gegenüber wichtig."

Neirynck 1979, 109-110: See Q 7:2, 3, 4-6a³ Luke = Q, Con (pp. 107-108).

Jeremias 1980, 152: See Q 7:2, 3, 4-6a⁶ Luke = Q, Con (p. 141).

Schweizer 1982, 86 (ET 1984, 131): See Q 7:2, 3, 4-6a³ Luke = Q, Con (p. 109).

Dauer 1984, 113-114: See Q 7:2, 3, 4-6a⁶ Luke = Q, Con (p. 141).

116: "Rückschauend läßt sich als lk Redaktion feststellen: ... ἐρωτῶν αὐτὸν ὅπως."

Schnelle 1987, 102: "Matthäus steht am Anfang der Q-Überlieferung näher als Lukas. Dies ergibt sich aus ... dem unmittelbaren Auftreten und der direkten Rede des Centurio."

Schnelle 1987, ET 1992, 88: "At the beginning, Matthew is closer to Q than is Luke. This is seen from ... the immediate appearance and direct address of the centurion."

Crossan 1991, 326, 328 (GT 1994, 431, 433): See Q 7:2, 3, 4-6a³ Luke = Q, Con (p. 112).

Catchpole 1992, 531 [297]: "Given so extensive a correspondence [between Mark 5:21-43 and Q 7:1-10] it is readily understandable that Luke should move over from the one story to the other a series of details. ... From ἵνα ἐλθὼν... σωθῇ (Mark 5,23) there develops the ὅπως ἐλθὼν διασώσῃ in Luke 7,3."

Jacobson 1992, 108-109: See Q 7:2, 3, 4-6a³ Luke = Q, Con (p. 113).

Dunderberg 1994, 85-89: See Q 7:2, 3, 4-6a³ Luke = Q, Con (pp. 114-116).

Gagnon 1994b, 137: "Luke's version cannot represent the original Q text since a request by the centurion that Jesus 'come' would stand in direct contradiction to the core Q saying (viz., 'Don't come to my house')."

Landis 1994, 21: Landis argues that ἐρωτάω with ὅπως comes from Lukan Sondergut.

Merklein 1994, 100: See Q 7:2, 3, 4-6a³ Luke = Q, Con (pp. 118-119).

Matt = Q: (καὶ λέγων· ... μου ... καὶ λέγει αὐτῷ· ἐγὼ ...-ω)⁷

Pro

Wellhausen 1904b, 27: "Bemerkenswert ist ἐλθών in 7,3: Jesus wird anfangs doch gebeten, er solle kommen. Dadurch wird die Auffassung von Mt. 8,6 als Frage bestätigt. Bei Lc sträubt sich Jesus aber nicht."

von Harnack 1907, 56: "Daß Matth. den in Q überlieferten Text geändert hat (man beachte das für Q so charakteristische ἐγώ in v. 7 und anderes), läßt sich nicht nachweisen."

91: Reconstruction. Harnack omits the second καί: "καὶ λέγων ... λέγει αὐτῷ· ἐγὼ ...-ω." For complete text see Q 7:1⁶ Luke = Q, Pro (p. 55).

von Harnack 1907, ET 1908, 77: "It cannot be shown that St. Matthew has altered the text of Q (note among other things the ἐγώ of verse 7, which is so characteristic of Q)."

131: Reconstruction. Harnack omits the second καί: "καὶ λέγων ... λέγει αὐτῷ· ἐγὼ ...-ω." For complete text see Q 7:1⁶ Luke = Q, Pro (p. 55).

B. Weiß 1908, 15: Reconstruction. Weiß omits the initial καί in accordance with his emendation of Matthew's participle παρακαλῶν to an aorist in Q, παρεκάλει. For complete text see Q 7:1⁰ In Q (p. 5).

Crum 1927, 138: Reconstruction. For complete text see Q 7:2, 3, 4-6a¹ Luke = Q, Pro (pp. 71-72).

Schlatter 1931, 252: "Die Rede des Hauptmanns muß in der Quelle nahe mit dem verwandt gewesen sein, was er bei Mat. sagt. Auch bei ihr bewog er Jesus durch die Weise, wie er bat, ihm die Heilung zu gewähren, und auch bei ihr kam zum Ausdruck, daß mit dem Wort Jesu dem Bittenden alles gegeben sei, was er bei Jesus suche. Wie aber im einzelnen das Gespräch formuliert war, ist nicht mehr erkennbar."

Jeremias 1956, 25-26: "Die Antwort Jesu auf die Bitte des Heiden ist, wie sich aus dem Vergleich [26] mit Joh 4,48 ergibt, als Frage zu lesen: ἐγὼ ἐλθὼν θεραπεύσω αὐτόν; (Mth 8,7). wieder lehnt Jesus also scharf ab."

Jeremias 1956, ET 1958, 30: "Jesus' answer to the request of the Gentile should be read as a question, as is shown by a comparison with John 4.48: ἐγὼ ἐλθὼν θεραπεύσω αὐτόν; (Matt. 8.7). Again Jesus brusquely refuses."

Haenchen 1959a, 23 [1965, 82]: "Zahn [1910, 340] und Wellhausen [1904b, 27] nahmen an, was heute fast zur Communis opinio geworden ist: Jesu Antwort sei in der ursprünglichen Überlieferung eine befremdete Frage gewesen.¹"

23-24¹ [82-83]: Haenchen refutes Bultmann's argument that Jesus' question (ἐγὼ ἐλθὼν θεραπεύσω αὐτόν;) derives from knowledge of Mark 7:24-30 par Matt 15:21-28, thereby indirectly arguing for the presence of the question in Q.

Siegman 1968, 192: "The original Q version contained a rebuff, if Mt 8,7 is to be read as a question. This also Jn preserves in a way that is also a lesson and a warning as to the role of miracles in the process of faith."

George 1972, 71: See Q 7:2, 3, 4-6a¹³ Luke = Q, Con (p. 224).

Schulz 1972, 237: "Aber wahrscheinlicher ist doch, daß die Umformung der direkten Rede zu einem bloß erzählenden Bericht das Werk des Lk ist und mit dem lk Einschub Vv 3-6 zusammenhängt. Daß in Q die Krankheit des Kindes vom Vater geschildert wurde, wie dies bei Mt der Fall ist, ist wahrscheinlich.⁴⁰⁷"

237⁴⁰⁷: "Das Wort des Vaters von seiner Unwürde (Mt V 8) setzt nämlich die Abweisung Jesu (Mt V 7) voraus, und diese wiederum ein entsprechendes Gesuch des Vaters. Dieses könnte zwar auch nur erzählt gewesen sein, aber da direkte Eingriffe des Mt nicht wahrscheinlich zu machen sind, wird man die direkte Rede in Mt V 6 für ursprünglich halten."

Lange 1973, 49: "Jesus beantwortet das Ansinnen des Heiden zunächst mit einer erstaunt oder entrüstet ablehnenden Frage (Mt 8,7), die wohl der ursprünglichen Form von Q entspricht."

Polag 1979, 38: Reconstruction. Apart from the omission of the initial καί, Polag gives Matthew's text. For complete text see Q 7:1⁰ In Q (pp. 9-10).

Schenk 1981, 37: Reconstruction. For complete text see Q 7:1⁰ In Q (p. 10).

Wegner 1985, 37-41: For Matthew's direct speech, see Q 7:2, 3, 4-6a⁶ Matt = Q, Pro (pp. 143-144).

134: For καί: "Der Befund im ersten Ev zeigt, daß das anreihende καί von Mt sehr selten red eingesetzt, dagegen aber häufig durch δέ, τότε oder andere Konstruktionen ersetzt wird. Daher wird man das καί in 8,6 wohl eher der Trad zuweisen müssen."

141: For καὶ λέγων: "Bei der Wendung καὶ λέγων ließ sich eine mt Red mit letzter Sicherheit nicht beweisen. Sie könnte dem ersten Evangelisten bereits trad vorgelegt haben."

154: For ἐγώ: "Was nun Mt 8,7 (QMt!) betrifft, so hängt viel davon ab, wie man Mt 8,7 gegenüber Lk 7,3ff beurteilt. Unter Forschern, die der Meinung sind, Mt habe die Lk-Version gekürzt, ist natürlich eine Vorentscheidung zugunsten einer mt Red des ἐγώ bereits gefallen. Bei anderen, die sich für die Ursprünglichkeit der kürzeren Fassung des Mt entscheiden, wird das Pronomen meistens für ursprünglich gehalten. Dieser letzteren Position wollen auch wir uns anschließen, zumal die Gesamtanalyse zeigen wird, daß Lk 7,3ff sehr wahrscheinlich überlieferungsgeschichtlich für sek gehalten werden kann. Hinzu kommt, daß die Verwendung des emphatischen ἐγώ, wie sie auSt sehr wahrscheinlich vorliegt, auch an anderen Stellen für Jesus belegt ist."

Catchpole 1992, 522 [1993, 286]: "Direct speech by the centurion in the presence of Jesus is suggested by (i) Matthew/Luke agreement in having *some* direct speech by someone, (ii) the greater suitability of Matt 8,8-9/Luke 7,6b.7b-8 as the speech of someone who is present, and (iii) the overall tendency of Q to reduce narrative to a minimum."

527 [292]: Reconstruction: "καὶ λέγων; ... λέγει αὐτῷ. ... -ω." For complete text see Q 7:1⁰ In Q (p. 14).

Sevenich-Bax 1993, 179: "Der Vers Mt 8,7 hat bei Lukas keine direkte Entsprechung. Dies kann allerdings nicht verwundern, da Lukas durch den Einschub von Lk 7,3-6b andere Akzente setzt. Da auf die Mt 8,6 ausgesprochene (implizite) Bitte des Hauptmanns erzähltechnisch eine Reaktion erfolgen muß, die ihrerseits erst die Vertrauensäußerung VV. 8b-9 evoziert, muß damit gerechnet werden, daß Matthäus hier den Wortlaut der Logienquelle wiedergibt.[4]"

179[4]: "So auch Schulz [1972, 238]. Ähnlich Wegner [1985, 149-157], der seine Ergebnisse allerdings nicht auf erzähltechnische bzw. kompositionelle Erfordernisse, sondern auf wortstatistische Beobachtungen stützt. Diese haben hier jedoch nur marginalen Aussagewert: Selbst wenn für die eine oder andere Vokabel matthäische Redaktion wahrscheinlich gemacht werden kann ..., bleibt die im Ersatz angebotene Rekonstruktion in hohem Maß unsicher, da nicht verifizierbar."

238: Reconstruction. For complete text see Q 7:1[0] In Q (p. 15).

Dunderberg 1994, 85-89: See Q 7:2, 3, 4-6a[3] Luke = Q, Con (pp. 114-116).

Gagnon 1994b, 135: Reconstruction: for καὶ λέγων only; for the remainder, see Gagnon 1994b at Matt = Q, Con (pp. 158-159). For complete text see Q 7:1[0] In Q (p. 15).

Landis 1994, 7: "Mt dürfte in diesem Vers recht genau den Q-Wortlaut wiedergeben. Schon die Einleitungswendung καὶ λέγων scheint traditionell zu sein, denn Mt zeigt durchaus keine besondere Vorliebe für diesen Ausdruck. Pleonastisches λέγων ist zwar für Q singulär, die Formulierung paßt aber gut zum vorangehenden παρακαλῶν αὐτόν.

"Auch die direkte Rede, in welcher der Hauptmann die Situation beschreibt, ist wohl ursprünglich. Daß in Q—anders als bei Lk—die Krankheit des Jungen vom ἑκατοντάρχης selbst geschildert wurde, ist deshalb wahrscheinlich, weil die sicher auf Q zurückgehende V.8 die abweisende Äußerung Jesu in V.7, diese aber wiederum ein Gesuch des Hauptmanns voraussetzt."

9: "In V.8,7 hält sich Mt wohl noch mehr als bisher an die Q-Vorlage. Schwierig zu entscheiden ist allerdings, ob der Versanfang im Praesens historicum (καὶ λέγει) redaktionell überarbeitet ist. Bezüglich des Praesens historicum ist der Befund beim sonstigen Vorgehen der mt Redaktion nicht eindeutig. So übernimmt es Mt zwar einerseits nur selten von Mk, fügt es aber andererseits recht oft von sich aus in den Mk-Stoff ein. In den Q-Texten verwendet oft nur Mt das Praesens historicum, was aber wohl damit zusammenhängt, daß es von Lk allgemein gemieden wird. Gegen einen redaktionellen Charakter des Ausdrucks spricht, daß Mt selbst wohl eher die asyndetische Konstruktion bevorzugt und nur λέγει eingesetzt hätte, wie er es häufig bei seinen Mk-Vorlagen tat. Die Parataxe καὶ λέγει scheint demgegenüber eher für Q typisch zu sein. Sie ist also wohl von Mt aus dieser Quelle übernommen worden."

9, 10, 17: Reconstruction: For complete text, see Q 7:1[6] Luke = Q, Pro (p. 57).

Meier 1994, 769[193]: "I think that Schulz [1972, 236-240] and Fitzmyer [1981, 648-649] make a good case for the position that, apart from the redactional insertion in Matt 8:11-12, Matthew's version of the story is closer to the Q form than is Luke's version. In particular: ... Matthew and John agree that the petitioner comes to Jesus and speaks face-to-face with him; neither knows anything of the two Lucan delegations."

International Q Project 1995, 478: Reconstruction. For complete text see Q 7:1⁰ In Q (p. 16).

Wiefel 1998, 161: "Der lineare Aufbau der Erzählung bei Matthäus (direkte Begegnung des Hauptmanns mit Jesus) stellt die ursprünglichere Form dar."

Con

Parker 1953, 63-65: See Q 7:1⁶ Matt = Q, Con (pp. 58-60).

Held 1960, 221-223: "3. Das Gespräch als die Mitte der Wundergeschichten.

"Viele der bisherigen Beobachtungen zur Form der matthäischen Wundergeschichten deuten darauf hin, daß für den Evangelisten die in ihnen gesprochenen Worte entscheidende Bedeutung haben im Unterschied zu den erzählen Teilen. Offenbar sind Rede und Gegenrede für ihn die Hauptsache in den Wundergeschichten.

"Freilich finden sich auch in der ihm vorgegebenen Überlieferung Erzählungen, in denen nicht das Wunder selbst im Mittelpunkt [222] steht, sondern das Gespräch, das ihm vorangeht. Das ist etwa der Fall in der Blindenheilung von Jericho (Mk. 10,46ff.), beim Hauptmann von Kapernaum (Mt. 8,8-10 = Lk. 7,7b-9) und bei der Kanaanitin (Mk. 7,24-30). Das Wechselgespräch Jesu mit dem Hilfesuchenden hat hier das Wunder an den Rand gedrängt. Aber es ist doch in allen drei Fällen Matthäus, der den Gesprächscharakter dieser Geschichten am reinsten zur Geltung bringt. Das kann am klarsten anhand der Geschichte vom Hauptmann gezeigt werden.

"Während Lukas das Gespräch zwischen Jesus und dem Hauptmann im Rahmen einer regelrechten Geschichte bringt, während er ihm einen rein erzählenden Anfang (Lk. 7,2-3) und einen ebenso erzählenden Abschluß (Lk. 7,10) gibt und novellistisch ausgestaltet,¹ berichtet Matthäus im ganzen nur einen Dialog von zwei Gesprächsgängen, dessen Einleitung und Schluß formelhaft sind, d.h. nicht erzählen wollen. Dem ersten Evangelisten geht es offensichtlich um das Gespräch zwischen dem Hilfesuchenden und Jesus. Auch in der Geschichte von der Kanaanitin und in den Blindenheilungen von Mt. 9 und 20 hat er das Gespräch völlig in den Mittelpunkt gestellt. Die Elemente der Wundergeschichte, die sich etwa Mk. 7,24b und in dem offenbar typischen Fernheilungsschluß² finden, hat er beseitigt bzw. durch seine stereotypen Formeln in Mt. 8,13 und 15,28 ersetzt. Gerade diese Formeln aber setzen im Zusammenhang mit der vorhergehenden ebenfalls stereotypen Formel vom Glauben die Konstatierung des Wunders mit dem Gespräch in Beziehung, das Jesus bei Matthäus in beiden Fällen als Ausdruck des Glaubens bezeichnet.

"Auch in den anderen Heilungsgeschichten legt Matthäus auf die Redeteile den Nachdruck. Fast alle seine Heilungswunder setzen nach kurzer formelhafter Einleitung mit einer direkten Rede ein: Mt. 8,2; 8,6; 9,18; 9,21; 9,27; 15,22; 17,15; 20,30. Die Tatsache der direkten Rede gewinnt an Gewicht, wenn man sich vor Augen stellt, daß Markus und Lukas mehrmals eine solche Bitte um Heilung in indirekter Rede bringen (Mk. 7,26.32; 8,22; Lk. 7,3; 8,41), Lukas sogar einmal die von Markus (5,28) und Matthäus (9,21) gebotene (Gedanken-) Rede der blutflüssigen Frau fortläßt (Lk. 8,44). So darf man zunächst feststellen, daß die in direkter Rede an Jesus [223] gerichtete Bitte ein wesentlicher Baustein der Wunderheilung im Matthäusevangelium ist."

222[1]: "Vgl. die Steigerung der Not (Lk. 7,2 ἤμελλεν τελευτᾶν) und die Hervorhebung des persönlichen Verhältnisses zwischen dem Hauptmann und seinem Knecht (Lk. 7,2 ὃς ἦν αὐτῷ ἔντιμος)."

222[2]: "Man beachte die Formelhaftigkeit und den Gleichlaut der beiden Sätze Mk. 7,30 und Lk. 7,10!"

Held 1960, ET 1963, 233-235: "3. *Conversation as the centre of the miracle stories.*

"Many of the observations so far made on the form of the Matthaean [234] miracle stories point to the fact that for the evangelist the words spoken in them carry decisive meaning as distinct from the descriptive portions. Obviously speech and counter-speech is the thing that matters most for him in the miracle stories.

"Of course, there are also in the tradition as it came to him narratives in which the miracle itself does not occupy the centre, but the conversation that precedes it. That is the case, for example, with the healing of the blind man of Jericho (Mark 10:46 ff.), with the centurion of Capernaum (Matt. 8:8-10 = Luke 7:7b-9) and with the Canaanite woman (Mark 7:24-30). The conversation of Jesus with the suppliant has here pushed the miracle to the side. It is Matthew, however, who in all three cases brings out the conversational character of these stories most clearly. This can be shown most effectively by means of the story of the centurion.

"Whereas Luke sets the conversation between Jesus and the centurion in the framework of a normal story and gives it a purely descriptive beginning (Luke 7:2-3) and a similarly descriptive ending (Luke 7:10) and arranges it in a novelistic fashion,[1] Matthew reports in all only one dialogue consisting of two pieces of conversation, the introduction and conclusion of which are formal, that is, are not intended as descriptive. What matters to the first evangelist is obviously the conversation between the suppliant and Jesus. In the story of the Canaanite woman and the healing of the blind men in Matthew 9 and 20 as well he has placed the conversation completely in the centre. The elements of the miracle story, such as are found in Mark 7:24b and in the clearly typical conclusion[2] of the case of healing from a distance, he has removed, or rather replaced by his stereotyped formulae in Matt. 8:13 and 15:28. But these very formulae, in association with the preceding, similarly stereotyped formula about faith, set the notice of a miraculous event in relationship with the conversation, which in both cases in Matthew Jesus denotes as an expression of faith.

"In the other healing stories, too, Matthew lays emphasis on the sections containing speeches. Nearly all his healing miracles begin, after a brief formal introduction, with direct speech: Matt 8:2; [235] 8:6; 9:18; 9:21; 9:27; 15:22; 17:15; 20:30. The fact of the direct speech gains in importance when it is remembered that Mark and Luke frequently present such a request for healing in indirect speech (Mark 7:26, 32; 8:22; Luke 7:3; 8:41), and in one case Luke even omits (Luke 8:44) the speech (thought) of the woman with the haemorrhage which is given in Mark (5:28) and Matthew (9:21). Hence one may conclude, in the first place, that the request addressed to Jesus in direct speech is an essential component in the construction of the healing miracle in Matthew's Gospel."

234[1]: "Cf. the heightening of the need (Luke 7:2 ἤμελλεν τελευτᾶν) and the underlining of the personal relationship between the centurion and his servant (Luke 7:2 ὃς ἦν αὐτῷ ἔντιμος)."

234[2]: "Note the formalistic nature and the similarity of the two sentences in Mark 7:30 and Luke 7:10."

Schulz 1972, 237: "Mt könnte den in seiner Vorlage als Feststellung formulierten V 6 unter Einfügung der κύριε-Anrede in direkte Rede umgeformt haben." But see Schulz at Luke = Q, Con (p. 149), and Matt = Q, Pro (pp. 151-152).

Frankemölle 1974, 112-113: See Q 7:2, 3, 4-6a[3] Luke = Q, Pro (p. 89).

Howard 1975, 172: "Das bedeutet, daß man hier, ohne lukanische Eingriffe in den Text bestreiten zu können, dem dritten Evangelisten wieder den Vorzug geben kann. Er steht der Q-Überlieferung am nächsten. Mt hat diese Überlieferung entsprechend seiner Behandlung der Wundererzählungen umgestaltet. Sein Satz V. 7 entspricht der Haltung Jesu nach Lk 7,6a und könnte auch der Haltung Jesu selber entsprechen. Aber die Formulierung in Mt 8,7 geht auf den Redaktor selber zurück."

Gundry 1982, 141: "Matthew omits the part of the story concerning the delegation of Jewish elders. The centurion now appears to approach Jesus directly. ...

"Παρακαλῶν and λέγων come from the account of the Jewish elders' plea to Jesus (see Luke 7:4)."

142: "In v 6 Matthew makes a request out of the description of the servant's illness (so Luke) in order to compensate for his omitting the Jewish elders' words to Jesus. In this direct discourse he inserts 'Lord.'"

142-143: "Verse 7 opens with a vivid historical present tense in λέγει (not in Luke). The word appears in this form often throughout chaps. 8-9 and typifies Matthew's style (47,11). It always has Jesus as its subject in these chapters, and it points up Matthew's emphasis on his authoritative words. Again Matthew makes a direct quotation ('I will come and heal him') out of a description ('and Jesus went with them,' so Luke). None of the words in the direct quotation is paralleled in Luke even though the thought corresponds. Matthew likes the emphatic ἐγώ (12-13,3), especially for Jesus. Here, as in the Sermon on the Mount, it emphasizes [143] Jesus' authority."

Dauer 1984, 101-102: See Q 7:2, 3, 4-6a¹ Matt = Q, Con (pp. 73-74).

Wegner 1985, 135-136: For λέγων: "1. Das Ptz. λέγων erscheint 179x im NT, davon zu fast einem Drittel im MtEv. Mt bringt λέγων/λέγοντες o.ä. unabhängig von Lk und als Eintragung in seinem Mk-Stoff 11x statt eines mk Verbum finitum mit καί, und 27x bei anderen Fällen unterschiedlicher Natur. Demgegenüber lassen sich lediglich 9 Fälle ermitteln, in denen Mt ein mk λέγων bzw. λέγοντες ersetzt. Sprechen schon diese Zahlen für die Wahrscheinlichkeit einer mt Red, so wird dies noch dadurch erhärtet, daß λέγειν in Mt 8,6 in Verbindung mit προσέρχεσθαι begegnet, zumal nach Held [1960, 215-216] 'die Verbindung von προσέρχεσθαι und λέγειν … eine stereotype Formel des Matthäus zur Einleitung von Reden und Gesprächen' ist.

"2. Das hier pleonastisch gebrauchte λέγων gehörte kaum urspr zu Q; sonst müßten ja beim hohen Q-Vorkommen von λέγειν weitere Belege vorliegen, was aber nicht der Fall ist. Lediglich in QMt erscheint es außer auSt noch 6x: Mt 3,2 (QMt?); 5,2 (Lk 6,20: ἔλεγεν); 7,21 (Lk 6,46: καλεῖτε); 22,1 (Einleitungsvers!); 22,4 und 25,20. Daß Lk es an all diesen Stellen kaum ausgelassen haben wird, geht schon daraus [136] hervor, daß auch von ihm pleonastisches λέγων/λέγοντες mit Vorliebe verwendet wird."

152-153: "Gibt die Verwendung von λέγειν als PH [*praesens historicum*; historical present] keine sicheren Indizien für Trad oder mt Red auSt, so führt vielleicht die Tatsache weiter, daß λέγει in Mt 8,7 möglicherweise in asyndetischer Konstruktion steht. In dieser Konstruktion wird λέγει nämlich mehrfach von Mt gegenüber dem Mk-Text red hinzugefügt[17], so daß von daher eine mt Red recht wahrscheinlich erscheint.

[153] "Dies wird auch dadurch bekräftigt, daß für asyndetisches λέγει kein sicherer Q-Beleg vorliegt. QMt und QLk haben es, von Mt 8,7 abgesehen, jeweils 1x: Mt 18,22 diff Lk 17,4 und Lk 19,22 diff Mt. Auch asyndetisches

ἔφη erscheint niemals in Q, aber 3x in QMt: Mt 4,7 und 25,21.23 diff Lk. Bedenkt man nun, daß Q demgegenüber deutlich die Parataxe bevorzugt, so liegt es nahe zu vermuten, Mt habe λέγει als Ersatz für eine ihm urspr durch Parataxe + Verbum finitum vorgelegenen Konstruktion benutzt. Danach hätte der ihm urspr vorgelegene Wortlaut etwa καὶ εἶπεν oder καὶ λέγει gelautet.

"Man wird daher bezüglich des λέγει mit mt Red einer vor-mt Konstruktion zu rechnen haben." But see Wegner at Matt = Q, Pro (p. 152).

152¹⁷: "Vgl. Mt 19,7.8.10.20.21 (v.l.); 20,21.22b.23a.33; 22,21; 26,35a.64; 27,22b und 16,15 diff Mk und dazu Neirynck [1974, 212-213, 206]. Besonders Schenk [1981; cf. 1987,465; 465³] hebt das asyndetisch konstruierte PH als für Mt charakteristisch hervor. Er stellt hierzu 29 Belege fest, die a) ausschließlich in lokutionären Verben, und b) 'nie in Anfangspositionen von Perikopen oder Abschnitten' (ebd.) vorkommen."

Luz 1990, 13⁶: "Matthäismen sind in V 5-7: Προσέρχομαι, λέγων, κύριε, λέγει (Präs. historicum bei Jesuswort, …) evt. βασανίζομαι, ἐλθών."

Luz 1990, ET 2001, 8⁶: "Mattheisms in vv. 5-7 are …: προσέρχομαι, λέγων, κύριε, λέγει (historical present when Jesus speaks …), perhaps βασανίζομαι, ἐλθών."

Davies and Allison 1991, 19: "Pace Schulz [1972, 237], Matthew has probably turned indirect speech (so Luke and Jn 4.47) into direct speech, as in 26.1-2 diff. Mk 14.1."

21: "Καὶ λέγει αὐτῷ· ἐγὼ ἐλθὼν θεραπεύσω αὐτόν; The formulation may be editorial."

Catchpole 1992, 525-527 [1993, 289-292]: Concerning ἐγώ alone, Catchpole summarizes arguments for and against understanding Jesus' response in Matt 8:7 (Q 7:3) as a deliberative question related to the issue of Jewish purity laws. He concludes that Jesus' response is not a deliberative question and that ἐγώ should not be over-interpreted. Noting several instances elsewhere of Matthew inserting ἐγώ into the narrative, on p. 527 (292) he concludes: "In view of the unconvincing character of the arguments for understanding Jesus' response as a deliberative question, better inferences can now be drawn. The first is that ἐγώ is MattR."

Gagnon 1994b, 135: Reconstruction. For complete text see Q 7:1⁰ In Q (p. 15).

136: "In my estimation, Matthew has … added an indignant or disbelieving question on the part of Jesus in order to heighten the literary tension and so to magnify the ultimate victory of faith."

137: "In favour of the contention that Matthew inserted Jesus' initial indignant response (v. 7, and thus also v. 8a) is Matthew's addition of the oppositional dialogue of the disciples and Jesus to Mark's story of the Syrophoenician woman, against which the faith of the 'Canaanite' woman shines the more brightly (15.23-4; cf. also the insertions and creation of dialogue in 3.14-15; 19.18; 21.11, 41-3; 22.7, 42-3; 26.25; 27.21, 24-5). ... If Matthew's version were original, ... one would have expected Luke to reproduce it between Luke 7.5 and 7.6 as a word of Jesus (especially since he had the option of interpreting the remark as a positive response). In addition, the pericope makes perfectly good sense without Matt 8.7-8a. Therefore, I think it preferable to regard the similarities between Matt 8.7 and Luke 7.3 as coincidental."

Emendation = Q: καὶ <εἶπεν>⁷ ...

Wegner 1985, 136: "Der Befund in Q deutet also darauf hin, daß λέγων auSt von Mt selbst eingetragen wurde. Da nun das vorangehende καί sehr wahrscheinlich traditionell ist, kommt ein Ersatz am ehesten in Frage. Vielleicht las Mt in seiner Vorlage einfach καί + Verbum finitum, etwa καὶ εἶπεν. Dafür spräche, daß die Wendung auch in Q auftaucht, wie aus Lk 4,6/Mt 4,9 und vielleicht Lk 4,9 und 9,58 diff Mt zu entnehmen ist."

152-153: See Wegner at Matt = Q, Con (pp. 157-158).

156: "Bei λέγει vermuteten wir einen Ersatz für urspr καί = Verbum finitum (etwa καὶ λέγει oder καὶ εἶπεν)." Elsewhere, Wegner decides for Matt = Q, Pro (p. 152).

270: Reconstruction: "καὶ εἶπεν." For complete text see Q 7:1⁰ In Q (pp. 11-12).

Emendation = Q: <ἵνα>⁷

Lindars 1992, 210: Reconstruction: "ἵνα." For complete text see Q 7:1⁶ Luke = Q, Pro (p. 56).

Evaluations

Johnson 2000: Matt = Q {B}, (καὶ λέγων· ... μου ... καὶ λέγει αὐτῷ· ἐγὼ ...-ω)⁷.

Nolland is not entirely correct about John's use of indirect speech. The initial plea of John 4:47 is in indirect speech, but Jesus' response in 4:48 is direct speech. Therefore, John does not provide persuasive support for Luke's indirect speech. On the contrary, Jeremias suggests that Jesus' negative statement in John is reminiscent of Jesus' negative question in Matthew (i.e., Q approximates the tradition behind John 4:48). Once again, there is little to speak for Luke's version except for the position that Matthew essentially created most or all of the variations from Q in 8:5b-8 when the double delegation was eliminated.

Cadbury gives several examples of Luke shortening dialogue by putting speech into indirect form. One can turn to a number of Markan miracle stories to see this demonstrated, such as Luke's versions of the Gerasene Demoniac and the Healing of Jairus' Daughter. Use of ἐρωτάω with ὅπως is distinctive of Luke (Schulz, Busse).

Matthew may prefer direct speech (Held), but Q's proclivity is toward lack of narrative and a propensity for dialogue in what little narrative it contains. Catchpole makes the observation that both narratives actually have some direct speech. However, Luke includes it in the worthiness speech of the elders, which must be judged redactional if the delegation of elders itself is redaction. With nothing to speak for Luke and with Matthew's text best approximating Q style, Matthew's direct speech is most likely from Q.

Robinson 2000: Matt = Q {C}, ⟦(καὶ λέγων· ... μου ... καὶ λέγει αὐτῷ· ἐγώ ...-ω)⁷⟧.

In the case of blind Bartimaeus (Mark 10:46-52), Held is not accurate to describe Matthew as reducing narration to make dialogue central. The reduction in Matthew does take place in both instances (Matt 9:27-31; 20:29-34), but Matt 9:27 omits Mark's repetition of a saying, "Son of David, have mercy on me!" (Mark 10:48). The following dialogue (Mark 10:49): "And Jesus stopped and said, 'Call him.' And they called the blind man, saying to him, 'Take heart; rise, he is calling you,'" is omitted both at Matt 9:28 and at Matt 20:32. The saying of Mark 10:52 is in Matt 9:29, but omitted in Matt 20:34, whereas in both cases Matthew adds the narrative detail absent from Mark that Jesus touched their eyes. Hence, what is clear in this instance is that Matthew does compress the stories (and has a vested interest in varying the one from the other, to obscure the duplication). What is not clear is the assumption that what gets cut is always narration and what gets augmented is always dialogue.

Held appeals to Mark 7:24b as the element of a miracle story, but it is not; rather it is part of Mark's motif of the messianic secret. The "hearing" motif in Mark 7:25 (which may be what Held intended) is indeed omitted by Matthew; see Q 7:2, 3, 4-6a² above. But Matt 15:22 enlarges the narrative opening by referring to the woman as a Canaanite from those regions, which Mark 7:26 inserts somewhat later ("Hellene, Syrophoenician by race"). The supplication put in Mark 7:26b in indirect discourse (ἵνα ...) becomes in Matt 15:25 a (much briefer) appeal in direct discourse. The most prominent ingredient of Matthew increasing the dialogue is Matt 15:23-24, which begins by Jesus not answering her at all ("dialogue"?), then the disciples saying he should dismiss her, then Jesus quoting Matt 10:6. This is not an instance of Matthew preferring dialogue, but of his desire to get that rejection of the Gentile mission into this story.

Thus the emphasis on Matthew changing narration into dialogue in healing stories should not be exaggerated. What is overlooked in the subsequent appeal to Held is his opening comment (ET 234):

"Of course, there are also in the tradition as it came to him narratives in which the miracle itself does not occupy the centre, but the conversation that precedes it. That is the case, for example, with the healing of the blind man of Jericho (Mark 10.46 ff.), with the centurion of Capernaum (Matt. 8.8-10 = Luke 7.7b-9) and with the Canaanite woman (Mark 7.24-30). The conversation of Jesus with the suppliant has here pushed the miracle to the side."

That is to say, Q already anticipated Matthew's preference for dialogue over narration in these healings. Hence it is quite inappropriate to postulate as the point of departure in Q the Lukan text, since Luke's form-critical tendencies follow Mark. (One notes he usually does not change healing stories, which just means he doesn't change Mark!) It is already clear that Matthew continues several of Q's distinctive vocabulary traits (see Q 7:1[0]), and probably also, as a text oriented to sayings collections, the priority of dialogue. So it would be inappropriate to postulate the Matthean Healing of the Centurion's Boy to have begun with a form-critically correct miracle story in the Lukan-Markan style in the Q text, which Matthew then reduced to an exclusively Matthean focus on dialogue. It is more probable that Q anticipated Matthew's focus on dialogue.

Jesus' negative reaction to the idea of coming (Q 7:3) explains Luke's interpolation of the second delegation of friends saying he does not need to come. Busse sees here the motivation for both delegations. Thus Matt 8:7 needs to be presupposed in Q to suggest the Lukan delegation(s). Luke replaces Jesus' negative reaction with an effort to have the centurion cope with it by means of the delegations.

Kloppenborg 2000: Matt = Q {B}, (καὶ λέγων· ... μου ... καὶ λέγει αὐτῷ· ἐγώ ...-ω)[7].

Hoffmann 2001: Matt = Q {C}, ⟦(καὶ λέγων· ... μου ... καὶ λέγει αὐτῷ· ἐγώ ...-ω)[7]⟧.

Helds These (1960, 222f, ET 1963, 234f), daß Matthäus "die in direkter Rede an Jesus gerichtete Bitte ein wesentlicher Baustein der Wunderheilung im Matthäusevangelium ist", bedarf der Präzisierung. Redaktionell hat sie Matthäus nur in 15,22 (diff. Mk 7,26) eingeführt. In 8,2 streicht er nur das in Mk 1,40 vorgegebene ὅτι recitativum (so auch Lukas in 5,12). Dagegen übernimmt Matthäus die direkte Rede aus Markus in Mt 9,18 (mit ὅτι recitativum), in 9,21 (ohne dieses), 9,27 und 20,30 sowie in 17,15. Dadurch aber werden die von ihm aufgeführten Beispiele für eine indirekte Rede bei Mar-

kus relativiert. Auch in der Markustradition finden sich Belege für die direkte
Rede. Insofern kommt nur Mk 7,26 diff. Mt 15,22 eine gewisse Relevanz zu.
In dem Sammelbericht Mk 7,31-37/Mt 15,29-31 übergeht jedoch Matthäus
die Bitte in Mk 7,32 ganz. Mk 8,22 fehlt bei Matthäus, da er die ganze Perikope nicht übernommen hat. In Lk 8,41 hat dagegen Lukas die direkte Rede
des Jairus (Mk 5,23) teils in indirekte Rede, teils in einen Bericht umgestaltet.
Ein analoges Verfahren könnte er also auch in Q 7,2.3 angewendet haben.

Wenn Matthäus die direkte Rede also auch bevorzugt, so übernimmt er sie
doch oft aus der Tradition. Die Entscheidung in Q 7,3 ist daher—von Matthäus her—offen: Tradition oder Redaktion? Von Lukas her geurteilt, spricht
gegen die Ursprünglichkeit seiner Textfassung, daß er auch in Lk 8,41 in ähnlicher Weise eine Vorlage in indirekte Rede und Bericht umsetzt.

Q 7:2, 3, 4-6a⁸: Matthew's κύριε.

Luke = Q: ( )⁸

Pro

Con

Matt = Q: (κύριε)⁸

Pro

> **von Harnack** 1907, 91 (ET 1908, 131): Reconstruction. For complete text see Q 7:1⁶ Luke = Q, Pro (p. 55).
> **B. Weiß** 1908, 15: Reconstruction. For complete text see Q 7:1⁰ In Q (p. 5).
> **Cadbury** 1920, 79-80: See Q 7:2, 3, 4-6a⁷ Luke = Q, Con (p. 148).
> **Crum** 1927, 138: Reconstruction. For complete text see Q 7:2, 3, 4-6a¹ Luke = Q, Pro (pp. 71-72).
> **Lange** 1973, 220: "Das κύριε in Mt 8,6 ist sehr wahrscheinlich mit dem Q-Text übernommen⁶."
> 220⁶: "Die mattäische Fassung der Hauptmannsperikope steht—abgesehen von Änderungen in V. 10 und abgesehen von der Einfügung V. 11f—der Q-Fassung wohl näher als Lk."
> **Polag** 1979, 38: Reconstruction. For complete text see Q 7:1⁰ In Q (pp. 9-10).
> **Crossan** 1991, 328 (GT 1994, 433): See Q 7:2, 3, 4-6a³ Matt = Q, Pro (p. 112).
> **Landis** 1994, 7: "Ungewiß ist, ob Mt den Vokativ κύριε redaktionell einge-fügt hat. Der Evangelist setzt diese Jesusanrede zwar häufig in seine Vorlagen ein. Hier könnte sie aber ebenso traditionell sein wie in V.8, wo sie durch die Lk-Parallele für Q gesichert ist."
> 9, 17: Reconstruction. For complete text see Q 7:1⁶ Luke = Q, Pro (p. 57).

Con

> **Castor** 1912, 223: Reconstruction. For complete text see Q 7:1⁰ In Q (p. 6).
> **Zuntz** 1945, 187³: "The addition, before Matt. viii. 6, of κύριε (on the model of vv. 2 and 8) betrays the … desire to emphasize the devotion due to the Saviour. It is rightly omitted by ℵ* syˢᶜ k vulgᴰ Origen (*In Joh.* II. 12) and Hilary."

Parker 1953, 63-65: See Q 7:1⁶ Matt = Q, Con (pp. 58-60).

Held 1960, 223: "Diese Bitte um Heilung weist häufig die gleichen Züge auf. So braucht Matthäus oft die Anrede κύριε (Mt. 8,2; 8,6; 15,22; 17,15; 20,30.31), die Markus nirgendwo und Lukas nur einmal (Lk. 5,12) in der Bitte verwenden."

Held 1960, ET 1963, 235: "This request for healing frequently exhibits the same traits. Thus Matthew often uses the form of address κύριε (Matt. 8:2; 8:6; 15:22; 17:15; 20:30, 31) which Mark never uses in a request and Luke only once (Luke 5.12)."

Schulz 1972, 237: "Daß Mt in den Wortlaut eingegriffen hat, zeigen gewisse mt Spracheigentümlichkeiten.⁴⁰⁶"

237⁴⁰⁶: "Die κύριε-Anrede könnte wie in V 8 ... trad sein, wird aber von Mt häufig auch red seinen Vorlagen eingefügt (mindestens 13mal; weiterhin findet sich die κύριε-Anrede 6mal im Sondergut des Mt)."

Schenk 1981, 37: Reconstruction. For complete text see Q 7:1⁰ In Q (p. 10).

Gundry 1982, 142: "In this direct discourse he [Matthew] inserts 'Lord' (not in the initial request reported by Luke). This anticipates and parallels the same address in v 8, where it appears also in Luke. The stress on Jesus as κύριος typifies Matthew's theology (34,15) and ties the story more closely to the preceding, where the leper addresses Jesus in the same way."

Wegner 1985, 137: "Als Anrede an Jesu begegnet der Vokativ κύριε in Mt: 3x in Q (7,21.22; 8,8 par Lk), 3x in QMt (8,6.21; 18,21 diff Lk) und 4x im Sg (14,28.30; 25,37.44). Mt bringt es außerdem noch 1x als acc (15,27 par Mk), dagegen aber 12x als add: vgl. 8,2.25; 9,28; 15,22.25; 16,22; 17,4.15; 20,30.31.33 und 26,22 diff Mk. Legen schon diese Zahlen die Wahrscheinlichkeit einer mt Red auSt nahe, so wird diese noch dadurch erhärtet, daß in Übereinstimmung mit Mt 8,6 rund fünf dieser eindeutig red Belege von Mt bei der Bitte um Heilung eingesetzt werden: vgl. 8,2; 15,22; 17,15 und 20,30f. Eine mt Red kann daher auch auSt für sehr wahrscheinlich gehalten werden."

270: Reconstruction. For complete text see Q 7:1⁰ In Q (pp. 11-12).

Geist 1986, 353: "Das MtEv verwendet die κύριε-Anrede 30 mal, davon 21 mal mit hoher Wahrscheinlichkeit redaktionell. Die übernommenen Stellen stammen überwiegend aus Q. In die mk Tradition wird diese Anrede in 8,2; 15,22.25; 16,22; 20,30f; 26,22, in die Q-Tradition höchstwahrscheinlich in 8,21, in 18,21 (mit Umgestaltung) und sicher in 8,6 eingefügt." Κύριε in Matt 8,21 is in minimal Q, however, since Luke 9:59 also has it.

Gnilka 1986, 301: "Die Kyrie-Anrede, von Mt verdoppelt (auch in V 8) entspricht der von V 2."

Sand 1986, 179: "Die Anrede 'Herr' sieht Mt aus V. 8 vor; sie steht ganz im Dienst der mt. Theologie (vgl. schon V. 2: Jesus ist einer, der Macht hat, er ist ein Kyrios mit Autorität."

Nolland 1989, 315-316: See Q 7:2, 3, 4-6a⁷ Luke = Q, Pro (p. 148).

Luz 1990, 13⁶: "Matthäismen ... sind in V 5-7: Προσέρχομαι, λέγων, χύριε, λέγει ... evt. βασανίζομαι, ἐλθών."

Luz 1990, ET 2001, 8⁶: "Mattheisms in vv. 5-7 are ...: προσέρχομαι, λέγων, χύριε, λέγει ..., perhaps βασανίζομαι, ἐλθών."

Davies and Allison 1991, 20: "As in 8:2, Matthew has added 'Lord'. Q itself had the word in 8:8 = Lk 7:6. Our evangelist very much likes to use 'Lord' in healing stories. When a supplicant addresses Jesus, more often than not the title appears.⁴²"

20⁴²: "8:2, 6, 8; 9:28; 15:22, 25, 27; 17:15; 20:30, 31."

Catchpole 1992, 522-523 [1993, 287]: "In spite of the linkage to Q 6,46, the only other χύριε address in Q outside this tradition, and the [523] agreement with Q 7,7, it is easier to attribute this term to MattR than to explain why Luke would have dropped it."

527 [292]: Reconstruction. For complete text see Q 7:1⁰ In Q (p. 14).

Lindars 1992, 210: Reconstruction. For complete text see Q 7:1⁶ Luke = Q, Pro (p. 56).

Sevenich-Bax 1993, 178-179: "Schließlich ist auch die χύριε-Anrede Mt 8,6b durch matthäische Redaktion entstanden. Matthäus setzt den Vokativ als Anrede Jesu gehäuft ein,⁸ insbesondere—auch verglichen mit Lukas—redaktionell [179] bei der Bitte um Heilung. Wahrscheinlich hat Matthäus die für Q durch Lk 7,6//Mt 8,8 ausgewiesene Titulatur von dort vorgezogen."

178⁸: "Allerdings nur verglichen mit Markus. Lukas frequentiert den Titel fast genauso oft wie Matthäus."

238: Reconstruction. For complete text see Q 7:1⁰ In Q (p. 15).

International Q Project 1995, 478: Reconstruction. For complete text see Q 7:1⁰ In Q (p. 16).

Evaluations

Johnson 2000: Luke = Q {B}, ()⁸.

Q uses the vocative on several occasions (Q 7:6). Luke often takes over the vocative from Q and *Sondergut*, but also adds it redactionally. If it had been in Q, it would have been omitted when Luke added the delegations and eliminated the dialogue between Jesus and the centurion.

However, statistics indicate Matthew's interest in adding χύριε, especially in requests (Held, Wegner, Geist)—even two or three times within a miracle story (Matt 14:28, 30; 15:22, 25, 27; 20:31, 33). It fits Matthew's leitmotif of presenting Jesus as Lord of the Church (also Zuntz, Gundry).

Robinson 2000: Luke = Q {B}, ()⁸.

The vocative title is often redactional in Matthew, especially in the request for healing.

Kloppenborg 2000: Luke = Q {B}, ()⁸.

Hoffmann 2001: Luke = Q {B}, ()⁸.

Die Anrede in Q 7,6 durch Matthäus und Lukas für Q sicher bezeugt; hier dürfte sie aber auf das Konto des Matthäus gehen, da er diese Anrede häufig verwendet und vor allem auch in die einleitende Bitte um Hilfe in Heilungs-geschichten redaktionell einführt (Mt 8,2 [par. Lk 5,12!]; 15,22.25; 17,15; 20,30[?].31, vgl. auch 9,28. Allgemein in Wundergeschichten auch Mt 8,25; 14,30). Allerdings ist zu bedenken, daß Lukas bei der Umgestaltung der direk-ten in eine indirekte Rede (ὅπως) eine solche Anrede nicht übernehmen konnte.

Q 7:2, 3, 4-6a⁹: Luke's δοῦλος..., ὃς ἦν αὐτῷ ἔντιμος or Matthew's ὁ παῖς.

Luke = Q: [δοῦλος..., ὃς ἦν αὐτῷ ἔντιμος]⁹

Pro

Castor 1912, 223: Reconstruction: for δοῦλος only. For complete text see Q 7:1⁰ In Q (p. 6).

Jeremias 1980, 152: "Trad ... ἔντιμος: in den Evangelien nur im Nicht-Markusstoff des LkEv: 7,2; 14,8."

Gundry 1982, 142: "Some think that Matthew switches from an alternation between δοῦλος and παῖς (so Luke) to a consistent use of παῖς in order to imply the meaning 'son' rather than 'servant'—this because of the centurion's affection for the boy (cf. John 4:46-53). But Matthew omits the clause that expresses that affection (Luke 7:2b)."

Wiefel 1988, 143: "Der Centurio ... hat einen Sklaven, offenbar zu seinen persönlichen Diensten, der ihm viel wert ist. Bei Matthäus wird er παῖς genannt, ein Ausdruck, der das nahe Verhältnis des Knechts zu seinem Herrn ('Bursche') oder auch das jugendliche Alter bezeichnen kann. Bei Johannes ist der παῖς der υἱός des Mannes im königlichen Dienst. Die Linie führt also von δοῦλος über den παῖς zum υἱός."

Con

Bleek 1862, 348: "Wir würden uns dann das δοῦλος des Lucas so zu erklären haben, daß er in der ihm vorliegenden Relation zwar auch, wie es bei Matth. ist, παῖς vorgefunden hätte, was er auch in den Worten des Hauptmannes V. 7 beibehält, daß er dieses aber in dem Sinne von δοῦλος gefaßt und darnach, wo er selbst redet, letztere Bezeichnung dafür gesetzt hätte."

Holtzmann 1863, 77-78: "Der mittlere Ausdruck παῖς (von Matthäus verstanden = υἱός, vgl. 17,15.18) wurde von Lucas falsch ausgelegt = δοῦλος. Nur Lucas 7,7 ist παῖς unvermerkt stehen geblieben, was deutlich genug die Abhängigkeit beweist. Die Sorge des Herrn um einen δοῦλος würde nicht blos voraussetzen, daß derselbe [78] der einzige Knecht des Hauptmanns gewesen, sondern auch, daß dieser ein besonderes Interesse an ihm gehabt, was daher Lucas ergänzt (ἔντιμος hat unter den Synoptikern blos Lucas 7,2 und 14,8)."

B. Weiß 1876, 229: "Lucas hat das παῖς der Quelle offenbar im Sinne von δοῦλος genommen, wie er es oft gebraucht (1,54.69; 12,45; 15,26 und 5mal in Act.), da v. 7 noch deutlich zeigt, daß er jenes las; und hat darum den Sklaven, dem sein Herr so große Theilnahme beweist, für einen von ihm besonders werthgeschätzten (ἔντιμος wie 14,8) erklärt."

B. Weiß 1878, 364: "Luk. hat das παῖς der Quelle im Sinne von δοῦλος genommen, wie er es 1,54.69 braucht, und darum den Sklaven, dem sein Herr so große Theilnahme beweist, als einen von ihm besonders werthgeschätzten (ἔντιμος, wie 14,8) bezeichnet."

365: "παῖς—gleich δοῦλος, V. 2. Daß Luk. das παῖς seiner Quelle hier unvermerkt stehen gelassen habe, ist eine unverdiente Anklage nach Baur [source not found]; nahm er einmal παῖς im Sinne von δοῦλος, wie freilich die Quelle nicht that, so konnte er es ja auch hier in diesem Sinne stehen lassen."

J. Weiß 1892, 398-399: "Den παῖς [399] des Centurio ... hat Lk als δοῦλος genommen (1,54.69 LQ)."

B. Weiß 1900, 322: "Den παῖς Mt. 8,6 hat Luk. von einem Knecht vestanden (vgl. 1,54.69), der ihm aber besonders wertgeschätzt ... war."

Holtzmann 1901, 344: "Weiterhin schreibt Lc (7,2) statt παῖς, welches gleichwohl 7,7 aus der Quelle stehen geblieben ist, δοῦλος, fühlt aber um so mehr das Bedürfniss, die außerordentliche Sorge des Herrn für ihn, die einem Sohne gegenüber eher zu begreifen wäre, zu motiviren: *welcher ihm werth war.*"

B. Weiß 1901, 383: "Der παῖς Mt 8,6 erscheint hier als δοῦλος, sei es, daß schon die Quelle des Lk ihn so bezeichnete, sei es, daß Lk das παῖς derselben (1,54.69) in diesem Sinne deutete."

B. Weiß 1904, 242 (ET 1906, 56): See Q 7:2, 3, 4-6a³ Luke = Q, Con (pp. 94-95).

von Harnack 1907, 56: "Bemerkt sei nur, daß ἔντιμος (v. 2), [et alia] in den Evangelien ausschließlich lukanisch sind."

von Harnack 1907, ET 1908, 76-77: "I would only remark that ἔντιμος (verse 2), [et alia] are, as far as the gospels [77] are concerned, exclusively Lukan."

Loisy 1907, 648: "Si la substitution du serviteur au fils n'a pas été voulue par Luc, elle pourrait s'expliquer soit par une méprise sur le sens du mot grec, que l'évangéliste aurait voulu remplacer par un synonyme non équivoque, mais mal choisi, soit par une double traduction d'un mot hébreu ou araméen, qui offrait le même double sens que le terme grec de Matthieu.⁸"

648⁸: "δοῦλος. Le mot παῖς est resté au v. 7, conformément à la source et à Mt. 8."

B. Weiß 1907, 242: "Bei Q ist es der Sohn des Hauptmanns, der an schmerzhafter Paralysis darniederliegt (Mt. 8,6), bei Lukas ein ihm besonders werter Knecht, der im Sterben liegt (7,2), eine Darstellung, die wieder merkwürdig, wie so oft in L, an die johanneische Überlieferung erinnert (vgl. Joh. 4,47: ἤμελλεν ἀποθνήσκειν); denn auch Lk. 7,3 (ἀκούσας περὶ τοῦ Ἰησ.) hat der Hauptmann nur von Jesu gehört, genau wie der Königische Joh. 4,47; es ist also bei beiden ein erster Besuch Jesu während seines öffentlichen Lebens in Kapharnaum, wo er nur gerüchtweise bekannt ist."

Castor 1912, 42: "In Luke 7:2b ἤμελλεν τελευτᾶν, ὃς ἦν αὐτῷ ἔντιμος are, perhaps, additions of Luke; so also ὄχλῳ in 7:9."

223: Reconstruction: for ὃς ἦν αὐτῷ ἔντιμος only. For complete text see Q 7:1⁰ In Q (p. 6).

Haupt 1913, 81: "Bei Wiedergabe der Erzählung weichen Mt und Lc stark von einander ab; es rührt das wohl daher, daß Lc neben dem Bericht von Q einen andern in seiner Sonderquelle vorfand, den er auch verwertete (vgl. δοῦλος v. 2.10; aber in [v.] 7 παῖς)."

Patton 1915, 144: "In Luke's vss. 3-6, which contain the account of the sending of the messengers, there are at least five Lucan words (ἔντιμος, παραγενόμενοι, σπουδαίως, μακράν, ἀπέχοντος). ... Of these Lucan words, ἔντιμος is used a second time by Luke (xiv, 8) in a passage not paralleled in Matthew."

Klostermann 1919, 448: "Lc unterscheidet sich besonders durch: ... die Ersetzung von παῖς durch δοῦλος, ... hier noch durch ὃς ἦν αὐτῷ ἔντιμος näher charakterisiert."

Cadbury 1920, 79-80: See Q 7:2, 3, 4-6a⁷ Luke = Q, Con (p. 148).

187: "The following changes [by Luke] may be recorded without more particular explanation. Many of them are probably improvements in clearness, or in elegance or exactness of expression: ... Mt. 8,5-13 παῖς—Lk 7,2-10 δοῦλος (once παῖς) (Q)."

Loisy 1924, 215: "La forme originale du récit a été beaucoup mieux conservée dans Matthieu (viii, 5-13), où le centurion lui-même intervient pour demander la guérison de son fils, tandis que dans notre évangile le centurion ne traite avec Jésus que par intermédiaire et en faveur d'un esclave qu'on dit lui être cher. Pour ce dernier point la variante résulte de l'interprétation, probablement fausse, donnée au mot 'enfant' (παῖς). ... A la lettre 'précieux' (ἔντιμος). C'est par cette affection que notre auteur veut expliquer l'intérêt particulier qui le centurion prend à la guérison de son serviteur."

Klostermann 1929, 86: "Δοῦλος: ersetzt Mt' παῖς, ebenso [v.] 10, dagegen [v.] 7 ist παῖς geblieben. ... ὃς ἦν αὐτῷ ἔντιμος: nähere Charakterisierung."

Bultmann 1931, 39¹: "Unbedingt ist παῖς Mt V. 6 als Kind zu verstehen; δοῦλος Lk V. 2 ist falsche Wiedergabe."

Bultmann 1931, ET 1968, 38⁴: "Unquestionably παῖς in Matt. 5:6 is to be understood as child: δοῦλος in Lk. 7:2 is an error in reproduction."

Manson 1937, 64: "Lk. having understood 'boy' in the sense 'slave' rather than 'son' produces a reason for the remarkable concern of the master, a concern which would be perfectly natural and would need no explanation, if it was a case of father and son."

Hirsch 1941, 88-89: "Anders steht es in unsrer Geschichte mit den Lukasabweichungen von der [89] vorauszusetzen gemeinsamen Grundlage.

Die Partien, in denen sie auftreten, sind daran kenntlich, daß es statt παῖς nun δοῦλος heißt."

Sparks 1941, 180: "I believe [Luke] read through the Centurion's παῖς in Q, and with δοῦλος impressed on his memory, formed a mental picture of the servant as subject of the cure, and accordingly introduced him as such into his narrative setting at Luke vii. 2 and 10. By so doing he has emphasized the centurion's moral worth in his solicitude for his servant, much as he has emphasized his humility in approaching the Lord through messengers. Consequently, in the first instance, the centurion's παῖς was identified with his δοῦλος, not so much by design as by accident; and I doubt if his παῖς would have ever been taken in any other sense than his 'son' had not his δοῦλος also been mentioned in the course of the Q conversation."

Zuntz 1945, 186-187[1]: "John, not Luke, interpreted correctly the notion of παῖς. The care for his only son could turn the man of authority into a petitioner. He would not have condescended to act as he did on behalf of one of the slaves whom [187] (v. 9b) he regarded as mere objects of his authority. Note that Luke's change necessitated the addition (vii. 2) 'whom he greatly valued'. Nothing of the kind is in Matthew; the anxiety for an only child suffers no qualification; that for a slave needs it."

188[1]: "[Luke] even retained καὶ γάρ (v.7), and also the word παῖς where it stood in the original (v. 7), though he wrote δοῦλος in the passages which he added to it. Such looseness is characteristic of Luke."

Haenchen 1959a, 25 [1965, 84]: "In dem Augenblick, wo mit V. 7b der alte Text erreicht wird, erscheint auch prompt das vorher durch δοῦλος ersetzte παῖς."

Held 1960, 183: See Q 7:2, 3, 4-6a[1] Luke = Q, Con (p. 67).

222: "Während Lukas das Gespräch zwischen Jesus und dem Hauptmann im Rahmen einer regelrechten Geschichte bringt, während er ihm einen rein erzählenden Anfang (Lk. 7,2-3) und einen ebenso erzählenden Abschluß (Lk. 7,10) gibt und novellistisch ausgestaltet[1], berichtet Matthäus im ganzen nur einen Dialog von zwei Gesprächsgängen."

222[1]: "Vgl. die Steigerung der Not (Lk. 7,2 ἤμελλεν τελευτᾶν) und die Hervorhebung des persönlichen Verhältnisses zwischen dem Hauptmann und seinem Knecht (Lk. 7,2 ὃς ἦν αὐτῷ ἔντιμος)."

Held 1960, ET 1963, 194: See Q 7:2, 3, 4-6a[1] Luke = Q, Con (pp. 67-68).

234: "Luke sets the conversation between Jesus and the centurion in the framework of a normal story and gives it a purely descriptive beginning (Luke 7:2-3) and a similarly descriptive ending (Luke 7:10) and arranges it in a novelistic fashion.[1]"

234[1]: "Cf. the heightening of the need (Luke 7:2 ἤμελλεν τελευτᾶν) and the underlining of the personal relationship between the centurion and his servant (Luke 7:2 ὃς ἦν αὐτῷ ἔντιμος)."

Grundmann 1961, 155: See Q 7:2, 3, 4-6a³ Luke = Q, Con (pp. 99-100).

Dodd 1963, 188-190²: "The part of the narrative common to Matthew and Luke calls the patient only παῖς. Luke, at the beginning and again at the end of the *pericopé*, uses the term δοῦλος. But the dialogue, which is common to both, appears to distinguish the [189—table of stories] [190] δοῦλος from the παῖς. The original intention was probably to represent him as the officer's son. Similarly in John the terms παῖς and υἱός are interchangeable."

Schnackenburg 1964, 74: See Schnackenburg 1964 at Matt = Q, Pro (p. 179).

Schnackenburg 1965, 504-505 (ET 1968, 474): See Schnackenburg 1965 at Matt = Q, Pro (p. 179).

Brown 1966, 193: "It was Luke or a Lucan forerunner who, in the Greek stage of the tradition, understood *pais* as servant boy and began to speak of a *doulos*. That Luke's use of *doulos* is secondary is suggested by the fact that it appears in those verses (2, 3, 10) where the Lucan story differs from that of Matthew."

Cadbury 1966, 93-94: "The peculiar stylistic combination of similarity and variation in phrase and vocabulary can be illustrated in great profusion. The likeness is most striking when found in widely sundered passages without any inner connection; the variation is most noteworthy when it occurs in passages adjacent in position and closely connected in thought. ...

"A few examples in related or adjacent passages from many that could be quoted are as follows: [94] ... Luke 7:2 δοῦλος 3 δοῦλον 7 παῖς 10 δοῦλον (Matt. 8:6, 8, 13 παῖς)." Cadbury's list includes variations in Luke 1:12, 29; 1:22, 62; 1:32, 35; 1:57 and 2:6; 1:58, 65; 1:58 and 2:44; 2:18, 33; 4:24, 25; 5:7, 10; 8:7, 14; 8:42, 45; 9:5 and 10:11; 9:10, 18.

Delobel 1966, 454: "La différence entre δοῦλος (vv. 2.3.10) et παῖς (v. 7b et *Mt.*, vv. 6.8.13) n'est évidemment pas d'ordre stylistique. Les deux recensions ont le terme δοῦλος là où le centurion parle de commandements à son serviteur. S'il s'agit ici de la même personne, à savoir le malade, παῖς a la signification de 'serviteur', ce qui est possible. S'il s'agit d'une autre personne, παῖς peut avoir sa signification ordinaire, l'enfant du centurion. Ceci paraît plus probable à la lumière de *Lc.*, IX, 41 (l'enfant épileptique) et *Lc.*, VIII, 51.54 (la fille de Jaïre). Comme dans ce dernier cas, notre péricope raconterait, à l'origine, la préoccupation du père pour son enfant malade; ce que *Mt.* a vraisemblablement conservé. H.F.D. Sparks [1941, 180] suppose un 'glissement' chez *Lc.* Impressionné par le terme δοῦλος (v. 8b: Q!) il a spontanément interprété παῖς dans le même sens. C'est un premier indice du fait que Luc accentue la valeur morale du centurion qui s'humilie devant Jésus, même pour sauver son esclave."

Schürmann 1969, 391¹²: "Luk hat 7,7 par Mt 8,8 παῖς stehen gelassen. (Er liebt Abwechslung in den Termini. ...) Diese Vokabel steht auch Joh 4,51 (aber in der Bedeutung παιδίον 4,49, υἱός 4,46f.50.53) wie Mt 8,6.8.13. Luk wurde vielleicht durch die Erwähnung eines δοῦλος V 8 par Mt veranlaßt, παῖς (richtig) als 'Sklave' zu verstehen und seinen Lesern zu verdolmetschen. ... Er vermeidet in Apg (außer für den παῖς θεοῦ) die Vokabel in der Bedeutung 'Sklave'. Auch 12,45 diff Mt hat Luk die Glieder der θεραπεῖα nicht als Sklaven charakterisieren wollen. 15,26 S handelt es sich möglicherweise—anders als 15,21—auch um einen μίσθιος (vgl. 15,17.19) nach dem Verständnis des Luk 7,7 par Mt 8,8 läßt Luk παῖς auch wohl darum durchgehen, weil er den Zenturio betont vertraulich von dem δοῦλος ἔντιμος reden lassen will. ... Mt 8,6.8.13 wird παῖς also wohl ursprünglich stehen."

391[15]: "῎Εντιμος scheint luk Redaktion zu entstammen (syn nur noch Lk 14,8 S) und durch den Ersatz des ursprünglicheren παῖς ... durch δοῦλος veranlaßt zu sein."

Schnider and Stenger 1971, 60-61: "Wenn man bedenkt, daß bei Johannes das zweideutige παῖς des Matthäus eindeutig als υἱός (Sohn) bezeichnet [61] wird, läßt sich durchaus erwägen, daß Lukas in ähnlicher Weise das mit Knecht oder Sohn übersetzbare παῖς in ein eindeutig mit Knecht zu übersetzendes δοῦλος verändert hat. Das hätte zudem den Erfolg gehabt, die Gestalt des Centurio um so tugendhafter erscheinen zu lassen, denn, daß sich jemand um die Heilung seines eigenen Kindes bemüht, ist nicht mehr als selbstverständlich; daß er sich aber so um seinen Knecht sorgt, läßt ein gutes Licht auf seinen Charakter fallen. Man beachte im übrigen, wie gerade dieser Zug bei Lukas unterstrichen ist durch den angehängten Relativsatz 'der ihm wert war' (Lk 7,2). Obwohl es sein Knecht ist, so ist er dem Herrn doch so wert und teuer, daß er sich bei Jesus um seine Heilung bemüht. Gerade dieser Relativsatz hebt den Centurio aus dem Bereich des allgemein Üblichen heraus. Das allgemein Übliche wird in Vers 8 dargestellt. Das Verhältnis von Herrn und Knecht ist das von Befehl und Gehorsam, von dem Vers 8 als von einer Selbstverständlichkeit spricht. Daß sich ein Herr so sehr um seinen ihm teuren Knecht bemüht, geht über das gerechte Maß der Fürsorge hinaus. Der Centurio erscheint so als ein guter Herr."

62: "Bis jetzt ist kein Grund sichtbar geworden, warum Lukas eine besondere, judenchristlich vorgeformte Vorlage benutzt haben soll; vielmehr weist die angewandte Erzählkunst auf Lukas selber, was auch wortstatistische Beobachtungen bestätigen.[10]"

62[10]: "Die wortstatistische Untersuchung zeigt folgendes: 1. das in Vers 2 benutzte Wort ἔντιμος kommt bei Lukas zweimal vor (Lk 7,2; 14,8), ansonsten findet es sich im Neuen Testament nur noch Phil 2,29 und 1 Pt 2,4.6."

Schramm 1971, 40-41: "Daß auch in Lk 7,1-10 Quellenkombination vorliegt, ist evident. In den Versen 6c-9, die bis in Einzelheiten mit Mt 8,8-10 übereinstimmen, ist ein Grundbericht [Q] greifbar, der vom παῖς (Lk 7,7; Mt 8,6.8.13) des Centurio erzählte. Lk 7,1-6b und 10 dagegen sind durch termi-

nologische [41] —hier ist durchweg vom δοῦλος des Hauptmanns die Rede—
und inhaltliche Charakteristika von diesem Grundbericht unterschieden und
als Teil einer abweichenden Ausprägung der Geschichte ausgewiesen."

Schulz 1972, 236[400]: "Mt liest immer παῖς (Vv 6.8.13), und Lk ebenfalls
dort, wo er mit Mt genau übereinstimmt (V 7b), dagegen hat Lk in Vv 2.10
und in seinem Zusatz Vv 3-6a δοῦλος eingeführt. Lk. liebt nach Cadbury
[1966, 94] Abwechslung in den Termini. Bei Lk entsteht eine gewisse Un-
klarheit dadurch, daß auch die Vorlage V 8 von einem δοῦλος in anderem
Zusammenhang sprach, so daß jetzt zwei verschiedene Personen mit δοῦλος
bezeichnet werden. Es ist unnötig, die Varianten παῖς-δοῦλος als Überset-
zungsvarianten eines ursprünglichen עבד zu erklären."

236-237: "Ἔντιμος ist zwar nicht lk, aber [237] der ganze Zusatz ὃς ἦν
αὐτῷ ἔντιμος hängt mit der Ersetzung des παῖς durch einen δοῦλος zusammen,
stammt also von Lk."

Achtemeier 1975, 549[7]: "Luke occasionally adds details that make the story
more colorful, e.g., a child healed becomes for Luke an only child (7:12;
8:42; 9:38; the latter two Luke himself has changed from his sources); a sick
youth is 'valued' (7:2); a man's crippled hand is his right one (6:6). Such
details have little apparent theological significance, except perhaps to make the
stories more gripping, and thus more memorable."

Pesch and Kratz 1976, 81: "Der Einsatz des Hauptmanns wird mit der
Angabe motiviert, daß ihm der Sklave 'wertvoll' war. Diese Motivation könnte
Lukas eingebracht haben, als er 'Knecht' (oder 'Sohn', vgl. oben a) und Joh
par) in 'Sklave' änderte."

Busse 1977, 146-147: "Daher versteht er [Lukas] παῖς (= Q) im Sinn von
δοῦλος. Das entspricht [147] erzählerisch einer 'objektiven' Berichterstattung
eher als das der direkten Rede angemessene παῖς, das eine besondere emotionale Bindung signalisiert. Aus diesem Grund behält Lukas auch παῖς in der
direkten Rede V 7 bei. Andererseits möchte er die emotionale Bindung des
Hauptmanns an den kranken Knecht nicht unterschlagen. Er fügt deshalb
einen Relativsatz mit den entsprechenden Angaben an."

Marshall 1978, 279: "The use of δοῦλος in 7:8 is natural in the context
of a command being given, and the use of παῖς in 7:7 stresses the affection of
the centurion for his slave. δοῦλος is, therefore, Luke's correct synonym for
παῖς. ...

"Luke adds that he was ἔντιμος to his master, a word that here means 'hon-
oured, respected' (14:8; Phil. 2:29), rather than 'precious, valuable' (1 Pet.
2:4, 5), and indicates why the centurion was so concerned over him; Luke's
own concern for the inferior members of society is perhaps also reflected."

Martin 1978, 15: "Matthew is consistent with his use of παῖς for the sufferer, while Luke varies between παῖς (v. 7, Q) and δοῦλος (normally), and 'in

v. 8 the centurion speaks of his "slave" as if the slave were another person than his "boy" [Manson 1937, 64]. But we should note that δοῦλος and ἄξιος are Luke terms,[11] while παῖς and ἱκανός are preferred in those passages where Matthew and Luke overlap (i.e., in Q). ... Luke has justified his preference for δοῦλος by adding ὃς ἦν αὐτῷ ἔντιμος, so 'boy' is to be taken in the military sense of subaltern, 'batman.'[13]"

20[11]: "And it is part of Luke's style to ring the changes stylistically by substituting closely similar or synonymous terms. ...

"The peculiarity of Lukan usage would support once again the originality of Matthew's consistent use of παῖς (from Q). Perhaps Luke's intention in departing from the Q designation was to highlight the military aspect of the centurion-slave relationship, in keeping with an underlying purpose to draw the parallel between the story here and that involving another Gentile centurion, Cornelius. See in particular Acts 10:1 (a centurion), 10:2, 22 (a Gentile God-fearer, pious and generous), 10:22 (well-spoken of by the entire Jewish people), and 10:24 (having 'friends'). Then, the bond mentioned in 7:2 of a slave 'who was valued by him' ... is meant to soften the harshness that otherwise could be associated with δοῦλος, a term in the sociological sense Luke avoids in the Acts of the Apostles."

20[13]: "Batman: 'an orderly of a British military officer' (*Webster's Dictionary*)."

Muhlack 1979, 41: For complete text of Lukan expansions, see Q 7:2, 3, 4-6a³ Luke = Q, Con (pp. 105-106).

45: "Wie Lukas 7,3 verwendet er das für Zusätze charakteristische δοῦλος."

Neirynck 1979, 109-110: See Q 7:2, 3, 4-6a³ Luke = Q, Con (pp. 107-108).

Fitzmyer 1981, 649: "Whereas [*pais*] has been understood as 'son' (*huios*) in John, it is interpreted as 'servant, slave' (*doulos*) by Luke in vv. 2,3 and even extended to v. 10."

651: "Luke's shift from *pais* in 'Q' to *doulos* is interpretative, but it is not clear why he shifted. ... *whom he prized highly*. Lit. 'who was valuable to him.' This is probably a Lucan redactional addition, since *entimos* is used by Luke alone among the evangelists."

Haapa 1983, 71: "Die lukanischen Erweiterungen sind in ganz anderem Geiste geschrieben. Hier spricht man von der Liebe zu 'unserem Volk', vom Synagogenbau und vom Ziehen Jesu mit den Ältesten der Juden zum Hause des Hauptmanns, um dessen schwerkranken Knecht aus dem Tode zu erretten.⁹"

71[9]: "Für den Redaktor ist der Kranke *doulos*, Knecht. Augenscheinlich hat er mit diesem Wort den Begriff *pais* der Logienquelle verdeutlichen wollen."

Dauer 1984, 95: "Außerdem ist ἔντιμος in Verbindung mit δοῦλος lk Ersatz für παῖς."

111: "Trotzdem ist V. 2 nicht ohne lk Bearbeitung. Hierher gehören: δοῦλος ... ὃς ἦν αὐτῷ ἔντιμος: Diese Wendung ist eine Umschreibung des aus Q stammenden παῖς. Lukas schreibt an dieser Stelle δοῦλος, weil er die sprachliche Abwechslung liebt; er vermeidet außerdem παῖς in der Bedeutung 'Sklave' in der Apg völlig. Den Anstoß für das Wort δοῦλος hat er wohl von V. 8 her bekommen. Zu ἔντιμος vgl. noch Lk 14,8; sonst im NT: Phil 2,29; 1 Petr 2,4; 2,6 (atl Zitat)."

Wegner 1985, 142: "Der Befund zeigt, daß Lk mit δοῦλος sehr wahrscheinlich den Wortlaut seiner Vorlage wiedergibt. Ob diese freilich Q—so Parker [1953, 64-65] bezüglich Lk 7,1-5 auf Grund der Verwendung zweier von ihm herausgestellten Q-Vorzugswörter, δοῦλος und ἄξιος—oder etwa eine Traditionsvariante aus dem Sg ist, muß später entschieden werden. Übrigens wird Mt, der in der entsprechenden Parallele παῖς bringt (Mt 8,6), kaum δοῦλος in seiner Vorlage gelesen haben, was durch die reichliche Übernahme dieses Wortes in seinem Ev nahegelegt wird."

148: "Diese Wendung [ὃς ἦν αὐτῷ ἔντιμος] erscheint innerhalb des gNT nur auSt. Meistens wird sie dem Lk selbst zugeschrieben. Wir können uns dieser Deutung nicht anschließen, denn der hier entscheidende Ausdruck ἔντιμος weist eher auf Sg hin. Das wird noch dadurch erhärtet, daß auch alle anderen Worte dieser Wendung im lk Sg durchaus gut belegt sind."

Schnelle 1987, 103: "Lukas hat in einem weit größeren Maß als Matthäus die Q-Vorlage umgestaltet. Auf seine Redaktion gehen die Situationsschilderung in V.2 [und] die Bezeichnung des Kranken als δοῦλος ... zurück."

Schnelle 1987, ET 1992, 89: "Luke has reshaped the Q version of the story much more thoroughly than Matthew. His redaction produced the description of the situation in v. 2 [and] the designation of the sick person as δοῦλος."

Wiefel 1988, 141: "Das legte die Folgerung nahe, daß bei Lukas zwei Berichte miteinander verbunden sind: der mit Matthäus gemeinsame Grundbericht aus Q und ein Sonderbericht. Diese Verbindung wird auch durch sprachliche Beobachtungen belegt. In dem beiden Evangelien gemeinsamen Grundbericht wird der Kranke als παῖς (Luk. 7,7; Matth. 8,6.8.13), in den nur Lukas eigenen Partien als δοῦλος (Luk. 7,2.3.10) bezeichnet, für den Ausdruck der Würdigkeit hat der Grundbericht ἱκανός (Luk. 7,6; Matth. 8,8), der Sonderbericht ἄξιος (Luk. 7,4)." But see Wiefel at Luke = Q, Pro (p. 167).

Nolland 1989, 316: "The use of δοῦλος, 'slave,' rather than Matthew's παῖς, 'servant'/'slave'/'son'/'child,' will be Lukan, as possibly is the final clause 'who was precious to him.'"

Crossan 1991, 326, 328 (GT 1994, 431, 433): See Q 7:2, 3, 4-6a³ Luke = Q, Con (p. 112).

Catchpole 1992, 523 [1993, 287]: "The sick person: ὁ παῖς μου (Matt 8,6) or δοῦλος ... ὃς ἦν αὐτῷ ἔντιμος (Luke 7,2). The final phrase in Luke, using a term which occurs elsewhere only at Luke 14,8, and conforming to the evangelist's tendency to make personal details more specific (cf. Luke 8,42 diff Mark 5,23), is necessary only when the concern of the centurion needs to be explained. This is so in the case of a servant, but not in the case of a son, so much hinges on whether παῖς is original and whether it stands for a son. The answer is probably 'yes' on both counts, for the following reasons: (i) Q 7,7 uses παῖς, and Luke's change would be explicable in terms of his 'studied variation of phrase and exchange of synonyms' [Cadbury 1966, 92]. For Luke,[26] as for a minority of instances in Josephus,[27] παῖς can stand for a servant. (ii) the terms παῖς and υἱός are equivalent in normal Josephus usage, and in Matt 17,15.18/Luke 9,38, the retelling of Mark 9,14-29. Significant above all is the use of παῖς/παιδίον with a clear sense of one's own child in the related traditions of Jairus and the Syro-Phoenician woman: Mark 5,39-41/Luke 8,51.54; Mark 7,30. The appeal of the parent, not the master, seems to be a standard feature of this family of traditions, so in this case the sick person should probably be taken to be a παῖς, that is, a son of the centurion."

523 [287][26]: "Luke 12,45 diff Matt 24,49 σύνδουλος; Luke 15,26 παῖς = Luke 15,22 δοῦλος = Luke 15,17.19 μίσθιος."

523 [287][27]: "*Ant.* 18.6.6 §192; *J.W.* 1.3.6 §82."

527 [292]: Reconstruction. For complete text see Q 7:1⁰ In Q (p. 14).

Lindars 1992, 211: "Luke has changed παῖς to δοῦλος, possibly for consistency with the centurion's speech (Lk 7,8), and added ὃς ἦν αὐτῷ ἔντιμος to explain why the centurion was specially interested in his welfare."

Gagnon 1993, 715: "It should be noted that Lucan redaction can ... be seen in ... the δέ τινος and δοῦλος of v 2a, '*now a slave of a certain* centurion' [and] the relative clause in v 2c which characterizes the slave's relationship to the centurion as one 'who was precious to him' (ὃς ἦν αὐτῷ ἔντιμος)."

716-717: "In the case of δοῦλος (vv 2-3,10), it is true that Luke shows no marked preference for the word and no strong aversion to it (30/5/26 + 3; the strongest cases of redaction are in 12:47 [L?], 14:23 [LQ], and in Acts), whereas the word occurs 5x in [S] material (2:29; 15:22; 17:7,9,10). Yet Luke's tendency to vary terms, including those for 'servant,' suggests that Luke is responsible for the use of the word δοῦλος (note Luke's retention of παῖς in the core sayings material, Luke 7:7 par.). The redactor also probably wanted to clarify the identity of the character for his audience and to emphasize that the slave to whom he gave orders (7:8) was the same slave who was 'precious to him' (so great was the centurion's humility and compassion for those of a lower socioeconomic class).

"The relative clause ὃς ἦν αὐτῷ ἔντιμος could stem from Luke's special source but more likely arises from Luke himself. ... Since the phrase coheres so well with the rest of the material found in vv 3-6a,7a (underscoring the centurion's godly behavior even to his servants), it no doubt belongs to the same author. Luke adds comparable details twice to his Marcan source when discussing the specialness of the sick person for whom intercession is made: in 8:42 Jairus pleads for his daughter 'because she was his only daughter' (ὅτι θυγάτηρ μονογενὴς ἦν αὐτῷ), and in 9:39 the father [717] pleads for the healing of his epileptic son 'because he is an only child to me.' The centurion's affection for his slave is also consistent with Luke's interest elsewhere in transforming relations between patron and client in his community. In a choice between Luke's special source or Luke himself, the latter has the edge."

Hagner 1993, 203: See Hagner at Matt = Q, Pro (p. 181).

Sevenich-Bax 1993, 166-167: "'Der stilistische Befund ist bei Lk, anders als in Mt, nicht einheitlich: Lk hat in 7,7 mit Mt 8,8 παῖς, dagegen aber in 7,2.3.10 δοῦλος; in 7,6c mit Mt 8,8 ἱκανός, in 7,4.7a aber ἄξιος/ἀξιοῦν; in 7,6 οἰκία, in 7,10 aber οἶκος. Dieser Befund [167] könnte auf eine sek Bearbeitung oder Quellenkombination hinweisen, ...' [Wegner 1985, 8]. Da Quellenkombination aber bereits als unwahrscheinlich zurückgewiesen wurde, muß die Frage nach der Ursache der uneinheitlichen Wortwahl im Sinne redaktioneller Tätigkeit entschieden werden."

176-177: "Auch die Designation des Kranken als δοῦλος ist Lukas anzulasten. Darauf deutet schon der Umstand, daß auch Lukas in bezug auf den Kranken zumindest einmal den Begriff παῖς als ursprünglich ausweist (Lk 7,7b//Mt 8,8bβ). Zudem entstehen bei Lukas durch die Einführung des δοῦλος anstelle des παῖς semantische Unschärfen. Es wird nämlich nicht nur der Kranke mit diesem Begriff belegt. In der Begründung seiner Bitte bezeichnet der Hauptmann auch den unter seiner Gewalt stehenden Untergebenen als 'δοῦλος': 'Es ist daher anzunehmen, daß bereits in Q die Erzählung in Bezug auf den Kranken ausschließlich παῖς verwendete, um eine eventuelle Gleichsetzung mit dem [177] δοῦλος des Hauptmannwortes (Mt 8,8 par Lk) zu vermeiden [Wegner 1985, 138].'"

178: "Die Aussage, daß der Knecht dem Bittsteller 'teuer' ist, wird gleichfalls von Lukas stammen. Sie hat ihre Ursache in der Substitution des παῖς durch δοῦλος."

Landis 1994, 20: Landis argues that δοῦλος here and ὃς ἦν αὐτῷ ἔντιμος come from a Lukan *Sonderquelle*.

Matt = Q: (ὁ παῖς)⁹

Pro

Strauss 1836, 104: "So wird man wohl schwerlich annehmen können, daß aus dem johanneischen υἱός in absteigender Linie zuerst unbestimmt ein παῖς, dann ein δοῦλος geworden sei, und auch die umgekehrte aufsteigende Richtung ist hier minder wahrscheinlich, als das Mittlere, daß aus dem zweideutigen παῖς (= נַעַר), welches wir im ersten Evangelium finden, in zwei Richtungen das einemal ein Knecht, wie bei Lukas, das andremal ein Sohn, wie bei Johannes, gemacht worden sein mag."

Strauss 1836, ET 1855, 517: "It can scarcely be supposed that the υἱός of John became in a descending line, first the doubtful term παῖς, and then δοῦλος; and even the reverse ascending order is here less probable than the intermediate alternative, that out of the ambiguous παῖς (= נַעַר) there branched off in one direction the sense of *servant*, as in Luke; in the other, of *son*, as in John."

Bleek 1862, 347-348: See Q 7:2̶, 3, 4̶-6a¹ Matt = Q, Pro (pp. 70-71).

B. Weiß 1876, 228: "Daß παῖς in der Quelle gleich υἱός gebraucht wird, zeigt 17,18, und daß es auch hier von δοῦλος unterschieden wird, v. 9; es ist also harmonistische Willkühr, es von einem Knechte ... zu nehmen."

B. Weiß 1878, 364: "Luk. hat das παῖς der Quelle im Sinne von δοῦλος genommen."

B. Weiß 1898, 167: "V. 2.—ὁ παῖς μου—mein Sohn, ... wie in derselben Quelle 17:9."

Wernle 1899, 64: "Lc hat den παῖς der Quelle durch δοῦλος ersetzt, freilich nicht konsequent (7,7)."

von Harnack 1907, 91 (ET 1908, 131): Reconstruction. For complete text see Q 7:1⁶ Luke = Q, Pro (p. 55).

B. Weiß 1907, 242: "Bei Q ist es der Sohn des Hauptmanns, der an schmerzhafter Paralysis darniederliegt (Mt. 8,6)."

B. Weiß 1908, 15: Reconstruction. For complete text see Q 7:1⁰ In Q (p. 5).

Klostermann 1919, 448: "Lc unterscheidet sich besonders durch: ... die Ersetzung von παῖς durch δοῦλος."

Cadbury 1920, 79-80: See Q 7:2̶, 3, 4̶-6a⁷ Luke = Q, Con (p. 148).

Bussmann 1929, 57: "In der einen Quelle (R) war vom παῖς, in der anderen vom δοῦλος die Rede; als L aber zu R zurückkehrt, da schreibt er auch παῖς, ein Zeichen, wie treu er diese Vorlage wiedergibt."

Klostermann 1929, 86: "Δοῦλος: ersetzt Mt' παῖς, ebenso [v.] 10, dagegen [v.] 7 ist παῖς geblieben."

Creed 1930, 101: "[Luke 7:2]. δοῦλος— Mt. παῖς, and this [παῖς] was probably the word used in the source, since it is also found in Lk. v. 7. The word, like the English 'boy,' is ambiguous, and might mean 'servant' or 'son.' Lk. interprets in the former sense, and Jo. apparently in the latter."

Manson 1937, 64: "The word used by Lk. means 'slave.' In Mt. 8:6 the Greek word may mean 'servant' or 'son,' much the same as the English word 'boy.' In John (4:46) the invalid is definitely the 'son' of the petitioner. In Lk. 7:7 the 'slave' of v. 2 has become 'boy' as in Mt.: and in v. 8 the centurion speaks of his 'slave' as if the slave were another person than his 'boy.' Taking all these facts into consideration, the balance of probability is in favour of 'son' rather than 'slave.'"

Hirsch 1941, 88: "Dem Matth ist die Geschichte vom Hauptmann in der Q-Fassung selbst überliefert worden. Beweis dafür ist, daß er das Wort παῖς, das in den wörtlich mit Luk übereinstimmenden Versen gebraucht ist, durch die ganze Geschichte hindurchführt."

Sparks 1941, 179: "In discussion of the section Matt. viii. 5-13/Luke vii. 1-10 it is now generally agreed: (1) that behind both Matt. and Luke lies a Q original, (2) that in Q the subject of the cure was described as παῖς, (3) that the word παῖς is ambiguous, meaning either 'son' or 'servant', and (4) that, although Matt. has retained the ambiguity by reference to παῖς throughout, John has interpreted it as 'son', while Luke has interpreted it as 'servant'."

Haenchen 1959a, 23 [1965, 82]: "Beginnen wir mit der *Vorlage des Matthäus.* ... Ein Centurio, Offizier des Herodes Antipas ... kommt zu Jesus: sein παῖς liegt gelähmt daheim in furchtbaren Schmerzen."

Held 1960, 183³ (ET 1963, 194¹): See Q 7:2, 3, 4-6a¹ Luke = Q, Con (p. 67).

Schnackenburg 1964, 74 (1965, 504-505): "Bei den Synoptikern könnte man vermuten, daß die zweifach deutbare Angabe bei Mt 'παῖς' bei Lk eindeutig zu 'Knecht' ('Bursche') präzisiert wurde. Geschah das vielleicht auf Grund des im *Vergleich* (auch bei Mt 8,9!) genannten δοῦλος, da Lk wiederum in 7,7 noch die Kenntnis eines ursprünglichen παῖς zu verraten scheint? Auch bei Joh 4,51 stoßen wir noch auf παῖς, das in dieser Tradition aber als 'Sohn' bestimmt wird."

Schnackenburg 1965, ET 1968, 474: "In the Synoptics, one might think that the ambiguous παῖς of Matthew was defined clearly in Luke as 'slave' ('servant'). Was this perhaps due to the mention of δοῦλος in the comparison (also in Mt 8:9), since in 7:7 Luke once more seems to show knowledge of an original παῖς? We also come upon παῖς in Jn 4:51, though in this tradition it is defined as meaning 'son'."

Schürmann 1969, 391¹²: "Mt 8,6.8.13 wird παῖς wohl ursprünglich stehen."

Schramm 1971, 40-41: See Schramm at Luke = Q, Con (pp. 172-173).

George 1972, 70: "Chez Matthieu, le malade est le *pais* du centurion (8,6.8.13), ce qui peut signifier soit son serviteur, soit son enfant; Luc le présente comme un esclave (*doulos*: 7,2.3.10), mais dans les paroles de Jésus en 7,7 il le qualifie de *pais*, comme son parallèle de Mt 8,8; ce doit être là le terme de la source grecque des deux évangélistes."

Martin 1978, 20[11]: "The peculiarity of Lukan usage would support once again the originality of Matthew's consistent use of παῖς (from Q)."

Gatzweiler 1979, 302: "Le terme utilisé par Mt (pais) est indéterminé et peut être interprété dans le sens du serviteur chez Lc (doulos) et éventuellement dans le sens de fils chez Jn (uios). On lit pour ainsi dire l'évolution du récit au cours de son histoire."

Polag 1979, 38: Reconstruction. For complete text see Q 7:1[0] In Q (pp. 9-10).

Schmithals 1980, 90: See Q 7:2, 3, 4-6a[3] Matt = Q, Pro (p. 119).

Fitzmyer 1981, 649: "The term used for the boy in Matt 8:6,8,13 is *pais* ... and it is found in the strictly 'Q' part of the Lucan episode (7:7c). It probably represents the more primitive (even pre-'Q') tradition."

Haapa 1983, 71[9]: "Für den Redaktor ist der Kranke *doulos*, Knecht. Augenscheinlich hat er mit diesem Wort den Begriff *pais* der Logienquelle verdeutlichen wollen."

Dauer 1984, 112: "Wenn es stimmt, daß ἤμελλεν τελευτᾶν auf Lukas zurückgeht, dann wird es in der lk Vorlage geheißen haben: ἑκατοντάρχου δέ τινος παῖς κακῶς ἔχει."

Wegner 1985, 138: "Für die Ursprünglichkeit von παῖς auSt spricht vor allem die Tatsache, daß παῖς durch Mt 8,8/Lk 7,7 mit Bezug auf den Kranken mindestens 1x innerhalb der Erzählung sicher belegt ist. Auch muß bedacht werden, daß die Erzählung das bei Lk entsprechende δοῦλος innerhalb der Antwort des Hauptmannes an Jesus (Mt 8,9/Lk 7,8) verwendet. Es ist daher anzunehmen, daß bereits in Q die Erzählung in Bezug auf den Kranken ausschließlich παῖς verwendete, um eine eventuelle Gleichsetzung mit dem δοῦλος des Hauptmannswortes (Mt 8,9 par Lk) zu vermeiden."

270: Reconstruction. For complete text see Q 7:1[0] In Q (pp. 11-12).

Bovon 1989, 349[29]: "Die Überlieferung las παῖς (Mt 8,6), das von Johannes als 'Sohn' (υἱός [Joh 4,46]) und von Lukas als 'Diener' (δοῦλος [Lk 7,2]) interpretiert wurde. Lukas bedient sich des Wortes δοῦλος als inclusio für seine Erzählung: Es erscheint zweimal zu Beginn (VV 2-3) und einmal am Schluß (V 10). Das traditionelle παῖς hat sich da erhalten, wo wenig verändert wurde: in einer Rede (V 7)."

Bovon 1989, FT 1991, 341[29]: "Dans la tradition παῖς (Mt 8,6) que Jean interprète comme un fils (υἱός, Jn 4,46) et Luc comme un serviteur (δοῦλος, Lc 7,2). Δοῦλος sert d'inclusion au récit de Luc: il apparaît deux fois au début (v. 2-3) et une fois à la fin (v. 10). Le mot traditionnel παῖς est resté accroché à ce qui change le moins, les sentences (v. 7)."

Davies and Allison 1991, 20-21: "Concerning ὁ παῖς μου: throughout the present pericope Matthew has only παῖς, Luke παῖς and δοῦλος. Is Luke's 'servant' redactional? Gundry [1982, 142] thinks not, arguing that Matthew changed 'servant' (so Q) in order to gain a parallel with 8:8, where ὁ παῖς μου appears. But (i) Matthew shows no avoidance of δοῦλος; (ii) John has υἱός, and granted his independence from the synoptics in the present instance, this would argue for the [21] originality of Matthew's ambiguous παῖς, which like the Hebrew *na'ar* or the Aramaic *talyā'* can mean either 'son' (cf. John) or 'servant' (cf. Luke); (iii) παῖς appears in Jn 4:49; (iv) παῖς did undoubtedly appear in Q (cf. Lk 7:7), at least at one point; (v) Luke may have been interested in the parallelism between Lk 7 and the story of Cornelius in Acts 10, and Cornelius had servants (Acts 10:7); (vi) Luke shows a tendency to substitute synonymous terms for one another. With all this in mind, the παῖς in Mt. 8:5 and 13 may very well be original."

Catchpole 1992, 523 [1993, 287]: Catchpole argues against Luke's δοῦλος … ὃς ἦν αὐτῷ ἔντιμος, but sets up the argument as a choice between Matthew's ὁ παῖς μου and Luke's δοῦλος … ὃς ἦν αὐτῷ ἔντιμος, thus indirectly arguing for Matt = Q. See Catchpole at Luke = Q, Con (pp. 175-176).

527 [292]: Reconstruction. For complete text see Q 7:1⁰ In Q (p. 14).

Lindars 1992, 204: "For the sick person it is widely held that Matthew preserves the original παῖς, varied to δοῦλος in Luke and υἱός in John, though both retain παῖς at other points in the story."

210: Reconstruction. For complete text see Q 7:1⁶ Luke = Q, Pro (p. 56).

Hagner 1993, 203: "That παῖς was the fundamental term in the tradition is indeed indicated by its occurrence in Luke 7:9 as well as in John 4:51 (cf. also τὸ παιδίον μου, 'my little child' [John 4:49]). When Luke thus took Q's παῖς as a δοῦλος, 'slave,' in itself a legitimate rendering, he removed the inherent ambiguity of παῖς from the tradition."

204: "Παῖς rather than υἱός may well have been used in the original Q tradition because of the young age of the child (cf. John's τὸ παιδίον, 'little child')."

Sevenich-Bax 1993, 238: Reconstruction. For complete text see Q 7:1⁰ In Q (p. 15).

Landis 1994, 7: "Die Bezeichnung παῖς für den Kranken ist durch Lk 7,7/Mt 8,8 mindestens einmal sicher für die Q-Fassung belegt. Auch hier in Mt 8,6 ist sie wohl traditionell. Jedenfalls hat Q an dieser Stelle gewiß nicht wie Lk den Begriff δοῦλος gebraucht, denn mit diesem Wort wird in der Q-Erzählung (Lk 7,8/Mt 8,9) eine andere Person bezeichnet."

9,17: Reconstruction. For complete text see Q 7:1⁶ Luke = Q, Pro (p. 57).

Meier 1994, 724: "It is possible that the earliest Q and Johannine versions of the healing story in Greek used only the ambiguous *pais*. The word occurs at some point in all three versions of the story we now have; that is not true of *huios, doulos,* or *paidion*. In fact, in the only verse of the story where the wording of Matthew and Luke is practically identical, the word used for the sufferer is *pais*: 'Say but the word and my *pais* will be healed' (Matt 8:8//Luke 7:7). Most probably, then, the primitive form of this tradition about the centurion or royal official spoke throughout only of the man's *pais*. As the tradition developed both orally and in writing, it was interpreted differently by different groups. John's Gospel represents those who took *pais* to mean son, and Luke's Gospel represents those who took it to mean servant or slave, while Matthew's Gospel alone preserves the original ambiguity."

769[193]: "I think that Schulz [1972, 236-240] and Fitzmyer [1981, 648-649] make a good case for the position that, apart from the redactional insertion in Matt 8:11-12, Matthew's version of the story is closer to the Q form than is Luke's version. In particular: (2) ... Matthew's ambiguous *pais* ... may be primitive, explaining the opposite interpretations of Luke ('servant') and John ('son')."

International Q Project 1995, 478: Reconstruction. For complete text see Q 7:1⁰ In Q (p. 16).

Kollmann 1996, 257: "Daß das mt παῖς (im Sinne von Kind) dem δοῦλος von Lk 7,1-10 vorzuziehen ist, zeigt neben dem 'Lapsus' παῖς in Lk 7,7 auch Joh 4,46-54 (υἱός)."

Con

McNeile 1915, 103: "Κύριε κτλ.: Lk. has δοῦλος for παῖς. Mt. may have understood παῖς to mean υἱός (so Jo.); contrast τ. δούλῳ μου (v. 9)."

Parker 1953, 63-65: See Q 7:1⁶ Matt = Q, Con (pp. 58-60).

65: "Matthew's ambiguous *pais* may have been chosen by the editor to cover both K's *huios* (son) and Q's *doulos* (slave)."

Gundry 1982, 141: "Matthew reduces the independent clause concerning Jesus' entering Capernaum (so Luke) to a genitive absolute and makes the centurion rather than his servant the subject of the sentence. In harmony with the latter change, the description of the servant as one 'who was highly regarded by him (the centurion)' drops out."

142: "Παῖς, which means 'servant, boy,' replaces δοῦλος, which means 'servant, slave.' The replacement avoids a confusing correspondence between Jesus as Lord and the servant as a slave—but a slave to the centurion rather than to Jesus. It also works a parallel, and thus consistency, with ὁ παῖς μου in v 8 (so also Luke)."

Emendation = Q: ὁ παῖς <αὐτοῦ>[7,9]

Gagnon 1994b, 135: Reconstruction: "ὁ παῖς <αὐτοῦ>." For complete text see Q 7:1[0] In Q (p. 15).

Evaluations

Johnson 2000: Matt = Q {B}, (ὁ παῖς)[9].

Q has παῖς for the boy at Q 7:7 (Dodd). Q likely had the more ambiguous παῖς here, which best explains the Lukan δοῦλος and the Johannine υἱός as redaction- and tradition-historical developments (Bovon, Meier; so also Strauss).

The argument that Matthew strives for consistency by replacing δοῦλος with παῖς throughout (Gundry) is not a particularly strong one. It is opposed by Luke's well-documented tendency to vary use of synonyms (Cadbury 1966). Even more forceful than Cadbury's argument for this variation unit is the observation that Luke keeps Q's παῖς in the relatively unedited portion of the story, but changes to δοῦλος in the sections that evidence a great degree of variation between the two Gospels (Schramm). While Gagnon 1993 correctly cautions that Luke has no particular preference for δοῦλος, it is appropriate here as a clarification of παῖς. Matthew does not show an aversion to δοῦλος, using it elsewhere (Davies and Allison).

Once Luke replaces παῖς with δοῦλος, the characterization of the servant as ὃς ἦν αὐτῷ ἔντιμος becomes necessary to explain the centurion's remarkable concern (Loisy). This necessity is intensified by Luke's sending of a delegation of Jewish elders in the centurion's place. To be clear, despite the observation that ἔντιμος is only in Luke (Harnack), it is elsewhere only found in *Sondergut* material (Jeremias) and so is not necessarily Lukan.

Robinson 2000: Matt = Q {B}, (ὁ παῖς)[9].

The word παῖς is attested for Q at Q 7:7 (where Matthew and Luke are almost identical). In Matt 8:13, though the verse is Matthean (see 7:?10?[0]), παῖς may be a reminiscence of the word in Q. Cf. παιδίον John 4:49; παῖς John 4:51; υἱός John 4:46, 47, 50, 53. Luke uses δοῦλος at Luke 7:2, 3, 13. But δοῦλος may have been avoided in Q, since it is used of a slave other than the sick person in Q 7:8.

Matthew uses δοῦλος sufficiently to make it clear he had no particular motivation to omit it, if it had been here in Q.

The Lukan comment that the servant was precious to him would not be necessary if it were παῖς (whose ambivalent meaning "son" or "servant" may be caught in the English term "boy"), but, once there is the Lukan shift to δοῦλος, the reason needs to be stated as to why the centurion is so concerned about no more than a slave. For otherwise one might expect a centurion to be quite callous about the health of a slave (unless ἔντιμος is meant in a purely financial sense). Of course, some slaves functioned almost as family members, which is what Luke has in mind. But when it is a slave rather than a son, this needs to be made clear.

Kloppenborg 2000: Matt = Q {B}, (ὁ παῖς)[9].

Hoffmann 2001: Matt = Q {B}, (ὁ παῖς)[9].

Q 7:2, 3, 4-6a¹⁰: Luke's κακῶς ἔχων or Matthew's βέβληται ἐν τῇ οἰκίᾳ παραλυτικός (See also Luke 7:6b ἀπὸ τῆς οἰκίας).

Luke = Q: [κακῶς ἔχων]¹⁰

Pro

H. Meyer 1864, 218: "Welchem der beiden Evangelisten der Vorzug der Ursprünglichkeit gebühre, ist zu Gunsten nicht des Matth., ... sondern des *Lukas* zu entscheiden."

H. Meyer 1864, ET 1884, 179: "The question as to which of the two evangelists the preference in point of originality is to be accorded, must be decided not in favor of Matthew ... but of *Luke*."

B. Weiß 1876, 229: "Daß die Krankheit in der Quelle als Paralysis bezeichet war, ist nach dem allgemeinen Ausdruck des Luc. (κακῶς ἔχων) sehr unwahrscheinlich; denn wenn derselbe auch wegen der damit verbundenen heftigen Schmerzen allenfalls an den Tetanus denken konnte, der oft schnellen Tod herbeiführt, so bleibt er doch bei dem tödtlichen Character der Krankheit (ἤμελλεν τελευτᾶν) in einer Weise stehen, die wohl nur die Dringlichkeit der Hülfe stärker motiviren soll."

Castor 1912, 223: Reconstruction. For complete text see Q 7:1⁰ In Q (p. 6).

Easton 1926, 96-97: "Κακῶς ἔχειν is not Lukan; it occurs only in 5:31, where it is from Mk."

Schlatter 1931, 252: "Κακῶς ἔχειν ist palästinisch und L. nicht geläufig."

Schürmann 1969, 391¹¹: "Κακῶς ἔχειν schreibt Luk noch 5,31 par Mk, vermeidet es aber diff Mk 1,32; er hat es auch diff Mk 1,34 nicht und nie in Apg. Es spricht hier also wohl die Vorlage."

Marshall 1978, 279: "The slave was ill: κακῶς ἔχω (5:31) is not a Lucan phrase and probably comes from the source."

Jeremias 1980, 151: "Trad κακῶς ἔχων: Die Wendung κακῶς ἔχω (Mt 5; Mk 4; Lk 2; sNT 0) findet sich im Lukas-Evangelium nur 5,31 und 7,2 (unsere Stelle). Lukas steht ihr mit Reserve gegenüber. Nur in einem von drei Fällen, in denen sie ihm durch die Markus-Vorlage angeboten wurde, übernahm er sie (Lk 5,31 par. Mk 2,17), während er sie Lk 4,40a (ὅσοι εἶχον ἀσθενοῦντας) diff. Mk 1,32 ersetzte und Lk 4,40b diff. Mk 1,34 ganz fortließ. Seinerseits bevorzugt er νόσος (→ 7,21 Red) und ἀσθένια (→ 8,2 Red). Da er κακῶς ἔχω sonst nicht verwendet, wird man die Wendung auch an unserer Stelle der Tradition zuzuschreiben haben."

Dauer 1984, 112: "Vor-lk ist ... die Wendung κακῶς ἔχειν: Lukas übernimmt es Lk 5,31 par Mk 2,17. Lk 4,40a diff Mk 1,32 ersetzt er es durch eine andere Wendung; Lk 4,40b om Mk 1,34 vermeidet er es ganz; in der Apg verwendet er es nie.

"Wenn es stimmt, daß ἤμελλεν τελευτᾶν auf Lukas zurückgeht, dann wird es in der lk Vorlage geheißen haben: ἑκατοντάρχου δέ τινος παῖς κακῶς ἔχει."

Wegner 1985, 143: "Lk, der sie 2x innerhalb des von ihm bearbeiteten Mk-Stoffes überging, wird sie kaum von sich aus auSt eingetragen haben. Man wird daher κακῶς ἔχειν auSt für trad halten müssen." In favor of Lukan *Sondergut*, Wegner goes on to argue, against Schulz (1972; see Luke = Q, Con [p. 188]), that the expression is not Lukan.

Bovon 1989, 349[30]: "Die volkstümliche Wendung κακῶς ἔχων in Lk 7,2 ist nicht lukanisch."

Bovon 1989, FT 1991, 341[30]: "L'expression populaire κακῶς ἔχων, Lc 7,2, n'est pas lucanienne."

Nolland 1989, 315-316: See Q 7:2, 3, 4-6a[7] Luke = Q, Pro (p. 148).

Davies and Allison 1991, 20: "Lk 7.2-5 is much longer. Matthew has, presumably, severely abbreviated Q.[41]"

20[41]: "A pre-Lukan basis for Lk 7.2-5 is indicated by several facts, including some expressions not typical of Luke (e.g. κακῶς ἔχων and ἤμελλεν τελευτᾶν)."

Lindars 1992, 204: "The description of the sickness in Matthew is not likely to be original. … The colloquial expression κακῶς ἔχων in Luke should be accepted, as he retains it in 5,31 when reproducing a source (i.e., Mk 2,17), but does not introduce it elsewhere, whereas John's ἠσθένει is his regular word for sickness (cf. 11,1-6)."

210: Reconstruction. For complete text see Q 7:1[6] Luke = Q, Pro (p. 56).

Gagnon 1993, 715: "I regard the description of the illness in Luke 7:2 (κακῶς ἔχων ἤμελλεν τελευτᾶν) to be an original part of the Q account rather than a revision by Luke's special source."

718: "The description of the slave's illness in 7:2 was probably not a product of Luke's special source or Lucan redaction (notwithstanding Luke 8:42), for three reasons: (1) κακῶς (7/4/2 + 1) and τελευτᾶν (4/2/1 + 2) appear nowhere else in Luke's special source material and rarely in Luke-Acts; (2) the parallel description of the illness in John 4:47 confirms Luke's version as a reproduction of Q; (3) Matthew's diagnosis of the illness is largely formulated in Matthean language, and it compensates for the displacement of the story of the paralytic."

Gagnon 1994b, 135: Reconstruction. For complete text see Q 7:1[0] In Q (p. 15).

137: "There is little in the word usage of Luke's description that would indicate redaction on his part (especially with regard to κακῶς ἔχων. … That Luke was influenced by the description of Jairus' daughter (ἐσχάτως ἔχει,

Mark 5.23; reproduced by Luke 8.42 as ἀπέθνῃσκεν) is not impossible given other points of contact between the two stories. However, if that were the case, we might have expected the more usual ἀπέθνῃσκεν (as in Luke 8.42). Luke would almost certainly have retained a report of paralysis as an illustration of the claim that 'the lame walk' (Luke 7.22). Finally, the parallel description in John 4.47 (ἤμελλεν γὰρ ἀποθνῄσκειν) confirms that Luke preserved the Q text."

Landis 1994, 20: "Κακῶς ἔχω ist für Lk untypisch." Landis is arguing, however, that Luke has used a *Sonderquelle*, not Q. See Matt = Q, Pro (p. 192).

International Q Project 1995, 478: Reconstruction. For complete text see Q 7:1⁰ In Q (p. 16).

Con

Cadbury 1920, 48: "In Luke 4,39 = Mark 1,31 = Matt. 8,15, Luke alone omits the fact that in curing the woman Jesus took ... her hand. In fact Luke frequently omits reference to touching or laying on of hands where Matthew and Mark mention it. Again with all his 'special interest in methods of healing' [Harnack 1906, 128-129; ET 184] Luke does not mention (9,6) as does Mark (6,13) that the twelve on their mission of preaching and practicing anointed their patients with olive oil. In Matthew (8,6) the patient healed at the request of a Capernaum centurion is plainly described as παραλυτικός, but in Luke (7,2) merely as one very sick and about to die."

79-80: See Q 7:2, 3, 4-6a⁷ Luke = Q, Con (p. 148).

Loisy 1924, 215-216: "Dans le récit original, les détails nécessaires sur la maladie étaient donnés par le centurion même parlant à Jésus. Matthieu (vii, 6): ... Les traits de notre récit [Luke] sont plus vagues, et celui de la mort imminente est emprunté à l'histoire de la fille de Jaïr (cf. viii, 42); il vient d'ailleurs beaucoup moins pour le relief du miracle que pour ménager une sorte de gradation dans les péricopes qui vont se succéder. Notre récit, en effet, montre un homme sur le point de mourir, qui va être guéri; suivra un mort, le fils de la veuve, qui sera ressuscité; après quoi, Jésus dira aux envoyés de Jean que les morts ressuscitent à sa voix. La combinaison n'est pas fortuite; c'est pourquoi il paraît possible que la substitution du serviteur au fils ait été voulue par l'évangéliste, [216] qui se contenterait ici d'un serviteur guéri, parce qu'il va présenter aussitôt un fils ressuscité, le second miracle étant en quelque façon dédoublé du premier. Mais on croira difficilement que Luc se soit livré à tous ces enfantillages: le remaniement du présent récit et l'invention du miracle de Naïn doivent être imputés au rédacteur évangélique."

Delobel 1966, 456: "Cette péricope lucanienne comporte, comme nous venons de signaler, plusieurs points de contact avec le récit de Jaïre, un texte que Luc trouve dans *Mc.*, et qu'il a foncièrement retravaillé. Il y a chaque fois allusion à la synagogue (*Lc.*, VII, 5; VIII, 41) et dans les deux récits, le malade est à la mort (VII, 2: κακῶς ἔχων ἤμελλεν τελευτᾶν; VIII, 42: ἀπέθνῃσκεν duratif, et seulement au v. 49 τέθνηκεν)."

Schulz 1972, 236: "Κακῶς ἔχειν kommt zwar bei Lk nur noch in 5,31 trad vor, könnte aber stilistische Anlehnung an mk Wundergeschichten sein.⁴⁰²"

236⁴⁰²: "Dort 4mal. Außerdem ist die Bezeichnung des Kranken als κακῶς ἔχων allgemeiner als die konkretere Angabe des Mt, wonach es sich um einen Gelähmten handelt, sie ist also sek."

237: "Erst Lk hat die Schilderung der Krankheit durch den Vater in einen bloßen Bericht über den kranken Knecht umgewandelt."

Busse 1977, 147: "Die veränderte Erzählweise veranlaßt Lukas, die Krankheit zu dramatisieren,¹ um die Transportunfähigkeit des Kranken sicherzustellen."

147¹: "Votiert Schulz [1972, 236-240] für die matth. als [der] Q-Fassung. – Schlatter [1931, 252] vermutet hinter κακῶς ἔχων palästinenischen Einfluß und hält deshalb die luk. für die ältere Version. Beide Thesen haben ihre Schwächen. Nach Schulz könnte stilistisch κακῶς ἔχων eine 'Anlehnung an mk Wundergeschichten' sein und formgeschichtlich muß man vom Konkreten auf das sekundär Allgemeinere schließen. Deshalb sei die allgemeinere Terminologie des Lk sekundär. Dagegen ist einzuwenden, daß das matth. Krankheitsbild in Mt 9,2 und 8,14 seine Entsprechung hat. Dabei ist vor allem παραλυτικός red., da es viermal bei mt vorkommt, wovon Mt 4,24 (Sammelbericht) sicherlich math. ist. Schon Cadbury [1920, 48] fiel auf, daß Lk, dem von Harnack Medizinkenntnisse zugetraut werden, hier keine exakte Terminologie wählt. Es liegt also die Vermutung nahe, κακῶς ἔχων sei eine Anpassung an mark. Ausdrucksweise. Es ist also anzunehmen, Lk hat keine klare Vorstellung von der Krankheit in seiner Vorlage vorgefunden und deshalb diese ergänzt."

Gatzweiler 1979, 308: "[Lc] dramatise sa narration en soulignant la gravité de la maladie du serviteur qui lui est cher (v. 4)."

Neirynck 1979, 109-110: See Q 7:2, 3, 4-6a³ Luke = Q, Con (pp. 107-108).

Wegner 1985, 143: "Kaum wird Mt, der die Wendung konsequent aus seinem Mk-Stoff übernahm, κακῶς ἔχειν in seiner Vorlage gelesen haben."

Schnelle 1987, 103: "Lukas hat in einem weit größeren Maß als Matthäus die Q-Vorlage umgestaltet. Auf seine Redaktion gehen die Situationsschilderung in V.2 ... [und] die dramatische Krankheitsschilderung ... zurück."

Schnelle 1987, ET 1992, 89: "Luke has reshaped the Q version of the story much more thoroughly than Matthew. His redaction produced the description of the situation in v. 2 ... [and] the dramatic depiction of the illness."

Gnilka 1990, 127³⁴: "Die Schilderung der Krankheit bei Lk 7,2: es ging ihm schlecht, und er war dabei zu sterben (vgl. Joh 4,47), ist sicher sekundär."

Gnilka 1990, ET 1997, 121⁹⁸: "The description of the disease in Luke 7:2, that he was sick and at the point of death (cf. John 4:47), is surely secondary."

Catchpole 1992, 523 [1993, 287-288]: "The phrase κακῶς [298] ἔχων cannot with safety be attributed to Q. Not a normal Lucan term,²⁹ it occurs elsewhere in Luke-Acts only at Luke 5,31/Mark 2,17. But in that context he also introduced ὑγιαίνειν, present also in Luke 7:10, so he may in both contexts be redactionally setting up a pairing."

523 [288]²⁹: "Statistics: 5—4—2 + 0."

Sevenich-Bax 1993, 177-178: "Zwar trifft umgekehrt zu, daß Lukas die Aussage κακῶς ἔχειν aus dem ihm mehrfach in dieser Form überlieferten Markus-Stoff nur einmal übernommen hat. Entgegen dem offensichtlichen lukanischen Desinteresse an dieser Formulierung mag die Wendung hier jedoch auf Lukas zurückgehen: Sie könnte eine 'stilistische Anlehnung an mk Wundergeschichten [178] sein' [Schulz 1972, 236]. Außerdem verrät die Formulierung mit μέλλειν die Hand des Lukas.²"

178²: "Daß dieser Erzählzug von Lukas sekundär in die Geschichte eingetragen sein wird, erweist sich umgekehrt wiederum daran, daß die Formulierung mit βασανίζω Matthäus aus der Tradition überkommen ist.'"

Matt = Q: (βέβληται ἐν τῇ οἰκίᾳ παραλυτικός)¹⁰

Pro

Strauss 1836, 100-101: "Nehmen wir zuerst die beiden Synoptiker für sich, so ist nur Eine Stimme der Erklärer, daß Lukas die genauere Darstellung gebe. Schon das will man unwahrscheinlich finden, daß der Kranke nach Matthäus ein Paralytischer gewesen sein sollte, da bei dem Ungefährlichen dieses Leidens der bescheidene Hauptmann schwerlich Jesum gleich beim Eintritt in die Stadt in Beschlag genommen haben würde: [101] als ob ein sehr schmerzhaftes Übel, wie das von Matthäus beschriebene, nicht möglichst schnelle Abhülfe wünschenswerth machte, und als ob es ein unbescheidener Anspruch gewesen wäre, Jesum noch vor seiner Nachhausekunft um ein heilendes Wort zu ersuchen. Vielmehr das umgekehrte Verhältniß zwischen Matthäus und Lukas wird durch die Bemerkung wahrscheinlich, daß das Wunder und also auch das Übel des wunderbar Geheilten in der Überlieferung sich nie verkleinert, sondern stets vergrößert, daher eher der arggeplagte Paralytische zum μέλλων τελευτᾶν gesteigert, als dieser zu einem bloß Leidenden herabgesetzt werden mochte."

Strauss 1836, ET 1855, 515-516: "If we take first the two synoptists by themselves, expositors with one voice declare that Luke gives the more correct account. First of all, it is thought improbable that the patient should have been as Matthew says, a paralytic, since in the case of a disease so seldom fatal the modest centurion would scarcely have met Jesus to implore his aid immediately on his entrance into the city: as if a very painful disease such as is described by Matthew did not render desirable the quickest help, and as if there were any want of modesty in asking Jesus before he reached home to utter a healing word. Rather, the contrary relation between Matthew and Luke seems probable from the observation, that the miracle, and consequently [516] also the disease of the person cured miraculously, is never diminished in tradition but always exaggerated; hence the tormented paralytic would more probably be heightened into one *ready to die*, μέλλων τελευτᾶν, than the latter reduced to a mere sufferer."

von Harnack 1907, 91 (ET 1908, 131): Reconstruction. For complete text see Q 7:1⁶ Luke = Q, Pro (p. 55).

Loisy 1907, 648-649: See Q 7:2, 3, 4-6a¹¹ Luke = Q, Con (p. 203).

B. Weiß 1908, 15: Reconstruction. For complete text see Q 7:1⁰ In Q (p. 5).

Crum 1927, 138: Reconstruction. For complete text see Q 7:2, 3, 4-6a¹ Luke = Q, Pro (pp. 71-72).

Haenchen 1959a, 23 [1965, 82]: "Beginnen wir mit der *Vorlage des Matthäus*. ... Ein Centurio, Offizier des Herodes Antipas ... kommt zu Jesus: sein παῖς liegt gelähmt daheim in furchtbaren Schmerzen."

Schulz 1972, 237: "Daß in Q die Krankheit des Kindes vom Vater geschildert wurde, wie dies bei Mt der Fall ist, ist wahrscheinlich. Die Beschreibung des Krankheitsbildes mit παραλυτικός bei Mt⁴⁰⁸ dürfte die Vorlage wiedergeben."

237⁴⁰⁸: "4,24 red; 9,2 (2mal).6 trad."

Pesch and Kratz 1976, 78: "Die Charakterisierung der Not drückt sich bei Mattäus in einer genaueren Krankheitsangabe aus: es handelt sich um einen Gelähmten."

Polag 1979, 38: Reconstruction. For complete text see Q 7:1⁰ In Q (pp. 9-10).

Schenk 1981, 37: Reconstruction. For complete text see Q 7:1⁰ In Q (p. 10).

Wegner 1985, 138-139: For βέβληται: "Gegen die mt Red auSt erheben sich indessen einige Bedenken, die eher zur Zurückhaltung raten. Als erstes muß der Befund in Q beachtet werden. Die fünf sicheren Belege (Mt 3,10; 4,6; 5,13.25 und 6,30 par Lk), die in dieser Überlieferung erscheinen, deuten darauf hin, daß auch die Verwendung in Mt 8,6 durchaus ursprünglich sein könnte. Ferner muß bedacht [139] werden, daß dieses Verb auch sonst in den Evv und in anderer Literatur für erkrankte Personen verwendet wird. Interessant ist schließlich, daß Mt in der Fernheilung der Tochter der Syrophoenizierin (Mk 7,24-30/Mt 15,21-28) das mk εὖρεν τὸ παιδίον βεβλημένον aus 7,30 gerade nicht übernimmt."

140: For οἰκία: "Was Mt 8,6 angeht, so vermutet Schürmann [1968, 121], das mt οἰκία enthalte eine Reminiszenz an Lk 7,6. Hat Lk 7,1ff gegenüber Q den urspr Wortlaut bewahrt, so könnte dies zutreffen. Ist jedoch die mt Perikope der Traditionsträger, dann könnte ebensogut das Gegenteil der Fall sein. Wie auch immer hierüber entschieden werden mag: Das οἰκία-Motiv in allen drei Fassungen der Erzählung ist kaum zufällig, so daß man mit relativer Wahrscheinlichkeit das Wort in der urspr Hauptmannsperikope vermuten kann."

Gnilka 1986, 299: "Bei einem Vergleich mit der lk Perikope ergeben sich folgende bemerkenswerte Unterschiede: Zunächst betreffen sie die Schilderung der Krankheit. Nach Mt. 8,6 liegt der Knecht gelähmt im Haus und leidet große Qualen. Nach Lk 7,2 ist er dem Tod nahe (vgl. Joh 4,47). ... Für die Rekonstruktion der Q-Vorlage wird man sich an Mt halten müssen. Die Steigerung zur Todeskrankheit ist sicher sekundär."

Schenk 1987, 419: For παραλυτικός: "Während Mk 2,3-10 alle Stellen in einer einzigen Episode vorgab, sind von Mt 9,2a.b.6 nur drei übernommen; gleichzeitig wurde dieses Segment zur mt Letztverwendung; die beiden andern stehen voran: 8,6 (+Q) dürfte die urspr. Q-Fassung bieten ...; Mt hat beide Stellen noch weiter durch labiale Alliteration mit →*liegend* aneinander angeglichen."

Schnelle 1987, 102: "Matthäus steht am Anfang der Q-Überlieferung näher als Lukas. Dies ergibt sich aus ... der Krankheitsbeschreibung mit παραλυτικός."

Schnelle 1987, ET 1992, 88: "At the beginning, Matthew is closer to Q than is Luke. This is seen from ... the description of the sickness with the term παραλυτικός (paralyzed)."

Crossan 1991, 328 (GT 1994, 433): See Q 7:2, 3, 4-6a³ Matt = Q, Pro (p. 120).

Catchpole 1992, 524 [1993 288]: "Οἶκος/οἰκία is a natural element in the story, especially since Q located the conversation with Jesus away from the centurion's home, and the occurrence of οἰκία in Luke 7,6 is better understood as a Lucan reminiscence of a Q detail than as evidence that Matthew know some text approximating to Luke 7,1-6." For Catchpole's argument against βέβληται, and for a prefacing argument against ἐν τῇ οἰκίᾳ, see Matt = Q, Con (p. 195).

Sevenich-Bax 1993, 177: "Nun läßt sich zwar nicht unmittelbar das Interesse des Lukas an der Eskalation begründen. Jedoch kann zunächt erwiesen werden, daß die Formulierung bei Matthäus traditionell ist: παραλυτικός verwendet Matthäus insgesamt nur fünfmal, und zwar außer an der vorliegenden Stelle dreimal in Abhängigkeit von seiner Markus-Vorlage (Mk 2,3-10 vgl. Mt 9,2a.b.6), einmal in dem Summarium Mt 4,24. Nur diese letzte Stelle ist mit einiger Sicherheit der redaktionellen Arbeit des Matthäus zu verdanken. Aber: 'Aus diesem stat Befund ist nicht mehr als eine negative Feststellung zu entnehmen: In 8,6 ist ein red Gebrauch von παραλυτικός nicht prinzipiell unmöglich; wahrscheinlich ist er aber keineswegs, da die Basis, die dafür durch 4,24 gegeben ist, zu schmal ist' [Wegner 1985, 47]. Gegen eine von Matthäus vorgenommene redaktionelle Substitution eines generellen κακῶς ἔχειν durch παραλυτικός spricht ferner, daß Matthäus die Wendung κακῶς ἔχειν immer übernimmt, wenn seine Tradition sie ihm vorgibt (vgl. besonders zu Mk 1,34; 2,17; 6,55 par. Mt). Matthäus zeigt also keine Tendenz, diese Diktion zu übergehen und hätte sie folglich kaum gestrichen, wenn er sie in der Logienquelle vorgefunden hätte."

238: Reconstruction. For complete text see Q 7:1[0] In Q (p. 15).

Landis 1994, 7: "Deutlichere Spuren einer mt Redaktion zeigen sich in einzelnen Teilen der Beschreibung der Krankheit des Jungen. Die Ortsangabe ἐν τῇ οἰκίᾳ dürfte allerdings traditionell sein. Dafür spricht schon der Umstand, daß das οἰκία-Motiv in allen drei Fassungen der Erzählung (Mt 8,6; Lk 7,6; Joh 4,53) auftaucht." However, Landis' reconstruction leaves out all of βέβληται ἐν τῇ οἰκίᾳ, replacing it with a hesitant emendation of Wegner's κατάκειται. See Landis at Matt = Q, Con (p. 196).

Con

H. Meyer 1864, 218: "Die Beschreibung der Krankheit ist nicht *gegen* Luk. 7,2., aber genauer."

H. Meyer 1864, ET 1884, 179: "The description of the disease is not at *variance* with Luke vii. 2, but more exact."

Castor 1912, 223[1]: "Matthew defines the disease as παραλυτικός, but this term seems to be very loosely employed in the First Gospel, and without the support of Luke cannot be credited to Q."

Parker 1953, 63-65: See Q 7:1[6] Matt = Q, Con (pp. 58-60).

Schnackenburg 1964, 74: For παραλυτικός: "Doch ließe sich darauf hinweisen, daß Matthäus bei Krankheitsangaben seine eigenen Wege geht. Aufschlußreich ist sein Sammelbericht in 4,24, wo er nach 'Besessenen' noch zusätzlich 'Mondsüchtige und Gelähmte (παραλυτικούς)' nennt; für beide Bezeichnungen scheint er eine Vorliebe zu haben, da er den 'besessenen' Knaben Mk 9, 17f, der epileptische Züge aufweist, betont als 'Mondsüchtigen' (der oft ins Feuer oder ins Wasser fällt) beschreibt (17, 15)—für den antiken Menschen, der die Epilepsie auf den Einfluß des Mondes zurückführte, sicher nichts Verwunderliches."

Schnackenburg 1965, 505: "Ähnlich unausgleichbar ist die Angabe der Krankheit bei Mt (Lähmung) und Joh (Fieber). … Doch ließe sich darauf hinweisen, daß Matthäus bei Krankheitsangaben seine eigenen Wege geht[1]. Sachlich möchte man in unserem Fall eher das bei Joh erwähnte 'Fieber' für zutreffend halten, da dies besser zu der akuten Lebensgefahr paßt, von der auch Lk 7,2 spricht."

505[1]: "Im Sammelbericht 4,24 nennt er nach 'Besessenen' noch zusätzlich 'Mondsüchtige und Gelähmte' (παραλυτικούς). Für beide Bezeichnungen scheint er eine Vorliebe zu haben (vgl. 17,15 mit Mk 9,17f)."

Schnackenburg 1965, ET 1968, 474: "It is … impossible to reconcile the nature of the illness as given by Matthew (paralysis) and John (fever). … There is … the factor that Matthew goes his own way in describing illnesses.[36] In the present case, the fever mentioned by John would seem to fit the facts better, as the danger of death is acute, as Lk 7:2 also says."

474[36]: "In the summary account 4:24 he mentions along with 'possessed' also 'lunatics and cripples' (παραλυτικούς). He seems to have a liking for these last two terms (cf. 17:15 with Mk 9:17f)."

Brown 1966, 193: "In Matthew the *pais* is lying paralyzed in terrible distress. In Luke the *doulos* is sick and at the point of death. In John the *huios* is ill and near death with fever. John's account is perfectly plausible here since fever would explain the crisis more easily than Matthew's paralysis. As Schnackenburg [1964], p. 74, points out, Matthew has a tendency to specify illnesses."

Schürmann 1969, 391[14]: "Matth bringt die παραλυτικοί (diff Mk 2,3 [4.5] 10 von Luk vermieden) auch 4,24 (diff Mk 1,32) ins Spiel. Er konkretisiert die Krankheit neben 8,1-4.14f—und vielleicht im Hinblick auf den Vergleich V 9?—zur Lähmung, wie er auch 17,15 diff Mk und 12,22 diff Lk 11,14 Krankheitsangaben ändert."

Schulz 1972, 236[402]: "Dort 4mal. Außerdem ist die Bezeichnung des Kranken als κακῶς ἔχων allgemeiner als die konkretere Angabe des Mt, wonach es sich um einen Gelähmten handelt, sie ist also sek."

237: "Daß Mt in den Wortlaut eingegriffen hat, zeigen gewisse mt Spracheigentümlichkeiten.[406]"

237[406]: "Das Verb βάλλειν ist bei Mt gehäuft (34mal; dagegen Mk 18mal; Lk 18mal)—βεβλημένος im Sinn von 'krank darniederliegend' findet sich bei Mt noch 8,14 red; 9,2 red."

Sabourin 1975, 153: "The nature of the illness, left undefined by Luke, is described as paralysis by Matthew who shows elsewhere his willingness to give sick people more concrete names, like 'lunatics and paralytics' (cf. 17:15)."

Pesch and Kratz 1976, 78: "Die Schwere der Krankheit wird unterstrichen durch die Erwähnung des Darniederliegens (im Griechischen ausdrucksstärker: 'hingeworfen sein'; vgl. 8,14; 9,2) im Zustandsperfekt und den Zusatz 'furchtbar gequält' (vgl. ähnlich 8,28; 15,22; 17,15); das Vokabular ist dämonistisch gefärbt."

Busse 1977, 147[1]: "Nach Schulz [1972, 236[402]] könnte stilistisch κακῶς ἔχων eine 'Anlehnung an mk Wundergeschichten' sein und formgeschichtlich muß man vom Konkreten auf das sekundär Allgemeinere schließen. Deshalb sei die allgemeinere Terminologie des Lk sekundär. Dagegen ist einzuwenden, daß das matth. Krankheitsbild in Mt 9,2 und 8,14 seine Entsprechung hat. Dabei ist vor allem παραλυτικός red., da es viermal bei mt vorkommt, wovon Mt 4,24 (Sammelbericht) sicherlich math. ist."

Beare 1981, 207: "It is possible that Matthew has introduced the notion of paralysis from a recollection of the Markan story which in Mark follows upon the healing of the leper."

Gundry 1982, 142: "The sending of a delegation from the centurion to Jesus is out of the picture. So Matthew almost necessarily inserts 'in the house,' i.e., 'at home,' as an indication of some distance between Jesus and the place where the servant lies prostrate. οἰκία typifies Matthew's diction (5,3). The identification of the servant's malady as paralysis is absent from Luke. It compensates for the delay of the story concerning the paralytic carried by four and makes specially appropriate the thought of prostration contained in βέβληται (not in Luke). Cf. Matthew's distinctive uses of βάλλω for the prostrations of Peter's mother-in-law (8:14) and the paralytic carried by four (9:2) as well as other distinctive occurrences (12,8)."

Dauer 1984, 104: "Man muß in diesem Fall sicher auch mit Überarbeitung des Lukas rechnen ..., aber auch Mt dürfte nicht die ursprüngliche Fassung haben, wie die folgenden Beobachtungen zeigen: βάλλεσθαι = krank darniederliegen, schreibt Matthäus auch Mt 8,14 diff Mk 1,30, hier freilich durch das mk κατακεῖσθαι angeregt.—Die Krankheitsangabe παραλυτικός aber nimmt er Mt 9,2.6 aus der Mk-Vorlage; Mt 4,24 aber fügt er sie diff Mk 1,39 (vgl. auch 1,32ff) zusammen mit 'Besessenen und Mondsüchtigen' von sich aus ein, wie er auch Mt 15,29f diff Mk 7,32; Mt 17,15 diff Mk 9,17; Mt 12,22 diff Lk 11,14 Krankheitsangaben ändert. So könnte auch hier die Änderung und Konkretisierung des Krankheitsbildes in 'Lähmung' durchaus ihm zugetraut werden."

Wegner 1985, 140: For παραλυτικός: "Alle fünf mk Belege kommen innerhalb der Heilung des Gelähmten Mk 2,1-12 vor. Mt übernimmt das Wort aus dieser Perikope 3x (9,2 [bis].6) und hat es außer Mt 8,6 nur noch 1x innerhalb des Summariums 4,23-25, V 24, hier wahrscheinlich red." Wegner includes παραλυτικός, however, in his reconstruction of Q. For a complete text of his reconstruction, see Q 7:1⁰ In Q (pp. 11-12).

Bovon 1989, 349[30]: "Matthäus, der eine Vorliebe für Gelähmte hat, änderte die von Lukas (vgl. Joh 4,46) weitergegebene Überlieferung."

Bovon 1989, FT 1991, 341[30]: "Matthieu, qui aime les paralytiques, a dû modifier la tradition que Luc véhicule (cf. Jn 4,46)."

Davies and Allison 1991, 21: "Matthew shows a tendency to specify sicknesses, and perhaps his formulation has been affected by Mk 2.1-12, a story which in Mark follows the healing of the leper (Mk 1.40-5 = Mt 8.2-4): 'paralytic' occurs there. 'In the house' has been added ... because, given the changes vis-à-vis Q, we would not otherwise know that Jesus was not near the sick servant and that healing occurred at a distance."

Catchpole 1992, 524 [1993 288]: "The same cannot be said for Matthew's παραλυτικός, derived directly from the related healing story in Mark 2,1-12, probably the source of all NT παραλυτικός references. ... The phrase ἐν τῇ οἰκίᾳ could certainly be a reminiscence of οἶκος in Mark 2,1.11, or even drawn from Mark 1,29 in view of the next tradition in Matthew's sequence being Mark 1,29-31/Matt 8,14-15. [See Matt = Q, Pro (p. 191), for Catchpole's position on ἐν τῇ οἰκίᾳ.] ... The use of βάλλειν in a description of a sick person before recovery is extremely rare in the gospels and confined to two cases of MattR, both in traditions adjacent to this one.³⁵ Therefore βέβληται seems likely to be MattR [289] as well."

524 [288]³⁵: "Matt 8,14 diff Mark 1,29; Matt 9,2 diff Mark 2,3."

Jacobson 1992, 112: "Q seems to have little interest in miracles. It has one miracle story (Q 7:1-10), but the nature of the illness is not specified.¹⁴⁴"

112¹⁴⁴: "Matthew's reference to paralysis in 8:6 is probably redactional; he inserts it in 4:25 also."

Lindars 1992, 204: "The description of the sickness in Matthew is not likely to be original. ... ἐν τῇ οἰκίᾳ may be taken from a sentence which [Matthew] has omitted." Lindars later indicates the source of this phrase, but the part of the sentence that indicates the source has been omitted inadvertently.

Gagnon 1993, 718: "Matthew's diagnosis of the illness is largely formulated in Matthean language, and it compensates for the displacement of the story of the paralytic."

Gagnon 1994b, 136: "In my estimation, Matthew has ... altered the original description of the boy's illness ... to one of paralysis in order to draw stronger ties with the themes of Mark's story of 'the healing of the paralytic' (faith, Christologically-based authority, and conflict with Israel's leaders)."

137: "With regard to the claim [of Gagnon himself] that Matthew's description of the boy's illness is secondary, note that Mark's story of the paralytic (Mark 2.1-12 par. Matt 9.1-8) follows immediately upon the story of the leper (Mark 1.40-5) which Matthew had just reproduced in 8.1-4. With the sole exception of δεινῶς, the diagnosis is formulated in Matthean language (...for βάλλω see esp. 8.14; 9.2; for παραλυτικός, the redactional summary in 4.24; for βασανίζω, the use of two cognates in 18.34 [βασανιστής] and again in 4.24 [βάσανος; cf. σεληνιάζεσθαι in 4.24 and 17.15]). Matthew elsewhere shows a willingness to embellish the details of the patient's condition (8.28; 12.22; 15.22; 17.15, 18)."

Landis 1994, 8: "Anders liegen die Dinge nun aber bei der Wendung βέβληται ... παραλυτικός. Schon das Verb βάλλω an sich tritt bei Mt gehäuft auf. V.a. aber wird βάλλομαι in der Bedeutung 'krank darniederliegen' vom ersten Evangelisten zweimal in markinischen Wundergeschichten eingefügt: In 8,14 ersetzt es κατάκειμαι (Mk 1,30), in 9,2 begegnet ἐπὶ κλίνης βεβλημένον anstelle von αἰρόμενον ὑπὸ τεσσάρων (Mk 2,3).[19] Dies legt die Vermutung nahe, daß Mt auch an unserer Stelle βέβληται als Ersatz für ein anderes Wort gebraucht haben könnte.

"Auch die Konkretisierung der Krankheit als Lähmung bei Mt wird kaum ursprünglich sein. Im Vergleich mit der lukanischen und der johanneischen Fassung, welche beide den Kranken als dem Tode nahe und damit transportunfähig schildern, fällt auf, daß bei Mt nicht mehr klar wird, warum der Junge nicht zu Jesus gebracht wird; bei Gelähmten war dies nämlich durchaus möglich, wie etwa Mk 2,1-12 zeigt. Daß erst Mt παραλυτικός in seine Vorlage eingetragen hat, erscheint deshalb als sehr wohl denkbar, weil der erste Evangelist ganz allgemein sehr frei mit Krankheitsangaben umgeht und gerne zusätzliche medizinische Begriffe einbringt: So trägt er z.B. in 12,22 (diff Lk 11,14) τυφλός ein, in 17,15 ergänzt er gegenüber Mk 9,17b die Mondsüchtigkeit des epileptischen Knaben, und in sein Summar 4,24 fügt er redaktionell die Begriffe 'Mondsüchtige' und 'Gelähmte' (παραλυτικούς) ein (diff Mk 1,32-34.39). Auch an unserer Stelle dürfte παραλυτικός der mt Redaktion entstammen. Ganz unwahrscheinlich ist dabei, daß Mt in seiner Vorlage eine Krankheitsbeschreibung wie jene von Lk oder Joh gelesen und diese dann durch seine eigene mit der Lähmung des Jungen ersetzt hätte."

8[19]: "Zwar übernimmt Mt in 15,21-28 die Wendung εὗρεν τὸ παιδίον βεβλημένον aus Mk 7,30 nicht. ... Das kann aber damit erklärt werden, daß Mk den Begriff auf einen bereits gesunden und nicht wie jeweils Mt auf einen kranken Menschen anwendet."

9: "Παραλυτικός ... ist redaktioneller Zusatz des ersten Evangelisten, nicht Ersatz für eine andere Formulierung seiner Quelle."

Meier 1994, 685: "We would have a fifth instance of Jesus curing a paralyzed person if we decided to take up at this point Matthew's version of the story of the centurion's servant (Matt 8:5-13 parr.). However, there is a reason for not doing so. Only in Matthew's account are we told that the servant lies at home paralyzed (*paralytikos*) and in extreme pain (v 6). This description is lacking in both the Lucan parallel (Luke 7:1-10) and in the distant parallel in John, the story of the cure of the royal official's son (John 4:46-54). In both Luke and John the problem is rather that the slave or son is near death from a grave but unspecified illness (Luke 7:2; John 4:46-47). This striking agreement of both the Lucan form of the Q story and the Johannine tradition over against Matthew inclines me to treat the story in a later category, namely, various *types* of healing that are attested only once in the Gospels. The primitive form of the story of the centurion's servant seems to have dealt with Jesus curing at a distance a servant or son who was near death.[30]"

733[30]: "Why Matthew would have introduced the term *paralytikos* into the story of the centurion's servant is by no means clear. It is curious, though, that there is a clear divide in the Gospel between Matthew's use of 'paralyzed' (*paralytikos*) before chap. 11 and his use of 'lame' (*chōlos*) from chap. 11 onwards. The word *paralytikos* occurs in Matthew only in 4:24; 8:6; 9:2(*bis*), 6, while *chōlos* occurs only in 11:5; 15:30-31; 18:8; 21:14."

764[179]: See Q 7:2, 3, 4-6a[11] Luke = Q, Pro (pp. 202-203).

Merklein 1994, 97: "Allerdings wird die Krankheit im Unterschied zu Lukas als Lähmung beschrieben. Das hängt wahrscheinlich wieder mit dem Summarium von Mt 11,2.5f zusammen."

Neirynck 1995, 177: "Je crois que Landis a raison de refuser παραλυτικός (v. 6). Pour renforcer son argument, il aurait pu signaler une influence possible de la séquence parallèle en Mc: Mt 8,2-4/Mc 1,40-45; Mt 8,5-13/Mc 2,1-12 (cf. Mt 9,1-8). D'autre part, il concède peut-être trop facilement le caractère traditionnel de βασανιζόμενος."

Kollmann 1996, 258: "Andererseits begegnet παραλυτικός Mt 4,24 redaktionell, und δεινῶς βασανιζόμενος Mt 8,6 deutet darauf hin, daß ursprünglich auch bei Mt von einer akuten Erkrankung die Rede war."

Emendation = Q: ὁ παῖς μου ... <κατάκειται>[10] δεινῶς βασανιζόμενος.

Wegner 1985, 139: "Βέβληται kann sowohl red—in diesem Falle könnte Mt es als Ersatz für eine Form von κατακεῖσθαι, εἶναι o.ä. verwendet haben—als auch trad sein. Um dieser Ungewißheit willen wird κατακεῖσθαι als v.l. zu βέβληται im Rekonstruktionsversuch der urspr Erzählung angegeben."

270[5]: "Statt βέβληται könnte auch κατάκειται o.ä. gestanden haben." Elsewhere, Wegner decides for Matt = Q, Pro (pp. 190-191).

Landis 1994, 8: "Welches Wort aber in der Quelle des Mt gestanden hat, ob z.B. das von Wegner vorgeschlagene κατάκειται der Fassung der Logienquelle entspricht, läßt sich kaum entscheiden."

9, 17: Reconstruction: "ὁ παῖς μου ... (κατάκειται?) δεινῶς βασανιζόμενος." For complete text see Q 7:1[6] Luke = Q, Pro (p. 57).

Emendation = Q: ὁ παῖς μου <>[10] ἐν τῇ οἰκίᾳ <>[10] δεινῶς βασανιζόμενος <μέλλει>[11] τελευτᾶν.

Catchpole 1992, 527 [1993, 292]: Reconstruction: "ὁ παῖς μου ἐν τῇ οἰκίᾳ δεινῶς βασανιζόμενος μέλλει τελευτᾶν." For complete text see Q 7:1[0] In Q (p. 14).

Evaluations

Johnson 2000: Luke = Q {B}, (κακῶς ἔχων)[10].

It is clear in the database that while κακῶς ἔχων is not Lukan (e.g. Easton, Jeremias; cf. Schulz), Matthew's παραλυτικός is probably taken from the Healing of the Paralytic in Mark 2:1-12, which in Mark immediately follows the Healing of the Leper (Matt 8:2-4), but which follows somewhat after The Centurion's Faith in Jesus' Word (Matt 9:2-8) in Matthew (Catchpole). Gundry correctly observes Matthew's distinctive use of βάλλω in the first half of the Gospel.

The ending of ἔχων is partly dependent upon a decision for Q 7:2, 3, 4-6a[11].

Robinson 2000: Luke = Q {C} (with emendation), [[(κακῶς ἔχ<ει>)[10]]].

Since the finite verb ἤμελλεν τελευτᾶν is Lukan redaction (see Q 7:2, 3, 4-6a[11]), one would have to postulate a finite verb instead of the Lukan participle. Thus the Lukan reading would require a conjectural emendation, which weakens its likelihood of being the Q reading.

In the case of the Matthean reading, the criticism has focused on the word paralytic as being typically Matthean. But if it is omitted, one has a text for Q that would be appropriate: βέβληται ἐν τῇ οἰκίᾳ.

The reference to a paralytic in Matt 9:2, 6 is simply derived from Mark 2:3, 10 (Luke 5:18, 24: παραλελυμένος/-ῳ). In Matt 8:14 βεβλημένην καὶ πυρέσσουσαν reflects Mark 1:30: κατέκειτο πυρέσσουσα. The Matthean usage is thus slight enough to leave open whether the term paralytic was in Q, but Luke 7:3 does not use the participle as he does in the case of Mark 2:3, 10. The Matthean βεβλημένην in Matt 8:14 may reflect βέβληται in Matt 8:6, which hence could reflect Q, rather than being a typically Matthean expression.

Κακῶς ἔχειν is in Mark 1:32, 34, in the latter case followed by Matt 8:16, but in neither case by Luke 4:40-41. It is used in Mark 6:55, adopted by Matt 14:35, but the context is missing from Luke. It is used in Mark 2:17, followed both by Matt 9:12 and Luke 5:31. It is also used in Matt 15:22; 21:41 without parallels. Therefore it is not obvious that Luke uses the term in 7:2 under Markan influence, since there is not a strong pattern of Luke following Mark in this regard, rather than avoiding the expression in Mark. If Luke did prefer more precise medical terminology, it is unclear why he would improve a Q reading that was already vague with the vague expression κακῶς ἔχων. It is more reasonable to conjecture that he found some vague expression in Q and did not make it more specific, but did (like Matthew) accentuate its gravity by saying the sick person was about to die (see Q 7:2, 3, 4-6a[11]).

Since the Matthean reading seems, by comparing it with Matt 9:2, to be redactional, and the Lukan reading is not Lukan (e.g. never in Acts), the Lukan reading is more likely to be that of Q.

Kloppenborg 2000: Luke = Q {C} (with emendation), [[(κακῶς ἔχ<ει>)¹⁰]].

Hoffmann 2001: Luke = Q {C} (with emendation), [[(κακῶς ἔχ<ει>)¹⁰]].
Ich folge Robinsons Argumentation. Daß βέβληται matthäisch ist legt auch Mt 9,2 nahe: παραλυτικὸν ἐπὶ κλίνης βεβλημένον statt Mk 2,3 παραλυτικὸν αἰρόμενον ὑπὸ τεσσάρων (Lukas vermeidet hier die ungeschickte Ausdrucksweise ganz: φέροντες ἐπὶ κλίνης ...). In 15,28 übernimmt Matthäus nicht Mk 7,30: εὗρεν τὸ παιδίον βεβλημένον ἐπὶ τὴν κλίνην καὶ τὸ δαιμόνιον ἐξεληλυθός, möglicherweise, weil das Partizip hier positiv gemeint ist?
Lukas meidet zwar παραλυτικός, scheut sich aber nicht vom Gelähmten zu sprechen (παραλελυμένος: Lk 5,18.24, Apg 8,7; 9,33, χωλοί: Lk 7,22 [Q]; 14,13.21; Apg 3,2; 8,7; 14,8). Er hätte also wahrscheinlich, wie in Mk 2,3, den sprachlichen Ausdruck geändert, aber nicht den Krankheitsbefund, hätte er ihn in Q vorgefunden. Matthäus bevorzugt in Sammelberichten den Hinweis auf Gelähmte, nicht nur in Mt 4,24 (παραλυτικούς redaktionell), sondern auch in Mt 15,30 (χωλούς ... diff. Mk 7,32), 15,31 (χωλοὺς περιπατοῦντας diff. Mk 7,37, unter dem Einfluß von Q 7,22?) und 21,14. War die Zuordnung von Kap. 8-9 auf die Anfrage des Johannes (11,2: "Werke des Messias") für Matthäus Anlaß, die allgemeine Krankheitsangabe der Q-Vorlage zu präzisieren?
Einige Bemerkungen zu κακῶς ἔχων: Die Wendung kommt bei Markus abgesehen von 2,17 dreimal in Sammelberichten vor (Mk 1,32.34; 6,55). Lukas übernimmt sie aus Mk 2,17 in 5,31, wie auch Matthäus in 9,12. Sonst findet sie sich bei ihm nur an unserer Stelle Lk 7,2. Mk 1,32 πάντας τοὺς κακῶς ἔχοντας καὶ τοὺς δαιμονιζομένους und Mk 1,34 πολλοὺς κακῶς ἔχοντας ποικίλαις νόσοις faßt er in Lk 4,40 durch ἀσθενοῦντας νόσοις ποικίλαις zusammen. Der Sammelbericht Mk 6,53-56 entfällt bei ihm. Matthäus folgt in den Sammelberichten Markus: Mk 1,34 übernimmt er in Mt 8,16; Mk 1,32 benutzt er zusammen mit Mk 3,7.8 für den die Bergpredigt einleitenden Sammelbericht Mt 4,24.25. Dabei wird das markinische πάντας τοὺς κακῶς ἔχοντας καὶ τοὺς δαιμονιζομένους von ihm präzisiert: πάντας τοὺς κακῶς ἔχοντας ποικίλαις νόσοις καὶ βασάνοις συνεχομένους [καὶ] δαιμονιζομένους καὶ σεληνιαζομένους καὶ παραλυτικούς. In Mt 14,35 übernimmt er die Wendung ohne Ergänzung aus Mk 6,55. Läßt sich daraus schließen, daß Matthäus die Wendung aufgrund ihrer Allgemeinheit zwar in Sammelberichten gebraucht, sie aber in der Geschichte von der Heilung des Knechtes des Centurio durch eine präzisere Krankheitsangabe ersetzt, weil sie ihm für eine Heilungserzählung zu

allgemein war? Das Genus der Erzählung braucht mehr Konkretion. Die Art wie er auch in dem Sammelbericht 4,24.25 die Wendung durch konkretere Krankheitsangaben präzisiert (vgl. auch Mt 15,30 diff. Mk 7,32), läßt solches vermuten. Matthäus ändert die Krankheitsangaben auch in 17,15 diff. Mk 9,17 und in Mt 12,22 diff. Lk 11,14. So könnte in der Tat "auch hier die Änderung und Konkretisierung des Krankheitsbildes in 'Lähmung' durchaus ihm zugetraut werden" (mit Dauer, 104).

Q 7:2, 3, 4-6a¹¹: Luke's ἤμελλεν τελευτᾶν or Matthew's δεινῶς βασανιζόμενος.

Luke = Q: [ἤμελλεν τελευτᾶν]¹¹

Pro

H. **Meyer** 1864, 218 (ET 1884, 179): See Q 7:2, 3, 4-6a¹⁰ Luke = Q, Pro (p. 185).

B. **Weiß** 1876, 229: See Q 7:2, 3, 4-6a¹⁰ Luke = Q, Pro (p. 185).

Schmid 1956, 163: "Der Bericht des Lukas erweist sich dabei als der genauere und vollständigere. Bei ihm ist von vornherein klar, daß der Hauptmann ... stehend zu denken ist, ein Heide war und daß sein Knecht bereits im Sterben lag."

Schnackenburg 1964, 74: "Sachlich möchte man in unserem Fall eher das bei Joh erwähnte 'Fieber' für zutreffend halten, da dies besser zu der akuten Lebensgefahr paßt, von der auch Lk 7, 2 spricht."

Jeremias 1980, 151-152: "Trad ... ἤμελλεν τελευτᾶν: Das Imperfekt von [152] μέλλω wird im NT teils mit dem Augment ἠ- (so LkEv 4mal/Apg 3, Joh 4, Hebr 1, Offb 1), teils mit dem Augment ἐ- (so Apg 1mal, Joh 3, Offb 1) geschrieben. Was das Doppelwerk anlangt, so bietet es mit Ausnahme von Apg 21,27 stets ἤμελλον (Lk 7,2; 9,31; 10,1; 19,4; Apg 12,6; 16,27; 27,33). Das Imperfekt von μέλλω mit folgendem Infinitiv schreibt von den Synoptikern nur Lukas. Vor allem die Belege aus der Apostelgeschichte zeigen, daß dieser Sprachgebrauch redaktionell ist; für Lk 9,31 kommt hinzu, daß wir es hier mit einem Zusatz zu Markus (9,4) zu tun haben, für Lk 10,1; 19,4 die lukanische Färbung des unmittelbaren Kontexts. Anders ist jedoch über die Kombination Imperfekt von μέλλω mit einem Verbum des Sterbens, Tötens etc. im Infinitiv zu urteilen. Denn diese Kombination stammt aus der Tradition, wie sich aus der breiten Streuung Lk 7,2; Apg 16,27; Joh 4,47; 11,51; 12,33; 18,32; Offb 3,2 ergibt und wie der Vergleich unserer Stelle Lk 7,2 (ἤμελλεν τελευτᾶν) mit Joh 4,47 (ἤμελλεν ἀποθνήσκειν) bestätigt, der auf den Schluß führt, daß die Kombination in der Heilungsgeschichte Lk 7,1ff. par Joh 4,46ff. verwurzelt war."

Gundry 1982, 142: See Q 7:2, 3, 4-6a¹¹ Matt = Q, Con (p. 209).

Schweizer 1982, 85: "Sprachlich erweisen sich als vorlukanisch der Zug, daß der Kranke am Sterben (und daher nicht transportfähig) ist (auch Joh 4,47)."

Schweizer 1982, ET 1984, 131: "There are several pre-Lukan features in the language of this episode: ([v.] 2) the sick slave is at the point of death (so that he cannot be transported; also John 4:47)."

Bovon 1989, 349³¹: "Die Parallele in Joh 4,47 erweist den Hinweis als traditionell."

Bovon 1989, FT 1991, 341[31]: "En raison du parallèle, Jn 4,47, l'indication doit être traditionnelle."

Nolland 1989, 315-316: See Q 7:2, 3, 4-6a[7] Luke = Q, Pro (p. 148).

Davies and Allison 1991, 20: "Lk 7.2-5 is much longer. Matthew has, presumably, severely abbreviated Q.[41]"

20[41]: "A pre-Lukan basis for Lk 7.2-5 is indicated by several facts, including some expressions not typical of Luke (e.g. κακῶς ἔχων and ἤμελλεν τελευτᾶν) and Jn 4.47, which agrees with Luke that the servant or son was at the point of death."

Catchpole 1992, 523-524 [1993, 288]: "More promising is the phrase ἤμελλεν τελευτᾶν. The verb μέλλειν is a Lucan favourite but, in view of Q 3,7 usage and its being needed here to qualify τελευτᾶν, not thereby shown to be LukeR. Much depends, therefore, on the verb τελευτᾶν itself. This is rare in the synoptic gospels:[31] leaving aside OT quotations there remain only the two non-relevant cases in Matt 9,18 diff Mark 5,23 and Luke 7,2, i.e., Matthew's Jairus [524] story and Luke's centurion story! Since Luke did not know Matt 9,18, the 'coincidental' overlap must be a reminiscence by Matthew of what was in the related tradition. This serves once again to confirm the flow of details between one and another member of this family of traditions. On this basis the same can be said of Matthew's παραλυτικός, derived directly from the related healing story in Mark 2,1-12, probably the source of all NT παραλυτικός references."

523 [288][31]: "Statistics: 4—2—1 + 2."

527 [292]: Reconstruction: See Q 7:2, 3, 4-6a[10] Emendation = Q (p. 197).

Lindars 1992, 204: "It is difficult to decide whether Luke's ἤμελλεν τελευτᾶν is correctly placed, or John's position is original, where it adds urgency to the man's request. But τελευτᾶν is not common in Luke (only here and Acts 2,29; 7,15)."

210: Reconstruction. For complete text see Q 7:1[6] Luke = Q, Pro (p. 56).

211: See Lindars at Matt = Q, Con (p. 209).

Gagnon 1993, 715, 718: See Q 7:2, 3, 4-6a[10] Luke = Q, Pro (p. 186).

Gagnon 1994b, 135: Reconstruction. For complete text see Q 7:1[0] In Q (p. 15).

Landis 1994, 20: "Bei ἤμελλεν τελευτᾶν ist zwar einzuräumen, daß ἤμελλεν = Infinitiv eine von Lk in der Apg bevorzugte Konstruktion ist." However, Landis is arguing that Luke has used a *Sonderquelle*, not Q. See Luke = Q, Con (pp. 206-207).

Meier 1994, 685: See Q 7:2, 3, 4-6a[1] Matt = Q, Con (pp. 196-197).

764[179]: "Schürmann [1969, 391[14]] points out that, without the mention of the servant or son being near death, Matthew's version has no adequate explanation of why the sufferer is not brought to Jesus, as are many other ill people in the Gospel miracles (e.g., Mark 2:1-12). Hence it may be that the element of the sufferer being near death belongs to the earlier tradition (reflected in both Luke and John), which Matthew has modified at this point."

Con

Wernle 1899, 86: "Ganz deutlich geht auf Lc zurück das ἤμελλεν τελευτᾶν (7,2), wodurch er eine Steigerung innerhalb der nächsten Erzählungsgruppe vorbereitet hat: 7,2 ἤμελλεν τελευτᾶν; 7,12 τεθνηκώς; 7,22 νεκροὶ ἐγείρονται."

Holtzmann 1901, 344: "Weiterhin schreibt Lc (7,2) statt παῖς, welches gleichwohl [7,]7 aus der Quelle stehen geblieben ist, δοῦλος, fühlt aber um so mehr das Bedürfniss, die außerordentliche Sorge des Herrn für ihn, die einem Sohne gegenüber eher zu begreifen wäre, zu motiviren: *welcher ihm werth war*; läßt ihn auch gegen Mt 8,6 bereits im Sterben liegen (ἤμελλεν = *in eo erat ut*; *Augmentum temporale*, wie 10,1), wie 8,42 die Jairustochter: Antecipation wie 6,19."

B. Weiß 1904, 242 (ET 1906, 56): See Q 7:2, 3, 4-6a³ Luke = Q, Con (pp. 94-95).

Loisy 1907, 648-649: "L'idée d'une substitution volontaire est peut-être moins invraisemblable qu'elle ne paraît. En d'autres détails, Luc est secondaire [649] par rapport à Matthieu, et les modifications qu'il introduit dans le récit primitif semblent réfléchies. Dès le début, au lieu de dire simplement que le malade était atteint de paralysie, il le représente comme étant sur le point de mourir: trait emprunté à l'histoire de la fille de Jaïr, mais qui vient ici beaucoup moins pour le relief du miracle, que pour ménager une sorte de gradation dans les péricopes qui vont se succéder. On trouve, en effet, dans l'histoire du centurion un homme sur le point de mourir, qui va être guéri; puis un mort, le fils de la veuve, sera ressuscité; après quoi Jésus dira aux envoyés de Jean-Baptiste que les morts ressuscitent à sa voix. Cette combinaison ne peut être fortuite: ne serait-il pas possible que Luc, ayant à présenter en second lieu un fils ressuscité, ait voulu se contenter, en premier lieu, d'un serviteur guéri, les deux faits qu'il raconte équivalant, en quelque façon, dans l'économie de sa relation, au fait unique de Matthieu?"

Castor 1912, 42: "In Luke 7:2b ἤμελλεν τελευτᾶν, ὃς ἦν αὐτῷ ἔντιμος are, perhaps, additions of Luke; so also ὄχλῳ in 7:9."

223: Reconstruction. For complete text see Q 7:1⁰ In Q (p. 6).

Klostermann 1919, 448: "Lc unterscheidet sich besonders durch: ... die Ersetzung von παῖς durch δοῦλος, ... hier noch durch ὃς ἦν αὐτῷ ἔντιμος näher charakterisiert ... und die Steigerung ἤμελλεν τελευτᾶν (= Joh 4,47), die der Jairuserzählung 8,42 Parr entspricht."

Cadbury 1920, 48: See Q 7:2, 3, 4-6a¹⁰ Luke = Q, Con (p. 187).

Loisy 1924, 215-216: See Q 7:2, 3, 4-6a¹⁰ Luke = Q, Con (p. 187).

Klostermann 1929, 86: "'Ημελλεν τελευτᾶν (= Jo 4,47): statt der Schilderung der Krankheit (Mt) vielmehr eine Steigerung, die der Jairuserzählung 8,42 Parr entspricht."

Held 1960, 183 (ET 1963, 194): See Q 7:2, 3, 4-6a[1] Luke = Q, Con (pp. 67-68).
222 (ET 234): See Q 7:2, 3, 4-6a[9] Luke = Q, Con (p. 170).

Grundmann 1961, 155: See Q 7:2, 3, 4-6a[3] Luke = Q, Con (pp. 99-100).
155-156: "Diese Erwägungen legen die Auskunft Hirschs [1941, 88-90] nahe, daß Lukas in einer überarbeiteten Ausgabe von Q, Hirschs Lu I, den Bericht bereits zusammengefügt vorgefunden hat. Die Zusammenfügung steigert den Wundercharakter: [156] Der Knecht liegt im Sterben, während er bei Matthäus gelähmt und von Schmerzen geplagt ist."

Delobel 1966, 456: See Q 7:2, 3, 4-6a[10] Luke = Q, Con (pp. 187-188).

Schürmann 1969, 391[14]: "Schwerlich steigert Luk (und Joh) als Vorbereitung … und in Angleichung an Mk 5,23 parr die Krankheit zur Todeskrankheit."

Miller 1971, 78: "There is still another kind of addition which Luke makes in his narratives, however. This is the kind which emphasizes the difficulty of the problem, or the seriousness of the situation. … In 7:2 the centurion's servant is *ēmellen teleutan* instead of *deinōs basanizomenos*.[2]"
78[2]: "This is only a "Q" comparison, but this is the same kind of change against Matthew that Luke also makes against Mark."

Schulz 1972, 236: "Ein sek Zug ist ferner die Steigerung der Krankheit zu einem Zustand der Todesnähe, der in der Formulierung durch μέλλειν die Hand des Lk verrät."
237: "Erst Lk hat die Schilderung der Krankheit durch den Vater in einen bloßen Bericht über den kranken Knecht umgewandelt."

Busse 1977, 146: "Lukas gestaltet die Bittrede des Hauptmanns (Mt 8,5) in eine Situationsschilderung V 2 um, die er stilistisch elegant mit dem Imperfekt von ihrem Kontext abhebt."
147[1]: "Dagegen ist einzuwenden, daß das matth. Krankheitsbild in Mt 9,2 und 8,14 seine Entsprechung hat. Dabei ist vor allem παραλυτικός red., da es viermal bei mt vorkommt, wovon Mt 4,24 (Sammelbericht) sicherlich math. ist. Schon Cadbury [1920, 48] fiel auf, daß Lk, dem von Harnack Medizinkenntnisse zugetraut werden, hier keine exakte Terminologie wählt. Es liegt also die Vermutung nahe, κακῶς ἔχων sei eine Anpassung an mark. Ausdrucksweise. Es ist also anzunehmen, Lk hat keine klare Vorstellung von der Krankheit in seiner Vorlage vorgefunden und deshalb diese ergänzt. Lk meidet weiterhin παραλυτικός und βασανιζόμενος."

Gatzweiler 1979, 308: "[Lc] dramatise sa narration en soulignant la gravité de la maladie du serviteur qui lui est cher (v. 4)."

Muhlack 1979, 41: For complete text of Lukan expansions, see Q 7:2, 3, 4-6a[3] Luke = Q, Con (pp. 105-106).

Neirynck 1979, 109-110: See Q 7:2, 3, 4-6a³ Luke = Q, Con (pp. 107-108).

Schmithals 1980, 90: See Q 7:2, 3, 4-6a³ Matt = Q, Pro (p. 119).

Schenk 1981, 37: Reconstruction. For complete text see Q 7:1⁰ In Q (p. 10).

Haapa 1983, 71: See Q 7:2, 3, 4-6a³ Luke = Q, Con (p. 109).

Dauer 1984, 111-112: "Von Lukas wird auch die Schilderung des *bedroh-lichen* Zustandes des Kranken mit ἤμελλεν τελευτᾶν stammen. Dafür spre-chen:

"(1) Sprachliche Beobachtungen: ἤμελλεν o.ä. kommt außer Joh 4,47; 7,39; 11,51; 12,33; 18,32 nur in den lk Schriften vor: Lk 7,2 u.St.; 9,31; 10,1; 19,4; Apg 12,6; 16,27; 27,33.—τελευτᾶν schreibt Lukas auch noch Apg 2,29; 7,15; sonst noch Mt 4mal; Mk 2mal; Joh 1mal; Hebr 1mal.

"(2) Beobachtungen zur lk Schriftstellerei: Lukas hat mit dieser zusätzlichen Bemerkung zwei Ziele im Auge:

"(a) Er will damit erklären, warum der kranke Knecht nicht zu Jesus gebracht wurde....

"(b) Er will weiterhin die Größe der Krankheit und damit [112] die Größe des anschließenden Wunders steigern. Ähnliche Steigerungen liegen vor: Lk 4,38 diff Mk 1,30: die Schwiegermutter des Petrus litt an *großem* Fieber; Lk 8,27 diff Mk 5,2: der Besessene hat Dämonen (Plural!), nicht einen unreinen Geist; Lk 8,42 diff Mk 5,23: das Töchterchen des Jairus ist nicht nur ganz schlecht dran, sondern liegt bereits im Sterben.

"Un-lk ist dagegen die Konstruktion Genitiv + dazugehöriges Substantiv + Prädikat am Anfang einer Perikope, wie überhaupt Genitiv am Anfang eines Satzes, vom Genitivus absolutus abgesehen, in den lk Schriften selten vor-kommen."

Wegner 1985, 145: "Was die Ursprünglichkeit der Wendung in Q anbe-langt, so gibt die Statistik allein kaum genügende Anhaltspunkte für eine sichere Entscheidung. Μέλλω ist zwar noch 1x in Q belegt (Lk 3,7/Mt 3,7), nicht aber τελευτάω. Doch besagt letzteres wenig, denn erstens wird τελευτάω überhaupt im gNT nur spärlich verwendet (11x), und zweitens begegnet das Synonym ἀποθνήσκω ebenfalls nicht in Q, woraus zu entnehmen ist, daß das Fehlen weiterer Belege eher sachlich bedingt ist. Immerhin läßt ein Blick auf die mt Verwendung beider Begriffe wenigstens eine negative Feststellung zu, nämlich, daß der erste Evangelist kaum die lk Wendung in seiner Vorlage las. Dies geht aus dem Befund von τελευτάω hervor, das Mt im Gegensatz zu Lk 2x in seinen Mk-Stoff einsetzt, und vor allem aus seiner Verwendung von μέλλω, das er nicht weniger als 6x in seinen Mk-Stoff einfügt, und zwar stets mit nachfolgendem Infinitiv (Mt 16,27; 17,12.22; 20,17 [v.l.].22 und 24,6). Aber auch die bereits erwähnte Tatsache, daß Mt unter den anderen Evange-listen Jesu Wundertätigkeit am deutlichsten hervorhebt, weist in dieselbe Richtung.

"Es bleibt die auffällige Berührung zwischen der Wendung und dem joh ἤμελλεν γὰρ ἀποθνήσκειν (Joh 4,47). Diese weist jedoch nicht unbedingt auf Q-Wortlaut hin, sondern deutet lediglich an, daß vielleicht Lk und Joh in diesem Punkte unter Einfluß eines gleichen Traditionsstranges stehen, was ja angesichts der auch sonst zu treffenden Verbindungslinien zwischen diesen beiden Evangelien nicht verwundert."

270: Reconstruction. For complete text see Q 7:1[0] In Q (pp. 11-12).

Schnelle 1987, 103: "Lukas hat in einem weit größeren Maß als Matthäus die Q-Vorlage umgestaltet. Auf seine Redaktion gehen die Situationsschilderung in V.2 ... [und] die dramatische Krankheitsschilderung ... zurück."

Schnelle 1987, ET 1992, 89: "Luke has reshaped the Q version of the story much more thoroughly than Matthew. His redaction produced the description of the situation in v. 2 ... [and] the dramatic depiction of the illness."

Gnilka 1990, 127[34]: "Die Schilderung der Krankheit bei Lk 7,2: es ging ihm schlecht, und er war dabei zu sterben (vgl. Joh 4,47), ist sicher sekundär."

Gnilka 1990, ET 1997, 121[98]: "The description of the disease in Luke 7:2, that he was sick and at the point of death (cf. John 4:47), is surely secondary."

Sevenich-Bax 1993, 177: "Die Darstellung der Krankheit und ihrer Folge (Qual/Todesgefahr) hängt eng zusammen: Wenn sich nachweisen läßt, daß Lukas an der Steigerung zur Todeskrankheit interessiert ist, dann leuchtet ein, daß er die Qualifizierung der Erkrankung als Lähmung bei Matthäus übergehen mußte, denn eine Lähmung impliziert nicht zugleich Todesgefahr." See Sevenich-Bax at Q 7:2, 3, 4-6a[10] Matt = Q, Pro (pp. 191-192).

178: "Außerdem verrät die Formulierung mit μέλλειν die Hand des Lukas."

Dunderberg 1994, 83: "Darüber hinaus verbietet die lk Parallele (Lk 7,2) es, die Wendung im Joh 4,47 ohne weiteres für redaktionell zu halten."

87: "Die Bezeichnung der Todesgefahr ist wiederum der lk Redaktion zuzuschreiben. Das ἤμελλεν mit Infinitiv kommt im lukanischen Doppelwerk sieben Mal vor (Lk 7,2; 9,31; 10,1; 19,4; Apg 12,6; 16,27; 27,33; vgl. auch Apg 21,27 (ἔμελλον). Darüber hinaus ist die Steigerung der Krankheit für Lk typisch (vgl. Lk 4,38 diff Mk 1,30; Lk 8,27 diff Mk 5,2; Lk 8,42 diff Mk 5,23)."

89: "Lk hat... die Krankheit bis zur Todesgefahr gesteigert."

Landis 1994, 8-9: "Denn abgesehen [9] davon, daß Mt keine Tendenz zeigt, die von Lk und Joh gebrauchten Wendungen zu meiden, ist es kaum glaubhaft, daß ausgerechnet Mt, bei dem die Wunderkraft Jesu mehr als bei allen anderen Evangelisten hervorgehoben wird, einen Erzählzug wie jenen der Todesnähe des παῖς weggelassen hätte. Dieser—wahrscheinlich ursprüngliche—Zug muß vielmehr bereits in der Quelle des Mt gefehlt haben, die Krankheitsschilderung in Q schon erheblich in Richtung des uns vorliegenden Mt-Textes umgestaltet gewesen sein."

20: "Im dritten Evangelium selbst kommt das Imperfekt ἤμελλεν fast aus-schließlich im Sondergut vor. Zudem wird das Verb τελευτάω von Lk im Ver-gleich zu den anderen Synoptikern eher gemieden; Lk hätte für eine redaktio-nelle Wendung wohl eher ἀποθνήσκω gebraucht."

Merklein 1994, 99-100: "Dem Wortlaut nach ist Matthäus (8,5-13) näher an der Fassung der Logienquelle. Doch kann darauf hier nicht weiter einge-gangen werden. Es sollen nur die lukanischen Besonderheiten herausgestellt werden:

"Der Knecht ... des Hauptmanns liegt im Sterben (V. 2; Mt: er hatte große Schmerzen). Lukas betont dies schon im Blick auf die folgende Geschichte (eine Totenerwek- [100] ung)."

International Q Project 1995, 478: Reconstruction. For complete text see Q 7:1⁰ In Q (p. 16).

Kollmann 1996, 257-258: "Lk und Joh, der speziell von Fieber spricht (4,52), schildern sie übereinstimmend als [258] lebenbedrohlich (Lk 7,2; Joh 4,47.49), was gegenüber dem mt παραλυτικός als sekundäre Steigerung wirkt."

Neirynck 1996, 455: "I can agree with D's [Dunderberg—see above] view on Lukan redaction in Lk 7,1-10 (87-89): ἤμελλεν τελευτᾶν (in v. 2), the two delegations (vv. 3-6) and the conclusion (v. 10)."

Matt = Q: (δεινῶς βασανιζόμενος)¹¹

Pro

von Harnack 1907, 91 (ET 1908, 131): Reconstruction. For complete text see Q 7:1⁶ Luke = Q, Pro (p. 55).

B. Weiß 1907, 242: See Q 7:2, 3, 4-6a⁹ Luke = Q, Con (p. 168).

B. Weiß 1908, 15: Reconstruction. For complete text see Q 7:1⁰ In Q (p. 5).

Crum 1927, 138: Reconstruction. For complete text see Q 7:2, 3, 4-6a¹ Luke = Q, Pro (pp. 71-72).

Haenchen 1959a, 23 [1965, 82]: See Q 7:2, 3, 4-6a¹⁰ Matt = Q, Pro (p. 190).

Schnackenburg 1964, 74: For δεινῶς βασανιζόμενος: "Ähnlich wie dort könnte Matthäus auch in 8,6 das ursprünglich vielleicht unbestimmte δεινῶς βασανιζόμενος konkret ausdeuten, diesmal auf eine schwere Lähmung." See also Schnackenburg 1964 at Luke = Q, Pro (p. 201).

Schnackenburg 1965, 505¹: "Vielleicht hat Matthäus in 8,6 das ursprüng-liche δεινῶς βασανιζόμενος konkret auf eine Lähmung gedeutet. Auch in 12,22 weicht er von Lk 11,14 ab."

Schnackenburg 1965, ET 1968, 474[36]: "In 8:6 Matthew has possibly interpreted the original δεινῶς βασανιζόμενος concretely as being crippled. In 12:22 he also departs from Lk 11:14."

Miller 1971, 78: See Miller at Luke = Q, Con (p. 204).

Polag 1979, 38: Reconstruction. For complete text see Q 7:1[0] In Q (pp. 9-10).

Schmithals 1980, 90: See Q 7:2, 3, 4-6a[3] Matt = Q, Pro (p. 119).

Dauer 1984, 104: "Dagegen dürften ihm δεινῶς und βασανίζομαι vorgegeben gewesen sein."

361[459]: "Vielleicht noch add δεινῶς βασανιζόμενος, vgl. Mt 8,6."

Wegner 1985, 141: "Δεινῶς: … kein Hinweis auf mt Red. … βασανίζω: … kein Hinweis auf mt Red.

"Wenn auch βάσανος in Mt 4,24 sehr wahrscheinlich vom ersten Evangelisten selbst stammt, wird man kaum aus dieser Stelle Indizien für eine mt Eintragung des βασανιζόμενος in 8,6 ableiten können."

270: Reconstruction. For complete text see Q 7:1[0] In Q (pp. 11-12).

Gnilka 1986, 299: See Q 7:2, 3, 4-6a[10] Matt = Q, Pro (p. 191).

Catchpole 1992, 524-525 [1993, 289]: "The extreme and striking phrase δεινῶς βασανιζόμενος probably did figure in Q. The word δεινῶς is expressive of great intensity. It occurs elsewhere in the NT only at Luke 11,53, so word statistics prove nothing. With βασανίζειν, however, more can be said. It occurs in Matt 8,29/Mark 5,7/Luke 8,28 and Matt 14,24/Mark 6,48, while βάσανος occurs at Matt 4,24 diff Mark 1,28.32.34. Its presence in Matthew can therefore derive from a source or from MattR. The former is more likely in Matt 8,6, for four reasons. First, the βάσανος group normally stands for extreme agony/torture/torment, which does not fit well content-wise with the MattR παραλυτικός. Second, the use of βασανίζειν to describe dangerous and potentially fatal illness not only goes beyond παραλυτικός but matches ἤμελλεν τελευτᾶν extremely well. It frequently occurs elsewhere in contexts involving fatal illness or suffering when the judgment of God or the torture of martyrs is in view.[37] Given the intensity conveyed by δεινῶς, the point is clear. Third, the use of such language would fit particularly well the exorcistic [525] pattern regarded by many as involved in Q 7,7b-8.[38] Fourth, some such language would go far to explain why, contrary to the norm, the sick person is not this time brought to Jesus."

524 [289][37]: "Wis 11,9; 12,23; 16,1; 2 Macc 7,15; 9,6; 4 Macc 6,5.10.11; 8,2.5.27; 9,7.15.27.30-31; 11,16.20; 12,4.13; 15,22; 16,3.15; Josephus, *Ant.* 2.14.4 §304; 9.5.2 §100-101; 12.10.6 §413."

525 [289][38]: "Cf. Mark 5,7; the exorcism involved in the related tradition Mark 7,24-30; *T.Asher* 6:5: βασανίζεται ὑπὸ τοῦ πονηροῦ πνεύματος." Concerning παραλυτικός, see Q 7:2, 3, 4-6a[10] Matt = Q, Con (p. 195).

527 [292]: Reconstruction: See Q 7:2, 3, 4-6a[10] Emendation = Q (p. 197).

Sevenich-Bax 1993, 178[2]: "Daß dieser Erzählzug von Lukas sekundär in die Geschichte eingetragen sein wird, erweist sich umgekehrt wiederum daran, daß die Formulierung mit βασανίζω Matthäus aus der Tradition überkommen ist."

238: Reconstruction. For complete text see Q 7:1[0] In Q (p. 15).

Landis 1994, 8: "Der Ausdruck δεινῶς βασανιζόμενος weist nicht auf mt Redaktion hin: δεινῶς kommt bei Mt nur hier vor, βασανίζω ist im Evangelium selten und immer aus Mk übernommen."

9, 17: Reconstruction. For complete text see Q 7:1[6] Luke = Q, Pro (p. 57).

Con

Castor 1912, 223: Reconstruction. For complete text see Q 7:1[0] In Q (p. 6).

Parker 1953, 63-65: See Q 7:1[6] Matt = Q, Con (pp. 58-60).

Brown 1966, 193: See Q 7:2, 3, 4-6a[10] Matt = Q, Con (p. 193).

Schenk 1981, 37: Reconstruction. For complete text see Q 7:1[0] In Q (p. 10).

Gundry 1982, 142: "The change from 'was about to die' (so Luke) to 'being terribly tortured' takes emphasis from the imminency of death and puts it on the severe tormenting of the servant by his paralysis, which is a malevolent force Jesus overcomes with his lordly authority. Matthew shows some fondness for words beginning with βασαν- (2,1)."

Wegner 1985, 141[45]: Wegner argues that Luke would not likely have eliminated βασανίζω from a source—however, Wegner appears to be arguing that Luke used L here, not Q.

Schenk 1987, 168: "Δεινῶς 8,6 (+Q—NT nur noch Lk 11,52 permutiert?)."

355: For βασανιζόμενος: "Red. dürfte im Zusammenhang mit der mt Labial-Alliteration auch die Verwendung des Pt.Pass. 8,6 (+Q) für den Kranken sein: *furchtbar gequält* (=die Lähmung schreitet bedenklich fort). Auf den Schmerz ist auch bei der Verwendung des subst. Adj."

Luz 1990, 13[6]: "Matthäismen ... sind in V 5-7: Προσέρχομαι, λέγων, κύριε, λέγει ... evt. βασανίζομαι, ἐλθών."

Luz 1990, ET 2001, 8[6]: "Mattheisms in vv. 5-7 are ...: προσέρχομαι, λέγων, κύριε, λέγει ..., perhaps βασανίζομαι, ἐλθών."

Davies and Allison 1991, 21: "Concerning δεινῶς βασανιζόμενος, the adverb (='terribly') is a Matthean hapax. It here serves to underline the severity of the affliction and so magnify the act of healing."

Lindars 1992, 211: "Δεινῶς βασανιζόμενος may be a substitute for ἤμελλεν τελευτᾶν. ... Matthew uses βασανίζω elsewhere only at 8,29; 14,24, both from Mark (5,7; 6,48)."

Gagnon 1994b, 137: See Q 7:2, 3, 4-6a[10] Matt = Q, Con (pp. 195-196).

International Q Project 1995, 478: Reconstruction. For complete text see Q 7:1[0] In Q (p. 16).

Kollmann 1996, 258: "Δεινῶς βασανιζόμενος Mt 8,6 deutet darauf hin, daß ursprünglich auch bei Mt von einer akuten Erkrankung die Rede war."

Emendation = Q: ὁ παῖς μου <>[10] ἐν τῇ οἰκίᾳ <>[10] (δεινῶς βασανιζόμενος)[11] [<>[11]μέλλε<ι>[11] τελευτᾶν] [11].

Catchpole 1992, 527 [1993, 292]: Reconstruction: "ὁ παῖς μου ἐν τῇ οἰκίᾳ δεινῶς βασανιζόμενος μέλλει τελευτᾶν." For complete text see Q 7:1[0] In Q (p. 14).

Evaluations

Robinson 2000: Neither is in Q {C}, ⟦[()]^11⟧.
The intensification of the illness is in both Matthew and Luke, but it is so widely divergent in its formulation that one may assume that neither was in Q.
The way in which δεινῶς βασανιζόμενος is appended makes it seem secondary, much like Luke's ἤμελλεν τελευτᾶν. The fact that both make the sickness worse is typical of healings, to accentuate the power of the healer.

Kloppenborg 2000: Neither is in Q {B}, [()]^11.

Hoffmann 2001: Neither is in Q {C}, ⟦[()]^11⟧.
Die in der Datenbasis gegen Lukas vorgebrachten Argumente halte ich für stringent. Daß Matthäus die Diagnose des Lukas abgeschwächt hat, ist kaum nachzuvollziehen. Zu überlegen ist, ob Lukas nicht das Motiv der Todesnähe hier in Korrespondenz zu der Geschichte von der Totenerweckung des Jünglings von Nain eingebracht hat, um so durch beide Wundergeschichten das der Antwort Jesu auf die Anfrage des Johannes (Lk 7,22) vorzubereiten, wie er ja auch in 7,21 die erste Aussage des Zitats veranschaulicht.
Βασανίζω verwendet Matthäus 3mal, in Bezug auf Krankheit an unserer Stelle in 8,6/Q 7,3. In Mt 14,24 par. Mk 8,29 dagegen werden die Jünger von den Wellen "gequält". In Mt 8,29 par. Mk 5,8 par. Lk 8,28 fürchtet der Dämon beim Exorzismus von Jesus "gequält" zu werden. Nur Matthäus bezieht also das Wort auf eine Krankheit. Das gleiche gilt für βάσανος. Nur Mt 4,24 wird es von ihm auf eine Krankheit bezogen. Lukas gebraucht das Wort in 16,23.28 von der Höllenqual des Reichen. Daher {C}.

Johnson 2001: Luke = Q {C}, ⟦[ἤμελλεν τελευτᾶν]^11⟧.
Apart from one use of μέλλω (Q 3:7), none of the vocabulary of this variation unit is found in Q outside of this pericope.

All three versions of this pericope contain a two-part description of the illness, the second part intensifying the first. If one uses John elsewhere as support for a Q reading—as many in the database do (cf., however, Dunderberg and Neirynck)—then the near-death aspect of the illness in John 4:47 is an argument for its presence in Q (Schnackenburg 1964, Jeremias, Bovon). Furthermore, since Matthew changes the vagueness of the Q illness to the specific case of paralysis, it should not be surprising that Matthew would replace nearness to death (in Q) with the "grievous torment" of paralysis.

The vagueness of κακῶς ἔχων alone does not provide a satisfactory rationale for the centurion's approach to Jesus in Q—though, admittedly, the non-urgency of κακῶς ἔχων does fit with Jesus' subsequent question to the centurion. However, two of the authors (Luke and John) describe the sick person as near death (though John doesn't have the Healing of Jairus' Daughter as a paradigm and John's Lazarus is already dead) and two of them (Matthew and Luke) coincidentally use adverb + participle constructions alongside finite verb constructions in their descriptions. For this reason, the argument that Luke, Matthew and John all represent a redactional heightening of the illness (e.g. Loisy, Gatzweiler) appears to be pushing considerations of genre tendency too far.

While μέλλω is commonly used by Luke (and Matthew and John), τελευτάω is not. Luke intensifies the illness on other occasions (Dunderberg), but the instances are not especially dramatic and do not provide a needed rationale for Jesus' action as does the additional phrase in the centurion pericope: Simon's mother-in-law has a *high* fever, the Gerasene demoniac is *naked* and *homeless* (already implied in the story—see esp. Mark 5:15; note that Luke abbreviates other parts of the long description), and Jairus' daughter is his *only* daughter.

Matthew's δεινῶς βασανιζόμενος is, by most accounts, redactional (Gundry; cf. Schnackenburg). Catchpole argues for its originality, but his observation that it matches Luke's ἤμελλεν τελευτᾶν cuts both ways. If Luke's κακῶς ἔχων is in Q, replaced by βέβληται ... παραλυτικός in Matthew, then ἤμελλεν τελευτᾶν provides a precursor to Matthew's δεινῶς βασανιζόμενος. Indeed, the adverb + participial construction of Q's κακῶς ἔχων may have been the inspiration for Matthew's similar construction in δεινῶς βασανιζόμενος. If this is so, then a finite verb, required in Q, is found in ἤμελλεν (τελευτᾶν).

In view of the lack of clear redactional tendencies with regard to vocabulary and the tendentious nature of the argument that Matthew, Luke and John all intensify the malady with further elaborations that coincidentally show distinctive similarities to each other (Matthew and John each agreeing with Luke, but in different ways), the observation that Luke redactionally intensifies illnesses is greatly outweighed by the commonalities of all three pericopes with regard to this variation unit.

Q 7:2, 3, 4-6a[12]: Luke's διασώσῃ τὸν δοῦλον αὐτοῦ· or Matthew's θεραπεύσ-αὐτόν;.

Luke = Q: [διασώσῃ τὸν δοῦλον αὐτοῦ·][12]

Pro

Castor 1912, 223: Reconstruction. For complete text see Q 7:1[0] In Q (p. 6).

Wiefel 1988, 143: For δοῦλος, see Q 7:2, 3, 4-6a[9] Luke = Q, Pro (p. 167).

Nolland 1989, 314: See Q 7:2, 3, 4-6a[2] Luke = Q, Pro (p. 80).

Con

Strauss 1836, 104 (ET 1855, 517): For δοῦλος, see Q 7:2, 3, 4-6a[9] Matt = Q, Pro (pp. 177-178).

Bleek 1862, 348: See Q 7:2, 3, 4-6a[9] Luke = Q, Con (p. 167).

B. Weiß 1876, 229: For δοῦλος, see Q 7:2, 3, 4-6a[9] Luke = Q, Con (p. 167).

J. Weiß 1892, 399: "Die Sendung der Stadt-πρεσβύτεροι ... gehört der Sonderüberlieferung an; ebenso ἐρωτᾶν = bitten, ... sowie διασώζειν (Act 5 Mal) = 'durchbringen'."

Plummer 1896, 195: "The compound διασώζειν, "to bring safe through," is almost peculiar to Lk. in N.T. (Acts xxiii. 24, xxvii. 43, 44 xxviii. 1, 4; Mt. xiv. 36; I Pet. iii. 20)."

Wernle 1899, 64: "Lc hat den παῖς der Quelle durch δοῦλος ersetzt."

von Harnack 1907, 56: "Διασώζειν kann als ein lukanisches Wort in Anspruch genommen werden."

von Harnack 1907, ET 1908, 77: "Διασώζειν can be claimed as Lukan."

Haupt 1913, 81: See Q 7:2, 3, 4-6a[9] Luke = Q, Con (p. 169).

Klostermann 1919, 448: "Lc unterscheidet sich besonders durch: ... die Ersetzung von παῖς durch δοῦλος."

Cadbury 1920, 79-80: See Q 7:2, 3, 4-6a[7] Luke = Q, Con (p. 148).

Klostermann 1929, 86: "Δοῦλος: ersetzt Mt' παῖς."

Manson 1937, 64: See Q 7:2, 3, 4-6a[9] Luke = Q, Con (p. 169) and Q 7:2, 3, 4-6a[9] Matt = Q, Pro (pp. 178-179).

Sparks 1941, 180: For δοῦλος, see Q 7:2, 3, 4-6a[9] Luke = Q, Con (p. 170).

Zuntz 1945, 186-187[1], 188[1]: For δοῦλος, see Q 7:2, 3, 4-6a[9] Luke = Q, Con (p. 170).

Jeremias 1956, 26[92] (ET 1958, 30[3]): See Q 7:2, 3, 4-6a[7] Luke = Q, Con (pp. 148-149).

Haenchen 1959a, 25 [1965, 84]: For δοῦλος, see Q 7:2, 3, 4-6a⁹ Luke = Q, Con (p. 170).

Grundmann 1961, 155: See Q 7:2, 3, 4-6a³ Luke = Q, Con (pp. 99-100).

Dodd 1963, 188-190²: For δοῦλος, see Q 7:2, 3, 4-6a⁹ Luke = Q, Con (p. 171).

Schnackenburg 1964, 74: For δοῦλος, see Q 7:2, 3, 4-6a⁹ Matt = Q, Pro (p. 179).

Schnackenburg 1965, 504-505 (ET 1968, 474): See Q 7:2, 3, 4-6a⁹ Matt = Q, Pro (p. 179).

Brown 1966, 193: "It was Luke or a Lucan forerunner who, in the Greek stage of the tradition, understood *pais* as servant boy and began to speak of a *doulos*. That Luke's use of *doulos* is secondary is suggested by the fact that it appears in those verses (2, 3, 10) where the Lucan story differs from that of Matthew."

Cadbury 1966, 93-94: For δοῦλος, see Q 7:2, 3, 4-6a⁹ Luke = Q, Con (p. 171).

Delobel 1966, 454: For δοῦλος, see Q 7:2, 3, 4-6a⁹ Luke = Q, Con (p. 171).

456-457: "On peut supposer que la péricope de Jaïre a été influencée par celle du centurion. Celui-ci se croyait indigne de recevoir Jésus dans sa maison, tandis que Jaïre l'y invite explicitement. Ce motif est même plus accentué [457] chez *Lc.* que chez *Mc.* (cf. *Lc.*, VIII, 41.51 diff *Mc*). Θυγάτηρ μονογενὴς ἦν αὐτῷ (VIII, 42 diff *Mc*) rappelle, aussi bien par la construction que par le contenu, *Lc.*, VII, 2: ὃς ἦν αὐτῷ ἔντιμος."

Schürmann 1969, 391¹²: See Q 7:2, 3, 4-6a⁹ Luke = Q, Con (pp. 171-172).

Schnider and Stenger 1971, 60-61: For δοῦλος, see Q 7:2, 3, 4-6a⁹ Luke = Q, Con (p. 172).

62: "Bis jetzt ist kein Grund sichtbar geworden, warum Lukas eine besondere, judenchristlich vorgeformte Vorlage benutzt haben soll; vielmehr weist die angewandte Erzählkunst auf Lukas selber, was auch wortstatistische Beobachtungen bestätigen.¹⁰"

62¹⁰: "Die wortstatistische Untersuchung zeigt folgendes: ... 2. das διασώζω von Vers 3 kommt bei Matthäus einmal vor (Mt 14,36), bei Lukas nur hier, aber in der Apostelgeschichte fünfmal, ansonsten nur noch in 1 Pt 3,20."

Schramm 1971, 40-41: For δοῦλος, see Q 7:2, 3, 4-6a⁹ Luke = Q, Con (pp. 172-173).

George 1972, 70: For δοῦλος, see Q 7:2, 3, 4-6a⁹ Matt = Q, Pro (p. 180).

Schulz 1972, 236: For δοῦλος, see Q 7:2, 3, 4-6a⁹ Luke = Q, Con (p. 173).

237-238: "Die Vv 3-6a bei Lk haben keine Parallele bei Mt und sind lk Erweiterung der Geschichte vom [238] Hauptmann.⁴¹⁰ Auch sachlich erweist sich der Einschub als sek."

238[410]: "Das Verb διασώζειν ist fast ganz auf das Lk Schrifttum konzentriert (5mal in Apg; sonst nur 1mal Mt und 1mal I Petr)."

Pesch and Kratz 1976, 81: For δοῦλος, see Q 7:2, 3, 4-6a⁹ Luke = Q, Con (p. 173).

Busse 1977, 148[1]: "Auch V 3b zeigt red. Beeinflussung. Die Verbindung von ἐρωτᾶν mit ὅπως findet sich bei ihm in 11,37 und Apg 23,10 und 25,3. Ebenso ist διασώζω (Apg 23,24; 27,43.44; 28,1.4) 'almost peculiar to Luke in NT' [Plummer 1896, 195]."

152-153: See Q 7:2, 3, 4-6a⁶ Luke = Q, Con (pp. 140-141).

Martin 1978, 15: "Matthew is consistent with his use of παῖς for the sufferer, while Luke varies between παῖς (v. 7, Q) and δοῦλος (normally), and 'in v. 8 the centurion speaks of his "slave" as if the slave were another person than his "boy".' [Manson 1937, 64] But we should note that δοῦλος and ἄξιος are Luke terms,[11] while παῖς and ἱκανός are preferred in those passages where Matthew and Luke overlap (i.e., in Q)."

20[11]: "And it is part of Luke's style to ring the changes stylistically by substituting closely similar or synonymous terms. ...

"The peculiarity of Lukan usage would support once again the originality of Matthew's consistent use of παῖς (from Q). Perhaps Luke's intention in departing from the Q designation was to highlight the military aspect of the centurion-slave relationship, in keeping with an underlying purpose to draw the parallel between the story here and that involving another Gentile centurion, Cornelius. See in particular Acts 10:1 (a centurion), 10:2, 22 (a Gentile God-fearer, pious and generous), 10:22 (well-spoken of by the entire Jewish people), and 10:24 (having 'friends'). Then, the bond mentioned in 7:2 of a slave 'who was valued by him' ... is meant to soften the harshness that otherwise could be associated with δοῦλος, a term in the sociological sense Luke avoids in the Acts of the Apostles."

Gatzweiler 1979, 302: See Q 7:2, 3, 4-6a⁹ Matt = Q, Pro (p. 180).

Neirynck 1979, 109-110: See Q 7:2, 3, 4-6a³ Luke = Q, Con (pp. 107-108).

Jeremias 1980, 152: "Red ... διασώσῃ: Es entspricht der Vorliebe des Lukas für Verbkomposita mit δια- (→ 1,65 Red ...), daß διασώζειν außer Mt 14,36; 1Petr 3,20 im NT nur bei ihm vorkommt (Lk 1/Apg 5mal)."

Fitzmyer 1981, 649: "Whereas [*pais*] has been understood as 'son' (*huios*) in John, it is interpreted as 'servant, slave' (*doulos*) by Luke in vv. 2,3 and even extended to v. 10."

Haapa 1983, 71⁹: See Q 7:2, 3, 4-6a⁹ Luke = Q, Con (p. 174).

Dauer 1984, 114: "Διασώζειν in der Bedeutung 'gesundmachen, heilen' kommt nur Mt 14,36 (diff Mk 6,56) und Lk 7,3 u.St. vor⁴⁷⁶."

363-364[476]: "Die 5 Fälle von διασώζειν in der Apg (23,24; 27,43.44; 28,1.4) sprechen von der Rettung des Paulus aus dem Volksaufruhr bzw. von der Rettung der Schiffbrüchigen. — Jeremias [1980, 152] scheint freilich διασώζειν [364] für lk zu halten, wenn er schreibt: 'Es entspricht der Vorliebe des Lukas für Verbkomposita mit δια-..., daß διασώζειν außer Mt 14,36; 1 Petr 3,20 im NT nur bei ihm vorkommt (Lk 1/Apg 5mal)'. ... In der Apg dürfte aber διασώζειν eine andere Nuance haben."

Wegner 1985, 169: For διασώσῃ: "Der Beleg im NtEv zeigt, daß das Verb auch außerhalb des lk Schrifttums innerhalb der Synoptiker Verwendung finden konnte. Daher muß auch die Möglichkeit, daß es das im urspr Text verwandte Wort wiedergibt, zumindest erwogen werden. Doch wird hier wohl tatsächlich mit lk Bearbeitung zu rechnen sein, was nicht nur durch die im Vergleich mit den anderen ntl. Schriften relativ hohe Zahl der Belege in der Apg, sondern durch die auch sonst bei Lk anzutreffende Vorliebe für Komposita mit διά nahegelegt ist."

171: "Lediglich bei διασώζω ist eine lk Stilisierung sehr wahrscheinlich."

Schnelle 1987, 103: "Lukas hat in einem weit größeren Maß als Matthäus die Q-Vorlage umgestaltet. Auf seine Redaktion gehen ... die Bezeichnung des Kranken als δοῦλος ... zurück."

Schnelle 1987, ET 1992, 89: "Luke has reshaped the Q version of the story much more thoroughly than Matthew. His redaction produced ... the designation of the sick person as δοῦλος."

Wiefel 1988, 141: For δοῦλος, see Q 7:2, 3, 4-6a⁹ Luke = Q, Con (p. 175).

Bovon 1989, 349²⁹: For δοῦλος, see Q 7:2, 3, 4-6a⁹ Matt = Q, Pro (p. 180).

351³⁷: "Das Vokabular bleibt im Bereich der physischen Gesundheit (ἰάομαι [V 7]; ὑγιαίνω [V 10]). Nur διασώζω (V 3) läßt vielleicht für christliche Ohren eine Errettung anklingen, die über die Wiederherstellung der körperlichen Krankheit hinausgeht."

Bovon 1989, FT 1991, 341²⁹: For δοῦλος, see Q 7:2, 3, 4-6a⁹ Matt = Q, Pro (pp. 180-181).

343³⁷: "Le vocabulaire reste au niveau de la santé physique (ἰάομαι, ici v. 7, et ὑγιαίνω, v. 10). Seul διασώζω, v. 3, suggère à une oreille chrétienne une délivrance dépassant la santé physique, mais Luc n'avait peut-être pas l'intention de suggérer ce dépassement."

Crossan 1991, 326, 328 (GT 1994, 431, 433): See Q 7:2, 3, 4-6a³ Luke = Q, Con (p. 120).

Catchpole 1992, 531 [297]: "Given so extensive a correspondence [between Mark 5,21-43 and Q 7,1-10] it is readily understandable that Luke should move over from the one story to the other a series of details: ... From ἵνα ἐλθὼν ... σωθῇ (Mark 5,23) there develops the ὅπως ἐλθὼν διασώσῃ in Luke 7,3."

Lindars 1992, 204: For δοῦλος, see Q 7:2, 3, 4-6a⁹ Matt = Q, Pro (p. 181).

205: "Luke's διασώζω, also found only here in the gospel, is used five times in Acts, and in both books σῴζω is common as an alternative (Matthew has διασῴζω only at 14,36 = Mk 6,56, σῴζω). Luke likes variation, and uses both ἰάομαι and θεραπεύω several times."

211: "The use of διασῴζειν seems to be a stylistic alteration to increase the sense of urgency (cf. Acts 23,24; 27,43-44; 28,1.4)."

Gagnon 1993, 716: For δοῦλος, see Q 7:2, 3, 4-6a⁹ Luke = Q, Con (pp. 176-177).

719: For διασῴζω, see Q 7:2, 3, 4-6a³ Luke = Q, Con (p. 113).

720: "Five out of the seven other occurrences of διασῴζω ... in the NT appear in Acts (23:24; 27:43,44; 28:1,4); otherwise one finds the word only in Matt 14:36 [M] and in 1 Pet 3:20. Given also Luke's preference for compounds with διά, the probability that this is Luke's term is extremely high."

721: "It is quite possible that the phrase 'come and heal' (Matt 8:7; Luke 7:3; cf. John 4:47) was already in Q and was put in the mouth of Jesus (as it is in Matt 8:7). [But see Gagnon 1993 at Matt = Q, Con, below (p. 218).] That the centurion might have uttered these words in a direct request to Jesus (as in John 4:47; cf. Luke 7:3) is highly unlikely, since such a request would stand in complete contradiction to the centurion's next request in Q that Jesus not come."

Hagner 1993, 203: See Q 7:2, 3, 4-6a⁹ Matt = Q, Pro (p. 181).

Sevenich-Bax 1993, 166-167, 176-177: For δοῦλος, see Q 7:2, 3, 4-6a⁹ Luke = Q, Con (p. 177).

Dunderberg 1994, 88: See Q 7:2, 3, 4-6a⁶ Luke = Q, Con (p. 142).

Landis 1994, 21: "Am ehesten wird man in diesem Vers Spuren lk Redaktion noch bei διασώσῃ erkennen können. Das Verb διασῴζω ist im NT fast ganz auf das Lk Schrifttum (allerdings sonst nur auf die Apg) konzentriert. Es ist denkbar, daß Lk mit seiner Vorliebe für Komposita mit διά hier διασῴζω anstelle des Simplex oder eines anderen sinnverwandten Wortes, das er in seiner Quelle vorfand, eingesetzt hat."

Meier 1994, 724, 769¹⁹³: For δοῦλος, see Q 7:2, 3, 4-6a⁹ Matt = Q, Pro (p. 182).

Matt = Q: (θεραπεύσ- αὐτόν;)¹²

Pro

von Harnack 1907, 91 (ET 1908, 131): Reconstruction. For complete text see Q 7:1⁶ Luke = Q, Pro (p. 55).

B. Weiß 1908, 15: Reconstruction. For complete text see Q 7:1⁰ In Q (p. 5).

Crum 1927, 138: Reconstruction. For complete text see Q 7:2, 3, 4-6a¹ Luke = Q, Pro (pp. 71-72).

Klostermann 1929, 86: "'Όπως ἐλθὼν διασώσῃ (luk.) κτλ.: hier will der Hauptmann noch, was er v. 6 nicht mehr will—natürlicher Mt."

Jeremias 1956, 25-26 (ET 1958, 30): See Q 7:2, 3, 4-6a⁷ Matt = Q, Pro (p. 151).

Haenchen 1959a, 23 [1965, 82]: See Q 7:2, 3, 4-6a⁷ Matt = Q, Pro (p. 151).

George 1972, 71: For the form of Jesus response, see Q 7:2, 3, 4-6a¹³ Luke = Q, Con (p. 224).

Schulz 1972, 238: "Eine Vergleichsmöglichkeit mit Lk fehlt. Einerseits verwendet Mt θεραπεύειν etwa 10mal red, andererseits muß dem V 8, der durch Lk Vv 6b.7b für Q ausgewiesen ist, ein die Bereitschaft oder das Befremden Jesu ausdrückender Satz vorangehen. Es ist deshalb mit der Möglichkeit zu rechnen, daß Mt V 7 Q wiedergibt."

Lange 1973, 49: "Jesus beantwortet das Ansinnen des Heiden zunächst mit einer erstaunt oder entrüstet ablehnenden Frage (Mt 8,7), die wohl der ursprünglichen Form von Q entspricht."

Muhlack 1979, 43: See Q 7:2, 3, 4-6a⁷ Luke = Q, Con (p. 150).

Polag 1979, 38: Reconstruction. For complete text see Q 7:1⁰ In Q (pp. 9-10).

Schenk 1981, 37: Reconstruction. For complete text see Q 7:1⁰ In Q (p. 10).

Wegner 1985, 155-156: "Für die Annahme einer Ursprünglichkeit auSt spricht (1) die Tatsache, daß das Verb in Q nicht unbekannt ist, und (2) der Hinweis von Schulz, daß θεραπεύω oder ein Synonym eigentlich [156] konstitutiv für die Antwort des Hauptmanns in Mt 8,8 (Lk 7,6b.7b) seien."

270: Reconstruction. For complete text see Q 7:1⁰ In Q (pp. 11-12).

Catchpole 1992, 525 [1993, 289]: "The tendency is to find Q in Matthew's wording, and this is perfectly safe in respect of θεραπεύειν.⁴⁰"

525 [289]⁴⁰: "When Matthew uses θεραπεύειν he normally draws it from a source; occasionally, when it is MattR, the context demands it or a comparable word. It occurs in Q at 10,9 and is probably original here, too."

527 [292]: Reconstruction. For complete text see Q 7:1⁰ In Q (p. 14).

Sevenich-Bax 1993, 238: Reconstruction. For complete text see Q 7:1⁰ In Q (p. 15).

Landis 1994, 9-10: "Θεραπεύω wird zwar [10] von Mt nicht selten redaktionell verwendet, doch ist es auch für die Logienquelle bezeugt. Außerdem setzt V.8, der durch die Lk-Parallele für Q gesichert ist, einen Satz Jesu in der Art von V.7 voraus. Daß aber Mt θεραπεύσω als Ersatz für ein synonymes Wort eingesetzt hätte, ist deshalb eher unwahrscheinlich, weil der Evangelist die in Frage kommenden Verben sonst keineswegs mied. θεραπεύσω ist also wohl wie der ganze übrige Ausspruch Jesu für traditionell zu halten."

10, 17: Reconstruction. For complete text see Q 7:1⁶ Luke = Q, Pro (p. 57).

International Q Project 1995, 478: Reconstruction: "θεραπεύσω αὐτόν [with a period, not a question mark]." For complete text see Q 7:1⁰ In Q (p. 16).

Con

Parker 1953, 63-65: See Q 7:1⁶ Matt = Q, Con (pp. 58-60).

Howard 1975, 172: See Q 7:2, 3, 4-6a⁷ Matt = Q, Con (p. 156).

Comber 1978, 431: "Although Matthew uses the verb *therapeuō* only twice in his miracles section, Matt 8:1–9:34, these uses are deliberate and indicate the importance Matthew attaches to the healing aspect of the ministry. In the episode of the healing of the centurion's servant, only Matthew has Jesus say, 'I will come and heal (*therapeusō*) him' (Matt 8:7; cf. Luke 7:1-10). And in Matt 8:16, Matthew concludes the first portion of his presentation of Jesus as miracle-worker with a summary statement, linguistically similar to Matt 4:24 [which Comber previously argues is an elaboration of the summary statement in 4:23]."

Gundry 1982, 143: "The nominative participle ἐλθών and θεραπεύσω characterize Matthew's diction (10,10: 10,0)."

Davies and Allison 1991, 21: "Καὶ λέγει αὐτῷ· ἐγὼ ελθων θεραπεύσω αὐτόν; The formulation may be editorial.⁵⁰"

21⁵⁰: "θεραπεύω: Mt: 16; Mk: 5; Lk: 14; with αὐτόν/αὐτούς as direct object: Mt: 8; Mk: 1; Lk: 1."

Lindars 1992, 205: "Of the three words for healing John's ἰάσηται may well preserve the original verb against the others. Matthew retains it in verses 8 and 13 (cf. Lk 7,7), but otherwise has it only in a quotation in 13,15 and in the ending of the Syrophoenician's Daughter, 15,28 probably dependent on 8,13. His usual word is θεραπεύω, as here."

Gagnon 1993, 721-722: "Matt 8:7, construed as a disbelieving question by Jesus, functions much like the Matthean insertion in 15:23-24. Furthermore, had something like Matt 8:7 stood in Luke's Q account, one would expect Luke to have reproduced it as a word [722] of Jesus."

Gagnon 1994b, 136: "In my estimation, Matthew has ... added an indignant or disbelieving question on the part of Jesus in order to heighten the literary tension and so to magnify the ultimate victory of faith."

137: See Q 7:2, 3, 4-6a⁷ Matt = Q, Con (pp. 158-159).

Fleddermann 1995, 43: "Τυφλός and θεραπεύω¹⁵ are both Matthean."

43¹⁵: "The verb is redactional at Matt 4,23.24; 8,7; 9,35; 10,1; 12,22; 14,14; 15,30; 17,16.18; 19,2; 21,14."

Emendation = Q: <ἵνα>⁷ ἐλθὼν <ἰάσηται>¹² αὐτοῦ <τὸν παῖδα>¹²

Lindars 1992, 210: Reconstruction. For complete text see Q 7:1⁶ Luke = Q, Pro (p. 56).

Emendation = Q: <>¹²

Gagnon 1994b, 135: Reconstruction. For complete text see Q 7:1⁰ In Q (p. 15).

Evaluations

Johnson 2000: Matt = Q {B}, (θεραπευσ- αὐτόν;)¹².

Q has one other occurrence of θεραπεύω (Q 10:9), but none of διασῴζω.
Διασῴζω is a Lukan term (e.g. Plummer). Matthew uses it once redactionally, replacing Mark's σῴζω, but Luke is notorious for the addition of prepositional prefixes to verbs (Dauer).

The arguments for or against δοῦλος are pretty much the same as those found in Q 7:2, 3, 4-6a⁹.

Matthew and Luke both use θεραπεύω with regularity over against Mark.

Robinson 2000: Matt = Q {B}, (θεραπευσ- αὐτόν;)¹².

Dauer provides the evidence, against his intention, that διασῴζειν is Lukan, and hence, in spite of the other nuance, is probably Lukan here.

The expression in Matthew and Q is intended as a question. It is part of the structure of the healings from a distance that Jesus initially acknowledges the Jewish custom of not associating with Gentiles. Hence, John 4:48 has Jesus first answer the appeal with a reproach, and Matt 15:23-24 first has Jesus give no answer at all to the woman's appeal, then has his disciples call on him to dismiss her, whereupon Jesus repeats the saying of Matt 10:6 that he does not go to the lost sheep of the house of Israel.

The presence of this implied rejection here in Q is needed to explain the Lukan redactional interpolation of the emissary of the Jewish elders to dissuade Jesus from taking the position expected at this point in the story. Luke substitutes the emissary, omitting completely the rejection by Jesus that Luke would be happy to forget, but betraying its presence in Q by the extent he goes to cancel it by means of the delegation.

Kloppenborg 2000: Matt = Q {B}, (θεραπευσ- αὐτόν;)¹².

Hoffmann 2001: Matt = Q {B}, (θεραπευσ- αὐτόν;)¹².

Vgl. zu Lukas—neben dem qualifiziert theologischem Gebrauch von σῴζω—auch dessen Gebrauch in Heilungsgeschichten, der ihm durch Markus vorgegeben ist: Lk 6,9; 8,36(R).50(R); 17,19(R); 18,42; 23,35; Apg 4,9.

Q 7:2, 3, 4-6a¹³: Is Luke 7:4-6a in Q?

Luke = Q: [οἱ δὲ παραγενόμενοι πρὸς τὸν Ἰησοῦν παρεκάλουν αὐτὸν σπουδαίως λέγοντες ὅτι ἄξιός ἐστιν ᾧ παρέξῃ τοῦτο· ἀγαπᾷ γὰρ τὸ ἔθνος ἡμῶν καὶ τὴν συναγωγὴν αὐτὸς ᾠκοδόμησεν ἡμῖν. ὁ δὲ Ἰησοῦς ἐπορεύετο σὺν αὐτοῖς.]¹³

Pro

H. Meyer 1864, 218 (ET 1884, 179): See Q 7:2, 3, 4-6a³ Luke = Q, Pro (p. 87).

Hawkins 1899, 195: "Luke may have retained the original narrative in its fullness, while Matthew, after his manner, shortened it: —Lk vi.17a(?); vii. 3a, 4, 5, 6, 7a; 10; 20, 21."

Castor 1912, 223: Reconstruction. For complete text see Q 7:1⁰ In Q (p. 6).

Schmid 1930, 252-253: See Q 7:2, 3, 4-6a³ Luke = Q, Pro (p. 88).

Schmid 1951, 118: See Q 7:2, 3, 4-6a³ Luke = Q, Pro (p. 88).

Schulz 1972, 238⁴¹⁰: "Σπουδαίως kommt bei den Synoptikern nur hier vor; sonst noch 3mal im NT."

Dauer 1984, 114-115: "Der Rest des Verses [Lk 7,4] wird aus Q sein: "παρακαλεῖν findet sich auch Mt 8,5—dort freilich, entsprechend [115] der mt Neugestaltung der Szene, vom Hauptmann selbst gesagt. Das zusätzliche pleonastische λέγοντες zur direkten Rede wird auf Lukas zurückgehen.— σπουδαίως kommt nur noch 2 Tim 1,17 und Tit 3,13 vor.—ἄξιος verwendet Lukas sonst immer nur mit dem Genitiv der Sache oder mit nachfolgendem Infinitiv. In der Konstruktion 'ἄξιός ἐστιν ᾧ παρέξῃ (Med.) τοῦτο ist das Relativum Latinismus: dignus qui mit Konj.'⁴⁸²
"*VERS 5*:
"Er stammt ebenfalls aus der Vorlage des Lukas: er soll ein Eingreifen Jesu motivieren. Die Argumentation wird ganz unter jüdischem (judenchristlichem) Gesichtspunkt geführt. ...
"*VERS 6*:
"Πορεύεσθαι ist zwar lk Vorzugswort; Lukas konstruiert aber nur noch Apg 10,20; 26,13 mit σύν. So könnte also trotzdem vor-lk Formulierung vorliegen. Wenn freilich die Wendung vom 3. Evangelisten stammen sollte, so muß doch schon in seiner Vorlage davon die Rede gewesen sein, daß Jesus sich auf den Weg zum Hauptmann machte; denn nach Mt 8,7 hat sich Jesus, nach der wahrscheinlicheren Deutung, bereit erklärt, mit dem Hauptmann zu gehen— mit dem Hauptmann allerdings selbst, da dieser ja auch, nach der mt Änderung, persönlich zu Jesus gekommen war."

364⁴⁸²: "[BDR] 307 A. 1 [BDF §379.1] (statt ἵνα und gleichbedeutend mit dem im Klassischen üblichen Infinitiv)."

Nolland 1989, 314: See Q 7:2, 3, 4-6a² Luke = Q, Pro (p. 80).

Lindars 1992, 211: "In v. 6 Luke is once more closer to the source. He has of course changed σὺν αὐτῷ to σὺν αὐτοῖς." See Lindars at Emendation = Q (p. 232).

Con

Strauss 1836, 101-102: "Den ersten Anstoß zu dieser Gesandtschaft scheint übrigens das andere Interesse gegeben zu haben, die Bereitwilligkeit Jesu, in des Heiden Haus zu gehen, durch eine vorgängige Empfehlung desselben zu motiviren. Das ist ja das Erste, was die πρεσβύτεροι τῶν Ἰουδαίων, nachdem sie Jesu den Krankheitsfall berichtet, hinzusetzen, ὅτι ἄξιός ἐστιν ᾧ παρέξει τοῦτο· ἀγαπᾷ γὰρ τὸ ἔθνος ἡμῶν κ.τ.λ., ähnlich, wie gleichfalls bei Lukas, in der A. G. 10,22., die Boten des Cornelius dem Petrus, um ihn zu einem Gang in dessen Haus zu vermögen, auseinandersetzen, daß er ein ἀνὴρ δίκαιος καὶ φοβούμενος τὸν θεόν, [102] μαρτυρούμενός τε ὑπὸ ὅλου τοῦ ἔθνους τῶν Ἰουδαίων sei."

Strauss 1836, ET 1855, 516: "The first embassy seems to have originated in the desire to introduce a previous recommendation of the centurion as a motive for the promptitude with which Jesus offered to enter the house of a Gentile. The Jewish elders after having informed Jesus of the case of disease, add, *that he was worthy for whom he should do this, for he loveth our nation and has built us a synagogue*: a recommendation the tenor of which is not unlike what Luke (Acts x. 22) makes the messengers of Cornelius say to Peter to induce him to return with them, namely, that the centurion was a *just man, and one that feareth God, and in good report among all the nation of the Jews.*"

Bleek 1862, 347-348: See Q 7:2, 3, 4-6a¹ Matt = Q, Pro (pp. 70-71).

Simons 1880, 42: "Lc. V. 3, 4, 5 sind vom Evangelisten eingeschoben."

Plummer 1896, 195: "Οἱ δὲ παραγενόμενοι. A favourite verb (ver. 20, viii. 19, xi. 6, xii. 51, xiv. 21, xix. 16, xxii. 52; and about twenty times in Acts): elsewhere in N.T. eight or nine times, but very freq. in LXX."

Hawkins 1899, 21: "Words and Phrases characteristic of St. Luke's Gospel: … παραγίνομαι."

Wernle 1899, 86: "Leider verrät gerade diese Einleitung so deutlich wie möglich den Lc als Verfasser durch den Ausdruck 'Die Ältesten der Juden' 7,3. Davon abgesehen spricht gegen Annahme einer ebjonitischen Vorlage: …

"Die Ähnlichkeit der Empfehlung des Hauptmanns v. 4f. mit der Empfehlung des Hauptmanns Cornelius Acta 10,2. Tatsächlich ist sie gar nicht judaistisch, sondern katholisch gemeint. Es liegt—populär gefaßt—der Begriff des spätern meritum de congruo vor. Der Heide und Sünder kann sich für Gottes Gnade vorbereiten durch gute Werke, die er Angehörigen der Kirche erweist. Das sind gerade Gedanken des Lc selber."

Holtzmann 1901, 344: "Gleich dem Cornelius Act 10,2 erscheint (7,5) der Centurio als Judenfreund (s. zu Act 13,16), daher (7,4) ἄξιος ᾧ παρέξῃ τοῦτο: in gut griech. Weise ein Relativsatz zur Angabe der Zweckbestimmung. Er hat den Juden *eine Synagoge erbaut* wie der Polizeihauptmann im ägyptischen Athribis. ... Auch das ἐπορεύετο σὺν αὐτοῖς (7,6) erinnert an Act 10,20."

von Harnack 1907, 56: "Bemerkt sei nur, daß ἔντιμος (v. 2), οἱ παραγενόμενοι (v. 4), σπουδαίως (v. 4), [et alia] in den Evangelien ausschließlich lukanisch sind."

91: Reconstruction. For complete text see Q 7:1[6] Luke = Q, Pro (p. 55).

von Harnack 1907, ET 1908, 76-77: "I would only remark that ἔντιμος (verse 2), οἱ παραγενόμενοι (verse 4), σπουδαίως (verse 4), [et alia] are, as far as the gospels [77] are concerned, exclusively Lukan."

131: Reconstruction. For complete text see Q 7:1[6] Luke = Q, Pro (p. 55).

Loisy 1907, 651: "Pour Luc, le centurion a bâti la synagogue de Capharnaüm, et ce n'est pas à l'évangéliste qu'il faut demander s'il n'y en avait pas auparavant, ni comment la charité d'un centurion a pu être indispensable pour une telle œuvre dans un milieu israélite. Ce centurion, ami des Juifs, ressemble beaucoup au centurion Cornelius, dont on dira tant de bien au livre des Acts [10,2]."

B. Weiß 1908, 15: Reconstruction. For complete text see Q 7:1[0] In Q (p.).

Easton 1910, 164: "Of the eight cases [of παραγίνομαι in Luke], one (8:19) seems to be a Lucan change in Mc. (3:31). One (11:6) is probably from Q. The other six cases (7:4, 20; 12:51; 14:21; 19:16; 22:52) are L. But the great number in [Acts] outweighs this evidence." In other words, they are more likely the result of Lukan redaction than L source material.

Castor 1912, 223: Reconstruction: Castor omits σπουδαίως only. For complete text see Q 7:1[0] In Q (p. 6).

223[2]: "Σπουδαίως is not a characteristic Lukan term: it occurs only here in Luke or Acts, but it may well have been added by the evangelist for dramatic effect."

Patton 1915, 144-145: "In Luke's vss. 3-6, which contain the account of the sending of the messengers, there are at least five Lucan words (ἔντιμος, παραγενόμενοι, σπουδαίως, μακράν, ἀπέχοντος). ... Of these Lucan words, ... παραγενόμενοι [145] is used once by Mark, three times by Matthew, eight times by Luke in his Gospel, and twenty times in the Book of Acts. Σπουδαίως is found here only in the Gospels, and not in Acts."

Easton 1926, 97: "Σύν is 'Lukan,' as is πέμπειν."

Crum 1927, 138: Reconstruction. For complete text see Q 7:~~2~~, 3, ~~4-6a~~[1] Luke = Q, Pro (pp. 71-72).

Montefiore 1927, 423-424: "Luke ... makes diverse changes [424] in the story of the centurion. The centurion sends the Jewish elders to Jesus instead of coming himself. Hence the addition of [vv.] 4 and 5."

Bussmann 1929, 56: "In [Lk 7:3-7a] ist ein Stück anscheinend einge-schoben, von dem Mt nichts hat."

Hauck 1934, 93: "Die Verse 2-6a (Bittgesandtschaft), welche eine Erweite-rung gegenüber Mt darstellen, sind wohl eine Überlieferungsvariante (Bericht II [= a Jewish-Christian source used by Luke]), welche Lk in den ersten Bericht (I [= Q]) eingearbeitet hat."

Kiddle 1935, 170¹: "Since Lk.'s account from vii 8 is almost exactly the same as that in Mt., it is probable that the long introduction which makes the narrative so clumsy was inserted by him."

Hirsch 1941, 89: "Sachlich bedeuten sie eine Veränderung der Geschichte, wie sie Luk sich an Markustexten da, wo nicht eine markusfremde Vorlage ihn bestimmte, nirgends erlaubt hat. Es find folgende: a) Der Hauptmann spricht nicht selbst mit Jesus, sondern schickt erst die jüdische Gemeindebehörde, dann Freunde zu Jesus (Luk 7,2-6a). Bei der Bestellung durch die Freunde fällt auf, daß sie in einer ausführlichen Darlegung so reden, als ob sie der Hauptmann selber wären. b) Die jüdischen Presbyter begründen, daß der heidnische Haupt-mann der Hilfe Jesu wert sei, mit seinen Opfern für die jüdische Gemeinde: er ist Judenfreund und hat der Gemeinde von Kapernaum die Synagoge gebaut."

Jeremias 1956, 25-26⁹⁷: "Lukas hat ... die Einleitung der Geschichte völlig neu gefaßt (7,2-6a.7a)."

Jeremias 1956, ET 1958, 30³: "Luke has completely recast the introduction to the story (7.2-6a,7a)."

Held 1960, 183 (ET 1963, 194): See Q 7:2, 3, 4-6a¹ Luke = Q, Con (pp. 67-68).

Grundmann 1961, 155: See Q 7:2, 3, 4-6a³ Luke = Q, Con (pp. 99-100).

Delobel 1966, 456: "Nous avons déjà remarqué que Luc aime les déléga-tions de personnes intermédiaires, tels les envoyés de Jean-Baptiste dans *Lc.*, VII, 24, et les envoyés aux Samaritains dans IX, 52. En plus, il faut signaler l'emploi lucanien de μέλλειν, εἶναι τινί, παραγίνεσθαι πρός, σὺν αὐτοῖς. L'imparfait des verbes: 'demander que', aussi longtemps que la demande n'est pas accordée, s'avère encore une fois être du style lucanien. Il n'y a aucune rai-son, à notre avis, pour considérer le verbe ἀγαπᾶν dans un tel contexte comme 'protolucanien'. L'expression τὸ ἔθνος ἡμῶν serait à tort alléguée comme indice contre l'usage lucanien. Luc n'a pas l'habitude de s'en servir pour le peuple Juif, mais il donne ici l'opinion d'un païen. C'est ainsi encore que parlent les Juifs lorsqu'ils veulent se faire comprendre par Pilate (*Lc.*, XXIII, 2)."

457: "La partie rédactionnelle du récit du centurion rappelle certains détails de la péricope de Jaïre. Au v. 6a, ὁ δὲ Ἰησοῦς ἐπορεύετο σὺν αὐτοῖς (après la question des Juifs) est à comparer avec *Mc.*, V, 24: καὶ ἀπῆλθεν μετ' αὐτοῦ (après la question de Jaïre)."

Schnider and Stenger 1971, 62: "Bis jetzt ist kein Grund sichtbar gewor-den, warum Lukas eine besondere, judenchristlich vorgeformte Vorlage benutzt haben soll; vielmehr weist die angewandte Erzählkunst auf Lukas selber, was auch wortstatistische Beobachtungen bestätigen.¹⁰"

62¹⁰: "Die wortstatistische Untersuchung zeigt folgendes: … 3. das in Vers 4 vorkommende παραγίνομαι mit πρός kommt im Neuen Testament nur bei Lukas vor: (Lk 7,4; 7,20; 8,19; 11,6; 22,52; Apg 20,18). Matthäus gebraucht παραγίνομαι überhaupt nur zweimal, Markus einmal, Johannes zweimal, Lukas achtmal, Apostelgeschichte zwanzigmal. 4. Das παρέχω von Vers 4 kommt in einer vom Markustext abhängigen Stelle vor (Mk 14,6; Mt 26,10). Sonst kennen es Markus und Matthäus nicht. Lukas gebraucht es im ganzen viermal (Lk 6,29; 7,4; 11,7; 18,5), außerdem fünfmal in der Apostelgeschichte (Apg 16,16; 17,31; 19,24; 22,2; 28,2)."

George 1972, 71: "En Mt 8,7, de nombreux auteurs jugent que Jésus commence par s'étonner de la demande du centurion, ou même par la rejeter (comme en Mt 15,26 et Mc 7,27). Ils traduisent: 'Moi! J'irais le guérir?'. Matthieu fait ainsi ressortir la difficulté que Jésus éprouve à entrer chez le centurion et il prépare par là la réponse de l'officier au v. 8. Chez Luc, par contre, Jésus accepte aussitôt de se rendre chez le païen. Cela répond bien à l'idéal missionnaire du troisième évangile."

Jervell 1972, 120-121: "When Jesus heals a non-Jew, or rather listens to and grants [121] a prayer from a Gentile, Luke must offer a defense, by referring to the Gentile's close relationship to Israel (7:5)."

Schulz 1972, 237-238: "Die Vv 3-6a bei Lk haben keine Parallele bei Mt und sind lk Erweiterung der Geschichte vom [238] Hauptmann.⁴¹⁰ Auch sachlich erweist sich der Einschub als sek."

238⁴¹⁰: "Παραγίνεσθαι ist bei Lk stark gehäuft (Ev ca 3mal trad; ca 4mal red; Apg 20mal; dagegen Mk 1mal; Mt 3mal); auch παρακαλεῖν ist bei Lk gehäuft (22mal in Apg); σπουδαίως kommt bei den Synoptikern nur hier vor; sonst noch 3mal im NT; ἄξιος ist durch die Häufung in Apg (7mal) auch als lk ausgewiesen; παρέχειν (-εσθαι) kommt ebenfalls öfters in Apg vor (5mal); ἔθνος (vom jüdischen Volk) ist ein Lk vertrauter Sprachgebrauch (Ev 23,2 red; 6mal in Apg); συναγωγή ist im lk Schrifttum gehäuft (Ev ca 30mal trad; ca 15mal red; Apg 37mal; dagegen Mk 3mal; Mt 29mal)."

Derrett 1973, 176: "Luke explains, as it were, why the Centurion was entitled to sympathetic treatment, as an exception in a life dedicated to service of the Jews; but Q probably did not have this feature, assuming that its hearers would already have known that a centurion who addressed Jesus as 'Lord' would have been favourably received."

Lange 1973, 42⁵⁰: See Q 7:2, 3, 4-6a⁷ Luke = Q, Con (p. 149).

Wilson 1973, 31: See Q 7:2, 3, 4-6a¹ Luke = Q, Con (p. 68).

Achtemeier 1975, 549: "Luke can adapt a miracle in such a way that interest is pointed away from the recipient of the miracle and toward Jesus … On the other hand, details about the one who requests the miracle can be added, thus heightening our interest in someone other than Jesus (cf. Luke 7:1-10 with Matt 8:5-13, and the added details about the kind of man the centurion was)."

Sabourin 1975, 154: See Q 7:6b-c² Matt = Q, Pro (p. 256).

170: "Une expansion du troisième évangile représente le centurion comme plein de dévotion (7,4-5), presque comme un 'craignant-Dieu', semblable au centurion de Ac 10,2."

Busse 1977, 148¹: "V 4 bringt statistisch gehäuft red. Vokabeln (nach Schulz [1972, 238⁴¹⁰]: παραγίνομαι, παρακαλέω, ἄξιος und παρέχω). Ebenso verdrängt παρεγένετο πρός in Lk 8,19 das mark. ἔρχομαι. Weiter ist zu beachten, daß in Apg 20,12 sich παρακαλέω mit einem Adverb verbindet, so daß auch σπουδαίως luk. ist.—Mit V 5 begründet Lk das Bitten der Ältesten der Juden. Auffällig ist der Gebrauch von ἀγαπάω in diesem Zusammenhang. Denn in der synoptischen Sprachregelung wird das Verb nur verwendet, 'wo es um die Auslegung des Gebotes der Liebe zu Gott (Dt 6,4f) und zum Nächsten (Lv 19,18) geht.' Doch hier wie in Lk 11,43 liegt wohl eher hellenistischer Sprachgebrauch vor, was wiederum auf Lk zurückschließen läßt.—Auch V 6 sollte man Lk zuweisen, da allein der Gebrauch des Verbs πορεύομαι (29—3—51) auf ihn schließen läßt."

France 1977, 254: "Luke ... is more leisurely and colourful in his telling of the story, including extra detail about the centurion's Jewish sympathies, and in particular the account of his having approached Jesus through his friends, rather than in person as in Matthew's version."

Marshall 1978, 280: "The participle of παραγίνομαι, 'to come, arrive, be present' (Lucan), is used adverbially."

Gatzweiler 1979, 308: For παρακάλουν: "Dans la version lucanienne la requête du centurion se voit à la fois amplifiée et dramatisée. Elle porte la marque de la prière: le verbe prier est utilisé à plusieurs reprises (vv. 3 et 4)."

Muhlack 1979, 41: 7:4b-5 only (ἄξιός ἐστιν ... ἡμῖν). For complete text of Lukan expansions, see Q 7:2, 3, 4-6a³ Luke = Q, Con (pp. 105-106).

Neirynck 1979, 109-110: See Q 7:2, 3, 4-6a³ Luke = Q, Con (pp. 107-108).

Polag 1979, 38: Reconstruction. For complete text see Q 7:1⁰ In Q (pp. 9-10).

Jeremias 1980, 152-153: "Red παραγενόμενοι πρὸς τὸν Ἰησοῦν: Die Statistik weist παραγίνομαι als markantes lukanisches Vorzugswort aus: Mt 3, Mk 1, Lk 8/Apg 20, Joh 1, sNT 3; Lukas schreibt das Verb im Ev 8, 19 [153] (παρεγένετο) gegen Mk 3,31 (ἔρχονται). Vorzugsweise benutzt er das Partizip von παραγίνομαι als Übergangswendung (Lk 7,4.20; 14,21/Apg 13 mal). Die Konstruktion παραγίνομαι πρός τινα findet sich außer Mt 3,13 nur im Doppelwerk (Lk 7,4.20; 8,19; 11,6/Apg 20,18). Alle diese Beobachtungen führen übereinstimmend zu dem Schluß, daß παραγενόμενοι πρὸς τὸν Ἰησοῦν in Lk

7,4 lukanisch ist.—παρεκάλουν ... λέγοντες: Lukas ergänzt παρακαλέω gern durch pleonastisches λέγων + direkte Rede (→ 1,63 Red ...), öfter auch durch Infinitiv (Lk 8,41/Apg elfmal), vereinzelt durch ὅπως (Apg 25,2f.); dagegen stammt die Ergänzung durch nicht-finales ἵνα aus Markus (Lk 8,31 par. Mk 5,10; Lk 8,32 par. Mk 5,12).

"Red ἀγαπᾷ: Im LkEv findet sich eine große Bedeutungsbreite der Wortgruppe ἀγαπάω κτλ. → 6,27 Trad.

"Red ἐπορεύετο σύν: Zu πορεύομαι → 1,56 Red. ...—ἔπεμψεν ... λέγων: Die Verbindung von πέμπω mit pleonastischem λέγων zur Einführung der direkten Rede (→ 1,63 Red ...) findet sich im NT nur Lk 7,6.19. Die Analogie des unmittelbar auf 7,19 folgenden ἀπέστειλεν ... λέγων (→ 7,20 Red ...) erweist die Wendung als lukanisch."

161: "παραγενόμενοι ... πρὸς αὐτόν: ist lukanisch → 7,4 Red."

Fitzmyer 1981, 649, 650: See Q 7:2, 3, 4-6a[3] Luke = Q, Con (p. 108).

Schenk 1981, 37: Reconstruction. For complete text see Q 7:1[0] In Q (p. 10).

Denaux 1982, 315: "Q: Mt 8,5-10.13—Lk 7,1b-3.6b-10."

Schweizer 1982, 86 (ET 1984, 131): See Q 7:2, 3, 4-6a[3] Luke = Q, Con (p. 109).

Haapa 1983, 71: See Q 7:2, 3, 4-6a[3] Luke = Q, Con (p. 109).

Dauer 1984, 114: "Die zu Beginn des Verses stehende Partizipkonstruktion παραγενόμενοι πρὸς τὸν Ἰησοῦν ist lk, wie eine Wortuntersuchung deutlich macht: παραγίνεσθαι ist lk Vorzugswort: Lk 8mal; Apg 20mal – sonst: Mt 3mal; Mk 1mal; Joh 1mal; Joh 8,2; Pls 2mal; Hebr 1mal." For Luke 7:4b-5, see Dauer at Luke = Q, Pro (p. 220).

Wegner 1985, 173-174: "Der Gesamtausdruck παραγίνομαι + πρός findet sich abgesehen von 22,52 (v.l.) und 8,19 (wo Lk zwar ἔρχεται durch παραγίνομαι ersetzte, doch πρός schon vorfand) nur noch außSt, 1x in QLk (7,20) und 1x im Sg (11,6). In der Apg taucht er nur in 20,18 auf, während Lk selbst dort eher παραγίνομαι + εἰς bevorzugt: vgl. Apg 9,26; 13,14; 15,4; 17,10 und 24,17.

[174] "Aus dem Befund ergibt sich, daß der Gesamtausdruck entweder aus der lk Red oder aus dem lk Sg stammt; zweifelhaft ist dagegen ein Ursprung in Q (vgl. Lk 7,20 om Mt)."

176: "Wörtlich erscheint die Wendung παρεκάλουν ... λέγοντες ὅτι innerhalb der Synoptiker und Apg nur außSt. Für eine lk Red dieses Gesamtausdruckes spricht: 1. Lk fügt von sich aus nach λέγοντες mehrmals ein ὅτι in der Apg (vgl. Apg 5,23 und 11,3: ὅτι rec.; ferner 15,5; 18,13 und 26,31) und 1x im Ev (20,5 om Mk 11,31) ein. 2. Παρακαλέω erscheint auch anderswo im lk Doppelwerk mit pleonastischem Ptz. von λέγειν verbunden (vgl. Apg 2,40; 16,9 und 27,33: λέγων; 16,15: λέγουσα)."

177: Wegner argues that παρακαλέω + pleonastic λέγοντες + ὅτι *recitativum* is not Lukan, but belongs to Lukan *Sondergut* material.

181-182: "Was Q betrifft, so kann zwar von der Stat her die Zugehörigkeit von Lk 7,4 zu dieser Quelle nicht gänzlich bestritten werden, doch scheint im Vergleich mit dem lk Sg die Wahrscheinlichkeit eines Q-Ursprungs weit geringer zu sein. Bei παραγίνομαι und παρέχω ist es zweifelhaft, ob außer auSt Q diese Verben überhaupt benutzt hat. Ἄξιος ist zwar noch an zwei weiteren Stellen belegt (vgl. Lk 3,8 und 10,7 par Mt), doch scheint Q selbst innerhalb der Hauptmannsperikope allein ἱκανός gebraucht zu haben, wie Mt 8,8/Lk 7,6c nahelegen. Hiermit stimmt überein, daß auch das pleonastische λέγοντες kaum aus Q stammen wird, zumal innerhalb dieser Quelle keine weiteren Belege für λέγειν mit diesem Gebrauch auftauchen. Demgegenüber wäre aber die Konstruktion von Artikel + nachgestelltes δέ, der Gebrauch von ὅτι recitativum u.a. in Q sehr wohl denkbar. Sehr wahrscheinlich ist sogar ein Q-Ursprung bei dem Verb παρακαλέω, da auch der erste Evangelist es innerhalb derselben Perikope (vgl. Mt 8,5) bietet.

[182] "Zusammend zu Lk 7,4 wird man daher wohl sagen können, daß dieser Vers sehr wahrscheinlich im Kern auf Sg-Stoff fußt, der von Lk mehr oder weniger bearbeitet wurde. Die Möglichkeit eines Q-Ursprungs ist zwar nicht ganz von der Hand zu weisen, doch ist im Vergleich mit dem Sg die Wahrscheinlichkeit dazu weit geringer."

189: "Auf eine nähere Angabe der Belege kann in diesem Falle verzichtet werden, da die Zahlen von sich aus schon genügende Anhaltspunkte für die stat Auswertung hergeben. ... Daß Lk dieses Verb tatsächlich mit Vorliebe benutzt, geht schon daraus hervor, daß von den insgesamt 154 Belegen im NT sich mehr als die Hälfte innerhalb seines Doppelwerkes befinden. Doch zeigt zugleich die Belegzahl des Sg, daß es auch für diese Schicht als charakteristisch angesehen werden muß."

241: "In einer ähnlichen Richtung weist die Beobachtung zur mt Verwendung von ἱκανός und ἄξιος hin. Wäre die Lk-Fassung die ursprünglichere, so müßte angenommen werden, daß bereits die Q-Erzählung die zwei Synonyma ἱκανός (vgl. Mt 8,8/Lk 7,6c) und ἄξιος (vgl. Lk 7,4; ferner Lk 7,7a: ἀξιοῦν!) urspr enthielt, was ja prinzipiell durchaus möglich wäre. Andererseits zeigt die mt Verwendung von ἱκανός (im MtEv 3x: 3,11 par Mk; 8,8: Q und 28,12: Sg) und ἄξιος (im MtEv 9x: 5x in QMt; 2x in Q; 1x im mt Sg und 1x [vgl. Mt 10,10b] sehr wahrscheinlich red), daß der erste Evangelist das letztere Adjektiv im Vergleich zu ἱκανός deutlich bevorzugt, was vor allem aus der hohen Zahl der QMt-Belege hervorgeht, deren wahrscheinliche Herkunft aus der mt Red sich schon alleine deshalb nahe legt, weil Lk gegenüber ἄξιος in der Apg keineswegs zurückhaltend ist (er gebraucht es dort 7x!) und es daher kaum aus Q gestrichen hätte, falls die QMt-Belege urspr wären. Angesichts dieses Befundes darf die Tatsache, daß Mt das von ihm bevorzugte ἄξιος in seiner Fassung der Hauptmannsperikope nicht verwendet, als Indiz dafür aufgefaßt werden, daß er dieses Adjektiv in seiner Vorlage wohl nicht gelesen und somit von Lk 7,4b keine Kenntnis gehabt hat."

270: Reconstruction. For complete text see Q 7:1⁰ In Q (pp. 11-12).

Evans 1990, 342: "That Luke is largely responsible for his narrative is suggested by the excellence of the Greek in vv. 2, 4-7a, and by similarities with the story of Cornelius in Acts 10."

343-344: "That these verses [7:4-6] are from Luke is suggested by (i) the idiomatic Greek, notably [344] *he is worthy to (axios estin hō)*, a Latinism found 'mostly in connection with Roman officials,' (BDF [BDR] §5.3) and (ii) the parallels with Acts 10:1-33."

Crossan 1991, 326, 328 (GT 1994, 431, 433): See Q 7:2, 3, 4-6a³ Luke = Q, Con (p. 120).

Catchpole 1992, 528-529 [1993, 293-294]: "The Lucan central section, describing the delegation which presses Jesus for help, has no parallel in Matthew 8, but has nevertheless occasionally been claimed for Q. Josef Schmid [1930, 252-254], for example, set the shorter version of the story in Matt alongside shortened versions of other stories and claimed that a similar shortening had happened here. His three parallels were Matt 8,28-34/Mark 5,1-20; Matt 9,18-26/Mark 5,21-43; and Matt 11,2-6/Luke 7,18-23. These three examples, the third of which [294] is particularly problematic, almost certainly do not suffice to establish Schmid's position. Luke 7,3-6a.7a is shot through with Lucan verbal and stylistic features, though that by itself is also not sufficient. After all, Luke often edits Mark drastically so that his verbal and stylistic tendencies are very much in evidence, but there is still the Marcan source in the background. More important as supplementary and confirming evidence are the conformity of the extra Lucan material here to Lucan theological concerns, and also the awkwardness in its relationship to its present context.

"More recently support has been attracted to the proposal that Luke [529] 7,3-6a.7a is a post-Q but pre-Lucan development. Uwe Wegner [1985, 161-188, 250-255], for example, believes that there were four stages in the evolution of Luke 7,1-10: (a) The primary formation in Q. (b) The adoption and modification of the Q tradition by the tradents of Lucan *Sondergut*. (c) The adoption and redactional modification by Luke of the version in the *Sondergut*. (d) The Lucan displacement of the Q version in favour of the *Sondergut* version. However, in an extended investigation of Luke 7,3-6a.7a Wegner is able to find almost no formulations to which the conclusions 'lk Red möglich' or 'lk Red nicht unmöglich' do not apply. His explanation of the choice made by Luke involves an appeal to the very considerations which would support the attribution of Luke 7,3-6a.7a to LukeR of Q, namely, the centurion's pious Jewish-style performance of good works and his humble demeanour."

531 [297]: "Given so extensive a correspondence [between Mark 5,21-43 and Q 7,1-10] it is readily understandable that Luke should move over from the one story to the other a series of details: ... From the ἀρχισυνάγωγος (Mark 5,22) there develops the συναγωγή reference in Luke 7,5."

Jacobson 1992, 108-109: See Q 7:2, 3, 4-6a³ Luke = Q, Con (p. 113).

141: "Worthiness language is introduced by Luke in 7:4."

Lindars 1992, 211: "In v. 4 there is virtual repetition ἀπῆλθεν πρὸς αὐτὸν καὶ παρεκάλει αὐτόν in οἱ δὲ παραγενόμενοι πρὸς τὸν Ἰησοῦν παρεκάλουν αὐτόν." See Lindars at Emendation = Q (p. 232).

Gagnon 1993, 722: "*1. Summary remarks.* In v 4, παραγίνομαι (+ πρός) is probably due to Lucan redaction. While the combination παρακαλέω + λέγων + ὅτι *recitativum* occurs nowhere else in Luke-Acts, the closest constructions (παρακαλέω + λέγων; παρακαλέω + ὅτι *recitativum*) point to Luke rather than to his special source. Pleonastic λέγων is a pronounced feature of Lucan style, frequent also in material usually relegated to the special source, while ὅτι *recitativum* seems to be a particular trait of the special source, not common for Luke himself but still possible for him. The combination of λέγων + ὅτι *recitativum* may be slightly more common for the special source than for Lucan redaction, though not in cases where the λέγων is pleonastic; on several occasions Luke alters such combinations in Mark. Luke's borrowing from Mark's story about Jairus (Mark 5:23) may account for the construction παρεκάλουν αὐτὸν σπουδαίως λέγοντες ὅτι. The adverb σπουδαίως and the construction ἄξιος ... ᾧ are found nowhere else in the Gospels or in Acts; otherwise, ἄξιος and παρέχω are equally plausible for Luke or for his special source. The Latinism ἄξιός ἐστιν ᾧ παρέξῃ τοῦτο (=*dignus est cui hoc praestes*) is perhaps to be explained by the fact that Luke conceives of the centurion as a Roman officer.

"*2. Statistical evidence.* In Luke, παραγίνομαι (3/1/8 + 20/1; elsewhere in the NT only 3x) appears in four [LQ] passages (7:20; 12:51; 14:21; 19:16; no probable Q occurrences), only once in [S] (11:16), but once in [L?] (22:52), and once in an especially telling [L] passage (8:19, where Luke's παρεγένετο δὲ πρὸς αὐτόν replaces Mark's καὶ ἔρχεται). The large number of occurrences in Acts confirms this word as indeed the product of Luke's redaction. The combination of παραγίνομαι πρός (τινα) occurs elsewhere in the NT only in Matt 3:17 [M]; Luke 7:20 [LQ]; 8:19 [L]; 11:6 [S]; 22:52 (as a variant reading; Acts 20:18 (however, 5x in Acts with εἰς)."

723-724: Further statistics on the use of παρακαλέω with complements in Luke are given to support Gagnon's argument for Lukan redaction.

724: "Παρέχω (1/1/4 + 5; only 5x more in the NT) occurs elsewhere in Luke in 6:29 [LQ]; 11:7 [S]; 18:5 [S]; its frequency in Acts makes Lucan redaction a strong possibility. The only other occurrence of the word in the middle voice is in Acts 19:24 (albeit in a different sense)."

725: "As for the reference to 'our nation' (τὸ ἔθνος ἡμῶν), the use of ἔθνος as a designation of Israel is extremely well established for Acts (and barely or not at all for [S]). The whole thought of v 5 coheres well with Luke's theological and social aims, namely, to undercut Jewish complaints to civil authorities that Christians are hostile to the Jews and, thus, a threat to the political order. ...

"Wegner [1985, 184, 186, 239] makes much of the paratactic construction in v 5 as being particularly un-Lucan. ... Although Luke often replaces Mark's paratactic construction with participles, he himself is not above inserting frequent paratactic constructions into his Marcan material. For example, a cursory review of some Lucan miracle stories with Marcan parallels reveals the following insertions which may be considered examples of parataxis: Luke 5:18,26; 6:11,19; 8:23,27,41,42,45,52; 9:34,39,42. Parataxis may be less characteristic of Luke than of Mark, but, compared to classical Greek, 'there is no doubt about Luke's paratactic style' [Turner 1976, 50].

"Outside of John 11:48-52; 18:35; and 1 Pet 2:9, the word ἔθνος appears in the NT with the referent 'Israel' only in Luke 23:2 [L? or S]: Acts 10:22; 24:2,10,17; 26:4; 28:19 (primarily in speeches in the second half of Acts). This is the truly important statistic, not (contra Wegner) the number of times the word is used with reference to Gentiles. Lucan redaction here is probable."

Sevenich-Bax 1993, 166-167: For ἄξιος, see Q 7:2, 3, 4-6a[9] Luke = Q, Con (p. 177).

166, 169: See Q 7:2, 3, 4-6a[3] Luke = Q, Con (p. 114).

238: Reconstruction. For complete text see Q 7:1[0] In Q (p. 15).

Dunderberg 1994, 60: "Die Erklärung, es gebe keinen Bedeutungsunterschied zwischen ἄξιος und ἱκανός, trifft bei Lk nicht zu. Lk verwendet das ἱκανός im Sinne von 'würdig, wert' nur zweimal, und zwar unter dem Einfluß von Q (Lk 3,16/Mt 3,11; Lk 7,6/Mt 8,8). Anderswo im lk Doppelwerk erscheint das Wort in Redewendungen, die einen längeren Zeitraum oder eine zahlreiche Volksmenge bezeichnen." The implication is for ἄξιος in the present variation unit being typically Lukan, in contrast to ἱκανός in Luke 7:6 being non-Lukan.

85-89: See Q 7:2, 3, 4-6a[3] Luke = Q, Con (pp. 114-116).

Gagnon 1994b, 135: Reconstruction. For complete text see Q 7:1[0] In Q (p. 15).

Landis 1994, 22-24: Landis argues that Luke 7:4-6a comes almost entirely from Lukan *Sondergut*.

International Q Project 1995, 478: Reconstruction. For complete text see Q 7:1[0] In Q (p. 16).

Neirynck 1995, 180: See Q 7:2, 3, 4-6a[1] Luke = Q, Con (p. 70).

Tuckett 1996, 395: "Catchpole's discussion [1992, 528-532 (1993, 293-298)] about the LkR nature of Luke's extra verses in Luke 7:3-6a, 7a seems to me fully convincing."

Matt = Q: [ ]¹³

Pro

    Strauss 1836, 101-103 (ET 1855, 516-517): See Q 7:2̶, 3, 4̶-6̶a̶³ Luke = Q, Con (pp. 90-93).
    Bleek 1862, 347-348: See Q 7:2̶, 3, 4̶-6̶a̶¹ Matt = Q, Pro (pp. 70-71).
    Sabourin 1975, 154: See Q 7:6b-c² Matt = Q, Pro (p. 256).
    Fitzmyer 1981, 649, 650: See Q 7:2̶, 3, 4̶-6̶a̶³ Luke = Q, Con (p. 108).
    Denaux 1982, 315: "Q: Mt 8,5-10.[1]3—Lk 7,1b-3.6b-10."
    Crossan 1991, 328 (GT 1994, 433): See Q 7:2̶, 3, 4̶-6̶a̶³ Matt = Q, Pro (p. 120).
    Dunderberg 1994, 85-89: See Q 7:2̶, 3, 4̶-6̶a̶³ Luke = Q, Con (pp. 114-116).
    Neirynck 1995, 180: See Q 7:2̶, 3, 4̶-6̶a̶¹ Luke = Q, Con (p. 70).

Con

    Burton 1904, 46: "A survey of the gospels in parallelism discloses two facts that seem to be of importance. The first of these is the condensed character of Matthew's narrative at certain points as compared with the accounts in the other gospels. Examples of shortening or condensation as compared with Mark are found in all the following sections:

A day in Capernaum:	Mark 1:21-34	Matt. 8:14-17.
Healing of a leper:	Mark 1:40-45	Matt. 8:1-4.
Healing of a paralytic:	Mark 2:1-12	Matt. 9:1-8.
The Gerasene Demoniac:	Mark 5:1-20	Matt. 8:28-34.
Jairus's daughter:	Mark 5:21-43	Matt. 9:18-26.
Rejection at Nazareth:	Mark 6:1-6a	Matt. 13:54-58.
Death of John the Baptist:	Mark 6:14-29	Matt. 14:1-12.
Feeding of the five thousand:	Mark 6:30-46	Matt. 14:13-23.
Eating with unwashen hands:	Mark 7:1-23	Matt. 15:1-20.

"In the few instances in which the narrative of Matt. is longer than Mark's, this arises from the addition of some saying of Jesus, or of some comment of the evangelist, the latter sometimes in the form of a reference to the fulfilment of prophecy.²⁵

"In the few narratives that are common to Matt. and Luke only, the relation of Matthew's account to Luke's is in general the same as to Mark's in the cases above enumerated. Thus in the story of the centurion's servant (Matt. 8.5-13; Luke 7:1-10), the narrative in Matt. is but two-thirds of the length of that in Luke, the apparent equality of the accounts being due to the inclusion by Matt. (vss. 11, 12) of certain *sayings* of Jesus found in Luke's Perean section (13:28, 29)."

46²⁵: "See Mark 1:14, 15 = Matt. 4:12-17; Mark 2:23-28 = Matt. 12:1-8; Mark 6:47-52 = Matt. 14:24-33."

Parker 1953, 63-65: See Q 7:1⁶ Matt = Q, Con (pp. 58-60).

Gundry 1982, 142: "In v 6 Matthew makes a request out of the description of the servant's illness (so Luke) in order to compensate for his omitting the Jewish elders' words to Jesus."

Dauer 1984, 105-106: See Q 7:2, 3, 4-6a³ Matt = Q, Con (pp. 123-124).

Davies and Allison 1991, 19: See Q 7:2, 3, 4-6a³ Matt = Q, Con (p. 124).

Hagner 1993, 202: See Q 7:2, 3, 4-6a³ Matt = Q, Con (p. 125).

204: "Matthew has removed the larger context referred to in Luke about the centurion's interest in Judaism so that no preparation is given for such a person approaching or having such confidence in Jesus."

Emendation = Q: <>¹³ ὁ δὲ ᾿Ιησοῦς ἐπορεύετο σὺν αὐτ<ῷ>¹³.

Lindars 1992, 208: "For ὁ δὲ ᾿Ιησοῦς ἐπορεύετο σὺν αὐτοῖς (adapted from an original αὐτῷ) in Lk 7,6 follows naturally from the centurion's appeal to Jesus to come in Lk 7,3 = Mt 8,7, and the further note, that it was not until Jesus was near the house (ἤδη δὲ αὐτοῦ οὐ μακράν ἀπέχοντος ἀπὸ τῆς οἰκίας) that the centurion spoke again, follows naturally on that. There is really a lacuna in Matthew's account, for the centurion asks Jesus to come, and then, as soon as Jesus agrees to do so, tells him not to come after all. ... The story makes ... sense if Jesus showed no unwillingness, but the centurion began to have doubts about the propriety of expecting him to enter his house when they had already gone part of the way. It is this delicacy of feeling which Luke has picked up and elaborated ... by making the centurion work entirely through messengers."

210: Reconstruction. For complete text see Q 7:1⁶ Luke = Q, Pro (p. 56).

Evaluations

Johnson 2000: Matt = Q {B}, []¹³.

The vocabulary of these verses is decidedly Lukan (e.g. Harnack, Plummer, Patton, Jeremias; Gagnon 1993 summarizes the statistical evidence well). The most vocal proponents of Matthean omission (Dauer) and Lukan *Sondergut* traditions (Wegner) both present overwhelming statistical evidence *against* their own positions. Even vocabulary that is not particularly Lukan is apparently pulled in by Luke from the Healing of Jairus' Daughter (Delobel).

This variation unit as a whole depends on the Jewish delegation being in Q, but is not essential to it. The worthiness speech serves to explain the presence of the elders as emissaries of a soldier and is particularly relevant for an urban audience (such as Luke's) that readily accepts and assumes the realities of the Roman patronage system. Despite the narrative "color" of the verses, there appears to be no reason for caution in deciding against this variant.

Robinson 2000: Matt = Q {B}, []̈[13].
The Lukanisms are decisive.

Kloppenborg 2000: Matt = Q {B}, []̈[13].

Hoffmann 2001: Matt = Q {B}, []̈[13].

Q 7:6b-c

Mark 7:28	Matt 15:27	Matt 8:8a
ἡ δὲ ἀπεκρίθη	ἡ δὲ εἶπεν·	(καὶ ἀποκριθεὶς)¹ [ ]²
καὶ λέγει αὐτῷ· κύριε·		ὁ ἑκατόνταρχ(ο)³ς (ἔφη)⁴ [ ]⁵· κύριε, [ ]⁶
	ναὶ κύριε,	
καὶ τὰ κυνάρια	καὶ γὰρ τὰ κυνάρια	οὐ(κ)⁷ [ ]⁷ ⌐ ⌐⁸ εἰμὶ ⌐ἱκανὸς⌐⁸
ὑποκάτω τῆς τραπέζης		ἵνα ⌐μου⌐⁹ ὑπὸ τὴν στέγην
ἐσθίουσιν ἀπὸ τῶν ψιχίων	ἐσθίει ἀπὸ τῶν ψιχίων τῶν πιπτόντων ἀπὸ τῆς τραπέζης	⌐ ⌐⁹ εἰσέλθῃς,
τῶν παιδίων.	τῶν κυρίων αὐτῶν.	

IQP 1994: ἑκατονταρχ[( )]³ς; JSK: ἑκατοντάρχ(η)³ς.
PH: (< >)⁴ indeterminate.
IQP 1994: ⌐ ⌐⁸.
IQP 1994: ⌐ ⌐⁹.

Text Critical Note: In Matt 8:8a ἀποκριθεὶς δέ is in ℵ* B 33 *pc* sa, but καὶ ἀποκριθείς is in ℵ¹ C L W Θ 0233 *f*¹·¹³ 𝔪 lat syʰ bo.

¹ Matthew's καὶ ἀποκριθείς.
² Luke's ἤδη δὲ αὐτοῦ οὐ μακρὰν ἀπέχοντος ἀπὸ τῆς οἰκίας ἔπεμψεν φίλους.
³ Luke's ἑκατοντάρχης or Matthew's ἑκατόνταρχος.
⁴ Luke's λέγων or Matthew's ἔφη.
⁵ Luke's αὐτῷ.
⁶ Luke's μὴ σκύλλου.
⁷ Luke's οὐ γάρ or Matthew's οὐκ.
⁸ The position of ἱκανός before (Luke) or after (Matthew) εἰμί.
⁹ The position of μου after (Luke) or before (Matthew) ὑπὸ τὴν στέγην.

Q 7:6b-c

Q 7:6b-c	Luke 7:6b-c	John 4:51a, 49
(καὶ ἀποκριθεὶς)¹ []²	( )¹ [ἤδη δὲ αὐτοῦ οὐ μακρὰν ἀπέχοντος ἀπὸ τῆς οἰκίας ἔπεμψεν φίλους]²	4:51a ἤδη δὲ αὐτοῦ καταβαίνοντος
ὁ ἑκατόνταρχ⟦(ο)³⟧ς (ἔφη)⁴ []⁵· {κύριε,} []⁶ οὐ(χ)⁷ []⁷ ∫ ²⁸ εἰμὶ ∫ἱκανὸς²⁸ ἵνα ∫μου²⁹ ὑπὸ τὴν στέγην ∫²⁹ εἰσέλθῃς,	ὁ ἑκατοντάρχ[η]³ς [λέγων]⁴ [αὐτῷ]⁵· κύριε, [μὴ σκύλλου]⁶, οὐ( )⁷ [γὰρ]⁷ ∫ἱκανός²⁸ εἰμι ∫ ²⁸ ἵνα ∫ ²⁹ ὑπὸ τὴν στέγην ∫μου²⁹ εἰσέλθῃς·	4:49 λέγει πρὸς αὐτὸν ὁ βασιλικός· κύριε, κατάβηθι πρὶν ἀποθανεῖν τὸ παιδίον μου.

Q 7:6b-c¹: Matthew's καὶ ἀποκριθείς.

Luke = Q: [ ]¹

Pro

Con

Matt = Q: (καὶ ἀποκριθείς)¹

Pro

von Harnack 1907, 91 (ET 1908, 131): For reconstruction, see Harnack at Emendation = Q (p. 238).

Polag 1979, 38: Reconstruction. For complete text see Q 7:1⁰ In Q (pp. 9-10).

Schenk 1981, 37: Reconstruction. For complete text see Q 7:1⁰ In Q (p. 10).

Wegner 1985, 157: For καί: "Der Befund zu καί zeigte, daß Mt es parataktisch nur selten von sich aus einfügt, dagegen überwiegend durch δέ, τότε oder andere Konstruktionen zu ersetzen pflegt."

157-158: For ἀποκριθείς: "1. In Q erscheint das Verb sicher belegt in Mt 4,4/Lk 4,4 und 11,4/Lk 7,22: An beiden Stellen wird ἀποκρίνομαι sehr wahrscheinlich mit vorangestelltem καί gestanden haben. [158] Dem urspr Q-Stoff dürfte auch noch das καὶ ἀποκριθείς von Lk 4,8.12 angehören, da Lk diese Wendung nicht in der Apg gebraucht und auch mehrfach gegenüber seiner Mk-Vorlage geändert hat. Von hieraus wäre sogar zu erwägen, ob nicht auch die in Lk 17,37 stehende Einleitungswendung zum Q-Spruch Lk 17,37c/Mt 24,28 auf Grund der Formulierung καὶ ἀποκριθέντες urspr der Q-Quelle angehörte."

158: "2. Man wird auf Grund dieses Befundes wohl sagen können, daß, trotz einer eindeutigen mt Vorliebe für ἀποκρίνομαι, dieses Verb sehr wohl auch in Mt 8,8 bereits durch Q vorgegeben sein konnte. Dem widerspricht keineswegs die Tatsache, daß in Lk 7,1-10 ἀποκρίνομαι nicht begegnet, da es dort infolge der Einführung einer zweiten Gesandtschaft (Lk 7,6a) notwendigerweise entfallen muß. Hinzu kommt noch, daß das Verb auSt auch sachlich berechtigt ist, da der Hauptmann in 8,8 auf eine ihm von Jesus gestellte Frage (Mt 8,7) antwortet."

159: "Ergab die isolierte Betrachtung von ἀποκρίνομαι und φημί für die Wahrscheinlichkeit einer mt Red einige Anhaltspunkte, so ändert sich jedoch dieser Eindruck entscheidend, sobald man die Wendung als Ganze betrachtet, da καὶ ἀποκριθεὶς ... ἔφη in dieser Formulierung weder woanders im MtEv noch an irgend einer andern Stelle im NT anzutreffen ist. Hinzu kommt, daß auch in anderen Formulierungen Mt ἀποκρίνομαι niemals in Verbindung mit ἔφη, wie es in 8,8 der Fall ist, bringt. Ganz überwiegend verwendet er dagegen ἀποκρίνομαι in Verbindung mit εἰπεῖν. Schließlich ist die Verwendung von ἀποκριθείς + Verbum finitum mit vorangestelltem καί in Mt auch recht selten: Bei 45maligem Vorkommen von ἀποκριθείς + Verbum finitum in Mt begegnet ausschließlich in 8,8 und 22,1 (Q?) ein vorangestelltes καί. Mt selbst benutzt vielmehr Wendungen wie ἀποκριθεὶς δέ oder ὁ δὲ ἀποκριθείς oder schließlich ἀποκριθείς mit vorangestelltem τότε."

160: "Der Befund ergibt, daß die Konstruktion καὶ ἀποκριθεὶς … ἔφη kaum von Mt selbst stammen wird und daher eher der Trad zuzurechnen ist."

270: Reconstruction. For complete text see Q 7:1⁰ In Q (pp. 11-12).

Schenk 1987, 338: "Die restl. Stellen haben alle den LXXismus ἀποκριθεὶς εἶπεν (bzw. 8,8 beim Zenturio ἔφη 25,40 das Fut. ἐρεῖ im Vorhersage-Text), der außerhalb der Synopt. nie verwendet ist (auch nicht bei Joh …). … Dabei ist Jesus nicht Handlungsträger in folgenden 13 Fällen: 8,8 (+Q—in dem Bescheidenheitsausdruck des Zenturio, der damit nichtsdestoweniger eine grundsätzliche Aussage macht)."

Catchpole 1992, 533 [1993, 299]: Reconstruction: "ἀποκριθεὶς δέ …." For complete text see Q 7:1⁰ In Q (p. 14).

Sevenich-Bax 1993, 179-180: "Ebenso ist Vers Mt 8,8a der Logienquelle zuzuschlagen. Das lukanische Pendant (Lk 7,6bβ) ist im Zusammenhang mit der Entsendung der Freunde formuliert, also sicher redaktionell. Zugunsten der matthäischen Version spricht ferner, daß Matthäus die Vokabel ἀποκριθείς mit vorangestelltem καί ausgesprochen selten verwendet und auch die [180] Verknüpfung von ἀποκρίνομαι und φημί in seinem Evangelium sonst nicht belegt ist."

238: Reconstruction. For complete text see Q 7:1⁰ In Q (p. 15).

Landis 1994, 10: "Die Redeeinleitung in Mt 8,8a, die bei Lk keine Entsprechung hat, weil der Erzählverlauf dort ganz anders ist, geht mit großer Wahrscheinlichkeit auf Q zurück; denn Mt hat zwar eine Vorliebe für die Einzelwörter ἀποκρίνομαι und φημί, der Gesamtausdruck καὶ ἀποκριθεὶς … ἔφη jedoch ist für den ersten Evangelisten, der das anknüpfende καί wohl vermieden und nach ἀποκριθείς eher εἶπεν verwendet hätte, ausgesprochen untypisch und daher kaum redaktionell."

11, 17: Reconstruction. For complete text see Q 7:1⁶ Luke = Q, Pro (p. 57).

International Q Project 1995, 478: Reconstruction. For complete text see Q 7:1⁰ In Q (p. 16).

Con

B. Weiß 1908, 15²⁴: "Wir können daher den Wortlaut des Matth. im Einzelnen nicht mehr kontrollieren, in dem aber höchstens das asyndetische λέγει

8,7 und das ἀποκριθείς … —ἔφη … so verdächtig sind daß ich sie im Text entfernt habe."

Castor 1912, 223: Reconstruction. For complete text see Q 7:1⁰ In Q (p. 6).

Crum 1927, 138: Reconstruction: "And the centurion said, …" For complete text see Q 7:2̶, 3, 4̶-6̶a̶¹ Luke = Q, Pro (pp. 71-72).

Gundry 1982, 143: "In place of the centurion's further sending of some friends and speaking through them (note the singular of λέγων in Luke 7:6), Matthew uses the stereotyped ἀποκριθείς with ἔφη. εἶπε(ν) always appears in the phrase elsewhere in his gospel (29,6). But here the recency of λέγει in v 7 leads him to use ἔφη."

Luz 1990, 12⁴: "Matthäismen … sind: ἀποκριθεὶς δέ, μόνον."

Luz 1990, ET 2001, 8⁴: "Mattheisms are: ἀποκριθεὶς δέ, μόνον."

Davies and Allison 1991, 22-23: "Although Q named the subject (see Lk 7.6), ἀποκριθείς and ἔφη may well be [23] Matthean—although καὶ ἀποκριθείς … ἔφη is found nowhere else in the First Gospel (or the NT)."

Lindars 1992, 210: Reconstruction. For complete text see Q 7:1⁶ Luke = Q, Pro (p. 56).

Gagnon 1994b, 137: See Q 7:2̶, 3, 4̶-6̶a̶⁷ Matt = Q, Con (p. 15).

137: "The expression in v. 8aα (καὶ ἀποκριθεὶς ὁ ἑκατόνταρχος ἔφη), though not the usual Matthean expression, is still possible for Matthew."

Emendation = Q: καὶ <>¹ ….

B. Weiß 1908, 15: Reconstruction: "καὶ ὁ ἑκατόνταρχος." For complete text see Q 7:1⁰ In Q (p. 5).

Emendation = Q: <>¹ ἀποκριθεὶς <δέ>¹ ….

von Harnack 1907, 91 (ET 1908, 131): Reconstruction: "ἀποκριθεὶς δέ …." For complete text see Q 7:1⁶ Luke = Q, Pro (p. 55).

Catchpole 1992, 533 [1993, 299]: Reconstruction: "ἀποκριθεὶς δέ …." For complete text see Q 7:1⁰ In Q (p. 14).

Evaluations

Robinson 2000: Matt = Q {B}, (καὶ ἀποκριθείς)¹.

The ἀποκριθείς gives some expression to the structure of the dialogue: The petitioner has just been rebuffed, and must produce a rejoinder that overcomes the objection. This is suggested by ἀποκριθείς, just as in Mark 7:28 ἡ δὲ ἀποκρίθη καὶ λέγει αὐτῷ.

Also καὶ ἀποκριθείς occurs in Q at 7:22.

Kloppenborg 2000: Matt = Q {B}, (καὶ ἀποκριθείς)[1].

Johnson 2001: Matt = Q {B}, (καὶ ἀποκριθείς)[1].
Though both argue against Matthew, Gundry and Davies and Allison seem at odds over whether Matthew's grammar is common to Matthew or not. The IQP has voted in καί with ἀποκρίνομαι at Q 4:4.

Hoffmann 2001: Matt = Q {B}, (καὶ ἀποκριθείς)[1].

Q 7:6b-c²: Luke's ἤδη δὲ αὐτοῦ οὐ μακρὰν ἀπέχοντος ἀπὸ τῆς οἰκίας ἔπεμψεν φίλους.

Luke = Q: [ἤδη δὲ αὐτοῦ οὐ μακρὰν ἀπέχοντος ἀπὸ τῆς οἰκίας ἔπεμψεν φίλους.]²

Pro

H. Meyer 1864, 218 (ET 1884, 179): See Q 7:2, 3, 4-6a³ Luke = Q, Pro (p. 87).

Hawkins 1899, 195: "Luke may have retained the original narrative in its fullness, while Matthew, after his manner, shortened it: —Lk vi.17a(?); vii. 3a, 4, 5, 6, 7a; 10; 20, 21."

Castor 1912, 41-42: See Q 7:2, 3, 4-6a³ Luke = Q, Pro (pp. 87-88).
223: Reconstruction. For complete text see Q 7:1⁰ In Q (p. 6).

Schmid 1930, 252-253: See Q 7:2, 3, 4-6a³ Luke = Q, Pro (p. 88).

Schmid 1956, 163: "Als sich Jesus auf den Weg zu seinem Hause macht, schickt der Hauptmann nochmals Freunde, die in seinem Auftrag das sagen, was er bei Mt 8,8f persönlich zu Jesus spricht."

Ellis 1966, 117: See Q 7:2, 3, 4-6a¹ Luke = Q, Pro (p. 67).

Jeremias 1980, 153: "Trad μακρὰν ἀπέχοντος: Die Wendung μακρὰν ἀπέχω findet sich im NT nur im Nicht-Markusstoff des Lukas-Evangeliums: 7,6 (unsere Stelle); 15,20. Da Lukas selbst μακρὰν ὑπάρχω schreibt (Apg 17,27) und da das Übliche μακρὰν εἰμί (Mk 12,34; Mt 8,30; Joh 21,8) war, wird μακρὰν ἀπέχω eine dritte vorlukanische Variation sein. —φίλους: Trotz der Alltäglichkeit der Vokabel φίλος wird man nicht unbeachtet lassen dürfen, daß sie in den Synoptikern (abgesehen von Mt 11,19) nur bei Lukas vorkommt, und zwar 15mal. Alle Belege (bis auf 21,16 = Zusatz zu Mk 13,12) stehen im Nicht-Markusstoff. Auch wenn Lukas die Vokabel in der Apg 3mal verwendet, so sind zum mindesten einige Fälle profilierten Gebrauchs wie Lk 7,34 (par. Mt 11,19) oder 16,9 typisch für die vorlukanische Tradition."

Schweizer 1982, 85: "Sprachlich erweisen sich als vorlukanisch der Zug … die Sendung der Freunde (V.6)."

Schweizer 1982, ET 1984, 131: "There are several pre-Lukan features in the language of this episode: … (6) the centurion sends his friends."

Dauer 1984, 94: See Q 7:2, 3, 4-6a³ Luke = Q, Pro (p. 89).
115: "Zur 2. Gesandtschaft gilt das, was oben schon zur 1. gesagt worden ist: sie stammt kaum von Lukas selbst, sondern ist aus der Quelle. Matthäus hat sie, wie die 1., gestrichen." But for the text of Q 7:6b-c², which Dauer omits from Q (with the exception of ἔπεμψεν φίλους), see Dauer at Luke = Q, Con (p. 249).

Sand 1986, 178: See Sand at Matt = Q, Con (p. 257).

Lindars 1992, 208: "John thus contributes to the reconstruction of this part of the story, because he has retained ἤδη δὲ αὐτοῦ from the source, though he has adjusted the verb to suit the distance and applied the phrase to the centurion, who alone goes to the house in his recasting of the story." See Lindars at Emendation = Q (p. 257).

Con

Strauss 1836, 101: "Hauptsächlich aber die doppelte Gesandtschaft bei Lukas ist nach Schleiermacher etwas, das nicht leicht erdacht wird. Wie, wenn sich dieser Zug vielmehr sehr deutlich als einen erdachten zu erkennen gäbe? Während bei Matthäus der Hauptmann Jesum auf sein Erbieten, mit ihm gehen zu wollen, durch die Einwendung zurückzuhalten sucht: κύριε, οὐκ εἰμὶ ἱκανός, ἵνα μου ὑπὸ τὴν στέγην εἰσέλθῃς, läßt er bei Lukas durch die abgesandten Freunde noch hinzusetzen: διὸ οὐδὲ ἐμαυτὸν ἠξίωσα πρὸς σὲ ἐλθεῖν, womit deutlich genug der Schluß angegeben ist, auf welchem diese Gesandtschaft beruht. Erklärte sich der Mann für unwürdig, daß Jesus zu ihm komme, dachte man, so hat er wohl auch sich selbst nicht für würdig gehalten, zu Jesu zu kommen; eine Steigerung seiner Demuth, durch welche sich auch hier der Bericht des Lukas als der secundäre zu erkennen gibt."

Strauss 1836, ET 1855, 516: "Especially the double message in Luke is, according to Schleiermacher, a feature very unlikely to have been invented. How if, on the contrary, it very plainly manifested itself to be an invention? While in Matthew the centurion, on the offer of Jesus to accompany him, seeks to prevent him by the objection: *Lord, I am not worthy that thou shouldest come under my roof,* in Luke he adds by the mouth of his messenger, *wherefore neither thought I myself worthy to come unto thee,* by which we plainly discover the conclusion on which the second embassy was founded. If the man declared himself unworthy that Jesus should come to him, he cannot, it was thought, have held himself worthy to come to Jesus; an exaggeration of his humility by which the narrative of Luke again betrays its secondary character."

Bleek 1862, 347-348: See Q 7:~~2~~, 3, ~~4-6a~~¹ Matt = Q, Pro (pp. 70-71).

Holtzmann 1863, 78, 220: See Q 7:~~2~~, 3, ~~4-6a~~³ Luke = Q, Con (p. 93).

B. Weiß 1876, 229: "Während nun Jesus in dieser nur seine Bereitwilligkeit zu kommen erklärt (Mtth. 8,7), ist er bei Luc. v. 6 bereits im Kommen begriffen, als wieder nicht der Vater selbst, sondern abgesandte Freunde dies sein Kommen abwehren; aber hier zeigt das μὴ σκύλλου noch deutlich genug, daß dies nur eine Reminiscenz an die Erzählung von dem Synagogenobersten Jair ist, wo auch eine zweite Botschaft aus dem Trauerhause jede weitere

Bemühung Jesu verhindern will (Mrc. 5,35). Denn so lebenswahr die Worte der Abwehr im Munde des Centurio selbst klingen, so unnatürlich erscheinen sie, namentlich wegen ihrer Begründung (v. 8), im Munde der Freunde."

B. Weiß 1878, 364: "Auch von dieser zweiten Sendung, die sehr an Mark. 5,35 erinnert, weiß die ältere Quelle nichts, und im Munde der Freunde klingt die Begründung V. 8 weniger natürlich, als im Munde des Hauptmanns selbst."

J. Weiß 1892, 398²: "Daß hier zwei Überlieferungen zusammenstoßen, zeigt sich daran, daß den Freunden des Hauptmanns die lange directe Rede desselben in den Mund gelegt wird, die doch nur Sinn hat in seinem Munde (6b-8), vgl. W. [B. Weiß 1876], 229f. Nach W. hätte Lk hier die Darstellung von Q mit einer anderen aus LQ verbunden. Wahrscheinlich aber hat bereits LQ die Darstellung von Q mit einer Sonderdarstellung (L) verbunden."

399-400: "Auch von der zweiten Sendung, die an Mk 5,35 erinnert, weiß Q (Mt) nichts und im Munde dieser Freunde klingt [400] die ausführliche Rede des Hauptmanns (aus Q), namentlich V. 8 sehr merkwürdig."

Plummer 1896, 195: "Οὐ μακράν. Comp. Acts xvii. 27. The expression is peculiar to Lk., who is fond of οὐ with an adj. or adv. to express his meaning. Comp. οὐ πολλοί (xv. 13; Acts i. 5), οὐ πολύ (Acts xxvii. 14), οὐκ ὀλίγος (Acts xii. 18, xiv. 28, xv. 2, xvii. 4, 12, xix. 23, 24, xxvii. 20), οὐκ ὁ τυχών (Acts xix. 11, xxviii. 2), οὐκ ἄσημος (Acts xxi. 39), οὐ μετρίως (Acts xx. 12)."

B. Weiß 1900, 322-323: "Die zweite Sendung ... erinnert stark an Mk. 5,35, namentlich wegen des folgenden μη σκυλλ. Zu φιλ. vgl. Act. 10,24. Mit dem οὐ γὰρ ἱκ. κτλ. setzt der Wortlaut von Mt. 8,8 ein, der sich freilich im Munde des Hauptmanns selbst viel natürlicher ausnimmt. Nur das διὸ ... οὐδὲ [323] ἐμ. ἠξίωσα ... πρὸς σὲ ἐλθ. mußte v. 7 wegen v. 3 eingeschoben werden."

Holtzmann 1901, 344: "Wie Cornelius bei seiner Begegnung mit Petrus Act 10,24 seine Freunde um sich hat, so schickt der Centurio die seinigen als eine Gesandtschaft, die jetzt in Folge der redactionellen Maassnahmen des Lc eine Modification der früheren Bitte zu überbringen, ... in Wirklichkeit nur dasselbe Wort auszurichten hat, welches der Centurio Mt 8,8 persönlich zu Jesus spricht."

B. Weiß 1901, 383: "Diese zweite Sendung (ἔπεμψ., wie 4,26) erinnert auffallend an Mk 5,35, besonders wegen des μὴ σκύλλου (doch bem. das Med.), und selbst an Joh 4,51, nur daß hier Freunde (φίλ., wie Act 10,24) gesandt werden. Wenn aber ihr Auftrag durch Mt 8,8 (wörtlich) motivirt wird, so paßt das nicht zu der bisherigen Erzählung, da der Hauptmann V. 3 allerdings um sein persönliches Kommen bitten ließ. Hat Lk darauf reflektirt, so hat er sich natürlich, warum derselbe seinen Entschluß geändert; aber die Erzählung weiß davon nichts, und so ist klar, daß hier eine andere Überlieferung einsetzt (vgl. das ἱκανὸς ἵνα mit dem ἄξιος ᾧ V. 4). Auch sind die Worte nur im Munde des Hauptmanns selbst, wie bei Mt., natürlich, im Munde der Freunde höchst unnatürlich."

384: See Q 7:~~2~~, 3, ~~4-6a~~³ Luke = Q, Con (p. 94).

B. Weiß 1904, 242: "Schon in der ältesten Überlieferung schloß sich an die Bergrede die Erzählung vom Hauptmann zu Kapernaum an (vgl. Mtth. 8,1.5). Auch hier geht Jesus unmittelbar nach Vollendung derselben nach Kapernaum. Aber Lukas befaß in der ihm eigentümlichen Überlieferung noch einen reicheren Bericht über diese Geschichte, dem er besonders in der ersten Hälfte folgt. ... Hier hält sich der heidnische Hauptmann nicht einmal für würdig, Jesus selbst mit seiner Bitte zu nahen, sondern sendet die Stadtältesten zu ihm, um die Errettung des Knechtes aus der letzten Todesnot zu erbitten. ... Aber selbst als Jesus seinem Hause zugeht, sendet der Hauptmann noch Freunde, die sein Kommen abwehren sollen, weil er sich dazu vollends nicht für gut genug hält."

B. Weiß 1904, ET 1906, 56-57: "In the oldest tradition the Sermon on the Mount was followed by the account of the centurion of Capernaum (cf. Matt. viii. 1-5). According to this tradition Jesus goes to the city immediately after finishing His address. But Luke possessed in his special source of information fuller details of this history which he follows, especially in the first part of his account. ... Here the Gentile centurion does not even consider himself worthy of approaching the Lord personally with his petition, but he sends the elders of the city to Him, to ask Him to save his servant in his great danger. ... [57] ... but even after Jesus starts to go to his house, the centurion sends other friends to restrain Him from coming because he considered himself entirely unworthy of this honor."

Wellhausen 1904b, 27: "Diese reden [Luke 6b-8], als wenn sie die Bestellung auswendig gelernt hätten, ihre Worte passen nur in den Mund des Hauptmanns selber, wie bei Mt. Auf Lc hat der §27 [Luke 8:40-56] eingewirkt, wo die Leute des Jairus hinter ihm herschicken und sagen, er solle den Meister nicht in sein Haus bemühen."

von Harnack 1907, 55-56: "Die beiden Gesandtschaften an Jesus (statt daß der Hauptmann selbst kommt) sind späterer Zusatz. Das geht schlagend 1. daraus hervor, daß die lange Rede, die nach Luk. angeblich die Freunde halten, schlechterdings nur in den Mund des Hauptmanns selbst paßt, 2. daß auch bei Joh. (4,46ff.) der Hauptmann (βασιλικός) selbst kommt. ... [56] ... Bemerkt sei nur, daß ἔντιμος (Verse 2), ... μακρὰν ἀπέχειν (Verse 6), [et alia] in den Evangelien ausschließlich lukanisch sind. ... Auch διασώζειν kann als ein lukanisches Wort in Anspruch genommen werden, sowie der Wechsel ἀπέστειλεν (v. 3) und ἔπεμψεν (v. 6)."

91: Reconstruction. For complete text see Q 7:1⁶ Luke = Q, Pro (p. 55).

von Harnack 1907, ET 1908, 76-77: "The two deputations to our Lord (in place of the personal interview of the centurion) are a later addition. This is strikingly shown (1) by the fact that the long speech which St. Luke assigns to the friends is intelligible and appropriate only if it was spoken by the centurion himself, and (2) because also in St. John (iv. 46ff.) the centurion (βασιλικός) comes himself. ... I would only remark that ἔντιμος (verse 2), ... μακρὰν ἀπέχειν (verse 6), [et alia] are, as far as the gospels [77] are concerned, exclusively Lukan. ... διασώζειν can be claimed as Lukan, as well as the alternation between ἀπέστειλεν (verse 3) and ἔπεμψεν (verse 6)."

131: Reconstruction. For complete text see Q 7:1⁶ Luke = Q, Pro (p. 55).

Loisy 1907, 651: "Le second message que le centurion dépêche à Jésus correspond, en effet, à celui que reçoit Jaïr pendant que le Sauveur se rend avec lui dans sa maison, et un même mot caractéristique se rencontre dans les deux, transposé de l'histoire de Jaïr dans celle du centurion."

B. Weiß 1907, 242-243: "Und während Mt. 8,8 der Hauptmann das Kommen Jesu ablehnt, weil er sich zu unwürdig fühlt, Jesum zu empfangen, begegnet Jesus nach Lk. 7,6, als er bereits mitgeht, anderen [243] vom Hauptmann abgesandten Freunden, welche sein Kommen abwehren. Auch diese zweite Botschaft (vgl. das ἤδη δὲ αὐτοῦ οὐ μακρὰν ἀπέχοντος mit 15,20 in einer Parabel aus L) erinnert merkwürdig an die zweite Botschaft in der Geschichte des Königischen, die ebenfalls auf ein ἐπορεύετο Joh. 4,50 folgt."

J. Weiß 1907, 448: "Die Bergrede wird fast wörtlich so beschlossen, wie bei Matthäus. Die Geschichte, die von V. 6 an ganz wie bei Matthäus ... verläuft, hat bei Lukas einige Zusätze: die doppelte Botschaft und die starke Zurückhaltung des Hauptmanns fügt zu dem kühnen Glauben des Mannes noch den Zug der außerordentlichen Demut hinzu. ... Die zweite Botschaft, die wie in der Geschichte des Jairus den Meister von persönlicher Bemühung zurückhalten soll, redet mit den Worten des Hauptmanns selber."

B. Weiß 1908, 15: Reconstruction. For complete text see Q 7:1⁰ In Q (p. 5).

Patton 1915, 144: See Q 7:~~2~~, 3, ~~4-6a~~³ Luke = Q, Con (pp. 95-96).

144-145: "Of these Lucan words, ... [145] ... μακράν is used once by Matthew, once by Mark, twice by Luke in his Gospel, and three times in Acts. Ἀπέχοντες (in the intransitive sense) occurs twice in Matthew, once in Mark, three times in Luke's Gospel, and not in Acts."

145: See Q 7:~~2~~, 3, ~~4-6a~~³ Luke = Q, Con (p. 96).

Klostermann 1919, 449: "(Οὐ μακράν: Lc liebt solche Umschreibungen), so ist für die Modifikation der früheren Bitte durch eine neue Botschaft des Hauptmanns kein äußerer Anlaß vorhanden ...; die Freunde [ἔπεμψεν φίλους] (vgl. Act 10,24) sagen fast wörtlich das, was bei Mt der Hauptmann selbst sagt, nur daß das Unwürdigkeitsgefühl jetzt zur Begründung der neuen Aufforderung μὴ σκύλλου (vgl. die Jairuserzählung 8,49 = Mc 5,35) dient, und daß der eingeschobene Satz 7,7a διὸ οὐδὲ ἐμαυτὸν ἠξίωσα πρὸς σὲ ἐλθεῖν ... nachträglich noch die erste Botschaft rechtfertigen muß."

Loisy 1924, 217: "Le second message correspond à celui que reçoit Jaïr pendant qui Jésus se rend avec lui à sa maison."

Bussmann 1925, 11: See Q 7:2̶, 3, 4̶-6̶a³ Luke = Q, Con (p. 96).

Easton 1926, 96: See Q 7:2̶, 3, 4̶-6̶a³ Luke = Q, Con (pp. 96-97).

97: "Σύν is 'Lukan', as is πέμπειν."

Crum 1927, 138: Reconstruction. For complete text see Q 7:2̶, 3, 4̶-6̶a¹ Luke = Q, Pro (pp. 71-72).

Montefiore 1927, 423-424: "Luke ... makes diverse changes [424] in the story of the centurion. ... friends are made to say the words, which are scarcely suitable except in the centurion's own mouth, in 6-8. Luke's version, whether its peculiarities are due to himself or to a special source, are clearly secondary as compared with Matthew."

424: "Jesus immediately agrees to go. The second embassy is thus really needless, and becomes a little clumsy. The idea is to show the great humility of the centurion. But the whole effect, both of the speech and of Jesus's reply, is weaker and less natural than in Matthew. The resemblance of the centurion to Cornelius in Acts x. is worthy of notice."

Klostermann 1929, 86-87: Same text as Klostermann 1919, 449, above.

Creed 1930, 100: See Q 7:2̶, 3, 4̶-6̶a³ Luke = Q, Con (p. 97).

Manson 1937, 64: "The second deputation is an expression of the humility of the man, and this is made explicit in v. 7, which has no parallel in Mt. and is not to be regarded as original."

Hirsch 1941, 89: "Sachlich bedeuten sie eine Veränderung der Geschichte, wie sie Luk sich an Markustexten da, wo nicht eine markusfremde Vorlage ihn bestimmte, nirgends erlaubt hat. Es find folgende: a) Der Hauptmann spricht nicht selbst mit Jesus, sondern schickt erst die jüdische Gemeindebehörde, dann Freunde zu Jesus (Luk 7:2-6a). Bei der Bestellung durch die Freunde fällt auf, daß sie in einer ausführlichen Darlegung so reden, als ob sie der Hauptmann selber wären."

Haenchen 1959a, 25-26 [1965, 84-85]: See Q 7:2̶, 3, 4̶-6̶a³ Luke = Q, Con (p. 99).

Grundmann 1961, 155: See Q 7:2̶, 3, 4̶-6̶a³ Luke = Q, Con (pp. 99-100).

Dodd 1963, 191: See Q 7:2̶, 3, 4̶-6̶a¹ Luke = Q, Con (p. 68).

Schnackenburg 1964, 75: "Die gleiche Rede, die der Hauptmann bei Mt unmittelbar an Jesus selbst richtet, wird nun von den Freunden fast wörtlich als Botschaft des Mannes an Jesus 'bestellt', und dieses Verfahren ist deutlich sekundär, erst nachträglich geschaffen, zerstört es doch die ursprüngliche Frische, die über der Szene bei Mt liegt."

Schnackenburg 1965, 505-506: "So ist die zweite Sendung, diesmal von 'Freunden' (Lk 7,6), auffällig und mit dem matthäischen Parallelbericht unvereinbar. Die gleiche Rede, die der Hauptmann bei Mt unmittelbar an Jesus selbst richtet, wird nun von den Freunden fast wörtlich als Botschaft des Mannes an Jesus 'bestellt', und dieses Verfahren ist deutlich sekundär, erst nachträglich geschaffen, zerstört es doch die [506] ursprüngliche Frische, die über der Szene bei Mt liegt. Die abweichende lukanische Darstellung läßt sich nicht bestreiten, und ohne auf die möglichen Gründe dafür einzugehen, müssen wir zur Kenntnis nehmen, daß die Tradition in dieser Weise erfahren ist."

Schnackenburg 1965, ET 1968, 475: "The second mission, that of the 'friends' (Lk 7:6), is remarkable and cannot be reconciled with the parallel account in Matthew. The words which the centurion addresses directly to Jesus in Matthew are now passed on almost word for word by his friends, in the form of a message. The procedure in Luke is obviously secondary, a subsequent manipulation which robs the scene of the spontaneity which it had in Matthew. The divergency of the Lucan presentation cannot be missed, and without going into the possible reasons for it, we must take cognizance of the fact that tradition has proceeded in this way."

Talbert 1967, 491-492: See Q 7:~~2~~, 3, ~~4-6a~~³ Luke = Q, Con (p. 101).

Siegman 1968, 189: "I submit that we may reconstruct the incident as follows: the centurion first sent the Jewish elders to Jesus; they persuade Him to come with them. As they near the house, the centurion *personally* comes out to meet Jesus and bids Him inconvenience Himself no further."

Schnider and Stenger 1971, 61-62: See Q 7:~~2~~, 3, ~~4-6a~~³ Luke = Q, Con (pp. 101-102).

62-63[10]: "Die wortstatistische Untersuchung zeigt folgendes: … 5. μακράν von Vers 6b kommt zweimal nur bei Lukas in der Verbindung [63] mit ἀπέχω vor, beidemale ist mit dem Genitivus absolutus konstruiert (Lk 7,6; 15,20). 6. Das πέμπω von Vers 6b kommt bei Matthäus viermal, bei Markus einmal, bei Lukas jedoch zehnmal und in der Apostelgeschichte elfmal vor."

Schramm 1971, 40-41: "Daß auch in Lk 7,1-10 Quellenkombination vorliegt, ist evident. In den Versen 6c-9, die bis in Einzelheiten mit Mt 8,8-10 übereinstimmen, ist ein Grundbericht [Q] greifbar, der vom παῖς (Lk 7,7; Mt 8,6.8.13) des Centurio erzählte. Lk 7,1-6b und 10 dagegen sind durch [41] terminologische[1]—hier ist durchweg vom δοῦλος des Hauptmanns die Rede—und inhaltliche Charakteristika von diesem Grundbericht unterschieden und als Teil einer abweichenden Ausprägung der Geschichte ausgewiesen."

41[1]: "Und 7,6 (ἤδη δὲ) αὐτοῦ (οὐ) μακρὰν ἀπέχοντος …—durch Lk 15,20 als Wendung des Lk-Sondergutes belegt."

41-42: "Besonderes Kennzeichen der 7,1-6b.10 [42] vorliegenden Lk-S-Fassung war der indirekte Verkehr zwischen Jesus und dem Hauptmann. Die jüdischen Ältesten erbitten die Hilfe (V 3), Freunde wehren Jesu Kommen ab (v 6b)."

George 1972, 70: See Q 7:~~2~~, 3, ~~4-6a~~³ Luke = Q, Con (p. 102).

71: "Mt 8,8-9 ne diffère guère de Lc 7,6b-8 que par les traits propres à ce dernier (l'envoi des amis en 7,6b, l'explication de l'absence du centurion en 7,7a) et par quelques différences de rédaction qui semblent dues à Luc."

Schulz 1972, 237-238: "Die Vv 3-6a bei Lk haben keine Parallele bei Mt und sind lk Erweiterung der Geschichte vom [238] Hauptmann.⁴¹⁰ Auch sachlich erweist sich der Einschub als sek.⁴¹¹"

238⁴¹⁰: "Ἤδη besagt nichts (Ev ca 6mal trad; ca 3mal red; Apg 3mal); μακράν (Ev noch 1mal trad) ist Lk vertraut (3mal Apg); πέμπειν wird relativ häufig von Lk selbst gebraucht (Ev ca 6mal trad; ca 3mal red; Apg 11mal; dagegen Mk 1mal; Mt 4mal); φίλος ist bei Lk stark gehäuft (allerdings ca 13mal trad; ca 1mal red; Apg 3mal; fehlt bei Mk; 1mal bei Mt)."

238⁴¹¹: See Q 7:~~2~~, 3, ~~4-6a~~³ Luke = Q, Con (p. 103).

Dupont 1973, 177: "Les Verbes 'envoyer', ... relèvent particulièrement du vocabulaire de l'évangéliste."

Wilson 1973, 31: See Q 7:~~2~~, 3, ~~4-6a~~¹ Luke = Q, Con (p. 68).

Theissen 1974, 183: "Ursprünglich sprach in Lk 7,6ff. der Hauptmann selbst, wie die Rede in der 1. Person zeigt. Lk hat hier das Gesandtschaftsmotiv in die Erzählung eingeführt. Es gehörte jedoch schon zur ursprünglichen Überlieferung: Jesus wurde durch eine erste Gesandtschaft ... geholt.

"Die Worte des Hauptmanns wurden kurz vor seinem Haus gesprochen: 'Ich bin nicht würdig, daß du unter mein Dach kommst ...' ist am ehesten in dieser Situation verständlich. In Lk 7,6a 'als er nicht weit von seinem Hause war', ist also ein zur alten Geschichte gehörender Zug enthalten. Danach wurde Jesus durch eine Gesandtschaft aus einem entfernteren Ort geholt, unmittelbar aber vor dem Haus durch den Hauptmann begrüßt.

"Lk hat wahrscheinlich das Gesandtschaftsmotiv wiederholt und damit einen wirkungsvollen Kontrast herausgearbeitet. Die erste Gesandtschaft betont, der Hauptmann sei 'würdig', die zweite aber läßt ausrichten, er habe sich nicht für 'würdig' erachtet, Jesus selbst zu begrüßen. Diese Dramatisierung der Erzählung ist freilich durch einige erzählerische Ungeschicklichkeiten erkauft. Zu deutlich ist nach wie vor, daß der Hauptmann einmal selbst an Stelle der zweiten Gesandtschaft sprach."

Theissen 1974, ET 1983, 182-183: "Originally the centurion spoke himself in Lk 7.6ff., as the wording in the first person shows. Luke has introduced the motif of sending messengers [183] here. This was, however, part of the original tradition: Jesus was sent for by a first group of messengers. ...

"The centurion's words were spoken not far from his house: 'I am not worthy to have you come under my roof,' makes most sense in this situation. Lk 7.6a: 'when he was not far from the house' thus contains an element of the old story. In this Jesus was brought from a distant place by messengers and met very close to the house by the centurion.

"Luke probably repeated the motif of messengers to produce an effective contrast. The first message stresses that the centurion is 'worthy,' but the second announces that he has not felt himself 'worthy' to meet Jesus himself. Nevertheless, the increase in drama is obtained only at the cost of some awkwardnesses in the narrative. It remains only too clear that the centurion previously spoke where there is now the second group of messengers."

Busse 1977, 147-149: "Die Schilderung der beiden Gesandtschaften V 3-6a, von Harnack [1907, 55; ET, 76] schon als späterer Zusatz erkannt, läßt sich stilkritisch [148] präzise als luk. Zusatz bestimmen.[1] Die stilistische Analyse wird besonders dort relevant, wo Lukas den [149] Hauptmann charakterisiert."

148[1]: "V 6 sollte man Lk zuweisen, da allein der Gebrauch des Verbs πορεύομαι (29—3—51) auf ihn schließen läßt. Das gleiche ist zu dem Verb von V 6b zu sagen. Dort gebraucht Lk ἀπέχω ἀπὸ τῆς οἰκίας, was er in Lk 24,13 wörtlich wiederholt. Ferner ist der Litotes οὐ μακράν eine nur dem Lk eigentümliche Wendung. ... Auch erinnert die Notiz, er sende nun seine Freunde, an Apg 10,5. Auch bringt Lk das Verb πέμπω außer 7,19 (Q) immer eigenständig in seine Vorlagen ein. Hartman [1963, 45] hat auf eine weitere Stileigentümlichkeit hingewiesen. Es sei bei Lk ungewöhnlich, das Subjekt des Gen. abs. in demselben Vers zu wiederholen. Wenn er es aber tut, dann unter der Bedingung, daß ein gewisser Zwischenraum zwischen dem wiederholten Auftreten ein- und derselben Person liegt. Dies ist ein Zeichen, daß Lk eine zweite Gesandtschaft in seine Erzählung von vornherein eingeplant hat. Da die Wendung ἔφη (Mt 8,8) von Lk häufig ausgewechselt wird (Lk 9,49 diff Mk 9,38; 18,21 diff Mk 10,20; 19,29 diff Mk 10,29; 20,34 diff Mk 12,24; Lk 4,12 diff Mt 4,7; 19,17.19 diff Mt 25,21.23), stammt die Redeeinleitung von ihm."

Ernst 1977, 238: "Mt bevorzugt die direkte Rede Jesu am Anfang (8,6ff.) und am Schluß der Perikope (8,13), Lk schaltet dagegen als Mittler die 'Ältesten der Juden' und Freunde ein."

France 1977, 254: See Q 7:2, 3, 4-6a[13] Luke = Q, Con (p. 225).

Jacobson 1978, 66: See Q 7:2, 3, 4-6a[3] Luke = Q, Con (p. 104).

Marshall 1978, 281: "Μακράν in an adverbial sense is not uncommon in Lk.-Acts (15:20; Acts 2:39; 17:27; 22:21; rest of NT, 5x), and the litotes is characteristic of him (Acts, 11x; Haenchen [1956, 70]). The centurion sent a group of his friends with a message to be delivered to Jesus as if he himself were actually saying it. φίλος is a favourite word of Luke (Mt. 11:19 par. Lk. 7:34; Mk., 0x; Lk., 15x; Jn., 6x ...).”

Martin 1978, 17-18: See Q 7:~~2~~, 3, ~~4 6a~~³ Luke = Q, Con (p. 105).

Gatzweiler 1979, 308: See Q 7:~~2~~, 3, ~~4 6a~~³ Luke = Q, Con (p. 105).

Neirynck 1979, 109-110: See Q 7:~~2~~, 3, ~~4 6a~~³ Luke = Q, Con (pp. 107-108).

Polag 1979, 38: Reconstruction. For complete text see Q 7:1⁰ In Q (pp. 9-10).

Jeremias 1980, 153: “Red ... ἔπεμψεν ... λέγων: Die Verbindung von πέμπω mit pleonastischem λέγων zur Einführung der direkten Rede (→ 1,63 Red ...) findet sich im NT nur Lk 7,6.19. Die Analogie des unmittelbar auf 7,19 folgenden ἀπέστειλεν ... λέγων (→ 7,20 Red ...) erweist die Wendung als lukanisch.”

Schmithals 1980, 91: See Q 7:~~2~~, 3, ~~4 6a~~³ Luke = Q, Con (p. 108).

Beare 1981, 207: “In Luke, the recognition of the centurion's inferiority is carried further by his use of intermediaries and his explanation—'I did not count myself worthy to come to you in person' (Lk. 7:7).”

Fitzmyer 1981, 649, 650: See Q 7:~~2~~, 3, ~~4 6a~~³ Luke = Q, Con (p. 108).

Schenk 1981, 37: Reconstruction. For complete text see Q 7:1⁰ In Q (p. 10).

Haapa 1983, 71: See Q 7:~~2~~, 3, ~~4 6a~~³ Luke = Q, Con (p. 109).

76: “Daß der alte Vokativ auch in der Hauptmannperikope (Lk 7,6) im Geiste der Fischfangperikope zu deuten ist—zumal in Verbindung mit dem redaktionellen Verbot *mē skullou* ('bemühe dich nicht')—dürfte sicher sein.”

Dauer 1984, 115-116: “Lk Redaktion ist aber der Genitivus absolutus ἤδη δὲ αὐτοῦ οὐ μακρὰν ἀπέχοντος ἀπὸ τῆς οἰκίας. Darauf weist jedenfalls [116] die sprachliche Analyse: zu ἀπέχειν (intransitiv) = 'entfernt sein' vgl. Lk 7,6 u.St.; 15,20; 24,13—sonst noch: Mk 7,6 par Mt 15,8 (atl Zitat [Isa 24:13 LXX]).—Zu μακράν vgl. Lk 7,6 u.St.; 15,20; Apg 2,39; 17,27; 22,21— sonst: Mt 8,30; Mk 12,34; Joh 21,8; Eph 2,13.17.—Zu οὐ in Verbindung mit einem Adjektiv oder Adverb vgl. die Wendungen wie οὐ πολλοί (Lk 15,13; Apg 1,5); οὐ πολύ (Apg 27,14); οὐκ ὀλίγος (Apg 12,18; 14,28; 15,2; 17,4.12; 19,23.24; 27,20); οὐκ ἄσημος (Apg 21,39); οὐ μετρίως (Apg 20,12).

“Eine gute Parallele zur vorliegenden Konstruktion haben wir in Lk 15,20.”

Schneider 1984, 165: “Bei Lk hingegen erscheint die Vermittlertätigkeit der 'Ältesten' (VV 3-5) und der 'Freunde' des Hauptmanns (V 6) als mögliche Erweiterung gegenüber Q.”

Zeller 1984, 37: “Er berichtete von Jesu Kommen nach Kafarnaum, dem Hauptmann und seinem schwerkranken Burschen, der Bitte des Haupt-manns—die beiden Gesandtschaften bei Lk sind redaktionell—um Heilung.”

Wegner 1985, 191-195: By means of word statistics and style analysis, Wegner argues that much of the language of Luke 7:6b is not Lukan but probably derives from *Sondergut*. He therefore does not include it in Q.

197: "Die Verwendung des Gen. abs. und die Formulierung οὐ μακρὰν ἀπέχοντος, die den Einfluß der bei Lk beliebten Litotes-Figur zu verraten scheint, könnten auf lk Stilisierung hinweisen."

270: Reconstruction. For complete text see Q 7:1⁰ In Q (pp. 11-12).

Gnilka 1986, 299: "Für die Rekonstruktion der Q-Vorlage wird man sich an Mt halten müssen. Die Steigerung zur Todeskrankheit ist sicher sekundär, ebenfalls die Delegation der Freunde."

Schnelle 1987, 103: "Lukas hat in einem weit größeren Maß als Matthäus die Q-Vorlage umgestaltet. Auf seine Redaktion gehen ... die zweifache Gesandtschaft in V. 3-6a und die Gestaltung des Schlußverses zurück. Vor allem durch die Einführung der zwei Gesandtschaften verlagert Lukas das Schwergewicht der Erzählung vom Dialog zwischen Jesus und dem Hauptmann auf eine mit dramatischen Elementen durchsetzte Schilderung der Handlungsabfolge."

103⁹⁶: "E. Haenchen [1959a, 25-27; 1965, 84-86] hält die doppelte Gesandtschaft für eine 'verunglückte Bearbeitung' der Q-Überlieferung durch judenchristliche Kreise auf vorlukanischer Ebene (auch A. Dauer [1984, 93-94] hält die doppelte Gesandtschaft für vorlukanisch). Diese Annahme ist unzutreffend, weil sowohl der sprachliche Befund als auch das theologische Interesse auf lukanische Redaktion schließen lassen."

Schnelle 1987, ET 1992, 89: "Luke has reshaped the Q version of the story much more thoroughly than Matthew. His redaction produced ... the two sets of messengers in vv. 3-6a, and the shape of the final verse.⁹⁶ Especially by the introduction of the second group of messengers, Luke shifts the focus of the narrative from the dialogue between Jesus and the centurion to a description of the sequence of events that is studded with dramatic elements."

89⁹⁶: "Haenchen [1959a, 25-27; 1965, 84-86] regards the two sets of messengers as a 'failed revision' of the Q tradition by Jewish Christian circles at a pre-Lukan stage of development. ... Dauer [1984, 93-94] also considers the two sets of messengers pre-Lucan. ... This idea is inaccurate, because both the language and the theological interest point to Lukan redaction."

Sato 1988, 55: "Zwischen V. 3 und V. 6b besteht eine inhaltliche Inkongruenz. Dies ist eindeutig durch sekundäres Auftreten der jüdischen 'Ältesten' sowie der Freunde des Hauptmanns verursacht worden. Auch die parallele Erzählung in Joh 4,46-53, die der Szenerie von Mt 8,5-10.13 entspricht, bestätigt den sekundären Charakter der Lukas-Version. Diese Erweiterung wird aber im ganzen kaum lukanisch sein; sie stammt wahrscheinlich von Q-Lukas."

Wiefel 1988, 141: See Q 7:2, 3, 4-6a³ Luke = Q, Con (pp. 110-111).

Bovon 1989, 346-347: "Doch wird die Rede der zweiten bei Lukas so ungeschickt eingeführt, daß ich sie als redaktionellen Zusatz betrachte¹¹.

Lukas vermeidet demnach den [347] direkten Kontakt zwischen Jesus und dem Heiden."

346-347[11]: "Vergleicht man Lk 7,6b-8 mit Mt 8,8, kommt man zur Überzeugung, daß die Überlieferung diese Worte dem Hauptmann selbst, der Jesus entgegengegangen war, in [347] den Mund legte, wie das noch Matthäus tut, der natürlich auch von der Rückkehr der Ausgesandten (Mt 8,13; vgl. Lk 7,10) nichts weiß."

350: "Lukas dramatisiert die Erzählung: Als Jesus schon (ἤδη) in der Nähe des Hauses steht, schickt der Hauptmann seine Freunde. Durch das im Neuen Testament seltene Wort φίλοι wie mit der schönen Beziehung zwischen Herrn und Sklaven suggeriert Lukas eine harmonische Atmosphäre im gastfreundlichen Haus des Hauptmannes."

352: "Wer die zurückkehrenden Boten sind, bleibt unbestimmt, vielleicht ein Zeichen dafür, daß die Urfassung nur eine Delegation [the first] kannte."

Bovon 1989, FT 1991, 339: "Le discours de la deuxième délégation est introduit de façon si artificielle chez Luc que je considère l'épisode de cette deuxième ambassade comme rédactionnel[11]. Luc veut ainsi éviter le contact entre Jésus et le païen."

339[11]: "A comparer Lc 7,6b-8 et Mt 8,8, on est convaincu que la tradition mettait ces mots sur les lèvres mêmes du capitaine sorti à la rencontre de Jésus, comme le fait encore Mt, qui naturellement ignore aussi tout retour de délégation en Mt 8,13 (comparé à Lc 7,10)."

342: "Luc accentue l'intensité dramatique du récit: Jésus est 'déjà' (ἤδη) près de la maison, lorsque le centurion lui envoie ses amis. Avec le mot, rare dans le Nouveau Testament, de φίλοι, 'amis', et, par ailleurs, l'affection qu'il dépeint entre maître et serviteur, Luc suggère l'harmonie qui règne dans cette maison hospitalière."

344: "On ne nous dit même pas quels sont les envoyés qui retournent à la maison, signe sans doute que la version primitive ne comprenait qu'une seule [the first] délégation."

Judge 1989, 487: "The Gentile's approach to Jesus through a delegation of respected Jews followed by the friends who come to say μὴ σκύλλου corresponds with Jairus' respectful request and the delegation from the house who say it is not necessary to bother Jesus further. Jesus' going to the house could have been suggested by the traditional saying, 'come under my roof', and he re-used the motif of the house from the Jairus story, where he has put more emphasis on Jesus' entry into the house vis-à-vis Mark (cf. Lk 8:41, 51)."

Nolland 1989, 314: See Nolland at Matt = Q, Pro (p. 256).

317: "The second delegation (of friends) also has no counterpart in Matthew. The awkwardness of the construction (although the friends are the messengers, the centurion does the speaking), the links with Luke 8:49 (message while journeying; use of σκύλλειν), and the way in which the alteration keeps Jesus from any suspicion of 'associating with or visiting anyone of another nation' (Acts 10:38; the evidence is mixed concerning how consistently such a hard line was ever in practice sustained) combine to suggest Lukan responsibility for the introduction of the second delegation. The use of litotes ('not far,' i.e., 'quite near') is characteristic of Luke."

Evans 1990, 342, 343-344: See Q 7:2̶, 3, 4̶-6a̶[13] Luke = Q, Con (p. 228).

344: "[Luke] 7:6-7a. An awkward turn in the story in two respects. (i) As a result of the success of the deputation of elders in closing the gap between Jesus and the Gentile through their commendation of his piety, a second deputation has to be sent of *friends* ... to reopen it from the centurion's side, so that it may then be overcome by his faith which Jesus is to commend. (ii) The highly personal *I am not worthy* ... and *say the word* are artificial when uttered by others on his behalf."

Gnilka 1990, 127-128[34] (ET 1997, 121[98]): See Q 7:2̶, 3, 4̶-6a̶[3] Luke = Q, Con (p. 111).

Riniker 1990, 62: See Q 7:2̶, 3, 4̶-6a̶[3] Luke = Q, Con (pp. 111-112).

63: "L'influence de la rédaction lucanienne se résume à ἤδη δέ avec un génitif absolu, qui a pour sujet le père (Jn 4,51) ou Jésus (Lc 7,6)."

Davies and Allison 1991, 22: "In Lk 7.6 the centurion himself does not directly address Jesus: 'When he was not far from the house, the centurion sent friends to him, saying to him: "Lord, do not trouble yourself, for I am not worthy to have you come under my roof; and for this reason I did not presume to come to you myself."' Because the words that follow (cf. 8.8-9) are more fitting coming from the centurion himself, it may be that Luke is responsible for artificially attributing the second speech of supplication to messengers, thus bringing it into line with the first speech (...).[54]"

22[54]: "In Luke the messengers have replaced the centurion in the second encounter, in order to illustrate the latter's 'authority' and to sound the theme of believing without seeing."

Schnackenburg 1991, 79: "Die unmittelbare Begegnung Jesu mit dem Hauptmann ist ihm wichtig, während Lk nochmals 'Freunde' intervenieren läßt (7,6, sicher redaktionell)."

Catchpole 1992, 529 [1993, 294-295]: "The effect of [Luke's redactional additions of] 7,3-6a.7a is to draw out and amplify ideas which were already given prominence in the Q version. In particular, the theme of the worthiness of the centurion is developed in a distinctive way. In v. 6b the centurion affirms through a second set of mediators that he is not worthy to have Jesus come into his house, but this is developed in a highly elaborate fashion: in v. 7a it is extended so that he states his unworthiness *even to come* to Jesus, which implies that he is in some way inferior to both the Jewish elders (v. 3) and the friends (v.6a). Since there is some content correspondence between the centurion's friends (φίλοι) and his love (ἀγαπᾷ) of [295] 'our nation' it is evident that the friends are as Jewish as the elders, and therefore that (un)worthiness does not relate to modesty and self-deprecation in general but to the Jew/Gentile distinction in particular. ... He has, in other words, to be regarded as typical of at least a trend towards the position of the godfearer. And Jesus, by responding to the plea of the elders, and therefore to the argumentation upon which it is based, already sets his own work within the continuity of the salvation history of Israel.

"The substance of all this is, of course, entirely in line with Luke's concept of salvation history, a fact which naturally reinforces the suspicion of LukeR."

530 [296]: "The theology which underlies the Lucan version of the tradition is wholly in line with the evangelist's outlook."

530-531 [296]: Catchpole observes several aspects of the Lukan narrative concerning the delegations that to him imply an artificial redaction of Luke's source.

531-532 [297-298]: "Given so extensive a correspondence [between Mark 5:21-43 and Q 7:1-10] it is readily understandable that Luke should move over from the one story to the other a series of details. ... [532, 298] From the double approach to Jesus, first by Jairus and then by members of his household (Mark 5,22.35), there develops the idea of the double approach by the elders and the friends in Luke 7,3.6."

533 [299]: Reconstruction. For complete text see Q 7:1⁰ In Q (p. 14).

Jacobson 1992, 108-109: See Q 7:~~2~~, 3, ~~4-6a~~³ Luke = Q, Con (p. 113).

Lindars 1992, 208: "It remains to be said that Luke's οὐ μακρὰν ἀπέχοντος ἀπὸ τῆς οἰκίας is a typically Lucan expression, and perhaps replaces a simpler phrase ἐγγίζοντος τῇ οἰκίᾳ in the source." See Lindars at Emendation = Q (p. 257).

Gagnon 1993, 713⁵: See Q 7:~~2~~, 3, ~~4-6a~~³ Luke = Q, Con (p. 113).

725-726: "In v 6a, πορεύομαι (σύν), ἤδη, μακράν, the litotes 'not far from,' and the use of a compound verb with the same preposition (here ἀπέχω + ἀπό) are all strongly attested as Lucan terminology and [726] style; ἀπέχω and φίλος are better attested in [S] than anywhere else in Luke-Acts (though the latter is also sufficiently attested for Luke), and the construction μακρὰν ἀπέχω is found in the NT only in Luke 15:20 [S]. Overall the case for Lucan redaction of v 6a, to judge from the choice of words and style, is relatively good."

727: "When a word [μακράν] is used so infrequently in the NT, one cannot assume [against Wegner 1985, 192] that an author's syntactical capacity is exhausted with a single use, or that one combination of words necessarily precludes another by the same author. It is certainly conceivable that Luke, not his source, was responsible for the expression in Luke 15:20 [S]. For examples of Lucan fondness for litotes, see Acts 12:18; 14:28; etc. (10x); in Luke's Gospel the only example is in 15:13 [S]."

730-731: "It is my opinion that the function of Luke 7:3-7a coheres well with Luke's redactional themes elsewhere. ...

"The insertion of a second delegation allows Luke both to emphasize the willingness of the Jews to have Jesus visit the house of this Gentile (v 3), with Jesus' own acquiescence in the matter (v 6a), and to confirm that the sending of delegations was a manifestation of the centurion's humility (v 7a). His humility in turn makes him a model to members of status in Luke's [731] community. The rich are not to lord it over the disadvantaged but rather are to maintain concern for the needy, even in the context of patronage (as the centurion does for his slave; note the significance of the theme of riches in Luke-Acts)."

Sevenich-Bax 1993, 166: "Die den Freunden in den Mund gelegte Bitte des Hauptmanns muß schon aufgrund der 1.Pers. Sgl. von diesem selbst gesprochen sein."

169: See Q 7:2̶, 3, 4̶-6̶a³ Luke = Q, Con (p. 114).

238: Reconstruction. For complete text see Q 7:1⁰ In Q (p. 15).

Dunderberg 1994, 85-89: See Q 7:2̶, 3, 4̶-6̶a³ Luke = Q, Con (pp. 114-116).

Gagnon 1994a, 124-125, 127: See Q 7:2̶, 3, 4̶-6̶a³ Luke = Q, Con (pp. 116-117).

139-140: "The primary reason for splitting up the messages among [140] two delegations is probably that Luke wants to first show that Jesus (like Peter in Acts 10) was perfectly willing to enter the house of a Gentile. For Luke's community, the Gentile mission is inconceivable apart from intimate fraterniza-tion with uncircumcised Gentiles. Once Jesus consents to this and indeed is well on his way (v. 6b: 'when he was not far distant ...'), then and only then is it time to report the Q saying which dismisses the need for a personal visit.⁴¹"

140⁴¹: "Hence, when Nolland [1989, 317] later adds that the second dele-gation 'keeps Jesus from any suspicion of "associating with or visiting anyone of another nation"', ... he overlooks the fact that Jesus has already assented to such a visit (*but*, Luke would add in defense of the church, so have the Jewish elders!). Schürmann [1969, 395⁴] suggests that had Luke composed vv. 3-6, he would probably have had Jesus go to the centurion's house, just as Peter does in the story of Cornelius. ... This, however, would have forced Luke to contradict the Q dialogue (which is quite clear in rejecting any visit to the centurion's home) and ruined the motif of the centurion's faith for a distance healing."

144: See Q 7:2̶, 3, 4̶-6̶a³ Luke = Q, Con (p. 118).

Gagnon 1994b, 141: "The door to Matthean shortening of a Q version with the double delegation is nailed shut by the fact that the double-delegation motif in Luke does not fit very smoothly over the common core dialogue in Q. By both linguistic and literary standards this motif looks secondary. ... On the literary level, the involvement of Jewish πρεσβύτεροι and φίλοι has an air of artificiality to it. The message that the 'friends' (φίλοι) carry to Jesus is in first-person speech (as in Matthew's account)—this in contrast to the third-person dialogue of the πρεσβύτεροι. This probably reflects a desire on an editor's part to faithfully record the Q-saying as it is while giving it a new spokesperson."

Landis 1994, 11, 17: Reconstruction. For complete text see Q 7:1⁶ Luke = Q, Pro (p. 57).

Meier 1994, 769¹⁹³: "I think that Schulz [1972, 236-240] and Fitzmyer [1981, 648-649] make a good case for the position that, apart from the redactional insertion in Matt 8:11-12, Matthew's version of the story is closer to the Q form than is Luke's version. In particular: ... (3) The second of Luke's delegations has an awkward 'feel' to it in the story. If the centurion went to all the trouble of sending a formal delegation to Jesus, and if from the beginning he used the mechanism of a delegation because he felt too unworthy to have Jesus enter his house (as the centurion affirms through his second delegation in Luke 7:7), why did he not instruct the first delegation to make this declaration and so obviate the need for a second delegation? The switch from third-person narrative by the first delegation ('he is worthy') to first-person confession of the centurion conveyed through the second delegation ('I am not worthy') also looks suspicious. Indeed, the whole two-part pattern of Jews confidently proclaiming worth and Gentiles confessing lack of worth may be part of Luke's theological message (cf. Acts 10:34-35)."

Merklein 1994, 100: See Q 7:~~2~~, 3, ~~4-6a~~³ Luke = Q, Con (pp. 118-119).

International Q Project 1995, 478: Reconstruction. For complete text see Q 7:1⁰ In Q (p. 16).

Neirynck 1995, 180: See Q 7:~~2~~, 3, ~~4-6a~~¹ Luke = Q, Con (p. 70).

Neirynck 1996, 455: "I can agree with D's [Dunderberg 1994, 85-89] view on Lukan redaction in Lk 7,1-10 (87-89): ἤμελλεν τελευτᾶν (in v. 2), the two delegations (vv. 3-6) and the conclusion (v. 10)."

Tuckett 1996, 395: "Catchpole's discussion [1992, 528-532 (1993, 293-298)] about the LkR nature of Luke's extra verses in Luke 7:3-6a, 7a seems to me fully convincing."

Brock 1997, 396-399: "It is not certain where the use of φίλοι as a designation for early Christians began, but in the New Testament this usage clearly predominates in Luke-Acts. Luke's writings contain seventeen of the twenty-nine occurrences of the word in the New Testament, as well as the one use of φίλη."

397-399: "Numerous instances of the Lukan Q material contain the word φίλοι while the same Q material occurring in Matthew does not. Compare, for example, Matt 10:28 and Luke 12:4-5. In this early saying tradition, Jesus addresses his disciples as a group, specifically referring to them with the epithet τοῖς φίλοις μου. In this case, it is explicitly clear that the Jesus saying incorporates φίλος as a designation for believers or followers, a designation absent from the parallel in Matthew.

[The texts of Matt 10:28 and Luke 12:4-5 are laid out side-by-side.]

"This dynamic occurs again when one compares the Q material preserved in Matt 8:8 and its parallel in Luke 7:6:

[397-398—Texts are laid out side-by-side].

"A third example of this pattern occurs in a comparison of Matt 18:13 with Luke 15:6, where φίλος appears in Luke, but not in the parallel tradition:

[The texts of Matt 18:12-13 and Luke 15:4-6 are laid out side-by-side.].

"One could argue that just because φίλοι appears in Luke and not in Matthew when material is taken from Q, one does not necessarily know whether it is Lukan to incorporate the term into the material or Matthean [399] to subtract it from the tradition. However, when the word φίλοι occurs in Luke, even when Luke has used Markan material, it seems that the tendency is becoming apparent." Brock goes on to compare the texts of Mark 13:12 and Luke 21:16.

Matt = Q: [ ]²

Pro

Strauss 1836, 101-103 (ET 1855, 516-517): See Q 7:~~2~~, 3, ~~4-6a~~³ Luke = Q, Con (pp. 90-93).

Sabourin 1975, 154: "In Matthew's version the freshness of the original encounter seems preserved: the centurion himself speaks to Jesus, while in Luke he communicates through interpreters. The laborious, even confusing narrative of Luke (esp. in v. 6) would indicate that he transmits a preexistent composite narrative he found in his source, while the Q version alone would be preserved in Mt. In Luke's tradition the Jairus story (8:40-56) seems to have literarily contaminated the centurion narrative."

Nolland 1989, 314: "Matthew frequently abbreviates and simplifies the tradition that he uses and may have omitted the delegation of Jewish elders. It is more difficult to attribute to him the omission of the delegation of the friends, where along with the consideration already adduced above we should note the similarity to Luke 8:49 (note in each case the use of μὴ σκύλλειν, 'not to trouble')."

Con

H. Meyer 1864, 218 (ET 1884, 179): See Q 7:~~2~~, 3, ~~4-6a~~³ Luke = Q, Pro (p. 87).

Hawkins 1899, 195: See 7:6b-c² Luke = Q, Pro (p. 240).

Castor 1912, 41-42: See Q 7:~~2~~, 3, ~~4-6a~~³ Luke = Q, Pro (pp. 87-88).

223: Reconstruction. For complete text see Q 7:1⁰ In Q (p. 6).

Schmid 1930, 252-253: See Q 7:~~2~~, 3, ~~4-6a~~³ Luke = Q, Pro (p. 88).

Schmid 1956, 163: See Q 7:~~2~~, 3, ~~4-6a~~³ Matt = Q, Con (p. 121).

Pesch and Kratz 1976, 77: See Q 7:~~2~~, 3, ~~4-6a~~³ Matt = Q, Con (p. 123).

Gundry 1982, 141: "Matthew ... omits the further delegation of the centurion's friends, though he retains almost all the conversation between Jesus and the centurion as represented by his friends (Luke 7:6-8)."

143: See Q 7:6b-c¹ Matt = Q, Con (p. 238).

Dauer 1984, 99-104, 105-106: See Q 7:~~2~~, 3, ~~4-6a~~¹,³ Matt = Q, Con (pp. 73-74, 123-124).

Sand 1986, 178: "Nicht zuletzt kommt darin die theologische Intention des Evangelisten gut zum Ausdruck: Nicht nur die Vereinfachung der Handlung (Streichung der zweifachen Gesandtschaft bei Lk), sondern vor allem die Konzentration auf die Hauptperson (Jesus und der Hauptmann) und noch mehr die Hervorhebung des Dialogs, des erkennenden und bekennenden Wortes also, offenbaren die gestaltende Absicht des Redaktors."

Lindars 1992, 208: "Once it is realized that Matthew has omitted this item [Jesus approaching the centurion's house], the argument for treating Mt 8,7 as a question becomes unnecessary, as we are dealing here, not with the original form of the story, but with Matthew's slightly inept abbreviation of it."

Hagner 1993, 202: See Q 7:~~2~~, 3, ~~4-6a~~³ Matt = Q, Con (p. 125).

Emendation = Q: ἤδη δὲ αὐτοῦ <ἐγγίζοντος τῇ οἰκίᾳ,>²

Lindars 1992, 210: Reconstruction. For complete text see Q 7:1⁶ Luke = Q, Pro (p. 56).

211: "We have the evidence of John's ἤδη δὲ αὐτοῦ καταβαίνοντος (Jn 4,51) to suggest that Luke preserves the original motif, which John has altered to suit his recasting of the story. But οὐ μακρὰν ἀπέχοντος is much too characteristic of Luke's style to be accepted as the original text, and so it has seemed probable that both Luke and John have altered the common verb ἐγγίζοντος with dative or εἰς. Luke uses this verb frequently, but his alteration of it here adds vividness to the narrative."

Evaluations

Johnson 2000: Matt = Q {B}, []².

Very little speaks in favor of Luke. Most arguments in favor of a tradition behind Luke's variant readings (Jeremias, Dauer) stop short of identifying that tradition with Q. Lindars makes the observation that John also has ἤδη δὲ αὐτοῦ. But John is tricky to use here because it is at this point that the Johannine story begins to deviate widely from the synoptic tradition. While servants do come from the house and meet the royal official on the way, it is to the royal official they come—Jesus has disappeared from the scene—and it is good news of healing that they bring.

The fact is, this variation unit is thoroughly Lukan in style and vocabulary: the use of litotes (Plummer); the alternation between πέμπω and ἀποστέλλω (Harnack); ἀπέχω (Busse); φίλοι (Brock), etc. Many authors have commented on the second delegation reciting the first person speech as being somewhat suspicious (e.g., B. Weiß 1876 et al.; especially in light of the first speech being narrated in the third person [Meier]).

The second delegation serves Luke's purpose of highlighting the centurion's god-fearing faith (cf. Cornelius in Acts 10, whom the centurion foreshadows), while keeping him from direct contact with Jesus and providing a basis for the subsequent unworthiness speech (Q 7:6c-8). While the double-delegation material as it stands in Luke is not as difficult and contradictory as some would make it out to be (cf. Strauss and Loisy at Q 7:~~2~~, 3, ~~4-6a~~³ Luke = Q, Con), many of the longer Lukan variant readings make sense if Luke is creating the physical distance between Jesus and the centurion (Bovon). For example, having the centurion send out Jewish elders requires an explanation as to why they are willing to do his bidding faithfully (Q 7:~~2~~, 3, ~~4-6a~~¹³). Having Jesus go with them then requires a second delegation to stop him before he gets to the house—otherwise the Q speech makes no sense (Q 7:6b-c²). Luke's μὴ σκύλλου softens the apparent contradiction and imperiousness of his sending out yet another delegation to Jesus (Q 7:6b-c⁶), while his justification for not coming out himself on both occasions (Q 7:7¹) softens what might mistakenly (?) be interpreted as a blatant and capricious display of patronal social power (sending out Jewish elders, calling Jesus to his home, sending out more friends, stopping Jesus before he even gets to his home—all without ever leaving his own home).

Robinson 2000: Matt = Q {B}, []².

In Luke 7:20 the disciples say precisely what John had said to them in Luke 7:19, just as in Luke 7:6-8 the second delegation of friends makes the speech that actually fits the centurion but hardly them; i.e., Luke repeats almost exactly what Q had the centurion himself say. The Lukan expression ἔπεμψεν ... λέγων is repeated in Luke 7:19 (Matt 11:2 πέμψας ... εἶπεν), and resumed with slight variation redactionally in Luke 7:20, ἀπέστειλεν ... λέγων. Thus the Lukan style is clear.

The many Lukanisms make clear the redactional nature of the second delegation.

The scholarly literature is more nearly unanimous in rejecting as redactional the second delegation than it is regarding the first delegation.

Kloppenborg 2000: Matt = Q {B}, []².

Hoffmann 2001: Matt = Q {B}, []².

Q 7:6b-c³: Luke's ἑκατοντάρχης or Matthew's ἑκατόνταρχος.

Luke = Q: ἑκατοντάρχ[η]³ς

Pro

Polag 1979, 38: Reconstruction. For complete text see Q 7:1⁰ In Q (pp. 9-10).
Wegner 1985, 129, 160, 195: See below, Matt = Q, Con.
270: Reconstruction For complete text see Q 7:1⁰ In Q (pp. 11-12).
Catchpole 1992, 533 [1993, 299]: Reconstruction. For complete text see Q 7:1⁰ In Q (p. 14).
Landis 1994, 11, 17: Reconstruction. For complete text see Q 7:1⁶ Luke = Q, Pro (p. 57).

Con

Neirynck 1979, 109-110: See Q 7:2̶, 3, 4̶-6a̶³ Luke = Q, Con (pp. 107-108).
Jeremias 1980, 153: "ὁ ἑκατοντάρχης: → 7,2 Red."

Matt = Q: ἑκατόνταρχ(ο)³ς

Pro

von Harnack 1907, 91 (ET 1908, 131): Reconstruction. For complete text see Q 7:1⁶ Luke = Q, Pro (p. 55).
B. Weiß 1908, 15: Reconstruction. For complete text see Q 7:1⁰ In Q (p. 5).
Schenk 1987, 205: See Q 7:2̶, 3, 4̶-6a̶⁵ Matt = Q, Pro (p. 136).
Lindars 1992, 210: Reconstruction. For complete text see Q 7:1⁶ Luke = Q, Pro (p. 56).
Sevenich-Bax 1993, 238: Reconstruction. For complete text see Q 7:1⁰ In Q (p. 15).

Con

Wegner 1985, 129: See Q 7:2̶, 3, 4̶-6a̶⁵ Matt = Q, Con (pp. 136-137).
160: "Gegenüber lk ἑκατοντάρχης schien uns ... die mt Endung -αρχος von Mt red gebildet worden zu sein."
195: "Die Q-Zugehörigkeit des Wortes auSt ist dadurch gesichert, daß auch die Mt-Fassung unmittelbar vor der Antwort des Hauptmanns ἑκατόν-ταρχος verwendet (vgl. Mt 8,8a). Wie bereits erwähnt, ist es wahrscheinlich, daß die in Mt 8,8a gegebene Endung -αρχος als sek anzusehen ist."

Gagnon 1994b, 137: "The expression in v. 8aα (καὶ ἀποκριθεὶς ὁ ἑκατόν-ταρχος ἔφη), though not the usual Matthean expression, is still possible for Matthew."

Undecided

International Q Project 1995, 478: Reconstruction. For complete text see Q 7:1⁰ In Q (p. 16).

Evaluations

Johnson 2000: Matt = Q {C}, ἑκατόνταρχ⟦(ο)⟧³ς.
The same arguments used in Q 7:~~2~~, 3, ~~4-6a~~⁵ apply here as well, except that here we clearly have a Lukan preference: use of the ending –ης.
In spite of Matt 27:54, Matthean redactional preference is not certain.

Robinson 2000: Matt = Q {C}, ἑκατόνταρχ⟦(ο)⟧³ς.
Matthew's redactional use of the ending -ης in Matt 8:13 suggests it was in the Q text itself, though he uses -ος in Matt 8:5, 8. Luke's use of -ης in Luke 7:6 of course supports Matt 8:13. But the fact that both Matthew and Luke use both endings, and Matthew in this pericope uses both, indicates that such a fluctuation could also have taken place in Q. Luke's clear preference for -ης could explain his use of -ης here as redactional, rather than Matthew's -ος (*bis*) as redactional. See Q 7:~~2~~, 3, ~~4-6a~~⁵.

Kloppenborg 2000: Luke = Q {B}, ἑκατοντάρχ[η]³ς.

Hoffmann 2001: Matt = Q {C}, ἑκατόνταρχ⟦(ο)⟧³ς.
Der Wechsel in der Endung bei Matthäus in Mt 8,5.8 und 8,13 spricht für Ursprünglichkeit. Wenn Matthäus einen Grund zur Änderung gehabt hätte, dann wäre dieser in allen drei Fällen gegeben gewesen. Lukas bevorzugt offenbar die Endung –ης (so auch Lk 23,47 [diff. Mk 15,39 κεντυρίων, Mt 27,54 ἑκατόνταρχος], Apg 10,22; 21,32; 22,26; 24,23; 27,1.6.11.31.43, nur Apg 22,25 ἑκατόνταρχος, die Genitive Apg 23,17.23 und Lk 7,2 können zu beiden Bildungen gehören, vgl. πατριάρχου in Apg 2,29; 7,8.9; πολιτάρχας in Apg 17,6.8 sowie Wegner 1985). Lukas folgt damit dem hellenistischen Sprachtrend (BDR [BDF] §50,1 mit Anm. 1). Bauer [1988, 477; 2000, 298-299] s.v. weist darauf hin, daß auch in Josephus, *Ant.* 14.69 "beide Formen unmittelbar nebeneinander" stehen.

Q 7:6b-c⁴: Luke's λέγων or Matthew's ἔφη.

Luke = Q: [λέγων]⁴

Pro

Castor 1912, 223: Reconstruction. For complete text see Q 7:1⁰ In Q (p. 6).
Gundry 1982, 143: See Q 7:6b-c¹ Matt = Q, Con (p. 238).

Con

Busse 1977, 153-154: "Kurz vor dem Ziel wird Jesus von einer zweiten Gesandtschaft, diesmal von persönlichen Freunden des Hauptmanns, ange-halten. Sie überbringen eine persönliche Nachricht. Lukas [154] deuten es mit einer singulären Partizipialwendung λέγων in V 6 (vgl V 3 ἐρωτῶν) an."
Neirynck 1979, 109-110: See Q 7:2, 3, 4-6a³ Luke = Q, Con (pp. 107-108).
Jeremias 1980, 253: See Q 7:6b-c² Luke = Q, Con (p. 249).
Wegner 1985, 197: "Für eine Red des dritten Evangelisten könnte die Ver-wendung des pleonastischen λέγων sprechen; zugleich muß aber bedacht wer-den, daß es auch im lk Sg des öfteren begegnet."

Matt = Q: (ἔφη)⁴

Pro

von Harnack 1907, 91 (ET 1908, 131): Reconstruction. For complete text see Q 7:1⁶ Luke = Q, Pro (p. 55).
Busse 1977, 148¹: "Da die Wendung ἔφη (Mt 8,8) von Lk häufig aus-gewechselt wird (Lk 9,49 diff Mk 9,38; 18,21 diff Mk 10,20; 19,29 diff Mk 10,29; 20,34 diff Mk 12,24; Lk 4,12 diff Mt 4,7; 19,17.19 diff Mt 25,21.23), stammt die Redeeinleitung von ihm."
Polag 1979, 38: Reconstruction. For complete text see Q 7:1⁰ In Q (pp. 9-10).
Wegner 1985, 159, 160: See Q 7:6b-c¹ Matt = Q, Pro (pp. 236-237).
270: Reconstruction. But see Wegner at Emendation = Q (p. 263). For complete text see Q 7:1⁰ In Q (pp. 11-12).
Sevenich-Bax 1993, 179-180: See Q 7:6b-c¹ Matt = Q, Pro (p. 237).
238: Reconstruction. For complete text see Q 7:1⁰ In Q (p. 15).
Landis 1994, 10: See Q 7:6b-c¹ Matt = Q, Pro (p. 237).
11, 17: Reconstruction. For complete text see Q 7:1⁶ Luke = Q, Pro (p. 57).

International Q Project 1995, 478: Reconstruction. For complete text see Q 7:1⁰ In Q (p. 16).

Con

B. Weiß 1908, 15²⁴: See Q 7:6b-c¹ Matt = Q, Con (pp. 237-238).

Gundry 1982, 143: See Q 7:6b-c¹ Matt = Q, Con (p. 238).

Davies and Allison 1988, 22-23: "Although Q named the subject (see Lk 7.6), ἀποκριθείς and ἔφη⁵⁵ may well be [23] Matthean—although καὶ ἀποκριθείς ... ἔφη is found nowhere else in the First Gospel (or the NT)."

22⁵⁵: "φήμι is often redactional."

Gagnon 1994b, 137: "The expression in v. 8aα (καὶ ἀποκριθεὶς ὁ ἑκατόνταρχος ἔφη), though not the usual Matthean expression, is still possible for Matthew."

Emendation = Q: ὁ ἑκατοντάρχης <εἶπεν>⁴

B. Weiß 1908, 15: Reconstruction: "ὁ ἑκατοντάρχης εἶπεν." For complete text see Q 7:1⁰ In Q (p. 5).

Catchpole 1992, 532 [1993, 298]: "The centurion's direct speech, like that of Jesus (Q 7,9), was probably introduced by εἶπεν (cf. λέγων, Luke 7,6), since Matthew's ἔφη is repeatedly attested in MattR⁵⁹ and never attested in Q."

532 [298]⁵⁹: "Matt 14,8; 21,27; 22,37; 26,34.61; 27,11."

533 [299]: Reconstruction: "ὁ ἑκατοντάρχης εἶπεν." For complete text see Q 7:1⁰ In Q (p. 14).

Emendation = Q: ὁ ἑκατοντάρχης <ἔλεγεν>⁴ or <εἶπεν>⁴

Wegner 1985, 161: "Lediglich hinsichtlich des Impf. ἔφη muß u.E. die Möglichkeit einer mt Stilisierung offen gelassen werden, und dies einfach wegen der hohen Zahl seiner feststellbaren Addierungen zur Mk-Vorlage. In diesem Falle könnte ἔφη sehr wohl als Ersatz für εἶπεν, ἔλεγεν o.ä. gebraucht worden sein. Sicheres läßt sich freilich nicht mehr feststellen, so daß wir auch zu uSt an dem Grundsatz 'in dubio pro traditione' festhalten wollen."

270⁸: "An Stelle von ἔφη könnte auch ἔλεγεν, εἶπεν o.ä. gestanden haben."

Emendation = Q: <λέγει>⁴ <πρὸς αὐτὸν>⁵ ὁ ἑκατοντάρχος·

Lindars 1992, 210: Reconstruction. For complete text see Q 7:1⁶ Luke = Q, Pro (p. 56).

Evaluations

Robinson 2000: Matt = Q {B}, (ἔφη)⁴.

Luke's participle depends on his redactional finite verb ἔπεμψεν. Yet, I agree that arguments against Luke as redactional do not vindicate the Matthean verb.

The IQP voted against ἔφη only when Luke read εἶπεν. Hence this does not encourage us much to emend to εἶπεν, since in this case εἶπεν is not in Luke. So I hesitate to emend to εἶπεν.

Kloppenborg 2000: Matt = Q {B}, (ἔφη)⁴.

Johnson 2001: Luke = Q {C} (with emendation), ⟦<εἶπεν>⁴⟧.

Q does not use φήμι elsewhere. On the other hand, various forms of λέγω—especially the aorist third person singular εἶπεν—are common in Q.

Luke's participle is occasioned by the sending of friends (Robinson).

Matthew's ἔφη is usually redactional.

Therefore, B. Weiß, Wegner, and Catchpole are probably correct in suggesting an emended reading of εἶπεν. The emendation involves only a change of mood and tense to Luke's (Q's) verb.

Hoffmann 2001: Indeterminate {U}, (< >)⁴.

Mit dem Nachweis, daß das Partizip λέγων auf die Redaktion des Lukas zurückgeht, ist die Ursprünglichkeit von matthäischen καὶ ἀποκριθεὶς … ἔφη noch nicht erwiesen. Für Q ist der Gebrauch von φημί nicht mit Sicherheit nachzuweisen. Denn nur Matthäus bietet es neben unserer Stelle noch in Q 4,12 und 19,17.19. Die Editio Critica [Robinson et al., 2000] entscheidet sich mit dem IQP in diesen drei Fällen gegen ihn für das von Lukas gebotene εἶπεν. Insgesamt finden sich für φημί bei Matthäus 16, bei Markus 6, bei Lukas 8 (je 4mal redaktionell in der Markusüberlieferung und im Sondergut, in 5 Markusstellen dagegen durch εἶπεν ersetzt) und in der Apostelgeschichte 25 Belege. Matthäus führt das Verb 8mal in seine Markusvorlage ein (Mt 14,8 für λέγουσα; 19,21 für λέγει; 21,27 für εἶπεν; 22,37 für ἀποκρίθη; 26,34 für λέγει; 26,61 für λέγοντος; 27,11 für λέγει; 27,23 für ἔλεγεν), 5mal streicht er es dort und 4mal wird es im Sondergut verwendet (Mt 13,28.29; 17,26; 27,65). Ein redaktioneller Eingriff durch Matthäus ist daher sehr wahrscheinlich.

Der ursprüngliche Q-Text läßt sich dann nur hypothetisch durch eine Konjektur rekonstruieren. Zwei Möglichkeiten bestehen: εἶπεν oder λέγει das wahrscheinlich auch in Q 7,3 stand. Für εἶπεν spricht, daß es in dialogischen Texten auch sonst in Q nachgewiesen ist und ἀποκριθεὶς … εἶπεν im synoptischen Sprachgebrauch stereotyp verwendet wird. Für λέγει spricht, daß es in Q wahrscheinlich bereits in Q 7,3 und auch in Q 19,22 verwendet wird (vgl. auch Q 11,24 sowie die Matthäusüberlieferung von Q 4,8.9; 9,58.60). Die Verwendung eines *Praesens historicum* in erzählenden Texten entspricht dem allgemeinen, vor allem volkstümlichen Sprachgebrauch (vgl. BDR §321,2 mit Anm. 4 [BDF §321 with notes]) und dient zur Hervorhebung der Haupt-handlung. In der synoptischen Überlieferung findet es sich vor allem bei Mat-thäus und Markus, Lukas "vermeidet es weitgehend" (BDR §321,1 [BDF §321]. F. Rehkopf [1959, 99] zählt für die allgemeine Anwendung des *Praesens historicum* in den Evangelien des Matthäus 78, des Markus 151, des Lukas 12 und in der Apostelgeschichte 13 Belege, zum Gebrauch von λέγει vgl. meine Evaluation zu Q 6,20⁷ i[m Erscheinen begriffen]: Hieke 2001, 68-77). Im Fall einer Emendation in Q 7,6 würden sowohl die Reaktion Jesu auf die Bitte des Centurio als auch dessen Antwort durch das Präsens hervorgehoben: καὶ λέγει αὐτῷ ... καὶ ἀποκριθεὶς ὁ ἑκατόνταρχος λέγει.

Um die Möglichkeit einer solchen Textgestalt abzusichern, ist zu prüfen, ob sich dafür in der synoptischen Überlieferung Analogien finden und wie die einzelnen Evangelisten mit einer solchen Redeeinleitung und mehrfacher Ver-wendung des Präsens umgehen. Da sich in Q nur wenige erzählende Stoffe finden und es sich hier um eine Wundererzählung handelt, empfiehlt es sich von der Markusüberlieferung auszugehen und zu prüfen, ob und wie analoge Fälle von Matthäus oder Lukas redigiert wurden.

Für die Redeeinleitung ἀποκριθεὶς ... λέγει finden sich in der Tat bei Mar-kus zahlreiche Belege, bei Matthäus findet sich dagegen kein Beleg, obwohl auch er sonst λέγει häufig gebraucht (s.o.), bei Lukas, der das *Praesens histori-cum* generell meidet, nur einer in der redaktionellen Überleitung Lk 17,37 καὶ ἀποκριθέντες λέγουσιν. In der Regel ersetzen beide das markinische ἀποκριθεὶς ... λέγει durch ein ἀποκριθεὶς ... εἶπεν (oder sie gebrauchen nur eines der bei-den Verben): Vgl. die Rezeption von Mk 3,33 in Mt 12,48 (Lk 8,31 nur εἶπεν); von Mk 9,5 in Mt 17,4 (Lk 9,33 nur εἶπεν); von Mk 9,19 in Mt 17,17 und Lk 9,41; von Mk 11,22 in Mt 21,21; von Mk 10,24 in Mt 19,24 (λέγω ὑμῖν Lk –); von Mk 11,33 in Mt 21,27 (Lk 20,7 ἀπεκρίθησαν). Von besonde-rem Interesse für Q 7,3 ist Mk 15,2, wo in Mt 27,11 die markinische Rede-einleitung durch ἔφη und in Lk 23,3 durch ἀποκριθεὶς ... ἔφη ersetzt wird. Ebenso formuliert Lukas in 23,40.

In der Wiedergabe eines Gesprächsverlaufs dient das *Praesens historicum* λέγει in der Redeeinleitung zur Dramatisierung der Darstellung. Lukas über-nimmt es niemals aus Markus, obwohl er es von sich aus 7mal redaktionell (Lk 5,39; 11,45; 17,37) und im Sondergut verwendet (Lk 13,8; 16,7.29; 24,36, vgl. auch Apg 12,8; 21,37). Von Markus und Matthäus wird das Prä-sens—gelegentlich wie in Q 7,3.6 auch mehrfach hintereinander innerhalb einer Gesprächssequenz—gebraucht. Auffallend ist jedoch, daß Matthäus in der Mehrzahl der Fälle die Markusvorlage abändert.

Ich nenne die relevanten Markusbelege mit ihren Matthäus- oder Lukasparallelen:

Mk 1,37.38 λέγουσιν ... λέγει: Matthäus ohne Parallele, Lk 4,43 εἶπεν; Mk 2,8.10 λέγει ... λέγει: Mt 9,4.6 εἶπεν ... λέγει, Lk 5,22.24 εἶπεν ... λέγει; Mk 3,3.4.5 λέγει ... λέγει ... λέγει: Mt 12,11.13 εἶπεν ... λέγει, Lk 6,8.9.10 εἶπεν ... εἶπεν ... εἶπεν; Mk 3,32.33.34 λέγουσιν ... λέγει ... λέγει: Mt 12,47.48.49 λέγουσιν ... λέγει ... εἶπεν, Lk 8,20.21 ἀπηγγέλη ... εἶπεν; Mk 5,36.39.41 λέγει ... λέγει ... λέγει: Mt 9,24 ἔλεγεν, Lk 8,45 εἶπεν ... εἶπεν ... εἶπεν; Mk 6,37.38 ὁ δὲ ἀποκριθεὶς εἶπεν ... λέγουσιν ... λέγει ... λέγουσιν: Mt 14,16 εἶπεν ... λέγουσιν, Lk 9,13 εἶπεν ... εἶπεν; Mk 8,17.19.20 λέγει ... λέγουσιν ... λέγουσιν: Mt 16,8 εἶπεν, Lk –; Mk 10,23.24.26.27 λέγει ... ἀποκριθεὶς λέγει ... ἐξεπλήσσοντο λέγοντες ... λέγει: Mt 19,23.24.25.26 εἶπεν ... λέγω ὑμῖν ... ἐξεπλήσσοντο λέγοντες ... εἶπεν, Lk 18,24.26 εἶπεν ... εἶπεν; Mk 11,33 ἀποκριθέντες ... λέγουσιν ... λέγει: Mt 21,27 ἀποκριθέντες ... εἶπεν ... ἔφη, Lk 20,7.8 ἀπεκρίθησαν ... εἶπεν; Mk 14,12.13 λέγουσιν ... ἀποστέλλει ... καὶ λέγει: Mt 26,17.18 προσῆλθον ... λέγοντες ... εἶπεν, Lk 22,8.9.10 ἀπέστειλεν ... εἰπών ... εἶπεν ... εἶπεν; Mk 14,32.33.34 ἔρχονται ... λέγει ... παραλαμβάνει ... ἤρξατο ἐκθαμβεῖσθει καὶ ἀδημονεῖν ... λέγει: Mt 26,36.37.38 ἔρχεται ... λέγει ... ἤρξατο λυπεῖσθαι καὶ ἀδημονεῖν ... λέγει, Lk 22,40 γενόμενος ... εἶπεν.

Bei Matthäus finden sich für den mehrfachen Gebrauch von λέγει in einer Texteinheit folgende Belege: Mt 19,7.8 λέγουσιν ... λέγει: Mk εἶπεν ... εἶπεν, Lk –; Mt 20,6.7.8 λέγει ... λέγουσιν ... λέγει ... λέγει (Sondergut); Mt 20,23.23 λέγουσιν ... λέγει: Mk 10,39 εἶπεν ... εἶπεν, Lk –; Mt 21,31 λέγουσιν ... λέγει (Sondergut); Mt 21,41.42 λέγουσιν ... λέγει: Mk 12,9.10 –; Mt 22,20.21 λέγει ... λέγουσιν ... λέγει: Mk 12,16.17 λέγει ... εἶπεν ... εἶπεν, Lk 20,24.25 εἶπεν ... εἶπεν; Mt 27,22.23 λέγει ... λέγουσιν ... ἔφη: Mk 15,12.13.14 ἀποκριθεὶς ἔλεγεν ... ἔκραξαν ... ἔλεγεν, Lk 23,20.21.22 προσεφώνησεν ... ἐρεφώνουν λέγοντες ... εἶπεν.

Diese Übersicht macht deutlich: Lukas vermeidet den Gebrauch von mehrfachen λέγει durchgehend. Matthäus hat offensichtlich keine Vorbehalte gegen den—auch mehrfachen—Gebrauch von λέγει. Wenn er trotzdem in der Mehrzahl der Fälle ein ihm bei Markus vorgebenes λέγει nicht übernimmt, wird deutlich, wie stark bei der redaktionellen Gestaltung einer Erzähleinheit die Wahl des Tempus vom individuellen stilistischen Empfinden des einzelnen Autors abhängig ist. Unter der Voraussetzung, daß Matthäus in Q λέγει vorgegeben war, ließe sich die matthäische Textfassung in Q 7,6 durch seine redaktionellen Tendenzen durchaus erklären.

Q 7:6b-c⁵: Luke's αὐτῷ.

Luke = Q: [αὐτῷ]⁵

Pro

Con

von Harnack 1907, 91 (ET 1908, 131): Reconstruction. For complete text see Q 7:1⁶ Luke = Q, Pro (p. 55).

B. Weiß 1908, 15: Reconstruction. For complete text see Q 7:1⁰ In Q (p. 5).

Castor 1912, 223: Reconstruction. For complete text see Q 7:1⁰ In Q (p. 6).

Crum 1927, 138: Reconstruction. For complete text see Q 7:~~2~~, 3, ~~4-6a~~¹ Luke = Q, Pro (pp. 71-72).

Polag 1979, 38: Reconstruction. For complete text see Q 7:1⁰ In Q (pp. 9-10).

Schenk 1981, 37: Reconstruction. For complete text see Q 7:1⁰ In Q (p. 10).

Wegner 1985, 270: Reconstruction. For complete text see Q 7:1⁰ In Q (pp. 11-12).

Catchpole 1992, 533 [1993, 299]: Reconstruction. For complete text see Q 7:1⁰ In Q (p. 14).

Sevenich-Bax 1993, 238: Reconstruction. For complete text see Q 7:1⁰ In Q (p. 15).

Landis 1994, 11, 17: Reconstruction. For complete text see Q 7:1⁶ Luke = Q, Pro (p. 57).

International Q Project 1995, 478: Reconstruction. For complete text see Q 7:1⁰ In Q (p. 16).

Matt = Q: [ ]⁵

Pro

Con

Emendation = Q: <λέγει>⁴ <πρὸς αὐτὸν>⁵ ὁ ἑκατοντάρχος·

Lindars 1992, 210: Reconstruction. For complete text see Q 7:1⁶ Luke = Q, Pro (p. 56).

Evaluations

Robinson 2000: Matt = Q {B}, []⁵.
In Luke, the αὐτῷ clarifies not only for λέγων, but also ἔπεμψεν. In Matthew and Q, ἀποκριθείς makes it less useful—indeed, even unnecessary. Thus it is part of the Lukan redaction.

Kloppenborg 2000: Matt = Q {B}, []⁵.

Johnson 2001: Matt = Q {B}, []⁵.
With the addition of the friends, there are now four groups of characters involved in Luke's story—Jesus, the centurion, and two delegations. Ἀυτῷ clarifies the one to whom the delegation speaks.
Matthew might have left it in had it been in Q, but Luke had good reason to add it when creating the two delegations.

Hoffmann 2001: Matt = Q {B}, []⁵.

Q 7:6b-c⁶: Luke's μὴ σκύλλου.

Luke = Q: [μὴ σκύλλου]⁶

Pro

Bovon 1989, 350³⁴: "Schramm, T. [1971, 42] ist der Ansicht, Lukas habe diesen Ausdruck aus der Geschichte der Tochter des Jairus (Mk 5,35//Lk 8,49) übernommen. Doch die Umstände sind dort ganz anders, da der Bote, der dem Vater den Tod seiner Tochter mitteilt, diesen auffordert, den Meister nicht mehr zu bemühen."

Bovon 1989, FT 1991, 342³⁴: "T. Schramm [1971, 42] estime que Luc puise l'expression dans l'histoire de la fille de Jaïrus (Mc 5,35//Lc 8,49). Mais la situation est toute différente, puisque là, c'est l'envoyé qui, apprenant au père la mort de sa fille, l'invite à ne pas déranger le maître."

Sevenich-Bax 1993, 180⁴: "Dies obgleich σκύλλειν nicht typisch lukanisch ist und von Lukas nur ein weiteres Mal aus Markus-Stoff übernommen wird (vgl. Lk 8,49 par. Mk 5,35)."

Con

Strauss 1836, 103: "Vielleicht erinnerte ihn auch der Hauptmann, welcher Jesum nicht in sein Haus bemühen will, an den Boten, der dem Jairus wehrte, den Lehrer in sein Haus zu bemühen, nachdem gleichfalls eine Aufforderung, in das Haus zu kommen, vorangegangen war, und er legte nun, wie zu Jairus, nach ihm und Markus, der Bote sagt: μὴ σκύλλε τὸν διδάσκαλον (Luc. 8,49), so auch hier der zweiten Gesandtschaft ein κύριε μὴ σκύλλου in den Mund; obwohl zu einer solchen Contre-ordre nur bei Jairus, in dessen Hause sich seit der ersten Aufforderung durch den Tod der Tochter die Lage der Dinge verändert hatte, ein Grund vorlag, keineswegs aber bei dem Centurio, dessen Knecht noch immer im gleichen Zustande sich befand."

Strauss 1836, ET 1855, 517: "Perhaps ... the centurion who was unwilling that Jesus should take the trouble to enter his house, reminded Luke of the messenger who warned Jairus not to trouble the master to enter his house, likewise after an entreaty that he would come into the house; and as the messenger says to Jairus, according to him and Mark, μὴ σκύλλε τὸν διδάσκαλον, *trouble not the master* (Luke viii. 49.), so here he puts into the mouth of the second envoys, the words, κύριε μὴ σκύλλου, *Lord, trouble not thyself,* although such an order has a reason only in the case of Jairus, in whose house the state of things had been changed since the first summons by the death of his daughter, and none at all in that of the centurion whose servant still remained in the same state."

Weiße 1838, 52: "Jene ablehnende Sendung aber eine, selbst in dem Gebrauch einzelner Worte erkennbare, ungehörige Nachbildung des ähnlichen Zwischenfalls in der Begebenheit mit der Tochter des Jairus ist."

B. Weiß 1876, 227-228[1]: "Die Berufung auf den Sprachcharacter des Mrc. stützt sich doch nur auf ... [228] ... das μὴ σκύλλου, das gar nicht der Urform der Erzählung, sondern ihrer Erweiterung bei Luc. (7,6) angehört und sich Mrc. 5,35 (Lc. 8,49) nur im Act. findet."

229: See Q 7:6b-c² Luke = Q, Con (pp. 241-242).

Holtzmann 1901, 344: "Dazu tritt das κύριε μὴ σκύλλου aus dem Munde der Jairusboten 8,49."

B. Weiß 1904, 242 (ET 1906, 56-57): See Q 7:6b-c² Luke = Q, Con (p. 243).

von Harnack 1907, 56: "Zu dem bei Luk. in Vers 6 stehenden μὴ σκύλλου ist Luk. 8,49 (Mark. 5,35) zu vergleichen [implying that μὴ σκύλλου is Lukan]."

91: Reconstruction. For complete text see Q 7:1⁶ Luke = Q, Pro (p. 55).

von Harnack 1907, ET 1908, 77: "With the μὴ σκύλλου of St. Luke verse 6, compare St. Luke viii. 49 (St. Mark v. 35) [implying that μὴ σκύλλου is Lukan]."

131: Reconstruction. For complete text see Q 7:1⁶ Luke = Q, Pro (p. 55).

B. Weiß 1907, 243[1]: "Übrigens zeigt das μὴ σκύλλου, das an die Totenerweckungsgeschichte Mk. 5,35 anklingt, daß hier die Hand des Lukas eingegriffen hat."

B. Weiß 1908, 15: Reconstruction. For complete text see Q 7:1⁰ In Q (p. 5).

Castor 1912, 223: Reconstruction. For complete text see Q 7:1⁰ In Q (p. 6).

223[3]: "Luke adds, 'Trouble not thyself.' But Matthew seems to have preserved this speech of the centurion very carefully."

Klostermann 1919, 449: See Q 7:6b-c² Luke = Q, Con (pp. 244-245).

Loisy 1924, 217: "Un mot caractéristique (ici, μὴ σκύλλου; viii, 49, μηκέτι σκύλλε τὸν διδάσκαλον) a été transposé de l'histoire de Jaïr dans celle du centurion."

Easton 1926, 97: "Μὴ σκύλλου may well be a further reminiscence of the Jairus story (Mk 5:35 = Lk 8:49), for Mt would scarcely have omitted it."

Crum 1927, 138: Reconstruction. For complete text see Q 7:~~2~~, 3, ~~4-6a~~[1] Luke = Q, Pro (pp. 71-72).

Klostermann 1929, 86-87: See Klostermann 1919 at Q 7:6b-c² Luke = Q, Con (pp. 244-245).

Creed 1930, 101: "The centurion forbears to come himself out of personal humility, and is only anxious to save Jesus the trouble of a journey to his house. The account of the healing of Jairus's daughter has perhaps influenced Luke's story at this point (cf. v. 6 Κύριε, μὴ σκύλλου with Mk. v. 35 τί ἔτι σκύλλεις τὸν διδάσκαλον;)."

Schlatter 1960, 492: "Das nach dem gemeinsamen κύριε eingelegte μὴ σκύλλου ist mit 8,49 identisch, wo es aus Mar. 5,35 stammt, zeigt also nicht die Hand der Quelle."

Delobel 1966, 454: "L'addition de μὴ σκύλλου nous rappelle le μὴ κλαίετε dont nous parlions plus haut, et surtout μηκέτι σκύλλε de *Lc.*, VIII, 49 (diff *Mc*)."

Schramm 1971, 42: "Um die mit diesem Personenwechsel sich ergebenden Härten zu mildern, fügt er V 6c μὴ σκύλλου ein,² ein Motiv, das ihm nach Inhalt und Formulierung aus Mk 5,35 (par Lk 8,49) vertraut war."

42²: "Im NT nur hier und Mk 5,35 par Lk 8,49; partizipial noch Mt 9,36."

George 1972, 71: "Mt 8,8-9 ne diffère guère de Lc 7,6b-8 que par les traits propres à ce dernier … et par quelques différences de rédaction qui semblent dues à Luc.¹¹"

71¹¹: "En Lc 7,6: *mè skyllou* et l'inversion d'*hikanos* et de *mou*."

Schulz 1972, 238: "Lk bietet über Mt hinaus μὴ σκύλλου und schließt die demütige Aussage des Hauptmannes mit γάρ an. Obwohl das Verb σκύλλειν für Lk nicht typisch ist (nur noch 8,49 trad), dürfte er die Wendung eingeführt und das folgende mit γάρ angeschlossen haben.⁴¹⁴"

238-239⁴¹⁴: "Das μὴ σκύλλου paßt zum Einschub Vv 3-6a und zu dem ebenfalls lk V 7a, … [239] wonach der Hauptmann den direkten Kontakt mit Jesus nicht gewagt hat, sondern durch Gesandte mit Jesus Verbindung aufnahm."

Busse 1977, 148¹: "Mit ihrem Beginn V 6 greift Lk wieder auf seine Vorlage zurück, wobei er μὴ σκύλλου (vgl Lk 8,49) mit dem dazugehörigen γάρ einbaut."

Marshall 1978, 281: "Schramm [1971, 42] regards the phrase [μὴ σκύλλου] as being based on Mk. 5:35, and designed to smooth the transition between the preceding piece of narrative (taken, on his view, from a special source) and the dialogue (taken from Q). This is probable enough, whatever view we take of the source problem."

Neirynck 1979, 109-110: See Q 7:2̶, 3, 4̶-̶6̶a̶³ Luke = Q, Con (pp. 107-108).

Polag 1979, 38: Reconstruction. For complete text see Q 7:1⁰ In Q (pp. 9-10).

Fitzmyer 1981, 652: "This is a Lucan addition to the material from 'Q'."

Schenk 1981, 37: Reconstruction. For complete text see Q 7:1⁰ In Q (p. 10).

Dauer 1984, 85: "Μὴ σκύλλου wird von Lukas stammen; es ist Reminiszenz an Lk 8,49 par Mk 5,35."

116: "Rückschauend läßt sich als lk Redaktion feststellen: … μὴ σκύλλου … γάρ."

Wegner 1985, 201: "Das Verb begegnet außer auSt nur noch Mk 5,35 par Lk 8,49 und Mt 9,36 als Hinzufügung zu Mk (vgl. Mk 6,34). Da es weder in Mt 8,8b noch in der joh Traditionsvariante der Hauptmannserzählung auftaucht, könnte es überlieferungsgeschichtlich sek sein. Ob es aber lk Red unter Einfluß von Mk 5,35 oder einer dem Lk schon vorgegebenen Erweiterung entstammt, läßt sich kaum noch entscheiden, da weitere Belege in Lk/Apg fehlen."

270: Reconstruction. For complete text see Q 7:1⁰ In Q (pp. 11-12).

Judge 1989, 487: See Q 7:6b-c² Luke = Q, Con (p. 251).

Davies and Allison 1991, 22: See Q 7:6b-c² Luke = Q, Con (p. 252).

Catchpole 1992, 532 [1993, 298]: "The influence of this material [Mark 5:31-43] is confirmed by μὴ σκύλλου in Luke 7,6, cf. τί ἔτι σκύλλεις (Mark 5,35): σκύλλειν occurs in the NT only at Mark 5,35/Luke 8,49, at Matt 9,36 which, in view of its proximity to Matthew's Jairus story (Matt 9,18-26), is clearly a reminiscence of Mark 5,35, and at Luke 7,6."

533 [299]: Reconstruction. For complete text see Q 7:1⁰ In Q (p. 14).

Lindars 1992, 208: "Cf. Mk 5,35 = Lk 8,49, which is responsible for Luke's insertion of μὴ σκύλλου."

210: Reconstruction. For complete text see Q 7:1⁶ Luke = Q, Pro (p. 56).

Gagnon 1993, 726: "The statement μὴ σκύλλου in v 6b was probably suggested to Luke by Mark 5:35 (note that Luke in 8:49 also changes Mark's rhetorical question to an imperative), but in any case it was mandated by the scenario posited in v 6a."

727: "Lucan redaction based on Mark's story about Jairus is suggested both by Luke's change of Mark's question 'Why are you bothering the teacher?' (Mark 5:35) to the imperative 'no longer bother (μηκέτι σκύλλε) the teacher' (Luke 8:49) and by the similar motif of people coming from Jairus' house to prevent an unnecessary visit by Jesus. Even Wegner [1985, 202] regards Lucan redaction as probable here, for he observes that 'the Third Evangelist, in his revision, repeatedly expands the Marcan material with explanations and reasons introduced by ὅτι or γάρ.'"

Sevenich-Bax 1993, 180: "Abgesehen von dem redaktionellen Nachtrag Lk 7,7a sind die Differenzen zwischen Matthäus und Lukas geringfügig, der Text also für die Logienquelle gut bezeugt: …

"Nur Lukas bietet unmittelbar nach der κύριε-Anrede den Zusatz 'μὴ σκύλλου'. Dieser wird in Zusammenhang mit der lukanischen Darstellung stehen, nach der der Hauptmann den direkten Kontakt mit Jesus vermeidet. Deshalb ist μὴ σκύλλου der lukanischen Redaktion anzulasten."

238: Reconstruction. For complete text see Q 7:1⁰ In Q (p. 15).

Landis 1994, 10: "In den Anfang der Rede des Hauptmanns, die Mt und Lk zum großen Teil wörtlich gleich wiedergeben, fügt Lk wahrscheinlich die Wendung μὴ σκύλλου ... γάρ ein; σκύλλω ist zwar nicht typisch für Lk (er hat es nur noch einmal, in 8,49, aus der Tradition), aber erstens ist ein Ursprung in Q daher unwahrscheinlich, weil Mt das Verb sonst nicht meidet (er fügt es sogar 9,36 in seine Mk-Vorlage ein), und zweitens paßt μὴ σκύλλου gut zu den von Lk eingefügten Versen 2-6b und zum ebenfalls lk V.7a."

11, 17: Reconstruction. For complete text see Q 7:1⁶ Luke = Q, Pro (p. 57).

International Q Project 1995, 478: Reconstruction. For complete text see Q 7:1⁰ In Q (p. 16).

Matt = Q: [ ]⁶

Pro

Con

Gundry 1982, 143: "Matthew drops 'do not trouble yourself' and, consequently, γάρ in the following clause. Thus the unworthiness of the centurion does not merely provide the reason why the Lord should not trouble himself to come to his house (so Luke)."

Evaluations

Johnson 2000: Matt = Q {B}, []⁶.
There is almost a consensus among critics (!) that Luke is influenced by Mark 5:35. Catchpole suggests that Matthew has done the same thing in Matt 9:36, using a term reminiscent of material omitted from the Healing of Jairus' Daughter.

It should be noted that if Matt 8:7a's ἐγὼ ἐλθὼν θεραπεύσω αὐτόν is to be interpreted as Jesus asking a question, and this question had been in Q, then the plea μὴ σκύλλου would not have made sense in Q. At the same time, if Q 7:3 par. Matt 8:7a was meant to be interpreted as a statement, then there would have been no good reason for Matthew to have omitted μὴ σκύλλου from Q. Ergo, if Q had ἐγὼ ἐλθὼν θεραπεύσω αὐτόν, then μὴ σκύλλου was most likely not in Q.

Robinson 2000: Matt = Q {B}, []⁶.
See Mark 5:35 τί ἔτι σκύλλεις τὸν διδάσκαλον par. Luke 8:49 μηκέτι σκύλλε τὸν διδάσκαλον. Here the same expression occurs for the same purpose, to dis-

suade Jesus from coming. In Luke 7:6c this is either imitation of Mark or Lukan vocabulary; in either case it is hardly Q. It is part of the Lukan redaction—the second delegation.

Kloppenborg 2000: Matt = Q {B}, []⁶.

Hoffmann 2001: Matt = Q {B}, []⁶.

Q 7:6b-c⁷: Luke's οὐ γάρ or Matthew's οὐκ.

Luke = Q: οὐ [γάρ]⁷

Pro

Gundry 1982, 143: See Q 7:6b-c⁶ Matt = Q, Con (p. 273).

Con

Schulz 1972, 238: See Q 7:6b-c⁶ Luke = Q, Con (p. 271).

Busse 1977, 148¹: "Mit ihrem Beginn V 6 greift Lk wieder auf seine Vorlage zurück, wobei er μὴ σκύλλου (vgl Lk 8,49) mit dem dazugehörigen γάρ einbaut."

Dauer 1984, 116: "Rückschauend läßt sich als lk Redaktion feststellen: ... μὴ σκύλλου ... γάρ."

Wegner 1985, 201-202: "Was den Gesamtausdruck μὴ σκύλλου ... γάρ betrifft, so ist u.E. ein Ursprung in Q dadurch unwahrscheinlich, weil Mt keine Tendenz aufweist das Verb σκύλλω zu vermeiden, wie seine Eintragung in Mt 9,36 gegenüber Mk 6,34 zeigt. Demgegenüber spricht für die Annahme einer lk Hinzufügung die Tatsache, daß der dritte Evangelist den Mk-Stoff in seiner Bearbeitung mehrfach durch mit ὅτι oder γάρ eingeleitete Erklärungen und Begründungen bereichert. Man wird daher die durch μὴ σκύλλου gegebene Begründung zur Aussage von Lk 7,6c wohl auf Lk selbst zurückführen dürfen, obwohl die Annahme eines vor-lk Ursprungs prinzipiell nicht ganz von der Hand zu weisen ist."

Davies and Allison 1991, 22: See Q 7:6b-c² Luke = Q, Con (p. 252).

Gagnon 1993, 727: See Q 7:6b-c⁶ Luke = Q, Con (p. 272).

Sevenich-Bax 1993, 180: "Die Modifikation der Aussage [with μὴ σκύλλου] nötigt Lukas dann zugleich, das Folgende mit (οὐ) γάρ anzuschließen."

Landis 1994, 10: See Q 7:6b-c⁶ Luke = Q, Con (p. 273).

Matt = Q: οὐ(κ)⁷

Pro

von Harnack 1907, 91 (ET 1908, 131): Reconstruction. For complete text see Q 7:1⁶ Luke = Q, Pro (p. 55).

B. Weiß 1908, 15: Reconstruction. For complete text see Q 7:1⁰ In Q (p. 5).

Castor 1912, 223: Reconstruction. For complete text see Q 7:1⁰ In Q (p. 6).

Crum 1927, 138: Reconstruction. For complete text see Q 7:~~2~~, 3, ~~4-6a~~¹ Luke = Q, Pro (pp. 71-72).

Polag 1979, 38: Reconstruction. For complete text see Q 7:1⁰ In Q (pp. 9-10).

Schenk 1981, 37: Reconstruction. For complete text see Q 7:1⁰ In Q (p. 10).

Wegner 1985, 270: Reconstruction. For complete text see Q 7:1⁰ In Q (pp. 11-12).

Catchpole 1992, 533 [1993, 299]: Reconstruction. For complete text see Q 7:1⁰ In Q (p. 14).

Lindars 1992, 210: Reconstruction. For complete text see Q 7:1⁶ Luke = Q (p. 56).

Sevenich-Bax 1993, 238: Reconstruction. For complete text see Q 7:1⁰ In Q (p. 15).

Landis 1994, 11, 17: Reconstruction. For complete text see Q 7:1⁶ Luke = Q, Pro (p. 57).

International Q Project 1995, 478: Reconstruction. For complete text see Q 7:1⁰ In Q (p. 16).

Con

Gundry 1982, 143: See Q 7:6b-c⁶ Matt = Q, Con (p. 273).

Evaluations

Johnson 2000: Matt = Q {B}, οὐ(x)⁷.
Γάρ is occasioned by the redactional interpolation of μὴ σκύλλου.

Robinson 2000: Matt = Q {B}, οὐ(x)⁷.
The γάρ is needed with μὴ σκύλλου, and hence shares with Q 7:6b-c⁶ in the classification as Lukan redaction.

Kloppenborg 2000: Matt = Q {B}, οὐ(x)⁷.

Hoffmann 2001: Matt = Q {B}, οὐ(x)⁷.

Q 7:6b-c[8]: The position of ἱκανός before (Luke) or after (Matthew) εἰμί.

Luke = Q: ⌜ἱκανός⌝[8] εἰμι ⌐ ⌐[8]

Pro

Con

B. Weiß 1876, 229: "Bem. nur die vereinfachte Stellung des εἰμί und μου v. 6."

Easton 1926, 97: "The centurion's words have been rearranged, so as to secure better emphasis."

George 1972, 71: "Mt 8,8-9 ne diffère guère de Lc 7,6b-8 que par les traits propres à ce dernier … et par quelques différences de rédaction qui semblent dues à Luc.[11]"

71[11]: "En Lc 7,6: *mè skyllou* et l'inversion d'*hikanos* et de *mou*."

Gagnon 1994a, 140[42]: "Note … how the ἱκανός εἰμι (the reverse order of Matthew's text … lays stress on the question of worthiness."

Matt = Q: ⌐ ⌐[8] εἰμί ⌜ἱκανός⌝[8]

Pro

von Harnack 1907, 91 (ET 1908, 131): Reconstruction. For complete text see Q 7:1[6] Luke = Q, Pro (p. 55).

B. Weiß 1908, 15: Reconstruction. For complete text see Q 7:1[0] In Q (p. 5).

Polag 1979, 38: Reconstruction. For complete text see Q 7:1[0] In Q (pp. 9-10).

Wegner 1985, 198-199: "Die Reihenfolge des Mt wird wohl mit Polag [1979, 38] als die ursprünglichere zu betrachten sein: man vergleiche dazu etwa [199] Mk 1,7. Bei Mt mag die Voranstellung des Verbs semitischem Einfluß unterliegen, so daß die lk Reihenfolge wohl als sek Gräzisierung zu interpretieren ist."

270: Reconstruction. For complete text see Q 7:1[0] In Q (pp. 11-12).

Davies and Allison 1991, 23: "Οὐκ εἰμί ἱκανός was a fixed expression.[56]"

23[56]: "Cf. LXX Exod 4.10; Mt 3.11; 1 Cor 15.9."

Catchpole 1992, 533 [1993, 299]: Reconstruction. For complete text see Q 7:1[0] In Q (p. 14).

Lindars 1992, 210: Reconstruction. For complete text see Q 7:1[6] Luke = Q, Pro (p. 56).

Sevenich-Bax 1993, 180: "Weitere Abweichungen in Vers Lk 7,6c//Mt 8,8bα betreffen v.a. die Stellung des (Hilfs)-Verbs εἰμί (bei Matthäus vor dem

Adjektiv, bei Lukas dahinter) sowie die Plazierung des Possessivpronomens (bei Matthäus wiederum vor dem Substantiv, bei Lukas nachgestellt).

"Hinsichtlich des ersteren wird man der matthäischen Konstruktion den Vorzug geben dürfen. Dafür spricht v.a. auch die vergleichbare und für Q in dieser Form belegte Redewendung Mt 3,11b//Lk 3,16bβ (vgl. dort)."

238: Reconstruction. For complete text see Q 7:1⁰ In Q (p. 15).

Landis 1994, 10: "Die Wortstellung ἱκανός εἰμι bei Lk dürfte wohl eine sekundäre Gräzisierung des—aus semitischem Einfluß erklärbaren—εἰμι ἱκανός sein, das sich bei Mt aus der Q-Vorlage erhalten hat."

11, 17: Reconstruction. For complete text see Q 7:1⁶ Luke = Q, Pro (p. 57).

International Q Project 1995, 478: Reconstruction. For complete text see Q 7:1⁰ In Q (p. 16).

Con

Evaluations

Johnson 2000: Matt = Q {B}, ⌜⁸ εἰμι ⌜ἱκανός⌝⁸.
Easton and Gagnon correctly interpret Luke's order as a redactional stress on the centurion's unworthiness.
Davies and Allison suggest that Matthew's order was a "fixed expression."

Robinson 2000: Matt = Q {B}, ⌜⁸ εἰμι ⌜ἱκανός⌝⁸.
The rearrangement of the sequence is part of the Lukan insertion of the delegation of the friends and μὴ σκύλλου ... γάρ, which puts the Q statement of humility in a new structure. The Lukan editing of the context probably involved the rearrangement of the sequence here.

Kloppenborg 2000: Matt = Q {B}, ⌜⁸ εἰμι ⌜ἱκανός⌝⁸.

Hoffmann 2001: Matt = Q {B}, ⌜⁸ εἰμι ⌜ἱκανός⌝⁸.

Q 7:6b-c⁹: Position of μου after (Luke) or before (Matthew) ὑπὸ τὴν στέγην.

Luke = Q: ἵνα ⌜²⁹ ὑπὸ τὴν στέγην ⌜μου²⁹ εἰσέλθῃς

Pro

Polag 1979, 38: Reconstruction. For complete text see Q 7:1⁰ In Q (pp. 9-10).

Wegner 1985, 200-201: "Immerhin könnte folgende Gründe für die Priorität der lk Reihenfolge sprechen: 1. Die Nachstellung von μου in Mt 11,27/Lk 10,22, wo es, wie auSt, in Verbindung mit ὑπό verwendet wird. 2. Die mt red Voranstellung von σου in 15,28, mit der der erste Evangelist vielleicht, wie auSt, die heidnische Abstammung des Angeredeten hervorheben will. 3. In der Hauptmannserzählung [201] begegnet auch sonst noch eine Anzahl mehrerer Semitismen, weshalb die dem Semitischen näherliegende Reihenfolge des Lk in unserem Falle die höhere Wahrscheinlichkeit für Ursprünglichkeit enthält. Unter diesen Voraussetzungen werden wir in dem später zu bringenden Rekonstruktionsversuch des urspr Q-Wortlautes der Erzählung die lk Reihenfolge bevorzugen."

270: Reconstruction. For complete text see Q 7:1⁰ In Q (pp. 11-12).

Sevenich-Bax 1993, 181: "In der Logienquelle findet sich das Pronomen zwar vereinzelt vor seinem Bezugswort (vgl. Mt 7,24//Lk 6,47; Mt 10,37f.//Lk 14,26f.), doch dominiert die Nachordnung. Könnte dies als ein erstes Indiz für die Prävalenz der lukanischen Formulierung gewertet werden, so kommt hinzu, daß in der Erzählung vom Hauptmann das Possessivpronomen insgesamt viermal verwendet wird (Mt 8,5b; Mt 8,8bα//Lk 7,6c; Mt 8,8bβ//Lk 7,7b; Mt 8,9bγ//Lk 7,8bγ). In allen Fällen—außer Mt 8,8bα diff. Lk—wird das Possessivpronomen nachgestellt. Die Konsistenz in der Überlieferung dieser Erzählung bietet so ein weiteres Argument zugunsten der lukanischen Fassung."

238: Reconstruction. For complete text see Q 7:1⁰ In Q (p. 15).

Landis 1994, 10-11: "Dagegen hat wahrscheinlich Lk im Nebensatz, der mit ἵνα eingeleitet wird, die ursprüngliche Wortreihenfolge mit Nachstellung von μου bewahrt; zwar hat Lk die Tendenz, die Voranstellung des Possessivpronomens zu vermeiden, aber umgekehrt wird diese von Mt ausgesprochen bevorzugt. Von daher ließe [11] sich also ein redaktioneller Eingriff sowohl beim ersten als auch beim dritten Evangelisten erklären. Den Ausschlag gibt, daß in der Logienquelle die Nachstellung des Possessivpronomens überwiegt, die demnach wohl auch an unserer Stelle für Q anzunehmen ist."

Con

B. Weiß 1876, 229: "Bem. nur die vereinfachte Stellung des εἰμί und μου v. 6."

B. Weiß 1908, 15[25]: "Ihnen ist noch hinzuzufügen die Nachstellung des μου hinter στέγην und die Hinzufügung des αὐτόν hinter ἐθαύμασεν; dagegen nicht das Fehlen des μόνον nach ἀλλά, das von Mt. 8,8 verstärkend hinzugefügt sein wird, da sich ein Grund der Weglassung bei Luk. nicht denken läßt."

Cadbury 1920, 152-153: "Luke comparatively seldom varies the order of words that he found in his sources, and the motives for such changes as he makes are not always apparent to us and were perhaps not always clearly defined in his own mind. He allows himself considerable freedom, and pays little regard to regularity. But, if we may judge from certain kinds of cases, the changes seem to be usually in the direction of a more normal order. …

[153] "The possessive normally follows; … Mt. 8,8 μου ὑπὸ τὴν στέγην Luke 7,6 ὑπὸ τὴν στέγην μου (Q)."

Easton 1926, 97: "The centurion's words have been rearranged, so as to secure better emphasis."

George 1972, 71: "Mt 8,8-9 ne diffère guère de Lc 7,6b-8 que par les traits propres à ce dernier … et par quelques différences de rédaction qui semblent dues à Luc.[11]"

71[11]: "En Lc 7,6: *mè skyllou* et l'inversion d'*hikanos* et de *mou*."

Wegner 1985, 199: "Eine Entscheidung ist schwierig, denn weder Q noch Mt verhalten sich hinsichtlich der Voran- oder Nachstellung des Possessivpronomens einheitlich. Anders ist es freilich bei Lk, wo eine deutliche Tendenz zu Tage tritt.

"1. Lk zeigt deutlich die Tendenz, die Voranstellung der Possessivpronomina zu vermeiden. Dies zeigt sich an seiner Bearbeitung des Mk-Stoffes, wo er kein einziges Mal ein vorangestelltes Possessivpronomen übernahm, sondern stets nachstellte: vgl. 5,20.23 und 8,45f diff Mk. Diese Tendenz wird durch den Befund im gesamten Ev (272 Nachstellungen gegenüber 22 Voranstellungen) und in der Apg (126 Nachstellungen gegenüber 9 Voranstellungen) vollends bestätigt, Als Faustregel könnte daher, was Q betrifft, angegeben werden: Immer dort, wo (a) innerhalb eines Q-Stoffes Lk gegenüber Mt eine Voranstellung des Possessivpronomens bietet (vgl. etwa 6,29; 11,19; 12,30; [14,23f; 19,23] und 14,26f diff Mt), ist mit hoher Wahrscheinlichkeit seine Reihenfolge die ursprünglichere; zumindest wird die Reihenfolge in diesen Fällen vor-lk sein. Dort aber, wo (b) Lk im Unterschied zur Mt-Parallele eine Nachstellung aufweist (vgl. etwa außer uSt noch 12,7 und 12,45), wird man mit seiner Red zu rechnen haben." But see Wegner at Luke = Q, Pro (p. 279).

Matt = Q: ἵνα ⌜μου⌝[29] ὑπὸ τὴν στέγην ⌐ [29] εἰσέλθῃς

Pro

von Harnack 1907, 91 (ET 1908, 131): Reconstruction. For complete text see Q 7:1[6] Luke = Q, Pro (p. 55).

B. Weiß 1908, 15: Reconstruction. For complete text see Q 7:1⁰ In Q (p. 5).

Catchpole 1992, 533 [1993, 299]: Reconstruction. For complete text see Q 7:1⁰ In Q (p. 14).

Lindars 1992, 210: Reconstruction. For complete text see Q 7:1⁶ Luke = Q, Pro (p. 56).

International Q Project 1995, 478: Reconstruction. For complete text see Q 7:1⁰ In Q (p. 16).

Con

Plummer 1909, 125[1]: "By placing μου before ὑπὸ τὴν στέγην, Mt. throws the emphasis on the substantive: 'enter under my *roof*.'"

Lagrange 1923, 165: "Le centurion, cela va sans dire, accepte avec reconnaissance l'offre de la guérison. Sa réponse exprime son humilité, mieux encore que dans Lc., puisqu'il a placé μου avant τὴν στέγην, pour mettre l'accent sur l'indignité de sa personne."

Gundry 1982, 143: "The centurion's unworthiness is the sole point—and it contrasts with Jesus' authority. To underline the contrast, Matthew moves μου away from στέγην and up to the beginning of the clause. There, ahead of the prepositional phrase to which it belongs, the centurion's unworthy μου gets heavy emphasis and acts as a foil to Jesus' authoritative ἐγώ (v 7)."

Wegner 1985, 200: "Mt zeigt, anders als Lk, eine Tendenz, das Possessivpronomen voranzustellen. Dies geht aus seiner Mk-Bearbeitung hervor, wo er zuweilen die mk Nachstellung durch Voranstellung ändert (vgl. 9,6; 12,13 [Mk 3,5: v.l.].50 und 17,15 diff Mk) oder von sich aus die Mk-Vorlage durch Voranstellung modifiziert (so etwa in 15,28 und 19,21 diff Mk). Dies bedeutet für den Q-Stoff, daß dort, wo Mt gegenüber der Lk-Parallele das Possessivpronomen in Voranstellung verwendet (vgl. außer uSt noch 7,26; 10,30 und 24,48 diff Lk), mit der Möglichkeit seiner Redaktionstätigkeit zu rechnen ist."

Evaluations

Robinson 2000: Matt = Q, {B}, ἵνα ⌜μου⌝⁹ ὑπὸ τὴν στέγην ⌞⌟⁹ εἰσέλθῃς.
Luke usually edits Mark to the Lukan position found here, as he would be expected to do, in order to improve the Greek. Luke's reading has less to do with being a Semitism than with improving the Greek, and hence is to be considered secondary.

The Q sequence ὑπὸ τοῦ πατρός μου (Matt 11:27 par. Luke 10:22) is not normative for Q in general, since it is standard usage with God (Pater Noster). The parallel to Matt 8:13, Matt 15:28 μ(σ?)ου ἡ πίστις to emphasize the problem of being a Gentile (cf. John 4:47b αὐτοῦ τὸν υἱόν), is not in Matt 15:28 specifically redactional regarding the issue at hand, since the context is absent from Mark 7:29, though of course it is Matthean usage. But there is not evidence for redaction regarding Q or Matthew that is as significant as that concerning Luke.

Kloppenborg 2000: Matt = Q, {B}, ἵνα ⌜μου⌝¹⁹ ὑπὸ τὴν στέγην ⌐¹⁹ εἰσέλθῃς.

Johnson 2001: Matt = Q, {B}, ἵνα ⌜μου⌝¹⁹ ὑπὸ τὴν στέγην ⌐¹⁹ εἰσέλθῃς. Robinson aptly summarizes the grammatical and stylistic issues.

Hoffmann 2001: Matt = Q, {B}, ἵνα ⌜μου⌝¹⁹ ὑπὸ τὴν στέγην ⌐¹⁹ εἰσέλθῃς. Vgl. Kloppenborgs response von 1994. ["Cadbury ... notes that Luke prefers pronouns to follow their substantives. Moreover Kloppenborg 1987, 64 n. 102 notes that Q has several instances of pronouns preceding substantives: 6:47; 9:60; 14:26 and several other instances where the pronoun-noun form is arguably from Q (based on Luke's tendency to prefer the other order, and the fact that the noun-pronoun order is more common in the LXX and NT Greek in general). Moreover, it has been Luke, not Matthew, who has intervened in this verse in other respects."]

Q 7:7

Matt 8:8b	Q 7:7	Luke 7:7
[ ]¹	[]¹	[διὸ οὐδὲ ἐμαυτὸν ἠξίωσα πρὸς σὲ ἐλθεῖν]¹.
ἀλλὰ (μόνον)² εἰπὲ λόγῳ, καὶ ἰαθή(σεται)³ ὁ παῖς μου.	ἀλλὰ [[()²]] εἰπὲ λόγῳ, καὶ ἰαθή[[[τω]]³] ὁ παῖς μου.	ἀλλὰ ( )² εἰπὲ λόγῳ, καὶ ἰαθή[τω]³ ὁ παῖς μου.

IQP 1994: ()².
IQP 1994: ἰαθή[[(σεται)³]].

¹ Luke's διὸ οὐδὲ ἐμαυτὸν ἠξίωσα πρὸς σὲ ἐλθεῖν.
² Matthew's μόνον.
³ Luke's ἰαθήτω or Matthew's ἰαθήσεται.

Q 7:7¹: Luke's διὸ οὐδὲ ἐμαυτὸν ἠξίωσα πρὸς σὲ ἐλθεῖν.

Luke = Q: [διὸ οὐδὲ ἐμαυτὸν ἠξίωσα πρὸς σὲ ἐλθεῖν]¹

Pro

H. **Meyer** 1864, 218 (ET 1884, 179): See Q 7:~~2~~, 3, ~~4-6a~~³ Luke = Q, Pro (p. 87).

Hawkins 1899, 195: "Luke may have retained the original narrative in its fullness, while Matthew, after his manner, shortened it: —Lk vi.17a(?); vii. 3a, 4, 5, 6, 7a; 10; 20, 21."

Gundry 1982, 143: See Gundry at Matt = Q, Con (p. 293).

Con

Holtzmann 1863, 220: See Q 7:~~2~~, 3, ~~4-6a~~³ Luke = Q, Con (p. 93).

B. **Weiß** 1876, 229: "Ohnehin zeigen die sichtlich von Luc. selbst in v. 7 eingeschalteten Worte (Vg. zu dem διό, das noch 10mal in Act. steht, 1,35, zu ἀξιοῦν Act. 15,38; 28,22), daß hier die Reflexion maßgebend war, er, der sich bei der ersten Bitte durch Andre vertreten ließ, werde auch die zweite nicht persönlich anzubringen gewagt haben."

J. **Weiß** 1892, 400: "V. 7 ist natürlich von Lk in den Bericht von Q einge-schoben.—διό ... οὐδέ: vgl. 1,35.—ἀξιοῦν: in dieser Bedeutung bei Lk nicht mehr vorkommend, ἄξιος noch 7 Mal, 5 Mal aus LQ."

B. **Weiß** 1900, 322-323: See Q 7:6b-c² Luke = Q, Con (p. 242).

B. **Weiß** 1901, 383-384: "V. 7. διό: wie 1,35 von der Hand des Lk (noch 10 mal in Act.), [384] leitet das Verbindungsglied zwischen beiden Überliefe-rungen ein: *darum habe ich mich auch nicht werth geachtet* (ἠξίωσα, wie II Th 1,11), *zu Dir zu kommen.*"

von Harnack 1907, 56: "Bemerkt sei nur, daß ἔντιμος (v. 2), ... διό (v. 7), ἀξιοῦν (v. 7), [et alia] in den Evangelien ausschließlich lukanisch sind (nur διό kommt einmal bei Matth. vor)."

von Harnack 1907, ET 1908, 76-77: "I would only remark that ἔντιμος (verse 2), ... διό (verse 7), ἀξιοῦν (verse 7), [et alia] are, as far as the gospels [77] are concerned, exclusively Lukan (διό alone occurs once in St. Mat-thew)."

B. **Weiß** 1907, 243¹: "Während Lk. 7,6f. bereits das Wort aus Mt. 8,8 auf-nimmt, das doch mit seinem οὐκ εἰμί im Munde der Freunde sehr unnatür-lich ist, ... zeigt das an das ἄξιός ἐστιν 7,4 anknüpfende (οὐδὲ) ἐμαυτὸν ἠξίωσα πρὸς σὲ ἐλθεῖν, das Lukas nur benutzt, um seine beiden Überliefe-run-gen durch das διὸ οὐδέ zu verbinden, noch deutlich, daß sie von Freunden im

Auftrage des Hauptmanns gesprochen sein sollen, in den aus Q (Mt. 8,9) übernommenen Worten Lk. 7,8."

Loisy 1907, 650: "Bien moins satisfaisante est la mise en scène du troisième Évangile. On sent que Luc a pour base de sa rédaction un récit identique à celui de Matthieu, où le centurion lui-même conversait avec Jésus, et qu'il a voulu le corriger en introduisant des détails qui ne sont pas en harmonie avec le cadre primitif. Le discours du centurion, même tel qu'il est reproduit dans Luc, n'a pu être tenu que par le centurion lui-même, et l'addition si singulière: 'C'est pour cela que je ne suis pas venu te trouver en personne,' qui veut expliquer la conduite du centurion, ne fait que trahir l'artifice du rédacteur."

Castor 1912, 223: Reconstruction. For complete text see Q 7:1⁰ In Q (p. 6).

233⁴: "Luke adds, 'Wherefore neither deemed I myself worthy to come to thee.' This attributes to faith what was more probably due to respect for Jewish prejudices."

Patton 1915, 144: See Q 7:2̶, 3, 4̶-6a̶³ Luke = Q, Con (pp. 95-96).

144-145: "Of these Lucan words, … [145] … διό occurs once in Mark, once in Matthew, twice in Luke's Gospel, and eight times in Acts. Ἀξιόω is found in Luke only among the Gospels, and twice in Acts."

145: See Q 7:2̶, 3, 4̶-6a̶³ Luke = Q, Con (p. 96).

Klostermann 1919, 449: See Q 7:6b-c² Luke = Q, Con (pp. 244-245).

Bussmann 1925, 11: See Q 7:2̶, 3, 4̶-6a̶³ Luke = Q, Con (p. 96).

Easton 1926, 97: "The first clause is an attempt to reconcile the centurion's words with his non-appearance."

Crum 1927, 138: Reconstruction. For complete text see Q 7:2̶, 3, 4̶-6a̶¹ Luke = Q, Pro (pp. 71-72).

Bussmann 1929, 56: "In Lk 7:3-7a ist ein Stück anscheinend eingeschoben, von dem Mt nichts hat."

Klostermann 1929, 86-87: See Klostermann 1919 at Q 7:6b-c² Luke = Q, Con (pp. 244-245).

Creed 1930, 102: "7. διὸ οὐδὲ … πρὸς σὲ ἐλθεῖν—These words are necessarily absent from Mt., where the centurion presents his own request. The man's personal humility gives the reason why he not only desires to prevent the entry of Jesus into his house, but has also chosen to approach Jesus through the elders and his friends. … Wellh [Wellhausen 1904b, 27] thinks that the sentence is an interpretative gloss. But in the Lucan form of the narrative they directly help the story, and are probably as old as the other modifications in Lk."

Schlatter 1931, 251: "Nun wird aber durch die Sendung neuer Boten, durch die der Hauptmann verhüten will, daß Jesus sein Haus betrete, die Situation der von Mat. beschriebenen ähnlich, und nun entsteht der seltsame Tatbestand, daß die Rede des Hauptmanns wörtlich dieselbe wie bei Mat. ist.

Sie wird nur durch eine kurze Einlage: διὸ οὐδὲ ἐμαυτὸν ἠξίωσα πρὸς σὲ ἐλθεῖν an das Erzählte angeheftet."

Manson 1937, 64: "The second deputation is an expression of the humility of the man, and this is made explicit in v. 7, which has no parallel in Mt. and is not to be regarded as original."

Jeremias 1956, 25-26: "Die Antwort Jesu auf die Bitte des Heiden ist, wie sich aus dem Vergleich [26] mit Joh 4,48 ergibt, als Frage zu lesen: ἐγὼ ἐλθὼν θεραπεύσω αὐτόν; (Mth 8,7). wieder lehnt Jesus also scharf ab.⁹⁷"

26⁹⁷: "Lukas hat, um diese scharfe Ablehnung zu umgehen, die Einleitung der Geschichte völlig neu gefaßt (7,2-6a.7a)."

Jeremias 1956, ET 1958, 30: "Jesus' answer to the request of the Gentile should be read as a question, as is shown by a comparison with John 4.48: ἐγὼ ἐλθὼν θεραπεύσω αὐτόν; (Matt. 8.7). Again Jesus brusquely refuses.³"

30³: "In order to avoid this harsh refusal, Luke has completely recast the introduction to the story (7.2-6a, 7a)."

Leaney 1958, 141: "Luke has also added an apology for the centurion's not coming to Jesus himself (7a), but it cannot be regarded as a very satisfactory explanation from a man with so earnest a request and so great respect for the Lord. The story in Matt. viii. 5-13 is free from these contradictions."

Held 1960, 183: "Lukas hat dem Gespräch aus einer anderen Quelle eine ausführliche und eigenartige Einleitung gegeben (Lk. 7,2-6a),³ die er durch einen eingeschobenen Satz (Lk. 7,7a) kunstvoll mit dem Dialog verknüpft.⁴"

183³: "Die Quelle des Lukas ist nach W. Bussmann [1929, 57] an der Verschiedenheit der verwandten Worte zu erkennen. Q (mit Mt. gemeinsam): παῖς, ἱκανός; Lukas-Sonderquelle: δοῦλος, ἄξιος."

183⁴: "Vgl. die Stichwortverbindung: (7,4) ἄξιος (7,7) ἠξίωσα."

185: "So kommt der Heide nicht selbst zu Jesus, da er sich nach seinen eigenen Worten für unwürdig hält (Lk. 7,7a, von Lukas selbst eingefügt)."

Held 1960, ET 1963, 194: "Luke, from another source, has given the conversation a detailed and unique introduction (Luke 7:2-6a)¹ which he has skillfully linked with the dialogue² by means of the insertion of a sentence (Luke 7:7a)."

194¹: "Luke's source can be recognized according to W. Bussmann [1929, 57] by the difference in the words he uses. Q (along with Matthew): παῖς, ἱκανός; Luke's special source: δοῦλος, ἄξιος."

194²: "Cf. the combination of the catchwords: (7:4) ἄξιος (7:7) ἠξίωσα."

195: "The Gentile man does not himself come to Jesus, since, according to his own words, he regards himself as unworthy (Luke 7:7a, inserted by Luke)."

Schlatter 1960, 492-493: "Ebenso zeigt das eingeschobene Sätzchen, das die Rede des Hauptmanns mit [493] der im Vorangehenden beschriebenen

Situation verbindet, διὸ οὐδὲ ἐμαυτὸν ἠξίωσα πρὸς σὲ ἐλθεῖν, in διό und in ἀξιοῦν den lukanischen Sprachgebrauch."

Grundmann 1961, 155: See Q 7:2, 3, 4-6a³ Luke = Q, Con (pp. 99-100).

Delobel 1966, 454-455: "Nous trouvons une deuxième indication de l'humilité du centurion dans l'addition: διὸ οὐδὲ ἐμαυτὸν ἠξίωσα πρὸς σὲ ἐλθεῖν. Ἀξιοῦν,—un *hapax* dans *Lc.*,—se retrouve deux fois dans *Act.*, tandis que le verbe manque dans *Mc.-Mt.* Le verbe reprend le motif du v. 4 (ἄξιος) et du v. 6 οὐ γὰρ ἱκανός εἰμι. On connaît en outre la [455] préférence de Luc pour la préposition πρός."

Siegman 1968, 188-189: "With a number of modern exegetes, ... it must be conceded that Lk's account is artificial. The protest of unworthiness is not natural when [189] spoken by proxy. In Lk 7,6 the centurion's words are quoted exactly as in Mt 8,8; it seems that Lk returns to the supposed Q source and neglects to smooth out the transition. But what reason would Lk have for expanding his source, if he was not utilizing additional sources of information? Wendland [1912, 209] notes Lk's preference for expansions of this kind (compare Lk 7,18-21 with Mt 11,2-3). In Lk 8,49 (= Mk 5,35-37; missing in Mt) as Jesus is on His way to the home of Jairus, messengers come from Jairus' home to bid Jesus trouble the Lord no further, since his daughter had already died. Possibly a detail from the Jairus story was transferred to the centurion story."

Schürmann 1969, 393²⁶: "Die Vokabel ἀξιόω ist luk (außer hier und Apg 15,38; 28,22 syn nicht) ebenso wie διό. ... ἐμαυτοῦ ist Reminiszenz an 7,8 = Mt 8,9, aber auch gut luk (syn sonst nicht, aber 4mal Apg, sonst im NT häufig nur bei Pls und Joh). So ist der Einschub V 7a vielleicht der luk Redaktion zuzuschreiben."

Schnider and Stenger 1971, 63: "Lukas fügte vor allem das Motiv von der zweifachen Gesandtschaft ein."

Schramm 1971, 42: "Es folgt ganz der an Mt kontrollierbaren Q-Fassung, bis auf einige unbedeutende Verbesserungen und den Zusatz V 7a: διὸ οὐδὲ ἐμαυτὸν ἠξίωσα πρὸς σὲ ἐλθεῖν, der Verklammerung⁴ der hier kombinierten Varianten dient. Er ist, wie der Sprachgebrauch zeigt, von Lk selbst formuliert.⁵"

42⁴: "Ἠξίωσα nimmt das ἄξιος aus V 4 betont auf."

42⁵: "Διό: Mt 1x, Mk—, Lk außer 7,7 noch 1,35; Act 8x, und zwar gehäuft im zweiten Teil der Apgsch und durchweg (bis auf 24,26) in Reden: damit sicher spezifisch luk. ἐμαυτόν: Mt 1x, Mk—, Lk außer 7,7 nur 7,8 par Mt 8,9; Act 4x: 20,24; 24,10; 26,2.9; d.h. nur im zweiten Teil und nur in Reden. ἀξιόω: Mt—, Mk—, Lk nur hier, offenbar durch ἄξιος V 4 veranlaßt; Act 2x; zur ganzen Wendung vgl. Act 26,2: ἥγημαι ἐμαυτὸν μακάριον; ... ἔρχεσθαι πρός + *Pers.*: Lk 9x, Act 6x (4,23; 17,15; 20,6; 21,11; 22,13;"

28,23): wie die Act, wiederum bes. die zweite Hälfte, zeigen, schätzt Lk diese Formulierung."

George 1972, 67: "Il explique par cette indignité le fait qu'il n'a pas osé aller jusqu'à Jésus (v. 7; le trait est propre à Luc, le seul évangéliste à montrer le païen traitant avec Jésus par des intermédiaires)."

71: "Mt 8,8-9 ne diffère guère de Lc 7,6b-8 que par les traits propres à ce dernier (l'envoi des amis en 7,6b, l'explication de l'absence du centurion en 7,7a) et par quelques différences de rédaction qui semblent dues à Luc."

Schulz 1972, 238-239: "Lk 7,7a: Der Vers hat keine Entsprechung bei Mt, [239] hängt inhaltlich aufs engste mit dem Einschub Vv 3-6a zusammen und weist zudem lk Sprachmerkmale auf, so daß Lk als Verfasser anzusehen ist."

239⁴¹⁵: "Διό ist durch Apg als lk ausgewiesen (Ev 1,35 trad; Apg 8mal; fehlt bei Mk; 1mal bei Mt); οὐδέ ist zwar im Ev vorwiegend trad (ca 16mal trad; ca 2mal red), wird aber von Lk in Apg oft gebraucht (12mal); ἀξιοῦν ist lk (fehlt sonst bei den Synoptikern; 2mal in Apg—reflexiver Gebrauch allerdings nur hier)."

Derrett 1973, 174: "From the discrepancies between the Matthaean and the Lucan versions we gather that Matthew stands closer to Q, the additions and modifications having been introduced by Luke for motives we can begin to reconstruct. The many textual puzzles may yield to a new interpretation: thus Lk. vii 7a (omitted by Mt. and by D, etc.) may well be Luke's own conception."

Schweizer 1973, 137: "Die Worte des Hauptmanns und die Jesu stimmen in V.8-10 fast wörtlich mit Lk. 7,6-9 überein, nur daß Lukas in V.7a in dem für ihn typischen Stil eine Bemerkung zufügt."

Schweizer 1973, ET 1975, 212: "The words of the officer and of Jesus in verses 8-10 agree almost word for word with Luke 7:6-9, except that in verse 7a Luke adds a comment in his typical style."

Wilson 1973, 31: See Q 7:2, 3, 4-6a¹ Luke = Q, Con (p. 68).

Achtemeier 1975, 549: See Q 7:?10?⁴ Luke = Q, Con (p. 379).

Pesch and Kratz 1976, 81: "Lukas fügt, den Gegensatz abmildernd, v 7a noch hinzu, der Hauptmann habe sich deshalb auch nicht für würdig gehalten, zu Jesus zu kommen."

Busse 1977, 143: "Trotz der Kritik von Haenchen an der literarischen Bearbeitung der Q-Fassung [1959a, 25-28 (1965, 84-87)] hat Held [1960, 183] die Verknüpfung von der Einleitung Lk 7,2-6a mit dem ursprünglichen Dialog Lk 7,7b-9 durch den eingeschobenen Satz (Lk 7,7a) als 'kunstvoll' empfunden."

148-149¹: "In V 7 ist luk. Bearbeitung spürbar. Der mit διό eingeleitete Satz ist red., da er sich inhaltlich [149] auf die Verse 3-6 zurückbezieht, die luk. sind. Dies läßt sich sprachlich an dem Tempuswechsel in den Aor ablesen. Zudem weist der Satz luk. Stileigentümlichkeiten auf. Nach Schulz [1972, 239⁴¹⁵] sind διό, ἀξιοῦν und οὐδέ red."

Marshall 1978, 281: "The first part of the verse is peculiar to Lk. and would be out of place in Mt. where nothing is said about the centurion's embassy to Jesus; it is, therefore, commonly regarded as due to Lucan redaction. The language is largely Lucan: διό (1:35); ἐμαυτόν (7:8 par. Mt. 8:9; Acts, 4x); ἀξιόω (Acts 15:38; 28:22; cf. καταξιόω, 20:35; Acts 5:41; 2 Thes. 1:5); ἔρχομαι πρός (Lk., 9x; Acts, 6x); and for the whole saying cf. Acts 26:2. The saying is parenthetic, and interrupts the connection between v. 6 and v. 7b (it is omitted by D pc it sy^s)."

Martin 1978, 15: "Matthew is consistent with his use of παῖς for the sufferer, while Luke varies between παῖς (v. 7, Q) and δοῦλος (normally), and 'in v. 8 the centurion speaks of his "slave" as if the slave were another person than his "boy".' But we should note that δοῦλος and ἄξιος are Luke terms,¹¹ while παῖς and ἱκανός are preferred in those passages where Matthew and Luke overlap (i.e., in Q)."

20¹¹: "And it is part of Luke's style to ring the changes stylistically by substituting closely similar or synonymous terms."

16: "In the Lukan version faith is not accented, but the reader's interest is attracted to the man's sense of unworthiness and the key phrase lies in verse 7a: διὸ οὐδὲ ἐμαυτὸν ἠξίωσα πρὸς σὲ ἐλθεῖν ([Luke]), i.e., the unworthiness and disadvantage of being a Gentile are stressed.¹⁵"

20¹⁵: "This conclusion is clinched by the Lukan insertion of αὐτόν into the statement of Jesus' reaction: 'He marveled (ἐθαύμασεν) at him.' The verb is found only once again in the synoptic tradition."

19⁷: "The point at issue in the question of defilement is emphasized in the centurion's perception: 'Lord, I am not worthy that *you should enter my roof.*' This sentiment is repeated in Luke 7:6 (Q), but then transformed in verse 7: 'nor did I esteem myself worthy (cf. v. 4) *to come to you,*' to explain why there is no direct contact between Jesus and the Gentile."

Gatzweiler 1979, 308: "Au v. 7 le centurion lui-même explique la raison de sa démarche. Impossible pour Lc d'invoquer des prescriptions juives pour interdire à Jésus l'accès à maison païenne. Pareil langage serait incompréhensible et inactualisable pour son public. Ce que Mt et sans doute le récit préévangélique mettent au compte du respect de la loi juive, Lc le met très simplement au compte de l'exigence de l'humilité dans la prière chrétienne."

Jeremias 1980, 51: "Διό findet sich in den Evangelien außer Mt 27,8 nur im LkEv: 1,35; 7,7. Lukas verwendet die Konjunktion im Doppelwerk außerdem noch 8mal in der Apg: 10,29; 15,19; 20,31; 24,26; 25,26; 26,3; 27,25.34."

154: "Διό: → 1,35 Red. ... ἐμαυτὸν ἠξίωσα; ἀξιόω und καταξιόω ('für angemessen erachten') mit nachfolgendem Infinitiv findet sich im NT ausschließlich im lk Doppelwerk (ἀξιόω: Lk 7,7; Apg 15,38; 28,22; καταξιόω: Lk 20,35; Apg 5,41). Die (klassische) Ergänzung durch den Infinitiv ist kennzeichnend für Lukas (→ 2,26 Red ...); dem entspricht, daß es sich, wie der Parallelenvergleich zeigt, sowohl Lk 7,7 (vgl. Mt 8,9) als auch Lk 20,35 (vgl. Mk 12,25) um lukanische Zusätze handelt. Mit ἐμαυτὸν ἠξίωσα ist die sinnverwandte, ebenfalls das Reflexivpronomen der 1. Pers. mit einem Verbum verbindende lukanische Wendung ἥγημαι ἐμαυτὸν μακάριον (Apg 26,2) zu vergleichen."

Schmithals 1980, 91-92: "Es war seine Demut gewesen, so [92] erfahren wir nun, die den Heiden zu jener durch die Ältesten der Juden vermittelten Begegnung mit Jesus bewogen hatte (V. 7a); damit macht Lukas die Umgestaltung seiner Vorlage psychologisch verständlich. Dementsprechend sind es auch die ausgesandten Freunde, die den Knecht gesund zu Hause antreffen."

Beare 1981, 207: "In Luke, the recognition of the centurion's inferiority is carried further by his use of intermediaries and his explanation—'I did not count myself worthy to come to you in person' (Lk. 7:7)."

Fitzmyer 1981, 649: "It is better to regard vv. 1a, 7a, and 10a as Lucan redaction."

Schweizer 1982, 86: "Hätte Lukas nach mündlicher Tradition oder in Angleichung an Apg 10,2.5.22 (s. zu Apg 10,1-48) V.3-6a gebildet und durch 7a (im Kontrast zu 4b) mit seiner Vorlage verbunden."

Schweizer 1982, ET 1984, 131: "Luke, drawing on oral tradition or Acts 10:2,5,22, composed vss. 3-6a and linked them with his archetype by means of vs. 7a (in contrast to vs. 4b)."

Haapa 1983, 72: "Der Lukastext ist Ergebnis einer zielbewußten Redaktionsarbeit. Auch in der älteren Erzählung liegt die Initiative auf Seiten des Bittstellers. Lukas benutzt diesen Zug, um den Kontaktverzicht zwischen den Hauptpersonen für seine Leser verständlich zu machen. Auch der Kontaktverzicht hängt nach der Lukasversion vom Verhalten des Heiden ab. Trotz seines guten Rufes bei den Juden fühlt sich der Mann unwürdig. So rückt die Selbsteinschätzung des Hauptmanns in die Mitte der Erzählung. Der Mann, dessen Würdigkeit von maßgebender Seite bezeugt wird, hält sich für wertlos, mit Jesus zu verkehren. Näheres läßt sich nicht von diesem Unwürdigkeitsgefühl auf Grund unserer Perikope sagen. Weil aber das Motiv redaktionell ist, hat man mit gutem Recht erwartet, vom lukanischen Großkontext aus zu einem besseren Verständnis zu gelangen."

Dauer 1984, 85: "Die Sprache deutet auf lk Einschub: zu ἀξιόω vgl. außer a.u.St. noch Apg 15,38; 28,22; bei den Syn begegnet es sonst nicht mehr.— διό kommt außer Mt 27,8 bei den Syn nur Lk 2mal und Apg 8mal vor.—

ἐμαυτόν könnte jenes von V. 8 (par Mt V. 9) vorausnehmen, ist aber auch gut lk: 4mal Apg, sonst im NT häufig nur im paulinischen Schrifttum und im 4. Evangelium.

"Lukas schiebt diese Zwischenbemerkung des Zenturio aber nicht deswegen ein, um damit geschickt zwei an sich selbständige Stücke—nämlich den Dialog aus Q und den Rahmen aus einer Sonder-Quelle—ineinander zu verarbeiten, sondern um damit die *Demut* des Mannes zu unterstreichen, die ihm hier neben dem Glauben besonders wichtig zu sein scheint, wie er die Demut als gottwohlgefällige Haltung auch sonst stark betont."

Wegner 1985, 202-205: Wegner provides detailed lexical data to support his argument that Q 7:7¹ does not represent Lukan redaction. He argues, however, that 7:7¹ derives, not from Q, but from Lukan *Sondergut*.

241: See Q 7:~~2~~, 3, ~~4-6a~~¹³ Luke = Q, Con (pp. 227-228).

270: Reconstruction. For complete text see Q 7:1⁰ In Q (pp. 11-12).

Bovon 1989, 350: "Die Wiederholung der Unwürdigkeitsbezeugung in V 7a (noch nicht in Matthäus und Q) suggeriert, daß der Heide sich auch dem Gesetz Gottes gegenüber für unwürdig hält."

Bovon 1989, FT 1991, 342: "Cette déclaration d'indignité, qui est répétée au v. 7a (qui ne se retrouve pas dans Matthieu, ni dans Q), laisse entendre que ce païen se sent indigne aussi devant la Loi de Dieu."

Nolland 1989, 317: "The opening clause of v 7 has no counterpart in Matthew. It explains the role of the delegation of friends and so is probably Lukan. The thought reflects that of the end of v 6, but the language is chosen to emphasize the personal humility of the centurion in the face of the generous evaluation by the Jewish elders in v 4. The clause is parenthetic and interrupts the development from v 6 to v 7b."

Davies and Allison 1991, 22: See Q 7:6b-c² Luke = Q, Con (p. 252).

Catchpole 1992, 528-529 [1993, 293-294]: See Q 7:~~2~~, 3, ~~4-6a~~¹³ Luke = Q, Con (p. 228).

530 [296]: "The centurion's sense of unworthiness in *both* its manifestations, his suggestion that Jesus should not enter his house and his decision not to come to Jesus in person, coupled together as they are by διὸ οὐδέ (v. 7a), is grounded not in an awareness of ethnicity but in a christological conviction about who Jesus is.

"The theology which underlies the Lucan version of the tradition is wholly in line with the evangelist's outlook."

533 [299]: Reconstruction. For complete text see Q 7:1⁰ In Q (p. 14).

Lindars 1992, 210: Reconstruction. For complete text see Q 7:1⁶ Luke = Q, Pro (p. 56).

Gagnon 1993, 726: "As for v 7a: with the possible exception of ἀξιόω (which at least has minimal attestation in Acts, but no references in [S]), no word or phrase can be excluded from at least the possibility of Lucan redaction. Note that οὐδέ and ἔρχομαι πρός are well, or better, attested in [S], διό less well so, and ἐμαυτοῦ not at all attested in [S])."

728: "For διό (1/0/2 + 8), see Luke 1:35 [S] and the frequent occurrences in Acts (all in the second half of Acts, and all but one in speeches). In Luke-Acts the oblique cases of ἐμαυτοῦ appear only 2x in Luke (here and in 7:8 [Q] [acc. case]) and 4x in Acts (only 26:2 in the acc. case, but all in the second part of Acts and in speeches). The use of the term here was probably suggested by its appearance in the Q dialogue."

Sevenich-Bax 1993, 166: "Die den Freunden in den Mund gelegte Bitte des Hauptmanns muß schon aufgrund der 1.Pers. Sgl. von diesem selbst gesprochen sein. Auf redaktionelle Tätigkeit weist ferner der Einschub Lk 7,7a der nicht nur den Auftritt einer zweiten Gesandtschaft motiviert, sondern darüberhinaus auch die Aussage der ersten Delegation ('er ist würdig, ...' Lk 7,4b) mit der durch die zweiten Boten überbrachten Selbstaussage ('ich habe mich nicht für würdig gehalten, ...' Lk 7,7a) kontrastiert."

166-167: For ἄξιος, see Q 7:2̶, 3, 4̶-̶6̶a⁹ Luke = Q, Con (p. 177).

169: See Q 7:2̶, 3, 4̶-̶6̶a³ Luke = Q, Con (p. 114).

238: Reconstruction. For complete text see Q 7:1⁰ In Q (p. 15).

Dunderberg 1994, 85-89: See Q 7:2̶, 3, 4̶-̶6̶a³ Luke = Q, Con (p. 114-116).

Gagnon 1994a, 139: "Luke 7:7a (not paralleled in Matthew) itself provides the literary rationale both for the centurion not coming to Jesus in the first place ('I did not even consider myself worthy to come to you,' viz., to make the initial request for healing) and for sending the (Q) message by way of a second delegation."

140: "Verse 7a adds an ethical dimension to the religious and political elements already interjected: the humility of the centurion (vv. 6b, 7a). To be sure, the dialogue in Q already introduces the element of humility (v. 6a: 'I am not fit to have you enter under my roof'). But Luke intensified it by (1) framing the motif of humility against the background of the extraordinary praise for this Gentile by Jewish elders and (2) showing that the centurion did not even consider himself worthy of meeting Jesus, let alone Jesus come to him (v. 7a)."

Landis 1994, 11: "Der Satz in Lk 7,7a fehlt bei Mt. Er geht mit Sicherheit nicht auf Q zurück; denn erstens hängt er inhaltlich eng mit dem Einschub Lk 7,2-6b zusammen (es wird begründet, warum der Hauptmann nicht wie bei Mt/Q selber zu Jesus gekommen ist), und zweitens zeigen eine Reihe lk Sprachmerkmale, daß Lk als Verfasser anzusehen ist. Typisch lk sind: διό,[38] ἀξιόω[39] und die von ἀξιόω abhängige Infinitivkonstruktion.[40] Auch die übrigen Wendungen von 7,7a sind alle für Lk/Apg bezeugt, so daß der Zuweisung des Satzes an die lk Redaktion nichts entgegensteht."

11[38]: "Διό ist besonders häufig in der Apg."

11[39]: "Das Wort fehlt sonst bei den Synoptikern; zur für das NT einzigartigen Verwendung von ἀξιόω mit Reflexivpronomen vgl. die sinnverwandte Konstruktion in Apg 26,2."

11[40]: "Infinitivkonstruktionen werden von Lk gegenüber Nebensätzen mit ὅτι oder ἵνα bevorzugt."

11, 17: Reconstruction. For complete text see Q 7:1[6] Luke = Q, Pro (p. 57).

Meier 1994, 769[193]: See Q 7:6b-c[2] Luke = Q, Con (p. 255).

International Q Project 1995, 478: Reconstruction. For complete text see Q 7:1[0] In Q (p. 16).

Neirynck 1995, 180: See Q 7:~~2~~, 3, ~~4-6a~~[1] Luke = Q, Con (p. 70).

Tuckett 1996, 395: "Catchpole's discussion [1992, 528-532 (1993, 293-298)] about the LkR nature of Luke's extra verses in Luke 7:3-6a, 7a seems to me fully convincing."

Matt = Q: [ ][1]

Pro

Con

Gundry 1982, 143: "Because he omitted the sending of the friends, Matthew naturally drops the centurion's statement 'For this reason I did not even consider myself worthy to come to you' (Luke 7:7) and skips to 'but say a word.'"

Evaluations

Johnson 2000: Matt = Q {B}, []¹.

This variation unit is dependent upon the sending of the first delegation (Q 7:~~2~~, 3, ~~4-6a~~[3]) as it explains the centurion's initial behavior (Loisy). In its present position, it justifies the second delegation as well, serving almost as a *mea culpa* for the centurion's refusal to meet Jesus in person.

The vocabulary and style of the clause is Lukan (Patton, Schramm, Schulz, Marshall, Gagnon 1993). Luke's preference for variation of synonyms comes into play here. As observed previously (Q 7:~~2~~, 3, ~~4-6a~~[9]) with παῖς and δοῦλος, so ἱκανός is used here in material paralleled in Matthew (hence Q), while ἄξιος and ἀξιόω are found in the additional Lukan material (Martin), an indication of redactional expansion. The two uses of ἀξιο- connect the first speech, which explains the Jewish elders serving as proxies for a Gentile soldier (Luke 7:4), to the second rationale, which focuses more on the behavior of the centurion in refusing to meet Jesus (Held). To the objection that Luke is not in the habit of expanding upon sources, Siegman reminds us of Luke 7:18-21 par. Matt 11:23 (Q). One might also include Luke 9:57-62 par. Matt 8:19-22 (the latter two verses in Luke being rejected by the IQP as a Lukan addition).

Some arguments against Luke's reading must be rejected as inadequate. Jeremias suggests that all of the additional material in Luke is added to avoid the impact of Jesus' initial refusal to come (Matt 8:7). Yet, a simple change in sentence structure would have removed the ambiguity and negativity of Jesus' response (ἐλεύσομαι καί for ἐλθών). One must also be hesitant in suggesting that Luke draws on the Cornelius story in Acts 10 for the verbal content of Luke 7:1-10. The connections between the stories, thematic and lexical, are undeniable. But *how* Luke redactionally creates these connections must be worked out before arguing the influence of Acts 10 on Luke 7:1-10. Finally, I would take issue with the argument that the primary reason for the insertion of Luke 7:7a is merely to emphasize the centurion's humility (Creed, Manson, Delobel, Gagnon 1994a). The statement is almost a necessary justification in light of his sending yet another embassy in his place. Furthermore, it clarifies that, while he is worthy of Jesus' help, he is not worthy of meeting Jesus in person.

In spite of these corrections, the clause is Lukan in style and closely bound to other redactional additions of Luke.

Robinson 2000: Matt = Q {B}, []¹.
This is clearly, in vocabulary and in the flow of the presentation, a Lukan interpolation justifying the interpolation in Luke 7:6b-c of the delegation of friends, who make the centurion's speech for him.

Kloppenborg 2000: Matt = Q {B}, []¹.

Hoffmann 2001: Matt = Q {B}, []¹.

Q 7:7²: Matthew's μόνον.

Luke = Q: ἀλλὰ ( )² εἰπὲ λόγῳ

Pro

Con

Schulz 1972, 239: "Lk hat μόνον (so Mt) wohl gestrichen, weil ja der Hauptmann nach Lk den direkten Kontakt mit Jesus gar nicht sucht, sondern Jesus von Anfang an eine Fernheilung zutraut, das μόνον also nicht gerechtfertigt ist.⁴¹⁶"

239⁴¹⁶: "Beyer [1962, 126⁴] meint allerdings, das μόνον sei bei Mt gräzisierend hinzugefügt; richtig Schmid [1930, 254]."

Busse 1977, 148-149¹: "[149] In den V 7b-9 folgt Lk dem Wortlaut der Vorlage. Einzelne Veränderungen sind als stilistische Verdeutlichungen zu verstehen. So paßt μόνον nicht in das luk. Konzept ... und fällt deshalb aus."

Matt = Q: ἀλλὰ (μόνον)² εἰπὲ λόγῳ

Pro

von Harnack 1907, 91 (ET 1908, 131): Reconstruction. For complete text see Q 7:1⁶ Luke = Q, Pro (p. 55).

Castor 1912, 223: Reconstruction. For complete text see Q 7:1⁰ In Q (p. 6).

Lindars 1992, 210: Reconstruction. For complete text see Q 7:1⁶ Luke = Q, Pro (p. 56).

Merklein 1994, 100: "Das aus der Tradition entnommene 'Sprich nur ein Wort!' geht konform mit dem lukanischen Konzept."

Con

B. Weiß 1876, 229-230: "Bei Mtth. nur das μόνον (wie 5,47) und das ἀμήν (wie 5,26) zugesetzt sein [230] dürfte."

Hawkins 1899, 6: "Words and Phrases characteristic of St. Matthew's Gospel: ... μόνον."

B. Weiß 1908, 15²⁵: See Q 7:6b-c⁹ Luke = Q Con (p. 280).

15: Reconstruction. For complete text see Q 7:1⁰ In Q (p. 5).

Cadbury 1920, 200: "Twice in parallels with Matthew Luke has no equivalent for μόνον: Mt. 5,47 ἐὰν ἀσπάσησθε τοὺς ἀδελφοὺς μόνον—Lk. 6,33 ἐὰν

ἀγαθοποιῆτε τοὺς ἀγαθοποιοῦντας ὑμᾶς (Q); Mt. 8,9 ἀλλὰ μόνον εἰπὲ λόγῳ—
Lk. 7,7 ἀλλὰ εἰπὲ λόγῳ (Q). ...

"Yet it is just as likely, or more so, that here [Matt 5:47; but by implication,
Matt 8:9 as well] Matthew added μόνον to the text of Q, as he three times
inserts μόνον in passages taken from Mark."

Lagrange 1923, 165: "La conviction est exprimée encore plus fortement
que dans Lc. par l'addition de μόνον et l'emploi du futur au lieu du subjonctif."

Easton 1926, 97: "'Only' would have appealed to Luke, had he read it."

Crum 1927, 138: Reconstruction. For complete text see Q 7:2, 3, 4-6a[1]
Luke = Q, Pro (pp. 71-72).

Schmid 1930, 254: "Zusatz des Mt ist zweifellos μόνον (V 8)."

Manson 1937, 64: "The word 'only' in Mt. 8:8 is editorial: cf. Mk. 2:26,
Mt. 12:4; Mk. 11:13, Mt. 21:19; Mk. 13:32, Mt. 24:36."

Delobel 1966, 455: "Μόνον peut-être ajouté par *Mt.*"

Lange 1973, 49: "Weiter ist zu erwähnen, daß Mattäus dem ἀλλὰ εἰπὲ
λόγῳ (Lk 7,7 Q) ein μόνον einfügt (Mt 8,8)."

Marshall 1978, 281: "After ἀλλά Matthew adds μόνον (so also Mt. 12:4;
21:19; 24:36 diff. Mk.)."

Martin 1978, 16: "Certain amplifications in Matthew contribute to the
purpose of this evangelist. For instance, he adds μόνον to Q's ἀλλὰ εἰπὲ λόγῳ,
and so emphasizes the importance of the Gentile's confidence in the mere
utterance of Jesus."

18: "Chiefly by [Matthew's] accentuation of faith in Jesus' naked word and
by his addition of the universalistic verses 11 and 12 he is a champion of the
Pauline gospel. ... We may remark on the way in which his addition of μόνον
and his conclusion at verse 10 correspond to the Pauline *sola fide.*"

Polag 1979, 38: Reconstruction. For complete text see Q 7:1[0] In Q (pp. 9-10).

Schenk 1981, 37: Reconstruction. For complete text see Q 7:1[0] In Q (p. 10).

Gundry 1982, 143: "Typically, [Matthew] inserts μόνον (7,0). This implies
that Jesus' authority needs only a little exercise for accomplishment of the
healing."

Dauer 1984, 86: "Μόνον ist mt Zusatz; vgl. außer a.u.St. noch Mt 9,21
(add Mk 5,28); 14,36 (add Mk 6,56); 21,19 (add Mk 11,13); ferner 5,47
und 21,21. Der Evangelist will durch das zusätzliche 'nur' die Wirk-
mächtigkeit des Wortes Jesu unterstreichen."

Wegner 1985, 207: "Liegt schon von der Stat her eine mt Red nahe, so
wird dies um so wahrscheinlicher, sobald man das adverbiale μόνον isoliert
betrachtet. Es erscheint nämlich 2x in Mk (5,36 und 6,8), 1x in Lk (8,50 par
Mk 5,36), 8x in Apg (8,16; 11,19; 18,25; 19,26f; 21,13; 26,29 und 27,10)
und 7x in Mt. Von diesen 7 Belegen innerhalb des ersten Ev gehören 2 zu

QMt (5,47 und 8,8), alle fünf anderen werden aber von Mt in seinen Mk-Stoff red hinzugefügt: vgl. Mt 9,21; 10,42; 14,36 und 21,19.21. Der Befund zeigt deutlich, daß das adverbiale μόνον auSt mit hoher Wahrscheinlichkeit aus der Hand des ersten Evangelisten stammt und kaum als urspr Q-Wort gedeutet werden kann, das Lk sek gestrichen hätte."

270: Reconstruction. For complete text see Q 7:1⁰ In Q (pp. 11-12).

Schenk 1987, 365: "Die pleonastische Verwendung des Adv. *nur* im Ausnahmesatz (nach εἰ μή) wurde Mt 21,19 (=Mk 6,8 permutiert) übernommen, doch bei Mk 5,36 ausgelassen; 21,21 (+Mk οὐ μ.—ἀλλὰ καί) wurde es dem Jesuswort ebenso gräz. unsemit. ... zugesetzt wie bei der Bitte des Centurio 8,8 (+Q οὐ—ἀλλὰ μ.)."

Luz 1990, 12⁴: "Matthäismen ... sind: ἀποκριθεὶς δέ, μόνον."

Luz 1990, ET 2001, 8⁴: "Mattheisms are: ἀποκριθεὶς δέ, μόνον."

Davies and Allison 1991, 23: "Luke does not have μόνον, an adverb which Matthew inserts to emphasize the ease with which Jesus exercises his power."

Catchpole 1992, 532 [1993, 298]: "It is theoretically possible to defend Matthew's μόνον, and to explain its absence from Luke, on the ground that in Luke's version, where the expectation is from the outset that a healing would take place at a distance, it would not be needed. But (i) in Luke the centurion only expects Jesus to heal from a distance from the time of the second delegation onwards, and μόνον would be wholly appropriate within a contrast between Jesus' *coming* to heal (v. 3) and his *speaking* to that effect (v. 7b); (ii) in contexts where a μόνος reference is appropriate Luke will insert it,⁶¹ so it would be odd for him to drop it here where it is so obviously useful and emphatic; (iii) MattR insertions are well attested.⁶²"

532 [298]⁶¹: "See Luke 5,21; 6,4; 9,18."

532 [299]⁶²: "See Matt 12,4; 18,15; 24,36."

533 [299]: Reconstruction. For complete text see Q 7:1⁰ In Q (p. 14).

Sevenich-Bax 1993, 181-182: "Die Zusetzung des adverbialen 'μόνον' ist mit großer Wahrscheinlichkeit auf Matthäus zurückzuführen: 'μόνον' ist im Matthäus-Evangelium siebenmal belegt (Mkev: zweimal; Lkev: einmal). Dabei fällt auf, daß Matthäus das Adverb an keiner Stelle einfach aus der Tradition übernimmt: Entweder wird das Adverb permutiert (vgl. etwa Mk 5,36—dort ausgelassen—mit Mt 9,21) oder es wird gegen seine Vorlage redaktionell zugesetzt (Mt 10,42 diff. Mk 9,41; Mt 14,36 diff. Mk 6,56; Mt 21,19 diff. Mk 11,13; Mt 21,21 [add. Mk 11,23]). Die beiden übrigen Belege finden sich in dem von Matthäus überlieferten Q-Stoff. [182] Dabei wurde in bezug auf μόνον auch schon für Mt 5,47 (diff. Lk 6,33) redaktionelle Tätigkeit vermutet. Da Lukas das Adverb nicht vermeidet (er hat es 8,50 = Mk 5,36 übernommen und bietet es darüberhinaus achtmal in der Apg), muß auch an dieser Stelle mit matthäischer Redaktion gerechnet werden."

238: Reconstruction. For complete text see Q 7:1⁰ In Q (p. 15).

Gagnon 1994b, 138: "As for Matthean alterations of the core dialogue in Q, we can probably attribute to him … the addition of μόνον in 8.8.¹⁹"

138¹⁹: "Matthew inserts the word five times into Markan material (9.21; 10.42; 14.36; 21.19, 21) and apparently once more into Q material (5.47). By adding the word in 8.8, Matthew sharpens the picture of the centurion's faith as well as the reader's estimate of Jesus' authority."

Landis 1994, 11: "Μόνον ist wahrscheinlich redaktioneller Zusatz des Mt; dieses Adverb ist nämlich ein ausgesprochenes Vorzugswort des ersten Evangelisten, das er gerne in seine Vorlagen einfügt."

11, 17: Reconstruction. For complete text see Q 7:1⁶ Luke = Q, Pro (p. 57).

International Q Project 1995, 478: Reconstruction. For complete text see Q 7:1⁰ In Q (p. 16).

Evaluations

Johnson 2000: Luke = Q {B}, ἀλλὰ ()² εἰπὲ λόγῳ.

It is not clear why Luke would omit μόνον from Q (cf. Schulz, Busse) since it emphasizes the centurion's faith in Jesus' word. This is especially problematic in light of the centurion having just changed his mind about having Jesus come to him (Easton, Catchpole). Luke is not averse to inserting μόνον for emphasis (Catchpole).

The interpolation of μόνον is, however, typical of Matthew (Cadbury, Manson, Wegner). It also fits with the change of the 2ⁿᵈ person imperative ἰαθήτω to the future indicative ἰαθήσεται (Q 7:7³); these two alterations change the centurion's plea to a statement of faith.

Robinson 2000: Luke = Q {C}, ἀλλὰ ⟦()²⟧ εἰπὲ λόγῳ.

The fact that Matthew adds the adverb 5 times to Mark (Matt 9:21; 10:42; 14:36; 21:19, 21) makes it probable that he does here as well (Wegner, 207).

Kloppenborg 2000: Luke = Q {C}, ἀλλὰ ⟦()²⟧ εἰπὲ λόγῳ.

Hoffmann 2001: Luke = Q {C}, ἀλλὰ ⟦()²⟧ εἰπὲ λόγῳ.

Q 7:7³: Luke's ἰαθήτω or Matthew's ἰαθήσεται.

Luke = Q: καὶ [ἰαθήτω]³ ὁ παῖς μου.

Pro

Lagrange 1923, 165: See Lagrange at Matt = Q, Con (p. 301).
Marshall 1978, 281: "The use of a second imperative (softened to a fut. indic. in Mt. and some MSS of Lk. ...) is equivalent to a conditional sentence, and, although it is possible in Classical Greek ([BDF (BDR) §]442.2), it may reflect a Hebrew or Aramaic construction."

Con

B. Weiß 1876, 229: "Bem. nur die vereinfachte Stellung des εἰμί und μου v. 6, das dem εἰπέ conformirte ἰαθήτω v. 7."
J. Weiß 1892, 400: "V. 7 ist natürlich von Lk in den Bericht von Q eingeschoben. ... ἰαθήτω) ist kräftiger als das Fut. des Mt."
Holtzmann 1901, 344: "Durch 7,3 veranlaßter, übrigens gleichfalls zur Hervorhebung der Demuth dienender, Zusatz liegt (7,7) vor in διὸ οὐδὲ κτλ., ... wo auch statt ἰαθήσεται Mt 8,8 das dem εἰπέ conformirte ἰαθήτω steht: *so werde er geheilt.*"
Klostermann 1919, 449: "Für die Modifikation ... ferner: ἰαθήτω für ἰαθήσεται."
Easton 1926, 97: "The mood of ἰαθήτω is conformed ... to εἰπέ."
Delobel 1966, 455: "Μόνον peut être ajouté par *Mt.*, tandis que l'impératif ἰαθήτω (diff *Mt*) est en accord avec toute une série d'impératifs dans cette section[162]."
455[162]: "Μὴ σκύλλου (réd!), εἶπε, πορεύθητι, ἔρχου, ποίησον."
George 1972, 71[11]: "En Lc 7,7, l'impératif *iathèto* semble une retouche du future *iathésétai* de Mt 8,8 pour uniformiser avec l'impératif précédent *eipé*."
Polag 1979, 38: Reconstruction. For complete text see Q 7:1⁰ In Q (pp. 9-10).
Schenk 1981, 37: Reconstruction. For complete text see Q 7:1⁰ In Q (p. 10).
Sevenich-Bax 1993, 182: "Lukas hat allerdings die futurische Aussage seiner Vorlage (vgl. Mt) in den Imperativ Aorist gesetzt. ...
"β) 'Im Rahmen ntl. Konditionalsätze, die unter semitischem Einfluß stehen, ist die Konstruktion Imp. + καί + fut. bei weitem häufiger angewendet als die Konstruktion Imp + καί + Imp [Wegner 1985, 207 (also 207³⁷)].' Die erstgenannte Struktur läßt sich im übrigen häufiger in der Logienquelle beob-

achten (vgl. etwa Lk 6,27f.35 par.; deutlicher Lk 6,37.38a par.; Lk 11,9//Mt 7,7 u.ä.; In einem weiteren Sinn könnte man auch die Seligpreisungen hierher rechnen). Auch dies spricht zugunsten der matthäischen Fassung.

"γ) Der von Lukas gesetzte Imperativ könnte unter Einfluß des vorangehenden Imperativs (εἰπέ) entstanden sein."

Matt = Q: καὶ (ἰαθήσεται)³ ὁ παῖς μου.

Pro

von Harnack 1907, 91 (ET 1908, 131): Reconstruction. For complete text see Q 7:1⁶ Luke = Q, Pro (p. 55).

B. Weiß 1908, 15: Reconstruction. For complete text see Q 7:1⁰ In Q (p. 5).

Castor 1912, 223: Reconstruction. For complete text see Q 7:1⁰ In Q (p. 6).

Crum 1927, 138: Reconstruction. For complete text see Q 7:~~2~~, 3, ~~4-6a~~¹ Luke = Q, Pro (pp. 71-72).

George 1972, 71¹¹: See George at Luke = Q, Con (p. 299).

Polag 1979, 38: Reconstruction. For complete text see Q 7:1⁰ In Q (pp. 9-10).

Schenk 1981, 37: Reconstruction. For complete text see Q 7:1⁰ In Q (p. 10).

Wegner 1985, 207-208: "Folgende Gründe scheinen uns jedoch für die Ursprünglichkeit des mt ἰαθήσεται zu sprechen: 1. Im Rahmen ntl. Konditionalsätze, die unter semitischem Einfluß stehen, ist die Konstruktion Imp. + καὶ + Fut. bei weitem häufiger angewendet als die Konstruktion Imp + καὶ + Imp. 2. Der bei Lk begegnende Imp. ἰαθήτω könnte unter dem Einfluß des vorangehenden Imp. εἰπέ entstanden sein. 3. Mt, der innerhalb seines Ev den Parallelismus membrorum mehrfach [208] verwendet, würde schwerlich eine ihm vorgegebene Parallelisierung—in unserem Falle durch zwei Imp.—sek von sich aus auflösen.

"Aus den erwähnten Gründen halten wir das von Mt im Fut. gegebene ἰαθήσεται für die urspr Q-Lesart."

270: Reconstruction. For complete text see Q 7:1⁰ In Q (pp. 11-12).

Catchpole 1992, 532 [1993, 299]: "Matthew's ἰαθήσεται is probably more original than Luke's ἰαθήτω: the latter fits the fact that now for the first time the centurion himself 'speaks' and voices his plea, but Matthew's verb form matches the following verbs πορεύεται, ἔρχεται, and ποιεῖ, which comment upon it."

533 [299]: Reconstruction. For complete text see Q 7:1⁰ In Q (p. 14).

Lindars 1992, 210: Reconstruction. For complete text see Q 7:1⁶ Luke = Q, Pro (p. 56).

Sevenich-Bax 1993, 182: 238: Reconstruction. For complete text see Q 7:1⁰ In Q (p. 15).

Landis 1994, 11: "Bei den unterschiedlichen Formen von ἰάομαι sprechen folgende Gründe für die Ursprünglichkeit des mt ἰαθήσεται: erstens ist der lk Imperativ ἰαθήτω möglicherweise unter dem Einfluß des vorangehenden εἰπέ entstanden; und zweitens hätte Mt den—bei ihm beliebten—Parallelismus membrorum wohl übernommen, wenn er ihm bereits vorgelegen hätte."

11, 17: Reconstruction. For complete text see Q 7:1⁶ Luke = Q, Pro (p. 57).

International Q Project 1995, 478: Reconstruction. For complete text see Q 7:1⁰ In Q (p. 16).

Con

Lagrange 1923, 165: "La conviction est exprimée encore plus fortement que dans Lc. par l'addition de μόνον et l'emploi du futur au lieu du subjonctif."

Gundry 1982, 143: "'And let my servant be healed' (so Luke) becomes the confident prediction 'and my servant will be healed.' Thus the emphasis [in Matthew] stays on Jesus' authoritative word, which will effect the healing."

Gagnon 1994b, 138: "As for Matthean alterations of the core dialogue in Q, we can probably attribute to him ... the transformation of the third person imperative ἰαθήτω to the future indicative ἰαθήσεται in 8.8.²⁰"

138²⁰: "*Contra* Wegner [1985, 207-208], note that Matthew elsewhere employs the future indicative as a replacement for another Markan form (Matt 20.26; 21.3); and that in the closest parallel to our passage (Luke 8.50, the story of Jairus) Luke adds the future passive καὶ σωθήσεται (not the third-person imperative) to Mark's imperative μόνον πίστευσον. Matthew's alteration puts stress on the centurion's firm conviction/faith in Jesus' power to heal."

Evaluations

Robinson 2000: Luke = Q {C}, καὶ [[ἰαθήτω]³] ὁ παῖς μου.

Jeremias makes it clear that Luke's passive use of the deponent is for him rare (4 out of 15 times), suggesting (as he does) that it is traditional; i.e., from Q.

Gagnon appeals to Luke 8:50 σωθήσεται to argue that Lukan style would have favored a future, and so its absence in Luke indicates it was not in Luke's source, Q. But Luke 8:50 does not really apply. Luke 8:50 uses the future in Jesus' statement that the child will be healed; it would not be appropriate for Jesus to say in the imperative: "Do not fear, only believe, and let him be healed." But in the present text it is fitting for the centurion to use two imperatives, "Say the word and let my boy be healed." Thus Luke 8:50 does not argue against Lukan style here and, hence, for redaction.

Wegner points out that Matthew is less likely to have eliminated the parallelism of two imperatives. Luke could have added it redactionally under the influence of the immediately preceding imperative εἰπέ. But the parallelism is subtle and in itself not compelling as an argument.

Matthew could have deferred the imperative for the climactic saying of Jesus (Matt 8:13), which is for him a standard conclusion (Matt 15:28). The language is performatory, effecting what it commands. Hence Matthew's future points toward this coming event, rather than letting the centurion anticipate it, as if the centurion's imperative could effect anything.

Kloppenborg 2000: Luke = Q {C}, καὶ [[ἰαθήτω]³]] ὁ παῖς μου.

Hoffmann 2000: Luke = Q {C}, καὶ [[ἰαθήτω]³]] ὁ παῖς μου.

Die Entscheidung ist nicht leicht, sie wird in der Diskussion aber—unnötig—verkompliziert. Es geht um die Frage: "futurischer Indikativ oder Imperativ". Wegner setzt richtig bei dem semitischen Sprachhintergrund an, allerdings mit falscher Konsequenz. Mit seinem den Ausschlag gebenden Argument, daß Matthäus schwerlich eine "vorgegebene Parallelisierung—in unseren Fall durch zwei Imperative—sekundär von sich auflösen würde", überinterpretiert er Lk 7,7. Denn die zwei Imperative lassen sich formal kaum als Parallelismus verstehen. Wegner bezieht sich in seinen Überlegungen auf K. Beyer (1962, 252; vgl. auch BDR [BDF] §442.7 Anm. 7).

Nach diesem ist die "Folge Imperativ-Futurum... wörtlich genommen sinnlos, da an eine Aufforderung nicht ein zukünftiges Ereignis logisch bruchlos angeschlossen werden kann". Vorauszusetzen ist hier eine im Semitischen ursprünglich konjunktionslose hypotaktische Konstruktion, in der der Imperativ die Stelle des bedingenden Satzes einnimmt (Beyer, 240). Im Hebräischen erscheint entsprechend dieser Verbindung von Imperativ und Futur "manchmal im Nachsatz syndetisches Kurzimperfekt (Jussiv), häufiger Kohortativ oder sogar ein zweiter Imperativ, und auch im Aramäischen wird gelegentlich das Partizip des Nachsatzes dem vorangehenden Imperativ als Imperfekt oder Imperativ angeglichen" (ebd. 140, Beispiele 241-251). Solche Verwendung des Imperativs (mit einem folgenden Futur) findet sich auch im Griechischen, allerdings weit seltener als im Semitischen (ebd. 251f: mit Beispielen. Vgl. dazu aber K-G I, 237: "Wie im Deutschen und Lat. wird oft der Imperativ auf nachdrückliche Weise st[att] eines hypothetischen Vordersatzes gebraucht; der zweite Satz wird dann gewöhnlich durch καί angereiht", und BDR [BDF] §442.2 "καί consecutivum... besonders nach Imperativen das Futur verbindend [klass.]").

Von den Synoptikern ist die konjunktionslose Konstruktion öfters in eine konjunktionale umgewandelt worden, häufig in einen Finalsatz (Beyer, ebd. 253f). Ausgesprochen semitisch sind nach Beyer jene Fälle, wo der Imperativ uneigentlich gemeint ist (z.B. Joh 2,19). "An den übrigen Stellen rät der Imperativ zugleich zur Ausführung, sei es, daß er mehr einen allgemeinen Rat, sei es, daß er (weniger typisch semitisch) einen konkreten Befehl gibt." (ebd.)

Für die Umschreibung eines konditionalen Verhältnisses mit zwei syndetischen Imperativen (wie bei Lukas) bringt Beyer (ebd. 253) nur drei Beispiele aus dem Johannesevangelium (1,46 = 11,34; 7,52). Nach Beyer (252²) könnte der doppelte Imperativ in Lk 7,7 "als zu wörtliche Übersetzung eines hebr. (aber nicht aus LXX) oder aram. dem vorangehenden Imperativ assimilierten Futurums" verstanden werden. "Doch ist wahrscheinlich, besonders bei Annahme einer aram. Vorlage, ..." ein konjunktionsloser hypotaktischer Finalsatz gemeint: "daß er geheilt werde". Beyer verweist in dieser Anmerkung auch auf Mk 8,34, wo sich der letzte Imperativ καὶ ἀκολουθείτω μοι in analoger Weise verstehen ließe: "Als Nachsatz zu den beiden vorangehenden Jussiven ("so wird er mir nachfolgen") kann der Jussiv καὶ ἀκολουθείτω μοι allerdings vom Sem. her auch verstanden werden" (ebd. S. 227² mit Verweis auf S. 240 und S. 252²). Schon Klostermann hat in seinem Markuskommentar (1950, 84) zu dem letzten Imperativ in Mk 8,34 vermerkt: "nicht eine dritte Voraussetzung, sondern die ersten beiden Imperative sind konditional, darauf folgt nach semitischer Art 'als Apodosis wiederum ein Imperativ oder Jussiv' [Zitat unbekannter Herkunft]". Sowohl Matthäus als auch Lukas übernehmen diese Konstruktion.

Werten wir Beyers Belegmaterial zu der im Neuen Testament häufig begegnenden Konstruktion Imperativ + Futur für die synoptische Überlieferung aus, so ergibt sich folgendes Bild:

Die Konstruktion findet sich in Q: Q 6,35c (falls man gegen das IQP Lukas folgt. Hat Matthäus durch ὅπως korrigiert?); 6,37 (diff. Mt 7,1: ἵνα); 10,5f (diff. Mt 10,12f, der hier zwei Imperative hat!); 11,9 (3x); 11,41 (Lukas ἐστίν, Mt 23,26: ἵνα); 12,31. So auch: Q 6,42b.

Die Konstruktion findet sich in matthäischen Sonderüberlieferungen: Mt 6,6.17f; 11,28.29; 17,27; 18,26.29; 20,4. Matthäus bildet die Konstruktion: Mt 27,42 (diff. Mk 15,32: ἵνα). Er übernimmt sie aus Markus: Mt 19,21 (par. Mk 10,21); 21,2 (par. Mk 11,2). Er ändert sie in der Markusvorlage: Mt 21,22 (diff. Mk 11,24); 21,24 (diff. Mk 11,29); 21,38 (diff. Mk 12,7); 26,18a (diff. Mk 14,13); 26,18b (diff. Mk 14,14f). Mk 6,22 übergeht Matthäus (vgl. 14,7).

Lukas bildet die Konstruktion: 6,35.37bc.38a; 8,50; 10,28; 14,13f; Apg 9,6; 16,31; 21,24. Er übernimmt sie aus Markus: Lk 18,22 (par. Mk 10,21); 19,30 (par. Mk 11,2); 22,11f (par. Mk 14,14f). Er ändert sie in der Markusvorlage: 19,30 (diff. Mk 11,2); 20,3 (diff. Mk 11,29); 20,14 (ἵνα diff. Mk 12,7); 22,10 (diff. 14,13).

Die Übersicht zeigt, daß die Konstruktion Imperativ + Futur allen drei Synoptikern sowie auch Q vertraut ist. Matthäus und Lukas folgen ihr in vielen Fällen, gelegentlich ändern sie diese griechischem Sprachempfinden folgend oder bilden sie selbst um. Für Mt 10,8 ergibt sich daraus, daß Matthäus die Konstruktion gebildet, aber auch übernommen haben kann. Andererseits hätte Lukas mit ihr keine Probleme gehabt, falls er sie in Q vorgefunden hätte. Das gleiche gilt nicht für die Konstruktion Imperativ + Imperativ, die in Lk 7,7 vorliegt. Sie ist offensichtlich seltener belegt. Aus Mk 8,34 übernehmen sie Matthäus und Lukas, in Mt 10, 12f findet sie sich 2mal bei Matthäus (aus Q? So das IQP und die Crit. Ed.). Hat sie Lukas in 7,7 gebildet? Oder hat Matthäus korrigiert?

Ist Beyer mit seiner Sprachanalyse im Recht, dann geht im NT, speziell in den Evangelien, die häufige Verwendung der Konstruktion Imperativ + Futur sowie auch die seltenere Verwendung der Konstruktion Imperativ + Imperativ auf semitischen Spracheinfluß zurück. Für die Konstruktion Imperativ (konditional verstanden) + Imperativ gibt es jedoch auch im griechischen Entsprechungen. Das vermag die relative Häufigkeit dieser semitisierenden Konstruktion in der griechischsprachigen Jesustradition zu erklären. Zugleich zeigt sich aber auch deutlich der Trend, diese "konjunktionslose Hypotaxe" im Sinne griechischen Sprachempfindens zu präzisieren, indem die konditionale oder finale Bedeutung durch eine entsprechende Konstruktion explizit gemacht wird (Konditionalsatz, Finalsatz, Partizip). Angesichts dieses Trends erklärt sich das relativ seltene Vorkommen des sprachlich noch ungewöhnlicheren doppelten Imperativs.

Auf unsere Stelle angewandt bedeutet dies: Matthäus hat wahrscheinlich einen ihm in Q vorgegebenen doppelten Imperativ in den in der synoptischen Sprachtradition und auch in Q üblicheren Imperativ + Futur geändert. Daß Lukas eine Konstruktion Imperativ + Futur in einen doppelten Imperativ abänderte, ist angesichts seines Umgangs mit jener Konstruktion und angesichts des erkennbaren gräzisierenden Gesamttrends in der Überlieferung höchst unwahrscheinlich.

Johnson 2001: Luke = Q {B}, καὶ [ἰαθήτω]³ ὁ παῖς μου.

Robinson and Hoffmann expose the weaknesses of several arguments against Luke's imperative that appear in the database (cf. Jeremias, Wegner [Sevenich-Bax]). It should be added that Delobel's argument compares apples and oranges. Luke's 2nd person imperative does not function in the same way as the previous prohibition (μὴ σκύλλου, which is probably Lukan) and subsequent 3rd person imperatives (πορεύθητι, ἔρχου, ποίησον), and so is probably not due to their influence. It functions as part of a plea, not a command, to Jesus.

For this reason, Marshall is not quite accurate in seeing Matthew's future as a softening to a conditional. On the contrary, the conviction of the centurion's faith is sharpened by this and the addition of μόνον (Lagrange, Gagnon 1994b). What in Q was a plea based on faith becomes in Matthew a statement of faith.

Q 7:8

Matt 8:9	Q 7:8	Luke 7:8
καὶ γὰρ ἐγὼ ἄνθρωπός εἰμι ὑπὸ ἐξουσίαν [ ]¹, ἔχων ὑπ' ἐμαυτὸν στρατιώτας, καὶ λέγω τούτῳ· πορεύθητι, καὶ πορεύεται, καὶ ἄλλῳ· ἔρχου, καὶ ἔρχεται, καὶ τῷ δούλῳ μου· ποίησον τοῦτο, καὶ ποιεῖ.	καὶ γὰρ ἐγὼ ἄνθρωπός εἰμι ὑπὸ ἐξουσίαν []¹, ἔχων ὑπ' ἐμαυτὸν στρατιώτας, καὶ λέγω τούτῳ· πορεύθητι, καὶ πορεύεται, καὶ ἄλλῳ· ἔρχου, καὶ ἔρχεται, καὶ τῷ δούλῳ μου· ποίησον τοῦτο, καὶ ποιεῖ.	καὶ γὰρ ἐγὼ ἄνθρωπός εἰμι ὑπὸ ἐξουσίαν [τασσόμενος]¹ ἔχων ὑπ' ἐμαυτὸν στρατιώτας, καὶ λέγω τούτῳ· πορεύθητι, καὶ πορεύεται, καὶ ἄλλῳ· ἔρχου, καὶ ἔρχεται, καὶ τῷ δούλῳ μου· ποίησον τοῦτο, καὶ ποιεῖ.

¹ Luke's τασσόμενος.

Q 7:8¹: Luke's τασσόμενος.

Luke = Q: [τασσόμενος]¹

Pro

Gundry 1982, 144: See Gundry at Matt = Q, Con (p. 311).

Allison 1997, 10: "In asking Jesus to perform a miracle the centurion lays claim to his own authority, albeit in words that are difficult to understand: 'I also am a man set under authority, ... with soldiers under me.'"

Con

B. Weiß 1876, 229: "Bem. nur ... die Hinzufügung des erläuternden τασσόμενος in v. 8."

Wernle 1899, 65: "Das τασσόμενος v. 8 ist Erleichterung des εἰμι ὑπ' ἐξουσίαν."

von Harnack 1907, 56: "Bemerkt sei nur, daß ἔντιμος (v. 2), ... das Pass. τάσσεσθαι (v. 8) in den Evangelien ausschließlich lukanisch sind."

91: Reconstruction. For complete text see Q 7:1⁶ Luke = Q, Pro (p. 55).

von Harnack 1907, ET 1908, 76-77: "I would only remark that ἔντιμος (verse 2) ... [and] the passive τάσσεσθαι (verse 8) are, as far as the gospels [77] are concerned, exclusively Lukan."

131: Reconstruction. For complete text see Q 7:1⁶ Luke = Q, Pro (p. 55).

B. Weiß 1907, 243¹ "Τασσόμενος [ist vom Lk] erläuternd hinzugesetzt."

B. Weiß 1908, 15: Reconstruction. For complete text see Q 7:1⁰ In Q (p. 5).

Castor 1912, 223: Reconstruction. For complete text see Q 7:1⁰ In Q (p. 6).

Patton 1915, 144: "But there are also three such Lucan words in the two following verses, where the story of Luke runs quite closely parallel to that of Matthew (διό, ἠξίωσα, τασσόμενος).

Klostermann 1919, 449: "Für die Modifikation ... ferner: ἰαθήτω für ἰαθήσεται, ... bei gleicher Bedeutung, vgl. zu Mc 8,34, und verdeutlichend τασσόμενος in v.8."

Cadbury 1920, 149: "Note the addition of the participles in the following cases: ... Mt. 8,9 ἄνθρωπός εἰμι ὑπὸ ἐξουσίαν; Lk. 7,8 adds τασσόμενος."

Easton 1926, 97: "Mt does not seem to have written τασσόμενος (despite B ℵ al), and τάσσειν belongs to Lk's vocabulary."

Crum 1927, 138: Reconstruction. For complete text see Q 7:~~2~~, 3, ~~4-6a~~¹ Luke = Q, Pro (pp. 71-72).

Klostermann 1929, 87: "Τασσόμενος (nicht im Mt): sprachlich besser."

Manson 1937, 64-65: "The words 'for I also am a man set under authority' are difficult; for the centurion goes on at once to say that he has men under him to whom he gives orders, whereas the opening phrase means one who [65] receives orders. Torrey [1933, 292] tries to get over the difficulty by supposing that the word 'set' is a misrendering of an Aramaic original, and that the true rendering would be something like 'exercising authority.' This is not convincing, because the word 'set' occurs only in Lk. Another and perhaps more likely explanation is that there has been confusion of the two senses of the Aramaic preposition *teḥōth*. This word means both 'under' and 'in place of.' What the centurion really said was, 'I am the representative of the government' or 'the deputy of the commander-in-chief.' This makes sense with what follows and also makes clear the analogy between the centurion's position and that of Jesus."

Zuntz 1945, 187-188: "In Luke's version the notion of ἐξουσία plays no part whatever. Like those editors who altered the text of Matthew on his model, Luke appears to have disliked the idea of any human being putting his authority on a level with that of Jesus and therefore seems to have put the applicant 'under authority' and, consequently, to have 'demoted' him. He transformed the dignified representative of secular authority into a pattern of that abject self-deprecation by which, in his view, a pagan could alone deserve the Saviour's condescension. Even so he felt that a great deal of excuse and intercession [188] by righteous Jews was needed. Consequently, something very near to flattery ('not even in Israel …') takes the place, in Luke vii. 9, of the threat of judgement against the unbelieving 'sons of the Kingdom' in Matt. viii. 10ff. The *centurion's* admission that he is only a subaltern (ὑπὸ ἐξουσίαν τασσόμενος) suits this revised picture. Luke did not bother to remove the incongruity caused by his taking over unchanged all the rest of the officer's words."

Schürmann 1955, 37: "Jedenfalls können diese beiden seltenen Stellen [Luke 23:38; 24:44] nicht aufkommen gegen die andern Fälle, in denen Luk in der gewöhnlichen Aussage eine fehlende Kopula irgendwie ergänzt: eine Form von εἶναι …; andere Verben auch Lk 3,22; 9,8.19; 20,24; 22,42 P; 23,50 P diff Mk; vgl. Lk 7,8 diff Mt."

Lohmeyer 1956, 158¹: "Lk fügt τασσόμενος hinzu, vgl. Diod. Sic. p. 210B: οὐκ ἦσαν ὑπὸ μίαν ἡγεμονίαν τεταγμένοι."

Jeremias 1960, 148: "Weglassung der Kopula aber ist nicht lukanischer Stil, vielmehr pflegt Lukas ein Verbum hinzuzufügen, wenn die Kopula in seiner Vorlage fehlte; in vier Fällen läßt sich das sicher nachweisen, in vier weiteren durch synoptischen Vergleich wahrscheinlich machen.⁵"

148⁵: "Lk. 3,22; 7,25; 17,35; 22,42 verglichen mit den synoptischen Parallelen. H. Schürmann [1955, 37] rechnet noch vier weitere Fälle (Lk. 6,3; 7,8; 22,3; 23,50) hierher, in denen bei Lukas ein Partizip ergänzt ist."

Jeremias 1960, FT 1972, 184: "L'omission de la copule toutefois n'est pas dans la manière de Luc; bien au contraire, Luc a l'habitude d'ajouter un verbe, si la copule fait défaut dans le document qu'il utilise. On peut le démontrer avec certitude dans quatre cas et avec probabilité dans quatre autres cas moyennant la comparaison avec les synoptiques.⁹⁰"

184⁹⁰: "Lc 3,22; 7,25; 17,35; 22,42 comparés avec les parallèles synoptiques. H. Schürmann [1955, 37] ajoute encore quatre autres cas (Lc 6,3; 7,8; 22,3; 23,50) où un participe est complété chez Luc."

Schlatter 1960, 493: "L. glättet, indem er beifügt τασσόμενος."

Delobel 1966, 455: "L'addition de τασσόμενος au v. 8 peut-être une troisième indication de l'effort de Luc pour montrer l'humilité du centurion."

Schnider and Stenger 1971, 58²: "Kleine Veränderungen, wie z. B. die Hinzufügung des Lukas τασσόμενος hinter ὑπὸ ἐξουσίαν (Lk 7,8) können das [wörtliche Übereinstimmung mit Matthäus] nicht verwischen."

George 1972, 71: "Mt 8,8-9 ne diffère guère de Lc 7,6b-8 que par les traits propres à ce dernier (l'envoi des amis en 7,6b, l'explication de l'absence du centurion en 7,7a) et par quelques différences de rédaction qui semblent dues à Luc¹¹."

71¹¹: "En Lc 7,8 le complément *hyp' exousian* est commandé par le participe *tassoménos*, absent de Mt 8,9."

Schulz 1972, 239: "Lk wird τασσόμενος verdeutlichend hinzugefügt haben,⁴¹⁷ da eine Streichung durch Mt unwahrscheinlich ist.⁴¹⁸"

239⁴¹⁷: "Lk fügt gerne ein Verb ein, wenn die Kopula in seiner Vorlage fehlt (3,22; 7,25; 17,35; 22,42; ein Partizip ist ergänzt in Lk 6,3; 22,3; 23,50)."

239⁴¹⁸: "Τάσσειν Ev nur hier; Apg 4mal; fehlt bei Mk; 1mal bei Mt)."

Busse 1977, 144: "In V 8 ergänzt Lukas τασσόμενος, das die Unterordnung des Hauptmannes noch stärker unterstreicht."

148-149¹: "[149] Dafür sind in V 8 τασσόμενος (Lk liebt den Einbau von Partizipien), in V 9 ταῦτα, αὐτὸν καὶ στραφείς ... und ὄχλος Verdeutlichungen."

Marshall 1978, 282: "The participle τασσόμενος, diff. Mt. is found 4x in Acts (cf. Luke's fondness for διατάσσω and ὑποτάσσω) and is probably a Lucan addition; the combination with ὑπό is classical."

Martin 1978, 15: "It is Luke who ... makes the man utter two strangely conflicting statements by the addition of τασσόμενος, namely, Luke thought that 'under authority' meant 'having superiors over me,' and completed the sentence with ὑπὸ ἐξουσίαν τασσόμενος. If this conclusion is sound, it indicates one further sign of Luke's editorializing work on a *Vorlage* which is better represented in Matthew."

19³: "Luke, with his ὑπὸ ἐξουσίαν τασσόμενος, has 'demoted' the Roman soldier whose higher rank should be restored in our translations."

Polag 1979, 38: Reconstruction. For complete text see Q 7:1⁰ In Q (pp. 9-10).

Fitzmyer 1981, 652: "Luke has added to the 'Q' material the ptc. *tassomenos*, 'subjected,' which clearly implies the centurion's subordination to superior officers and then his delegated authority over others."

653: "The Syriac variants [of Matt 8:9] … reflect an attempt to cope with the implication of the Greek text, made even more pronounced by Luke's addition of *tassomenos*, that Jesus too was somehow under authority and subordinated."

Dauer 1984, 85-86: "Τασσόμενος dürfte Lukas entsprechend seiner korrekteren Sprache ergänzt haben. Das Partizip soll wohl, wie schon die Zwischenbemerkung in V. 7a, noch stärker die Demut des Zenturio unterstreichen: er weiß [86] sich wirklich nur als ein Untergebener."

Wegner 1985, 208: "Was τάσσειν betrifft, so erscheint dieses Verb 1x in Mt (28,16) in Mk nicht, 2x im paulinischen Schrifttum (IKor 16,15 und Röm 13,1) und sonst innerhalb des NT außer auSt nur noch 4x in der Apg (13,48; 15,2; 22,10 und 28,23). Sprechen schon diese Zahlen für die Möglichkeit einer sek Hinzufügung des Ptz. durch Lk, so kann diese Annahme noch dadurch erhärtet werden, daß ja Lk an mehreren anderen Stellen Sätze seiner Vorlagen durch Hinzufügung von Hilfsverben ergänzt: vgl. in Bezug auf Q außer uSt noch Lk 10,13 (Lk add καθήμενοι zu Mt 11,21) und 17,35 (Lk add ἔσονται zu Mt 24,41). Hinzu kommt, daß die Einfügung von Partizipien und Partizipialwendungen durch Lk gegenüber dem Mk- und Q-Stoff mehrfach belegbar ist. Da nun andererseits für eine sek-mt Streichung des Ptz. keinen einleuchtenden Grund zu geben scheint, ist u.E. τασσόμενος auSt mit hoher Wahrscheinlichkeit als sek-lk zu betrachten."

270: Reconstruction. For complete text see Q 7:1⁰ In Q (pp. 11-12).

Nolland 1989, 317: "The centurion's words here are reported identically in Matthew and Luke, except that Luke adds the participle 'set.'"

Evans 1990, 345: "*Set* (*tassein*, Lukan) *under authority* may be Luke's alteration to further the picture of a self-effacing junior officer. The argument for the effective word of command then has to proceed entirely out of the next words *with soldiers under me*."

Davies and Allison 1991, 23⁶¹: "Redactional: so Wegner … [1985, 208]."

Catchpole 1992, 533 [1993, 299]: "The Lucan τασσόμενος is probably a redactional clarification.⁶³"

533 [299]⁶³: "It reinforces the subordination of the centurion; cf. also the correlation of τάσσειν and ἐξουσία in Tob 1,21 (aleph)."

533 [299]: Reconstruction. For complete text see Q 7:1⁰ In Q (p. 14).

Lindars 1992, 210: Reconstruction. For complete text see Q 7:1⁶ Luke = Q, Pro (p. 56).

Burchard 1993, 283²⁹: "Falls jemand ... τασσόμενος zugesetzt und nicht Matthäus es gestrichen hat (was exegetisch beachtlich wäre), ist das der älteste Kommentar."

Gagnon 1993, 715: "It should be noted that Lucan redaction can ... be seen in ... the occurrence of τασσόμενος in v 8, 'a man *who is put* under authority.'"

Sevenich-Bax 1993, 183: "Innerhalb der Vertrauensäußerung Mt 8,8b-9//Lk 7,6c-8 liegt eine letzte Deviation in Vers Mt 8,9a//Lk 7,8a vor: Gegen Matthäus bringt Lukas das Partizip τασσόμενος in den Text ein. Daß es tatsächlich Lukas war, der das Partizip verdeutlichend hinzugefügt hat, ergibt sich schon aus dem statistischen Befund, nach dem Lukas das Verb τάσσειν insgesamt 5mal benutzt, Matthäus aber nur einmal (28,16 redaktionell). Bei Markus ist das Verb als Simplex gar nicht belegt. Überdies läßt sich für Lukas eine Neigung nachweisen, durch die Einfügung von Hilfsverben, Partizipien oder Partizipialwendungen in seine Q- bzw. Markus-Vorlage konkretisierend einzugreifen."

238: Reconstruction. For complete text see Q 7:1⁰ In Q (p. 15).

Landis 1994, 12: "Die Versionen der beiden Evangelien stimmen hier wörtlich überein bis auf das nur bei Lk erscheinende τασσόμενος. Dieses Partizip ist wohl vom dritten Evangelisten verdeutlichend hinzugefügt worden, denn eine Streichung durch Mt wäre kaum zu begründen. Außerdem ergänzt Lk häufig seine Vorlagen durch Partipialwendungen. Das Verb τάσσω schließlich, im NT sonst äußerst selten, ist durch die Apg als lk ausgewiesen."

12, 17: Reconstruction. For complete text see Q 7:1⁶ Luke = Q, Pro (p. 57).

International Q Project 1995, 478: Reconstruction. For complete text see Q 7:1⁰ In Q (p. 16).

Matt = Q: [ ]¹

Pro

Con

Gundry 1982, 144: "Since Jesus is 'God with us' (1:23), Matthew wants to show the immediacy and supremacy of Jesus' authority. He therefore drops 'being placed (under)' and thereby suggests that the initial καί does not mean 'too,' but 'even' ('for even I [a centurion!] am a man under authority') and, moreover, that the centurion stands under the authority of Jesus, with whom he is talking. In Matthew, then, only Jesus' authority comes in view. The centurion's following statements do not imply, as in Luke, that the centurion's authority stands beside Jesus' authority in a comparison. Rather, the centurion's speaking and being obeyed stand in subordination to the only true authority there is, that of Jesus."

Burchard 1993, 283²⁹: "Übrigens lesen ℵ B *pc* it vg^{cl} τασσόμενος auch in Mt 8,9. Gäbe es Lukas nicht, würde man das womöglich für ursprünglichen Matthäustext halten, weil *difficilior,* obwohl *longior.*" But see Burchard at Luke = Q, Con (p. 311).

Evaluations

Johnson 2000: Matt = Q {B}, []¹.

Luke's τασσόμενος is certainly the *lectio difficilior* of the two variant readings (Burchard—though he is speaking of Matthew's text-critical issue here). While most authors consider this to be a case of Luke intensifying the humility of the centurion (Zuntz, Delobel, Busse), how τασσόμενος works in an analogy to Jesus himself is not at all clear, unless Luke also sees Jesus as a man *placed* under God's authority (which would seem to contradict his divine-man birth—Luke 1-2). The Matthean analogy is more precise: Just as Jesus has the implicit authority to command the demons of illness, so also a centurion has implicit authority to command his 100 soldiers (understanding ὑπὸ ἐξουσίαν with the meaning of "with a granted authority to command" rather than "under the authority of a superior"—see examples of the accusative of accompaniment in LSJ under "ὑπό" C.IV.2 [p. 1875a]). Is this a case of clarification on Matthew's part, sharpening the analogy and correcting Q's implication that Jesus has been placed under God's authority, rather than assuming that authority as God's son?

The problem with this argument is that an analogy has to make some sense for it to be passed down over time, and Luke's analogy doesn't quite work. It seems, rather, that Luke abandons the strict analogy of Q (which can but need not have a divine-son or christological implication) in order to emphasize the centurion's subordination to others. This would be in keeping with Luke's clarification of παῖς as δοῦλος, a servant or slave who is placed under a centurion's authority (though the Q version probably assumed παῖς meant serving boy in this story).

It is clear from the database that τάσσω is Lukan vocabulary and is redactionally inserted elsewhere (Schürmann, Jeremias, Wegner).

Robinson 2000: Matt = Q {B}, []¹.

The arguments of Busse and Wegner carry force, whereas the christological argument of Gundry does not.

Kloppenborg 2000: Matt = Q {B}, []¹.

Hoffmann 2001: Matt = Q {B}, []¹.

Q 7:9

Matt 8:10	Q 7:9	Luke 7:9
ἀκούσας δὲ [ ]¹	ἀκούσας δὲ []¹	ἀκούσας δὲ [ταῦτα]¹
ὁ Ἰησοῦς ἐθαύμασεν	ὁ Ἰησοῦς ἐθαύμασεν	ὁ Ἰησοῦς ἐθαύμασεν
[ ]²	[]²	[αὐτὸν]²
καὶ [ ]³	καὶ []³	καὶ [στραφεὶς]³
⌐εἶπεν⌐⁴	⌐εἶπεν⌐⁴	⌐ ⌐⁴
τ(οῖς)⁵ ἀκολουθοῦ(σιν)⁵	τ(οῖς)⁵ ἀκολουθοῦ(σιν)⁵	τ[ῷ]⁵ ἀκολουθοῦ[ντι αὐτῷ ὄχλῳ]⁵
⌐ ⌐⁴.	⌐ ⌐⁴.	⌐εἶπεν⌐⁴.
(ἀμὴν)⁶ λέγω ὑμῖν,	()⁶ λέγω ὑμῖν,	( )⁶ λέγω ὑμῖν,
(παρ᾽)⁷ οὐδε(νὶ)⁷	()⁷ οὐδὲ()⁷	( )⁷ οὐδὲ( )⁷
⌐ ⌐⁸	⌐ἐν τῷ Ἰσραὴλ⌐⁸	⌐ἐν τῷ Ἰσραὴλ⌐⁸
τοσαύτην πίστιν	τοσαύτην πίστιν	τοσαύτην πίστιν
⌐ἐν τῷ Ἰσραὴλ⌐⁸	⌐ ⌐⁸	⌐ ⌐⁸
εὗρον.	εὗρον.	εὗρον.

IQP 1994: τ⟦(οῖς)⁵⟧ ἀκολουθοῦ⟦(σιν)⁵⟧.

¹ Luke's ταῦτα.
² Luke's αὐτόν.
³ Luke's στραφείς.
⁴ The position of εἶπεν after (Luke) or before (Matthew) the reference to the followers.
⁵ Luke's τῷ ἀκολουθοῦντι αὐτῷ ὄχλῳ or Matthew's τοῖς ἀκολουθοῦσιν.
⁶ Matthew's ἀμήν.
⁷ Luke's οὐδέ or Matthew's παρ᾽ οὐδενί.
⁸ The position of ἐν τῷ Ἰσραήλ before (Luke) or after (Matthew) τοσαύτην πίστιν.

Q 7:9¹: Luke's ταῦτα.

Luke = Q: ἀκούσας δὲ [ταῦτα]¹.

Pro

Bussmann 1929, 56: "L. hat in v. 9 ταῦτα und αὐτόν, die ursprünglicher wohl sind als die absoluten Ausdrücke."

Gundry 1982, 144: See Gundry at Matt = Q, Con (p. 316).

Lindars 1992, 210: Reconstruction. For complete text see Q 7:1⁶ Luke = Q, Pro (p. 56).

Con

B. Weiß 1876, 229: "Bem. nur ... die Hinzufügung ... der fehlenden Objecte (ταῦτα—αὐτόν—αὐτῷ), sowie das näher bestimmende στραφείς—ὄχλῳ in v. 9."

B. Weiß 1901, 384: "Ταῦτα ist naheliegender Zusatz."

von Harnack 1907, 56: "Es dem Stil des Luk. entspricht, die Objekte zu ergänzen (vgl. Matth. 8,10 und Luk. 7,9)."

91: Reconstruction. For complete text see Q 7:1⁶ Luke = Q, Pro (p. 55).

von Harnack 1907, ET 1908, 77: "It is in the style of St. Luke to supply objects to the verbs (cf. St. Matthew 8:10 and St. Luke 7:9)."

132: Reconstruction. For complete text see Q 7:1⁶ Luke = Q, Pro (p. 55).

B. Weiß 1908, 15: Reconstruction. For complete text see Q 7:1⁰ In Q (p. 5).

Castor 1912, 224: Reconstruction. For complete text see Q 7:1⁰ In Q (p. 6).

Klostermann 1919, 449: "Für die Modifikation ... ferner: verdeutlichend ταῦτα, αὐτόν und malend στραφείς."

Cadbury 1920, 151: "Object of verb supplied [by Luke]: Mt. 8,10 ἀκούσας δέ—Lk. 7,9 ἀκούσας δὲ ταῦτα (Q)."

Crum 1927, 138: Reconstruction. For complete text see Q 7:2̶, 3, 4̶-6a¹ Luke = Q, Pro (pp. 71-72).

Klostermann 1929, 87: "Verdeutlichend gegenüber Mt: ταῦτα, αὐτόν, und malend στραφείς (14,25)."

Schlatter 1960, 493: "L. glättet, indem er beifügt τασσόμενος. Die Verba ohne Objekt ἀκούσας und ἐθαύμασεν erhalten die Objekte ἀκούσας ταῦτα und ἐθαύμασεν αὐτόν."

Delobel 1966, 455: "*Lc.* est le seul à donner l'expression ἀκούσας δὲ ταῦτα et l'emploi transitif du verbe θαυμάζειν."

George 1972, 71: "Mt 8,10 semble plus primitif que Lc 7,9. Luc paraît avoir introduit quelques retouches littéraires[12] et surtout deux modifications significatives."

71[12]: "Addition de *tauta.*"

Schulz 1972, 239: "Lk dürfte ταῦτα und αὐτόν eingefügt haben, ... alles Ergänzungen, deren Streichung durch Mt nicht verständlich wäre."

Busse 1977, 148-149¹: See Q 7:8¹ Luke = Q, Con (p. 309).

Marshall 1978, 282: "The addition of ταῦτα and αὐτόν, diff. Mt. may be Lucan."

Polag 1979, 38: Reconstruction. For complete text see Q 7:1⁰ In Q (pp. 9-10).

Schenk 1981, 37: Reconstruction. For complete text see Q 7:1⁰ In Q (p. 10).

Dauer 1984, 86: "Ταῦτα bei ἀκούειν (oder λέγειν o.ä.) ist häufig Ergänzung des Lukas; vgl. Lk 8,8 add Mk 4,9; Lk 9,34 add Mk 9,7; Lk 18,23 diff Mk 10,22; ferner die vermutlich redaktionellen Bemerkungen Lk 4,28; 11,27; 11,45; 13,17; 14,15; 16,14; 19,11.28; 24,9.10.36."

Wegner 1985, 209-210: "Lk übernahm es aus Q in 10,21; 11,42 und 12,30f par Mt und aus Mk in 18,21; 20,2.8 und 21,7bis.31. In QLk bringt er es außer auSt noch 12,4 und 14,15.21 om Mt. Er hat es mehrfach dem Mk-Stoff hinzugefügt (5,27; 8,8; 9,34; 18,23 und 21,6.9 om Mk) und bringt es gehäuft innerhalb seines Sg: vgl. 1,19f.65; 2,19; 4,28; 10,1 QLk?; 11,27.45 QLk?; 13,2.17; 14,6; 15,26; 16,14; 17,8; 18,4.11; 19,11.28; 21,36; 23,31.49 und 24,9.10.11.21.26.36.

"Der Befund zeigt, daß eine sichere Entscheidung für lk Red oder Trad des Sg kaum noch möglich ist. Das ergibt sich letztlich auch daraus, daß der Gebrauch von ταῦτα in Verbindung mit ἀκούω sowohl dem Lk selbst (vgl. Lk 18,23 mit Mk [210] 10,22; ferner Apg 5,11; 7,54; 11,18; 17,8 und 21,12) als auch seinem Sg (vgl. 4,28; 14,15 QLk?; 16,14 und 19,11) geläufig ist. Bedenkt man jedoch, daß Hinzufügungen des Verbobjektes überhaupt mehrfach von Lk gegenüber seinem Mk-Stoff gemacht werden, so könnte das ταῦτα in Lk 7,9a durchaus aus seiner eigenen Feder stammen. Negativ kann nur soviel gesagt werden, daß ταῦτα sehr wahrscheinlich nicht aus Q stammt, denn Mt, der es mehrmals in seinen Mk-Stoff red einfügt, würde es kaum streichen, falls es in seiner Vorlage gestanden hätte. Ergebnis: lk Red möglich/wahrscheinlich: Sg!"

271: Reconstruction. For complete text see Q 7:1⁰ In Q (pp. 11-12).

Nolland 1989, 318: "The Lukan text differs from the Matthean in a number of minor details. Most look like Lukan additions ('these things,' 'at him,' 'having turned,' 'crowd' [Luke has the singular form for 'following' rather than Matthew's plural form])."

Davies and Allison 1991, 24: "Ταῦτα ... could be Lukan, since the Third Evangelist has sometimes added it to Mark.[64]"

24⁶⁴: "E.g. 5.27; 8.8; 9.34; 18.23; 21.9."

Catchpole 1992, 539 [1993, 307]: Reconstruction. For complete text see Q 7:1⁰ In Q (p. 14).

Gagnon 1993, 715: "It should be noted that Lucan redaction can ... be seen in ... the occurrence ... of ταῦτα, αὐτόν, and, perhaps, στραφείς in v 9."

Sevenich-Bax 1993, 183: "Lk 7,9aα bietet gegenüber Matthäus zunächst zusätzlich ταῦτα sowie αὐτόν. Beides wird von Lukas ergänzt sein, da er sowohl ταῦτα als auch transitives θαυμάζειν gerne verwendet, darüberhinaus aber auch eine redaktionelle Tendenz zeigt, seinen Verben ein Objekt beizugeben."

238: Reconstruction. For complete text see Q 7:1⁰ In Q (p. 15).

Landis 1994, 12: "In 7,9a hat Lk einige bei Mt fehlende Ausdrücke, die alle seiner Redaktion entstammen dürften: —Das Objekt ταῦτα zu ἀκούσας. Die lk Redaktion ergänzt oft Akkusativobjekte. Außerdem wäre ταῦτα, hätte es in der Logienquelle gestanden, von Mt wohl übernommen worden."

13, 17: Reconstruction. For complete text see Q 7:1⁶ Luke = Q, Pro (p. 57).

International Q Project 1995, 479: Reconstruction. For complete text see Q 7:1⁰ In Q (p. 16).

Matt = Q: ἀκούσας δὲ [ ]¹

Pro

Con

Gundry 1982, 144: "Three omissions occur at the start of v 10. Matthew drops 'these things.' As an introductory participle in Matthew, ἀκούσας normally lacks a direct object. Here the omission steers attention away from the centurion's words. Similarly, the omission of 'him' diverts attention from the centurion himself. And the dropping of 'turning' avoids notice of Jesus' physical movement. Together, these omissions allow the authoritative speaking of Jesus—'he said'—to stand out."

Evaluations

Johnson 2000: Matt = Q {B} ἀκούσας δὲ []¹.

Luke often supplies objects to verbs in Markan material (Harnack); more specifically, ταῦτα to ἀκούω (Wegner, Dauer [also to λέγω]).

Gundry's argument that Matthew omits ταῦτα to divert attention from the centurion's words to Jesus seems rooted in his overall argument of thoroughgoing Matthean redaction.

Robinson 2000: Matt = Q {B} ἀκούσας δὲ [][1].

Wegner points out both that Luke is inclined to add the object ταῦτα, indeed specifically to ἀκούω, and that Matthew also adds ταῦτα at times to Mark, so would not be inclined here to delete it.

Kloppenborg 2000: Matt = Q {B} ἀκούσας δὲ [][1].

Hoffmann 2001: Matt = Q {B} ἀκούσας δὲ [][1].

Q 7:9²: Luke's αὐτόν.

Luke = Q: ὁ Ἰησοῦς ἐθαύμασεν [αὐτὸν]²

Pro

Bussmann 1929, 56: "L. hat in v. 9 ταῦτα und αὐτόν, die ursprünglicher wohl sind als die absoluten Ausdrücke."

Lampe 1965, 168: "Luke seems to have made an artificial reconstruction of the tradition and to have failed to carry it through to the end of the story, for the phrase 'Jesus marveled at him' ('at him' is not paralleled in Matthew) strongly suggests that at this point the centurion is present in person." Lampe is arguing against the priority of Luke at this variation unit, but the logic of his statement would appear to argue for Luke = Q, Pro.

Lindars 1992, 210: Reconstruction. For complete text see Q 7:1⁶ Luke = Q, Pro (p. 56).

Con

Bleek 1862, 351: "Luc. mit hinzugefügtem αὐτόν: habe sich über ihn verwundert, ihn angestaunt."

B. Weiß 1876, 229: "Bem. nur ... die Hinzufügung ... der fehlenden Objecte (ταῦτα—αὐτόν—αὐτῷ), sowie das näher bestimmende στραφείς—ὄχλῳ in v. 9."

von Harnack 1907, 56: "Es dem Stil des Luk. entspricht, die Objekte zu ergänzen (vgl. Matth. v. 10 und Luk. v. 9)."

91: Reconstruction. For complete text see Q 7:1⁶ Luke = Q, Pro (p. 55).

von Harnack 1907, ET 1908, 77: "It is in the style of St. Luke to supply objects to the verbs (cf. St. Matthew verse 10 and St. Luke verse 9)."

132: Reconstruction. For complete text see Q 7:1⁶ Luke = Q, Pro (p. 55).

B. Weiß 1908, 15²⁵: See Q 7:6b-c⁹ Luke = Q, Con (p. 280).

15: Reconstruction. For complete text see Q 7:1⁰ In Q (p. 5).

Castor 1912, 224: Reconstruction. For complete text see Q 7:1⁰ In Q (p. 6).

Klostermann 1919, 449: "Für die Modifikation ... ferner: verdeutlichend ταῦτα, αὐτόν und malend στραφείς."

Cadbury 1920, 151: "Object of verb supplied [by Luke]: ... Mt. 8,10 ἐθαύμασεν—Lk. 7,9 ἐθαύμασεν αὐτόν (Q)."

Crum 1927, 138: Reconstruction. For complete text see Q 7:2, 3, 4-6a¹ Luke = Q, Pro (pp. 71-72).

Klostermann 1929, 87: "Verdeutlichend gegenüber Mt: ταῦτα, αὐτόν, und malend στραφείς (14,25)."

Jeremias 1960, 144: "θαυμάζειν mit Akk. findet sich im NT nur Lk. 7,9; 24,12; Apg. 7,31; Joh. 5,28; Jud. 16."

Jeremias 1960, FT 1972, 178: "*Thaumazein* avec l'accusatif ne se trouve dans le NT que chez Lc 7,9; 24,12; Ac 7,31; Jn 5,28; Jude 16."

Schlatter 1960, 493: "L. glättet, ... Die Verba ohne Objekt ἀκούσας und ἐθαύμασεν erhalten die Objekte ἀκούσας ταῦτα und ἐθαύμασεν αὐτόν."

Fuchs 1971, 78-79: "Als Hinweis kann man werten, daß θαυμάζειν mit direktem Object bei Mk und Mt nicht vorkommt, bei Jo nur 5,28, jedoch dreimal in den Lk-Schriften: [79] (Lk 7,9), 24,12 (θαυμάζων τὸ γεγονός), Apg 7,31 (ἐθαύμασεν τὸ ὅραμα)."

George 1972, 71: "Mt 8,10 semble plus primitif que Lc 7,9. Luc paraît avoir introduit quelques retouches littéraires et surtout deux modifications significatives: en donnant un complément (*auton*) au verbe *éthaumasén*, il lui donne le sens '(Jésus) l'admira', tandis que chez Matthieu ce verbe sans complément signifie '(Jésus) s'étonna' (Luc semble avoir voulu éviter l'étonnement de Jésus et marquer la beauté de la foi du païen)."

Schulz 1972, 239: "Lk dürfte ταῦτα und αὐτόν eingefügt haben,[419] ... alles Ergänzungen, deren Streichung durch Mt nicht verständlich wäre."

239[419]: "θαυμάζειν mit folgendem Akkusativ findet sich im NT nur Lk 7,9; 24,12; Apg 7,31; Joh 5,28; Jud 16."

Busse 1977, 148-149[1]: See Q 7:8[1] Luke = Q, Con (p. 309).

Légasse 1977, 240[40]: "En ajoutant le pronom *auton*, Luc (7,9) modifie le sens du passage parallèle. Selon lui, Jésus 'admire le païen'. Pour Matthieu, Jésus 's'étonne'. Luc aura voulu, par scrupule christologique, bannir un sentiment qu'il juge indigne de Jésus et, en outre, satisfaire au projet d'édification qu'il poursuit tout au long de la péricope."

Marshall 1978, 282: "The addition of ταῦτα and αὐτόν, diff. Mt. may be Lucan."

Martin 1978, 16: See Q 7:7[1] Luke = Q, Con (p. 289).

Polag 1979, 38: Reconstruction. For complete text see Q 7:1[0] In Q (pp. 9-10).

Jeremias 1980, 155: "Red ἐθαύμασεν αὐτόν: Transitives θαυμάζω ('sich wundern über') kommt im NT nur im Doppelwerk (Lk 7,9; 24,12; Apg 7,31) und Joh 5,28; Jud 16 vor. Daß die Konstruktion lukanisch ist, ergibt sich für Lk 24,12 aus dem Objekt τὸ γεγονός (→ 24,12 Red ...), für Apg 7,31 aus dem typisch lukanischen τὸ ὅραμα (Mt 1, Apg 10) und für unsere Stelle aus dem Vergleich mit der Parallelstelle Mt 8,10 an der θαυμάζω absolut gebraucht wird."

Schenk 1981, 37: Reconstruction. For complete text see Q 7:1[0] In Q (p. 10).

Dauer 1984, 86: "Das zusätzliche αὐτόν zu θαυμάζειν wird lk Korrektur im christologischen Sinne sein: Jesus wundert sich nicht, sondern bewundert den Mann; zugleich liegt darin auch wieder eine Anerkennung des Zenturio wegen seiner Demut und seines Glaubens."

Dupont 1985, 341⁹: "En Lc 7,9, il ne s'agirait plus d'étonnement mais d'admiration selon A. George … [1972, 71] …: 'En donnant un complément (*auton*) au verbe *éthaumasén* (Luc) lui donne le sens '(Jésus) l'admira', tandis que chez Matthieu ce verbe sans complément signifie '(Jésus) s'étonna' (Luc semble avoir voulu éviter l'étonnement de Jésus et marquer la beauté de la foi du païen)'. … Elle nous paraît dépourvue de fondement: nous ne voyons pas pourquoi l'addition du complément direct changerait le sens du verbe."

Wegner 1985, 210: "Für die red Einfügung dieses Pronomens spricht die Tatsache, daß transitives θαυμάζειν, abgesehen von Joh 5,28 und Jud 16, innerhalb des NT sonst nur noch im lk Schrifttum vorkommt: vgl. außer auSt noch Lk 24,12 und Apg 7,31. Wenn darüber hinaus bedacht wird, daß Lk überhaupt mehrfach seinen Verben ein Objekt hinzufügt, dann dürfte der Annahme einer lk Eintragung des αὐτόν auSt kaum etwas entgegenzusetzen sein. Ergebnis: lk Red wahrscheinlich."

271: Reconstruction. For complete text see Q 7:1⁰ In Q (pp. 11-12).

Nolland 1989, 318: See Q 7:91¹ Luke = Q, Con (p. 315).

Catchpole 1992, 539 [1993, 307]: Reconstruction. For complete text see Q 7:1⁰ In Q (p. 14).

Gagnon 1993, 715: "It should be noted that Lucan redaction can … be seen in … the occurrence … of ταῦτα, αὐτόν, and, perhaps, στραφείς in v 9."

Sevenich-Bax 1993, 183: See Q 7:91¹ Luke = Q, Con (p. 316).

238: Reconstruction. For complete text see Q 7:1⁰ In Q (p. 15).

Landis 1994, 12: "In 7,9a hat Lk einige bei Mt fehlende Ausdrücke, die alle seiner Redaktion entstammen dürften: … —Das Akkusativobjekt αὐτόν zu ἐθαύμασεν. Transitives θαυμάζω ist typisch für Lk. Es findet sich innerhalb des NT fast nur im lk Schrifttum."

13, 17: Reconstruction. For complete text see Q 7:1⁶ Luke = Q, Pro (p. 57).

International Q Project 1995, 479: Reconstruction. For complete text see Q 7:1⁰ In Q (p. 16).

Matt = Q: ὁ Ἰησοῦς ἐθαύμασεν [ ]²

Pro

Con

Bussmann 1929, 56: See Bussmann at Luke = Q, Pro (p. 318).

Gundry 1982, 144: See Q 7:9¹ Matt = Q, Con (p. 316).

Davies and Allison 1991, 24: "In line with his tendency to abbreviate miracle stories, Matthew has probably omitted 'him' as unnecessary."

Evaluations

Johnson 2000: Matt = Q {B}, ὁ Ἰησοῦς ἐθαύμασεν []².

As I have indicated in the database, Lampe's observation should lead to a Luke = Q conclusion.

However, Luke's substantial additions that focus on the centurion, his good deeds, and his humbleness are an argument that Luke continues that emphasis here. George and Légasse perhaps overplay the issue of Jesus' amazement, but are probably correct that Luke focuses Jesus' reaction on the centurion since Luke has done this already with the many additions to the text. Transitive use of θαυμάζω is an instance of Lukan style (Jeremias).

Robinson 2000: Matt = Q {B}, ὁ Ἰησοῦς ἐθαύμασεν []².

The transitive use of θαυμάζω is predominantly Lukan. It is unclear if Luke was motivated to ascribe to Jesus less awe (which would use the verb as an intransitive), as unworthy of Jesus' exalted status, than surprise over the centurion's faith, where the verb would be used transitively.

Kloppenborg 2000: Matt = Q {B}, ὁ Ἰησοῦς ἐθαύμασεν []².

Hoffmann 2001: Matt = Q {B}, ὁ Ἰησοῦς ἐθαύμασεν []².

Q 7:9³: Luke's στραφείς.

Luke = Q: καὶ [στραφείς]³

Pro

Marshall 1978, 282: "It is less easy to be certain about the inclusion of στραφείς which is frequent in non-Marcan sections in Lk. (7:44; 9:55; 10:23; 14:25; 22:61; 23:28) but is not found in Acts; it may be pre-Lucan."

Jeremias 1980, 155: "Trad στραφείς: Im Lukas-Evangelium wird στρέφω stets als Participium pass. in reflexiver Bedeutung verwendet, um die Hinwendung Jesu zu Personen zu beschreiben. Alle 7 Belege finden sich im Nicht-Markusstoff (Lk 7,9.44; 9,55; 10,23; 14,25; 22,61; 23,28). Lukas selbst schreibt statt dessen das Kompositum ἐπιστρέψας (Apg 9,40; 16,18)."

Lindars 1992, 210: Reconstruction. For complete text see Q 7:1⁶ Luke = Q, Pro (p. 56).

Con

B. Weiß 1876, 229: "Bem. nur ... die Hinzufügung ... der fehlenden Objecte (ταῦτα—αὐτόν—αὐτῷ), sowie das näher bestimmende στραφείς—ὄχλῳ in v. 9."

Hawkins 1899, 22, 46: "Words and Phrases characteristic of St. Luke's Gospel: ... στραφείς."

Holtzmann 1901, 344: "Lc bringt (7,9) sein malendes στραφείς an, wie 7,44; 9,55; 10,23; 14,25; 22,61; 23,28, und steigert vielleicht (falls nämlich bei Mt παρ' οὐδενί statt οὐδέ zu lesen wäre) die Aussage: nicht einmal in Israel."

B. Weiß 1901, 384: "Auffallend ist nur das στραφείς, das allerdings häufig in L vorkommt."

von Harnack 1907, 56: "Διασώζειν kann als ein lukanisches Wort in Anspruch genommen werden, ... und das pleonastische στραφείς."

91: Reconstruction. For complete text see Q 7:1⁶ Luke = Q, Pro (p. 55).

von Harnack 1907, ET 1908, 77: "Διασώζειν can be claimed as Lukan, ... and the pleonastic στραφείς (verse 9)."

132: Reconstruction. For complete text see Q 7:1⁶ Luke = Q, Pro (p. 55).

Loisy 1907, 652¹: "Le στραφείς, qui vient ensuite et fait image, pourrait être un écho de Mc. v, 30; cette expression est d'ailleurs familière à Luc (cf. vii, 44; ix, 55, etc.)."

B. Weiß 1908, 15: Reconstruction. For complete text see Q 7:1⁰ In Q (p. 5).

Castor 1912, 224: Reconstruction. For complete text see Q 7:1⁰ In Q (p. 6).

Klostermann 1919, 449: "Für die Modifikation … ferner: verdeutlichend ταῦτα, αὐτόν und malend στραφείς."

Easton 1926, 97: "The first clause is easily understood as a Lukan revision of Q, but it has a curious similarity to the opening of the L section in 14:25. στραφείς is an L term."

Crum 1927, 138: Reconstruction. For complete text see Q 7:~~2~~, 3, ~~4-6a~~¹ Luke = Q, Pro (pp. 71-72).

Bussmann 1929, 56: "L. hat in v. 9 ταῦτα und αὐτόν, die ursprünglicher wohl sind als die absoluten Ausdrücke, aber στραφείς und ὄχλῳ (darum τῷ ἀκολουθοῦντι) gehen auf Stilisierung des L zurück."

Klostermann 1929, 87: "Verdeutlichend gegenüber Mt: ταῦτα, αὐτόν, und malend στραφείς (14,25)."

Knox 1957, 87²: "Καὶ στραφεὶς εἶπεν is a favourite Lucan method of introducing a saying; it is not found in Mark. It is necessitated by the scene in Luke vii. 44 and xxiii. 28, both of which are peculiar to Luke; in vii. 9 (=Matt. viii. 10), ix. 55, x. 22 (in many MSS.) and 23 and here, it is a piece of stylistic editing which improves the description of the scene but is quite unnecessary."

Delobel 1966, 455: "L'expression: στραφεὶς τῷ ἀκολουθοῦντι αὐτῷ ὄχλῳ εἶπεν, rappelle *Mc.*, V, 30: ἐπιστραφεὶς ἐν τῷ ὄχλῳ ἔλεγεν, d'autant plus que cette péricope sur l'hémorroïsse et son contexte sur la fille de Jaïre semblent avoir influencé plus largement notre récit du centurion."

Schürmann 1968, 226: "Στραφείς (außer bei Jo immer von Jesus gebraucht) begegnet in lukanischem Sondergut 7,44; 9,55; 23,28, aber auch Lk 7,9 diff Mt. Vielleicht ist matthäische Streichung hier angesichts der matthäischen Zusätze 9,22; 16,23 diff Mk nicht so wahrscheinlich."

Fuchs 1971, 79: "Weiters ist στραφείς eine bei Lk sehr beliebte Form (7,9.44; 9,55; 10,22.23; 14,25; 22,61; 23,28) während sie bei Mk nicht, bei Mt nur (7,6 -έντες) 9,22; 16,23 vorkommt (Jo 1,38; 20,16 -εῖσα). Es fällt besonders auf, daß das Wort στρέφειν bei Lk überhaupt nur in der Form στραφείς (ohne Abwandlung) vorkommt."

George 1972, 71: "Mt 8,10 semble plus primitif que Lc 7,9. Luc paraît avoir introduit quelques retouches littéraires¹² et surtout deux modifications significatives."

71¹²: "Addition de … *strapheis tōi … ochlōi* (ce participe se trouve 2 fois chez Mt, 0 chez Mc, 7 chez Lc, 2 chez Jn)."

Schulz 1972, 239: "Lk dürfte ταῦτα und αὐτόν eingefügt haben, ebenso στραφείς⁴²⁰ und ὄχλος, alles Ergänzungen deren Streichung durch Mt nicht verständlich wäre."

239⁴²⁰: "Ev ca 3mal trad; ca 3mal red—immer in der Form στραφείς; Apg 3mal."

Wilckens 1973, 411⁵⁶: "Denn ... ist στραφείς εἶπεν o.ä. eine von Lukas beliebte Einführungsformel (vgl. 7,9; 9,55; 14,25; 22,61; 23,28 sowie 10,23 στραφείς πρός τινα ... εἶπεν; sonst im NT nur noch Mt 16,23; Joh 1,38; 20,14.16."

Busse 1977, 148-149¹: See Q 7:8¹ Luke = Q, Con (p. 309).

154: "Die Bedeutsamkeit der Situation auskostend fügt Lukas das pleonastisch wirkende στραφείς hinzu und läßt Jesus vor der ihn begleitenden Menge sein Urteil über den Hauptmann fällen, das zugleich einen Tadel an Israel beinhaltet."

Polag 1979, 38: Reconstruction. For complete text see Q 7:1⁰ In Q (pp. 9-10).

Fitzmyer 1981, 653: "The ptc. *strapheis* is a Lucan favorite (7:44; 9:55; 10:22,23; 14:25; 22:61; 23:28)."

Schenk 1981, 37: Reconstruction. For complete text see Q 7:1⁰ In Q (p. 10).

Dauer 1984, 86: "Στραφείς ist lk: vgl. außer Mt 9,22 (add Mk 5,34); Mt 16,23 (diff Mk 8,33: ἐπιστραφείς) und Joh 1,38; 20,16; Lk 7,9 u.St.; 7,44; 9,55; 10,23; 14,25; 22,61; 23,28."

Wegner 1985, 210-211: "Das Verb begegnet 6x in Mt, in Mk nicht und in Lk/Apg 7/3x. Was Mt betrifft, so bringt er es 1x in QMt (5,39 diff Lk), 3x in seinem Sg (7,6; 18,3 und 27,3) und 2x als Hinzufügung [211] zu Mk (9,22 om Mk 5,34 und 16,23 diff Mk 8,33: ἐπιστραφείς), jeweils in der Partizipialform στραφείς. Während in 5,39; 7,6 und 18,3 das Verb innerhalb von Spruchtradition erscheint, taucht es in 27,3 und in den zwei red Hinzufügungen zu Mk in erzählendem Rahmen auf.

"Im LkEv erscheint στρέφω stets in der Partizipialform στραφείς, und zwar außer auSt noch 2x innerhalb von Svv (10,23a und 14,25) und 4x im Sg (7,44; 9,55; 22,61 und 23,28). Im LkEv begegnet das Verb ausschließlich in erzählendem Rahmen. Obwohl στρέφω auch 3x in der Apg auftaucht (7,39.42 und 13,46), erscheint es dort aber niemals in der Partizipialform στραφείς.

"Die Tatsache, daß Lk στραφείς nicht in der Apg verwendet und auch niemals als Einfügung in seinen Mk-Stoff benutzt, deutet darauf hin, daß der Gebrauch des Verbs in dieser Partizipialform vor-lk ist. Zu Q wird es auSt kaum gehört haben, denn Mt, der es in erzählerischem Rahmen 2x in seinen Mk-Stoff einfügte, hätte es kaum sek gestrichen. Scheiden die Annahmen einer lk Bildung und eines Q-Ursprungs aus, so steht u.E. kaum etwas im Wege, στραφείς auSt für eine trad Wendung des lk Sg zu halten, da es in dieser Traditionsschicht ja mehrfach erscheint."

271: Reconstruction. For complete text see Q 7:1⁰ In Q (pp. 11-12).

Nolland 1989, 318: See Q 7:9¹ Luke = Q, Con (p. 315).

Catchpole 1992, 537[85] [1993, 304[85]]: "Note ... the occurrence of ἐπισ-τραφείς in Mark 5,30."

539 [307]: Reconstruction. For complete text see Q 7:1⁰ In Q (p. 14).

Gagnon 1993, 715: "It should be noted that Lucan redaction can ... be seen in ... the occurrence ... of ταῦτα, αὐτόν, and, perhaps, στραφείς in v 9."

717: "In the case of στραφείς (6/0/7 + 3), Wegner [1985, 210-211] believes that Luke's special source is responsible for the insertion. The facts of the case are: (1) in Luke, only this nom. sg. ptc. is used, Jesus is always the subject, and, with the exception of 22:61, all are of the 'turning, Jesus said' variety (7:44 [S]; 9:55 [S]; 10:23 [LQ]; 14:25 [LQ] 22:61 [L?]; 23:28 [S]); (2) in Acts, the word is used three times, but never as a participle, and never in conjunction with speaking: ἐπιστρέψας, though, is employed on two occasions for the expression 'turning, (someone) said' (Acts 9:40; 16:18); (3) Matthew shows no reluctance in reproducing the word: both in Matt 9:22 and in Matt 16:23 he replaces Mark's ἐπιστραφείς with στραφείς in the combination 'turning, (someone) said,' indicating that he would have retained it had it appeared in his Q text. In my opinion, the three instances of its occurrence in [LQ] or [L?] certainly leave the door open for Lucan redaction (perhaps, then the three [S] examples derive from Luke as well), though, given the situation in Acts, it is also possible that the word in Luke 7:9 derives from Luke's special source."

Sevenich-Bax 1993, 183-184: "In Lk 7,9aβ ist im Verhältnis zum matthäischen Text das Partizip στραφείς und wiederum ein Objekt (αὐτῷ) samt der dem Partizip [184] ἀκολουθοῦντι zugeordneten substantivischen Näherbestimmung ὄχλῳ zugefügt. Auch hier wird man mit Ergänzung aus lukanischer Hand zu rechnen haben. Das ergibt sich für αὐτῷ schon aus den zu Lk 7,9aα angeführten Beobachtungen. Die Formulierung 'τῷ ἀκολουθοῦντι αὐτῷ ὄχλῳ' verrät zudem lukanischen Stil, 'da die attributive Stellung des Ptz. (...) zwischen Artikel und Substantiv eine vom dritten Evangelisten mehrmals verwendete Konstruktion darstellt' [Wegner 1985, 212]. Ebenso wird das Verb στρέφω als traditionelles Motiv in der Jüngerunterweisung (vgl. dazu auch Lk 9,55) von Lukas redaktionell gesetzt sein."

238: Reconstruction. For complete text see Q 7:1⁰ In Q (p. 15).

Landis 1994, 12: "In 7,9a hat Lk einige bei Mt fehlende Ausdrücke, die alle seiner Redaktion entstammen dürften: ... —Das Partizip στραφείς. Es gehörte kaum zum Q-Text, denn seine Streichung durch Mt wäre nicht verständlich. Für einen redaktionellen Ursprung spricht auch das recht häufige Vorkommen von στρέφω in der Apg und im LkEv, in dem es immer in der Partizipialform στραφείς erscheint und etwa in der Hälfte der Fälle redaktionell eingesetzt ist."

13, 17: Reconstruction. For complete text see Q 7:1⁶ Luke = Q, Pro (p. 57).

International Q Project 1995, 479: Reconstruction. For complete text see Q 7:1⁰ In Q (p. 16).

Matt = Q: καὶ [ ]³

Pro

Con

Gundry 1982, 144: See Q 7:9¹ Matt = Q, Con (p. 316).

Evaluations

Johnson 2000: Matt = Q {B}, καὶ []³.
Marshall and Jeremias argue that στράφεις might be traditional because it only occurs in Luke in non-Markan material. Knox counters with the argument that four of these seven cases are examples of stylistic editing. Sevenich-Bax finds the addition of στράφεις to be part of a larger Lukan construction in Luke 7:9a (her argument for this variation unit is prefaced upon her argument that Luke ≠ Q at 7:9⁵). Luke also uses ἐπιστρέφω in the sense of "turning, he said" two times in Acts (Gagnon 1993).
Matthew had no reason to omit the word, having added it to Markan material at Matt 9:22 and having omitted Mark 8:33's ἐπι- prefix at Matt 16:23.

Robinson 2000: Matt = Q {B}, καὶ []³.
There would be no reason for Matthew to omit it, had it stood in Q, since he even added it at Matt 9:22.
This participial form is distinctive of the Gospel of Luke (not Acts), and so could be Lukan (though Luke does not insert it into Mark).

Kloppenborg 2000: Matt = Q {B}, καὶ []³.

Hoffmann 2001: Matt = Q {B}, καὶ []³.

Q 7:9⁴: The position of εἶπεν after (Luke) or before (Matthew) the reference to the followers.

Luke = Q: ⌐ ⌐⁴ τ[ῷ]⁵ ἀκολουθοῦ[ντι αὐτῷ ὄχλῳ]⁵ ⌐εἶπεν⌐⁴

Pro

B. Weiß 1908, 15: Reconstruction. For complete text see Q 7:1⁰ In Q (p. 5).

Lindars 1992, 210: Reconstruction. For complete text see Q 7:1⁶ Luke = Q, Pro (p. 56).

Con

Delobel 1966, 455: See Q 7:9³ Luke = Q, Con (p. 323).

Sevenich-Bax 1993, 183-184: See Q 7:9³ Luke = Q, Con (p. 325).

Matt = Q: ⌐εἶπεν⌐⁴ τ(οῖς)⁵ ἀκολουθοῦ(σιν)⁵ ⌐ ⌐⁴

Pro

von Harnack 1907, 91 (ET 1908, 132): Reconstruction. For complete text see Q 7:1⁶ Luke = Q, Pro (p. 55).

Polag 1979, 38: Reconstruction. For complete text see Q 7:1⁰ In Q (pp. 9-10).

Wegner 1985, 271: Reconstruction. For complete text see Q 7:1⁰ In Q (pp. 11-12).

Catchpole 1992, 539 [1993, 307]: Reconstruction. For complete text see Q 7:1⁰ In Q (p. 14).

Sevenich-Bax 1993, 238: Reconstruction. For complete text see Q 7:1⁰ In Q (p. 15).

Landis 1994, 13, 17: Reconstruction. For complete text see Q 7:1⁶ Luke = Q, Pro (p. 57).

International Q Project 1995, 479: Reconstruction. For complete text see Q 7:1⁰ In Q (p. 16).

Con

Gundry 1982, 144: "Those who follow become the indirect objects of Jesus' speaking rather than of his turning (as in Luke)."

Evaluations

Johnson 2000: Matt = Q {B}, ^{S}εἶπεν^{L4} τ(οἷς)^5 ἀκολουθοῦ(σιν)^5 ^{SL4}.

Robinson 2000: Matt = Q {B}, ^{S}εἶπεν^{L4} τ(οἷς)^5 ἀκολουθοῦ(σιν)^5 ^{SL4}.
Luke's introduction of στραφείς makes it necessary to state to whom he turns (which also leads to the introduction of the reference to the crowd; see Q 7:9⁵). This dative phrase originally modified the verb εἶπεν, but in Luke comes to modify στραφείς (and only secondarily also εἶπεν). Thus the Lukan position of the verb between the two verbs it conditions comes from the Lukan redaction of the context.

Kloppenborg 2000: Matt = Q {B}, ^{S}εἶπεν^{L4} τ(οἷς)^5 ἀκολουθοῦ(σιν)^5 ^{SL4}.

Hoffmann 2001: Matt = Q {B}, ^{S}εἶπεν^{L4} τ(οἷς)^5 ἀκολουθοῦ(σιν)^5 ^{SL4}.

Q 7:9⁵: Luke's τῷ ἀκολουθοῦντι αὐτῷ ὄχλῳ or Matthew's τοῖς ἀκολουθοῦσιν.

Luke = Q: τ[ῷ]⁵ ἀκολουθοῦ[ντι αὐτῷ ὄχλῳ]⁵

Pro

B. Weiß 1908, 15: Reconstruction. For complete text see Q 7:1⁰ In Q (p. 5).

Marshall 1978, 282: "The reference to the crowds, diff. Mt., may be original (cf. Mt. 8:1)."

Lindars 1992, 210: Reconstruction. For complete text see Q 7:1⁶ Luke = Q, Pro (p. 56).

Con

B. Weiß 1876, 229: "Bem. nur ... die Hinzufügung ... der fehlenden Objecte (ταῦτα—αὐτόν—αὐτῷ), sowie das näher bestimmende στραφείς—ὄχλῳ in v. 9."

B. Weiß 1901, 384: "Wie nie sonst, c. dat. steht, und das τ. ἀκολ. ὄχλ. (6,17.19), das das allgemeine τ. ἀκολ. bei Mt erklärt, aber eben darum nicht ausreicht zu der Annahme, daß wir hier noch eine Reminiscenz an die Erzählung aus L haben."

Castor 1912, 42: "In Luke 7:2b ἤμελλεν τελευτᾶν, ὃς ἦν αὐτῷ ἔντιμος are, perhaps, additions of Luke; so also ὄχλῳ in 7:9."

Bussmann 1929, 56: "L. hat in v. 9 ταῦτα und αὐτόν, die ursprünglicher wohl sind als die absoluten Ausdrücke, aber στραφείς und ὄχλῳ (darum τῷ ἀκολουθοῦντι) gehen auf Stilisierung des L zurück."

Rehkopf 1959, 72-73: "Die attributive Stellung zwischen Artikel und Substantiv liebt Lukas, auch auf die Gefahr hin, daß die Periode dadurch zu lang wird und die attributive Stellung mit wieder aufgenommenen Artikel empfehlenswerter wäre."

Delobel 1966, 455: See Q 7:9³ Luke = Q, Con (p. 323).

Fuchs 1971, 79: "Man wird also eher den Singular des Lk für sekundär halten müssen als den Plural bei Mt."

George 1972, 71: "Luc paraît avoir introduit quelques retouches littéraires¹² et surtout deux modifications significatives."

71¹²: "Addition de ... *strapheis tōi* ... *ochlōi* (ce participe se trouve 2 fois chez Mt, 0 chez Mc, 7 chez Lc, 2 chez Jn)."

Schulz 1972, 239: "Lk dürfte ταῦτα und αὐτόν eingefügt haben, ebenso στραφείς und ὄχλος,⁴²¹ alles Ergänzungen deren Streichung durch Mt nicht verständlich wäre."

239[421]: "Ev ca 20mal trad; ca 20mal red; Apg 22mal."

Busse 1977, 148-149[1]: See Q 7:8[1] Luke = Q, Con (p. 309).

Jeremias 1980, 155: "Red ... τῷ ἀκολουθοῦντι αὐτῷ ὄχλῳ: Lukas setzt gelegentlich das Partizip zwischen Artikel und Substantiv: 1,1; 7,9 (diff. Mt 8,10); 21,1 (diff. Mk 12,41); 22,52 (diff. Mk 14,48); 23,48."

Dauer 1984, 116: "Rückschauend läßt sich als lk Redaktion feststellen: ... (ἐθαύμασεν) αὐτόν—στραφεὶς τῷ—ὄχλῳ."

Wegner 1985, 212: "Daß ὄχλος kaum urspr in der Q-Vorlage stand, zeigt die mt Vorliebe für dieses Wort bei seiner Bearbeitung des Mk-Stoffes, woraus zu schließen ist, daß Mt es auSt kaum gestrichen hätte, falls es in seiner Vorlage stünde. Demgegenüber steht der Annahme einer sek Einfügung durch Lk nichts entgegen. Dafür spricht: 1. Lk fügt ὄχλος mehrfach in seinen Mk-Stoff ein. 2. Die Formulierung τῷ ἀκολουθοῦντι αὐτῷ ὄχλῳ verrät lk Stil, da die attributive Stellung des Ptz. (ἀκολουθοῦντι) zwischen Artikel und Substantiv eine vom dritten Evangelisten mehrmals verwendete Konstruktion darstellt. Ist ὄχλος daher mit hoher Wahrscheinlichkeit auSt von Lk selbst eingefügt worden, so wird man auf Grund der lk Stilisierung dieses Versteiles auch bzgl. des αὐτῷ mit einer Einfügung durch den dritten Evangelisten zu rechnen haben. ...

"Die in Lk 7,9a über Mt 8,10a hinausgehenden Worte erwiesen sich in ihrer Mehrzahl als sek-lk Eintragungen gegenüber der Q-Vorlage. Keine Anzeichen lk Red zeigte aber das Ptz. στραφείς, das auf Sg-Einfluß hindeutet. Da die Formulierung τῷ ἀκολουθοῦντι αὐτῷ ὄχλῳ sich in stilistischer Hinsicht als lk erweist, wird das mt τοῖς ἀκολουθοῦσιν wohl den urspr Q-Wortlaut wiedergeben. Ob hinter τοῖς ἀκολουθοῦσιν urspr noch ein αὐτῷ stand, ist kaum noch mit Sicherheit zu entscheiden. Auf Grund der lk Stilisierung des Versteiles scheint es uns wahrscheinlich, daß dieser pronominal Dativ von Lk selbst stammt."

Nolland 1989, 318: See Q 7:9[1] Luke = Q, Con (p. 315).

Catchpole 1992, 537 [1993, 304]: See Catchpole at Matt = Q, Pro (p. 331).

537 [304] [84]: "Matt 4,25; 8,1; 19,2; 20,29; 21,9."

Gagnon 1993, 715: "It should be noted that Lucan redaction can ... be seen in ... the replacement of τοῖς ἀκολουθοῦσιν, 'to those who were following him,' with τῷ ἀκολουθοῦντι αὐτῷ ὄχλῳ, 'to the crowd that was following him,' in v 9."

Sevenich-Bax 1993, 183-184: See Q 7:9[3] Luke = Q, Con (p. 325).

Landis 1994, 12: "In 7,9a hat Lk einige bei Mt fehlende Ausdrücke, die alle seiner Redaktion entstammen dürften: ... —Die Wendung (τ)ῷ (ἀκολουθοῦ)ντι αὐτῷ ὄχλῳ. Die ganze Formulierung mit der attributiven Stellung des Partizips zwischen Artikel und Substantiv zeigt lk Stil. ὄχλος wird von Lk mehrmals in den Mk-Stoff eingefügt; von Mt wird es keinesfalls gemieden, so daß eine Streichung durch den ersten Evangelisten unwahrscheinlich wäre. Angesichts der allgemein intensiven Überarbeitung des Versteils durch Lk ist wohl auch αὐτῷ für eine lk redaktionelle Einfügung zu halten."

Matt = Q: τ(οῖς)⁵ ἀκολουθοῦ(σιν)⁵

Pro

B. Weiß 1876, 229: See Q 7:9¹ Luke = Q, Con (p. 314).

von Harnack 1907, 56: "Also ist ... τοῖς ἀκολουθοῦσιν ([Luke:] τῷ ἀκολουθοῦντι αὐτῷ ὄχλῳ) ursprünglich."

91: Reconstruction. For complete text see Q 7:1⁶ Luke = Q, Pro (p. 55).

von Harnack 1907, ET 1908, 77: "Τοῖς ἀκολουθοῦσιν (St. Luke, τῷ ἀκολουθοῦντι αὐτῷ ὄχλῳ) is also original."

132: Reconstruction. For complete text see Q 7:1⁶ Luke = Q, Pro (p. 55).

Castor 1912, 224: Reconstruction. For complete text see Q 7:1⁰ In Q (p. 6).

Crum 1927, 138: Reconstruction. For complete text see Q 7:~~2~~, 3, ~~4-6a~~¹ Luke = Q, Pro (pp. 71-72).

George 1972, 71: "Mt 8,10 semble plus primitif que Lc 7,9."

Polag 1979, 38: Reconstruction. For complete text see Q 7:1⁰ In Q (pp. 9-10).

Schenk 1981, 37: Reconstruction. For complete text see Q 7:1⁰ In Q (p. 10).

Wegner 1985, 212, 271: Reconstruction. For complete text see Q 7:1⁰ In Q (pp. 11-12).

Catchpole 1992, 537 [1993, 304]: "The specific audience for that pronouncement was probably οἱ ἀκολουθοῦντες without further qualification, for two reasons. (i) An association between ἀκολουθεῖν and ὄχλος (thus Luke 7,9) occurs sufficiently often in MattR[84] to make it unlikely that Matthew would pass over such an association if he had found it in his source. (ii) Such an association occurs just once in Mark, specifically in the Jairus story (Mark 5,24) whose influence upon the centurion story has already been detected. The most likely explanation for the combination used in Luke 7:9a is therefore LukeR."

537 [304][84]: "Matt 4,25; 8,1; 19,2; 20,29; 21,9."

539 [307]: Reconstruction. For complete text see Q 7:1⁰ In Q (p. 14).

Sevenich-Bax 1993, 238: Reconstruction. For complete text see Q 7:1⁰ In Q (p. 15).

Landis 1994, 12: "Das mt τοῖς ἀκολουθοῦσιν den genauen Wortlaut der Q-Vorlage wiedergeben dürfte."

13, 17: Reconstruction. For complete text see Q 7:1⁶ Luke = Q, Pro (p. 57).
International Q Project 1995, 479: Reconstruction. For complete text see Q 7:1⁰ In Q (p. 16).

Con

B. Weiß 1908, 16: "Das τῷ ἀκολουθοῦντι αὐτῷ ὄχλῳ mußte nach Mt. 8,1 in τοῖς ἀκολουθοῦσιν geändert werden."

Gundry 1982, 144: "We have already read that 'many crowds followed him' (v 1, peculiar to Matthew). Therefore Matthew omits τῷ ἀκολουθοῦντι αὐτῷ ὄχλῳ (so Luke) and refers simply to τοῖς (supply ὄχλοις from v 1) ἀκο-λουθοῦσιν. The plural contrasts with Luke's singular and derives from v 1."

Evaluations

Johnson 2000: Matt = Q {B}, τ(οῖς)⁵ ἀκολουθοῦ(σιν)⁵.

Luke stylistically prefers the construction of article + attributive + substantive (Rehkopf, Jeremias). Luke inserts ὄχλος into Markan material in other instances, demonstrating a redactional preference for it (Wegner).

Matthew, on the other hand, has a strong preference for ὄχλος and never omits it from Markan material (Wegner). Catchpole observes the use of ὄχλος with ἀκολούθειν in MattR, further strengthening the argument that Matthew would not likely omit it here.

Gundry offers the only argument for Luke's version, noting that Matt 8:1 already speaks of crowds following Jesus and suggesting that mention of the crowds would be redundant here. He attributes Matthew's plural to the influence of Matt 8:1. Despite the plausibility of Gundry's argument, the evidence is weighted heavily against the originality of Luke's reading.

Robinson 2000: Matt = Q {B}, τ(οῖς)⁵ ἀκολουθοῦ(σιν)⁵.

The fact that the *explicit* of Q refers to the Jesus people as οἱ ἀκολουθήσαν-τες, used by Matt 19:28a (but not by Luke 22:28), suggests that here, too, the plural substantive participle is in Q, also used by Matthew but not by Luke. Both texts are brought together by the invidious reference to Israel Q 22:30. ("Israel" is used only in these two places in Q, which underscores their interconnectedness.) This would suggest that "those following" Jesus are intended by Q more as the inner circle of disciples and less as the amorphous outer cluster of the crowd. In Q 7:9, the present participle indicates they are currently following Jesus, while in Q 22:28, they are identified, in retrospect, as those who have followed him.

The Lukan sequence is Lukan (Jeremias).

Kloppenborg 2000: Matt = Q {B}, τ(οῖς)⁵ ἀκολουθοῦ(σιν)⁵.

Hoffmann 2001: Matt = Q {B}, τ(οῖς)⁵ ἀκολουθοῦ(σιν)⁵.

Da Matthäus selbst häufig redaktionell schreibt, daß Jesus die ὄχλοι o.ä. folgen (8,1; 12,15; 19,2; 20,29; mit Markus 4,25; 21,9), hätte er hier ihre Erwähnung kaum gestrichen.

Q 7:9⁶: Matthew's ἀμήν.

Luke = Q: ( )⁶ λέγω ὑμῖν

Pro

Con

Cadbury 1920, 157: "With regard to ἀμήν Luke's practice varies, but he seems often to change or omit it. It is omitted in: ... Mt. 8,10 ἀμὴν λέγω ὑμῖν—Lk. 7,9 λέγω ὑμῖν (Q)."

George 1972, 71: "Luc paraît avoir introduit quelques retouches lit-téraires[12] et surtout deux modifications significatives."

71[12]: "Omission d'*Amen* qui se trouve 31 fois chez Mt, 13 chez Mc, 6 chez Lc, 50 chez Jn, 0 en Ac)."

Fitzmyer 1981, 653: "Luke has omitted the introductory *amen* (cf. Matt 8:10)."

Dauer 1984, 86: "Ἀμήν, das, im Gegensatz zu Mt, in Lk fehlt, wird der 3. Evangelist ausgelassen haben, wie er es öfters tut."

Stuiber 1985, 312: "Lukas hat Amen nur noch sechsmal beibehalten; sonst übersetzt er A[men] mit ναί (Lc. 7,26; 11,51; 12,5), ἀληθῶς (9,27; 12,44; 21,3), ἐπ᾽ ἀληθείας (4,25); er ersetzt Amen durch γάρ (20,24; 22,16.18) oder er läßt es ganz fort (7,9.29; 10,12; 12,59; 15,7.10; 22,34)."

Matt = Q: (ἀμὴν)⁶ λέγω ὑμῖν

Pro

von Harnack 1907, 56: "Also ist ... τοῖς ἀκολουθοῦσιν ([Luke:] τῷ ἀκολουθοῦντι αὐτῷ ὄχλῳ) ursprünglich, wahrscheinlich auch das ἀμήν."

91: Reconstruction. For complete text see Q 7:1⁶ Luke = Q, Pro (p. 55).

von Harnack 1907, ET 1908, 77: "Τοῖς ἀκολουθοῦσιν (St. Luke, τῷ ἀκολουθοῦντι αὐτῷ ὄχλῳ) is also original, probably also the ἀμήν."

132: Reconstruction. For complete text see Q 7:1⁶ Luke = Q, Pro (p. 55).

Castor 1912, 224: Reconstruction. For complete text see Q 7:1⁰ In Q (p. 6).

224[1]: "Ἀμήν seems to have been avoided by Luke. He frequently omits it from Mark."

Crum 1927, 138: Reconstruction. For complete text see Q 7:~~2~~, 3, ~~4-6a~~[1] Luke = Q, Pro (pp. 71-72).

Hasler 1969, 60: "Mt 8,10 führt das Logion aus Q mit der Amen-Formel, Lk 7,9 mit der Kurzformel ein."

George 1972, 71: "Mt 8,10 semble plus primitif que Lc 7,9."

Polag 1979, 38: Reconstruction. For complete text see Q 7:1⁰ In Q (pp. 9-10).

Gundry 1982, 144: "The tradition probably supplied ἀμήν, which Luke dropped."

Wegner 1985, 215: "Betrachtet man … das Vorkommen von ἀμήν im Q-Stoff, so ist es recht auffällig, daß alle Belege ausschließlich in den Mt-Parallelen vorkommen, wobei die entsprechenden Lk-Stellen es entweder gar nicht bringen, oder aber dafür ein ναί bzw. ἀληθῶς haben²⁴. Angesichts dieses Q-Befundes wird man kaum Mt eine sek Hinzufügung des ἀμήν an allen Q-Belegen zuschreiben dürfen, es sei denn, eine zurückhaltende red Tätigkeit gegenüber den ἀμήν-Worten des Mk hätte sich seltsamerweise gegenüber Q ins Uferlose gesteigert."

215²⁴: "Ersatzlos steht mt ἀμήν bei folgenden Lk-Parallelen: Lk 7,9.28; 10,12.24; 12,59; 15,7; 16,17 und 17,6 (wobei an den zwei letztgenannten Stellen auch die mit ἀμήν zusammen erscheinende Formel λέγω ὑμῖν entfiel); in Lk 11,51 erscheint das mt ἀμήν durch ναί und in 12,44 durch ἀληθῶς wiedergegeben."

271: Reconstruction. For complete text see Q 7:1⁰ In Q (pp. 11-12).

Lindars 1992, 210: Reconstruction. For complete text see Q 7:1⁶ Luke = Q, Pro (p. 56).

Con

B. Weiß 1876, 229-230: "Bei Mtth. nur das μόνον (wie 5,47) und das ἀμήν (wie 5,26) zugesetzt sein [230] dürfte."

B. Weiß 1908, 15: Reconstruction. For complete text see Q 7:1⁰ In Q (p. 5).

16²⁶: "Das so häufig von Mtth. hinzugefügte ἀμήν … kann auch Mt. 8,10 nicht ursprünglich sein (gegen Harnack [1907, 56; ET, 77])."

Bussmann 1929, 56: "L. hat in v. 9 ταῦτα und αὐτόν, die ursprünglicher wohl sind als die absoluten Ausdrücke, aber στραφείς und ὄχλῳ (darum τῷ ἀκολουθοῦντι) gehen auf Stilisierung des L zurück, während das ἀμήν von Mt zugesetzt ist."

Delobel 1966, 455-456: "Le jugement sur ἀμήν dans la matière Q est délicat. Connaissant la préférence prononcée de *Mt.* pour cette formule, nous nous sentons porté pour l'hypothèse [456] de l'addition, sans toutefois exclure tout à fait la possibilité d'une omission par Luc."

Schulz 1972, 239: "Auch ἀμήν wird von Mt stammen.⁴²⁴"

239⁴²⁴: "Mt zeigt allgemein eine Tendenz, ἀμήν seinen Vorlagen gelegentlich einzufügen."

Lange 1973, 131¹¹²: "Ἀμὴν λέγω ὑμῖν ist nachweislich redaktionell in Mt 19,23 (vgl. Mk 10,23) und Mt 24,2 (vgl. Mk 13,2), mit mehr oder minder großer Sicherheit aber auch in den Stellen Mt 5,18; 5,26; 8,10; 10,15; 11,11; 13,17; 17,20; 18,13; 23,36; 24,47 und häufig im Sondergut."

Schenk 1981, 37: Reconstruction. For complete text see Q 7:1⁰ In Q (p. 10).

Neirynck 1982, 69: "The Matthaean origin of ἀμήν is highly probable in passages which are heavily redacted: 8,10 (+ 8,11-12 λέγω δὲ ὑμῖν ὅτι) [et alia]."

Wegner 1985, 214: "Demnach hat Mt es 9x aus Mk übernommen, 2x in seinen Mk-Stoff eingefügt und 2x aus dem Mk-Stoff gestrichen. Eine bei Mt verstärkt festzustellende Tendenz, das ἀμήν zu tilgen, trifft entgegen der Meinung Jeremias nicht zu."

215: "Aus dem Vergleich mit Mk ergibt sich, daß das lk Verfahren hinsichtlich der ihm vorgegebenen ἀμήν-Belege 'konservativ' ist, so daß man angesichts des Befundes in Mt und Lk dazu geneigt ist, auSt eher an eine sek Interpolation des Mt als an eine red Streichung des Lk zu denken." But see Wegner at Matt = Q, Pro (p. 335).

Schenk 1987, 334-335: "Eine Grauzone der traditionsgeschichtlichen Analyse liegt in den 6 Logien aus Q vor, bei denen Lk zwar die explizit-performative Redeeinleitung, jedoch nur Mt ein zusätzliches Amen hat: ... 8,10 (= Lk 7,9—mt die lehrhafte Quintessenz der Heilungsgeschichte für die nachfolgenden)."

Nolland 1989, 318: "The 'amen' in Matthew's text is probably Matthean redaction."

Davies and Allison 1991, 24: "Matthew has probably added 'amen'. It makes for solemnity."

Catchpole 1992, 537 [1993, 304]: "As for the pronouncement itself two decisions have to be made. The first concerns Matthew's ἀμήν, a disputed matter but perhaps just more likely to have been inserted by Matthew than excised by Luke."

539 [307]: Reconstruction. For complete text see Q 7:1⁰ In Q (p. 14).

Gagnon 1994b, 138: "As for Matthean alterations of the core dialogue in Q, we can probably attribute to him ... the addition of ἀμήν to the introductory formula λέγω ὑμῖν in 8.10."

Landis 1994, 13: "Am Anfang von 8,10b bietet Mt über Lk 7,9b hinaus ἀμήν vor λέγω ὑμῖν. Die Frage, ob ἀμήν bereits im Text der Logienquelle gestanden hat, ist schwer zu entscheiden. Es sprechen aber doch einige Anzeichen für einen redaktionellen Ursprung des Wortes an unserer Stelle: so etwa eine

gewisse Tendenz des Mt, ἀμήν seinen Vorlagen einzufügen; die im allgemeinen 'konservative' Haltung des Lk zu diesem Ausdruck sowie seine
Zurückhaltung gegenüber der Neuschöpfung asyndetischer Konstruktionen
deuten darauf hin, daß dem dritten Evangelisten in der Logienquelle λέγω
ὑμῖν ohne vorangehendes ἀμήν vorgelegen hat."

    13, 17: Reconstruction. For complete text see Q 7:1⁶ Luke = Q, Pro (p. 57).
International Q Project 1995, 479: Reconstruction. For complete text see
Q 7:1⁰ In Q (p. 16).
    Neirynck 1995, 177: "Au v. 10, il [Landis 1994, 13] a sans doute raison de
supprimer ἀμήν."

Evaluations

Johnson 2000: Luke = Q {C}, [[()⁶]] λέγω ὑμῖν.
    The evidence on the redactional addition or omission of ἀμήν by Matthew
and Luke respectively is mixed (Johnson 1997 and Robinson 1997, 400-401
[see Bibliography]). As a preference, Matthew adds it and Luke omits it or
uses a synonymous expression.
    On the other hand, Matthew's sharpening of Q's subsequent οὐδέ to παρ'
οὐδενί and interpolation of Matt 8:11-12 raise the possibility of Matthean
insertion here. Matt 8:11 also has the λέγω ὑμῖν formula, but without ἀμήν
(Luke 13:28-29 does not have the λέγω ὑμῖν formula). In light of the subsequent interpolation, an ἀμήν at Matt 8:10b further sets apart and highlights
the central saying of the pericope. The added λέγω ὑμῖν formula without ἀμήν
in 8:11 distinguishes what follows as a separate saying, but one that specifies
the ramifications of the relative lack of faith in Israel described by Matt 8:10b.
    Because of Luke's preference for omitting ἀμήν, a cautious decision is
appropriate.

Robinson 2000: Luke = Q {B}, ()⁶ λέγω ὑμῖν.
    Though ἀμήν is not doubly attested in Q, it seems to have been in Q at
times, though eliminated by Luke. So its absence from Q here is not certain.

Kloppenborg 2000: Luke = Q {B}, ()⁶ λέγω ὑμῖν.

Hoffmann 2001: Luke = Q {B}, ()⁶ λέγω ὑμῖν.
    Da eine ersatzlose Streichung durch Lukas ungewöhnlich ist, Matthäus aber
Amen häufig einfügt, ist {B} berechtigt.

Q 7:9⁷: Luke's οὐδέ or Matthew's παρ' οὐδενί.

Luke = Q: ( )⁷ οὐδέ( )⁷

Pro

B. Weiß 1876, 230: "Gewiß ... sollte das οὐδὲ ἐν τῷ 'Ισραήλ bei Luc das Lob des Heiden noch stärker hervorheben."

von Harnack 1907, 91 (ET 1908, 132): Reconstruction. For complete text see Q 7:1⁶ Luke = Q, Pro (p. 55).

B. Weiß 1908, 15: Reconstruction. For complete text see Q 7:1⁰ In Q (p. 5).

Crum 1927, 138: Reconstruction. For complete text see Q 7:2, 3, 4-6a¹ Luke = Q, Pro (pp. 71-72).

Jacobson 1978, 67: "A striking difference between the Johannine and Q accounts is the 'punchline' in Q: 'I tell you, not even in Israel have I found such faith.'"

Polag 1979, 38: Reconstruction. For complete text see Q 7:1⁰ In Q (pp. 9-10).

Schenk 1981, 37: Reconstruction. For complete text see Q 7:1⁰ In Q (p. 10).

Jacobson 1992, 109: "A striking difference between the Johannine and Q accounts is the 'punchline' in Q: 'I tell you, not even in Israel have I found such faith.'¹³⁰"

109¹³⁰: "Or, 'I tell you, with no one is Israel ...' ... is the more probable reading in Matt 8:10. ... However, the Matthean reading is secondary, and Luke more nearly represents Q."

Gagnon 1993, 715-716: "The reading in Luke 7:9, '*not even* (οὐδέ) in Israel have I found such faith,' probably [716] reproduces the Q text."

Sevenich-Bax 1993, 185-186: "Da sich die sprachlichen Unterschiede zwischen Matthäus und Lukas nicht durch wortstatistische Beobachtungen klären lassen, muß danach gefragt werden, ob Matthäus oder Lukas an einer Modifizierung der ursprünglichen Aussage theologisch interessiert ist. Auch hier ergeben sich Probleme, da beide Standpunkte mit guten Argumenten vertreten werden:

"α) Eine Änderung durch Matthäus läßt sich damit begründen, daß Matthäus offensichtlich um eine deutliche Grenzziehung zwischen Juden und Heiden bemüht ist, wie v.a. der sekundäre Eintrag Mt 8,11+12 (par. Lk 13,28f.) zu erkennen gibt.

"β) Ebenso läßt sich aber auch eine Umarbeitung durch Lukas vertreten, weil er bereits durch die Einfügung der Verse Lk 7,3-6b eine pro-jüdische Tendenz dokumentiert.

"Eine Entscheidung hinsichtlich der Originalität der matthäischen oder lukanischen Fassung kann in diesem Fall also nur über die Frage nach der Vereinbarkeit des Wortlautes mit der Aussage der Erzähleinheit getroffen werden: Beide Evangelisten stimmen in der Pointe überein, daß nämlich solcher Glaube in 'Israel' nicht gefunden, in Nicht-Israel aber gefunden wird. Diese Paradoxie, die in dem Kontrastschema <'Israel'—sonstige> entwickelt wird, ist für die Erzählung konstitutiv und wird in dem Wort Jesu reflektiert. Daß Matthäus [186] nun—wie dargestellt—die Größe 'Israel' in der vorliegenden Form negiert, paßt nicht in das Muster der Erzählung, da er auf diese Weise die als 'Israel' bezeichnete kollektive Größe relativiert und damit zugleich das grundlegende und die Schilderung bestimmende Schema <'Israel'—sonstige> aufhebt. Umgekehrt entspricht die im lukanischen Text vorausgesetzte Vorstellung von dem Glauben Israels als dem Maßstab, an dem der Glaube der Völker gemessen wird, nicht allein lukanischen Anschauungen, sondern v.a. traditionellen weisheitlichen Ansichten seit Sir 24. Dabei kann die 'Ausnahme', nämlich der Glaube der 'anderen', durchaus die 'Regel', d.i. Israel als heilsgeschichtlicher Träger von Glaube überhaupt, bestätigen. Daß diese Sichtweise mit der von Q vertretenen Theologie übereinstimmt, daß mithin der lukanische Wortlaut der mutmaßlich ursprüngliche ist, läßt sich im weiteren Kontext unserer Perikope vertiefend auch an den Texten zeigen, die sich mit 'dieser Generation' auseinandersetzen. Im engeren Sinn zählen hierzu die Worte über 'dieses Geschlecht' (Lk 7,31//Mt 11,16; Lk 11,29//Mt 12,39; Lk 11,31f.//Mt 12,42f.; Lk 11,51//Mt 23,36), im weiteren Sinn sind hier aber auch die Weherufe über die jüdischen Städte Jerusalem (Lk 13,34-35//Mt 23,37-39) sowie Betsaida und Chorazin (Lk 10,13f.//Mt 11,21f.), also die sogenannten Gerichtsworte, von Interesse."

238: Reconstruction. For complete text see Q 7:1⁰ In Q (p. 15).

Landis 1994, 13: "Ein noch mehr diskutiertes Problem bietet die bei Mt 8,10b und Lk 7,9b unterschiedlich formulierte negative Aussage über Israel. Die mt Version (παρ' οὐδενί ... ἐν τῷ Ἰσραήλ) betont den schroffen Unterschied zwischen Juden und Heiden, stellt antithetisch den Glauben des Heiden dem absoluten Unglauben Israels gegenüber. Der Lk-Text (οὐδὲ ἐν τῷ Ἰσραήλ) hingegen impliziert, daß normalerweise Jesus bei den Juden die größere Empfänglichkeit voraussetzen könnte; diese Version hält also am Vorrang Israels fest. Hat hier Lk einer scharfen, gegen Israel gerichteten Aussage die Spitze brechen wollen, oder hat umgekehrt erst Mt den Gegensatz zwischen Juden und Heiden polemisch akzentuiert? Letzteres erscheint deshalb wahrscheinlicher, weil die verschärfte Formulierung bereits die mt Interpretation der Geschichte im Einschub von V.11f ... vorwegnimmt. Demnach ist in diesem Fall die lk Wendung als ursprünglich anzusehen."

13, 17: Reconstruction. For complete text see Q 7:1⁶ Luke = Q, Pro (p. 57).

International Q Project 1995, 479: Reconstruction. For complete text see
Q 7:1⁰ In Q (p. 16).

Con

B. Weiß 1878, 365: "V. 9. (οὐδὲ ἐν τ. 'Ισρ.) nicht einmal ist Israel, hebt das
Lob des Heiden noch stärker hervor, als die ursprüngliche Lesart bei Matth."

Hirsch 1941, 89: "Jesus sagt Luk 7,9 nicht wie bei Matth: 'Bei keinem in
Israel hab ich solchen Glauben gefunden', sondern (nach der besseren Lesart):
'Nicht einmal in Israel hab ich solchen Glauben gefunden'. D.h. die Veränderungen setzen es als das Normale voraus, daß Jesus allein mit den Juden
umgeht, daß die Fürsprache einer jüdischen Gemeindebehörde und ein Synagogenbau in Jesu Augen eine Empfehlung sind, daß Jesus im jüdischen Volk
die größere Empfänglichkeit zu erwarten hat. Damit ist die Begegnung Jesu
mit dem heidnischen Hauptmann in judenchristliche Logik eingeordnet."

90: "In [vs.] 9 gibt Luk nicht eine andre Vorlage, sondern die von andrer
Hand korrigierte Q-Fassung wieder ('Nicht einmal in Israel' usw.), und diese
Korrektur hat die gleiche Richtung wie die andre Fassung der Einleitung."
Hirsch argues here for pre-Lukan recensions of Q.

Zuntz 1945, 187-188: See Q 7:8¹ Luke = Q, Con (p. 308).

P. Meyer 1970, 410-411: "The central παρ' οὐδενί etc. (Matt 8:10b), however, is found in significantly different form in Luke 7:9b; Strecker [1962,
100; see Matt = Q, Con (pp. 344-345)], for one, thinks Luke's version is original and Matthew's redactional. Several reasons exist for disputing this. First,
Luke had reason to change Q's antagonistic challenge to one expressing only
a 'gradual contrast' (Strecker's phrase). Luke has structured Jesus' ministry
according to theological presuppositions, and this phase of that ministry was
one of popular acclaim and miracles (cf. chs. 4-6), one marked by division
within Israel between the true people of God and unbelievers (beginning with
John, cf. Luke 7:29f. and Conzelmann [1954, 173; ET,] 186). Most important, Jesus' ministry was *unto Israel*; Luke 'deliberately removes the time of the
mission to the Gentiles from the period of Jesus' (Conzelmann, [31;] 37).
Luke has emphasized Jesus' solicitous concern for Israel by excising Mark's
narrative of the accursed fig tree (Mark 11:12ff., 20-25) but adding a parable
allegorically stressing Jesus' nurture of Israel (Luke 13:6-9). For this same reason he substituted οὐδέ for παρ' οὐδενί, at one and the same time preserving
the impression of rapport between Jesus and Israel (if not her leaders) and (by
emphasizing the exceptional character of the Gentile and his faith) minimiz-
ing the implicit contradiction to *Heilsgeschichte* engendered by Jesus' minister-
ing to a Gentile. Second, if Luke's version represents Q, it is the only pericope
in that source implying anything like a favorable view of 'this generation,'

much less of the Gentiles. This is in sharp contrast to an abundance of texts condemning the faithlessness of 'this generation' (e.g., Matt 12:38-42/Luke 11:29-32; Matt 11:16-19/Luke 7:31-35, besides others ...). At best, Q views Gentiles as instruments by which Jews may be convicted and repent. Therefore to suppose Luke's version reflects Q in this matter implies a considerable contradiction [411] in the views reflected in that source. Lastly, it must be conceded that Matthew imported 8:11f. from another place in Q (and created vs. 13). But this by no means proves he altered the text of vs. 10; indeed, in its Matthean context the verse is somewhat contradictory, since Jesus has just healed a leper on confession of faith in his ability to do so, Matt 8:1-4. The sum of the evidence would indicate that Matthew has rightly interpreted the challenge in Jesus' saying as found in Q, and brought in the other saying (8:11f.) because it represented the same point of view: the Jews' unbelief was subject to condemnation when compared with the faith Gentiles were manifesting. On this point, at least, Matthew's and Q's theology coincide."

George 1972, 68: "Devant ce message, Jésus est rempli d'admiration (v. 9). Ce trait ne se trouve que chez Luc, et aucun autre passage des évangiles ne rapporte explicitement une telle réaction du Maître (on peut toutefois comparer son exclamation: 'Oh femme! ta foi est grande!' devant la confiance de la Cananéenne en Mt 15,28). Dans l'attitude du centurion, sûr de la puissance de sa parole, il reconnaît la foi véritable. Il se tourne vers la foule de Juifs qui le suit (ce trait est propre à Luc). Il compare la foi du païen à celle qu'il a rencontrée jusqu'ici: pas même en Israël il n'en a trouvé une aussi profonde. La phrase est moins dure pour Israël que son parallèle en Mt 8,10 puisqu'elle place Israël au-dessus des autres peuples; elle semble aussi indiquer que l'Évangile a été prêché ailleurs qu'en Israël et que Luc pense à la situation de son temps où le message de Jésus est prêché et aux Juifs et aux Gentils."

71: "Luc paraît avoir introduit quelques retouches littéraires et surtout deux modifications significatives: ... le jugement sur la foi d'Israël semble adouci par Luc, qui suggère en même temps qui l'évangile a déjà été prêché à d'autres."

Derrett 1973, 176: "The climax is Jesus's approval of the man's faith, greater than he had found in Israel, and Luke may well be right in placing the emphasis so, 'not even in Israel.'"

Martin 1978, 18: "Luke has phrased the Lord's word in 7:9 in a way that could conceivably be an implied compliment to Israel: 'Not even in Israel (where I would most expect it) have I found such faith'."

19²: "The reading [of Matt 8:10] offered in the other body of [textual] witnesses ... conforms to Luke 7:9, reading οὐδὲ ἐν τῷ Ἰσραήλ in place of παρ' οὐδενί. The standard comparison is less severe, and the former reading may even contain a tribute to the man as exemplifying such faith as Jesus expected to find within the Jewish nation. It says nothing about the presence or absence of faith, and this reading probably reflects Luke's redaction of the Matthean 'radicalized form' (W. Grundmann, [1968, 252]).

"In this way Luke has made it possible to include the faith of 'the elders' and the 'friends' (7:6) who presumably shared the Gentile's confidence in Jesus' ability to heal. The alternative Matthean reading demonstrates the tendency to osmosis with the 'easier reading,' and it attempts to soften the stark original form: παρ' οὐδενὶ τοσαύτην πίστιν, κτλ."

Fitzmyer 1981, 649: "Lucan redaction would be further responsible for the omission of 'Amen' (see Matt 8:10b) and for the use of the negative 'not even' (Luke 7:9)."

650: "The main point in the Lucan story is not so much the worthiness of this particular Gentile, a point stressed by the elders, but rather his 'faith' (*pistis*, 7:9). Its importance is seen ... in the Lucan emphasis ('*not even in Israel* have I found such faith as this')."

Wegner 1985, 218: "Die Möglichkeit einer red Bildung ist dadurch gegeben, daß Lk das Wort 12x in der Apg und 2x als Hinzufügung zu Mk benutzt. ... Bei Mt fällt auf, daß er οὐδέ mit Vorliebe red in seinen Mk-Stoff einfügt—insgesamt 8x. Das aber bedeutet, daß rein stat eine durch Mt sek unternommene Streichung des οὐδέ zugunsten von παρ' οὐδενί unwahrscheinlich ist."

Matt = Q: (παρ')[7] οὐδε(νί)[7]

Pro

Hirsch 1941, 89: See Hirsch at Luke = Q, Con (p. 340).
P. Meyer 1970, 410-411: See Meyer at Luke = Q, Con (p. 340-341).
George 1972, 71: "Mt 8,10 semble plus primitif que Lc 7,9."
Marshall 1978, 282: "Matthew states more simply that Jesus has not found such faith among anybody in Israel, which may be original."
Wegner 1985, 216-218: "Παρά: ... Ein bevorzugter Gebrauch von παρά in Verbindung mit dem Dativ ist bei Mt nicht festzustellen: Mt bringt es mit dem Dativ außer auSt noch 2x in seinem Sg (6,1 und 28,15), 2x als Übernahme von Mk (19,26 bis), und lediglich 1x setzt er diese Präposition mit dem Dativ red ein (22,25 diff Mk). Auch Lk bringt die Konstruktion παρά + Dativ mehrfach in seinem Ev: vgl. 18,27 bis par Mk; 9,47 diff Mk 9,36 und 1,30; 2,52; 11,37 und 19,7 Sg.

"Da von einer Bevorzugung des παρά durch den ersten Evangelisten kaum die Rede sein kann, wird man die Präposition hier für trad halten können, obwohl die Möglichkeit einer red Bildung nicht ganz ausgeschlossen werden kann. Demgegenüber zeigt aber der Befund im dritten Ev, daß Lk diese Präposition [217] kaum streichen würde, falls sie in der von ihm verarbeiteten Vorlage der Hauptmannserzählung gestanden hätte, denn Lk fügt nicht nur παρά mehrmals in seinen Mk-Stoff ein, sondern steht auch der Konstruktion παρά + Dativ keineswegs abweisend gegenüber. Stand παρά dennoch in der urspr Hauptmannserzählung, so bleibt es immerhin auffällig, daß diese Präposition in Q sonst nirgendwo mehr auftaucht.

"οὐδείς: ... Die drei Q-Belege sind Mt 6:24/Lk 16,13; 10,26/Lk 12,2 (οὐδέν) und 11,27/Lk 10,22. Zu QMt und QLk gehören nach Gaston [1973, 5] folgende Stellen: Mt 5,13; 8,10; 17,20 (QMt) und Lk 4,2b; 7,28; 11,33 (QLk). In Lk 11,33 par Mt 5,15 haben im Gegensatz zu uSt Lk οὐδείς und Mt οὐδέ. Für QLk käme noch Lk 14,24 (Sv om Mt 22,10) in Frage. Dieser Beleg ist für uSt insofern von Belang, als auch hier οὐδείς sich auf die Juden (als die zum Gastmahl Erstgeladenen) in Kontrast zu den Heiden (?) (als die Letzteingeladenen) bezieht. Innerhalb des LkEv wird οὐδείς zur Kennzeichnung des Juden im Kontrast zu den Heiden nur noch 2x im Sg gebraucht, nämlich in 4,26f; im MkEv kommt das Wort in diesem Gebrauch niemals und im MtEv—außer Mt 8.10—auch an keiner weiteren Stelle vor.

"Aus dem stat Befund ergibt sich kein sicherer Anhaltspunkt, οὐδείς für mt-red zu halten. Da es mehrfach in Q auftaucht, ist es wahrscheinlich, daß Mt es aus dieser Quelle übernommen hat. Andererseits zeigt der Befund im LkEv, daß mit einer Streichung des Wortes durch den dritten Evangelisten kaum zu rechnen ist.

"Der Gesamtausdruck παρ' οὐδενί erscheint außer in Mt 8,10 sonst niemals in den Evv und Apg. Der erste Evangelist, der weder παρά noch οὐδείς mit Vorliebe verwendet, wird ihn [218] nicht selbst gebildet haben. Lk, der dafür οὐδέ bringt, wird die Wendung kaum in seiner Vorlage gelesen haben, da ja gerade er in seinem Ev das Juden und Heiden kontrastierende οὐδείς am häufigsten verwendet (Lk 4,26.27 und 14,24)."

220: "Mit Strecker [1962, 100] wird wohl eine Akzentverschiebung in der mt Fassung festzuhalten sein. Ob dies aber auf das Konto der mt Red zurückzuführen ist, scheint uns fraglich. Das verschärfte παρ' οὐδενί muß von dem Hintergrund anderer gegen Israel zugespitzter Aussagen[39] gesehen werden, wo Jesus ebenfalls in äußerster Schärfe das von Gott auserwählte Volk tadelt und zugleich die Demut und den Glauben der Heiden als Kontrast-beispiele hervorhebt. Die mit παρ' οὐδενί gegebene Verschärfung paßt übrigens auch gut zu Q, wo ja mehrmals die Anklage gegen Israel in scharfen Tönen formuliert erscheint.

"Bestehen daher auch in sachlicher Hinsicht keine grundsätzlichen Bedenken gegen die Annahme einer Ursprünglichkeit des mt παρ' οὐδενί, so scheint uns, was οὐδέ anbelangt, die bessere Erklärung immer noch die der sekundären Ableitung aus derselben pro-jüdischen Tendenz zu sein, die auch für die Gestaltung von Lk 7,3-6ab."

220[39]: "Vgl. die Q-Stellen Mt 8,11f; 11,20-24; 12,38-42 und 22,1-10 par Lk; ferner Lk 4,26f (Sg)."

221: "Zwischen παρ' οὐδενί und οὐδέ war eine Entscheidung auf Grund der Stat allein nicht möglich. Aus sachlichen Erwägungen ergab sich aber, daß das mt παρ' οὐδενί für ursprünglicher gehalten werden kann, während οὐδέ vermutlich mit der Lk 7,3-6ab.(7a?)10 festzustellenden Bearbeitung der Erzählung zusammenhängt. Mit dieser Entscheidung für die Fassung des ersten Evangelisten hängt auch zusammen, daß die von ihm gebotene Wortakoluthie in diesem Versteil für die ursprünglichere gehalten wurde."

271: Reconstruction. For complete text see Q 7:1[0] In Q (pp. 11-12).

Schenk 1987, 380: "οὐδείς, -μία, -έν: 8,10 (+Q)."

Catchpole 1992, 539 [1993, 306]: "The slightest of slight preferences may favour Matthew's παρ' οὐδενί, given the overall closeness of the Matthaean text to Q, the correspondence with Lucan formulations in similar setting (Luke 4,25-27; 14,24), and the agreement between Luke's οὐδὲ ἐν τῷ Ἰσραήλ and the LukeR intervention in his vv. 3-6a.7a."

539 [307]: Reconstruction. For complete text see Q 7:1[0] In Q (p. 14).

Lindars 1992, 210: Reconstruction. For complete text see Q 7:1[6] Luke = Q, Pro (p. 56).

Dunderberg 1994, 85: "Obwohl Mt und Lk das Lob Jesu recht ähnlich wiedergeben, ist auch hier eine wichtige Abweichung vorhanden. Während Mt 8,10 betont, Jesus habe *bei niemandem in Israel* so einen festen Glauben gefunden (παρ' οὐδενὶ τοσαύτην πίστιν ἐν τῷ Ἰσραὴλ εὗρον), drückt Lk den Gegensatz zwischen dem Glauben eines Heiden und dem Verhalten Israels nicht so scharf aus. Denn nach Lk 7,9 habe Jesus *nicht einmal in Israel* einen solchen Glauben gefunden (οὐδὲ ἐν τῷ Ἰσραὴλ τοσαύτην πίστιν εὗρον)."

87: "Außerdem entspricht die drastische Kritik an dem Volk Gottes in diesem Zusammenhang der matthäischen Fassung vom Lob Jesu (8,10), in der sich ein schrofferer Gegensatz zu Israel anmeldete als bei Lk. Doch ist daraus nicht zu folgern, daß Mt den ursprünglichen Wortlaut von Q in 8,10 verschärft habe."

Con

B. Weiß 1908, 16[26]: "Dann aber wird auch das verstärkende παρ' οὐδενί Mt. 8,10 nicht aus Q herrühren, da es offenbar durch die eingeschalteten Sprüche v. 11.12 (bem. das ganz allgemeine οἱ υἱοὶ τῆς βασιλ.) veranlaßt ist."

Easton 1926, 97: "Παρ' οὐδενὶ τοσαύτην in Mt ... is a heightening, either by Mt himself or by some copyist."

Strecker 1962, 100: "Während Jesus nach Lukas 'noch nicht einmal (οὐδέ) in Israel solchen Glauben' gefunden hat (Lk. V. 9), heißt es Mt. V. 10: 'bei niemandem ...' (παρ' οὐδενί); letzteres ist sekundär, denn es nimmt die folgende matthäische Interpretation vorweg, wie sich gleich zeigen wird. Ursprünglich ist also die Perikope vom Standpunkt Israels aus geschrieben, indem sie am israelitischen Vorrang festhielt. Betont war zwar der außergewöhnliche Glaube des Centurio, aber das οὐδέ charakterisierte Israel nicht als ungläubig, sondern bezeichnete nur einen graduellen Gegensatz zwischen dem Glauben des Heiden und dem Israels. Anders die matthäische Darstellung. Hier ist der Akzent deutlich antithetisch-ausschließend gesetzt."

Walker 1967, 49: "So schreibt der harte Griffel des Redaktors in [Matt] 8,10: Bei *niemandem* habe ich so großen Glauben in Israel gefunden."

Grundmann 1968, 252: "Ihnen sagt er—in einer gegenüber Lukas radikalisierten Form: παρ' οὐδενί ... statt οὐδέ—mit einem Amen-Wort, er habe bei keinem in Israel so großen Glauben gefunden."

Schulz 1972, 239: "Mt hingegen wird ursprüngliches οὐδέ bei Lk durch παρ' οὐδενί ersetzt haben.⁴²³"

239⁴²³: "Mt will durch den folgenden Einschub der Vv 11f (aus Q) den schroffen Unterschied zwischen Israel und Heiden markieren und unterstreicht durch das παρ' οὐδενί diese Intention; ... Kann man Lk noch im Sinn eines bloß graduellen Unterschiedes zwischen dem Glauben Israels und demjenigen des Heiden verstehen, so verschärft die Mt-Fassung die Aussage durch das παρ' οὐδενί zu einer grundsätzlichen Antithese zwischen dem Glauben des Heiden und dem Glauben Israels."

Lange 1973, 50: "Mattäus formuliert sie, verglichen mit Lk 7,9 (= Q), zugleich mit einer merkwürdig einschneidenden und abschließenden Härte."

Jacobson 1978, 115¹²⁹: "The Matthaean reading is secondary, and Luke more nearly represents Q. Even if the 'not even in Israel' implies that hitherto the best examples of faith were to be found in Israel, the point is not to extol Israel's faith but to shame Israel for its lack of faith."

Gundry 1982, 144: "The emphatic 'not even' vanishes. In its stead appears 'with no one,' which is characteristic of Matthew's style in the use of παρά with the dative (2,2). He is implying that Jesus could hardly expect to find such faith as the centurion's in Israel as a nation, though he might have found it among individual Israelites."

Dauer 1984, 106: "Weiterhin wird auf diese mt Kritik die etwas anders und viel stärker formulierte Anerkennung des Glaubens des heidnischen Mannes durch Jesus zurückgehen: Während Jesus nach Lk V. 9 spricht: 'Ich sage euch, nicht einmal in Israel habe ich einen so großen Glauben gefunden' und damit zugesteht, doch Glauben unter seinen Landsleuten gefunden zu haben, urteilt er nach Mt V. 10 wesentlich schärfer: 'Wahrlich, ich sage euch, bei niemandem in Israel habe ich einen so großen Glauben gefunden.' Damit stellt er den Glauben als einzigartig dar und übt zugleich herbe Kritik an den Juden selbst."

Nolland 1989, 318: "Matthew's stronger and negatively slanted 'with no one' (Luke: 'not even') prepares for the extra material he inserts in Matt 8:11-12 and is therefore to be seen as Matthean redaction."

Luz 1990, 12[4]: "Παρ' οὐδενί (V 10) ist nicht aus sprachlichen, sondern aus inhaltlichen Gründen mt."

Luz 1990, ET 2001, 8[4]: "Παρ' οὐδενί (v. 10) is Matthean not for linguistic reasons but by virtue of its meaning."

Catchpole 1992, 537-539 [1993, 304-306]: "The case for παρ' οὐδενί has been put by Paul Meyer [1970, 410-411], and again more recently by Uwe Wegner [1985, 220]. (i) Luke's οὐδέ conforms to the scheme which gives priority to Jesus' mission to Israel and positive acclaim there, rather than a scheme involving sharp antagonism towards Israel. (ii) Matthew's version is in line with many other Q texts—10,13-15; 11,29-32; 13,28-29; 14,15-24 [Wegner, 220]—condemning the faithlessness of 'this generation' and viewing Gentiles as 'instruments by which the Jews may be convicted and repent' [Meyer, 410]. (iii) The Matthaean importation of Q [305] 13,28-29 does not prove that a MattR alteration has occurred in Matt 8,10, but rather indicates a Matthew/Q theological agreement that 'the Jews' unbelief was subject to condemnation when [538] compared with the faith Gentiles were manifesting' [Meyer, 411]. In the Matthaean context the παρ' οὐδενί saying is 'somewhat contradictory' because faith in Jesus' ability to work miracle has been confessed in the healing of the leper (Matt 8,1-4).

"By way of comment, several observations may be made: (i) The difference between Matthew and Luke has been greatly exaggerated. The key to the saying must be the agreed word τοσοῦτος, representing for both Matthew (cf. Matt 15,33 diff Mark 8,4) and Luke (cf. Luke 15,29; Acts 5,8) one amount rather than another. By 'another' neither evangelist would understand 'nothing'. Therefore neither evangelist would take ἡ τοσαύτη πίστις to mean that no faith at all had previously been encountered. Consequently, far from a discrepancy between Matt 8,1-4 and 8,10 there is a simple consistency. By way of confirmation, the faith which is shown in 'bringing' (προσφέρειν) the sick to Jesus in Matt 9,2/Mark 2,5 is also anticipated in advance of the centurion episode in the same 'bringing' in Matt 4,24/Mark 1,32. Similarly for Luke the faith of those who bring the sick to Jesus has already been on view in Luke 5,20/Mark 2,5. Consequently, whichever of παρ' οὐδενί and οὐδέ stood in Q, the implication is not that faith has been absent thus far in Israel. It is rather that in the context of a mission to Israel faith has indeed been present, but never on the scale or of the quality presently being exercised. (ii) What then of the argument from parallel material in Q, including that which refers to 'this generation'? Here again exaggeration is all too liable to occur. Q certainly envisages the present generation in general as misguided or obdurate, but there are qualifications and many exceptions. How otherwise can the criticism of 'this generation' as 'evil' (Q 11,29) and unrepentant (Q 11,32) coexist with the testimony of Q that the call for repentance (Q 3,8) has been heeded (Q 3,16b), as well as the implication that general human 'evil' (Q 11,13) by no means excludes all true goodness? How otherwise can a denunciation of 'this generation' in Q 7,31-32 [306] be interjected in a seemingly unqualified fashion as the rejection of John (Q 7,33) as well as Jesus (Q 7,34), and yet the preceding tradition make abundantly plain that 'crowds' (Q 7,24) have recognized him as a prophet (Q 7,26), and the concluding affirmation end on a resoundingly positive note in recording the recognition accorded by Wisdom's children (Q 7,35)? (iii) As to the Matthew/Q theological agreement centered on the use of Q 13,28-29, there is more than a little evidence that the saying in question referred to the diaspora Jews who would come 'from east and west' and displace certain other persons. [539] The 'sons of the kingdom', almost certainly the term used by Q to describe those persons,[93] cannot stand for all Jews resident within the boundaries of the land but rather for those Jews who have witnessed the mission of Jesus and kept their distance. Alongside them must be set those who, according to Q, receive the revelation as 'babes' (Q 10,21-22), or see and hear the present eschatological realities (Q 10,23-24), or address God as 'Father' (Q 11,2-4), or have some faith even if it is 'little faith' (Q 12,28). Indeed, one might add, even in the present story the audience consists of οἱ ἀκολουθοῦντες, and who are they but persons, Jewish persons indeed, who satisfy the conditions of discipleship (cf. Q 9,57-60; 14,27)? (iv) Word-statistical evidence is not decisive: παρά + dative formulations are attested in MattR,[95] while οὐδέ formulations are well attested in LukeR.[96]"

539 [306][93]: "Its synoptic usage is confined to Matt 8,12 diff Luke 13,28 and Matt 13,38. The two cases are related in that Matthew is in both contexts drawing on Q 13,18-30, but unrelated in that the sense of the term varies between those who participate in the kingdom and those who are excluded from it. One (Matt 8,12), but not the other (Matt 13,38), is therefore pre-Matthaean."

539 [306][95]: "Matt 6,1; 22,25; 28,15."

539 [306][96]: "Luke 6,3; 12,26; 20,36; 23,15.40."

Jacobson 1992, 109[130]: "'I tell you, with no one in Israel …' … is the more probable reading in Matt 8:10. … However, the Matthean reading is secondary, and Luke more nearly represents Q. Even if 'not even in Israel' implies that hitherto the best examples of faith were to be found in Israel, the point is not to extol Israel's faith but to shame Israel for its lack of faith."

Gagnon 1993, 715: "Matt 8:10, *'with no one* (παρ᾽ οὐδενί) in Israel have I found such faith,' is to be viewed as Matthew's polemically oriented sharpening of the Q text."

Gagnon 1994b, 138: "As for Matthean alterations of the core dialogue in Q, we can probably attribute to him ... the intensification of the less strident indictment of the Jews in Luke 7.9 (οὐδὲ ἐν τῷ Ἰσραὴλ τοσαύτην πίστιν εὗρον, 'not even in Israel did I find such faith') to the biting 'with no one did I find such faith in Israel' (παρ᾽ οὐδενὶ τοσαύτην πίστιν ἐν τῷ Ἰσραὴλ εὗρον) in Matt 8.10."

139: "Matthew was certainly capable of inserting the construction παρά + dative (5-6 times in Matthew, once in Mark, 14 times in Luke-Acts) into his source as he does in 22.25 (cf. Mark 12.20) and probably also in 28.15 (where Matthew alone notes that the story of the stolen body 'is still told among the Jews ... today'—a remark which in terms of tone and content bears striking resemblances to 8.10). Moreover, Luke shows no special aversion to using παρά + dat.; and παρά (+ any case!) never appears elsewhere in Q. Statistical evidence thus points to Matthean redaction. With regard to redactional motive, both Evangelists would have had good reason to alter the wording of the text: Matthew because of a tendency both here and elsewhere in his Gospel to polarize the debate with Judaism; Luke (or a pre-Lukan reviser of the Q story) because of the more positive presentation of the Jews in 7.3-5. On the whole, since it is doubtful that the *primary* intent of Luke 7.3-5 is to paint a more flattering picture of the Jews (see esp. Luke's account of Jesus' reception at the Nazareth synagogue in 4.16-30), the argument for deliberate Matthean redaction appears stronger. ...

"The reference to 'not even in Israel' would be quite consistent with the warning of John the Baptist in Q 3.8 against Jewish presumptuousness *vis-à-vis* their inheritance in Abraham."

Evaluations

Robinson 2000: Luke = Q {B}, ()⁷ οὐδέ()⁷.

The Lukan formulation "not even in Israel" shows the high esteem in which Israel is held, as a kind of ideal, to which empirical Israel does not live up— more like what the Q redaction would say. For the Matthean language ("with no one") seems to suggest there are no Jews at all who have faith in Jesse's word. This was not the case in the time of Q, for the Q community was Jewish Christian. The Q redactor was probably Jewish. The Matthean formulation seems to eliminate even one Jewish Christian. It would probably fit better Matthew's situation: Matthew, somewhat hesitantly, presupposed Mark's presentation of Jesus not keeping the law, and so accepted the Gentile

Christian practice of baptism and the Gentile mission in the Great Commission, which was in effect a repudiation of Jews (who wanted to stay Jews) as future members of the community (though Jewish members of the Matthean community who had earlier entered the Q community may have still been active, at the cost of their Jewishness).

Luke's formulation does not exclude Jews, but puts them down as having less faith than the centurion. Q knows of Q members with "little faith," and so Luke's language could fit the Q situation better than Matthew's. Q 13:28-29, like the generalizing rejection of "this generation," does reflect the eschatological replacement of a Jewish community with a non-Jewish community; i.e., it anticipates the failure of the Jewish mission by the Q community. But the future orientation does not go as far as Matthean redaction seems to go here.

Matthew's interpolation of Q 13:28-29 at this juncture, with its rejection of Israel in favor of the Gentiles, fits the Matthean redaction here. The Q formulation still implicitly venerates Israel: Israel is where one should expect such faith, but even in the venerated Israel it does not match the centurion's faith. Matthew here has in view the negative outcome of Q regarding Israel (see Q 7:9⁵), as well as Q 13:28-29, and hence moves to the exclusive contrast: No one in Israel. This of course does not fit the earlier history of the Q community, which consisted only of Jews. But it fits the hard reality about prospects for the future to which the redactor of Q and Matthew had been forced.

Kloppenborg 2000: Luke = Q {B}, ()⁷ οὐδέ()⁷.

Johnson 2001: Luke = Q {B}, ()⁷ οὐδέ()⁷.

Hoffmann 2001: Luke = Q {B}, ()⁷ οὐδέ()⁷.

Wenn auch in der Diskussion allgemein mit großer Selbstverständlichkeit Matthäus für sekundär gehalten wird, ist zu bedenken, daß auf der Ebene der Endredaktion von Q das matthäische "bei keinem" durchaus denkbar wäre. In Q folgt die Johannes-Rede, in der die Kinder der Weisheit dieser Generation, die Johannes wie Jesus abgelehnt hat, krass entgegengestellt werden. Matthäus könnte also das "bei keinem" in Q vorgefunden und durch die Einfügung des Logions expliziert haben. Umgekehrt scheint mir aufgrund der heilsgeschichtlichen Bedeutung, die Israel bei Lukas hat, es durchaus denkbar zu sein, daß er die radikale Formulierung abmilderte. Auch in 22,28-30 hat er das Gericht über Israel zur Herrschaft über Israel uminterpretiert.

Q 7:9⁸: The position of ἐν τῷ Ἰσραὴλ before (Luke) or after (Matthew) τοσαύτην πίστιν.

Luke = Q: ⌐ἐν τῷ Ἰσραὴλ⌐⁸ τοσαύτην πίστιν ⌐ ⌐⁸ εὗρον.

Pro

von Harnack 1907, 91 (ET 1908, 132): Reconstruction. For complete text see Q 7:1⁶ Luke = Q, Pro (p. 55).
B. Weiß 1908, 15-16: Reconstruction. For complete text see Q 7:1⁰ In Q (p. 5).
Polag 1979, 38: Reconstruction. For complete text see Q 7:1⁰ In Q (pp. 9-10).
Jacobson 1992, 109: "A striking difference between the Johannine and Q accounts is the "punchline" in Q: "I tell you, not even in Israel have I found such faith.¹³⁰"
109¹³⁰: "Or, 'I tell you, with no one is Israel ...' This is the more probable reading in Matt 8:10. ... However, the Matthean reading is secondary, and Luke more nearly represents Q."
Sevenich-Bax 1993, 238: Reconstruction. For complete text see Q 7:1⁰ In Q (p. 15).
Landis 1994, 13, 17: Reconstruction. For complete text see Q 7:1⁶ Luke = Q, Pro (p. 57).
International Q Project 1995, 479: Reconstruction. For complete text see Q 7:1⁰ In Q (p. 16).

Con

Matt = Q: ⌐ ⌐⁸ τοσαύτην πίστιν ⌐ἐν τῷ Ἰσραὴλ⌐⁸ εὗρον.

Pro

Wegner 1985, 220: "Was die Wortfolge betrifft, so sind die Unterschiede hinreichend aus dem Ersatz von παρ' οὐδενί durch οὐδέ erklärbar: letzteres zog ἐν τῷ Ἰσραὴλ nach sich. Die mt Wortakoluthie kann daher für die ursprünglichere gehalten werden."
271: Reconstruction. For complete text see Q 7:1⁰ In Q (pp. 11-12).
Catchpole 1992, 539 [1993, 307]: Reconstruction. For complete text see Q 7:1⁰ In Q (p. 14).
Lindars 1992, 210: Reconstruction. For complete text see Q 7:1⁶ Luke = Q, Pro (p. 56).

Con

Gundry 1982, 144: "In the statement about faith, the reference to Israel moves far back in the clause, where it lacks emphasis."
Gagnon 1994b, 138: See Q 7:9[7] Matt = Q, Con (p. 348).

Evaluations

Johnson 2000: Luke = Q {B}, ⌜ἐν τῷ Ἰσραὴλ⌝[8] τοσαύτην πίστιν ⌐⌐[8] εὖρον.

Robinson 2000: Luke = Q {B}, ⌜ἐν τῷ Ἰσραὴλ⌝[8] τοσαύτην πίστιν ⌐⌐[8] εὖρον. Wegner is right to sense that Q 7:9[7] influences the decision here. But since Luke = Q there, it is also the case here.

Kloppenborg 2000: Luke = Q {B}, ⌜ἐν τῷ Ἰσραὴλ⌝[8] τοσαύτην πίστιν ⌐⌐[8] εὖρον.

Hoffmann 2001: Luke = Q {B}, ⌜ἐν τῷ Ἰσραὴλ⌝[8] τοσαύτην πίστιν ⌐⌐[8] εὖρον. Die Verurteilung hängt von der Entscheidung in Var. 7 ab.

Matt 8:11-12 is to be found at Q 13:28-29

Q 7:?10?

Mark 7:29	Matt 15:28	Matt 8:13	Q 7:?10?
		[0]/	< >[0]
καὶ	τότε ἀποκριθεὶς	(καὶ εἶπεν)[1]	
εἶπεν	ὁ Ἰησοῦς εἶπεν	(ὁ Ἰησοῦς)[2]	
αὐτῇ·	αὐτῇ·	(τῷ ἑκατοντάρχῃ)[3]·	
διὰ τοῦτον τὸν λόγον	ὦ γύναι,		
ὕπαγε,		(ὕπαγε,	
	μεγάλη σου ἡ πίστις·	ὡς ἐπίστευσας	
	γενηθήτω σοι ὡς θέλεις.	γενηθήτω σοι.	
ἐξελήλυθεν	καὶ ἰάθη	καὶ ἰάθη	
ἐκ τῆς θυγατρός σου	ἡ θυγάτηρ αὐτῆς	ὁ παῖς αὐτοῦ	
τὸ δαιμόνιον			
.	ἀπὸ τῆς ὥρας ἐκείνης.	ἐν τῇ ὥρᾳ ἐκεινη)[4].	.
		[0]/	

Q 7:?10?

Luke 7:10	Mark 7:30	John 4:50-53
0/		
( )¹		4:50 λέγει αὐτῷ
( )²		ὁ Ἰησοῦς·
( )³		
		πορεύου, ὁ υἱός σου ζῇ.
[Καὶ	καὶ	ἐπίστευσεν ὁ ἄνθρωπος
ὑποστρέψαντες	ἀπελθοῦσα	τῷ λόγῳ ὃν εἶπεν αὐτῷ
εἰς τὸν οἶκον	εἰς τὸν οἶκον αὐτῆς	ὁ Ἰησοῦς καὶ ἐπορεύετο.
		4:51 ἤδη δὲ αὐτοῦ
		καταβαίνοντος
οἱ πεμφθέντες		οἱ δοῦλοι αὐτοῦ
		ὑπήντησαν αὐτῷ
		λέγοντες ὅτι
		ὁ παῖς αὐτοῦ ζῇ.
		4:52 ἐπύθετο οὖν
		τὴν ὥραν παρ' αὐτῶν
		ἐν ᾗ κομψότερον ἔσχεν·
		εἶπαν οὖν αὐτῷ
		ὅτι ἐχθὲς ὥραν ἑβδόμην
εὗρον	εὗρεν	ἀφῆκεν
τὸν δοῦλον	τὸ παιδίον	αὐτὸν
	βεβλημένον ἐπὶ τὴν κλίνην	
	καὶ τὸ δαιμόνιον	ὁ πυρετός.
ὑγιαίνοντα]⁴	ἐξεληλυθός	4:53 ἔγνω οὖν ὁ πατὴρ
	.	ὅτι ἐν ἐκείνῃ τῇ ὥρᾳ
0/		ἐν ᾗ εἶπεν αὐτῷ
		ὁ Ἰησοῦς·
		ὁ υἱός σου ζῇ,
		καὶ ἐπίστευσεν αὐτὸς
		καὶ ἡ οἰκία αὐτοῦ ὅλη.

Q 7:?10?

IQP 1994: καὶ [] < >⁰; JSK: < >⁰ something was in Q {B}; JMR: < >⁰ something was in Q {D}; PH: < >⁰ indeterminate.

⁰ Is there in Q some concluding statement?
¹ Matthew's καὶ εἶπεν.
² Matthew's ὁ Ἰησοῦς.
³ Matthew's τῷ ἑκατοντάρχῃ.
⁴ The form of the statement about the centurion's or his delegation's departure and the confirmation of the healing, including Matthew's statement about faith.

Q 7:?10?⁰: Is there in Q some concluding statement?

In Q

B. Weiß 1876, 230: "Nach dieser Einschaltung nimmt der Evangelist [Matthäus] den Faden der Quelle wieder auf, welche nach dem Worte Jesu an seine Begleiter noch eins an den Centurio berichtete: Gehe hin (8,4); wie du geglaubt hast, so geschehe dir (γενηθήτω, wie 6,10)."

von Harnack 1907, 91 (ET 1908, 132): Reconstruction. Harnack includes Q 7:10 with hesitation—elsewhere he rejects Matthew's ending (See B. Weiß below). For complete text see Q 7:1⁶ Luke = Q, Pro (p. 55).

B. Weiß 1908, 16²⁶: "Die Vermutung Harnacks (1907, 147; ET, 210-211; see Harnack at Undecided [p. 361]), daß Mt. 8,13 in Q gefehlt habe, … scheint mir unhaltbar, da in ihm gerade die Pointe liegt, um derentwillen diese Erzählung in Q aufgenommen, wie die vorige wegen des Wortes 8,4. Harnack ist dazu veranlaßt durch die Ähnlichkeit desselben mit Mt. 15,28; aber daraus folgt doch nur, daß auch die Erzählung vom kananäischen Weibe (vgl. [Harnack] 157f [ET, 227-228]) aus Q stammt. Es ist eben ganz undenkbar, daß eine Quelle, die den Hauptmann von Kapharnaum brachte, nicht auch andere Heilungsgeschichten enthalter haben sollte."

16: Reconstruction. For complete text see Q 7:1⁰ In Q (p. 5).

Castor 1912, 224: Reconstruction. But see Castor at Not in Q (p. 357). For complete text see Q 7:1⁰ In Q (p. 6).

Loisy 1924, 218: "Matthieu (viii, 13): … Ainsi finit l'histoire de la cananéenne (xv, 28; cf. Mc. vii, 29-30). Mais ce n'est pas motif pour supposer que le récit n'avait pas de conclusion dans la source et que les deux évangélistes ont suppléé à cette lacune chacun de son côté. Une conclusion était indispensable."

Crum 1927, 138: Reconstruction. For complete text see Q 7:~~2, 3, 4-6a~~¹ Luke = Q, Pro (pp. 71-72).

George 1972, 70, 72: See Q 7:?10?⁴ Luke = Q, Con (p. 378).

Schulz 1972, 240: "Beide Verse [Luke 7,10; Matt 8,13] zeigen zwar starke Eingriffe der Evangelisten, stimmen aber dennoch inhaltlich darin überein, daß die Konstatierung der Heilung den Abschluß der Geschichte bildet. Das legt die Annahme nahe, daß schon Q die eingetretene Heilung berichtet hat und nicht mit dem Wort über den Glauben schloß."

Theissen 1974, 183 (ET 1983, 182): See Q 7:?10?⁴ Luke = Q, Pro (p. 375).

Achtemeier 1975, 549: See Q 7:?10?⁴ Luke = Q, Con (p. 379).

Polag 1979, 38: Reconstruction: "καὶ ἰάθη ὁ παῖς αὐτοῦ ἐν τῇ ὥρᾳ ἐκείνῃ." For complete text see Q 7:1⁰ In Q (pp. 9-10).

Fitzmyer 1981, 653: "Luke changed the first part of the verse, omitting the impv. of Matt 8:13."

Schenk 1981, 37: Reconstruction. For complete text see Q 7:1⁰ In Q (p. 10).

Wegner 1985, 221: "Während einige Forscher jedoch dahin tendieren, einen erzählenden Schluß für die Perikope überhaupt zu bestreiten, halten andere einen solchen durchaus für möglich, wenn er auch nicht mehr mit Sicherheit rekonstruiert werden kann."

Bovon 1989, 352⁴⁴ (FT 1991, 344⁴⁴): See Q 7:?10?⁴ Luke = Q, Con (p. 381).

Nolland 1989, 318: "Presumably in the tradition the conclusion of the account mentioned the healing."

Davies and Allison 1991, 32: See Q 7:?10?⁴ Matt = Q, Pro (p. 385).

Catchpole 1992, 522 [1993, 286]: "A good case could be made on the basis of general Matthew/Luke agreement in content, and Matthew's overall tendency to be faithful to Q in this tradition, for the following as the conclusion: καὶ εἶπεν ὁ Ἰησοῦς τῷ ἑκατοντάρχῃ· ὕπαγε, ὡς ἐπίστευσας γενηθήτω σοι. καὶ ἰάθη ὁ παῖς ἐν τῇ ὥρᾳ ἐκείνῃ."

Lindars 1992, 210: Reconstruction. For complete text see Q 7:1⁶ Luke = Q, Pro (p. 56).

212: "At least ὕπαγε, ἐπίστευσας, ἰάθη ὁ παῖς, and ἐν τῇ ὥρᾳ ἐκείνῃ, which are paralleled in John, can well be accepted as original."

Gagnon 1993, 717: "I agree with Wegner's reconstruction of the conclusion to the original Q account: καὶ ἀπελθὼν εἰς τὴν οἰκίαν εὗρεν τὸν παῖδα ἰαθέντα (cf. Mark 7:30)."

Sevenich-Bax 1993, 238: Reconstruction. For complete text see Q 7:1⁰ In Q (p. 15).

Dunderberg 1994, 85: "Außerdem stimmen die beiden Evangelisten in der Schilderung der Heilung nicht überein. Mt zufolge stellt Jesus den Glauben des Mannes fest und mahnt ihn, zurückzukehren, wonach die Heilung des Jungen nur kurz erwähnt wird (Mt 8,13). Bei Lk folgt der Aussage Jesu dagegen noch eine kürzere Szene, in der *die zweite Gesandtschaft* das Wunder konstatiert (Lk 7,10)."

87: "Wegen der redaktionellen Tätigkeit von Mt und Lk läßt sich das ursprüngliche Ende der Erzählung nicht mehr rekonstruieren.⁶² Da beide die Erzählung mit der Konstatierung des Wunders beenden, ist doch anzunehmen, daß schon in Q ein entsprechendes Teil vorhanden war. Es ist zudem nicht glaubhaft, daß die Q-Fassung nur durch das Lob Jesu (Mt 8,10/Lk 7,9) abgeschlossen worden wäre, ohne daß das Wunder konstatiert würde."

87⁶²: "Wegner [1985, 271] versucht, das Ende der Erzählung folgenderweise zu rekonstruieren: καὶ εἶπεν τῷ ἑκατοντάρχῃ· ὕπαγε, [ὁ παῖς σου ἐσώθη.] [καὶ ἀπελθὼν εἰς τὴν οἰκίαν εὗρεν τὸν παῖδα ἰαθέντα]. So eine Rekonstruktion weicht allerdings von Mt sowie von Lk ab." Brackets are Wegner's.

Gagnon 1994b, 136-137: "In my estimation, Matthew has ... [137] ... replaced Q's confirmation of the healing with one of his own formulaic conclusions (cf. 9.22; 15.28; 17.18)."

Landis 1994, 14: "Wenn … auch aus all diesen Gründen anzunehmen ist, daß der Vers Mt 8,13 auf einen Bericht der Logienquelle über die Heilung des παῖς zurückgeht, so ist doch der genaue Wortlaut dieses erzählenden Schlusses der Q-Perikope kaum mehr zu rekonstruieren. Nur einzelne Elemente sind noch zu fassen."

17: Reconstruction. For complete text see Q 7:1[6] Luke = Q, Pro (p. 57).

Merklein 1994, 97: "Bereits in der Logienquelle schloß sich an die programmatische Rede eine Wundererzählung an: Lk 7,10."

International Q Project 1995, 479: Reconstruction. For complete text see Q 7:1[0] In Q (p. 16).

Not in Q

Hawkins 1911, 119[2]: "It is quite possible that the narrative in Q ended with the saying to which it led up, and did not record the cure; for that is related in totally different words by Mt (viii. 13) and by Lk (vii. 10)."

Castor 1912, 42-43: "Matt 8:13 [43] might seem to be more original than Luke 7:10 if we did not find that he changes the text of Mark 7:19, 30 in the same way.[1]"

43[1]: "Harnack [see Undecided (p. 361)] may be right in affirming that neither verse stood in Q. The interest to Q is not in the miracle, but in the saying of Jesus."

224[2]: "This last verse may not have been in Q."

Haupt 1913, 80: "Ob die Erzählung in Q überhaupt einen Schluß gehabt hat, kann zweifelhaft sein. Q[3] bringt die Erzählungsstücke lediglich als Einleitung für die folgenden Reden: wie es bei dem Abschnitt über die verschiedenen Nachfolger nichts davon sagt, ob sie sich durch Jesu Wort haben abschrecken lassen oder nicht, wie es über den Erfolg der Johannesfrage nichts erwähnt, so wird es auch die Hauptmannserzählung nur bis zu dem Punkte geführt haben, wo dann die Rede Jesu über die Annahme der Heiden einsetzte (Mt 8,10)."

Dibelius 1919, 245: "Die Evangelisten sind es, die den erzählenden Anfang und den erzählenden Schluß schufen [Matt 4,3; Luke 4,3], jeder auf seine Art. Eine ähnliche Beobachtung läßt sich endlich auch an der 'Erzählung' vom Hauptmann von Kapernaum machen. Auch hier reicht die Übereinstimmung nur bis Mt 8,10 = Lk 7,9, umfaßt also die Heilung nicht mit. Der Text der Quelle, der die Heilung wohl als selbstverständlich voraussetzt (wie Mt 8,22; Lk 9,60 den Anschluß des Fragers an Jesus), schloß wahrscheinlich mit dem Worte Jesu, das die Rede des Hauptmanns als Beweis eines Glaubens preist, wie er auch in Israel nicht zu finden sei."

Dibelius 1919, ET 1935, 244-245: "It is the Evangelists who invented the beginning and the conclusion of the narrative [Matt 4:3; Luke 4:3], each in his own manner. A similar observation can be made in regard to the Tale of the Centurion of Capernaum. The complete agreement [245] extends only to Matthew viii,10 = Luke vii,9, and thus does not include the cure. The text of the source which probably assumes the cure without question (just as Matthew viii,22 = Luke ix,60, assumes that the questioner became a disciple of Jesus) concluded with the word of Jesus which praises what the centurion had said because it is the evidence of a faith which is not to be found in Israel."

Easton 1926, 97: "This verse [Luke 7:10] has practically nothing in common with Mt v. 13, and ὑποστρέφεν and πέμπειν are 'Lukan,' while only Lk uses ὑγιαίνειν. Hk [Harnack—see Undecided (p. 361)] thinks that Q ended with v. 9, to which Lk and Mt have supplied independent conclusions, telling what Q took for granted."

Manson 1937, 63: "It is almost certain that the dialogue alone belongs to Q. The narrative framework is supplied independently by Mt. and Lk."

65: "With this comment [Luke 7:9 par Matt 8:10] the original Q section closes. ..."

"The most probable conclusion of the whole matter would seem to be that the dialogue is the original kernel, which belonged to Q and probably stood later in the document. This original has been furnished with two different narrative settings, which appear in Mt. and Lk. These narrative settings agree in stating that the cure was effected; and this was probably implied in the original Q story. But the interest of the compiler of Q was not in the cure of the boy, but in the contrast between the faith of the Gentile and the unbelief of Israel."

P. Meyer 1970, 411: "It must be conceded that Matthew imported 8:11f. from another place in Q (and created vs. 13)."

Fuchs 1971, 150-151: See Q 7:?10?⁴ Matt = Q, Con (p. 387).

Schweizer 1973, 137: "In Q war also offenkundig nur der Dialog V.8-10 überliefert, wohl mit einer überschriftartigen Angabe über die Krankheit des 'Jungen' des 'Hauptmanns von Kapernaum.'"

Schweizer 1973, ET 1975, 212-213: "It is clear ... that Q contained only the dialogue [213] in verses 8-10, probably with a kind of title mentioning the sickness of the 'boy' of the 'officer at Capernaum.'"

Busse 1977, 149-150: "Ganz verschieden haben die Korreferenten auch den Schlußvers gestaltet. Stilkritisch geurteilt steht Lukas als Verfasser außer Zweifel⁴. Es liegt aber der Verdacht nahe, Lukas [150] habe ihn mit Hilfe von Mk 7,30 formuliert, also mit dem Schlußvers der ausgefallenen Perikope von der Syrophönizierin. Dabei ist das Wortspiel zwischen πίστιν εὖρον in V 9 und εὖρον τὸν δοῦλον ὑγιαίνοντα zu beachten. Es ist redaktionelle Absicht, εὖρον in V 10 mit der Wendung πίστιν εὖρον korrespondieren zu lassen, um den engen

Zusammenhang zwischen dem Glauben des Hauptmanns und der erfolgreichen Heilung des Knechtes zu betonen."

149⁴: "Den abschließenden V 10 hat Lk eigenständig formuliert. Dazu zwang ihn seine eigene Ausführung in V 2-6a. Aber auch rein stilistisch lassen sich luk. Eigentümlichkeiten ausmachen. Die Verben πέμπω, ὑποστρέφω wie εὑρίσκω sind red. Vorzugsvokabeln. ... Zudem versucht er mit εὗρον ... ein Wortspiel, das mit V 9 πίστιν εὗρον korrespondiert."

Marshall 1978, 282: "Matthew ... includes a saying of Jesus assuring the centurion that the healing will take place according to his faith, but this is probably editorial (cf. Mt. 17:18 diff. Mk.).

"Luke simply notes, in accordance with his own form of the story, that the messengers returned home and found the slave well. ... The language (including ὑγιαίνω, 5:31; 15:27; Mt., 0x; Mk., 0x) suggests Lucan formulation."

Dauer 1984, 78: "Hier stellt sich heraus, daß Mt 8,13 und wahrscheinlich auch Lk 7,10 redaktionell sind."

Judge 1989, 487-489: "No one fails to see the conceptual correspondence between Lk 7:10 and Mk 7:30; it appears to be more than coincidental. At the same time the vocabulary and style are clearly Lukan: ὑποστρέφω, εὑρίσκω and ὑγιαίνω (in the medical sense) are Lukan, as is the theme of 'returning', even beyond specific vocabulary; οἱ πεμφθέντες derives from v. 6, and δοῦλος links with the same word in vv. 2 and 3 where Luke has altered the παῖς of v. 7; and the play-on-words between εὗρον in vv. 9 and 10 does not seem clumsy ... but purposeful and effective. It does not seem necessary to conclude that Luke employed a conclusion that was like Mk 7:30 from Q or a special source; rather, Luke composed a conclusion for his story in characteristic manner.

"The suggestion that Q contained only the dialogue with a brief introduction is appealing. A good amount of composition by the evangelists can be recognized in the story of the centurion from Capernaum. Moreover, the influence of Mark on their redaction of this Q saying seems to be quite evident. ...

"The redactional character of Mt 8:13 is also widely accepted, not only by those who defend the originality of Luke's version but also by many who hold that Matthew's account is otherwise closer to the tradition. For Wegner [1985, 104-127], this is the only verse where significant Matthean redaction is detected, and he proposes that the original ending was καὶ εἶπεν τῷ ἑκατοντάρχῃ· ὕπαγε, ὁ παῖς σου ἐσώθη [ἰάθη/ἰαθήσεται]. καὶ [488] ἀπέλθων εἰς τὴν οἰκίαν εὗρεν τὸν παῖδα ἰαθέντα (cf. Jn 4:50; Mk 7:30). The similarity of Mt 8:13 to Mk 7:29-30/Mt 15:28 (the Syrophoenician woman) is noted by many commentators. Some suppose that the original conclusion to the centurion pericope could have been something similar to Mk's conclusion of that story. Thus Gnilka's [1986, 299-300] is a representative statement: 'Wegen der weitgehenden Übereinstimmung mit Mt 15:28b kann man vermuten, daß der Schluß (V. 13) mt gestaltet ist. Vielleicht berichtete er einmal davon, daß der Hauptmann den Knecht gesund zu Hause vorfand.'

"We can compare Mt 8:13 not only with 15:28 but also with 9:22 (cf. Mk 5:34), 9:29 (cf. Mk 10:52), and 17:18b (cf. Mk 9:27), all conclusions to miracle stories where Matthew is working directly with Mark. The whole expression ὡς ἐπίστευσας γενηθήτω σοι resembles 9:29 and 15:28; the confirmation καὶ ἰάθη ὁ παῖς αὐτοῦ ἐν τῇ ὥρᾳ ἐκείνῃ is close to 9:22; 15:28 and 17:18. These are generally recognized Matthean changes to Mark, in which the first evangelist simplifies Mark's ending and, in the case of the first example, brings the theme of faith clearly to the fore even when it is already present in Mark. Neirynck [1981, 485-487] has drawn attention to the equivalence of the two expressions with ἐν and ἀπο in Matthew's typical conclusion formula.

"With v. 13, Matthew characteristically creates a parallel with v. 8, describing the cure in terms of the request. The evangelist seems to have similarly linked v. 13 to v. 10 with Jesus' comment on the man's faith, first to the crowd and then to the man himself. The healing word, requested by the centurion in v. 8, that Jesus pronounces in v. 13a takes up the theme of faith from v. 10, while 13c expresses the result in the very words of the centurion.

"Gundry [1982, 147] and Dauer [1984, 79] note that ὕπαγε is Matthean, and Polag [1979, 38] omits it from his reconstruction; Schenk [1981, 37], on the other hand, retains it, while Wegner [1985, 226-227] thinks it is a remnant of the original conclusion and not redactional chiefly because of Matthew's handling of the word in Markan miracle stories: he takes it over from Mk 1:44 (Mt 8:4) and Mk 2:11 (Mt 9:6), but does not use it in parallel with Mk 5:19 (Mt diff.); 5:34 (om.); 7:29 (diff.); and 10:52 (om.). In other words, Wegner argues that if ὕπαγε were a favorite word of Matthew he would not have omitted it when employing these Markan miracle stories. An examination of the Matthean pericopes vis-à-vis their Markan counterparts, however, can provide a more nuanced insight into Matthew's treatment of them (cf. Mt 8:28-34; 9:20-22; 15:21-28; 20:29-34 with 9:27-31). Wegner's rejection of Polag's suggestion that the word is Matthean redaction in the three so-called Q-Mt occurrences (Mt 4:10; 8:13; 18:15) appears questionable. ὕπαγε is Matthean enough to have been used in 8,13 by the evangelist himself. The use of ὕπαγε anticipates Matthew's postponed cure of the paralytic (cf. Mk 2:11 par. Mt 9:6) [489] and recalls 8:4 (cf. Mk 1:44; see also Mt 8:32). It also corresponds with his desire to align Jesus' response to the request: the centurion tells Jesus he does not need to come; Jesus sends him away without accompanying him. Matthew saw the similarity between the centurion and the Syrophoenician woman, and composed 8:13 himself in the same style as his redaction upon Mk 7:29-30."

Hagner 1993, 205: "The weighty statement (and concluding statement in the Q pericope) now given is prefaced by ἀμήν." But see Hagner at Q 7:?10?[4] Matt = Q, Con (p. 393), which implies a text for Q 7:10.

Undecided

von Harnack 1907, 56: "Hier nur so viel, daß Matth. 8,13 ganz wie c. 15,28 lautet (kananäisches Weib), während Luk. den Schluß in konventioneller Form summarisch abmacht."

147: "Matth. schließt sie fast wie die des kananäischen Weibes: καὶ εἶπεν ὁ Ἰησοῦς τῷ ἑκατοντάρχῃ· [ὕπαγε], ὡς ἐπίστευσας γενηθήτω σοι· καὶ ἰάθη ὁ παῖς ἐν τῇ ὥρᾳ ἐκείνῃ. Luk. schreibt ganz summarisch (und mit drei Partizipien, also in seinem Stil): καὶ ὑποστρέψαντες εἰς τὸν οἶκον οἱ πεμφθέντες εὗρον τὸν δοῦλον ὑγιαίνοντα. Kein Wort in diesen beiden Berichten ist identisch. Das ist sehr auffallend. Wie soll der Schluß in Q also gelautet haben? Ich halte, da das nicht auszumachen, die Hypothese nicht für zu kühn, daß in Q über die Heilung überhaupt nichts oder etwas ganz anderes gestanden hat, als was wir bei Matth. und Luk. lesen. Beides ist möglich und wäre nicht befremdlich; sicher ist jedenfalls, das der Schlußvers sowohl bei Matth. wie auch bei Luk. verdächtig ist. Daß sie aber beide unabhängig von einander so geschrieben haben, wie sie schrieben, ist nicht auffallend."

von Harnack 1907, ET 1908, 77: "Here I would only point out that St. Matt. viii. 13 is almost exactly like St. Matt. xv. 28 (Canaanitish woman), while St. Luke winds up the passage with a conclusion of conventional character."

210-211: "St. Matthew concludes it much in the same way as the story of the Canaanitish woman: καὶ εἶπεν ὁ Ἰησοῦς τῷ ἑκατοντάρχῃ· [ὕπαγε], ὡς ἐπίστευσας γενηθήτω σοι· καὶ ἰάθη ὁ παῖς ἐν τῇ ὥρᾳ ἐκείνῃ. St. Luke writes quite summarily (and with three participles, thus in his own style): καὶ ὑποστρέψαντες εἰς τὸν οἶκον οἱ πεμφθέντες εὗρον [211] τὸν δοῦλον ὑγιαίνοντα. *Not a single word in these two conclusions is identical.* This is very strange. What then may we suppose was the conclusion of Q? We cannot tell. Since this is so, it seems to me to be not too bold an hypothesis to assume that in Q either nothing at all was said about the cure, or that in this source there stood something quite different from what we read in St. Matthew and St. Luke. Either alternative is possible, and not improbable; it is at all events certain that the concluding verse, both in St. Matthew and also in St. Luke, is suspicious. Neither is it surprising that they have both independently of one another given the story the conclusion which we now read."

Evaluations

Hoffmann 2001: Indeterminate {U}, < >⁰.

Da wir nicht wissen, ob in Q eine Heilungszusage an den Hauptmann wie bei Matthäus oder nur eine Feststellung der Heilung wie bei Lukas erfolgte oder beides verbunden war, muß die Variante unentschieden bleiben.

"Spekulativ" gebe ich zu erwägen, ob nicht eine Schlußbemerkung möglich wäre, die das Glaubensmotiv erneut thematisiert. Auch wenn die Formulierung bei Matthäus sehr nach einer redaktionellen Bildung aussieht (vgl. 15,28; 9,25), könnte doch ein Kern auf Q zurückgehen. Matthäus könnte ja, wie es auch für die Redeschlußformel in Q 7,1 erwogen wird, durch Q zu den zwei weiteren (nicht ganz identischen) Formulierungen angeregt worden sein. Deswegen braucht die Heilung nicht berichtet worden zu sein. Lukas mußte ändern, weil bei ihm der Centurio nicht anwesend ist. [Hoffmann's final evaluation did not differ in any significant way from his preliminary evaluation. It is positioned here because his preliminary evaluation provided stimulus for part of Robinson's and Johnson's evaluations. Hoffmann's {U} votes at Q 7:?10?¹⁻⁴ reflect his decision here.]

Robinson 2000: In Q {D}, < >⁰.

Whether there is to be conjectured some text (which in any case cannot be reconstructed) is a weak possibility.

This variation unit is needed only when it becomes clear that neither Matthew nor Luke has preserved a conclusion that can be ascribed to Q. This is in fact the case (see Q 7:?10?¹⁻⁴). Each variation unit reflects the probability of Matthean and Lukan redaction or composition, so that nothing remains that can be ascribed to Q. In that case there either was no conclusion, other than the highlighting of the Gentile centurion's faith in Jesus' word (Q 7:9b), or there was in Q a conclusion affirming that the healing has taken place— even though it cannot be reconstructed (Harnack).

Wegner's conjectural reconstruction is so uncertain that it is prudent not to propose it or an alternative to it, but to limit oneself to the uncertain possibility that there was some conclusion affirming that the healing had taken place.

Though neither the Matthean nor the Lukan verse can be readily ascribed to Q, they nonetheless agree that there was some such final statement. But this minimal abstract agreement does not make it obvious that there was in Q such a final confirmation. It belongs to the genre of miracle story that the story culminates in such a confirmation, normally followed by some acclamation (which no one conjectures here). But if Q does not make use of the standard form of a miracle story at the beginning of the present pericope (see Q

7:~~2~~, 3, ~~4-6a~~¹ᶠᶠ), the standard form of a miracle story need not be conjectured at the end (*pace* Schulz and those who repeat his view). The Gentile centurion's faith in Jesus' word may be the intended climax, toward which the whole presentation in Q moves.

Of course it is assumed the healing did take place. That was what the centurion trusted in, and that faith is commended. Obviously the centurion was not let down. But this may be for Q so obvious that it need not be said, if for Q the genre of the story was not a healing story, but a faith/word story:

The scholarly concept of the form-critical outline of a miracle story is formed by Mark and John. How Q would have shaped such a story is an open question. The healing is not the point of the story for Q. It might have been a distraction, an anticlimax, had it been appended there! The flow of the context in Q suggests that the climax, faith in Jesus' word, is quite appropriate.

The pericope is then followed by John's delegation, where faith in Jesus' healings, alongside the Sermon, is involved in believing in him as the Coming One (Q 7:22). The pericope about the centurion's faith in Jesus' word reconciles nicely the two alternatives: Faith in Jesus' healings is also faith in Jesus' word. Indeed Q 7:22 lists not only healings, but evangelizing the poor. Perhaps Q 7:22, "Go and tell what you hear and see," would function better if it presupposed a statement that the healing had taken place in Q 7:10. But one may recall the reproach in John 4:48 of the insistence on seeing signs and wonders before one will believe (ascribed redactionally inappropriately to the father of the sick person). In any case, Jesus and those following him (Q 7:9), i.e., the Q community, never see the boy, sick or well. The Q text, however, could have reported that the cure did take place, which would in effect be an instance not of what one sees, but of what one hears.

Both Harnack and Dibelius say there was no conclusion affirming the healing had taken place. But on p. 91 (ET 132), Harnack includes Matt 8:13 in the reconstructed Q text!

Hoffmann poses the speculative question of whether Matt 8:13 may be Q, if its language is echoed later by Matthean redaction. The data seems to be as follows:

There are in fact in Matt 8:13 two formulae: ὡς ἐπίστευσας γενηθήτω σοι and ἰάθη ὁ παῖς αὐτοῦ ἐν τῇ ὥρᾳ ἐκείνῃ. The fact that the two formulae, in other usage in Matthew, are not, as here, side by side, weakens the assumption that other passages are echoing this text.

The ascription of the healing to faith is three times in Matthew:

8:13:	ὡς ἐπίστευσας	γενηθήτω σοι
9:29:	κατὰ τὴν πίστιν ὑμῶν	γενηθήτω ὑμῖν
15:28:	μεγάλη σου ἡ πίστις·	γενηθήτω σοι ὡς θέλεις.

Matt 8:13 and 15:28 are in the form-critically parallel Gentile healings from a distance. Matt 15:28 could not have been derived from Mark 7:29, his source of the Syro-Phoenician story, since it is absent there. Hence it could be borrowed from Matt 8:13 and put by Matthew into 15:28. But it could just be a motif typical of such stories. For Matt 9:29; 15:28 are not even closely identical in wording with Matt 8:13. If Matt 9:29 is Matthew quoting from memory, i.e. from his stock of phrases, this could be true of Matt 15:28, without postulating it to have been in Q 7:10/Matt 8:13, where he could also have derived it from his stock of phrases.

Hence the other alternative, that this is just Matthean redaction of a similar kind in all three cases, seems equally plausible. For the association of healing with faith is widespread; e.g., the formula ἡ πίστις σου σέσωχέν σε is in Mark 5:34 par. Matt 9:22 par. Luke 8:48; Mark 10:52 par. Luke 18:42; Luke 7:50; 17:19. Here the spread of the references suggests that the identity of language cannot be explained as one text dependent on another. (The identity of the language in this formula, incidentally, stands in contrast to the fluidity of language for the formula in Matt 8:13; 9:26; 15:28.)

Regarding the second formula, Hawkins (p. 34) lists Matt 8:13; 9:22; 15:28; 17;18 as instances of "that hour" in instantaneous cures in narrative.

8:13:	καὶ ἰάθη	ὁ παῖς αὐτοῦ	ἐν τῇ ὥρᾳ ἐκείνῃ.
9:22:	καὶ ἐσώθη	ἡ γυνὴ	ἀπὸ τῆς ὥρας ἐκείνης.
15:28:	καὶ ἰάθη	ἡ θυγάτηρ αὐτῆς	ἀπὸ τῆς ὥρας ἐκείνης.
17:18:	καὶ ἐθεραπεύθη	ὁ παῖς	ἀπὸ τῆς ὥρας ἐκείνης.

John 4:53, in the same concluding position of the same story, uses the expression ἐν ἐκείνῃ τῇ ὥρᾳ .... This suggests either that John was influenced by Matthew (which no doubt would be Neirynck's solution), or that the time reference was in the pre-Matthean, i.e. Q, tradition. But, if Matthew could add it to his (Markan) source in the case of the Syro-Phoenician story (Matt 15:28, absent from Mark 7:29), he could add it to his Q story also, if it was just a stock phrase.

It is of course possible that the Q language of Matt 8:13 influenced the Matthean language of the other three cases, as Hoffmann suggests. Yet the phrase is widespread:

Luke 7:21 reads ἐν ἐκείνῃ τῇ ὥρᾳ ἐθεράπευσεν πολλοὺς ..., which is Lukan redaction. But it is possible that it could echo Q 7:10/Matt 8:13, which Luke omits there.

Matt 18:1 begins ἐν ἐκείνῃ τῇ ὥρᾳ ... not in a healing story, but to begin a dialogue about who is greatest. Matt 26:55 uses the same phrase to introduce Jesus' saying in Gethsemane. It occurs in narration also in Matt 10:19; 24:36; Mark 13:55; Luke 7:21; Acts 16:33; John 19:27. (The references are all in

Hawkins, p. 34.) Thus the idiom is common, and hence its use in Matthew is not necessarily derived from the one Q instance.

Hawkins (p. 168) lists Matt 11:25; 12:1; 14:1 (similarly Luke 13:1; Acts 12:1; 19:23) reading ἐν ἐκείνῳ τῷ καιρῷ. This indicates that the idiom with "hour" or "time" is so widespread one can hardly use it to argue for a Q reading in Q 7:?10?.

Kloppenborg 2000: In Q {B}, < >⁰.

Johnson 2001: In Q {B}, <[[(εἶπεν·)¹]] ()² [( )³] [[(< > ὡς ἐπίστευσας γεν-ηθήτω σοι. καὶ ἰάθη ὁ παῖς < > ἐν τῇ ὥρᾳ ἐκείνῃ)⁴]]>⁰.

Elements in John 4:50-53 and Matthew 8:13 that include Jesus' command to "go," the belief of the centurion/royal official (in Jesus' word—John) and references to the healing of the boy in "that hour," if not evidence of John's use of Matthew, are evidence of such a notification of healing in pre-Johannine and Q traditions of this pericope. Since the latter phrase is not found in Mark 7:24-30 (Syro-Phoenician's Daughter), it cannot be considered a stock phrase in a *Fernheilung*.

The problem of turning to the form-critical structure of a miracle story for help in deciding this variation unit is that Matthew does not appear to treat this as a miracle story any more or less than does the Q redactor. Admittedly, Matthew surrounds this story with shorter healing stories (Matt 8:1-4; 14-15; and, a summary of healings in 8:16-17), a sign that this pericope has something to do with healing(!). At the same time, however, Matthew expands upon the centurion story in a manner quite unlike Matthew's treatment of miracle stories elsewhere. By enlarging the story through the insertion of Matt 8:11-12 (Q 13:28-29) Matthew uses the story—especially Jesus' pronouncement in Matt 8:10 (Q 7:9)—as an occasion for further teaching (in this case, on eschatology). With this interpolation, it is less likely that Matthew would further add a conclusion of healing; indeed, Matt 8:13 appears far more anti-climactic and out of place than it would be in Q.

The transition formula in Q 7:1 suggests a change in the direction of the Q text (which Matthew obviously perceives, since the formula is used repeatedly later in the Gospel). The subsequent Q pericope (John's Inquiry about the One to Come—Q 7:18-19, ~~20-21~~, 22-23) assumes that a healing story has preceded it, even though the *Fernheilung* nature of the story precludes the disciples of John "*seeing* and hearing" the result of the interaction between the centurion and Jesus—i.e., the actual healing. Therefore, the lack of verbal agreement between Matthew and Luke and the Lukanisms in Luke 7:10 remain the only real obstacles to the obvious—that Q concluded with some comment to the centurion and/or reference to healing.

Hoffmann's "speculation" is not much more "speculative" than the argument that Q 7:1a serves as the basis for Matthew's transition formula in other places. With the Matthean and Lukan variants of Q 7:1 we face the same problem of similar content but utter lack of verbal agreement. Admittedly, the structural correspondence between Matthew and Luke is not as close in Q 7:10 as it is in Q 7:1, nor are the verbal agreements between Matt 8:13 and later healing statements in Matthew (9:22; 9:29; 15:18; 17:18) when compared to Matt 7:28a and later transition formulas (11:1; 13:53; 19:1; 26:1). Note that this is the first instance in Matthew of both of the phrases noted in Hawkins and presented by Robinson. Overall, though, this is an argument for the text of Q and goes beyond the question of whether Q had an ending.

In the end, it is "speculative" on the part of Harnack and Dibelius to suggest that Q didn't have any kind of an ending after Jesus' pronouncement. It would be natural for Jesus, after commenting about the centurion's faith to those following him, to then turn to the centurion for one last word—one that confirms Jesus' help in the matter.

Q 7:?10?¹: Matthew's καὶ εἶπεν.

Luke = Q: ( )¹

Pro

Con

Matt = Q: (καὶ εἶπεν)¹

Pro

B. Weiß 1876, 230: See Q 7:?10?⁰ In Q (p. 355).

von Harnack 1907, 91 (ET 1908, 132): Reconstruction. Harnack includes Q 7:10 with hesitation. For complete text see Q 7:1⁶ Luke = Q, Pro (p. 55).

B. Weiß 1908, 16: Reconstruction. For complete text see Q 7:1⁰ In Q (p. 5).

Crum 1927, 138: Reconstruction. For complete text see Q 7:~~2~~, 3, ~~4-6a~~¹ Luke = Q, Pro (pp. 71-72).

Schenk 1981, 37: Reconstruction. For complete text see Q 7:1⁰ In Q (p. 10).

Wegner 1985, 223: "Die Wendung καὶ εἶπεν dürfte auf die vor-mt Trad zurückgehen, denn ihre red Verwendung durch Mt ist allzu schwach belegt: In Mt 8,32 und 14,2 war dem ersten Evangelisten das καὶ schon vorgegeben; in Mt 19,5, wo noch eher eine mt red Einfügung der Gesamtwendung vorliegen könnte, muß mit Einfluß der LXX (vgl. Gn 2,23) gerechnet werden. Wir halten daher die Einleitung mit καὶ εἶπεν entsprechend einer Vorlage für wahrscheinlicher."

223, 271: Reconstruction. For complete text see Q 7:1⁰ In Q (pp. 11-12).

Catchpole 1992, 522 [1993, 286]: See Q 7:?10?⁰ In Q (p. 356).

Landis 1994, 14: "Bei der Einleitungswendung in V.13a ist der Satzanfang καὶ εἶπεν für Mt eher untypisch; er dürfte also traditionell sein."

17: Reconstruction. For complete text see Q 7:1⁶ Luke = Q, Pro (p. 57).

Con

von Harnack 1907, 147 (ET 1908, 210-211): See Q 7:?10?⁰ Undecided (p. 361).

Castor 1912, 224: Reconstruction. For complete text see Q 7:1⁰ In Q (p. 6).

Klostermann 1927, 75: "Der von Mt gebotene Abschluß entspricht 15,28, weicht aber von Lc [v.] 10 völlig ab."

Parker 1953, 63-65: See Q 7:1⁶ Matt = Q, Con (pp. 58-60).

Held 1960, 183: "Der Schlußvers bei Matthäus trägt unzweifelhaft matthäische Züge. Das ergibt der Vergleich von Mt. 8,13 mit anderen dem ersten Evangelisten eigentümlichen Sätzen (Mt. 9,22b; 9,29; 15,28; 17,18b)."

224-225, 227: Held indirectly argues for Matthean creation of 8:13 based on catchword linkage to Matt 8:8b (Q 7:7b).

Held 1960, ET 1963, 193-194: "The [194] concluding verse in Matthew undoubtedly bears Matthaean traits. This is shown by the comparison of Matt. 8:13 with other statements peculiar to the first evangelist (Matt. 9:22b; 9:29; 15:28; 17:18b)."

237, 239: Held indirectly argues for Matthean creation of 8:13 based on catchword linkage to Matt 8:8b (Q 7:7b).

P. Meyer 1970, 411: "It must be conceded that Matthew imported 8:11f. from another place in Q (and created vs. 13)."

George 1972, 71: "Le début de Mt 8,13 (où Jésus reprend la parole, alors qu'il parlait déjà: cf. 8,10 et 13) semble une suture rédactionnelle."

Schweizer 1973, 137-138 (ET 1975, 213): See Q 7:?10?⁴ Matt = Q, Con (p. 388).

Polag 1979, 38: Reconstruction. For complete text see Q 7:1⁰ In Q (pp. 9-10).

Dauer 1984, 79: "Zu (καὶ) εἶπεν (-αν) c. Dat. Pers. vgl. [Matt] 8,32 (diff Mk 5,13); 11,3 (diff Lk 7,19); 12,2 (diff Mk 2,24); 12,3 (diff Mk 2,25); 12,11 (red.); 12,48 (diff Mk 3,33); 13,10 (diff Mk 4,10); 13,57 (diff Mk 6,4) u.ö." Dauer therefore considers καὶ εἶπεν to be Matthean redaction.

Wegner 1985, 222: "Der Gesamtausdruck καὶ εἶπεν begegnet bei Mt nur selten: 1. Am Anfang eines Satzes übernimmt Mt es 1x aus Mk (Mt 9,15) und fügt es 3x in den Mk-Stoff ein (8,32 diff Mk 5,13: καὶ ἐπέτρεψεν; 14,2 diff Mk 6,14: καὶ ἔλεγον und 19,5 diff Mk 10,7). Außerdem bringt er es in dieser Stellung auch 1x in Q (Mt 4,9). 2. Inmitten eines Satzes bringt er es nur 3x, und zwar 1x in Q (8,10), 1x im Sg (18,3) und 1x als Übernahme von Mk (26,18 par Mk 14,14). 3. Mehrmals streicht Mt aber diese Wendung in der Bearbeitung seiner Mk-Vorlage, wobei er sie entweder ganz ausläßt (so gegenüber Mk 4,40 und 5,33) oder durch eine andere Wendung ersetzt: so durch καὶ λέγει in 4,19; τότε ἀποκριθείς ... εἶπεν in 15,28; ὁ δὲ λέγει in 17,20; ὁ δέ ... εἶπεν in 19,14 und durch ἔφη in 19,21 (vgl. ferner 9,29 und 24,2 diff Mk)."

"Der Befund zeigt, daß von einer Bevorzugung der Wendung in Mt nicht die Rede sein kann. Daher lautet unser Ergebnis: mt Red möglich." But see Wegner at Matt = Q, Pro (p. 367).

Judge 1989, 487-488: See Q 7:?10?⁰ Not in Q (pp. 359-360).

Gnilka 1990, 128³⁴: "Der ursprüngliche Abschluß ist kaum noch einiger-maßen sicher zu rekonstruieren. Mt 8,13 is mt gestaltet, wie die übereinstimmung mit 15,28b nahelegt. Vielleicht fand sich noch ein Satz wie: Und zum Hauptmann sprach er: Dein Knecht ist gesund."

Gnilka 1990, ET 1997, 121[98]: "The original conclusion can no langer be reconstructed adequately. Matt 8:13 is shaped by Matthew, as the agreement with 15:28b suggests. Perhaps there was a sentence such as 'And he said to the centurion, "Your servant is healed."'"

Dunderberg 1994, 89: "Auf das Konto der mt Redaktion gehen die Anordnung des anderen Q-Abschnittes in diesen Kontext (Mt 8,11-12) sowie das Ende des Berichtes (Mt 8,13)."

International Q Project 1995, 479: Reconstruction: "καὶ [[]] < >." For complete text see Q 7:1⁰ In Q (p. 16).

Evaluations

Robinson 2000: Indeterminate {U}, [( )]¹.

If the Matthean quotation in Matt 8:13b is redactional (see Q 7:?10?⁴ below), the quotation formula in Matt 8:13a should also be considered redactional.

Matthew's interpolation of Q 13:28-29 (Matt 8:11-12) between Q 7:9 and Q 7:10 made it necessary for him to introduce at the beginning of Q 7:10 some transition back to the centurion story. Though this might explain the presence here of ὁ Ἰησοῦς (see Q 7:?10?² below), it does not explain the whole quotation formula. But in any case some redactional quotation formula is necessary itself after Q 7:9, where Jesus spoke in the plural to his followers about the centurion, to introduce the statement in the singular addressed to the centurion himself, if, as in Matthew, there were some confirming saying. καὶ εἶπεν serves this purpose. εἶπεν is frequent in Q.

To be sure, these same two words at Mark 7:29a introduce the conclusion to the similar faith healing of the Syrophoenician woman's daughter, which may have influenced Matthew here. For when one notes (see Q 7:?10?⁴ below) the way in which the Matthean editing of Mark 7:29b-30 at Matt 15:28b is similar to Matt 8:13, it becomes clear that Matthew was aware of the parallel in the two faith healings.

The καί of Luke 7:10a is derived from Mark 7:30, in view of the other parallels between the two verses (see Q 7:?10?⁴ below). The opening καί in both Matt 8:13 and Luke 7:10 seems to be coincidental, each dependent on different Markan verses (7:29 and 30). In the case of Matthew, the καί is moved forward from 7:30 to a position between 7:29a and 7:29b—i.e., to introduce the fact of the healing, since Matt 8:13, like Matt 15:28, has no equivalent to Mark 7:30, the finding the sick person well at home.

If there were a quotation formula in Q, the Lukan text, lacking a quotation, would not be in place.

Kloppenborg 2000: Indeterminate {U}, [( )]¹.

Johnson 2001: Matt = Q {C}, ⟦(καὶ εἶπεν·) ¹⟧.

Εἶπεν is common in Q. It is quite natural in this passage as Jesus first speaks to his followers, then to the individual.

A *redactional* transition formula back to the centurion after Q 7:9 is only necessary if Matt 8:13 was not in Q in the first place—a circular argument. The problem with appealing to Matt 15:28 par Mark 7:29(-30) is that Matthew has largely altered Mark 7:29-30 and so is not likely to be influenced by Mark there. On the contrary, as the Syro-Phoenician/Canaanite story is a later text in Mark and Matthew, unless Matthew is moving backward and forward between the texts, it is more likely that Matt 8:13 (Q 7:10!) has influenced Matthew's redactional alteration of Mark 7:29-30 than the reverse. Verbal parallels between Matt 8:13 and Mark 7:29 are also far less obvious than between Luke 7:10 and Mark 7:29, where there appears to be a good case for Markan influence on Luke's redaction of the Q story.

Hoffmann 2001: Indeterminate {U}, [( )]¹.

Q 7:?10?²: Matthew's ὁ Ἰησοῦς.

Luke = Q: ( )²

Pro

Con

Matt = Q: (ὁ Ἰησοῦς)²

Pro

    B. Weiß 1876, 230: See Q 7:?10?⁰ In Q (p. 355).
    B. Weiß 1908, 16: Reconstruction. For complete text see Q 7:1⁰ In Q (p. 5).
    Crum 1927, 138: Reconstruction. For complete text see Q 7:~~2~~, 3, ~~4-6a~~¹ Luke = Q, Pro (pp. 71-72).
    Schenk 1981, 37: Reconstruction. For complete text see Q 7:1⁰ In Q (p. 10).
    Catchpole 1992, 522 [1993, 286]: See Q 7:?10?⁰ In Q (p. 356).

Con

    Castor 1912, 224: Reconstruction. For complete text see Q 7:1⁰ In Q (p. 6).
    Klostermann 1927, 75: "Der von Mt gebotene Abschluß entspricht 15,28, weicht aber von Lc [v.] 10 völlig ab."
    Parker 1953, 63-65: See Q 7:1⁶ Matt = Q, Con (pp. 58-60).
    Held 1960, 183 (ET 1963, 193-194): See Q 7:?10?¹ Matt = Q, Con (p. 368).
    224-225, 227 (ET 237, 238): Held indirectly argues for Matthean creation of 8:13 based on catchword linkage to Matt 8:8b (Q 7:7b).
    P. Meyer 1970, 411: "It must be conceded that Matthew imported 8:11f. from another place in Q (and created vs. 13)."
    George 1972, 71: "Le début de Mt 8,13 (où Jésus reprend la parole, alors qu'il parlait déjà: cf. 8,10 et 13) semble une suture rédactionnelle."
    Schweizer 1973, 137-138 (ET 1975, 213): See Q 7:?10?⁴ Matt = Q, Con (p. 388).
    Polag 1979, 38: Reconstruction. For complete text see Q 7:1⁰ In Q (pp. 9-10).
    Wegner 1985, 111: "Das relativ häufige Auftauchen von Ἰησοῦς in QMt (9x) stimmt mit dem mt Verfahren gegenüber Mk überein, wo die Zahl der mt Eintragungen ebenfalls sehr hoch ist (59x!). Die mt Bearbeitung der Mk-Vorlage berechtigt also, auch in QMt weitgehend mit mt Red zu rechnen, wo

immer die Lk-Parallele Ἰησοῦς nicht enthält. Dies legt sich auch dadurch nahe, daß Mt überhaupt das Subjekt gegenüber Mk des öfteren präzisiert."

222: "Die Verteilung der Belege innerhalb des ersten Ev (In Q 5; QMt 4; Sg 37 (red 16); + 59; – 19; acc 47) führt zu folgendem Ergebnis: mt Red wahrscheinlich."

223: "Sehr wahrscheinlich ist u.E. auf die mt Red das ὁ Ἰησοῦς zurück-zuführen."

223, 271: Reconstruction. For complete text see Q 7:1⁰ In Q (pp. 11-12).

Judge 1989, 487-488: See Q 7:?10?⁰ Not in Q (pp. 359-360).

Gnilka 1990, 128³⁴ (ET 1997, 121⁹⁸): See Q 7:?10?¹ Matt = Q, Con (pp. 368-369).

Dunderberg 1994, 89: "Auf das Konto der mt Redaktion gehen die Anord-nung des anderen Q-Abschnittes in diesen Kontext (Mt 8,11-12) sowie das Ende des Berichtes (Mt 8,13)."

Landis 1994, 14: "Die Nennung von ὁ Ἰησοῦς als Subjekt hingegen, die an unserer Stelle eigentlich überflüssig ist, da ja Jesus schon vorher gesprochen hat, ist wohl redaktionell; Mt präzisiert häufig das Subjekt seiner Vorlagen, und Ἰησοῦς fügt er besonders oft redaktionell ein."

17: Reconstruction. For complete text see Q 7:1⁶ Luke = Q, Pro (p. 57).

International Q Project 1995, 479: Reconstruction. For complete text see Q 7:1⁰ In Q (p. 16).

Evaluations

Robinson 2000: Luke = Q {B}, ()².

The need to identify Jesus by name in Matthew is due to his having intro-duced Q 13:28-29 (Matt 8:11-12) between Q 7:9 and Q 7:10. There Abra-ham, Isaac and Jacob are named, and those coming from east and west and the sons of the kingdom are mentioned, so that it is fitting to mention Jesus to bring the reader back to the context of the centurion story.

Mark 7:29a did not name Jesus, but Matt 15:28a, in editing Mark, intro-duced the name of Jesus, without intervening material to make it all the more necessary. This indicates Matthew's tendency clearly.

Kloppenborg 2000: Luke = Q {B}, ()².

Johnson 2001: Luke = Q {B}, ()².

Hoffmann 2001: Indeterminate {U}, [( )]¹.

Q 7:?10?³: Matthew's τῷ ἑκατοντάρχῃ.

Luke = Q: ( )³

Pro

Con

Matt = Q: (τῷ ἑκατοντάρχῃ)³

Pro

> **B. Weiß** 1876, 230: See Q 7:?10?⁰ In Q (p. 355).
> **B. Weiß** 1908, 16: Reconstruction. For complete text see Q 7:1⁰ In Q (p. 5).
> **Crum** 1927, 138: Reconstruction. For complete text see Q 7:2, 3, 4-6a¹ Luke = Q, Pro (pp. 71-72).
> **Schenk** 1981, 37: Reconstruction. For complete text see Q 7:1⁰ In Q (p. 10).
> **Wegner** 1985, 223: "Für die Traditionalität des Wortes auSt könnte sprechen, daß es hier mit dem Dat. der ersten Deklination auftaucht, da Mt selbst—wie 27,54 gegenüber Mk 15,39 zeigt—die Endung -αρχος zu bevorzugen scheint. Ferner könnte diese durch ἑκατοντάρχῃ gegebene Spezifizierung des Dativobjektes schon im urspr Q-Bericht dadurch bedingt worden sein, daß in Mt 8,10/Lk 7,9 Jesus sich mit (ἀμὴν) λέγω ὑμῖν ja an eine breitere Zuhörerschaft wendete. …
> "… könnte τῷ ἑκατοντάρχῃ schon vor-mt sein, obwohl diesbezüglich eine letzte Sicherheit nicht mehr möglich ist."
> 223, 271: Reconstruction. For complete text see Q 7:1⁰ In Q (pp. 11-12).
> **Catchpole** 1992, 522 [1993, 286]: See Q 7:?10?⁰ In Q (p. 356).
> **Landis** 1994, 14-15: "Anders steht es mit dem Dativobjekt τῷ ἑκατοντάρχῃ: Seine Nennung [15] hat bereits in der ursprünglichen Q-Erzählung ihren Sinn, denn in Lk 9b/Mt 8,10b hatte sich Jesus an einen weiteren Zuhörerkreis gewandt, während er nun wieder ausschließlich den Hauptmann anredet. Für einen traditionellen Ursprung des Ausdrucks spricht auch die Verwendung des Dativs der ersten Deklination, weil Mt selbst eher die Endung -ος bevorzugt (s. 8,5 diff Lk 7,6; 27,54 diff Mk 15,39)."
> 17: Reconstruction. For complete text see Q 7:1⁶ Luke = Q, Pro (p. 57).

Con

> **Castor** 1912, 224: Reconstruction. For complete text see Q 7:1⁰ In Q (p. 6).

Klostermann 1927, 75: "Der von Mt gebotene Abschluß entspricht 15,28, weicht aber von Lc [v.] 10 völlig ab."

Parker 1953, 63-65: See Q 7:1[6] Matt = Q, Con (pp. 58-60).

P. Meyer 1970, 411: "It must be conceded that Matthew imported 8:11f. from another place in Q (and created vs. 13)."

George 1972, 71: "Le début de Mt 8,13 (où Jésus reprend la parole, alors qu'il parlait déjà: cf. 8,10 et 13) semble une suture rédactionnelle."

Schweizer 1973, 137-138 (ET 1975, 213): See Q 7:?10?[4] Matt = Q, Con (p. 388).

Polag 1979, 38: Reconstruction. For complete text see Q 7:1[0] In Q (pp. 9-10).

Schenk 1987, 205: See Q 7:~~2~~, 3, ~~4-6a~~[5] Matt = Q, Pro (p. 136).

Judge 1989, 487-488: See Q 7:?10?[0] Not in Q (pp. 359-360).

Gnilka 1990, 128[34] (ET 1997, 121[98]): See Q 7:?10?[1] Matt = Q, Con (p. 369).

Dunderberg 1994, 89: "Auf das Konto der mt Redaktion gehen die Anordnung des anderen Q-Abschnittes in diesen Kontext (Mt 8,11-12) sowie das Ende des Berichtes (Mt 8,13)."

International Q Project 1995, 479: Reconstruction. For complete text see Q 7:1[0] In Q (p. 16).

Evaluations

Robinson 2000: Indeterminate {U}, [( )][3].
The reference to the centurion would disappear along with the quotation formula (see Q 7:?10?[1,2]).

Kloppenborg 2000: Indeterminate {U}, [( )][3].

Johnson 2001: Indeterminate {U}, [( )][3].
The relative preponderance of the $-\eta\varsigma$ ending in this era suggests that Matthew's redaction at 27:54 might be a reminiscence of Q 7:3, 6 and that Matthew and Luke redactionally conform to standard usage here (Matthew) and at Q 7:6 (Luke). It is also possible that Q is responsible for altering the endings and that Matthew is merely following the source.

At the same time, while inclusion of the word isn't necessary, Matthew may have felt it to be helpful to include mention of Jesus and the centurion after the significant interruption of Q 13:28-29 (Matt 8:11-12).

Hoffmann 2001: Indeterminate {U}, [( )][3].

Q 7:?10?⁴: The form of the statement about the centurion's or his delegation's departure and the confirmation of the healing, including Matthew's statement about faith.

Luke = Q: [καὶ ὑποστρέψαντες εἰς τὸν οἶκον οἱ πεμφθέντες εὗρον τὸν δοῦλον ὑγιαίνοντα]⁴.

Pro

Castor 1912, 224: Reconstruction. But see Castor at Q 7:?10?⁰ Not in Q (p. 357). For complete text see Q 7:1⁰ In Q (p. 6).

Schürmann 1969, 395: "Jedenfalls hat die Perikope in Lk richtig in der Feststellung Jesu V 9 ihren einzigen Höhepunkt, und es ist ursprünglich, daß V 10—anders als Mt 8,13—das Wunder als geschehen nur kurz konstatiert wird."

Theissen 1974, 183: "Die Auffindung des gesunden Knechtes bei der Rückkehr, wie sie Lk berichtet, ist ein ursprünglicher Zug. Mt bemerkt nur, der Kranke sei von jener Stunde an gesund geworden. Eben dies Motiv hat er aber in Mt 15,28b für Mk 7,30 (die Auffindung der gesunden Tochter nach der Rückkehr) gesetzt. Ebenso wird er in Mt 8,13 verfahren sein."

Theissen 1974, ET 1983, 182: "Finding the slave cured on the return to the house, as Luke describes it, is an original feature. Matthew only notes that the slave was healed from that time on, but he has introduced this motif in Mt 15.28b (for Mk 7.30, where the mother finds the daughter recovered on her return), and probably did the same in Mt 8.13."

Gundry 1982, 144: See Gundry at Matt = Q, Con (p. 389).

Dauer 1984, 82-83: "Wir werden also doch annehmen können, daß schon in der vor-mt bzw. vor-lk Tradition (=Q) am Schluß der Erzählung von der Erfüllung der Bitte des Hauptmanns, d.h. vom erfolgten Wunder, die Rede gewesen ist. Läßt sich auch noch sagen, mit welchen Worten diese Konstatierung getroffen wurde? Bei aller Vorsicht, ja! Mit großer Wahrscheinlichkeit steht die [83] Formulierung bei Lk, trotz der Überarbeitung durch den 3. Evangelisten, der ursprünglichen Formulierung am nächsten."

Wegner 1985, 232-233: "Da Lk dieses Verb 5x in seiner Bearbeitung des Mk-Stoffes sek einfügt, könnte auch auSt lk Red vorliegen. Für Trad aus dem lk Sg spricht die hohe Belegzahl, die εὑρίσκειν in dieser [233] Traditionsschicht aufweist. Beachtet man nun noch, daß auch in Q das Verb relativ gut belegt ist, so wird deutlich, daß auf Grund der Stat allein sichere Entscheidungen nicht mehr möglich sind. Weiter hilft aber Mk 7,30. Denn aus diesem Vers, der wie Lk 7,10 ebenfalls den Abschluß einer Fernheilung wiedergibt, geht hervor, daß die Begegnung mit der genesenen Person (Mk

7,30: εὗρεν τὸ παιδίον βεβλημένον κτλ.) durchaus auch im Abschluß der Fernheilung von Mt 8,5-10.13/Lk 7,1-10 urspr berichtet sein könnte (Lk 7,10:
εὗρον τὸν δοῦλον ὑγιαίνοντα.). Mt, der gegenüber Mk 7,30 den εὗρεν-Satz
zugunsten einer von ihm redigierten formelhaften Wendung ausläßt, dürfte
auf ähnliche Weise auch in 8,13c verfahren haben, da die Formulierung dieses
Verses ganz seinen Stil verrät. So ergibt sich, daß εὑρίσκειν auSt sehr
wahrscheinlich dem Lk schon trad vorgelegen haben wird, wobei als Trad
sowohl Q als auch das lk Sg in Frage kommen."
    234: "Gut in Q belegt sind das anreihende καί, εὑρίσκειν und δοῦλος."
    235: "Auch εὑρίσκειν wird letztlich nicht aus der lk Red, sondern schon aus
der Trad stammen: Lk fügt es zwar mehrfach red in seinen Mk-Stoff ein, doch
ist es in Lk 7,10 wahrscheinlich trad, da (a) es sowohl in Q als auch in Traditionen des lk Sg mehrfach belegt ist, (b) es auch am Schluß der Fernheilung
der Tochter der Syrophoenizierin (Mk 7,24-30: vgl. V 30!) benutzt wird, und
(c) Mt es in 8,13 sehr wahrscheinlich sek zugunsten der durch ihn geprägten
Formel καὶ ἰάθη ὁ παῖς ἐν τῇ ὥρᾳ ἐκείνῃ (vgl. noch 9,22 und 17,18) ausließ."

Con

Bleek 1862, 348: For δοῦλος, see Q 7:~~2~~, 3, ~~4-6a~~⁹ Luke = Q, Con (p. 167).
    Holtzmann 1863, 77-78: For δοῦλος, see Q 7:~~2~~, 3, ~~4-6a~~⁹ Luke = Q, Con
(p. 167).
    B. Weiß 1876, 228: For δοῦλος, see Q 7:~~2~~, 3, ~~4-6a~~⁹ Matt = Q, Pro (p. 178).
    231: "Der Schluß der Erzählung vom Centurio musste bei Luc. (7,10)
natürlich ein ganz andrer werden, wenn der Vater nicht anwesend war, und
soll doch ebenfalls nur die sofortige Genesung constatiren (Bem. das echt luc.
ὑποστρέφειν, wie 4,1, und zu ὑγιαίνειν 5,31; 15,27)."
    Wernle 1899, 65: "Das entscheidende heilende Wort Jesu hat er ausfallen
lassen. Da anderseits die wörtliche Übereinstimmung mit Mt in v. 6-9 so groß
ist, so ließe sich auf Grund dieses Stücks die Abhängigkeit direkt von Mt
behaupten. Natürlich spricht gegen die Annahme gemeinsamer Quelle, der
Mt treu folgte, während Lc sie umgestaltete, keine der gemachten Beobachtungen."
    Holtzmann 1901, 344: "Der Erfolg wird (7,10) in sachlich gleicher, aber
im Vergleich mit Mt 8,13 vereinfachter Form berichtet."
    B. Weiß 1907, 243: "Ja, es muß durchaus in L noch ein Wort Jesu wie Joh.
4,50 gestanden haben, das den sein Kommen abwehrenden Freunden zugab,
daß dasselbe auch nicht nötig sei, da, völlig abweichend von Mt. 8,13, dort
die Erzählung damit schloß, daß die Abgesandten bei ihrer Rückkehr den
Knecht gesund fanden (Lk. 7,10). So hat also auch hier Lukas in der Erzählung aus L eine willkommene Ergänzung der Geschichte aus Q gefunden,

diesmal freilich ohne die Inkongruenz beider … ganz verwischen zu können und ohne zu sehen, daß der Abschluß aus L bei ihm unmotiviert bleibt."

B. Weiß 1908, 16[26]: "Lk. 7,10 ist natürlich der Schluß der Erzählung aus L."

Haupt 1913, 81: For δοῦλος, see Q 7:~~2~~, 3, ~~4-6a~~[9] Luke = Q, Con (p. 169).

Klostermann 1919, 448: "Lc unterscheidet sich besonders durch: … die Ersetzung von παῖς durch δοῦλος (ebenso 7,10)."

Cadbury 1920, 173: "The form ὕπαγε is especially common in Matthew and Mark, but occurs nowhere in Luke. Very likely it seemed to him vulgar. In the following cases he has probably changed or omitted it: … Mt. 8,13 ὕπαγε Lk. 7,10 entirely different (Q).[2]"

173[2]: "Perhaps this verse is not from Q at all; see Harnack [1907, 56, 147; ET, 77, 210-211)—see Q 7:?10?[0] Undecided (p. 361).]."

Loisy 1924, 218-219: "Notre évangéliste ne pouvait garder la conclusion qu'a retenue Matthieu, le centurion n'étant pas là pour entendre l'assentiment [219] de Jésus à sa requête; et c'est pour un motif analogue qu'il fait constater la guérison par les envoyés du centurion, au lieu de dire qu'elle s'accomplit à la parole de Jésus (il a pu d'ailleurs imiter Mc. vii, 30)."

Easton 1926, 97: "Ὑποστρέφειν and πέμπειν are 'Lukan.'"

Klostermann 1929, 86: "Δοῦλος: ersetzt Mt' παῖς, ebenso [v.] 10, dagegen [v.] 7 ist παῖς geblieben."

Hirsch 1941, 88-89: For δοῦλος, see Q 7:~~2~~, 3, ~~4-6a~~[9] Luke = Q, Con (pp. 169-170) and Matt = Q, Pro (p. 179).

Sparks 1941, 180: For δοῦλος, see Q 7:~~2~~, 3, ~~4-6a~~[9] Luke = Q, Con (p. 170).

Grundmann 1961, 155: See Q 7:~~2~~, 3, ~~4-6a~~[3] Luke = Q, Con (pp. 99-100).

155-156: "Diese Erwägungen legen die Auskunft Hirschs [1941, 88-90] nahe, daß Lukas in einer überarbeiteten Ausgabe von Q, Hirschs Lu I, den Bericht bereits zusammengefügt vorgefunden hat. Die Zusammenfügung steigert den Wundercharakter: [156] Der Knecht liegt im Sterben, während er bei Matthäus gelähmt und von Schmerzen geplagt ist; die Heilung erfolgt auf die Mitteilung der Worte des Centurio hin ohne Heilwort Jesu und ohne Berührung mit dem Bittsteller; zum Glauben des Centurio tritt seine Demut hinzu."

Dodd 1963, 188-190[2]: For δοῦλος, see Q 7:~~2~~, 3, ~~4-6a~~[9] Luke = Q, Con (p. 171).

191: See Q 7:~~2~~, 3, ~~4-6a~~[1] Luke = Q, Con (p. 68).

Schnackenburg 1964, 74-75: See Schnackenburg at Matt = Q, Pro (pp. 383-384).

Schnackenburg 1965, 504-505 (ET 1968, 474): For δοῦλος, see Q 7:~~2~~, 3, ~~4-6a~~[9] Matt = Q, Pro (p. 179).

Brown 1966, 193: "It was Luke or a Lucan forerunner who, in the Greek stage of the tradition, understood *pais* as servant boy and began to speak of a *doulos.* That Luke's use of *doulos* is secondary is suggested by the fact that it appears in those verses (2, 3, 10) where the Lucan story differs from that of Matthew."

Cadbury 1966, 93-94: For δοῦλος, see Q 7:2̶, 3, 4̶-6̶a̶⁹ Luke = Q, Con (p. 171).

Delobel 1966, 453: "*Le v. 10.*—La construction ὑποστρέψαντες εὗρον,—un participe aoriste avec verbe en mode personnel,—est très fréquent dans *Lc.* Le terme ὑποστρέφειν se trouve 21 fois dans *Lc.* et 11 fois dans *Act.*, tandis qu'on ne compte que trois cas dans les autres écrits du N.T."

454: For δοῦλος, see Q 7:2̶, 3, 4̶-6̶a̶⁹ Luke = Q, Con (p. 171).

454: "Ὑγιαίνειν est absent des autres synoptiques. Nous retrouvons ce verbe à deux endroits chez *Lc.* (V, 31 diff *Mc.*; XV, 27 S*Lc*). Il n'est pas impossible que le verset dans son ensemble contienne des réminiscences de *Mc.*, VII, 30, verset final de la péricope sur la Syrophénicienne."

Siegman 1968, 193: "*The Healing Word* (Jn 4,50; Mt 8,13)—Lk omits this altogether and concludes the story anti-climactically with the bare information that the elders and friends found the slave recovered, when they returned to the centurion."

Schürmann 1969, 391¹²: For δοῦλος, see Q 7:2̶, 3, 4̶-6̶a̶⁹ Luke = Q, Con (pp. 171-172).

Schnider and Stenger 1971, 60-61: See Q 7:2̶, 3, 4̶-6̶a̶⁹ Luke = Q, Con (p. 172).

Schramm 1971, 40-41: For δοῦλος, see Q 7:2̶, 3, 4̶-6̶a̶⁹ Luke = Q, Con (pp. 172-173).

George 1972, 68: "Luc rédige à sa manière⁶ le retour des 'envoyés' (v. 10), qui sont sans doute les amis du centurion ('envoyés' au v. 6), plutôt que les anciens."

68⁶: "Les caractéristiques lucaniennes s'accumulent dans le v. 10: *hypostrephein* (Mt: 0—Mc: 0—Lc: 21—Jn: 0—Ac: 11), *oikos* (respectivement: 10—12—33—4—25), *pempein* (4—1—10—32—11), *hygiainein* (0—0—3—0—0)."

70: For δοῦλος, see Q 7:2̶, 3, 4̶-6̶a̶⁹ Matt = Q, Pro (p. 180).

70: "Comme on va le voir, c'est sans doute l'absence du centurion qui amène Luc à ne pas rapporter la 'parole de guérison' de Mt 8,13."

Schulz 1972, 239: "Vokabelstatistisch ist Lk V 10 red.⁴²⁶"

239-240⁴²⁶: "Inhaltlich hängt V 10 aufs engste mit dem Einschub Vv 3-6a zusammen: Das Gespräch findet zwischen den vom Hauptmann ausgesandten Freunden und Jesus statt. Sie kehren jetzt ins Haus zurück und finden den δοῦλος gesund. Das Vokabelmaterial zeigt stark lk Einschlag: ὑποστρέφειν ist ausgesprochen lk (Ev ca 8mal trad; ca 11mal red; Apg 11mal; fehlt sonst bei den Synoptikern—nur noch 2mal im NT); οἶκος bezieht [240] sich eindeutig auf V 6a zurück; πέμπειν bezieht sich ebenfalls auf V 6a zurück; εὑρίσκειν ist bei Lk gehäuft (Ev ca 32mal trad; ca 12mal red; Apg 23mal); ὑγιαίνειν (in den Synoptikern nur bei Lk [15,27 trad; 5,31 red]); wie 7,2.3 spricht auch V 10 vom δοῦλος, während Q offenbar παῖς bietet (vgl Lk 7,7b/Mt 8,8b)."

Dupont 1973, 177: "Les Verbes 'envoyer', ... relèvent particulièrement du vocabulaire de l'évangéliste."

Achtemeier 1975, 549: "A third way of approaching the Lucan miracle stories is by way of formal analysis, i.e., to see at what points the stories no longer fit the typical form of a gospel miracle-story, which in turn may give us clues about the point Luke wants to make. To take Luke 7:1-10 again as an example, our analysis of the form will show that the 'solution' has, in fact, been omitted. That is, we are never told how, or even that, Jesus healed the boy (that the story once contained such a solution can be seen in Matt 8:13). The major point has thus become the fact that the centurion was worthy to receive the requested miracle (vs. 4), a point confirmed by his own humility (vs. 7; both points are absent in Matthew). Thus, while Matthew's point concerns the power of faith in healing, Luke emphasizes the worthiness of a non-Jew to receive the benefits of Jesus' power."

Pesch and Kratz 1976, 77: For δοῦλος, see Q 7:2, 3, 4-6a⁹ Luke = Q, Con (p. 173).

Busse 1977, 149-150: See Q 7:?10?⁰ Not in Q (pp. 358-359).

Marshall 1978, 282: "The language (including ὑγιαίνω, 5:31; 15:27; Mt., 0x; Mk., 0x) suggests Lucan formulation."

Martin 1978, 15, 20¹⁰, ¹¹: See Q 7:2, 3, 4-6a¹² Luke = Q, Con (p. 214).

Gatzweiler 1979, 302: For δοῦλος, see Q 7:2, 3, 4-6a⁹ Matt = Q, Pro (p. 180).

Muhlack 1979, 45: "Wie Lukas 7,3 verwendet er das für Zusätze charakteristische δοῦλος. Wieder liegt eine Erweiterung der Matthäus vergleichbaren ursprünglichen Geschichte vor, die Lukas' Erzählung selbst erfordert."

Polag 1979, 38: Reconstruction. For complete text see Q 7:1⁰ In Q (pp. 9-10).

Jeremias 1980, 156: "Red ὑποστρέψαντες εἰς τὸν οἶκον: ist eine lukanische Wendung → 1,56 Red ...—ὑγιαίνοντα: ὑγιαίνω im eigentlichen Sinn kommt im NT außer 3Joh 2 nur im LkEv vor: Lk 5,31; 7,10; 15,27. Das Verbum wird auch dadurch als redaktionell erwiesen, daß Lukas es in seiner Bearbeitung des Markusstoffs verwendet (Lk 5,31 ὑγιαίνοντες diff. Mk 2,17 ἰσχύοντες)."

Fitzmyer 1981, 649: "Whereas [*pais*] has been understood as 'son' (*huios*) in John, it is interpreted as 'servant, slave' (*doulos*) by Luke in vv. 2,3 and even extended to v. 10. ... it is better to regard vv. 1a,7a and 10a as Lucan redaction."

653: "Luke changed the first part of the verse, omitting the impv. of Matt 8:13; the indirect reporting of the miracle's effect is preferred and has its own literary purpose. It does not concentrate on the cure itself, but on the pronouncement of Jesus."

Schenk 1981, 37: Reconstruction. For complete text see Q 7:1⁰ In Q (p. 10).

Haapa 1983, 71⁹: For δοῦλος, see Q 7:2, 3, 4-6a⁹ Luke = Q, Con (p. 174).

73: "Das heilende Wort Jesu fehlt (vgl. Mt 8,13). Statt dessen wird die Erzählung von den Gesandtschaften zu Ende geführt durch den Schlußvers, in dem die Genesung von den heimgekehrten Abgesandten bezeugt wird (Lk 7,10)."

Dauer 1984, 80: "Für lk Bildung von Lk 7,10 sprechen:

"(1) Lukas hat eine ausgesprochene 'Vorliebe ... für das Motiv der Rückkehr. Denn es ist ein fester Zug seiner Erzähltechnik, die Rückkehr von Personen oder Personengruppen eigens zu vermerken', ja, das 'Motiv der Rückkehr [bildet] oft den Perikopenabschluß' [Lohfink 1971, 174].

"(2) Die verwendeten Wörter tragen lk Sprachkolorit: ὑποστρέφειν ist lk Vorzugswort: Lk 21mal und Apg 11mal; davon ist es sicher redaktionell in Lk 4,1 (diff Mk 1,12); 4,14 (diff Mk 1,14); 8,37 (add Mk 5,18); 8,40 (diff Mk 5,21); 9,10 (diff Mk 6,30); 24,9 (diff Mk 16,8)³⁰⁵.—Ähnliches gilt für die ganze Wendung ὑποστρέφειν εἰς τὸν οἶκον: Lk 1,56; 7,10 u.St.; 8,39 (diff Mk 5,19); 11,24 (diff Mt 12,44).

"Ὑγιαίνειν als medizinischer Ausdruck kommt nur Lk 5,31; 7,10 u.St.; 15,27 (Sg.) vor, wovon Lk 5,31 (diff Mk 2,17) sicher redaktionell ist; 3 Joh 2 hat ὑγιαίνειν die allgemeinere Bedeutung von 'sich wohl befinden'. οἱ πεμφθέντες ist Wiederaufnahme von V. 6: ἔπεμψεν φίλους.

"Δοῦλος stammt aus V. 2 bzw. V. 3, wo es wahrscheinlich lk Änderung des ursprünglicheren παῖς ist. ...

"(3) Möglicherweise ist Lukas zu dieser Schlußbemerkung in V. 10 durch Mk 7,30 angeregt worden, wo das erbetene Wunder nach der Begegnung der Bittstellerin mit Jesus mit ganz ähnlichen Worten konstatiert wird." But see Dauer at Q 7:?10?⁴ Luke = Q, Pro (p. 375).

342³⁰⁵: "Die Häufigkeit von ὑποστρέφειν bei Lukas hängt natürlich mit seiner Vorliebe für das Motiv der Rückkehr zusammen."

116: "Rückschauend läßt sich als lk Redaktion feststellen: ... ὑποστρέψαντες (statt ἀπῆλθον?)—δοῦλος (statt παῖς)—ὑγιαίνειν."

Wegner 1985, 230: For ὑποστρέφω: "Dieses Verb kommt weder in Mk noch in Mt vor, dagegen aber 21x in Lk, 11x in der Apg und nur noch 3x im übrigen NT. ... Innerhalb seines Ev bringt es Lk 4x als add (8,37.39.40 und 9,10 om Mk), 2x in QLk (4,1 om Mt und 11,24 diff Mt 12,44: ἐπιστρέφω) und 15x in seinem Sg. Das Verb ist somit eindeutig als Vorzugswort des lk Sg zu bewerten. Dies führt zu folgendem stat Ergebnis: lk Red möglich; hohes Vorkommen im Sg."

231: "Die Gesamtwendung ὑποστρέφειν + εἰς τὸν οἶκον begegnet außer auSt noch in 1,56 (Sg); 8,39 (diff Mk 5,19 ...) und 11,24 (diff Mt 12,44 ...). Von

1,56 einmal abgesehen, zeigt der Vergleich von Lk 8,39 und 11,24 mit den Parallelen aus Mk und Mt, daß Lk das Hausmotiv jeweils übernimmt, während sich seine red Tätigkeit auf den Ersatz der vorgegebenen Verben durch ὑποστρέφειν beschränkt. Daher wird auch bzgl. des ὑποστρέφειν in Lk 7,10 mit der Möglichkeit gerechnet werden müssen, daß der dritte Evangelist dieses Verb als Ersatz für ein urspr ὑπάγω, ἐπιστρέφω, πορεύομαι oder dergleichen gebraucht hat."

231-234: Wegner argues for the preceding material coming from Lukan *Sondergut* rather than Lukan redaction.

234: "Daß der gesamte Vers aber kaum aus Q stammt, ist der Verwendung von ὑποστρέφειν, ὑγιαίνειν und οἶκος zu entnehmen: Während die zwei Verben sonst an keiner anderen Stelle von Q gebraucht werden, taucht der Mask. οἶκος zwar 2x in anderen Q-Perikopen auf, doch zeigen Mt 8,6 und Lk 7,6, daß die urspr Q-Erzählung der Hauptmannsperikope sehr wahrscheinlich für 'Haus' die Femininform οἰκία verwendet hat."

271: Reconstruction. For complete text see Q 7:1⁰ In Q (pp. 11-12).

Schnelle 1987, 103: "Lukas hat in einem weit größeren Maß als Matthäus die Q-Vorlage umgestaltet. Auf seine Redaktion gehen ... die Gestaltung des Schlußverses zurück."

Schnelle 1987, ET 1992, 89: "Luke has reshaped the Q version of the story much more thoroughly than Matthew. His redaction produced ... the shape of the final verse."

Bovon 1989, 349²⁹: For δοῦλος, see Q 7:~~2~~, 3, ~~4-6a~~⁹ Matt = Q, Pro (p. 180).

352⁴⁴: "Lukas kann zwar die passivische Formulierung, die in Q vorliegt (ἰάθη, Mt 8,13), vermeiden, doch gelingt es ihm nur auf Kosten einer unglücklichen Wiederholung von εὗρον (dritte Person Plural [Lk 7,10]; vgl. die erste Person Singular in 7,9)."

Bovon 1989, FT 1991, 341²⁹: For δοῦλος, see Q 7:~~2~~, 3, ~~4-6a~~⁹ Matt = Q, Pro (pp. 180-181).

344⁴⁴: "Luc évite la formule de Q au passif (ἰάθη, Mt 8,13), mais il n'y parvient pas sans une malheureuse répétition de εὗρον (troisième personne du pluriel, v. 10; première personne du singulier, v. 9)."

Judge 1989, 487: See Q 7:?10?⁰ Not in Q (pp. 360-361).

Nolland 1989, 318: "Presumably in the tradition the conclusion of the account mentioned the healing, but both Matthew's and Luke's conclusions are strongly marked by the evangelists' activity (... Luke's conclusion depends upon the second embassy material)."

Riniker 1990, 62: "La forme que ce texte avait dans la source Q est pour l'essentiel mieux conservée chez Matthieu (8,5-10.13), qui ne l'a que peu retouchée.⁶⁰"

62⁶⁰: "La finale lucanienne dépend déjà de l'introduction des envois."

Davies and Allison 1991, 20-21: For δοῦλος, see Q 7:~~2~~, 3, ~~4-6a~~⁹ Matt = Q, Pro (p. 181).

31: "If Q had a conclusion to the story about the centurion it cannot now be reconstructed. Lk 7.10 has this: 'and returning to the house those who had been sent found the sick servant healed'. This appears redactional."

Catchpole 1992, 522 [1993, 286]: See Q 7:?10?⁰ In Q (p. 356).

Lindars 1992, 211: For δοῦλος, see Q 7:~~2~~, 3, ~~4-6a~~⁹ Luke = Q, Con (p. 176).

212: "Luke's ending ... has no words in common with John, and is clearly an adaptation of the source to accommodate the deputations. He has taken words from his previous text (οἶκον, cf. οἰκίαν, v. 6, πεμφθέντες, v. 6, εὗρον, v. 9, δοῦλον, v. 2), and reduced the original definite statement of the servant's recovery to the feeble and colourless ὑγιαίνοντα (cf. Lk 5,31 ὑγιαίνοντες for Mt/Mk ἰσχύοντες)."

Gagnon 1993, 715: "It should be noted that Lucan redaction can ... be seen in ... the words ὑποστρέψαντες, οἱ πεμφθέντες, δοῦλον, and ὑγιαίνοντα in v 10."

716: For δοῦλος, see Q 7:~~2~~, 3, ~~4-6a~~⁹ Luke = Q, Con (p. 176).

717-718: "According to Wegner [1985, 234], the substitute phrasing of Luke 7:10 could stem either from Luke or from his special source, but more likely stems from the latter; but the fact that ὑποστρέφω, ὑγιαίνω, and πέμπω are attested in redactional materials as strongly as they are in the so-called special-source material—or more strongly than they are in such material—puts the burden [718] of proof on those who presume that Luke has not also redacted his special source. Of the twenty other occurrences in Luke of ὑποστρέφω, 'to return' (0/0/21 + 11/0; only 3x more in the NT), six are clearly the product of Lucan redaction ([L]: 4:1,14; 8:37,39,40; 9:10), six probably are ([L?]: 23:48,56; [LQ]: 11:24; 19:12; 24:9), and nine may very well be ([S]: 1:56; 2:20,43,45; 10:17; 17:15,18; 24:33,52). The circumstantial participle appears in 9:10 [L]; 17:18 [S]; 23:56 [L?]; and 24:9 [L?]. The combination of ὑποστρέφω + εἰς τὸν οἶκον occurs in 1:56 [S]; 8:39 [L]; and 11:24 [LQ]. Given the high percentage of clear or probable instances of Lucan redaction, as well as the almost exclusive monopoly on NT use of the term held by Luke-Acts, it would be precarious to trace the occurrences of ὑποστρέφω in material peculiar to Luke back to Luke's special source. The verb ὑγιαίνω, 'to be in good health, healthy,' appears in the Gospels and Acts only in Luke: 5:31 [L] replacing Mark's οἱ ἰσχύοντες, and 15:27 [S]. In the case of the former, it is clearly a word chosen by Luke; in the case of the latter, it may derive either from Luke's source or from Luke himself. Finally, πέμπω, 'to send' (4/1/10 + 11) occurs three times as [L] (20:11-13, for Mark's ἀποστέλλω); frequently in Acts; once as [L?] (4:26); three times as [S] (15:15; 16:24,27); and only once in [Q] (7:19). ... The wording of v 10 favors Lucan redaction over derivation from Luke's special source."

Sevenich-Bax 1993, 166-167: For δοῦλος and οἶκος, see Q 7:~~2~~, 3, ~~4-6a~~⁹ Luke = Q, Con (p. 177).

176-177: For δοῦλος, see Q 7:~~2~~, 3, ~~4-6a~~⁹ Luke = Q, Con (p. 177).

Dunderberg 1994, 86-87: "Der lukanische Abschluß des Berichtes verrät redaktionelle Spuren. Die Wendung ὑποστρέφειν εἰς τὸν οἶκον wird bei Lk außer 7,10 noch dreimal (1,56; 8,39; 11,24) verwendet. Während es bei 1,56 kein Vergleichsmaterial bei Mk und Mt gibt, wird durch das ὑποστρέφειν in 8,39 das ὑπάγειν (Mk 5,19) ersetzt. Aufgrund dieser Änderung ist auch Lk 11,24 für redaktionell zu halten, weil die Parallele in Mt 12,44 mit ἐπιστρέφειν formuliert [87] ist. Über diese Wendung hinaus wird das Verb ὑγιαίνειν im NT als medizinischer Ausdruck nur von Lk verwendet."

89: "Außerdem hat auch Lk die Konstatierung des Wunders selbstständig formuliert (7,10)."

Landis 1994, 25: Landis argues that εὗρον τὸν δοῦλον comes from Lukan *Sondergut*, while the rest of Luke 7:10 is Lukan redaction.

Meier 1994, 724, 769¹⁹³: For δοῦλος, see Q 7:~~2~~, 3, ~~4-6a~~⁹ Matt = Q, Pro (p. 182).

International Q Project 1995, 479: Reconstruction. For complete text see Q 7:1⁰ In Q (p. 16).

Neirynck 1996, 455: "I can agree with D's [Dunderberg; see above] view on Lukan redaction in Lk 7,1-10 (87-89): ἤμελλεν τελευτᾶν (in v. 2), the two delegations (vv. 3-6) and the conclusion (v. 10)."

Matt = Q: (ὕπαγε, ὡς ἐπίστευσας γενηθήτω σοι. καὶ ἰάθη ὁ παῖς αὐτοῦ ἐν τῇ ὥρᾳ ἐκείνῃ)⁴.

Pro

von Harnack 1907, 91 (ET 1908, 132): Reconstruction. Harnack includes Q 7:10 with hesitation. For complete text see Q 7:1⁶ Luke = Q, Pro (p. 55).

Haupt 1913, 80: "Bem. auch, wie Mt den Schluß der Hauptmannserzählung genau nach dem der Kananäerin gestaltet 8,13 = 15,28."

Klostermann 1919, 448: "Lc unterscheidet sich besonders durch: ... die Ersetzung von παῖς durch δοῦλος (ebenso 7,10)."

Crum 1927, 138: Reconstruction. For complete text see Q 7:~~2~~, 3, ~~4-6a~~¹ Luke = Q, Pro (pp. 71-72).

Klostermann 1929, 86: "Δοῦλος: ersetzt Mt' παῖς, ebenso [v.] 10, dagegen [v.] 7 ist παῖς geblieben."

Hirsch 1941, 88: For παῖς, see Q 7:~~2~~, 3, ~~4-6a~~⁹ Matt = Q, Pro (p. 179).

Schnackenburg 1964, 74-75: "Das Zusammentreffen der Knechte mit dem Vater noch auf dessen Heimweg und ihr Bericht von der plötzlichen

Besserung des Kranken werden nur bei Joh erzählt. Das steht zwar in einer
[75] gewissen Spannung zu der Schlußbemerkung bei Lk 7,10, ist aber keine
ernstliche Schwierigkeit, da das lukanische Schlußwort—entsprechend der
Anlage dieses Berichtes—kaum anders lauten konnte und nur summarisch die
wunderbare Heilung konstatieren will. Die für einen Wunderbericht unent-
behrliche Konstatierung der Heilung ist bei Mt 8,13 wieder anders formuliert
und hier so, daß sie nicht nur dem joh Bericht näher steht, sondern auch für
die Zwischenszene auf dem Wege Raum läßt."

Schramm 1971, 40-41: For παῖς, see Q 7:~~2~~, 3, ~~4-6a~~[9] Luke = Q, Con
(pp. 172-173).

George 1972, 72: "Mt 8,13 présente une réponse de Jésus à la demande du
centurion. On a déjà noté que l'absence de ce trait chez Luc est étonnante.
Elle s'explique si l'on pense que Luc ne peut reproduire la phrase de Matthieu
(ou plus exactement de leur source commune) parce qu'il a exclu la présence
de l'officier. D'autre part, Luc doit conclure son récit. Il le fait en rédigeant
son v. 10 qui rapporte le retour des envoyés."

Schulz 1972, 240[428]: "Diese Annahme wird weiterhin dadurch gestützt, daß
die verwandte Perikope von der Syrophönizierin in der Mk-Fassung (Mk 7,24-
30) die Heilung berichtet. Hinzu kommt, daß der Abschlußvers bei Mt durchaus auch trad Züge aufweist: ὕπαγε ist durch 8,4; 9,6 als trad ausgewiesen;
die πίστις dem Wundertäter gegenüber begegnet ebenfalls in der Tradition
9,2.22; Konstatierung der eingetretenen Heilung findet sich allgemein in trad
Wundergeschichten." But see Schulz at Matt = Q, Con (pp. 387-388).

Martin 1978, 15, 20[10, 11]: See Q 7:~~2~~, 3, ~~4-6a~~[12] Luke = Q, Con (p. 214).

Muhlack 1979, 45: See Q 7:?10?[4] Luke = Q, Con (p. 379).

Fitzmyer 1981, 653: "Luke changed the first part of the verse, omitting the
impv. of Matt 8:13."

Wegner 1985, 226: For ὕπαγε: "Dieser gesamte Versteil erwies so eindeutig
Markmale einer mt Bearbeitung—Mt 8,13b ist vor allem mit 9,29 und 15,28
zu vergleichen—, daß es kaum berechtigt ist, ihn als Wiedergabe der urspr
Hauptmannsperikope anzusehen. Die einzige Ausnahme bildet u.E. der Imp.
ὕπαγε. Mt, der ihn sowohl gegenüber Mk 7,29 als auch 10,52 ausläßt, wird ihn
kaum in unserem mit Mt 9,29 und 15,28 so ähnlichen Vers eingefügt haben."

227: For καί: "Obwohl Mt sonst anreihendes καί mehrmals zu ersetzen
pflegt, verhält er sich am Schluß der Wundergeschichten äußerst zurückhaltend, denn er übernimmt bei der Konstatierung der Heilung stets das καί,
sofern die mk Vorlage es anbietet: vgl. Mt 8,3c; 9,7a.22c.25b.30a (vgl.
20,34b); 12,13c; 15,28c und 17,18c par Mk. Diese ausnahmslose Übernahme des mk καί bei Konstatierungen von Heilungen macht auch in diesem
Vers die Herkunft des parataktischen καί aus einer vor-mt Trad wahrscheinlich."

Davies and Allison 1991, 32: "καὶ ἰάθη ὁ παῖς ἐν τῇ ὥρᾳ ἐκείνῃ. Despite the parallels in 9.22; 15.28 diff. Mk 7.29-30; and 17.18 diff. Mk 9.25-6, the redactional use of ἰάομαι (cf. 8.8 = Lk 7.7) in 15.28, and Matthew's fondness for ὥρα + ἐκείνῃ, our line could have some basis in the tradition, for Jn 4.53 ('The father knew that was the hour when Jesus had said to him, "Your son will live"') is similar."

Catchpole 1992, 522 [1993, 286]: See Q 7:?10?[0] In Q (p. 356).

Lindars 1992, 209: "John here obviously agrees with Matthew. He has already represented ὕπαγε, ὡς ἐπίστευσας in πορεύου ... ἐπίστευσεν in v. 50, and the last word is repeated in the final sentence of v. 53."

212: "The concluding paragraph cannot be reconstructed with confidence, because Matthew has to be used as basis, and we cannot tell how far he has abbreviated what lay before him. Matthew has very similar conclusions in 9,22b; 9,29; 15,28; 17,18b. As he tends to repeat himself, it is arguable that the present passage lies behind all of these. At least ὕπαγε, ἐπίστευσας, ἰάθη ὁ παῖς, and ἐν τῇ ὥρᾳ ἐκείνῃ, which are paralleled in John, can well be accepted as original. It is noteworthy that Matthew has ἐν τῇ ὥρᾳ ἐκείνῃ only here, as he uses the preposition ἀπό in the other passages."

Hagner 1993, 203: For δοῦλος, see Q 7:~~2~~, 3, ~~4-6a~~[9] Matt = Q, Pro (p. 181).

Con

Hawkins 1899, 30: "Words and Phrases characteristic of St. Matthew's Gospel: ... γενηθήτω ... Mt vi. 10; viii. 13*; ix. 29*; xv. 28*; xxvi. 42. ... *These three times with reference to miracles of healing."

34: "Words and Phrases characteristic of St. Matthew's Gospel: ... ὥρα with ἐκείνῃ, in narrative. Mt viii. 13*; ix. 22*; xv. 28*; xvii. 18*; xviii. 1; xxvi. 55. ... *In these four cases used of spontaneous cures: cf. also Jn iv. 53."

von Harnack 1907, 76: "Das ὕπαγε ist wohl in allen drei Fällen (c. 4,10; 8,13; 18,15) von Matth. eingesetzt."

146-147: See Q 7:?10?[0] Undecided (p. 361).

von Harnack 1907, ET 1908, 109: "The ὕπαγε in all three cases of its occurrence (iv. 10, viii. 13, xviii. 15) is probably inserted by St. Matthew."

210-211: See Q 7:?10?[0] Undecided (p. 361).

Castor 1912, 42-43: "Matt 8:13 [43] might seem to be more original than Luke 7:10 if we did not find that he changes the text of Mark 7:29, 30 in the same way."

224: Reconstruction. For complete text see Q 7:1[0] In Q (p. 6).

Loisy 1924, 218: "Matthieu a pu d'autant plus facilement y conformer la conclusion de la cananéenne, que les deux histoires avaient le même sens."

Klostermann 1927, 75: "Der von Mt gebotene Abschluß entspricht 15,28, weicht aber von Lc [v.] 10 völlig ab."

Bussmann 1929, 57: "Aber das wird wesentlich durch den Schluß des Mt nahegelegt, der sekundär ist und mit Mt 15:28 fast wörtlich übereinstimmt."

Bacon 1930, 280: Matt 5:13 is printed in boldface and noted as "R" (redaction).

Manson 1937, 65: "Mt. (8:13) makes Jesus speak the word asked for: 'As thou hast believed, so be it done unto thee,' and the cure takes place forthwith."

Parker 1953, 63-65: See Q 7:1⁶ Matt = Q, Con (pp. 58-60).

Schmid 1956, 164: "V. 13 läßt in der Formulierung die Hand des Matthäus erkennen."

Held 1960, 183: "Hinaus erhält die Bitte des Hauptmanns bei Matthäus auch die erwartete Hilfe, indem Jesus das erbetene Wort spricht, das den Kranken heilt (Mt. 8,13). Der erzählende Schluß des Evangelisten stellt sich somit als die folgerichtige Ergänzung des Gespräches dar, die sozusagen aus ihm selber genommen ist. Anders ausgedrückt: der Abschluß ist vom Thema des Glaubens her gestaltet."

224-225, 227: Held indirectly argues for Matthean creation of 8:13 based on catchword linkage to Matt 8:8b (Q 7:7b).

273: "Wie sehr es dem ersten Evangelisten auf den Sachverhalt des bittenden Glaubens ankommt, kann besonders gut an der Geschichte vom Hauptmann zu Kapernaum verdeutlicht werden. Hier findet sich eine deutliche Entsprechung zwischen der Bitte des Hauptmanns (Mt. 8,8) und ihrer Erhörung durch Jesus (Mt. 8,13). ... Wie Lk. 7,7 zeigt, war die Bitte um ein Machtwort dem Matthäus vorgegeben. Er hat dann zwar die deutliche Entsprechung zwischen Bitte und Erhörung hergestellt, die bei Lukas fehlt, aber hat es so getan, daß an die Stelle des erwarteten Machtwortes das Wort vom Glauben getreten ist."

Held 1960, ET 1963, 194: "The centurion's request is met in Matthew by the expected help in that Jesus speaks the desired word which heals the sick man (Matt. 8:13). In this way the narrative conclusion of the evangelist depicts the logical expansion of the conversation and is derived, so to speak, from the conversation itself. In other words: the conclusion is fashioned in the light of the theme of faith."

237, 239: Held indirectly argues for Matthean creation of 8:13 based on catchword linkage to Matt 8:8b (Q 7:7b).

285-286: "How important to the first evangelist was the fact of supplicating faith can be made clear especially well from the story of the centurion of Capernaum. Here there is a clear correspondence between the request of the centurion (Matt. 8:8) and the answer to it by Jesus (Matt. 8:13). ... [286] ...

As Luke 7:7 shows, the request for a word of authority lay before Matthew. He has then established the clear correspondence between the request and its answer, which is absent from Luke, but he has done it in such a way that the saying about faith has taken the place of the expected word of authority."

Lohmeyer 1962, 158¹: "Zu γενεθήτω vgl. 6,10; 26,42 matthäische Formel. ὕπαγε V[v].4,10; 5,24.41; 8,4.13.32; 9,6; 16,23; 18,15; 19,21; 21,28; 27,65; 28,10. ἐν τῇ ὥρᾳ ἐκείνῃ 8,13 (10,19) ἀπό: 9,22; 15,28; 17,18. ἰάθη noch 15,28."

Grundmann 1968, 249-250: "Matthäus gibt der Erzählung in V. 13 einen von ihm geformten Abschluß, dessen Matthäische Ausdrucksweise [250] deutlich erkennbar ist."

254: "Nach diesem Wort [Matt 8,11-12] setzt Evangelist noch einmal ein mit einer Anrede Jesu an den Centurio, und zwar mit einem Wort, das 9,29 und 15,28 wiederkehrt."

Lührmann 1969, 57⁶: "Mt wiederholt die Erwähnung des Glaubens in 8,13."

P. Meyer 1970, 411: "It must be conceded that Matthew imported 8:11f. from another place in Q (and created vs. 13)."

Fuchs 1971, 150-151: "Der Text ist Sondergut des Evangelisten. Die vorausgehenden VV. 11-12 sind ein Einschub des Mt, wie aus dem parallelen Aufbau der Gesamtperikope bei Mt und Lk ersichtlich ist. Dieser Einschub schließt an die Feststellung Mt 8,10 par Lk 7,9 an, daß Jesus in Israel keinen solchen Glauben wie den des Hauptmanns gefunden habe und führt das Thema vom Unglauben der Juden weiter. Obwohl dieser Text auch bei Lk (13,28-29) vorliegt, steht er auch dort nicht in [151] ursprünglichem Zusammenhang. Bei Mt ist aber der sekundäre Charakter der Einordnung deutlicher, weil das Thema des Glaubens sehr gut beide Stoffe verbindet. Aus diesen Beobachtungen ergibt sich, daß auch Mt 8,13 redaktionell ist und vom Evangelisten stammt."

152: "Diese Verse [8,13; 15,28] haben einen parallelismus des Vokabulars und der Konstruktion, der auch sonst Merkmal der Mt-Redaktion ist. Besonders weist aber auf Mt noch die Wortverbindung ὥρα ἐκείνη, die in dieser Reihenfolge im ganzen NT nur bei Mt 8,13; 9,22; 15,28 und 17,18 vorkommt."

Strecker 1962, 99: "Der Schluß (V. 13) scheint dagegen matthäisch zu sein; er wurde wohl infolge des Einschubs (V. 11-12 ...) neu gebildet; eine Parallele findet sich in dem gleichfalls redaktionellen Vers 15,28."

George 1972, 71: "Le début de Mt 8,13 (où Jésus reprend la parole, alors qu'il parlait déjà: cf. 8,10 et 13) semble une suture rédactionnelle."

Schulz 1972, 240: "Aber auch Mt wird in V 13 eingegriffen haben.⁴²⁷"

240⁴²⁷: "Strecker [1962, 99] scheint den ganzen V 13 für mt zu halten; Grundmann [1968, 249]: 'Matthäus gibt der Erzählung in V 13 einen von ihm geformten Abschluß'; ähnlich Klostermann [1927, 75]; ὑπάγειν ist für Mt allerdings nicht typisch, sondern ist in Heilungsgeschichten stilgemäß (z.B. Mt 8,4 trad; 9,6 trad; mehrmals bei Mk); γενηθήτω in Verbindung mit πιστεύειν/πίστις ist ausgesprochen mt (vgl 9,29 red; 15,24 red...); ἰᾶσθαι findet sich in 8,8 in der von Mt übernommenen Q-Tradition, andererseits verwendet Mt das Verb red 15,28, wie überhaupt die Feststellung der erfolgten Heilung formelhafte Sprache aufweist, die für Mt typisch ist. ... Ähnliche Wendungen, die die Heilung konstatieren, finden sich in 9,22b; 15,28b; 17,18b. Harnack [1907, 56, 147; ET, 77, 210-211)] und Dibelius [1919, 245, 261; ET, 244-245, 261¹)] setzen sich dafür ein, daß die Geschichte in Q mit V 10 geschlossen habe; Held [1960, 183] läßt die Entscheidung offen, betont aber den mt Charakter des Verses."

Lange 1973, 50-51: "Nach solch massiver und langer Rede hat man das Anliegen des Hauptmanns nahezu vergessen. Doch wird von der Heilung des Knechtes schließlich noch gesprochen (Mt 8,13b). Matthäus nimmt aber die Gelegenheit wahr, dabei zu sagen, worauf es ihm eigentlich ankommt: hier hat einer geglaubt und dementsprechend [51] ist ihm geschehen (Mt 8,13a)⁷⁵."

51⁷⁵: "Die gleiche oder ähnliche redaktionelle Wendung Mt 9,29; 15,28."

Schweizer 1973, 137-138: "Matthäus selbst bildet das Wort von der dem Glauben entsprechenden Heilung. ... [138] Auffällig ist die sachliche Verwandtschaft mit 15,21-28; nur Heiden gegenüber wird von Fernheilungen berichtet."

Schweizer 1973, ET 1975, 213: "Matthew himself composed the saying about the healing that corresponds to belief. ... The similarity in content to 15:21-28 is striking; we hear of healings at a distance only in the case of gentiles."

Frankemölle 1974, 112: "Das Thema des Glaubens hat Mt gegenüber dem Stoff in der Logienquelle Q entschieden herausgestellt, indem er die Tradition—wie auch an anderen Stellen—strafft und kürzt, sie zugleich aber durch einen redaktionell bearbeiteten Einleitungs- (8,5 παρακαλῶν) und Schlußvers (8,13 ὡς ἐπίστευσας), vor allem durch den Zusatz 8,11f ... von der Wundergeschichte weg in verstärktem Maße zu einer Glaubensperikope gestaltet."

Theissen 1974, 183 (ET 1983, 182): See Theissen at Luke = Q, Pro (p. 375).

Howard 1975, 172: "Das καὶ ἰαθήσεται ὁ παῖς μου von V. 8 wird in V. 13 wieder aufgenommen: καὶ ἰάθη ὁ παῖς.¹ Ebenso wird das Stichwort Glaube von V. 10 in V. 13 wieder aufgegriffen: ὡς ἐπίστευσας γενηθήτω σοι."

172¹: "Vgl. 9,22b; 9,29; 15,28b; 17,18b."

Pesch and Kratz 1976, 79: "In v 13 setzt Mattäus mit der Hinwendung an den Hundertschaftsführer nochmals neu ein: Jesu Wort gewährt dem großen Glauben des Hauptmanns Erfüllung (vgl. 9,29; 15,28). Die Konstatierung der Heilung (vgl. 9,22; 17,18) entspricht dem vertrauensvollen Wort des Hauptmanns v 8 (welches das nicht ausgesprochene Heilwort Jesu mit umgreift—vgl. Joh 4,50). Der Schluß verrät in Formulierungen und theologischem Gehalt die gestaltende Hand des mattäischen Redaktors."

France 1977, 263: "Matthew alone inserts the healing word of Jesus for which the centurion had asked; taking up the theme of verse 10, it focuses on his remarkable faith: 'As you have believed let it be done for you.' In the Synoptic accounts healing frequently depends on faith; how much more healing at a distance, paralleled only in Matthew 15:21-28 and John 4:46-54. The parallel with Matthew 15:27 is here very close, just as the themes of the two stories have run parallel throughout, both concerned with Jesus' encounter with a Gentile supplicant, both focusing on the trial and the triumph of faith despite the racial barrier, both culminating in healing at a distance."

Gundry 1982, 147: "Where Luke gives only the finding of the servant well, Matthew first gives Jesus' authoritative words that effected the healing. The Mattheanism ὕπαγε (5,6) echoes the healing use of ὕπαγε in 8:4 and anticipates the same use in 9:6 (cf. 8:32). 'As you have believed' recalls attention to the centurion's faith. The whole expression, 'as you have believed, let it happen to you,' comes close to 'according to your faith let it happen to you' in 9:29, where, as here, Matthew will insert the expression in common tradition (cf. 15:28, to which add 6:10; 26:42 for all Matthew's insertions of the form γενηθήτω). Similarly, 'and (his) servant was healed at that hour' comes close to like statements in 9:22 (so Matthew alone right before a reference to faith and with a rejection, as here, of the stem ὑγι-, 'well,' in Mark 5:34); 15:28 (again alone, right after a reference to faith, and, as here with a combination of γενηθήτω σοι and ὡς); and 17:18 (referring to a παῖς, as here). All these passages contain references to 'that hour.' Cf. Matthew's insertions of 'in that hour' in 10:19; 18:1; 26:55. 'Was healed' replaces 'well' (so Luke) for a parallel with 'will be healed' in v 8. And '(his) servant' replaces 'the slave' for consistency with 'my servant' in vv 6 and 8. Matthew's stating the healing in a way that matches the centurion's request highlights the effectiveness of Jesus' authoritative word."

Dauer 1984, 78-80: "Für mt Bildung von Mt 8,13 sprechen:

"(1) Charakteristisch für mt Komposition ist die *Stichwortverbindung* innerhalb einer Wundergeschichte. Man vergleiche etwa Mt 8,2.3a.3b (Stichwort καθαρίζειν); 9,21.22 (Stichwort σῴζειν); 14,28a.29a.29b (Stichwort ἐλθεῖν). In unserer vorliegenden Erzählung zeigt sich diese Stichwortverbindung in der Weise, daß 'der Bitte des Hauptmanns von Kapernaum... das Handeln Jesu [entspricht], wie es im letzten Verse dargestellt wird' [Held 1960, 225; ET, 237)]: [79]

"Mt 8,8b: μόνον εἰπὲ λόγῳ,

καὶ ἰαθήσεται ὁ παῖς μου.

8,13: καὶ εἶπεν ὁ Ἰησοῦς ...

καὶ ἰάθη ὁ παῖς [αὐτοῦ].

"'Das Heilungswort Jesu greift das Stichwort des Glaubens auf, mit dem Jesus in 8,10 die Bitte des Hauptmanns gekennzeichnet hat. Das Wunder selbst erfolgt wie erbeten: ein Wort, und der Knecht wird gesund. Darüber hinaus aber gibt das Heilungswort dem formalen Befund der Stich-wortverbindung seine Rechtfertigung: dem Bittenden geschieht nach seinem Glauben'. [Held 1960, 225; ET, 237)]

"(2) Matthäus verwendet öfters für den Abschluß von Heilungswundern solche formelhaften Wendungen wie die vorliegende—vgl. außer a.u.St. noch Mt 9,22b; 15,28b; 17,18b—, um damit häufig eine ausführlichere Erzählung von Mk (par Lk) zu ersetzen.

"(3) V. 13 entspricht sachlich und z. T. auch wörtlich Mt 9,29 und 15,28, wovon sich besonders die letztgenannte Stelle (diff Mk 7,29) als mt Änderung erweist:

8:13:   ὡς   ἐπίστευσας   γενηθήτω   σοι

9:29:   κατὰ   τὴν   πίστιν ὑμῶν   γενηθήτω   ὑμῖν

15:28:   γενηθήτω   σοι ὡς θέλεις."

"Zu (καὶ) εἶπεν (-αν) c. Dat. Pers. vgl. [Matt] 8,32 (diff Mk 5,13); 11,3 (diff Lk 7,19); 12,2 (diff Mk 2,24); 12,3 (diff Mk 2,25); 12,11 (red.); 12,48 (diff Mk 3,33); 13,10 (diff Mk 4,10); 13,57 (diff Mk 6,4) u.ö.

"Zu ὕπαγε (ὑπάγετε) vgl. außer jenen Stellen, die Matthäus aus seiner Mk-Vorlage übernommen hat[297], noch 4,10 (add Lk 4,8); 5,24 (Sg.); 5,41 (Sg.); 8,13 u.St.; 8,32 (diff Mk 5,13); 18,15 (diff Lk 17,3): 21,28 (Sg.). Nur einmal ersetzt er es aus seiner Mk-Vorlage: 21,2 diff Mk 11,2.

[80] "Zu ἐν τῇ ὥρᾳ ἐκείνῃ vgl. außer u. St. noch [Matt] 10,19 (vgl. Mk 13,11); 18,1; 26,55 (= mt Übergangsfloskel). Zu vergleichen ist auch ἀπὸ τῆς ὥρας ἐκείνης: Mt 9,22 (diff Mk 5,34); 15,28 (diff Mk 7,30); 17,18 [... καὶ ἐθεραπεύθη ὁ παῖς ἀπὸ τῆς ὥρας ἐκείνης] (add Mk 9,27)."

341[297]: "8,4; 9,6; 16,23; 19,21; 26,18; 28,10."

82: "Unter Beachtung des zum redaktionellen Charakter von Mt 8,13 und Lk 7,10 Erarbeiteten wird man dann sagen können:

"(1) Die Erzählung enthielt kein eigentliches Heilungswort Jesu[315]."

343[315]: "Mt 8,13a ist ja mt Bildung."

Wegner 1985, 156: "'Ιάομαι fügt Mt red in 8,13 und 15,28 ein."

226-227: For ὡς ἐπίστευσας γενηθήτω σοι, see Wegner at Emendation = Q (p. 396).

227-229: For ἰάομαι: "Mt bringt das Verb 1x in Q (8,8/Lk 7,7), 1x in seinem Sg (13,15:Zitat) und außer auSt nur noch 1x als Hinzufügung [228]

zu Mk (15,28 diff Mk 7,29), wobei es in 15,28 in derselben Passivform konstruiert ist. Spricht schon diese Beobachtung für die Wahrscheinlichkeit einer
mt Red auSt, so kann diese Vermutung noch dadurch erhärtet werden, daß
der erste Evangelist in 8,13c sehr wahrscheinlich ein bei ihm beliebtes Stilmittel—die Stichwortverbindung—anwendet, wie der Vergleich mit 8,8 naheLegt
(8,8: καὶ ἰαθήσεται ὁ παῖς μου; 8,13c: καὶ ἰάθη ὁ παῖς κτλ.). Schließlich weist
Held [1960, 218; ET, 230)] auf die sprachliche Ähnlichkeit von V 13c mit
den mt Schlußformulierungen anderer Heilungswunder, wie 9,22b; 15,28b
und 17,18b, hin, die alle eine ähnliche formelhafte Sprache aufweisen und die
u.a. dadurch gekennzeichnet sind, daß sie—was aus den Parallelstellen hervorgeht—'ausführliche Erzählung' verdrängen.

"Aus den Beobachtungen geht hervor, daß ἰάθη auSt mit hoher Wahrscheinlichkeit auf Mt selbst zurückzuführen ist.

[For ἐν τῇ ὥρᾳ ἐκείνῃ:] "Diese Wendung ist zweifellos charakteristisch für
Mt. Er bringt sie in dieser Reihenfolge (ὥρα[ς] + ἐκείνη[ς]) in 8,13 diff Lk
7,10³³; 9,22 diff Mk 5,34; 15,28 diff Mk 7,30 und 17,18 diff Mk 9,27, also
stets im Abschluß der entsprechenden Wundergeschichten als Konstatierung
der Heilung. Die Reihenfolge ὥρα + ἐκείνη ist, abgesehen vom MtEv, weder
in den Synoptikern noch an anderer Stelle im NT zu belegen: dort erscheint
ὥρα vielmehr immer nachgestellt. Man wird daher auch für diese Wendung
eine mt Red mit großer Wahrscheinlichkeit annehmen können. ... [229] ...

[For ἰάθη ὁ παῖς αὐτοῦ ἐν τῇ ὥρᾳ ἐκείνῃ:] "Dieser Versteil ist eindeutig mt
Gestaltung, wie sich aus der Stat und aus dem Vergleich von V 13c mit dem
Abschluß anderer Wundergeschichten im MtEv ergibt. Nicht red schien uns
lediglich das anreihende καί zu sein. Da nun Mt, wie Held zeigt, gegenüber
Mk beim Abschluß seiner Wundergeschichten das Erzählte seiner Vorlage
mehrmals verdrängt und durch von ihm geprägte und kurz formulierte Wendungen zu ersetzen pflegt, ist damit zu rechnen, daß auch hinter dem καί in
V 13c urspr Erzählung stand, die von Mt sek durch ἰάθη ὁ παῖς αὐτοῦ ἐν τῇ
ὥρᾳ ἐκείνῃ ersetzt wurde."

228³³: "Vgl. aber Joh 4,53 in anderer Reihenfolge: ἐκείνη τῇ ὥρᾳ."

235: For καὶ ἰάθη ὁ παῖς αὐτοῦ ἐν τῇ ὥρᾳ ἐκείνῃ, see Wegner at Luke = Q,
Pro (p. 376).

Gnilka 1986, 299-300: "Wegen der [300] weitgehenden Übereinstimmung
mit Mt 15,28b kann man vermuten, daß der Schluß (V.13) mt gestaltet ist.
Vielleicht berichtete er einmal davon, daß der Hauptmann den Knecht
gesund zu Hause vorfand."

Sand 1986, 178: "Neben dieser besonders auffälligen Veränderung der Vorlage hat Mt auch sonst red. in die Überlieferung eingegriffen und so (wie auch
in 15,21-28) der Heilungsgeschichte eine Form und einen Aufbau verliehen,
die sich von der zweiten Textüberlieferung (Mk und Lk, vgl. auch Joh) deut-

lich abheben. Vor allem unterscheidet sich der jeweilige Abschluß der Erzählungen (8,13a; 15,28a gegenüber Lk 7,10 und Mk 7,30) in auffallender
Weise: Die Heilung selbst (das Ergebnis des Heilungsgeschehens) wird nicht
erzählt; vielmehr wird in direkter Rede die Heilung als folge des Glaubens
ausgesprochen."

Schenk 1987, 389: "Ἐκείνη ὥρᾳ: wurde vorangestellt im Logion 10,13
(=Mk ἐν) von der Stunde der gerichtlichen Verhandlung übernommen und
nachgestellt im Erzählkontext Q-Mt 8,13."

450: "Ὕπαγε: Sonst geht es um die positiv Ausführung eines Sendungsauf-
trags Jesu: ... 8,13 (+Q nach V.4 dupl. bzw. Mk 7,29 permutiert)."

468: "Γίνομαι ὡς: Neben den 8 Stellen mit zusätzlichem Nom bei → γίνομαι noch satzergänzend im Gebet 6,10 (+Q) und in den mt Heilungszusage-
formeln 8,13 (+Q)."

Judge 1989, 487-489: See Q 7:?10?⁰ Not in Q (pp. 359-360).

Nolland 1989, 318: "Presumably in the tradition the conclusion of the
account mentioned the healing, but both Matthew's and Luke's conclusions
are strongly marked by the evangelists' activity (for Matthew compare 9:22;
15:28; 17:18; ...)."

Gnilka 1990, 128³⁴ (ET 1997, 121⁹⁸): See Q 7:?10?¹ Matt = Q, Con (p. 369).

Luz 1990, 13⁶: "Matthäismen sind ... in V 13: ὑπάγω, πιστεύω, γενηθήτω,
ὥρα ἐκείνη."

13: "In V 13 hat Mt, wie der Vergleich mit 15,28 zeigt, weitgehend selbst
formuliert."

Luz 1990, ET 2001, 8⁶: "Mattheisms ... in v. 13: ὑπάγω, πιστεύω, γενηθήτω, ὥρα ἐκείνη."

9: "As a comparison with 15:28 shows, in v. 13 Matthew has worked quite
independently."

Davies and Allison 1991, 31-32: "Matthew's final verse equally seems to
contain redactional traits.

"Καὶ εἶπεν ὁ Ἰησοῦς τῷ ἑκατοντάρχῃ. 'Centurion' harks back to 8.5 and
forms an inclusio. εἶπεν ὁ Ἰησοῦς + dative appears only here in Matthew.

"Ὕπαγε. Compare 8.4, 32; 9.6 (all addressed by Jesus to people he has
healed).

[32] "Ὡς ἐπίστευσας γενηθήτω σοι. Compare 9.29; 15.28. ... γίνομαι +
dative: Mt: 5; Mk: 2; Lk: 1."

Jacobson 1992, 109: "The peculiar features of the Q story can be deter-
mined in part by a comparison with the parallel account in John 4:46-54; a
similar story is told of R. Hanina ben Dosa in b. Ber. 34b. Most obvious is the
fact that in Q the miracle itself so far recedes in importance that it becomes
unclear whether Q told of a miracle at all. That 'the servant was healed at that
very moment' (Matt 8:13, lacking in Luke) may be merely a feature typical of

healings at a distance (cf. John 4:42-43; b. Ber. 34b; Mark 7:30)."

Lindars 1992, 209: "Unfortunately we have no access to the full detail of the original conclusion in the source, because Matthew can be expected to have abbreviated it."

Burchard 1993, 284[36]: "V. 13 diff. Lk 7,10 kann Matthäus formuliert haben, vgl. 15,28 diff. Mk 7,30."

Hagner 1993, 202: "Luke 7:10, which is quite different from Matthew, lacks Matthew's ἐν τῇ ὥρᾳ ἐκείνῃ, 'in that hour,' probably added by Matthew to stress the immediacy of the remote healing (cf. 8:3c)."

Dunderberg 1994, 86: "In jedem Fall haben sowohl Mt als auch Lk den Abschluß der Erzählung stark bearbeitet. Mt 8,13 ist mit der erwähnten anderen Fernheilungsgeschichte zu vergleichen, wo sich aus der mt Bearbeitung ein Abschluß ergibt, der stark an Mt 8,13 erinnert:

"Mk 7,29-30	Mt 15,28	Mt 8,13
καὶ εἶπεν αὐτῇ	εἶπεν αὐτῇ·	καὶ εἶπεν ὁ Ἰησοῦς
	ὦ γύναι,	τῷ ἑκατοντάρχῃ·
διὰ τοῦτον τὸν λόγον	μεγάλη σου ἡ πίστις·	ὕπαγε,
ὕπαγε, ἐξελήλυθεν ἐκ	γενηθήτω σοι ὡς	ὡς ἐπίστευσας
τῆς θυγατρός σου τὸ	θέλεις.	γενηθήτω σοι.
δαιμόνιον.		
καὶ ἀπελθοῦσα		
εἰς τὸν οἶκον αὐτῆς		
εὗρεν τὸ παιδίον	καὶ ἰάθη	καὶ ἰάθη
βεβλημένον ἐπὶ τὴν	ἡ θυγάτηρ αὐτῆς	ὁ παῖς [αὐτοῦ]
κλίνην καὶ τὸ	ἀπὸ τῆς ὥρας ἐκείνης.	ἐν τῇ ὥρᾳ ἐκείνῃ.
δαιμόνιον ἐξεληλυθός.		

"Es lassen sich noch weitere Parallelen für den mt Abschluß der beiden Berichten finden. In Mt 9,22 ist der Satz ἡ πίστις σου σέσωκέν σε von Mk 5,34 (=Lk 8,48) vorhanden; doch streicht Mt die Mahnung Jesu ὕπαγε εἰς εἰρήνην καὶ ἴσθι ὑγιὴς ἀπὸ τῆς μάστιγός σου (Mk 5,34; vgl. Lk 8,48), fügt aber auch hier eine ähnliche Konstatierung des Wunders hinzu wie in 8,13; 15,28: καὶ ἐσώθη ἡ γυνὴ ἀπὸ τῆς ὥρας ἐκείνης. In Mt 9,29 wird die mk Formulierung ὕπαγε, ἡ πίστις σου σέσωκέν σε (Mk 10,52/Lk 18,42) durch κατὰ τὴν πίστιν ὑμῶν γενηθήτω ὑμῖν ersetzt. Diese Stellen zeigen deutlich den Zusammenhang von Mt 8,13 mit der mt Redaktion, durch die sowohl die Ankündigung des Glaubens des Bittstellers als auch das Stundenmotiv unterstrichen worden ist. Von daher ist das Ende der matthäischen Erzählung vom Hauptmann (8,13) als Ganzes der redaktionellen Tätigkeit von Mt zuzuschreiben."

89: "Auf das Konto der mt Redaktion gehen die Anordnung des anderen

Q-Abschnittes in diesen Kontext (Mt 8,11-12) sowie das Ende des Berichtes (Mt 8,13)."

Gagnon 1994b, 136-137: "In my estimation, Matthew has ... added to Jesus' message a word of dismissal and a characteristically Matthean word of [137] assurance regarding the petitioner's faith (cf. 15.28; 9.29);[16] and ... replaced Q's confirmation of the healing with one of his own formulaic conclusions (cf. 9.22; 15.28; 17.18)."

137[16]: "It is possible that the Q account may have read something like 'and he said to the centurion, "Go in peace."' ... However, such a reconstruction appears unlikely in view of the fact that Luke nowhere omits from his Markan healing stories *both* a word of dismissal *and* a message of assurance; ... and Luke's version of the centurion says nothing of either. Note, too, that Matthew adds the imperatival form of ὑπάγω to the story of the Gadarene demoniac (Matt 8.32), but three times omits it from Markan miracle stories."

Landis 1994, 15: "Der Rest des Versteils 13b [for text following ὕπαγε, see Landis at Emendation = Q (pp. 397-398)] ist durchweg durch die mt Redaktion geprägt. V.a. der Imperative γενηθήτω ist eine Vorzugswendung des Mt, die außerhalb des ersten Evangeliums im NT nur ganz selten begegnet. Ebenfalls ausgesprochen mt ist die Verbindung von γενηθήτω mit πίστις/πιστεύω. Der Gesamtausdruck ὡς ἐπίστευσας γενηθήτω σοι erinnert stark an das ebenfalls redaktionell überarbeitete Jesuswort am Schluß der Perikope über die Syrophönizierin Mt 15,28 diff Mk 7,29: γενηθήτω σοι ὡς θέλεις."

Meier 1994, 310: "It seems that Matthew himself noticed that his polemical insertion disrupted the miracle story's major theme of faith. He attempted to bring back the major theme at the end of the story by having Jesus' praise of the centurion's faith in 8:10 echoed in Jesus' final words of dismissal and promise (not present in Luke): 'Go. As *you have believed*, let it be done unto you' (8:13)."

International Q Project 1995, 479: Reconstruction. For complete text see Q 7:1⁰ In Q (p. 16).

Neirynck 1995, 178-179: "Landis [1994, 16-17] compare ἐν τῇ ὥρᾳ ἐκείνῃ avec ἀπὸ τῆς ὥρας ἐκείνης en Mt 9,22; 15,28; 17,18, et insiste sur la différence entre cette formule rédactionnelle 'von jener Stunde an' et le *Stundenmotiv* 'in jener Stunde' qui serait traditionnel ('ein kleines Reststück aus der Tradition'). Cela le mène tout droit à la conclusion que la source Q 'im Ausdruck ἐν τῇ ὥρᾳ ἐκείνῃ die Erinnerung daran bewahrt (hat), daß der Junge in der ursprünglichen Erzählung genau in jenem Moment gesund wurde, in dem Jesus zum Hauptmann sprach'. Landis n'y fait pas mention de Jn 4,53, mais, avant même d'examiner le parallèle johannique, le lecteur est fixé: le motif est pré-johannique. ... Le sens de l'expression ἀπό + gén. ne diffère guère de celui de ἐν + dat.: 'instantly' (NRSV), 'zu derselben Stunde' (Luther)' et 'les [179] parallèles matthéens sont là pour nous rappeler qu'en Mt il s'agit d'une formule typique de conclusion, *Fernheilung* (15,28) ou non (9,22; 17,18). Ce n'est qu'en Jn 4,52-53 que la formule de Mt 8,13 devient l'expression caractéristique de la constatation d'une guérison à distance'. [Neirynck 1981, 105 n. 59]

"Landis [15] retient le mot ὕπαγε dans sa reconstruction de Q: 'der einzige traditionelle Ausdruck' en 8,13b. ... Il me semble qu'il se fie ici trop facilement à la statistique de Wegner [1985, 224] qui, pour sa part, souligne le fait que, des six emplois dans des récits de miracle en Mc, Matthieu n'en reprend que deux. Et Landis [15] de généraliser: 'oft streicht er es aus seinen Mk-Vorlagen'. ... Les deux participes en Mc 6,31.33 mis à part, on compte treize emplois (dont douze à l'impératif): 1,44 (= Mt 8,4); 2,11 (= Mt 9,6); 5,19 (vv. 18-20 sans par.); 5,34 (phrase sans par.); 6,38 (phrase sans par.); 7,29 (cf. infra); 8,33 (= Mt 16,23); 10,21 (= Mt 19,21); 10,52 (phrase sans par.); 11,2 (Mt 21,1 πορεύεσθε; voir 26,18); 14,13 (= Mt 26,18); 14,21 indic. (= Mt 26,24); 16,7 (Mt 28,7 πορευθεῖσαι; = Mt 28,10). Dans deux cas seulement, Matthieu remplace un ὑπάγετε par un autre verbe: πορεύεσθε in 21,2 (mais une phrase similaire en Mc 14,13 est laissée inchangée); πορευθεῖσαι en 28,7 (mais il écrit ὑπάγετε dans le doublet au v. 10). Les 'omissions' dans les récits de miracle ne concernent jamais le seul verbe ὕπαγε (Mc 5,19.34; 6,38; 7,29; 10,52; Matthieu introduit un ὑπάγετε en 8,32, diff. Mc 5,13). Le ὕπαγε de Mc 7,29 n'est pas repris en Mt 15,28, mais on aurait tort de restreindre le rapprochement entre Mt 8,13 et 15,28 au seul motif de l'heure (καὶ ἰάθη ὁ παῖς ἐν τῇ ὥρᾳ ἐκείνῃ / καὶ ἰάθη ἡ θυγάτηρ αὐτῆς ἀπὸ τῆς ὥρας ἐκείνης) Comparer le motif de la foi et ὡς ... γενηθήτω σοι/γενηθήτω σοι ὡς ... Il n'est nullement téméraire de voir dans le ὕπαγε en Mt 8,13 le parallèle secondaire de Mc 7,29 (διὰ τοῦτον τὸν λόγον) ὕπαγε. D'ailleurs, Landis lui-même [49] le dira lorsqu'il fait le rapprochement entre ὕπαγε (Q) et πορεύου (SQ): 'ὕπαγε (scheint) sekundär zu sein, da es wahrscheinlich Mk 7,29 nachgebildet wurde'. ... On cherche donc en vain les traces d'une conclusion traditionnelle au v. 13 et, comme l'ont proposé M. Dibelius e.a.[1919, 245; ET, 244-245], la péricope dans la source Q n'a probablement jamais eu une telle conclusion au-delà du v. 10. Quoi qu'il en soit, c'est le caractère entièrement rédactionnel de Mt 8,13 qui nous intéresse ici."

Emendation = Q: ὕπαγε, ὡς ἐπίστευσας γενηθήτω σοι. καὶ ἰάθη ὁ παῖς <>⁴ ἐν τῇ ὥρᾳ ἐκείνῃ.

B. Weiß 1908, 16: Reconstruction: Matthew's text without αὐτοῦ. For complete text see Q 7:1⁰ In Q (p. 5).

Lindars 1992, 210: Reconstruction: Matthew's text without αὐτοῦ. For complete text see Q 7:1⁶ Luke = Q, Pro (p. 56).

Sevenich-Bax 1993, 238: Reconstruction: Matthew's text without αὐτοῦ. For complete text see Q 7:1⁰ In Q (p. 15).

Emendation = Q: <>⁴ καὶ ἰάθη ὁ παῖς αὐτοῦ ἐν τῇ ὥρᾳ ἐκείνῃ.

Polag 1979, 38: Reconstruction: "καὶ ἰάθη ὁ παῖς αὐτοῦ ἐν τῇ ὥρᾳ ἐκείνῃ." For complete text see Q 7:1⁰ In Q (pp. 9-10).

Emendation = Q: ὕπαγε. <>⁴ καὶ ἰάθη ὁ παῖς αὐτοῦ.<>⁴

Schenk 1981, 37: Reconstruction: "'Geh!' Und sein Sklave wurde geheilt." For complete text see Q 7:1⁰ In Q (p. 10).

Emendation = Q: ὕπαγε, <ὁ παῖς σου ἐσώθη καὶ ἀπελθὼν εἰς τὴν οἰκίαν εὗρεν τὸν παῖδα ἰαθέντα.>⁴

Wegner 1985, 226-227: For ὡς ἐπίστευσας γενηθήτω σοι: "Ist ὕπαγε aber urspr, so kann vermutet werden, daß diesem Imp. urspr irgendeine Heilungszusage Jesu folgte, die Mt—entsprechend seinem Interesse an der Hervorhebung des Glaubens—ähnlich wie in 15,28 (vgl. Mk 7,29) sek durch seine Formulierung ὡς ἐπίστευσας γενηθήτω σοι wiedergab. Wie nun der genaue Wortlaut dieser urspr Heilungszusage Jesu gelautet haben mag, kann natürlich nicht mehr ermittelt werden. Vielleicht stand urspr statt der mt For- [227] mulierung einfach ὁ παῖς σου ἐσωθη/σωθήσεται oder ὁ παῖς σου ἰάθη/ ἰαθήσεται o.ä. Wichtig scheint uns hier freilich primär nicht der eventuelle Wortlaut zu sein, sondern lediglich die Tatsache, daß angesichts der mt Bear- beitung von Mk 7,29 damit gerechnet werden muß, daß mt eine im urspr Text enthaltene Zusage der Heilung infolge seiner red Bearbeitung durch die Glaubensformel ὡς ἐπίστευσας γενηθήτω σοι wiedergab. Daß diese Annahme durchaus berechtigt ist, zeigen nicht nur andere, die jeweilige Heilung ver- heißende und vorwegkonstatierende Worte Jesu, wie Mk 7,29; 10,52 und Lk 17,14, sondern auch die Verwendung desselben Motivs in Fernheilungen, die außerhalb des NT berichtet sind."

229-230: "Fragt man sich nun, was urspr nach dem καί gestanden haben könnte, so liegt es von Mk 7,30 her gesehen nahe, an eine Konstatierung der Heilung durch dir Rückkehr des Hauptmanns in sein Haus zu denken. Polag [1979, 38] bietet dazu einen interessanten Rekonstruktionsvorschlag, der dem urspr Wortlaut der mt Vorlage nahe stehen mag: ἀπελθὼν εἰς τὸν οἶκον εὗρεν τὸν δοῦλον ἰαθέντα. Diese Konjektur könnte u.E. noch dahin verbessert wer- den, daß statt τὸν οἶκον die Femininform τὴν οἰκίαν und statt τὸν δοῦλον der Ausdruck τὸν παῖδα angenommen würde. Danach könnte der urspr Abschluß folgenden Wortlaut gehabt haben: καὶ ἀπελθὼν εἰς τὴν οἰκίαν εὗρεν τὸν παῖδα ἰαθέντα. Dieser Rekonstruktionsvorschlag scheint uns auch insofern angemessen, als er nicht nur durch Mk 7,30 (vgl. Mt 15,28c), sondern auch indirekt durch Lk 7,10 nahegelegt wird, obwohl an der letzteren Stelle— [230] entsprechend Lk 7,3-6—nicht von einem παῖς, sondern einem δοῦλος, und nicht von der Rückkehr des Fürbittenden, sondern seiner Gesandten die Rede ist."

232-233: See Wegner at Luke = Q, Pro (pp. 375-376).

234: See Wegner at Luke = Q, Con (p. 381).

235: See Wegner at Luke = Q, Pro (p. 376).

271: Reconstruction: "ὕπαγε, [ὁ παῖς σου ἐσώθη] [καὶ ἀπελθὼν εἰς τὴν οἰκίαν εὗρεν τὸν παῖδα ἰαθέντα]." For complete text see Q 7:1⁰ In Q (pp. 11-12).

Gagnon 1993, 717: "I agree with Wegner's reconstruction of the conclusion to the original Q account: καὶ ἀπελθὼν εἰς τὴν οἰκίαν εὗρεν τὸν παῖδα ἰαθέντα (cf. Mark 7:30)."

Gagnon 1994a, 135: Reconstruction. For complete text see Q 7:1⁰ In Q (p. 15).

Emendation = Q: The centurion (or his friends) finds the servant at home, physically sound.

Dauer 1984, 82: "Unter Beachtung des zum redaktionellen Charakter von Mt 8,13 und Lk 7,10 Erarbeiteten wird man dann sagen können:
"(2) Sie schloß aber mit einer Konstatierung des Wunders. Diese wird ähnlich wie in Mk 7,30 gelautet haben, womit sich die oben geäußerte Vermutung, Lukas habe 7,10 Mk 7,30 nachgebildet, erledigt³¹⁶."

343³¹⁶: "Vielleicht hat es im ursprünglichen lk Traditionsbericht θεωροῦσιν τὸν δοῦλον ὑγιαίνοντα o.ä. statt εὗρον κτλ. geheißen, da Lukas auch Lk 8,35 θεωρεῖν aus Mk 5,15 durch εὑρίσκειν ersetzt. Diese Vermutung liegt umso näher, wenn Busse [1977, 150] recht hat, daß der Evangelist hier ein Wortspiel zwischen πίστιν εὗρον in V. 9 und εὗρον τὸν δοῦλον ὑγιαίνοντα in V. 10 beabsichtigt hat."

Gnilka 1986, 299-300: "Wegen der [300] weitgehenden Übereinstimmung mit Mt 15,28b kann man vermuten, daß der Schluß (V.13) mt gestaltet ist. Vielleicht berichtete er einmal davon, daß der Hauptmann den Knecht gesund zu Hause vorfand."

Landis 1994, 15: "In V.13b dürfte ὕπαγε der einzige traditionelle Ausdruck sein. Das Entlassungsmotiv ist in Heilungsgeschichten stilgemäß, seine Formulierung mit ὕπαγε etwa bei Mk ausgesprochen häufig. Für Mt ist ὕπαγε nicht typisch. Der erste Evangelist setzt es nur ganz selten redaktionell ein; oft streicht er es aus seinen Mk-Vorlagen. ...

"Die Frage, was denn in der Logienquelle nach ὕπαγε gestanden hat, ist nur in allgemeiner Form zu beantworten: Es wird mit großer Wahrscheinlichkeit irgendeine Heilungszusage gewesen sein, die der erste Evangelist in ähnlicher Weise umgestaltete wie in 15,28 die Mk-Vorlage von 7,29. Ihr Wortlaut kann nicht mehr eruiert werden."

16-17: "Dieses 'Stundenmotiv', das in der Wendung ἐν τῇ ὥρᾳ ἐκείνῃ erscheint, gehört formgeschichtlich zum ursprünglichen Motivbestand von Fernheilungsgeschichten, ist also kaum redaktionell wie die mt Formel ἀπὸ τῆς ὥρας ἐκείνης. ... Bereits die Vorlage des Mt in der Logienquelle hat also wahrscheinlich nur noch im Ausdruck ἐν τῇ ὥρᾳ ἐκείνῃ die Erinnerung daran [17] bewahrt, daß der Junge in der ursprünglichen Erzählung genau in jenem Moment gesund wurde, in dem Jesus zum Hauptmann sprach." For the rest of Matt 8:13, see Landis at Matt = Q, Con (p. 394).

17: Reconstruction: "ὕπαγε ... (Heilungszusage, Bericht von der Heilung) ... ἐν τῇ ὥρᾳ ἐκείνῃ." For complete text see Q 7:1⁶ Luke = Q, Pro (p. 57).

Evaluations

Robinson 2000: Indeterminate {U}, [( )]⁴.

Matthew's formulation ὕπαγε, ὡς ἐπίστευσας γενηθήτω σοι is similar to Matthew's almost complete revision of Mark 7:30 (Matt 15:28): ὦ γύναι, μεγάλη σου ἡ πίστις· γενηθήτω σοι ὡς θέλεις. Only ὕπαγε, omitted in Matt 15:28; 20:34 = 9:29, hence not favored by Matthew (though added Matt 8:32), is shared by Matt 8:13 with Mark 7:30. This would argue for the Matthean formulation being dependent on Mark. To be sure, ὕπαγε is the standard dismissal after a cure (John 4:50: πορεύου), see Mark 5:34: ὕπαγε (Luke 8:48: πορεύου) εἰς εἰρήνην (Matt 9:22 omits); Mark 1:44 par. Matt 8:4; Mark 2:11 // Matt 9:6 (Luke 5:24 πορεύου); etc. But it is far from obvious that the Q story can be reconstructed on the model of the way miracle stories are told in Mark and John.

In Matt 9:29, Matthean redaction of Mark 10:52 also introduces quite new language κατὰ τὴν πίστιν ὑμῶν γενηθήτω ὑμῖν that is similar to Matt 8:13; 15:28. These three instances of the order for the healing being associated with faith with only slight variations of wording indicate Matthean style.

In Matt 15:28 καὶ ἰάθη ἡ θυγάτηρ αὐτῆς is (apart from the opening καί) a complete revision of Mark 7:30. It could betray Matthean style also responsible for καὶ ἰάθη ὁ παῖς αὐτοῦ in Q 7:10.

Matt 15:28 adds ἀπὸ τῆς ὥρας ἐκείνης to Mark 7:30. This could suggest that ἐν τῇ ὥρᾳ ἐκείνῃ in Matt 8:13 would be Matthean redaction. Matthew prefers ἀπό to ἐν in this phrase (Matt 9:22; 15:28; 17:18). Indeed one may note the corruption to standard Matthean usage in many manuscripts. The presence in John 4:53 of ἐν ἐκείνῃ τῇ ὥρᾳ suggests that this was in the oral form of this healing story, and perhaps of healing stories in general (as Matthew might suggest). A slight variation of word order is typical of oral transmission; only Matthew prefers the word order of ὥρᾳ preceding ἐκείνῃ (Matt 8:13; 9:22; 15:28; 17:18), with ἐν ἐκείνῃ τῇ ὥρᾳ attested only in Matt 18:1, though not in connection with a healing.

The absence of any parallel between John 4:50-53 and Luke 7:10, together with the apparent dependence of Luke 7:10 on Mark 7:30, weakens correspondingly the case for (even a modified form of) Luke 7:10 reflecting Q.

Luke's language contains Lukanisms, and the exclusion of Luke 7:10a from Q is necessitated by the plural referring to the members of the redactional delegation. The exclusion of Luke 7:10b is suggested by his secondary use of δοῦλος (see Luke 7:2, 3).

Luke's syntax is dependent on Mark 7:30: The opening participial expression modifying the subject is like Mark's ἀπελθοῦσα εἰς τὸν οἶκον αὐτῆς. The verb and its object are formed after Mark's εὗρεν τὸ παιδίον βεβλημένον ... ἐξεληλυθός. Also εὗρον shares vocabulary with Mark 7:30. There is nothing in Luke 7:10 to be ascribed to Q.

Kloppenborg 2000: Indeterminate {U}, [( )]⁴.

Johnson 2001: Matt = Q {C} (with emendations), [[(< > ὡς ἐπίστευσας γενηθήτω σοι. καὶ ἰάθη ὁ παῖς < > ἐν τῇ ὥρᾳ ἐκείνῃ)⁴]].

Arguments for Luke's notification of healing are not persuasive (Theissen, Wegner; cf. Delobel, George, Jeremias, Dauer, Wegner, Gagnon 1993).

John 4:50 has the imperative, but as a synonym to Matt 8:13's ὕπαγε: πορεύου. John's imperative suggests that Q may have had such an imperative, but the choice of imperatives in question. I include an imperative with the above text, but I cannot think of a persuasive reason to choose one synonym over the other and am therefore undecided.

Αὐτοῦ is to be omitted on text-critical grounds. It is omitted in texts of every text-family except the Koine, and in the earliest extant texts, possibly as early as the 2ⁿᵈ–3ʳᵈ c. (latt; as well as the 4ᵗʰ c. codicies ℵ and B). It appears to be a scribal improvement, re-clarifying the relationship of the boy to the centurion.

For the rest of the text, see my evaluations of Q 7:?10?⁰,¹ above (pp. 365, 370). The issue of faith is common to miracle stories, but Matthew's subsequent uses of γενηθήτω suggest a possible source in the first instance—Matt 8:13 (Q 7:10) (Lindars). Robinson observes several non-miracle story cases of "in that hour" in Matthew and other Gospel texts, and so doesn't see the necessity of arguing it for Q. Yet, its common usage elsewhere in the Synoptic tradition is suggestive of its presence in pre-Gospel sources as well—as indicated by John 4:53.

Intriguing is Harnack's hesitant inclusion of Matthew's text as Q in his reconstruction.

Hoffmann 2001: Indeterminate {U}, [( )]⁴.

The Critical Text of Q 7:1, 3, 6b-9,?10? with Translations

The Centurion's Faith in Jesus' Word

1 ⟦καὶ ἐγένετο ὅτε⟧ ἐ⟦πλήρω⟧σεν .. τοὺς λόγους τούτους, εἰσῆλθεν εἰς Καφαρναούμ. 3 <>ἦλθεν αὐτῷ ἑκατόνταρχ⟦ο⟧ς παρακαλῶν αὐτὸν ⟦καὶ λέγων·⟧ ὁ παῖς ⟦μου κακῶς ἔχ<ει>. καὶ λέγει αὐτῷ· ἐγὼ⟧ ἐλθὼν θεραπεύσ⟦ω⟧ αὐτόν; 6b-c καὶ ἀποκριθεὶς ὁ ἑκατόνταρχος ἔφη· κύριε, οὐκ εἰμὶ ἱκανὸς ἵνα μου ὑπὸ τὴν στέγην εἰσέλθῃς, 7 ἀλλὰ εἰπὲ λόγῳ, καὶ ἰαθή⟦τω⟧ ὁ παῖς μου. 8 καὶ γὰρ ἐγὼ ἄνθρωπός εἰμι ὑπὸ ἐξουσίαν, ἔχων ὑπ' ἐμαυτὸν στρατιώτας, καὶ λέγω τούτῳ· πορεύθητι, καὶ πορεύεται, καὶ ἄλλῳ· ἔρχου, καὶ ἔρχεται, καὶ τῷ δούλῳ μου· ποίησον τοῦτο, καὶ ποιεῖ. 9 ἀκούσας δὲ ὁ Ἰησοῦς ἐθαύμασεν καὶ εἶπεν τοῖς ἀκολουθοῦσιν· λέγω ὑμῖν, οὐδὲ ἐν τῷ Ἰσραὴλ τοσαύτην πίστιν εὗρον. ?10? <..>

The Centurion's Faith in Jesus' Word

1 ⟦And it came to pass when⟧ he.. ended these sayings, he entered Capernaum. 3 There came to him a centurion exhorting him ⟦and saying: My⟧ boy ⟦<is> doing badly. And he said to him: Am I⟧, by coming, to heal him? 6b-c And in reply the centurion said: Master, I am not worthy for you to come under my roof; 7 but say a word, and ⟦let⟧ my boy ⟦be⟧ healed. 8 For I too am a person under authority, with soldiers under me, and I say to one: Go, and he goes, and to another: Come, and he comes, and to my slave: Do this, and he does «it». 9 But Jesus, on hearing, was amazed, and said to those who followed: I tell you: Not even in Israel have I found such faith. ?10? <..>

Der Glaube des Zenturio an Jesu Wort

1 ⟦Und es geschah, als⟧ er.. diese Worte beendete, ging er nach Kafarnaum. 3 Ein Zenturio kam zu ihm, bat ihn ⟦und sagte: Mein⟧ Bursche ⟦<ist> krank. Und er sagt zu ihm: Soll ich⟧ kommen und ihn heilen? 6b-c Und der Zenturio antwortete «und» sprach: Herr, ich bin nicht würdig, daß du unter mein Dach gehst, 7 aber sage ein Wort, und ⟦laß⟧ meinen Burschen gesund ⟦werden⟧. 8 Denn auch ich bin ein Mensch unter einer Autorität, und ich habe unter mir Soldaten, und ich sage diesem: Geh, und er geht, und einem anderen: Komm, und er kommt, und meinem Sklaven: Tu dies, und er tut «es». 9 Als er aber das hörte, staunte Jesus und sagte zu denen, die ihm nachfolgten: Ich sage euch, nicht einmal in Israel habe ich solchen Glauben gefunden. ?10? <..>

La foi du centurion en la parole de Jésus

1 ⟦Et il arriva que lorsqu'⟧il.. acheva ces paroles, il entra dans Capharnaüm. 3 Un centurion vint à lui, le suppliant ⟦et disant: Mon⟧ fils ⟦<est> malade. Et il lui dit: Moi⟧ je vais venir le guérir? 6b-c Et en réponse, le centurion dit:

Seigneur, je ne suis pas digne que tu entres sous mon toit, 7 mais ne dis qu'une parole et ⟦fais que⟧ mon fils ⟦soit⟧ guéri. 8 Car je suis aussi une personne soumise à une autorité, avec des soldats sous mes ordres, et je dis à l'un: Va, et il va; et à un autre: Viens, et il vient; et à mon esclave: Fais ceci, et il «le» fait. 9 En entendant «cela», Jésus s'étonna et dit à ceux qui l'accompagnaient: Je vous «je» dis, même en Israël, je n'ai trouvé une si grande foi. ?10? <..>

Q 7:1-10 Bibliography

Achtemeier, P.J. 1975. "The Lucan Perspective on the Miracles of Jesus." *Journal of Biblical Literature* 96:547-562.

Allen, W.C. 1907. *A Critical and Exegetical Commentary on the Gospel according to S. Matthew.* ICC. Edinburgh: T&T Clark. 3ʳᵈ ed. 1912. Reprinted 1972.

Allison, D.C., Jr. 1997. *The Jesus Tradition in Q.* Harrisburg, PA: Trinity Press International.

Bacon, B.W. 1930. *Studies in Matthew.* London: Henry Holt.

Bartlett, J.V. 1911. "The Sources of St. Luke's Gospel." *Oxford Studies in the Synoptic Problem,* ed. W. Sanday, 315-366. Oxford: Clarendon.

Bartsch, H.W. 1960. "Feldrede und Bergpredigt. Redaktionsarbeit in Lukas 6." *Theologische Zeitschrift* 16:5-18.

Bauer, W. 1988. *Griechisch-deutsches Wörterbuch zu den Schriften des Neuen Testaments und der frühchristlichen Literatur.* 6. völlig neu bearbeitete Auflage im Institut für neutestamentliche Textforschung/Münster unter besonderer Mitwirkung von Viktor Reichmann herausgegeben von Kurt Aland und Barbara Aland. Berlin and New York: de Gruyter. English edition: *A Greek-English Lexicon of the New Testament and other Early Christian Literature.* 3ʳᵈ ed. Revised and edited by F.W. Danker. Based on Walter Bauer's *Griechisch-deutsches Wörterbuch zu den Schriften des Neuen Testaments und der frühchristlichen Literatur,* sixth edition, ed. Kurt Aland and Barbara Aland, with Viktor Reichmann, and on previous English editions by W.F. Arndt, F.W. Gingrich, and F.W. Danker. Chicago and London: University of Chicago Press, 2000.

Beare, F.W. 1981. *The Gospel According to Matthew: A Commentary.* Oxford: Blackwell.

Beyer, Klaus. 1962. *Semitische Syntax im Neuen Testament.* SUNT 1. Göttingen: Vandenhoeck & Ruprecht.

Blass, F. and A. Debrunner. 1990. *Grammatik des neutestamentlichen Griechisch,* ed. F. Rehkopf. 17ᵗʰ ed. Göttingen: Vandenhoeck & Ruprecht. English edition: *A Greek Grammar of the New Testament and Other Early Christian Literature.* A Translation and Revision of the ninth–tenth German edition incorporating supplementary notes of A. Debrunner by Robert W. Funk. Chicago, London: University of Chicago Press, 1961.

Bleek, F. 1862. *Synoptische Erklärung der drei ersten Evangelien.* Vol. 1. Ed. H.J. Holtzmann. Leipzig: W. Engelmann.

Boismard, M.E. 1972. (Benoit, P. and M.-E. Boismard) *Synopse des quatre Évangiles en français.* Vol. 2: *Commentaire par M.-E. Boismard.* Paris: Cerf.

Bovon, F. 1989. *Das Evangelium nach Lukas.* Vol. 1, *Lk 1,1-9,50.* EKKNT 3/1. Zürich: Benziger; Neukirchen-Vluyn: Neukirchener Verlag. FT: *L'Évangile selon saint Luc (1,1-9,50).* CNT 3a. Genève: Labor et Fides, 1991.

Brock, A.G. 1997. "The Significance of φιλέω and φίλος in the Tradition of Jesus Sayings and in the Early Christian Communities." *Harvard Theological Review* 90:393-409.

Brooks, S.H. 1987. *Matthew's Community: The Evidence of his Special Sayings Material.* JSNTSS 16. Sheffield: JSOT.

Brown, R.E. 1966. *The Gospel According to John, i-xii.* AB 29. Garden City, NY: Doubleday. 2nd ed. 1982.

Bultmann, R. 1931. *Die Geschichte der synoptischen Tradition.* 2nd rev. ed. FRLANT 29. Göttingen: Vandenhoeck & Ruprecht. 1st ed. 1921; 8th ed. 1970; 9th ed. 1979, 10th ed. 1995 [with a *Nachwort* by G. Theissen]. [The 3rd through the 10th eds. were not changed from the 2nd.] ET: *The History of the Synoptic Tradition.* Rev. ed. Oxford: Blackwell; New York and Evanston: Harper, 1968.

Burchard, C. 1993. "Zu Matthäus 8,5-13." *Zeitschrift für die neutestamentliche Wissenschaft* 84:278-288. Reprinted in *Studien zur Theologie: Sprache und Umwelt des Neuen Testaments*, ed. D. Sänger, 65-76. WUNT 107. Tübingen: Mohr-Siebeck, 1998.

Burton, E.D. 1904. *Some Principles of Literary Criticism and Their Application to the Synoptic Problem.* Decennial Publications. Chicago: University of Chicago Press.

Busse, U. 1977. *Die Wunder des Propheten Jesus: Die Rezeption, Komposition und Interpretation der Wundertradition im Evangelium des Lukas.* FB 24. Stuttgart: Katholisches Bibelwerk.

Bussmann, W. 1925. *Synoptische Studien.* Vol. 1, *Zur Geschichtsquelle.* Halle: Waisenhaus.

—. 1929. *Synoptische Studien.* Vol. 2, *Zur Redenquelle.* Halle: Waisenhaus.

Cadbury, H.J. 1920. *The Style and Literary Method of Luke.* HTS 6. Cambridge, MA: Harvard University Press. Reprinted in 1960 and 1969.

—. 1966. "Four Features of Lucan Style." *Studies in Luke-Acts: Essays Presented in Honor of Paul Schubert, Buckingham Professor of New Testament Criticism and Interpretation at Yale University*, ed. L.E. Keck and J.L. Martyn, 87-102. Nashville: Abingdon.

Castor, G.D. 1912. *Matthew's Sayings of Jesus: The Non-Marcan Common Source of Matthew and Luke.* Chicago: University of Chicago Press, 1918.

This book, which is based upon the author's Ph.D. dissertation at the University of Chicago (1907), was published under the auspices of S.J. Case exactly as left by the author in 1912. Therefore, we quote it with the year 1912.

Catchpole, D.R. 1992. "The Centurion's Faith and Its Function in Q." *The Four Gospels 1992: Festschrift Frans Neirynck*, ed. F. van Segbroeck et al., 517-540. BETL 100. Leuven: University Press and Peeters. Reprinted in idem., *The Quest for Q*, 280-308. Edinburgh: T&T Clark, 1993. [As *Quest* is usually cited in the literature, dates and pagination are given for both editions.]

Comber, J.A. 1978. "The Verb *Therapeuō* in Matthew's Gospel." *Journal of Biblical Literature* 97:431-434.

Conzelmann, H. 1954. *Die Mitte der Zeit: Studien zur Theologie des Lukas.* BHT 17. Tübingen: J.C.B. Mohr (Paul Siebeck). 3., überarbeitete Auflage 1960. 4., verbesserte und ergänzte Auflage 1962. ET: *The Theology of St. Luke.* London: Faber & Faber; New York: Harper & Row, 1960.

Creed, J.M. 1930. *The Gospel According to St. Luke: The Greek Text with Introduction, Notes and Indices.* London: Macmillan. Reprinted 1953, 2nd ed. 1965.

Crossan, J.D. 1991. *The Historical Jesus: The Life of a Mediterranean Jewish Peasant.* San Francisco: HarperCollins. GT: *Der historische Jesus.* München: Beck, 1994.

Crum, J.M.C. 1927. *The Original Jerusalem Gospel: Being Essays on the Document Q.* London: Constable; New York: Macmillan. The reconstructed Q text was originally published in *Hibbert Journal* 24 (1926) 537-562.

Danker, F.W. 1972. *Jesus and the New Age according to St. Luke: A Commentary on the Third Gospel.* St. Louis, MO: Clayton Publishing House.

Dauer, A. 1984. *Johannes und Lukas: Untersuchungen zu den johanneisch-lukanischen Parallelperikopen Joh 4,46-54/Lk 7,1-10—Joh 12,1-8/Lk 7,36-50, 10,38-42—Joh 20,19-29/Lk 24,36-49.* FB 50. Würzburg: Echter.

Davies, W.D. and D.C. Allison. 1988. *A Critical and Exegetical Commentary on the Gospel According to Saint Matthew.* Vol. 1, *Introduction and Commentary on Matthew I-VII.* ICC. Edinburgh: T&T Clark.

—. 1991. *A Critical and Exegetical Commentary on the Gospel According to Saint Matthew.* Vol. 2, *Commentary on Matthew VIII-XVIII.* ICC. Edinburgh: T&T Clark.

Delobel, J. 1966. "L'onction par la pécheresse. La composition littéraire de Lc., VII, 36-50." *Ephemerides Theologicae Lovanienses* 42:415-475.

Denaux, A. 1982. "Der Spruch von den zwei Wegen im Rahmen des Epilogs der Bergpredigt (Mt 7,13-14 par. Lk 13,23-34). Tradition und Redaktion." *Logia: Les Paroles de Jésus—The Sayings of Jesus: Mémorial Joseph Coppens*, ed. J. Delobel, 305-335. BETL 59. Leuven: University Press and Peeters.

Derrett, J.D.M. 1973. "Law in the New Testament: The Syro-Phoenician Woman and the Centurion of Capernaum." *Novum Testamentum* 15:161-186.

Dibelius, M. 1919. *Die Formgeschichte des Evangeliums*. Tübingen: J.C.B. Mohr (Paul Siebeck). Rev. 2nd ed. 1933; 4th ed. 1961. ET: *From Tradition to Gospel*. New York: Scribners, 1935. [Translated from the 2nd ed.]

von Dobschütz, E. 1928. "Matthäus als Rabbi und Katechet." *Zeitschrift für die neutestamentliche Wissenschaft* 27:338-348.

Dodd, C.H. 1963. *Historical Tradition in the Fourth Gospel*. Cambridge: Cambridge University Press.

Dunderberg, I. 1994. *Johannes und die Synoptiker: Studien zu Joh 1–9*. Annales Academiae Scientiarum Fennicae Dissertationes Humanarum Litterarum 69. Helsinki: Suomalainen Tiedeakatemia.

Dupont, J. 1973. *Les Béatitudes*. Vol. 3, *Les Évangélistes*. Ebib. Paris: Gabalda.

—. 1985. *Études sur les évangiles synoptiques*. 2 vols. Ed. F. Neirynck. BETL 70. Leuven: University Press and Peeters.

Easton, B.S. 1910. "Linguistic Evidence for the Lucan Source L." *Journal of Biblical Literature* 29:139-180.

—. 1926. *The Gospel According to St. Luke: A Critical and Exegetical Commentary*. Edinburgh: T&T Clark; New York: Scribners.

Ellis, E.E. 1966. *The Gospel of Luke*. The Century Bible. London: Nelson. Rev. ed., New Century Bible Commentary; Grand Rapids, MI: Eerdmans, 1974. [Citations to p. 117 in this volume are found on p. 118 in the rev. 1974 ed.]

Ernst, J. 1977. *Das Evangelium nach Lukas*. RNT 3. Regensburg: Pustet. Rev. ed. 1993.

Evans, C.F. 1990. *Saint Luke*. Trinity Press International New Testament Commentaries. London: SCM; Philadelphia: Trinity Press International.

Fitzmyer, J.A. 1981. *The Gospel According to Luke, I-IX: Introduction, Translation and Notes*. AB 28. Garden City, NY: Doubleday.

Fleddermann, H.T. 1995. *Mark and Q: A Study of the Overlap Texts*. With an Assessment by F. Neirynck. BETL 122. Leuven: University Press and Peeters.

France, R.T. 1977. "Exegesis in Practice: Two Samples." *New Testament Interpretation: Essays on Principles and Methods*, ed. I.H. Marshall, 252-281. Exeter: Paternoster.

Frankemölle, H. 1974. *Jahwebund und Kirche Christi: Studien zur Form- und Traditionsgeschichte des "Evangeliums" nach Matthäus*. NTAbh 10. Münster: Aschendorff.

Fuchs, A. 1971. *Sprachliche Untersuchungen zu Matthäus und Lukas: Ein Beitrag zur Quellenkritik—Die Blindenheilung: Mt 9,27-31; Das Zeugnis der Christen in der Verfolgung: Lk 21,14-15.* AnBib 49. Rome: Biblical Institute Press.

Gagnon, R.A.J. 1993. "Statistical Analysis and the Case of the Double Delegation in Luke 7:3-7a." *Catholic Biblical Quarterly* 55:709-731.

—. 1994a. "Luke's Motives for Redaction in the Account of the Double Delegation in Luke 7:1-10." *Novum Testamentum* 36:122-145.

—. 1994b. "The Shape of Matthew's Q Text of the Centurion at Capernaum: Did it Mention Delegations?" *New Testament Studies* 40:133-142.

Gaston, L. 1973. *Horae Synopticae Electronicae: Word Statistics of the Synoptic Gospels.* Missoula, MT: Society of Biblical Literature.

Gatzweiler, K. 1979. "L'exégèse historico-critique: une guérison à Capharnaüm." *La Foi et le Temps* 4:297-315.

Geist, H. 1986. *Menschensohn und Gemeinde: Eine redactionskritische Untersuchung zur Menschensohnprädikation im Matthäusevangelium.* FB 57. Würzburg: Echter.

George, A. 1972. "Guérison de l'esclave d'un centurion: Lc 7,1-10." *Assemblées du Seigneur; deuxième série* 40:66-77.

Gnilka, J. 1986. *Das Matthäusevangelium.* Erster Teil, *Kommentar zu Kap. 1,1-13,58.* HTKNT 1/1. Freiburg, Basel, and Wien: Herder. 2nd ed. 1988.

—. 1990. *Jesus von Nazaret: Botschaft und Geschichte.* HThKS 3. Freiburg, Basel and Wien: Herder. ET: *Jesus of Nazareth: Message and History.* Peabody, MA: Hendrickson, 1997.

Grundmann, W. 1961. *Das Evangelium nach Lukas.* 2. Auflage, 1. Auflage dieser neuen Fassung. THKNT 3. Berlin: Evangelische Verlagsanstalt.

—. 1968. *Das Evangelium nach Matthäus.* THKNT 1. Berlin: Evangelische Verlagsanstalt. 2nd ed. 1971.

Guelich, R.A. 1982. *The Sermon on the Mount: A Foundation for Understanding.* Waco, TX: Word.

Gundry, R.H. 1982. *Matthew. A Commentary on his Literary and Theological Art.* Grand Rapids, MI: Eerdmans.

Haapa, E. 1983. "Zur Selbsteinschätzung des Hauptmanns von Kapharnaum im Lukasevangelium." *Glaube und Gerechtigkeit: In Memoriam Rafael Gyllenberg,* ed. J. Kiilunen et al., 69-76. Helsinki: Vammalan Kirjapaino.

Haenchen, E. 1956. *Die Apostelgeschichte.* 10th ed. MeyerK 3. Göttingen: Vandenhoeck & Ruprecht. [The 1st through the 4th editions were written by H.A.W. Meyer, the 5th through 9th editions by H.H. Wendt, and the 10th through 16th editions by E. Haenchen. Significant revisions are made to the 12th (1959) and 15th (1968) editions.] ET: *The Acts of the Apostles: A Commentary.* Oxford: Blackwell, 1971. [Translated from the 14th (1965) ed.]

—. 1959a. "Johanneische Probleme." *Zeitschrift für Theologie und Kirche* 56:19-54. Reprinted in idem., *Gott und Mensch: Gesammelte Aufsätze*, 78-113. Tübingen: J.C.B. Mohr (Paul Siebeck), 1965. [As both editions are cited in the literature, dates and pagination for both editions are given.]

—. 1959b. "Faith and Miracle." *Studia Evangelica: Papers presented to the International Congress on "The Four Gospels in 1957" held at Christ Church, Oxford, 1957*, ed. K. Aland et al., 495-498. TU 73. Berlin: Akademie.

Hagner, D.A. 1993. *Matthew*. 2 vols. *1-13. 14-28*. WBC 33A/B. Dallas: Word.

Hahn. G.L. 1892. *Das Evangelium des Lucas*. Vol. 1. Breslau: Morgenstern.

von Harnack, A. 1906. *Lukas der Arzt: Der Verfasser des dritten Evangeliums und der Apostelgeschichte*. Beiträge zur Einleitung in das Neue Testament 1. Leipzig: J.C. Hinrichs'sche Buchhandlung. ET: *Luke the Physician: The Author of the Third Gospel and the Acts of the Apostles*. New Testament Studies 1. London: Williams & Norgate; New York: Putnam, 1907.

—. 1907. *Sprüche und Reden Jesu: Die zweite Quelle des Matthäus und Lukas*. Beiträge zur Einleitung in das Neue Testament 2. Leipzig: J.C. Hinrichs'sche Buchhandlung. ET: *The Sayings of Jesus: The Second Source of St. Matthew and St. Luke*. New York: Putnam; London: Williams & Norgate, 1908.

Harrington, W.J. 1967. *The Gospel according to St. Luke: A Commentary*. Westminster, MD, et al.: Newman.

Hartman, L. 1963. *Testimonium linguae: Participial Constructions in the Synoptic Gospels: A Linguistic Examination of Luke 21,13*. ConNT 19. Lund: Gleerup; Copenhagen: Munksgaard.

Hasler, V. 1969. *Amen: Redaktionsgeschichtliche Untersuchung zur Einführungsformel der Herrenworte "Wahrlich ich sage euch."* Zürich and Stuttgart: Gotthelf.

Hauck, F. 1934. *Das Evangelium des Lukas (Synoptiker II)*. THKNT 3. Leipzig: Deichertsche Verlagsbuchhandlung.

Haupt, W. 1913. *Worte Jesu und Gemeindeüberlieferung: Eine Untersuchung zur Quellengeschichte der Synopse*. UNT 3. Leipzig: J.C. Hinrichs'sche Buchhandlung.

Hawkins, J.C. 1899. *Horae Synopticae: Contributions to the Study of the Synoptic Problem*. Oxford: Clarendon. 2nd ed., rev. and supplemented 1909. Reprinted 1968.

—. 1911. "Probabilities as to the So-Called Double Tradition of St. Matthew and St. Luke." *Oxford Studies in the Synoptic Problem*, ed. W. Sanday, 95-140. Oxford: Clarendon.

Held, H.-J. 1960. "Matthäus als Interpret der Wundergeschichten." *Überlieferung und Auslegung im Matthäusevangelium*, ed. G. Bornkamm et al., 155-287. WMANT 1. Neukirchen-Vluyn: Neukirchener Verlag. ET:

"Matthew as Interpreter of the Miracle Stories." *Tradition and Interpretation in Matthew*, ed. G. Bornkamm et al., 165-299. NTL. Philadelphia: Westminster; London: SCM, 1963.

Hieke, T. 2001. *Q 6:20-21: The Beatitudes for the Poor, Hungry, and Mourning*, ed. T. Hieke. Documenta Q. Leuven: Peeters.

Hirsch, E. 1941. *Frühgeschichte des Evangeliums*. Vol. 2, *Die Vorlagen des Lukas und das Sondergut des Matthäus*. Tübingen: J.C.B. Mohr (Paul Siebeck).

von Hofmann, K. 1878. *Die heilige Schrift: Neuen Testaments*. Vol. 8 *Das Evangelium des Lukas*. Nördlingen: Beck.

Holtzmann, H.J. 1863. *Die synoptischen Evangelien, ihr Ursprung und geschichtlicher Charakter*. Leipzig: W. Engelmann.

—. 1901. *Die Synoptiker*. 3., gänzlich umgearbeitete Auflage. HKNT 1/1. Tübingen and Leipzig: J.C.B. Mohr (Paul Siebeck). 1st ed. 1889, 2nd ed. 1892.

Howard, V.P. 1975. *Das Ego Jesu in den synoptischen Evangelien: Untersuchungen zum Sprachgebrauch Jesu*. MThSt 14. Marburg: Elwert.

International Q Project. 1995. See Moreland, M.C.

Jacobson, A.D. 1978. *Wisdom Christology in Q*. Unpublished Ph.D. diss. The Claremont Graduate School. Claremont, CA.

—. 1992. *The First Gospel: An Introduction to Q*. FFNT. Sonoma, CA: Polebridge.

Jeremias, J. 1956. *Jesu Verheissung für die Völker*. Stuttgart: Kohlhammer. 2nd ed. 1959. ET: *Jesus' Promise to the Nations*. SBT 24. Naperville, IL: A. R. Allenson, 1958.

—. 1960. *Die Abendmahlsworte Jesu*. Dritte völlig neu bearbeitete Auflage. Göttingen: Vandenhoeck & Ruprecht. 1st ed. 1935; 2nd ed. 1949; 4th ed. 1967. FT: *La dernière cène: les paroles de Jésus*. Lectio Divina 75. Paris: Cerf, 1972. [Translated from the 4th ed.]

—. 1980. *Die Sprache des Lukasevangeliums: Redaktion und Tradition im Nicht-Markusstoff des dritten Evangeliums*. MeyerK Sonderband. Göttingen: Vandenhoeck & Ruprecht.

Jervell, J. 1972. *Luke and the People of God: A New Look at Luke-Acts*. Minneapolis: Augsburg.

Johnson, S.R. 1997. "Q 12:57-59 Evaluations." (J.E. Amon) *Q 12:49-59: Children against Parents; Judging the Time; Settling out of Court*, ed. S. Carruth, 269-413. Documenta Q. Leuven: Peeters.

Judge, P. J. 1989. "Luke 7,1-10: Sources and Redaction." *L'Évangile de Luc: Problèmes littéraires et théologiques*, ed. F. Neirynck, 473-489. BETL 32. Leuven: University Press and Peeters.

Kiddle, M. 1935. "The Admission of the Gentiles in St. Luke's Gospel and Acts." *Journal of Theological Studies* 36:160-173.

Kloppenborg, J.S. 1987. *The Formation of Q. Trajectories in Ancient Wisdom Collections*. Studies in Antiquity and Christianity. Philadelphia: Fortress. Reprinted Harrisburg, PA: Trinity Press International, 2000.

—. 1988. *Q Parallels: Synopsis, Critical Notes, and Concordance*. FFNT. Sonoma, CA: Polebridge.

Klostermann, E. 1919. *Das Lukasevangelium*. HNT 2/1. Tübingen: J.C.B. Mohr (Paul Siebeck).

—. 1927. *Das Matthäusevangelium*, 2., völlig neubearbeitete Auflage. HNT 4. Tübingen: J.C.B. Mohr (Paul Siebeck). 1st ed. 1909; 3rd ed. 1938; 4th ed. 1971.

—. 1929. *Das Lukasevangelium*, 2., völlig neubearbeitete Auflage. HNT 5. Tübingen: J.C.B. Mohr (Paul Siebeck). 1st ed. 1919; 3rd ed. 1975.

Knox, W.L. 1957. *The Sources of the Synoptic Gospels*. Vol. 2, *St. Luke and St. Matthew*. Cambridge: Cambridge University Press.

Kollmann, B. 1996. *Jesus und die Christen als Wundertäter: Studien zu Magie, Medizin und Schamanismus in Antike und Christentum*. FRLANT 170. Göttingen: Vandenhoeck & Ruprecht.

Kosch, D. 1989. *Die eschatologische Tora des Menschensohnes: Untersuchungen zur Rezeption der Stellung Jesu zur Tora in Q*. NTOA 12. Freiburg, Switzerland: Universitätsverlag; Göttingen: Vandenhoeck & Ruprecht.

Kühner, R. and B. Gerth. 1898. *Ausführliche Grammatik der griechischen Sprache*. Zweiter Teil, *Satzlehre*. 2 vols. Hannover and Leipzig: Hahn. Reprinted, Darmstadt: Wissenschaftliche Buchgesellschaft, 1966.

Ladd, G.E. 1967. *The New Testament and Criticism*. Grand Rapids, MI: Eerdmans.

Lagrange, M.J. 1921. *Évangile selon Saint Luc*. Ebib. Paris: Librairie Lecoffre.

—. 1923. *Évangile selon Saint Matthieu*. Ebib. Paris: Librairie Lecoffre.

Lampe, G.W.H. 1965. "Miracles in the Acts of the Apostles." *Miracles: Cambridge Studies in their Philosophy and History*, ed. C.F.D. Moule, 163-178. London: Mowbray.

Landis, S. 1994. *Das Verhältnis des Johannesevangeliums zu den Synoptikern: Am Beispiel von Mt 8,5-13; Lk 7,1-10; Joh 4,46-52*. BZNW 74. Berlin and New York: de Gruyter.

Lange, J. 1973. *Das Erscheinen des Auferstandenen im Evangelium nach Mattäus: Eine traditions- und redaktionsgeschichtliche Untersuchung zu Mt 28,16-20*. FB 11. Würzburg: Echter.

Leaney, A.R.C. 1958. *A Commentary on the Gospel According to Luke*. HNTC. New York: Harper. [also published in Black's New Testament Commentaries; London: Black] 2nd ed. 1966. Reprinted 1971.

Légasse, S. 1977. "Les miracles de Jésus selon Matthieu." *Les miracles de Jésus selon le Nouveau Testament*, ed. X. Leon-Dufour, 227-247. Paris: Seuil.

Liddell, H.G., and R. Scott. 1940. *A Greek-English Lexicon.* 9th ed. Revised and augmented by H.S. Jones. Oxford: Clarendon. With a supplement, 1968.

Lindars, B. 1992. "Capernaum Revisited: John 4,46-53 and the Synoptics." *Essays on John: Festschrift für Franz Neirynck,* ed. C.M. Tuckett, 199-214. SNTA 17. Leuven: University Press and Peeters.

Lohfink, G. 1971. *Die Himmelfahrt Jesu: Untersuchungen zu den Himmelfahrts- und Erhohungstexten bei Lukas.* SANT 26. München: Kösel. 2nd ed. Kleine Reihe zur Bibel 18. Stuttgart: Katholisches Bibelwerk, 1980.

Lohmeyer, E. 1956. *Das Evangelium des Matthaus: Nachgelassene Ausarbeitungen und Entwurfe zur Übersetzung und Erklärung.* MeyerK Sonderband. Göttingen: Vandenhoeck & Ruprecht. 2nd ed. 1958; 3rd ed. 1962.

Loisy, A. 1907. *Les Évangiles synoptiques.* Vol. 1. Ceffonds: Loisy.

—. 1924. *L'Évangile selon Luc.* Paris: Émile Nourry. Reprinted Frankfurt: Minerva, 1971.

Lührmann, D., 1969. *Die Redaktion der Logienquelle.* WMANT 33. Neukirchen-Vluyn: Neukirchener Verlag.

Luz, U. 1985. *Das Evangelium nach Matthäus.* Vol. 1, *Mt 1—7.* EKKNT 1/1. Zürich: Benziger; Neukirchen-Vluyn: Neukirchener Verlag. ET: *Matthew 1—7: A Commentary.* Minneapolis: Augsburg, 1989.

—. 1987. "Die Wundergeschichten von Mt 8-9." *Tradition and Interpretation in the New Testament: Essays in Honor of E. Earle Ellis for his 60th Birthday,* ed. G. F. Hawthorne with O. Betz, 149-165. Grand Rapids, MI: Eerdmans; Tübingen: J.C.B. Mohr (Paul Siebeck).

—. 1990. *Das Evangelium nach Matthäus.* Vol. 2, *Mt 8—17.* EKKNT 1/2. Zürich: Benziger; Neukirchen-Vluyn: Neukirchener Verlag. ET: *Matthew 8—20.* Hermeneia. Minneapolis: Fortress, 2000.

Manson, T.W. 1937. *The Sayings of Jesus: As Recorded in the Gospels according to St. Matthew and St. Luke arranged with Introduction and Commentary.* London: SCM. Originally published as *The Mission and Message of Jesus.* Book 2, *The Sayings of Jesus.* London: SCM, 1937; New York: E.P. Dutton, 1938. 301-639. Re-issued as a separate volume 1949; reprinted 1957, 1964, 1977.

Marriott, H. 1925. *The Sermon on the Mount.* London: SPCK; New York and Toronto: Macmillan.

Marshall, I.H. 1978. *The Gospel of Luke: A Commentary on the Greek Text.* NIGTC. Exeter: Paternoster; Grand Rapids, MI: Eerdmans.

Martin, R.P. 1978. "The Pericope of the Healing of the 'Centurion's Servant/Son (Matt 8:5-13 par. Luke 7:1-10): Some Exegetical Notes." *Unity and Diversity in New Testament Theology: Essays in Honor of George E. Ladd,* ed. R.A. Guelich, 14-22. Grand Rapids, MI: Eerdmans.

McNeile, A.H. 1915. *The Gospel according to St. Matthew*. London: Macmillan. Reprinted 1961 and 1965.

Meier, J.P. 1994. *A Marginal Jew: Rethinking the Historical Jesus*. Vol. 2, *Mentor, Message, and Miracles*. ABRL. New York: Doubleday.

Merklein, H. 1994. *Die Jesusgeschichte—synoptisch gelesen*. SBS 156. Stuttgart: Katholisches Bibelwerk.

Metzger, B.M. 1971. *A Textual Commentary on the Greek New Testament*. Stuttgart: United Bible Societies. Corrected ed. 1975; 2nd ed. 1994.

Meyer, H.A.W. 1864. *Kritisch-exegetisches Handbuch über das Evangelium des Matthäus*. 5th ed. MeyerK 1/1. Göttingen: Vandenhoeck & Ruprecht. 1st ed. 1832. [The 6th ed. 1876 was edited by A. Ritschl but revised by H.A.W. Meyer himself.] ET: *Critical and Exegetical Hand-Book to the Gospel of Matthew*. New York, London: Funk & Wagnalls, 1884.

—. 1867. *Kritisch-exegetisches Handbuch über die Evangelien des Markus und Lukas*. 5th ed. MeyerK 1/2. Göttingen: Vandenhoeck & Ruprecht. [The 1st ed. (1832) and the 5th ed. differ essentially.] ET: *Critical and Exegetical Hand-Book to the Gospels of Mark and Luke*. New York and London: Funk & Wagnalls, 1884.

Meyer, P.D. 1970. "The Gentile Mission in Q." *Journal of Biblical Literature* 89:405-417.

Miller, M.H. 1971. *The Character of Miracles in Luke-Acts*. Th.D. diss. Graduate Theological Union. Berkeley, CA.

Montefiore, C.G. 1927. *The Synoptic Gospels*. 3 parts in 2 vols. 2nd ed., revised and partly rewritten. London: Macmillan. 1st ed. 1909.

Moreland, M.C. and J.M. Robinson. 1995. "The International Q Project: Work Sessions 23-27 May, 22-26 August, 17-18 November 1994." *Journal of Biblical Literature* 114:475-485.

Morgenthaler, R. 1971. *Statistische Synopse*. Zürich and Stuttgart: Gotthelf.

Mouson, J. 1959. "De sanatione peuri Centurionis (Mt. VIII, 5-13)." *Collectanea mechliniensia* 29:633-636.

Muhlack, G. 1979. *Die Parallelen von Lukas-Evangelium und Apostelgeschichte*. Theologie und Wirklichkeit 8. Frankfurt am Main, Bern, and Las Vegas: Lang.

Müller, G.H. 1908. *Zur Synopse: Untersuchung über die Arbeitsweise des Lk und Mt und ihre Quellen, namentlich die Spruchquelle, im Anschluss an eine Synopse Mk—Lk—Mt*. FRLANT 11. Göttingen: Vandenhoeck & Ruprecht.

Mullins, Y.T. 1962. "Petition as a Literary Form." *Novum Testamentum* 5:46-54.

Neirynck, F. 1974. *The Minor Agreements of Matthew and Luke against Mark with a Cumulative List*, ed. F. Neirynck, T. Hansen and F. van Segbroek. BETL 37. Leuven: University Press and Peeters.

—. 1979. *Jean et les synoptiques: Examen critique de l'exégèse de M.-É. Bois-mard.* BETL 49. Leuven: University Press and Peeters.

—. 1981. "La traduction d'un verset johannique: Jn 19,27b." *Ephemerides Theologicae Lovanienses* 57:83-106. Reprinted in *Evangelica: Gospel Studies —Études d'Évangile: Collected Essays,* ed. F. van Segbroek, 465-488. BETL 60. Leuven: University Press and Peeters, 1982.

—. 1982. "Recent Developments in the Study of Q." *Logia: Les Paroles de Jésus—The Sayings of Jesus: Mémorial Joseph Coppens,* ed. J. Delobel, 29-75. BETL 59. Leuven: University Press and Peeters.

—. 1995. "Jean 4,46-54. Une leçon de méthode." *Ephemerides Theologicae Lovanienses* 71:176-184.

—. 1996. "Recension de I. Dunderberg, *Johannes und die Synoptiker. Studien zu Joh 1-9.*" *Ephemerides Theologicae Lovanienses* 72:454-56.

Nolland, J. 1989. *Luke 1-9:20.* WBC 35A. Dallas: Word.

O'Donnell, P.J. 1988. *A Literary Analysis of Matthew 8: Jesus' First Gentile Mission.* Unpublished Th.D. diss. Iliff School of Theology. Denver, CO.

Parker, P. 1953. *The Gospel Before Mark.* Chicago: University of Chicago Press.

Patton, C.S. 1915. *Sources of the Synoptic Gospels.* New York and London: Macmillan.

Pesch, R. and R. Kratz. 1976. *So liest man synoptisch: Anleitung und Kommentar zum Studium der synoptischen Evangelien.* Vol. 3, *Wundergeschichten.* Frankfurt am Main: Josef Knecht.

Plummer, A. 1896. *A Critical and Exegetical Commentary on the Gospel According to St. Luke.* ICC. Edinburgh: T&T Clark. 5th ed. 1922.

—. 1909. *An Exegetical Commentary on the Gospel according to St. Matthew.* London: Elliot Stock. Reprinted, London: Robert Scott, 1915; Grand Rapids, MI: Baker, 1982.

Polag, A. 1977. *Die Christologie der Logienquelle.* WMANT 45. Neukirchen-Vluyn: Neukirchener Verlag.

—. 1979. *Fragmenta Q: Textheft zur Logienquelle.* Neukirchen-Vluyn: Neukirchener Verlag. 2nd ed. 1982. ET: I. Havener: *Q: The Sayings of Jesus. With a Reconstruction of Q by Athanasius Polag,* 109-165. GNS 19. Wilmington, DE: Glazier, 1987. Reprinted, Collegeville, MN: Liturgical Press, 1990.

Reed, J.L. 1995. "The Social Map of Q." *Conflict and Invention: Literary, Rhetorical, and Social Studies on the Sayings Gospel Q,* ed. J.S. Kloppenborg, 17-36. Valley Forge, PA: Trinity Press International.

Rehkopf, F. 1959. *Die lukanische Sonderquelle: Ihr Umfang und Sprachgebrauch.* WUNT 5. Tübingen: J.C.B. Mohr (Paul Siebeck).

Rengstorf, K.H. 1949. *Das Evangelium nach Lukas.* 4th rev. ed. NTD 3. Göttingen: Vandenhoeck & Ruprecht. 1st ed. 1937; 9th rev. ed. 1962; 17th ed. 1978. [The 4th ed. marks a significant revision of the 1st ed.]

Riniker, C. 1990. "Jean 6,1-21 et les évangiles synoptiques." *La communauté johannique et son histoire: La trajectoire de l'évangile de Jean aux deux premiers siècles*, ed. J.-D. Kaestli, J.-M. Poffet and J. Zumstein, 41-67. Geneva: Labor et Fides.

Robinson, J.M. 1997. "Q 12:57-59 Evaluations." (J.E. Amon) *Q 12:49-59: Children against Parents; Judging the Time; Settling out of Court*, ed. S. Carruth, 269-413. Documenta Q. Leuven: Peeters.

Robinson, J.M., P. Hoffmann, and J.S. Kloppenborg, eds. 2000. *The Critical Edition of Q: Synopsis including the Gospels of Matthew and Luke, Mark and Thomas, with English, German, and French Translations of Q and Thomas*. Leuven: Peeters. Hermeneia. Minneapolis: Fortress.

Sabourin, L. 1975. "The Miracles of Jesus (III): Healings, Resuscitations, Nature Miracles." *Biblical Theology Bulletin* 5:146-200.

Sand, A. 1986. *Das Evangelium nach Matthäus*. RNT 1. Regensburg: Pustet.

Sato, M. 1988. *Q und Prophetie: Studien zur Gattungs- und Traditionsgeschichte der Quelle Q*. WUNT 2/29. Tübingen: J.C.B. Mohr (Paul Siebeck).

Schenk, W. 1981. *Synopse zur Redenquelle der Evangelisten: Q-Synopse und Rekonstruktion in deutscher Übersetzung mit kurzen Erläuterungen*. Düsseldorf: Patmos.

—. 1987. *Die Sprache des Matthäus: Die Text-Konstituenten in ihren makro- und mikrostrukturellen Relationen*. Göttingen: Vandenhoeck und Ruprecht.

Schlatter, A. 1929. *Der Evangelist Matthäus*. Stuttgart: Calwer Vereinsbuchhandlung. 2nd ed. 1933.

—. 1931. *Das Evangelium des Lukas aus seinen Quellen erklärt*. Stuttgart: Calwer Vereinsbuchhandlung. 2nd ed. 1960.

Schleiermacher, F.D.E. 1817. *Über die Schriften des Lukas*. Erster Teil: *Ein kritischer Versuch*. Berlin: Georg Reimer. ET: *A Critical Essay of the Gospel of St. Luke*. London: J. Taylor, 1825.

Schmid, J. 1930. *Matthäus und Lukas: Eine Untersuchung des Verhältnisses ihrer Evangelien*. BibS(F) 23. Freiburg: Herder.

—. 1951. *Das Evangelium nach Lukas: Übersetzt und erklärt*. 2. erweiterte Neuauflage. RNT 3. Regensburg: Pustet. 1st ed. 1940; 3rd ed. 1955; 4th ed. 1960. [The 3rd and 4th eds. are identical to the 2nd ed.]

—. 1956. *Das Evangelium nach Matthäus: Übersetzt und erklärt*. 3. von neuem umgearbeitete Auflage. RNT 1. Regensburg: Pustet. 1st ed. 1948; 2. umgearbeitete Aufl. 1952; 4. durchgesehene Aufl. 1959; 5. durchgesehene Aufl. 1965. [The 4th and 5th eds. are identical to the 3rd.]

Schmithals, W. 1980. *Das Evangelium nach Lukas*. ZBK.NT 3. Zürich: Theologischer Verlag.

Schmitz, O. 1954. "παρακαλέω, παράκλησις." *Theologisches Wörterbuch zum Neuen Testament*, ed. G. Friedrich, 5:771-797. Stuttgart: Kohlhammer.

ET: *Theological Dictionary of the New Testament.* 5:773-799. Grand
Rapids, MI: Eerdmans, 1967.

Schnackenburg, R. 1964. "Zur Traditionsgeschichte von Joh 4,46-54." *Biblische Zeitschrift* 8:58-88.

——. 1965. *Das Johannesevangelium.* Vol. 1, *Einleitung und Kommentar zu Kap. 1—4.* HTKNT 4. Freiburg, Basel, and Wien: Herder. ET: *The Gospel according to St. John.* Vol. 1: *Introduction and Commentary on Chapters 1—4.* New York: Crossroad, 1968.

——. 1991. *Matthäusevangelium 1,1—16,20.* 2nd ed. Würzburg: Echter.

Schneider, G. 1977. *Das Evangelium nach Lukas.* 2 vols. ÖTBK 3. Gütersloh: Gerd Mohn; Würzburg: Echter. 2nd ed. 1984; 3rd ed. of the first vol. 1992.

Schnelle, U. 1987. *Antidoketische Christologie im Johannesevangelium: Eine Untersuchung zur Stellung des vierten Evangeliums in der johanneischen Schule.* FRLANT 144. Göttingen: Vandenhoeck & Ruprecht. ET: *Antidocetic Christology in the Gospel of John: An Investigation of the Place of the Fourth Gospel in the Johannine School.* Minneapolis: Fortress, 1992.

Schnider, F. and W. Stenger. 1971. *Johannes und die Synoptiker: Vergleich ihrer Parallelen.* BiH 9. München: Kösel.

Schniewind, J. 1914. *Die Parallelperikopen bei Lukas und Johannes.* Hildesheim: G. Olms. 2nd ed. 1958 an "unveränderter fotomechanischer Nachdruck der 1. Aufl. von 1914."

Schramm, T. 1971. *Der Markus-Stoff bei Lukas: Eine literarkritische und redaktionsgeschichtliche Untersuchung.* SNTSMS 14. Cambridge: Cambridge University Press.

Schulz, S. 1972. *Q: Die Spruchquelle der Evangelisten.* Zürich: Theologischer Verlag.

Schürmann, H. 1955. *Der Einsetzungsbericht, Lk 22,19-20: Zweiter Teil einer quellenkritischen Untersuchung des lukanischen Abendmahlsberichtes, Lk 22,7-38.* NTAbh 20/4. Münster: Aschendorff. Reprint 1970.

——. 1968. *Traditionsgeschichtliche Untersuchungen zu den synoptischen Evangelien.* KBANT. Düsseldorf: Patmos.

——. 1969. *Das Lukasevangelium.* Erster Teil, *Kommentar zu Kap. 1,1—9,50.* HTKNT 3/1. Freiburg, Basel, Wien: Herder. 3rd ed.. 1984; 4th ed. 1990.

——. 1982. "Das Zeugnis der Redenquelle für die Basileia-Verkündigung Jesu." *Logia: Les Paroles de Jésus—The Sayings of Jesus: Mémorial Joseph Coppens,* ed. J. Delobel, 121-200. BETL 59. Leuven: University Press and Peeters.

Schweizer, E. 1973. *Das Evangelium nach Matthäus.* 13. Auflage, 1. Auflage dieser neuen Fassung. NTD 2. Göttingen: Vandenhoeck & Ruprecht. 4th ed. of this version 1986. ET: *The Good News According to Matthew.* Atlanta: John Knox, 1975.

——. 1982. *Das Evangelium nach Lukas.* 18. Auflage, 1. Auflage dieser neuen Fassung. NTD 3. Göttingen: Vandenhoeck & Ruprecht. 2nd ed. of this version 1986; 3rd ed. 1993. ET: *The Good News According to Luke.* Atlanta: John Knox, 1984.

Sellin, G. 1987. "Review of A. Dauer, *Untersuchungen zu den johanneisch-lukanischen Parallelperikopen Joh 4,46-54/Lk 7,1-10—Joh 12,1-8/Lk 7,36-50; 10,38-42—Joh 20,19-29/Lk 24,36-49.*" *Theologische Literaturzeitung* 112:30-31.

Sevenich-Bax, E. 1993. *Israels Konfrontation mit den letzten Boten der Weisheit: Form, Funktion und Interdependenz der Weisheitselemente in der Logienquelle.* MThA 21. Altenberge: Oros.

Siegman, E.F. 1968. "St. John's Use of the Synoptic Material." *Catholic Biblical Quarterly* 30:182-198.

Simons, Eduard. 1880. *Hat der dritte Evangelist den kanonischen Matthäus benutzt?* Bonn: Carl Georgi.

Sparks, H.F.D. 1941. "The Centurion's παῖς." *Journal of Theological Studies* 42:179-180.

Strauss, D.F. 1836. *Das Leben Jesu, kritisch bearbeitet.* Stuttgart: P. Balz'sche Buchhandlung. 4th ed. Tübingen: Osiander. ET: *The Life of Jesus, Critically Examined.* New York: Calvin Blanchard, 1855. [Trans. from the 4th ed.] Reprinted Philadelphia: Fortress, 1973.

Strecker, G. 1962. *Der Weg der Gerechtigkeit: Untersuchung zur Theologie des Matthäus.* 3rd ed. 1971. FRLANT 82. Göttingen: Vandenhoeck & Ruprecht.

—. 1984. *Die Bergpredigt: Ein exegetischer Kommentar.* Göttingen: Vandenhoeck & Ruprecht.

Streeter, B.H. 1911. "On the Original Order of Q." *Oxford Studies in the Synoptic Problem*, ed. W. Sanday, 140-164. Oxford: Clarendon.

—. 1924. *The Four Gospels: A Study of Origins*, London: Macmillan. Reprinted 1926 and 1964.

Stuiber, A. 1985. "Amen." *Reallexikon für Antike und Christentum. Sachwörterbuch zur Auseinandersetzung des Christentums mit der antiken Welt*, ed. T. Klauser et al., 310-323. Supplement-Lieferung 1/2-3. Stuttgart: Hiersemann.

Syreeni, K. 1987. *The Making of the Sermon on the Mount: A Procedural Analysis of Matthew's Redactional Activity.* Helsinki: Soumalainen Tiedeakatemia.

Talbert, C.H. 1967. "The Lucan Presentation of Jesus' Ministry in Galilee: Luke 4:31-9:50." *Review and Expositor* 64:485-497.

Theissen, G. 1974. *Urchristliche Wundergeschichten: Ein Beitrag zur formgeschichtlichen Erforschung der synoptischen Evangelien.* SNT 8. Gütersloh: Gerd Mohn. ET: *The Miracle Stories of the Early Christian Tradition*, ed. J. Riches. Studies of the New Testament and its World. Philadelphia: Fortress, 1983.

Torrey, C.C. 1933. *The Four Gospels: A New Translation*. New York: Harper.

Tuckett, C.M. 1996. *Q and the History of Early Christianity: Studies on Q*, Edinburgh: T&T Clark.

Turner, N. 1976. *A Grammar of New Testament Greek*. Vol. 4, *Style*. Edinburgh: T&T Clark.

Vassiliadis, P. 1982. "The Original Order of Q: Some Residual Cases." *Logia: Les Paroles de Jésus—The Sayings of Jesus: Mémorial Joseph Coppens*, ed. J. Delobel, 379-387. BETL 59. Leuven: University Press and Peeters. Reprinted in idem., *ΛΟΓΟΙ ΙΗΣΟΥ: Studies in Q*, 61-70. USF International Studies in Formative Christianity and Judaism 8. Atlanta: Scholars Press, 1999.

Walker, R. 1967. *Die Heilsgeschichte im ersten Evangelium*. FRLANT 91. Göttingen: Vandenhoeck & Ruprecht.

Wegner, Uwe. 1985. *Der Hauptmann von Kafarnaum (Mt 7,28a; 8,5-10.13 par Lk 7,1-10): Ein Beitrag zur Q-Forschung*. WUNT 2/14. Tübingen: J.C.B. Mohr (Paul Siebeck).

Weiß, B. 1876. *Das Matthäusevangelium und seine Lucas-Parallelen*. Halle: Waisenhaus.

—. 1878. *Die Evangelien des Markus und Lukas*. 6th rev. ed. MeyerK 1/2. Göttingen: Vandenhoeck & Ruprecht. 7th ed. 1885; 8th ed. [together with J. Weiß; see below] 1892; rev. 9th ed. 1901.

—. 1898. *Das Matthäus-Evangelium*. 9th rev. ed. MeyerK 1/1. Göttingen: Vandenhoeck & Ruprecht.

—. 1900. *Die vier Evangelien im berichtigten Text*. 2nd part of *Das Neue Testament: Textkritische Untersuchungen und Textherstellung*. Vol. 3, *Die vier Evangelien*. Leipzig: J.C. Hinrichs'sche Buchhandlung.

—. 1901. *Die Evangelien des Markus und Lukas*. 9th rev. ed. MeyerK 1/2. Göttingen: Vandenhoeck & Ruprecht. [This edition includes comments against J. Weiß' commentary on Luke in MeyerK 1/2, 8th ed. 1892.]

—. 1904. *Das Neue Testament*. Erste Hälfte: *Evangelien und Apostelgeschicht*. Leipzig: J.C. Hinrichs'sche Buchhandlung. ET: *A Commentary on the New Testament*. Vol. 2, *Luke—The Acts*. New York: Funk & Wagnalls, 1906.

—. 1907. *Die Quellen des Lukasevangeliums*. Stuttgart and Berlin: J.G. Cotta.

—. 1908. *Die Quellen der synoptischen Überlieferung*. TU 32/3. Leipzig: J.C. Hinrichs'sche Buchhandlung.

Weiß, J. 1892. "Evangelium des Lukas." *Die Evangelien des Markus und Lukas*, B. Weiß and J. Weiß, 271-666. 8th ed. MeyerK 1/2. Göttingen: Vandenhoeck & Ruprecht.

—. 1907. "Die drei älteren Evangelien." *Die Schriften des Neuen Testaments: Neu übersetzt und für die Gegenwart erklärt* 1. Zweite, verbesserte und vermehrte Auflage, ed. J. Weiß, 31-525. Göttingen: Vandenhoeck & Ruprecht. 1st ed., 1906.

Weiße, C.H. 1838. *Die evangelische Geschichte kritisch und philosophisch bearbeitet.* 2nd vol. Leipzig: Breitkopf und Härtel.

Wellhausen, J. 1904a. *Das Evangelium Matthaei übersetzt und erklärt.* Berlin: Georg Reimer. 2nd ed. 1914. Reprinted *Evangelienkommentare.* Berlin and New York: de Gruyter, 1987.

—. 1904b. *Das Evangelium Lucae übersetzt und erklärt.* Berlin: Georg Reimer. Reprinted *Evangelienkommentare.* Berlin and New York: de Gruyter, 1987.

Wendland, P. 1912. *Die urchristlichen Literaturformen.* 2nd ed. HNT 1/3. Tübingen: J.C.B. Mohr (Paul Siebeck).

Wendling, E. 1908. "Synoptische Studien: II. Der Hauptmann von Kapernaum." *Zeitschrift für die neutestamentliche Wissenschaft* 9:96-109.

Wernle, P. 1899. *Die synoptische Frage.* Freiburg: J.C.B. Mohr (Paul Siebeck).

Wiefel, W. 1988. *Das Evangelium des Lukas.* THKNT 3. Berlin: Evangelische Verlagsanstalt.

—. 1998. *Das Evangelium nach Matthäus.* THKNT 1. Leipzig: Evangelische Verlagsanstalt.

Wilckens, U. 1973. "Vergebung für die Sünderin (Lk 7,36-50)." *Orientierung an Jesus. Zur Theologie der Synoptiker. Für Josef Schmid,* eds. P. Hoffmann, N. Brox and W. Pesch, 394-424. Freiburg, Basel, Wien: Herder.

Wilson, S.G. 1973. *The Gentiles and the Gentile Mission in Luke-Acts.* SNTSMS 23. Cambridge: Cambridge University Press.

Zahn, T. 1910. *Das Evangelium des Matthäus.* 3rd ed. Kommentar zum Neuen Testament 1. Leipzig: A. Deichert.

Zeller, D. 1982. "Redaktionsprozesse und wechselnder 'Sitz im Leben' beim Q-Material." *Logia: Les Paroles de Jésus—The Sayings of Jesus: Mémorial Joseph Coppens,* ed. J. Delobel, 395-409. BETL 59. Leuven: University Press and Peeters. ET: "Redactional Processes and Changing Settings in the Q-Material." *The Shape of Q: Signal Essays on the Sayings Gospel,* ed. J.S. Kloppenborg, 116-130. Minneapolis: Fortress, 1994.

—. 1984. *Kommentar zur Logienquelle.* SKK.NT 21. Stuttgart: Katholisches Bibelwerk.

Zuntz, G. 1945. "The 'Centurion' of Capernaum and his Authority (Matt. viii. 5-13)." *Journal of Theological Studies* 46:183-190. Reprinted in *Opuscula Selecta: Classica, Hellenistica, Christiana.* Manchester: Manchester University Press, 1972.

PRINTED ON PERMANENT PAPER • IMPRIME SUR PAPIER PERMANENT • GEDRUKT OP DUURZAAM PAPIER - ISO 9706

N.V. PEETERS S.A., WAROTSTRAAT 50, B-3020 HERENT